If You Use Outlook As a PIM

Copy your Calendar, Contacts, and Tasks folders onto your laptop.

When You Get to Your Destination

- Never leave your laptop out of your sight.
- Set up Outlook to show the local time zone as well as your h
- When you get to your location, try connecting to the Interne̲ ̲̲̲ ̲̲̲̲̲g ̲̲̲̲̲̲ into your Exchange server. (Don't wait until you really need a connection to do that.)
- Don't leave sensitive or valuable information on your laptop's drive. It's bad enough if someone steals your laptop. It's far worse if your information is stolen.
- If your laptop has a removable hard drive, keep the laptop and the hard drive in separate places.

Outlook Shortcut Keys

The following tables list some commonly used Outlook shortcut keys. See Appendix E, "Outlook Shortcut Keys," for a comprehensive list of shortcut keys.

Shortcuts for Creating Items

Task	Shortcut
Create an appointment	Ctrl+Shift+A
Create a contact	Ctrl+Shift+C
Create a folder	Ctrl+Shift+E
Create a journal entry	Ctrl+Shift+J
Create a distribution list	Ctrl+Shift+L
Create a message	Ctrl+Shift+M
Create a meeting request	Ctrl+Shift+Q
Create a note	Ctrl+Shift+N
Find people	Ctrl+Shift+P
Create a task	Ctrl+Shift+K
Post in this folder	Ctrl+Shift+S
Create a task request	Ctrl+Shift+U

Dialog Box Shortcuts

Task	Shortcut
Switch to next tab stop	Ctrl+Tab
Switch to previous tab stop	Ctrl+Shift+Tab
Move to next option or option group	Tab
Move to previous option or option group	Shift+Tab
Move to next item in drop-down list	Down arrow
Move to previous item in drop-down list	Up arrow
Move to first item in drop-down list	Home
Move to last item in drop-down list	End
Perform action assigned to button	Spacebar
Select or clear check box	Spacebar
Open a drop-down list	Alt+Down arrow
Close a drop-down list	Alt+Up arrow or Esc

HINTS AND TIPS ABOUT USING OUTLOOK ON THE ROAD

Before You Leave Your Office

The list below offers some suggestions on what you should do, or at least check, before you leave on a business trip.

Make sure your laptop is in good working order.

- Verify that all the applications you might need are installed.
- Carry CDs for principal applications in case you need to reinstall any.
- Ensure your antivirus software is installed and up to date.
- Copy all the data files you might need onto the laptop's hard drive.
- Check to see whether you have sufficient free space on the hard drive.
- Carry a few spare floppy disks.
- Charge the batteries and make sure they are in good condition.
- Collect all power, modem, and peripheral cables and make sure those cables work.
- Take any power and phone adapters needed in the countries you plan to visit.
- Consider using a laptop that has a removable hard drive.
- If you're traveling abroad, be sure you have purchase receipts or other evidence of ownership to avoid customs problems.

Outlook for Internet E-mail Users

If you use Outlook for retrieving your Internet e-mail, read through the following list to keep yourself out of a jam while travelling.

- Become familiar with downloading message headers only, particularly if you won't have a local connection to your ISP.
- Copy existing messages you might want to refer to onto your laptop.
- Does your Outlook Contacts folder contain e-mail addresses for everyone to whom you might want to send e-mail?
- Check out using your laptop for Internet e-mail before you leave the office.
- If you do not have local phone numbers to connect to your ISP in the places you'll visit, consider setting up accounts with local ISPs in those places.

Outlook for Exchange E-mail Users

If you use Outlook with Exchange, read through the following list to keep yourself out of a jam while travelling.

- Set up offline folders on your laptop.
- Synchronize your offline folders with your Exchange server.
- Set up an out-of-office reply on the server.
- Arrange for a delegate to handle e-mail while you're away.
- If you want to be able to dial in to your Exchange server, ask the server administrator to set up dial-in facilities for you.
- Practice dialing in to your Exchange server from outside your office.
- If you intend to access your Exchange server remotely, make sure you know how to download message headers only.

Special Edition
Using
Microsoft®
Outlook®
2002

Gordon Padwick

201 W. 103rd Street
Indianapolis, Indiana 46290

SPECIAL EDITION USING MICROSOFT® OUTLOOK® 2002

Copyright © 2001 by Que

International Standard Book Number: 0-7897-2514-2

Library of Congress Catalog Card Number: 20-001087729

Printed in the United States of America

First Printing: June 2001

04   03   02   01   4   3   2   1

Trademarks

Warning and Disclaimer

Associate Publisher
Greg Wiegand

Acquisitions Editor
Stephanie McComb

Development Editor
Nicholas J. Goetz

Managing Editor
Thomas F. Hayes

Project Editor
Tricia S. Liebig

Copy Editor
Megan Wade

Indexer
Larry Sweazy

Proofreaders
Angela Boley
Jessica McCarty

Technical Editors
Patricia Cardoza
Milly Staples

Team Coordinator
Sharry Lee Gregory

Interior Designer
Ruth Harvey

Cover Designers
Dan Armstrong
Ruth Harvey

Page Layout
Susan Geiselman
Liz Patterson
Gloria Schurick

CONTENTS

ABOUT THE AUTHOR

Gordon Padwick is a consultant who specializes in Microsoft Office applications and Visual Basic. In addition to training and supporting Office users, Gordon develops custom applications based on the Office suite. He has been working with computers for more years than he cares to remember in engineering, management, support, and marketing positions and has been using Windows since Microsoft introduced the first version some 12 years ago.

Gordon has authored and contributed to many books about Windows and other PC-based applications, including *Special Edition Using Microsoft Office 97 Professional*, *Microsoft Office 97 User Manual*, *Special Edition Using Microsoft Outlook 97*, *Building Integrated Office Applications*, *Using Microsoft Outlook 98*, *Platinum Edition Using Microsoft Office 97*, *Platinum Edition Using Microsoft Office 2000*, *Special Edition Using Microsoft Outlook 2000*, *Programming Microsoft Outlook 2000*, and *Creating Microsoft Access 2000 Solutions*.

He is a graduate of London University, has completed postgraduate studies in computer science and communications, and is a senior member of the Institute of Electrical and Electronics Engineers. Gordon currently lives in Washington state.

DEDICATION

To Katie, my wife, inspiration, and best friend.—Gordon Padwick

ACKNOWLEDGMENTS

Writing the acknowledgments page for a new book is one of my favorite tasks—for two reasons. It's the last thing to be written for the book, so I can heave a huge sigh of relief that the project is almost complete. Also, it's my opportunity to look back over the last few months and gratefully remember the many people who have willingly helped me write the book.

Readers of this book owe a big vote of thanks to the two technical editors, Patricia Cardoza and Milly Staples. They carefully checked and corrected everything I'd written and made many detailed suggestions for additional material. I offer my personal thanks to Patricia and Milly; I prefer to think of them as technical advisors, rather than as technical editors.

I also offer my thanks to many people at Microsoft: To the people who conceived and developed Outlook and to others who've answered my many questions.

Thank you, Stephanie McComb, Aquisitions Editor, for inviting me to work on this book and for guiding me through the process of writing the book from start to finish. Nick Goetz has made a major contribution to this book as Development Editor. Thank you, Nick, for helping me organize and clarify the book, and for all your attention to detail. My thanks also go to the many people in Que Publishing, whose names I don't know, who have performed the miracle of converting my original text into a book in an amazingly short period of time.

As always, I want to acknowledge my gratitude to my wife, Katie, for her support and patience while I've been writing this book. She has been willing to put up with me spending most of my evenings and weekends pounding away at my computer. Her encouragement has made it possible for me to write this book.

TELL US WHAT YOU THINK!

As the reader of this book, *you* are our most important critic and commentator. We value your opinion and want to know what we're doing right, what we could do better, what areas you'd like to see us publish in, and any other words of wisdom you're willing to pass our way.

As an Associate Publisher for Que, I welcome your comments. You can fax, e-mail, or write me directly to let me know what you did or didn't like about this book—as well as what we can do to make our books stronger.

Please note that I cannot help you with technical problems related to the topic of this book, and that due to the high volume of mail I receive, I might not be able to reply to every message.

When you write, please be sure to include this book's title and author as well as your name and phone or fax number. I will carefully review your comments and share them with the author and editors who worked on the book.

Fax: 317-581-4666

Email: feedback@quepublishing.com

Mail: Greg Wiegand
          Que
          201 West 103rd Street
          Indianapolis, IN 46290 USA

INTRODUCTION

In this introduction

It has been my good fortune to work with Outlook since before Outlook 97 was released. I have seen Outlook develop from pre-birth (the early Outlook 97 betas) through childhood (the release of Outlook 97), adolescence (Outlook 98), the beginning of maturity (Outlook 2000), and now moving into adulthood (Outlook 2002). This book is my attempt to provide a comprehensive, up-to-date account of Outlook 2002 so you can take advantage of as much of what Outlook has to offer as helps you be productive.

Understanding Outlook's Scope

It's not easy to write about Outlook because it can be different things to different people. For example, you can choose to use Outlook only as a Personal Information Manager (PIM)—it's one of the best available—to keep track of your calendar, contacts, and tasks.

Going beyond that, you can use Outlook to send and receive Internet e-mail, as well as to access Web sites and to participate in Internet newsgroups. Within a corporation or work-group, you can use Outlook as a client for Exchange Server, Microsoft's messaging and collaboration system, to send and receive e-mail and to share information of many types.

The chapters near the beginning of this book describe how you can use Outlook more or less as it comes out of the box, without any customization. Subsequent chapters describe how you can customize Outlook in many ways to suit your specific needs and preferences. At a simple, interactive level, you can do such things as modify menus and toolbars and create additional toolbars. At a slightly more advanced level, you can set up Outlook to be your primary desktop environment instead of the normal Windows desktop.

An additional chapter that's not printed in the book, but available for downloading from http://www.quehelp.com, shows how developers can use Outlook's programmability to create specialized applications that employ Outlook's built-in capabilities and interact with other Office and Office-compatible applications.

If you're new to Outlook, you should initially learn how to use it without much customization. When you're comfortable with Outlook at that level, take the time to explore; learn how you can, quite easily in many cases, customize Outlook so that it exactly satisfies your needs. You can, for example, modify Outlook's forms (the screens you use to input and display Outlook information) into customized forms.

Microsoft and other organizations have developed many add-ins and add-ons for Outlook—some available at no charge, some available as shareware for a small amount, and some available as commercial applications. You might find that some of these provide the extended Outlook capabilities you need, so you don't have to develop your own.

What's New in Outlook 2002

Let me start by saying what isn't new in Outlook 2002. Outlook 2002 uses the same formats for storing data as Outlook 97, Outlook 98, and Outlook 2000. If you've been using a previous version of Outlook, you can switch to Outlook 2002 without modifying data formats. In most cases, you can share data between people who are using the four Outlook versions.

The list of enhancements in Outlook 2002 is too long to list in detail here, so I'll just highlight a few of them. Many of Outlook 2002's enhancements are shared with other applications in the Office XP suite.

One of the first enhancements you'll notice in Outlook 2002 is the integrated e-mail environment. No longer do you have to choose a service option—No E-Mail, Internet Mail Only, or Corporate/Workgroup—when you install Outlook. You can set up accounts to handle Internet, Exchange Server, and Hotmail e-mail. You can also use Outlook as a client for other messaging systems, including Lotus Notes, if you have appropriate transports available from third-party sources.

The preceding paragraph mentioned the ability to send and receive Hotmail e-mail messages, something new in Outlook 2002.

The ability to display appointments in color on Outlook's calendars is now available. You can assign one of 10 predefined colors to each calendar item, using each color to signify a particular type of appointment. You also can use rules to automatically assign colors to appointments.

Reminders are now displayed in a more convenient format. In previous versions of Outlook, each reminder was displayed in a separate window, which meant that if several reminders were current, you had to cycle through a series of reminder windows. In Outlook 2002, all current reminders are displayed in a single window, making it much faster to examine your reminders.

If you use Outlook as a client for Exchange, you probably make frequent use of its ability to help schedule meetings at times when the people who should attend are available. This capability is improved in Outlook 2002. Now, when you receive an invitation to attend a meeting, you can respond by suggesting an alternative time.

The Preview pane, used to preview messages and appointments without having to open them, is improved in several ways. In Outlook 2002, you can double-click an address in the Preview pane to see the properties of that address. The InfoBar, previously displayed only in forms, is now displayed in the Preview pane. If you receive a message with attachments, the Preview pane now displays those attachments as individual icons; you can open attachments directly from the Preview pane. When you receive a message inviting you to attend a meeting, the Preview pane now contains Accept and Decline buttons you can click without having to open the message.

These are just some of the more obvious enhancements you'll notice as you begin working with Outlook 2002. The chapters of this book contain information about many more enhancements.

OPERATING SYSTEM SUPPORT

Outlook 2002, in common with the other Office XP applications, runs under any of these operating systems:

- Windows 98
- Windows Me
- Windows NT (with Service Pack 6a or later installed)
- Windows 2000

You can expect Outlook 2002 to be compatible with Windows XP when Microsoft releases that operating system.

Notice that Office XP applications are not designed to run under Windows 3.x, Windows 95, or Windows 3.5x.

→ For more information about system requirements, **see** "System Requirements," **p. 734**.

WHO SHOULD READ THIS BOOK

This book is for almost everyone who uses, or plans to use, Outlook 2002. If you use Outlook much as it comes out of the box, you'll find many answers to problems that arise from time to time. At the other extreme, if you use Outlook as a development environment, you'll find information you need that either isn't available elsewhere or is difficult to find. The vast majority of Outlook users who fit somewhere between these extremes will find this book to be an indispensable resource to which they frequently refer.

The many detailed examples of the exact steps necessary to achieve what you want to do make exploring Outlook capabilities you haven't worked with before easy.

The book assumes you are generally familiar with one or more versions of Windows, and that you have some previous experience working with Office applications, such as Word.

HOW THIS BOOK IS ORGANIZED

The book contains seven major parts, six appendices, and a glossary.

PART I, "OUTLOOK BASICS"

The two chapters (Chapters 1 and 2) in this part provide a description of how Outlook works and information about the various ways you can run Outlook.

Part II, "Sending and Receiving Messages"

Chapter 3, "Managing E-mail Accounts," describes how to set up accounts with Outlook so you can send and receive e-mail messages by way of various types of servers. Chapter 4, "Sending Messages," is all about creating and sending e-mail messages. Chapter 5, "Receiving Messages," covers receiving e-mail messages. Chapter 6, "Accessing the Internet," contains information about using Outlook to access the Internet.

Part III, "Using Outlook As a Personal Information Manager"

This part contains separate chapters that describe how to manage specific types of personal information:

- Chapters 7 and 8—Contacts (people and organizations)
- Chapters 9 and 10—Calendar (appointments, events, and meetings)
- Chapter 11—Tasks (tasks you create for yourself, tasks you create for other people, and tasks other people create for you)
- Chapter 12—Journal (keeping a record of your daily activities)
- Chapter 13—Notes (usually temporary information)

In addition, Chapter 14, "Managing Outlook Folders," explains how Outlook saves information in folders, and how you can manage those folders. Chapter 15, "Using Outlook to Manage Your Windows Files," shows how Outlook can manage Windows files.

Part IV, "Organizing Outlook Items"

This part contains five chapters that cover various aspects of managing Outlook on your computer, as well as managing the information Outlook saves:

- Chapter 16, "Using Outlook Templates"—By becoming familiar with Outlook templates, you can save yourself a lot of time.
- Chapter 17, "Finding and Organizing Outlook Items"—What other reason for saving information is there than you subsequently need to find it? Learn about Outlook's powerful tools for retrieving information in this chapter.
- Chapter 18, "Importing and Exporting Outlook Items"—You can import information saved in many formats into Outlook, and export information from Outlook in many formats.
- Chapter 19, "Compacting Folders and Archiving Outlook Items"—If you don't learn and use the techniques described in this chapter, the space Outlook occupies can soon fill your hard disk.
- Chapter 20, "Using Categories and Entry Types"—You should get into the habit of assigning categories to all Outlook items so you can group items by category. Entry types enable you to extend the use of Outlook's Journal.

PART V, "USING OUTLOOK AS A CLIENT FOR EXCHANGER SERVER AND OTHER INFORMATION SYSTEMS"

Separate chapters in this part cover using Outlook as a client for e-mail servers:

- Chapter 21—Provides an overview of messaging systems
- Chapters 22–24—Describe how to set up and use Outlook as a client for Microsoft Exchange Server

PART VI, "CUSTOMIZING OUTLOOK"

The many ways you can customize Outlook interactively (without programming) are described in this part:

- Chapter 25, "Customizing the Outlook Bar"—You can modify Outlook's default Outlook Bar so that it contains shortcut buttons to Outlook folders, Windows, files, and Web pages.
- Chapter 26, "Customizing Command Bars"—You can customize Outlook's menu bar, menus, and toolbars to suit your needs.
- Chapter 27, "Setting Outlook's Options"—This chapter explains what you can do by making selections in the various tabs of the Options dialog box.
- Chapter 28, "Creating and Using Rules"—Rules are primarily used to automate the way Outlook handles e-mail you send and receive.
- Chapter 29, "Customizing Outlook Today"—Here, you learn about some simple changes you can make to the Outlook Today window. The chapter contains an introduction to working with HTML code to customize Outlook Today.
- Chapter 30, "Customizing the Folder List"—You're not limited to Outlook's 2002 standard folders. This chapter explains how to create and organize your own folders.
- Chapter 31, "Creating Views and Print Styles"—Learn how to modify the information views that come with Outlook and how to create your own. Also, learn how to take control over how Outlook prints information.

PART VII, "SECURITY CONSIDERATIONS"

This part contains a single chapter (Chapter 32) that provides information about keeping your Outlook information secure. In addition to basic security issues, the chapter provides information about obtaining and using a certificate (Digital ID) to authenticate and encrypt your Internet and intranet e-mail.

APPENDIXES

The book contains six appendixes:

- Appendix A, "Installing and Maintaining Outlook 2002"—You'll probably initially install Outlook as a component of Office XP. This appendix describes how you can modify the initial installation.

- Appendix B, "Outlook's Files, Folders, Fields, and Registry Keys"—Here, you'll find lists of many of the places where Outlook saves information and settings.
- Appendix C, "Outlook's Symbols"—Outlook uses symbols to identify information about items. Many of these symbols are listed in this appendix.
- Appendix D, "Outlook Resources"—There's a wealth of information and add-on capabilities available for Outlook. Some of these are listed in this appendix.
- Appendix E, "Outlook Shortcut Keys"—Most of this book explains how to use your mouse to perform operations in Outlook. The shortcut keys listed here can help you to work more quickly with Outlook.
- Appendix F, "Working with the Windows Registry"—Many of Outlook's settings are saved in the Windows registry. This appendix shows you how to access and change these settings.

GLOSSARY

The Glossary contains definitions of acronyms and terms used in Outlook and related subjects.

WEB CONTENT

Most readers of this book will be content to use Outlook exactly as it comes out of the box. Therefore, many chapters deal only with customization that can be done simply by making choices in dialog boxes. But for those using Outlook as a development environment, we have a special introduction chapter to creating custom forms, writing Visual Basic Scripting Edition code to enhance forms, and using Visual Basic for Applications to enhance Outlook's overall capabilities. You can find this information at `http://www.quehelp.com`.

CONVENTIONS USED IN THIS BOOK

The special conventions used throughout this book are designed to help you get the most from the book as well as Outlook 2002.

TEXT CONVENTIONS

Different typefaces are used to convey various things throughout the book. They include the following:

Type	Meaning
Italic	A new term or phrase when it is initially defined
`Monospace`	Web addresses and onscreen messages
`Bold Monospace`	Text the reader types
Initial Caps	Menu names, dialog box names, and dialog box elements

In this book, key combinations are represented with a plus sign. If the action you need to take is to press the Ctrl key and the S key simultaneously, the text tells you to press Ctrl+S.

SPECIAL ELEMENTS

Throughout this book, you'll find Tips, Notes, Cautions, Cross-References, and Troubleshooting Tips. These elements provide a variety of information, ranging from warnings you shouldn't miss to ancillary information that will enrich your Office experience but isn't required reading.

"SIGNATURE" TIPS

Tip from

Tips point out special features, quirks, or software tricks that will help you increase your productivity with Outlook 2002.

NOTES

Note

Notes highlight things you should be aware of. If your time is at a premium, you can skip these notes. Generally, you'll find that they uncover extra information that sheds additional light on a topic.

CAUTIONS

Caution

Cautions are the hazard lights of this book and could save you precious hours in lost work—not to mention any associated headaches or ulcers.

TROUBLESHOOTING

At the end of most chapters, you'll encounter a "Troubleshooting" section. This is where you learn how to solve or avoid common problems you might typically face with Outlook 2002.

CROSS-REFERENCES

Cross-references direct you to other locations in this book that provide supplemental or supporting information. They look like:

→ For information about configuring Outlook so the Outlook Today window appears each time you start Outlook, **see** "Other Options," **p. 572**.

AUTHOR'S FINAL COMMENT

As I always do in the books I write, I invite readers to send me their suggestions, comments, and questions. Send e-mail to me at

`gpadwick@earthlink.net`

I value all messages I receive and have, so far, been able to respond personally to almost all of them. While it's gratifying when people tell me they've found one of my books useful (some do), I also appreciate comments and questions that prompt me to think about things I've previously missed (many do that).

I hope you enjoy and benefit from this book.

Gordon Padwick

OUTLOOK BASICS

CHAPTER 1

HOW OUTLOOK WORKS

In this chapter

PUTTING OUTLOOK INTO PERSPECTIVE

This chapter puts Outlook 2002 into perspective and provides an overall understanding of what Outlook is, how it works, and what you can do with it. The chapter also summarizes the differences between Outlook 2002 and the preceding version, Outlook 2000.

INTRODUCING THE OUTLOOK FAMILY

This book is primarily about Microsoft Outlook 2002 (subsequently referred to in this book as Outlook), one of the applications included in the various versions of Microsoft Office XP. Outlook is also supplied with Microsoft Exchange Server.

With Outlook, you can

- Send and receive e-mail
- Maintain information about the people and organizations whom you contact
- Keep a calendar of your appointments, events, and meetings
- Keep track of your to-do list
- Maintain a journal of your activities
- Save miscellaneous notes
- Directly access Web pages

You can also use Outlook as an enhanced version of Windows Explorer. As a bonus, Outlook is tightly integrated with Internet Explorer so you can access Internet sites and Internet newsgroups from within Outlook.

Outlook is the primary client for Microsoft Exchange Server. Although you can use Outlook on standalone computers and on computers that use messaging systems other than Exchange, the Exchange environment offers sophisticated collaboration facilities. With Outlook as a client for Exchange, you can benefit from such capabilities as group scheduling and public folders.

Although Microsoft offers Outlook primarily to satisfy the needs of business users, it's an excellent Personal Information Manager (PIM) that you can use at home as well as at the office. Why pay extra for a PIM when Outlook 2002 comes as part of the Office XP package?

Microsoft also offers Outlook Express, which you get when you install Internet Explorer, Windows 98, Windows Me, Windows 2000, or Office for Macintosh. It is intended to satisfy home users. You can use Outlook Express to send and receive Internet e-mail, maintain an address book, and communicate with Internet newsgroups. Outlook uses facilities within Outlook Express to provide access to newsgroups.

In addition, Outlook Web Access is available, which Microsoft offers to people who use Exchange Server as an information store, but who don't have Outlook. With Outlook Web Access, you can use your Web browser to gain secure access to your e-mail and calendar you maintain on Exchange, and also to use group scheduling and have access to public folders.

Outlook Web Access is mentioned here only to complete the coverage of the Outlook family of products; it isn't covered in detail elsewhere in this book.

Windows CE Pocket Outlook, which runs on Windows CE–based handheld computers, is yet another member of the Outlook family. You can synchronize Outlook data between a palmtop computer running Pocket Outlook and a desktop or laptop computer running Outlook. Although Pocket Outlook doesn't have all the capabilities of Outlook, it provides what you need for personal information management.

OUTLOOK AND OUTLOOK TODAY

Outlook is the name of the application this book is about. Outlook Today is the name of an Outlook window that displays a summary of the information stored in Outlook that's relevant to today and the next few days.

Most people configure Outlook so that the Outlook Today window, such as that shown in Figure 1.1, is displayed each time Outlook starts.

Figure 1.1
The Outlook Today window shows a summary of your current activities.

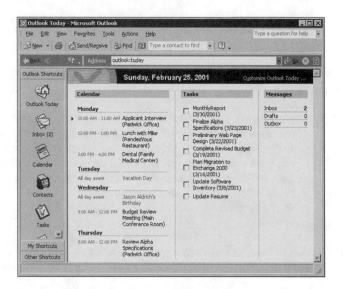

Note

If you don't see the Outlook Today window when you start Outlook, select Outlook Today in the column of icons (the Outlook Bar) at the left side of the Outlook window. If you still don't see the Outlook Today window, select View, Show Folder Home Page. Show Folder Home Page is only available in the menu when you've selected Outlook Today in the Outlook Bar.

→ For information about configuring Outlook so that the Outlook Today window appears each time you start Outlook, **see** "Other Options," **p. 572.**

The top of the Outlook Today window displays today's date, based, of course, on the date in your computer's internal clock.

The left side of the Outlook Today window shows a list of items on your calendar for today and the next few days. You can click any item on the list to see details about that item, as shown in Figure 1.2.

Figure 1.2
Outlook displays the details of a typical calendar item. Click the Close button (marked with an X) at the right end of the title bar to return to the Outlook Today window.

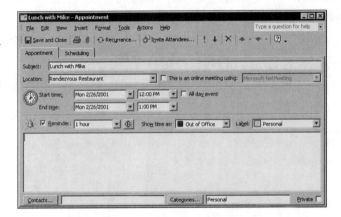

You can use the vertical scrollbar at the right side of the Outlook Today window to scroll down to items that aren't initially shown in the window.

Tip from

You can delete an appointment, an event, or a meeting from within Outlook Today. As you'll learn in Chapter 10, "Managing Calendars," you can use Outlook to create recurring appointments, events, and meetings. If the calendar item you delete from Outlook Today is recurring, you'll delete the entire recurring sequence, not just the item displayed in Outlook Today. Outlook Today doesn't tell you that a Calendar item is recurring, so be very careful about deleting calendar items in this way.

The center section of the Outlook Today window contains a list of your current tasks with the date each task is due. You can click any task to see the details of that task.

The upper-right side of the Outlook Today window shows how many unread messages are in your Inbox folder, how many drafts of messages are in your Drafts folder, and how many messages are waiting to be sent in your Outbox folder. You can click Messages to open your Inbox folder and start reading your messages.

The extreme left of the Outlook Today window contains the Outlook Bar, a set of shortcut icons you can click to go directly into parts of Outlook. After you do so, you see an Information viewer that displays specific types of Outlook items. Each of those viewers contains the same Outlook Bar. Click Outlook Today in an Information viewer to return to the Outlook Today window.

That's a quick explanation of the Outlook Today window as it appears after you first install Outlook. You can make some changes to the window by clicking Customize Outlook Today, to the right of the date at the top of the window.

You don't have to use the default Outlook Today window, nor are you limited to the choices made available when you click Options. The Outlook Today window is, in fact, defined by Hypertext Markup Language (HTML) code that you can customize.

➜ For information about enhancing Outlook Today, **see** "Customizing Outlook Today," **p. 611**.

HOW OUTLOOK SAVES DATA ITEMS

Data items are the units of information Outlook saves. All the information about a single contact is a data item, as is a message you send or receive. As an Outlook user, you need to have a basic understanding of how Outlook saves data items. If your job is to support Outlook users and, perhaps, to develop applications based on Outlook, you need to have a detailed understanding of this subject.

> **Note**
>
> If you've used previous versions of Outlook, one of the first things you'll notice about Outlook 2002 is that service options are gone. Outlook now has an integrated environment; no longer do you have to choose among the No E-mail, Internet Mail Only, or Corporate/Workgroup service options.

Outlook saves data items in a Personal Folders file that is usually on your local hard disk (but can be on any accessible disk on your network) or, if you're using Outlook as a client for an Exchange server, in a store on the server.

Whether you're using a Personal Folders file on your local disk or a store in Exchange Server, that storage location contains what Outlook calls *folders*. A separate folder exists for each type of data item Outlook saves.

> **Note**
>
> A folder is space on a disk that contains data items. You're probably used to thinking of folders as spaces on disks that contain files—you can use Windows Explorer to see these folders. In Outlook and Exchange, a folder is space that contains data items—you can't see these folders in Windows Explorer but you can, of course, see them in Outlook. Outlook folders are contained within files and are similar to tables in a database.

➜ For information about controlling where Outlook saves data items, **see** "Saving Data Items," **p. 57**.

YOUR PERSONAL FOLDERS FILE

The file Outlook uses to save items of information on your local hard drive is known as your Personal Folders file. This file can have any name you choose, but it always has the file name extension .pst. If you choose to save Outlook items on your hard drive, Outlook provides one Personal Folders file and saves all Outlook items in that file. You can create additional Personal Folders files. When you're using Outlook, you designate one Personal Folders file to be the default file in which all Outlook items are saved.

A Personal Folders file contains certain default folders. You can add any number of other folders and subfolders to a Personal Folders file.

→ For information about adding folders and subfolders to a Personal Folders file, **see** "Managing Outlook Folders," **p. 308**.

The default folders in a Personal Folders file are listed in Table 1.1. The same folders are normally available in an Exchange store.

TABLE 1.1   DEFAULT FOLDERS IN A PERSONAL FOLDERS FILE

Folder Name	Contains Information About
Calendar	Appointments, events, and meetings
Contacts	People and organizations
Deleted Items	Items deleted from other folders
Drafts	Messages not ready to be sent
Inbox	Messages received
Journal	Activities
Notes	Miscellaneous topics
Outbox	Messages waiting to be sent
Sent Items	Messages sent
Tasks	Personal tasks, tasks assigned to other people, and tasks received from other people

Each item of information within a folder is appropriately called an *item*. Each appointment, event, meeting, contact, received message, sent message, and so on is an Outlook item.

FIELDS WITHIN AN ITEM

Each Outlook item contains units of information. A Contact item, for example, contains a contact's first name, middle name, last name, and much more. In fact, a Contact item can contain more than 100 separate pieces of information about a contact. Each of these units of information is saved in a field. When you create a new Contact item, you can enter information into whichever fields are appropriate.

Outlook provides space for certain standard fields for each type of item. If you need to, you can create custom fields for additional information.

SAVING OUTLOOK SETTINGS

As described previously in this chapter, Outlook saves items of information either in a Personal Folders file or in the Exchange store. Additionally, a lot of information about how Outlook works—often referred to as Outlook's *settings*—is saved. Most of this is saved in the Windows registry. If you're using Outlook to get your work done, you don't need to be concerned with the registry. Just let it do its job, and get on with your work. However, if you're supporting Outlook users, or have problems with how Outlook works on your computer, you might have to modify the registry contents, at least somewhat.

PART

I

CH

1

Windows 98, Windows Me, Windows NT, and Windows 2000 all use a set of files, collectively known as the *registry*, to maintain information about your Windows configuration, about how applications are set up to run under Windows, and about people who use Windows. Many of the settings you establish in the Windows Control Panel are saved in the registry. Similarly, many of the settings you set for Outlook 2002 (and other Office XP applications) when you select Tools, Options are saved in the registry.

As much as possible, you should avoid making direct changes to the registry. However, for some purposes, the only way you can achieve what you need to do to is to batten down the hatches, grab the tiller, and steer into the storm. Various chapters in this book contain information about Outlook-related information in the registry.

→ To find out how to access the Windows registry, **see** "Working with the Windows Registry," **p. 799**.

In addition to saving settings in the registry, Outlook saves certain information in other files on your hard disk. Appendix B, "Outlook's Files, Folders, Fields, and Registry Keys," lists many of these files.

DISPLAYING ITEMS IN INFORMATION VIEWERS

Outlook keeps each type of item in a separate folder within your Personal Folders file or within your Exchange store. For example, all your Calendar items are kept in a Calendar folder, all your Contact items are kept in a Contact folder, and so on.

Note

When you first run Outlook after it has been installed, sample items are automatically installed in some Outlook folders. If you install Outlook 2002 on a computer on which a previous version of Outlook has been used, Outlook 2002 recognizes all previously created Outlook items.

Outlook displays the items in a folder in an Information viewer. By default, that Information viewer is appropriate for the type of items in a folder. For example, Calendar items in a Calendar folder are displayed in a Calendar Information viewer, such as that shown in Figure 1.3.

Figure 1.3
The Calendar Information viewer displays Calendar items. In addition to the monthly calendar shown here, Outlook can display weekly and daily calendars.

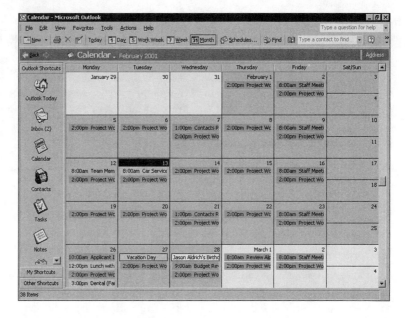

By default, Contact items are displayed in the Contacts Information viewer, which displays information about contacts much as information appears on index cards.

The way Outlook displays information in an Information viewer is referred to as a *view*. The view shown in Figure 1.3 is only one of several views you can choose to display Calendar items. In addition to the views supplied with Outlook, you can create your own custom views.

→ For information about creating custom views, **see** "Creating Views and Print Styles," **p. 651**.

An Information viewer displays only some of the information contained in Outlook items. To display detailed information about an item, double-click the item in the Information viewer. When you do so, the item is displayed in the form in which it was created. To return to the Information viewer from the form, click the Close button at the right end of the form's title bar.

USING THE OUTLOOK BAR

Each Information viewer contains the Outlook Bar at its left edge. You can click a shortcut icon in the Outlook Bar to select which Information viewer you want to see. If the Outlook Bar isn't displayed at the left side of an Information viewer, select View, Outlook Bar.

The Outlook Bar initially contains three groups named Outlook Shortcuts, My Shortcuts, and Other Shortcuts. Only one group is displayed at a time. Click the name of a group to display the shortcut icons in that group.

You can

- Create additional Outlook Bar groups
- Add shortcut icons to the initial three groups and to groups you've created
- Move shortcut icons from one group to another

→ For information about customizing the Outlook Bar, **see** "Customizing the Outlook Bar," **p. 489**.

OUTLOOK SHORTCUTS OUTLOOK BAR GROUP

The Outlook Shortcuts group in the Outlook Bar contains shortcut icons that provide access to most of Outlook's folders. The name of each shortcut identifies an Outlook folder and the name of the Information viewer used to display the contents of that folder. The shortcut icons in this group are listed in Table 1.2.

TABLE 1.2   SHORTCUTS IN THE OUTLOOK SHORTCUTS GROUP

Shortcut	Purpose
Outlook Today	Displays the Outlook Today window that summarizes your current activities.
Inbox	Displays the Inbox Information viewer that lists the headers of messages you've received and are saved in the Inbox folder. The number in parentheses at the right of the icon name in the Outlook Bar is the number of messages in your Inbox folder that you haven't read.
Calendar	Displays the Calendar Information viewer that shows Calendar items saved in the Calendar folder.
Contacts	Displays the Contacts Information viewer that shows Contact items saved in the Contacts folder.
Tasks	Displays the Tasks Information viewer that shows Tasks items (personal tasks, tasks you've assigned to others, and tasks assigned to you) saved in the Tasks folder.
Notes	Displays the Notes Information viewer that shows Note items saved in the Notes folder.
Deleted Items	Displays the Deleted Items Information viewer that shows items you've deleted from other Outlook folders and are saved in the Deleted Items folder.

Depending on your monitor's resolution, you might not see all these icons. If some icons are hidden below the visible Outlook Bar group, click the button that's marked with a down-pointing triangle near the bottom of the group. Similarly, if some icons are hidden above the visible Outlook Bar group, click the button that's marked with an up-pointing triangle near the top of the group.

MY SHORTCUTS OUTLOOK BAR GROUP

The My Shortcuts group of the Outlook Bar contains five shortcut icons. These icons are listed in Table 1.3.

TABLE 1.3   SHORTCUTS IN THE MY SHORTCUTS GROUP

Shortcut	Purpose
Drafts	Displays the Drafts Information viewer that lists the headers of message drafts you haven't yet sent and are saved in the Drafts folder. The number in parentheses at the right of the icon name in the Outlook Bar is the number of drafts in the Drafts folder.
Outbox	Displays the Outbox Information viewer that lists headers of messages you've told Outlook to send but are still in your Outbox folder waiting to be sent. The number in parentheses at the right of the icon name in the Outlook Bar is the number of messages waiting to be sent.
Sent Items	Displays the Sent Items Information viewer that lists headers of messages that Outlook has sent to your mail server.
Journal	Displays the Journal Information viewer that shows Journal items saved in the Journal folder.
Outlook Update	If you have a connection to the Internet, or if Outlook is set up to automatically connect to the Internet, this shortcut accesses a Microsoft Web page that provides information about Outlook.

Note

A number in parentheses at the right of the icon indicates the number of unread sent items, something that you don't normally see. However, if you use WinFax Pro (an Outlook add-on available from Symantec) to send and receive faxes, that application can automatically move sent faxes into the Sent Items folder and classify them as unread.

OTHER SHORTCUTS OUTLOOK BAR GROUP

The shortcuts in this group provide the capability to use Outlook to manage Windows folders and files, but with some capabilities that aren't easily accessible within Windows Explorer.

The shortcut icons you might see in the Other Shortcuts group of the Outlook Bar are listed in Table 1.4.

TABLE 1.4   SHORTCUTS IN THE OTHER SHORTCUTS GROUP

Shortcut	Purpose
My Computer	Displays your Windows environment. The information provided is similar to that provided when you select My Computer from the Windows desktop. You can use this Information viewer to print lists of folders and files.
My Documents	This shortcut is available if you're running Outlook under Windows 98, Windows Me, or Windows 2000. It displays a list of files in your My Documents folder, the default folder in which applications running under these versions of Windows save files.

Shortcut	Purpose
Personal	This shortcut is available if you're running Outlook under Windows NT. It displays a list of files in your Personal folder, the default folder in which applications running under Windows NT save files.
Favorites	Displays uniform resource locators (URLs), folders, and files in your Windows Favorites folder.

USING FORMS TO CREATE AND DISPLAY OUTLOOK ITEMS

The preceding sections of this chapter provide an introduction to how you can see items of information that already exist in Outlook—items you or other people have created. Now it's time to consider how you create Outlook items.

Outlook contains forms you use to create items; a separate form exists for each type of Outlook item. There's a form for creating Calendar items, a form for creating Contact items, a form for creating message items, and so on. Each of these forms is similar to a paper form. It contains boxes in which you enter information and lists from which you can select information.

It doesn't matter which type of item you want to create; you proceed in much the same way. Let's suppose you want to create an item to remind yourself of an appointment. One way you can do that is by entering information in the Appointment form.

With any Information viewer displayed, click the Calendar shortcut in the Outlook Bar to display the Calendar Information viewer. Select Actions, New Appointment to display the Untitled - Appointment form shown in Figure 1.4.

Figure 1.4
The form is shown here in a reduced form. You might have to click the Maximize button near the right end of the form's title bar to see the entire form.

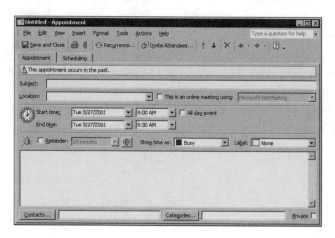

As you can see, this form contains various boxes in which you can enter information. Entering information into this form is fairly intuitive, so we won't go into details at this stage.

→ You can find detailed information about creating a one-time appointment later in this book. **See** "Creating a One-Time Appointment in the Calendar Information Viewer," **p. 196**.

After you've entered information into the various boxes in the form, select Save and Close in the form's Standard toolbar to save the information as an Outlook item.

Having saved the information, you can open the appropriate Information viewer (the Calendar Information viewer in this case) to display basic information about the item. Double-click the item in the Information viewer to display the form that contains all the information you originally entered in the form.

This short introduction to Outlook's forms refers only to the standard forms available after you first install Outlook. You can modify these forms and create your own.

OUTLOOK'S COMMAND BARS

Office applications previously dealt with menu bars and toolbars separately. Microsoft has now combined menu bars and toolbars, and the way you work with them, into the single concept of command bars. Outlook 2002 is similar to other Office XP applications. Each Information viewer and form has a menu bar at the top and, under that, one or more toolbars.

The menu bar at the top of most Information viewers are almost identical, although the menu items available in each menu vary as appropriate for the type of item displayed by the viewer. Also, in some cases, menu items vary according to the actual view selected. The menu bars at the top of Outlook's forms contain menus appropriate to each form.

After you install Outlook, each Information viewer has one toolbar, the Standard toolbar, under the menu bar. To display an Advanced toolbar, select View, move the pointer onto Toolbars, and select Advanced to display a toolbar that contains additional Outlook icons. You can also select View, Toolbars, Web to display a toolbar that contains Web-related icons.

You can customize Outlook's menus by adding menus to, or deleting menus from, the menu bar; you can also add menu items to menus and remove menu items from menus. You can create additional toolbars that contain buttons you choose, and add buttons to—or delete buttons from—the Standard, Advanced, and Web toolbars.

→ For information about creating and modifying menus and toolbars, **see** "Customizing Command Bars," **p. 505**.

CHAPTER 2

RUNNING OUTLOOK

In this chapter

CONTROLLING HOW OUTLOOK STARTS

You can start Outlook in several ways, the most obvious of which is to click the Microsoft Outlook icon on the Windows desktop.

STARTING OUTLOOK FROM THE OFFICE SHORTCUT BAR

Instead of starting Outlook and then choosing what you want to do, you can create a new Outlook item by clicking a button in the Office shortcut bar. If you've installed Outlook by itself (not as an Office component), you won't have an Office shortcut bar. You can select

- New Message to open Outlook's Message form
- New Appointment to open Outlook's Appointment form
- New Task to open Outlook's Task form
- New Contact to open Outlook's Contact form
- New Note to open Outlook's Note form

Note

To display the Office shortcut bar, in the Windows taskbar select Start, move the pointer onto Programs, move the pointer onto Microsoft Office Tools, and then select Microsoft Office Shortcut Bar.

You can also start Outlook by clicking the Launch Microsoft Outlook button in the Quick Launch section next to the Start button in the Windows taskbar.

STARTING OUTLOOK AUTOMATICALLY WHEN YOU TURN ON YOUR COMPUTER

After you start using Outlook, you'll probably get into the habit of opening Outlook at the beginning of each day. It's convenient, then, for Outlook to open automatically when you turn on your computer.

Tip from

If you have sufficient system resources, it's a good idea to leave Outlook running while you work with other applications. By doing so, you'll always see Outlook's reminders at the time they're scheduled to appear. If Outlook isn't running, reminders don't appear until you start Outlook. You'll also have Outlook immediately available for making quick notes.

To set Outlook to open automatically when you turn on your computer:

1. If Outlook is running, select File, Exit to close Outlook.
2. Select Start on the Windows taskbar, move the pointer onto Settings, and then select Taskbar & Start Menu (Windows 98, Windows Me, and Windows 2000) or Taskbar (Windows NT) to open the Taskbar Properties dialog box.

3. Select the Start Menu Programs (Windows 98, Windows NT) or Advanced (Windows Me and Windows 2000) tab.

4. Select Add to display the Create Shortcut dialog box.

5. Click Browse to display the Browse dialog box.

6. Navigate to the folder that contains Outlook (probably C:\Program Files\Microsoft Office\Office10). This folder is similar to that shown in Figure 2.1.

Figure 2.1
Make sure to find the file named Outlook or Outlook.exe (the one that's marked with the Outlook icon).

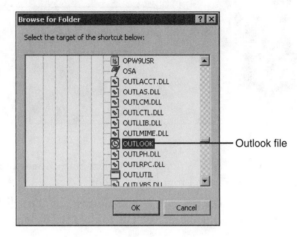

Outlook file

Note

Depending on how your computer is set up, executable files such as Outlook.exe might be displayed with or without the file name extension.

The window in Figure 2.1 shows Windows Me. If you're running Outlook under a different operating system, your window will be slightly different.

7. Select Outlook.exe or Outlook and click OK or Open to return to the Create Shortcut dialog box shown in Figure 2.2.

Figure 2.2
The command line box contains the complete path of the file that runs to start Outlook.

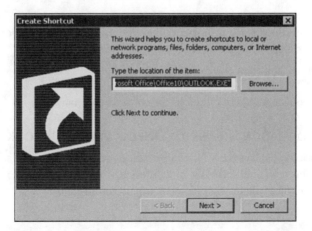

8. Click Next to display the dialog box shown in Figure 2.3.

Figure 2.3
The folder named
StartUp contains
applications that run
automatically when
Windows starts.

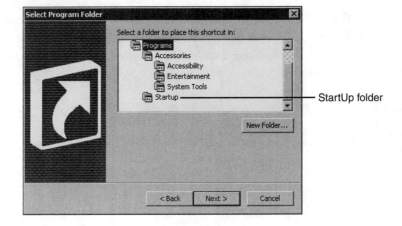

StartUp folder

9. Select the StartUp folder (make sure you don't select Start Menu) and click Next to display the Select a Title for the Program dialog box.

10. Enter a name, such as Outlook Startup, for the shortcut and then click Finish to return to the Taskbar Properties dialog box. Click OK to close the dialog box.

The next time you start Windows, Outlook will start automatically.

CANCELING AUTOMATIC OUTLOOK STARTUP

If you've followed the steps in the preceding section and then decide you don't want Outlook to start automatically, you can easily do that.

To cancel automatic Outlook startup:

1. Follow the first three steps in the preceding procedure.

2. Click Remove to display the Remove Folders/Shortcuts dialog box.

3. Expand the Startup menu; then select Outlook Startup (or whatever other name you gave to the Outlook startup shortcut). The Remove button at the bottom of the dialog box becomes active.

4. Click Remove, and then close the dialog box.

The next time you start Office, Outlook will not start automatically.

CHOOSING AN INFORMATION VIEWER TO DISPLAY WHEN OUTLOOK STARTS

By default, Outlook displays the Inbox Information viewer when it starts. You can choose to display the Outlook Today window of a different Information viewer instead, and you can make other choices about what happens when Outlook starts.

To select a default Information viewer:

1. Start Outlook, select Tools, Options, and select the Other tab. Then click Advanced Options to display the Advanced Options dialog box shown in Figure 2.4.

Figure 2.4
Use this dialog box to choose which Information viewer Outlook displays when it opens.

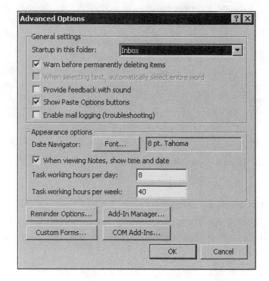

2. Open the Startup in This Folder drop-down list and select the Outlook folder that contains what you want Outlook to initially display.

3. Click OK twice to close the dialog boxes.

After you've done this, when you next start Outlook, it will display the Information viewer you selected.

You can also choose to display Outlook Today when Outlook starts from within the Outlook Today window:

1. Click the Outlook Today shortcut in the Outlook Bar to display the Outlook Today window.

2. Click Customize Outlook Today at the upper-right of the Outlook Today window to display the window shown in Figure 2.5.

Figure 2.5
You can select various
Outlook Today options
in this window.

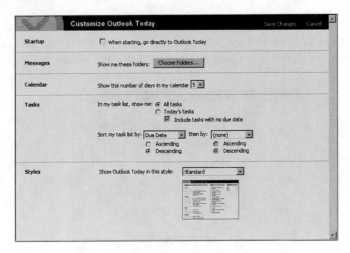

3. Check the box labeled When Starting, Go Directly to Outlook Today if you want
    Outlook to open with Outlook Today displayed. This overrides any choice you might
    have previously made in the Options dialog box (as previously described).

4. Click Save Changes.

The other choices available in the Customize Outlook Today window are described in
Chapter 29, "Customizing Outlook Today."

→ For information about customizing Outlook Today, **see** "Choosing Outlook Today's Options," **p. 613**.

MAKING OTHER OUTLOOK STARTUP CHOICES

Whether you start Outlook by clicking its icon on your Windows desktop or have Outlook
start automatically when you start Windows, Windows executes a command line to run
the Outlook.exe program file. You saw an example of such a command line previously in
Figure 2.2.

To make Outlook behave in various ways when it starts, you have to modify the properties
of an Outlook shortcut. One of these properties is the command line. By modifying a shortcut's properties you can, for example, make Outlook always open in a maximized window.

Before continuing, you must have a clear understanding of the icons on your Windows
desktop—not all of them are shortcuts. The next section gives you more information about
creating shortcuts.

CREATING SHORTCUTS

We often think of all the icons on the Windows desktop as shortcuts because they seem
to act as shortcuts. In fact, some of these icons represent programs or files themselves,
although others represent shortcuts to those programs or files. Each icon that is truly a
shortcut has a small square containing an up-and-to-the-right-pointing arrow (known as an

overlay) in its bottom-left corner. Look closely at your desktop—you'll probably see that the Microsoft Outlook icon isn't a shortcut, whereas the Outlook Express icon is a shortcut.

Note

> The information in the preceding paragraphs isn't infallible because you can use Tweak UI to remove the overlay from an icon so that a shortcut icon appears to be an icon representing a program or file.

➔ For information about Tweak UI, **see** "Troubleshooting Outlook," **p. 41**.

PART

I

CH

2

Normally, whether an icon on your desktop is or isn't a shortcut is not a matter of concern. You just click an icon to start an application or open a file. When you want to work with Outlook command-line options, however, you must be working with an Outlook shortcut, not with an icon that represents Outlook itself.

Because the Outlook installation process creates an icon on your desktop, rather than a shortcut, you have to create the shortcut yourself. Close Outlook if it's running; then open Windows Explorer. Navigate to the folder that contains `Outlook.exe` (probably `C:\Program Files\Microsoft Office\Office10`). Right-click `Outlook.exe` to display its context menu, and then click Create Shortcut. After doing that, you'll see Shortcut to OUTLOOK.EXE at the bottom of the list of files in the folder. Drag Shortcut to OUTLOOK.EXE onto the Windows desktop, and then close Windows Explorer.

On the Windows desktop, right-click the Shortcut to OUTLOOK.EXE icon to display its context menu and select Properties to display the dialog box shown in Figure 2.6.

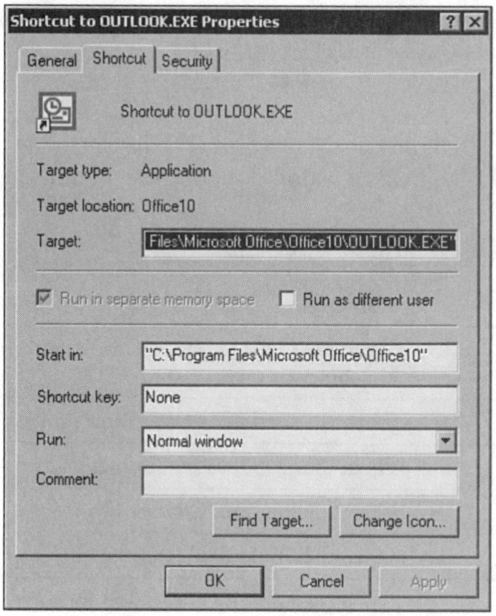

Figure 2.6
You can control how Outlook starts by making choices in this dialog box.

To enable you to choose among several ways for Outlook to open, create several Outlook shortcuts on your Windows desktop and set different properties for each.

If you always want Outlook to be maximized when it starts, open the Run drop-down list box near the bottom of the Outlook Properties dialog box and select Maximized.

You can make other changes to the way Outlook starts by appending a switch to the text in the Target box. By default, the text in this box contains the complete path of the program that starts Outlook—something similar to this:

```
"C:\Program Files\Microsoft Office\Office\outlook.exe "
```

You can add switches to this text. For example, if you want Outlook to open without displaying the Outlook Bar, place the insertion point at the right end of the text in the Target box (after the double quotation mark), press the spacebar once, and then type **/folder**. Now the command line in the Run box looks something like this:

```
"C:\Program Files\Microsoft Office\Office\outlook.exe " /folder
```

Caution

If the path includes long folder names (such as `Program Files` and `Microsoft Office`), the complete path must be within quotation marks, as shown in this example.

Subsequently, when you start Outlook, it's displayed without the Outlook Bar—this might be the way you'd like to initially see Outlook Today.

Note

After you've opened Outlook without the Outlook Bar displayed, you can select View, Outlook Bar to display the Outlook Bar.

In addition to the `/folder` switch just described, several other switches are available that you should know about. Table 2.1 contains a list of Outlook's command-line switches.

TABLE 2.1 OUTLOOK'S COMMAND-LINE SWITCHES

Command-Line Switch	Purpose
/a file name	Open the Outlook Message form with the specified file as an attachment
/c ipm.activity	Open the Outlook Journal Entry form
/c ipm.appointment	Open the Outlook Appointment form
/c ipm.contact	Open the Outlook Contact form
/c ipm.note	Open the Outlook Message form
/c ipm.post	Open the Outlook Discussion form
/c ipm.stickynote	Open the Outlook Note form
/c ipm.task	Open the Outlook Task form

Command-Line Switch	Purpose
/c message class	Create an item of the specified message class
/CheckClient	Prompt for the default manager of e-mail, news, and contacts
/CleanFreeBusy	Clean and regenerate free/busy information
/CleanReminders	Clean and regenerate reminders
/CleanSchedPlus	Delete all Schedule+ data from the server and allow the free/busy information in the Outlook calendar to be used by Schedule+ users
/CleanViews	Restore default views
/Folder	Hide the Outlook Bar (and also the folder list if that was displayed when you previously closed Outlook)
/NoPreview	Turn off the Preview pane and remove the option from the View menu
/Profiles	Offer a choice of profiles at startup (regardless of the setting in the Options dialog box)
/Profile profile name	Open using the specified profile (regardless of the setting in the Options dialog box)
/ResetFolders	Restore missing folders for the default delivery location
/ResetOutlookBar	Rebuild the Outlook Bar
/select folder name	Open with the contents of the specified Outlook folder displayed

PART

I

CH

2

Note

More command-line switches might be available by the time you read this book. For information about command-line switches, look in online Help for the Switch keyword, and then select the topic "WEB: Customize the way Outlook starts by using command-line switches." That opens your browser and connects you to a Microsoft Web site to display the topic.

You can append more than one switch to a command line.

Tip from

If you frequently open Outlook and go immediately to a particular folder or form, consider creating a shortcut on your Windows desktop for that purpose. You can create as many shortcuts as you need.

If you want to run Outlook regularly based on a command-line switch, create a shortcut on your Windows desktop as previously explained. However, if you want to use a command-line switch only occasionally, starting Outlook from the Run dialog box is more convenient. The following example shows how you can use the /CleanViews switch to restore the default Outlook views.

Close Outlook if it's currently running. Click Start in the Windows taskbar, and then select Run in the start menu to display the Run dialog box. In the Run dialog box, enter `Outlook.exe /CleanViews`.

You can use the same technique to start Outlook with any command-line switch.

HAVING TWO OR MORE OUTLOOK WINDOWS VISIBLE

You might be one of those fortunate people who has a large monitor—17 inches or more. If that's the case, you can often speed your work by having two or more Outlook windows visible at the same time. For example, it's often convenient to display your Inbox and Calendar simultaneously, or Contacts and Calendar simultaneously.

To display your Contacts and Calendar simultaneously:

1. Open Outlook as you normally do and select Contacts in the Outlook Bar to display your Contacts Information viewer.

2. If your Outlook window is maximized, click the Maximize/Restore button in the title bar and drag the borders of the window so that it occupies about half of your screen— make sure the Outlook Bar is visible.

3. Right-click Calendar in the Outlook Bar to display its context menu.

4. Click Open in New Window to display the Calendar Information box in a separate window.

5. If the new window is maximized, click the Maximize/Restore button in its title bar. Then position and size the window so that it occupies the remainder of the screen, as shown in Figure 2.7.

Figure 2.7
With two Outlook windows displayed, click either window to activate it. Alternatively, press Alt+Tab to switch from one window to the next.

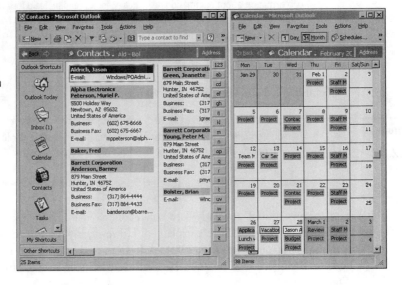

Now you can refer to your contacts while you look at your calendar. Instead of having the windows side by side on your screen, you can maximize them and press Alt+Tab to bring each window up in turn. You can display other Outlook Windows in the same way.

You're not limited to having just two Outlook windows open. You can use the technique described in this section to open additional Outlook windows.

ACCESSING INTERNET EXPLORER FACILITIES FROM OUTLOOK

When you're working in Outlook and decide to use an Internet Explorer facility, such as accessing newsgroups or Web sites, you can easily do so. For example, in Outlook you can

- Click View, move the pointer onto Go To, and click News to access Outlook Express's capability of interacting with Internet newsgroups.
- Click View, move the pointer onto Go To, and click Web Browser to open Internet Explorer so you can access Web sites.
- Click View, move the pointer onto Go To, and click Internet Call to call up NetMeeting and start an electronic conference.

This book is primarily about Outlook, rather than Internet Explorer, so we won't go into detail here about using these facilities. For detailed information about these subjects look for a *Special Edition Using* title tailored to your operating system, such as *Special Edition Using Microsoft Windows 2000 Professional* (ISBN: 0-7897-2125-2) or *Special Edition Using Microsoft Windows Me* (ISBN: 0-7897-2446-4), both published by Que.

UNDERSTANDING PROTOCOLS

A *protocol* is a set of rules that control how computers communicate.

Outlook supports the major Internet messaging, directory, security, scheduling, and collaboration protocols. In addition, Outlook fully supports the Messaging Application Programming Interface (MAPI), which provides rich messaging, scheduling, and collaboration facilities when Outlook is used as a client for Exchange Server and other MAPI-compliant mail and collaboration servers.

Table 2.2 lists the Internet protocols supported by Outlook.

TABLE 2.2 INTERNET PROTOCOLS SUPPORTED BY OUTLOOK	
Protocol	**Description**
Hypertext Markup Language (HTML)	The standard format for information on the Web
iCalendar	A means of sending and receiving free/busy calendar information over the Internet

TABLE 2.2   CONTINUED

Protocol	Description
Internet Mail Access Protocol 4 (IMAP4)	A format for sending and receiving Internet e-mail messages that provides facilities beyond those in POP3 and SMTP
Lightweight Directory Access Protocol (LDAP)	Used to provide access to directories on the Internet
Multipurpose Internet Mail Extensions (MIME)	An extension that allows binary attachments to e-mail messages
Multipurpose Hypertext Markup Language (MHTML)	An extension of HTML that allows images to be embedded within e-mail messages
Network News Transport Protocol (NNTP)	Used to post and retrieve newsgroup messages
Post Office Protocol 3 (POP3)	The most widely used format for sending and receiving Internet e-mail
Secure Multipurpose Internet Mail Extensions (S/MIME)	An extension that allows e-mail messages to be digitally signed and encrypted
Simple Mail Transport Protocol (SMTP)	Another widely used format for sending and receiving Internet e-mail
vCalendar	A means of sending and receiving calendars and schedules over the Internet
vCard	A means of sending and receiving information (including pictures) about people over the Internet

CHOOSING WINDOWS SETTINGS

To use Outlook properly, you should make sure that certain Windows settings are set correctly:

- Your monitor should have a resolution of at least 600×800 pixels to display Outlook's Information viewers and forms.

- Outlook depends on your computer's real-time clock (RTC) to properly date- and time-stamp items, so you must make sure the clock is set correctly.

- You should also ensure that Windows Regional Settings is correct, so Outlook uses appropriate date and time formats. Having the correct regional setting is particularly important if you send messages to, and receive messages from, time zones other than your local time zone.

- When setting Windows Regional Settings, check Automatically Adjust Clock for Daylight Saving Changes if that's appropriate for your region. Also, within Outlook Calendar options, make sure the Adjust for Daylight Saving Time setting matches the setting in Windows Regional Settings.

Note

For detailed information on Windows settings, refer to books such as *Using Microsoft Windows 98* (ISBN: 0-7897-1516-3), *Special Edition Using Microsoft Windows 2000 Professional* (ISBN: 0-7897-2125-2), or *Special Edition Using Microsoft Windows Me* (ISBN: 0-7897-2446-4), all published by Que.

GETTING HELP FOR OUTLOOK

Many sources of help are available to aid you in using Outlook. In addition to books such as this one, you can turn to the following sources:

- An experienced colleague
- The Office Assistant
- Outlook's online Help
- Internet Web sites and newsgroups

ASKING A COLLEAGUE

If you have a colleague who's an Outlook expert and has the time and patience to sit down with you in front of your computer, you're very fortunate. This one-on-one approach to problem-solving is usually the fastest way of getting answers to your questions.

The fact that you're reading this book, though, indicates that you are the Outlook expert in your organization, or intend to become the expert. If that's the case, you have to go elsewhere for help.

GETTING HELP FROM THE OFFICE ASSISTANT

When you first start Outlook, the Office Assistant usually appears on your screen. In Outlook 2002 and other Office XP applications, the Office Assistant is much less intrusive than it was in previous Office applications.

Note

If the Office Assistant isn't visible, select Help, Show the Office Assistant.

You can select any of the items listed in the Office Assistant balloon. Alternatively, you can enter a question and then click Search. As an example, if you enter the question "How do I send a message?" and click Search, the Office Assistant responds by displaying a list of relevant topics.

If you select a topic, the Office Assistant opens a pane that provides detailed information about that topic. The Office Assistant displays more topics if you click See More.

After you've started Outlook a few times, you might become weary of having the Office Assistant in front of you while you work. To hide the Office Assistant, select Help, Hide the Office Assistant.

Click Options in the Office Assistant pane to customize it. Outlook displays the dialog box shown in Figure 2.8.

Figure 2.8
Use the Options tab to specify how you want the Office Assistant to work.

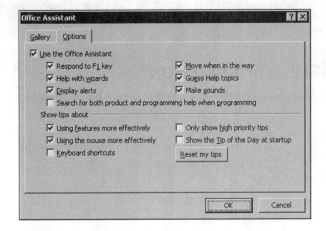

Check the boxes in the Options tab to choose the Office Assistant facilities you want to use.

If you don't want to see the Office Assistant anymore, uncheck Use the Office Assistant.

> **Note**
>
> You can also select the Gallery tab to add a little variety to your life by choosing various animated icons to represent the Office Assistant. To conserve disk space, only the default Office Assistant is installed at the time you install Office. When you choose an icon that isn't already installed, Outlook asks whether you want to install it. If you click Yes, you must install the new icon from the Office CD-ROM or download it from your server.

If you right-click the Office Assistant, a context menu appears that contains these menu items:

- **Hide**—Click this to temporarily hide the Office Assistant.
- **Options**—Click this to display the Office Assistant dialog box with the Options tab selected, as shown previously in Figure 2.8.
- **Choose Assistant**—Click this to display the Office Assistant dialog box with the Gallery tab selected.
- **Animate**—Start the Office Assistant performing some animation tricks—cute entertainment if you're bored!

> **Note**
>
> Any changes you make to the way the Office Assistant behaves in Outlook affects all the Office Applications. Likewise, any change you make to the Office Assistant in another Office Application affects Outlook.

USING ONLINE HELP

Initially, when you select Help, Microsoft Outlook Help, Outlook displays the Office Assistant. You can make a change that results in this command displaying Online Help. After you do so, you can select Help, Show the Office Assistant to use the Office Assistant. To make this change, right-click the Office Assistant to display its context menu; then click Options to display the dialog box previously shown in Figure 2.8. In that dialog box, uncheck Use the Office Assistant. Now you can directly access Online Help.

To use Online Help, disable the Office Assistant and then select Help, Microsoft Outlook Help to display the Microsoft Outlook Help window shown in Figure 2.9.

PART

I

CH

2

Figure 2.9
Use this window to look up specific information topics.

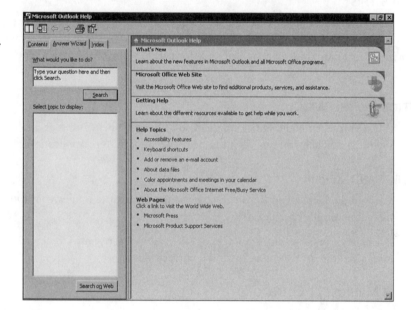

The Microsoft Outlook Help window has two panes. The left pane is where you select topics; the right pane shows information about the selected topic.

The left pane has three tabs:

- **Contents tab**—Select this tab to select general areas of information. You can expand each area of information by clicking the + at the left of the information name. Then select one of the listed subjects to see information about that subject in the right pane.

- **Answer Wizard tab**—Select this tab if you want to ask a question in your own words. Enter your question into the What Would You Like to Do box, and then click Search. Outlook lists topics based on the words in your question. Select a topic to see information about that topic in the right pane.

- **Index tab**—Select this tab to see an alphabetical list of major help topics. You can enter a keyword, or keywords, in the Type Keywords box and then click Search to find corresponding topics. Alternatively, you can scroll down the list of topics. Double-click a topic to see subtopics in the Choose a Topic box. Select a subtopic to see details about it in the right pane.

You also can click the Search On Web button at the bottom of the Help window to access various Web sites supported by Microsoft in which you can find answers to Outlook questions.

What's This?

When you select Help, What's This?, a question mark is added to the pointer. Using this question-mark pointer, point onto any menu item and click to get information about that item, or point onto any region of an Information viewer or form and click to get information about that region.

Office on the Web

When you select Help, Office on the Web, Outlook opens Internet Explorer and opens a Web site in which you can obtain information about Office applications, including Outlook.

Detect and Repair

Select Help, Detect and Repair to activate a utility that examines your Office installation and automatically corrects errors.

If it finds errors in your installation, it asks you to insert your Office CD into the drive. After you do that, the utility loads the correct files.

About Microsoft Outlook

Select Help, About Microsoft Outlook to display a dialog box that provides information about the version of Outlook you're using. The top line in this dialog box shows the version and build numbers of Outlook you have installed.

Click one of the four buttons at the bottom-right of the dialog box:

- **OK**—Closes the dialog box.
- **System Info**—Displays information about your computer hardware and the installed operating system.
- **Tech Support**—Displays information about resources for Outlook technical support.
- **Disabled Items**—Displays a list of Office components that have become disabled. You can select items to re-enable.

TROUBLESHOOTING OUTLOOK

One of the problems you might experience is that Windows and Windows applications on your computer might be somewhat, or very, different from what's described in this chapter. That's because Windows and many Windows applications are highly customizable. If you inherit a computer on which Outlook is already installed, you might find that Outlook looks quite different from the descriptions in this chapter and elsewhere in this book.

Also, if you install Outlook on a computer that has previously had Outlook installed, what you see might be quite different from what you see in this book. That's because the Office installation procedure attempts to install Outlook (and other Office applications) in a manner that's as similar as possible to any previous installation.

Many of the settings for Windows and Windows applications are set by values in the Windows registry, some of which you can change from the Control Panel. However, many registry settings can't be changed from the Control Panel. That's where Tweak UI, a utility supplied with Windows 98 (and also available for downloading from a Microsoft Web site), comes in very useful for fine-tuning the Windows user interface.

Note

The version of Tweak UI supplied with Windows 98 is compatible only with that version of Windows. You can download a more recent version of Tweak UI that's compatible with Windows 2000, Windows NT, Windows Me, Windows 98, and Windows 95 from `http://www.Microsoft.com/ntworkstation/downloads/powertoys/` `networking/nttweakui.asp`.

DOWNLOADING AND INSTALLING TWEAK UI

Download Tweak UI from the Web site mentioned in the preceding note and save the file `Tweakui.exe`. Double-click the file to extract five files from it, one of which is `Tweakui.inf`. Right-click `Tweakui.inf` to display its context menu, and then click Install.

The installation process creates an icon named Tweak UI in your Windows Control Panel. Double-click that icon to display the Tweak UI dialog box, shown in Figure 2.10, which contains 13 tabs, each tab containing a variety of related options.

Figure 2.10
The Tweak UI dialog box has many tabs, each giving access to certain aspects of the Windows user interface.

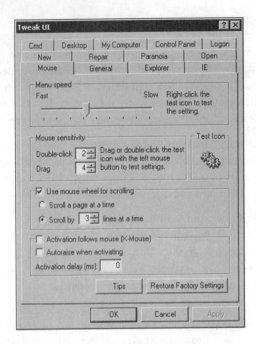

Many, but not all, of Tweak UI's tabs contain a Restore Factory Settings button you can use to return the Windows user interface to its original state.

The Tweak UI tabs are

- Mouse
- General
- Explorer
- IE
- New
- Repair
- Paranoia
- Open
- Cmd
- Desktop
- My Computer
- Control Panel
- Logon

It's a few minutes well spent to open each of the tabs and gain an idea of what's there. The purpose of many of the items in the Tweak UI tabs is fairly obvious. If you need help, click the Help button near the right end of the title bar, and then click the item in the tab for which you need help to see information about that item.

USING OTHER WAYS TO CUSTOMIZE OUTLOOK

This book contains a great deal of information about customizing Outlook, much of which is in Chapters 25 through 31. If Outlook isn't working the way you think it should, you'll probably find the answer to your problem in those chapters.

SENDING AND RECEIVING MESSAGES

CHAPTER 3

MANAGING E-MAIL ACCOUNTS

In this chapter

WHAT'S NEW ABOUT E-MAIL ACCOUNTS

Among the most significant improvements in Outlook 2002 is the merging of the Corporate/Workgroup and Internet Mail Only service options so that, in a single Outlook installation, you have access to POP3 and IMAP Internet e-mail as well as to Exchange Server and other messaging system accounts. You no longer have to choose between installing Outlook with the Corporate/Workgroup or Internet Mail Only service option.

With Outlook 2002, you can also access Hotmail accounts.

CONNECTING TO A NETWORK

Before you can use Outlook for e-mail or to share information with people who use other computers, you must have a connection to some sort of network and have the protocol the network uses installed on your computer. This book doesn't provide information about connecting Outlook to an Exchange server or other LAN-based messaging system because those connections are usually managed by administrators and their staffs. However, the next few paragraphs do provide some basic information about connecting Outlook to the Internet that is likely to be useful to people who use Outlook at home or in a small office.

Note

> Refer to a book such as *Special Edition Using Microsoft Exchange Server 2000* (ISBN: 0-7897-2278-0) for detailed information about administering Exchange Server 2000.

One of the common mistakes people make when they first try to connect to an Internet service provider (ISP) is not making sure that the Transmission Control Protocol/Internet Protocol (TCP/IP) protocol is installed on their computers. All Internet communication depends on the TCP/IP protocol, so you must have it installed to send and receive e-mail, access Web sites, or interact with newsgroups. You don't need to understand TCP/IP; just make sure it's installed.

The most common way to connect to the Internet is by way of a dial-up connection over a telephone line. You also might consider using a high-speed Digital Subscriber Line (DSL) or cable connection, although you should take precautions about the security issues involved with these always-on connections.

Note

> Refer to TCP/IP and Dial-up topics in Windows help for information about these subjects. Alternatively, refer to such books as *Special Edition Using Microsoft Windows 98*, *Special Edition Using Microsoft Windows Me*, or *Special Edition Using Microsoft Windows 2000 Professional*, all published by Que.
>
> For information about connecting to the Internet using DSL or cable, consult the companies who provide these services.

CREATING E-MAIL ACCOUNTS

If a previous version of Outlook is installed on your computer, the process of installing Outlook 2002 automatically creates e-mail accounts equivalent to those you previously had. Unless you need additional e-mail accounts, you won't have to go through the process of creating e-mail accounts for Outlook 2002.

This chapter assumes you've just installed Outlook 2002 on a computer that didn't have a previous version of Outlook installed. The first time you run Outlook, the E-mail Accounts Wizard leads you through the process of creating an e-mail account. You can subsequently select Tools, E-mail Accounts to create additional e-mail accounts. In either case, you see the window shown in Figure 3.1.

Figure 3.1
Use this window to start creating a new e-mail account.

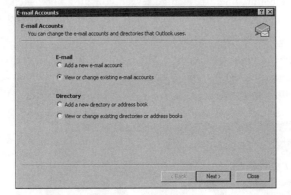

Note

> The E-mail Accounts item is available in the Tools menu when you have most Information viewers displayed. The item isn't available when you have Outlook Today, Outlook Update, My Computer, My Documents, or Favorites displayed.

In the window shown in Figure 3.1, select Add a New E-mail Account and click Next to display the window shown in Figure 3.2.

Figure 3.2
This window lists the types of e-mail accounts you can create.

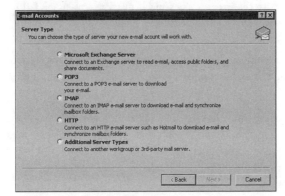

The next few sections separately describe the process of creating each type of e-mail account. You need to read only those sections that apply to the types of accounts you want to create.

CREATING A MICROSOFT EXCHANGE SERVER ACCOUNT

Outlook can be used as a client for Exchange Server 5.5 or Exchange Server 2000. The process of creating an e-mail account in Outlook to access an Exchange Server account is the same for both versions of Exchange Server.

Before you can create an Exchange Server account in Outlook, you must already have an account on your Exchange server. The process of creating an account on the server is the responsibility of the Exchange administrator and is not covered in this book. For information about creating accounts on an Exchange server, consult a book such as *Special Edition Using Microsoft Exchange 5.5* or *Special Edition Using Microsoft Exchange 2000*, both published by Que.

To create an account in Outlook to access a Microsoft Exchange Server account, in the window shown in Figure 3.2, select Microsoft Exchange Server and then click Next to display the window shown in Figure 3.3.

Figure 3.3
This dialog box is shown here after the server and user names have been entered.

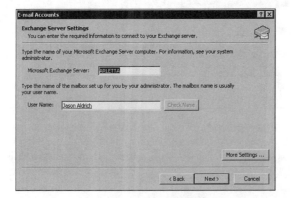

Note

Outlook can support only one Exchange Server account at a time. If you already have an Exchange Server account set up, a message explains this fact.

The information you enter in the window shown in Figure 3.3 is supplied by your Exchange administrator. Enter the name of your Exchange server, and enter your username on the server.

After entering your username, click Check Name to verify that the name you entered is for a valid account on the server. When you do that, Outlook displays a message reminding you that the new account you're creating will not be available until you close and restart Outlook. Click OK to acknowledge that message. After a short delay, if you entered the correct server name and a valid username, Outlook underlines the username you entered to verify that the account exists on the server.

If the username you entered does not correspond to the name of an existing account on the server, Outlook displays a message stating The name could not be matched to a name in the address list. That can happen because you didn't correctly enter the username supplied by the administrator or, perhaps, because the administrator didn't tell you the correct name. Try reentering the username. If, after that, the problem still exists, contact the administrator for help in solving the problem.

Another possible problem is that you didn't enter the server name correctly, or the server is not accessible. If that happens, Outlook displays a message stating that Outlook could not log on. Check that you entered the server name correctly. If the problem still exists, contact your administrator for help.

At this stage, you can click More Settings to refine your Exchange Server account but you probably don't need to do so. Click Next to display the next window. In that window, click Finish to complete the process of setting up the account. Before you can use the account, select File, Exit to close Outlook. Then restart Outlook.

→ For information about refining an Exchange Server account, **see** "Refining an Exchange Server E-mail Account in Outlook," **p. 429**.

After restarting Outlook, you can select Tools, E-mail Accounts to display the window previously shown in Figure 3.1. In that window, select View or Change Existing E-mail Accounts and then click Next to display a window in which the Exchange account you just created is listed.

CREATING A POP3 ACCOUNT FOR INTERNET E-MAIL

Post Office Protocol 3 (POP3) is the protocol used by many Internet and intranet e-mail servers. You can create as many POP3 accounts in Outlook as you need. The accounts you create in Outlook access accounts that already exist on a POP3 server. Before setting up a POP3 account in Outlook, contact an ISP or other POP3 server administrator to have an account set up for you.

Note

Post Office Protocol 3 (POP3) is a protocol used to receive e-mail from a server. Simple Mail Transport Protocol (SMTP) is a protocol used to send e-mail to a server.

CREATING AN ACCOUNT WITH AN INTERNET SERVICE PROVIDER

Establishing an account with an Internet service provider usually involves choosing an ISP and then making a phone call to that ISP, or using your Web browser to connect to that ISP's Web site. Either way, you must give the ISP your name, suggest a name for your account, provide a password, and agree to some way that the ISP will bill you (usually via a monthly charge to one of your credit cards). After you've done that, the ISP will provide whatever information is necessary for you to log on to your account.

Don't choose your ISP lightly. Although you can change your ISP at any time, when you change your ISP, your Internet e-mail address changes.

You can choose from many ISPs, many of whom offer different services. Consider the following:

- Some ISPs have local access telephone numbers in many parts of the country, whereas others have local access numbers only for one city or region. If you're likely to want to connect to your ISP while traveling, choose an ISP that has local access numbers in the places you expect to visit.
- Some ISPs allow you to have more than one e-mail address for your account so that people who share the account can keep their e-mail separate. This is particularly useful for a family or small business. Not all ISPs offer this service.
- Some ISPs accommodate various types of connections, including DSL, ISDN, and others. If you expect to become a frequent Internet user, choose an ISP that offers high-speed connections, even if you don't use those connections initially.
- Some ISPs offer free or low-cost disk space you can use to create your own Web site; others don't. If you anticipate having your own Web site, investigate the cost of it being hosted by the ISP before you make your choice.
- Most ISPs provide access to Internet newsgroups. If there are some newsgroups you need to use, make sure the ISP you choose provides access to them.

After you've evaluated ISPs based on these criteria, ask around to get the opinions of local people who use the services you're interested in. What you need is an ISP that provides the services you require and that gives you fast, reliable access. Only people's experience can give you the information you need to make your choice.

CREATING AN INTERNET ACCOUNT IN OUTLOOK

To create an Outlook account to access a POP3 account on a server, select Tools, E-mail Accounts to display the window previously shown in Figure 3.1. Select Add New E-mail Account and click Next to display the window previously shown in Figure 3.2. Select POP3 and click Next to display the window shown in Figure 3.4.

Figure 3.4
This is where you set up a POP3 e-mail account. The window is shown here with information entered.

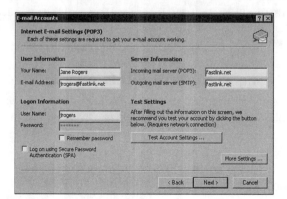

The administrator of the POP3 server provides the information you have to enter into the boxes in the window shown in Figure 3.4. The information you enter in these boxes must be correct; otherwise, you won't be able to connect to the server.

Caution

I strongly recommend you leave the Remember Password box unchecked. Check this box only if you are totally confident that you are the only person who has access to your computer. By leaving this box unchecked, you have the minor inconvenience of having to enter your e-mail password each time you log on to the server. On the other hand, if you check this box, anyone who has access to your computer can download e-mail addressed to you and, what might be of even more concern, send e-mail on your behalf.

After completing the six text boxes in this window, the Test Account Settings button becomes enabled. You have more work to do before you click that button. Click More Settings to display the dialog box shown in Figure 3.5.

Tip from

It's particularly important to make the correct choices in the Internet E-mail Settings dialog box's Connection tab before you attempt to test your account settings.

CHOOSING GENERAL SETTINGS

The Internet E-mail Settings dialog box is initially displayed with the General tab selected.

Figure 3.5
Enter some basic information about the account here.

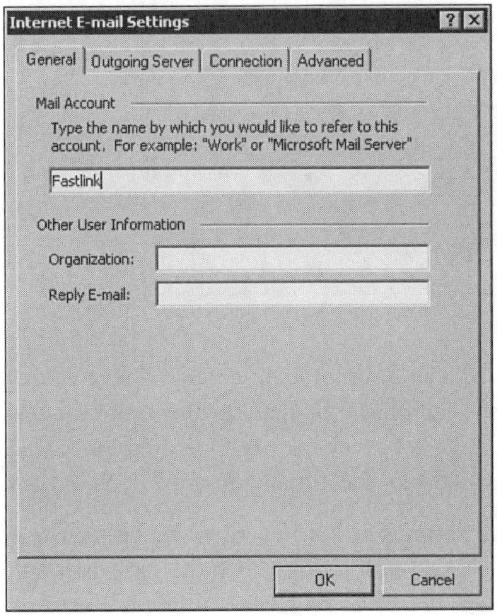

PART

II

CH

3

By default, Outlook proposes to give the new account a name that corresponds to the name of your POP3 mail server. You can change the proposed name to anything you prefer. The name you choose is the name by which you'll subsequently select the account elsewhere in Outlook. If you have several accounts on the same server, you should give each of those accounts a different name so you can easily identify them.

You can, if you like, enter the name of your organization in the Organization box. Although you might expect that name to appear in messages you send, it doesn't. There appears to be no reason to enter a name in this box.

When people reply to messages you send, those messages are normally sent to the e-mail address from which you sent the original messages. If you want replies to be sent to a different e-mail address, enter that address in the Reply E-mail box.

CHOOSING OUTGOING SERVER SETTINGS

Select the Outgoing Server tab, shown in Figure 3.6, to refine the account.

Figure 3.6
Use this dialog box to refine the account.

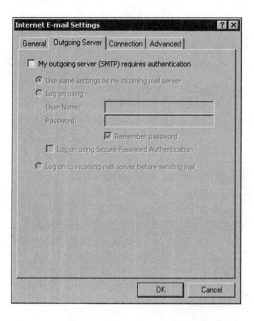

In most cases, you can log on to an Internet mail server and receive and send messages without much ado. However, you might have to separately log on to the SMTP server to which you send messages. If that's the case, check the My Outgoing Server (SMTP) Requires Authentication box. When you do so, the initially dimmed parts of the tab become enabled.

Leave the default, Use Same Settings as My Incoming Mail Server selected if you have to separately log onto the SMTP server, but do so with the same username and password as for the POP3 server. If the SMTP server requires a different username and password, select Log on Using, and then enter the required username and password in the two boxes.

Tip from

As mentioned previously, leaving the Remember Password box checked defeats the purpose of having a password. Uncheck that box to ensure your security.

Check the Log on Using Secure Password Authentication box only if instructed to do so by the e-mail administrator. This is required only if the server has a second level of security. In that case, when you log in, the server requires you to enter another password. Don't check this box unless the server requires you to do so.

By default, when you log on to an e-mail server, Outlook sends any messages currently in your Outbox folder to the server and then downloads messages from the server to your Inbox folder. If you prefer Outlook to download messages before it sends messages, check the Log on to Incoming Mail Server Before Sending Mail box.

CHOOSING CONNECTION SETTINGS

Select the Connection tab to display the dialog box shown in Figure 3.7.

Figure 3.7
Use this dialog box to specify how you want to connect to an e-mail server.

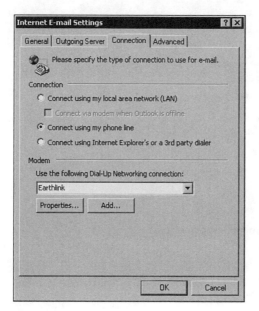

By default, Outlook proposes to connect to the mail server using your local area network (LAN), which is appropriate if you're using an intranet server. Most likely, you're setting up an account to access an Internet server that you access by way of a phone line. If you have a DSL connection, consult your DSL provider for information about setting up and using that connection.

If you're not connecting by way of your LAN, select Connect Using My Phone Line or Connect Using Internet Explorer's or a 3rd Party Dialer, whichever is appropriate. If you select Connect Using My Phone Line, the Modem section in the lower part of the dialog box becomes enabled. Use that section to select the dial-up connection you want to use and, optionally, to set the properties of that connection or to create a new connection.

CHOOSING ADVANCED SETTINGS

Select the Advanced tab to display the dialog box shown in Figure 3.8.

Figure 3.8
These are the Internet e-mail advanced settings.

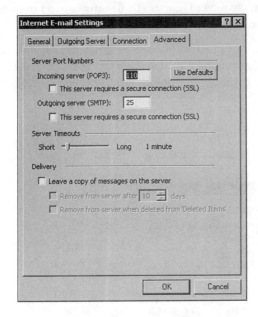

By default, Outlook proposes the Server Port Numbers that most servers use. Similarly, the two check boxes are unchecked. Change these settings only if you're instructed to do so by the server administrator.

By default, the Server Timeouts slider is set to 30 seconds. This is the time Outlook waits before telling you it hasn't been able to make a connection to the server. If you have a problem establishing a server connection, try increasing the time by dragging the slider to the right.

The Delivery section at the bottom of the dialog box is something you might find useful. By default, the Leave a Copy of Messages on the Server box is unchecked. This means that messages for you on the server are deleted as soon as you've downloaded them. When you're working from your office or home, that's a reasonable thing to do. There's no reason to clutter up your server's storage with messages you've already downloaded. However, if you're traveling and download messages to your laptop, you might want to leave messages on the server so that, when you return home, you can download those messages to your principal computer. Check the box to leave messages you've downloaded on the server.

Note

Your ISP or other mail server probably sets a limit to the space you can use to save messages and also might have a limit on the time for which you can save messages.

TESTING ACCOUNT SETTINGS

After you've completed entering information into the four tabs described in the preceding four sections, click OK to return to the E-mail Accounts window shown previously in Figure 3.4. Then click Test Account Settings. Outlook displays the dialog box shown in Figure 3.9.

Figure 3.9
This dialog box lists the five steps used to test account settings.

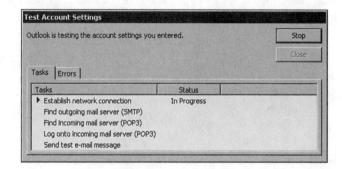

Depending on your dial-up settings, Outlook either starts to attempt making a connection to your mail server or displays a dialog box in which you have to click Dial to start the attempt. If the account is correctly configured, check marks appear at the left of each step displayed in the dialog box shown in Figure 3.9 and the word Completed appears at the right of each step when that step is completed satisfactorily. When all five steps have been completed (a process that normally takes only a few seconds), a message at the top of the dialog box states Congratulations! All tests completed successfully. Click Close to continue.

If a step in the test process doesn't complete successfully, an error message appears describing the nature of the problem. You can use the information in this message to deduce which setting has caused the problem. Close the message box to return to the window previously shown in Figure 3.4 so you can correct the settings.

FINALIZING THE ACCOUNT SETUP

After successfully testing the account, click Next in the windows previously shown in Figure 3.4. Outlook displays a window that states you have successfully entered all the information required to set up your account. Click Finish to close that window.

The first time you download messages from the account, you'll see a message with the content This is an e-mail sent automatically by Microsoft Outlook's Account Manager while testing the settings for your POP3 account.

Creating an IMAP Account for Internet E-mail

Internet Message Access Protocol (IMAP) is a protocol that offers more capabilities than POP3. At present, it's not generally available from ISPs; you're more likely to require an IMAP account to access e-mail on an intranet. Follow the procedure described in the section "Creating a POP3 Account for Internet E-mail," p. 49 for information about setting up an IMAP account.

No provision exists to automatically test an IMAP account.

Creating an HTTP Account for Hotmail

Hypertext Transport Protocol (HTTP) is a protocol for sending hypertext documents by way of the Internet. It is the protocol used by Hotmail and some other e-mail systems.

Note

You must have a Hotmail account before you can create an account within Outlook to access a Hotmail account. One way to create a Hotmail account is to open Internet Explorer and select `http://www.hotmail.com`. With that page displayed, click Sign Up Now.

The procedure for setting up an account within Outlook for accessing a Hotmail account is quite similar to that described in the section "Creating a POP3 Account for Internet E-mail," p. 49. The principal differences are

- Instead of specifying separate incoming and outgoing mail servers, you have to specify only a single mail service provider.
- After clicking More Settings, instead of four tabs the dialog box has only two.
- No provision exists to test an HTTP account.

When you create a Hotmail account, Outlook automatically creates a Personal Folders file for use by Hotmail messages.

Creating Accounts for Other Mail Servers

Open the window previously shown in Figure 3.2, select Additional Server Types and then click Next. Outlook displays a window that lists other server types for which a transport is installed on your computer.

Outlook is supplied with the capability to create accounts for accessing e-mail on an Exchange server, in POP3 and SMTP Internet and intranet servers, and in HTTP servers such as Hotmail. You can install so-called transports available from various companies that enable you to use Outlook as a client for other systems. For example, Lotus supplies a transport you can install in Outlook so you can access Lotus Notes. Such transports are not described in this chapter because they are not part of Outlook. You can obtain information about installing these transports from their suppliers.

Accessing E-mail Accounts

If you have two or more e-mail accounts, one of these accounts is the default Outlook normally uses to send outgoing messages and receive incoming messages. You can, of course, specify an account other than the default account at the time you instruct Outlook to begin processing (sending and receiving) messages.

To identify and possibly change the default e-mail account used for processing messages, select Tools, E-mail Accounts to display the window previously shown in Figure 3.1. In that window, select View or Change Existing E-mail Accounts and click Next to display the window shown in Figure 3.10.

Figure 3.10
This window lists all your e-mail accounts.

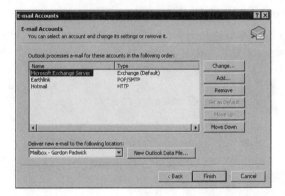

PART

II

CH

3

The window shown in Figure 3.10 shows the default account at the top with the word "default" at the right of the account name. To make a different account the default, select that account and click Set as Default. As soon as you do that, Outlook reorders the list so that the new default account is at the top of the list.

If you instruct Outlook to process messages from all accounts, it processes messages from the default account first and then messages from other accounts in the order those accounts are listed in the window previously shown in Figure 3.10. You can change the order in which accounts are listed by selecting an account in that window and then clicking Move Up or Move Down. If you move an account to the top of the list, that account becomes the default.

Saving Data Items

The section "How Outlook Saves Data Items" in Chapter 1, "How Outlook Works," explained that Outlook saves data items either in a Personal Folders file on a hard disk or in the Exchange store. You can control where Outlook saves data items.

If you set up Outlook for use only as a client for an Exchange server, Outlook assumes you want to save data items in a store on the Exchange server. If you prefer, you can create a Personal Folders file on your hard disk and save data items there. Although there's usually not a reason to do so, you can create several Personal Folders files and select one of them to be the place where Outlook saves data items.

If you set up Outlook for use only to send and receive e-mail from the Internet or an intranet, Outlook creates a Personal Folders file in which all data items are stored.

The next two sections explain what happens after you've set up Outlook for use as a client for an Exchange Server as well as to send and receive Internet or intranet e-mail.

Note

If your administrator has set up Exchange Server appropriately, you can use Outlook to send and receive Internet and intranet messages by way of the server. I'm talking here, though, of sending Internet and intranet messages directly from Outlook.

IDENTIFYING THE DEFAULT STORAGE LOCATION

With Outlook set up for use as a client for an Exchange server and to send and receive Internet or intranet messages, you have two possible places—your Exchange store and your Personal Folders file—in which Outlook can store data items. One of these is the default in which Outlook saves all data items, not only messages, but also all calendar, contact, deleted items, drafts, journal, note, and task data items.

To see which location is the default, select View, Folder List to display the folder list, which should look similar to the one in Figure 3.11.

Figure 3.11
This is a typical folder list for Outlook set up as a client for an Exchange server and for Internet or intranet e-mail.

This folder list contains four storage locations:

- Hotmail
- Outlook Today - [Mailbox - Gordon Padwick]
- Personal Folders - Gordon
- Public Folders

The first is a Personal Folders file that was automatically created at the time a Hotmail account was created. The second is an Exchange store, identified as such by the word Mailbox. The third—Personal Folders – Gordon—is a Personal Folders file. The fourth—Public Folders—is a location you can use to share information by way of Exchange Server.

→ For information about public folders, **see** "Using Public Folders," **p. 454**.

The second storage location (the Exchange store) shown in Figure 3.11 is identified as the default store by the image of a house over the icon at the left of the location's name. With Outlook set up in this way, all messages you receive (whether from the Exchange Server or from the Internet) are saved in the Exchange store. Likewise, all other Outlook data items you create or receive are saved in the Exchange store.

CHANGING THE DEFAULT STORAGE LOCATION

This section assumes you have set up Outlook as a client for an Exchange server and also to send and receive Internet or intranet e-mail, so that you have an Exchange store and a Personal Folders file available as storage locations.

However many storage locations are available, it's important to understand that one of these is the default location in which Outlook saves all data items. This section explains how you can select the storage location you want Outlook to use.

PART

II

CH

3

Tip from

Gordon Padwick

If you use Outlook as a client for Exchange and are desk-bound, you normally should save all your data items on the server. By doing that, you can take full advantage of Outlook's capability to share information with other people.

Select Tools, E-mail Accounts to display the E-mail Accounts window previously shown in Figure 3.1. In that window, select View or Change Existing E-mail Accounts and click Next to display the window previously shown in Figure 3.10.

The Deliver New E-mail to the Following Location box near the bottom of the window shows the default location in which Outlook currently saves all data items, your Exchange Server store in this case. Although the name of the box seems to apply only to e-mail messages, in fact, the named location is where Outlook saves all data items.

Open the drop-down Deliver New E-mail to the Following Location list to see the names of all available storage locations.

If you want to change to a different storage location, select that location in the list, and then click Finish. Outlook displays a message stating You have changed the default delivery location for your e-mail. This will change the location of your Inbox, Calendar, and other folders. These changes will take effect the next time you start Outlook.

Click OK to accept the change. Select File, Exit to close Outlook; then restart Outlook.

When Outlook restarts, it displays a message stating that The location messages are delivered to has changed.... Read the message carefully because you might need to follow the recommendations included in it. Click Yes to continue. When an Outlook Information viewer appears, you can, if you want, select View, Folder List. Now, in the Folder List, you'll see the Personal Folders file indicated as the default storage location by the house image superimposed over that folder's icon.

After doing this, Outlook saves all the data items you create or receive in the new default location.

CREATING STORAGE LOCATIONS

To create an additional storage location, select Tools, E-mail Accounts to display the window previously shown in Figure 3.1. Select View or Change Existing E-mail Accounts and click Next to display the window previously shown in Figure 3.10. In that window, click New Outlook Data File to display a dialog box similar to the one shown in Figure 3.12.

Figure 3.12
This dialog box offers the ability to create a Personal Folders file.

This list doesn't include storage locations not under your control, such as your account on an Exchange server. That's because you can't create storage locations on the server from within Outlook. Only the Exchange Server administrator can create storage locations within Exchange Server.

With the dialog box shown in Figure 3.12 displayed, click OK to display the Create or Open Outlook Data File dialog box. Here you can select the location within the Windows file structure where you want to save the file and enter a name for the file. Click OK to display the dialog box shown in Figure 3.13.

Figure 3.13
Use this dialog box to customize the new Personal Folders file.

The dimmed File box at the top of the dialog box shown in Figure 3.13 contains the path of the new file. Enter a name by which Outlook will identify the new file in the Name box. Select an encryption setting and, optionally, protect the file with a password.

Click OK to close the Create Microsoft Personal Folders dialog box and return to the Outlook Data Files dialog box previously shown in Figure 3.12. The list of data files in this dialog box now contains the name of the new data file. Close that dialog box to return to the E-mail Accounts dialog box previously shown in Figure 3.10. In that dialog box, you can open the Deliver New E-mail to the Following Location drop-down list and, if you want, select the new data file as the default in which Outlook saves all new items.

You can select View, Folder List to see the new data file as one of your folders. If you do this without making the new data file your default, that data file contains only a Deleted Items folder. If you do make the new data file your default and follow the instructions to close and then restart Outlook, the Folder List shows the new data file with a complete set of Outlook's standard folders.

→ For more information about working with data files and Outlook's folders, **see** "Managing Outlook Folders," **p. 299**.

GROUPING E-MAIL ACCOUNTS

Prior to Outlook 2002, Outlook handled all accounts separately. By default, Outlook 2002 still handles all accounts separately, but it does enable you to create groups of accounts. If you have only a few accounts, as many people do, the ability to create groups of accounts is of little practical value. However, if you have a substantial number of accounts, creating groups can save you a lot of time. By grouping your accounts, you can specify settings for a group instead of having to specify settings for each account separately.

To work with groups of accounts, select Tools, Options, select the Mail Setup tab in the Options dialog box, and click Send/Receive. The Send/Receive dialog box is where you can create account groups and specify group settings.

→ For information about creating account groups, **see** "Sending and Receiving Messages," **p. 555**.

TROUBLESHOOTING

E-MAIL ACCOUNTS

Many people seem to have few problems in creating and using e-mail accounts in Outlook. Unfortunately, other people experience many difficulties.

When you're creating e-mail accounts in Outlook, it's very important to get detailed information about server requirements from the server administrator and to exactly follow the instructions the administrator provides.

If you work in a large organization and are using Outlook as a client for Exchange Server, the administrator and support staff are likely to be very experienced in creating e-mail accounts in Outlook. Problems are likely to arise, though, in a small organization that doesn't have a full-time server administrator. Setting up Exchange Server is not all that difficult if you stay with the basics, but it can become quite complex if you go beyond the basics. I recommend that, if you run into Exchange Server problems that are beyond your experience, you should seek the help of an experienced consultant.

To set up Outlook to send and receive Internet e-mail, you need information from your ISP. Well-established ISPs should have exactly the information you need, but I've come across some ISPs who offer no help for Outlook users. In that case, you should at least be able to get some basic setup information that, with some thought, you can translate into Outlook settings.

Drop-outs are a common problem for people who use a dial-up connection to an ISP. You might find that you can connect to your ISP, start sending and receiving messages, and then suddenly become disconnected. One possible cause for this problem is a poor-quality telephone line, something that's more likely in rural areas than in cities. If you experience this problem more than just occasionally, you should ask your telephone company to test the line. The result of this test might result in the discovery of a problem the company is willing to remedy.

If the telephone line seems to be satisfactory, your ISP might be the culprit. Some ISPs have a reputation for frequent drop-outs—that's why I suggested previously in this chapter that you should inquire about local people's experience with an ISP before signing up. The only solution to an unreliable ISP is to change to one that has a better reputation.

CHAPTER 4

SENDING MESSAGES

In this chapter

Most of the material covered in this chapter applies specifically to sending e-mail by way of the Internet, an intranet, and Hotmail, although much applies also to sending e-mail by way of an Exchange server. A section at the end of the chapter covers using Outlook to send faxes.

→ For additional information that applies only to sending e-mail by way of an Exchange server, **see** "Using Exchange Server for E-mail," **p. 427**.

→ For information about sending faxes, **see** "Sending Faxes," **p. 93**.

SENDING MESSAGES DIRECTLY FROM WORD AND OTHER OFFICE APPLICATIONS

With Office XP installed on your computer, you don't necessarily need to have Outlook open to send e-mail. Suppose you have a document in Word, a workbook in Excel, a presentation in PowerPoint, or a database in Access and you want to send it to someone by e-mail. One way to do that is to create a message in Outlook, insert the appropriate Office file, and send the message. A simpler way is to send it directly from the original application.

→ For information about inserting files into an Outlook message, **see** "Inserting a File," **p. 80**.

Consider a Word document, for example. If the Word document is already open, simply select File and move the pointer onto Send To. Word offers you several ways to send the file, as shown in Figure 4.1.

Figure 4.1
Select one of these ways to send the document.

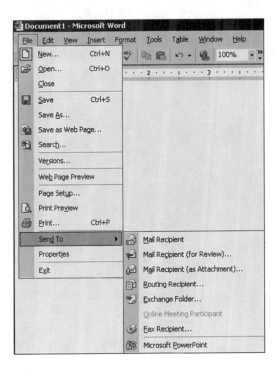

If you select Mail Recipient, Word displays the dialog box shown in Figure 4.2.

Figure 4.2
Fill in the four boxes
near the top of this
dialog box.

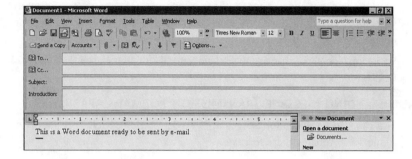

Address the message in the same manner as you address an Outlook message, enter an appropriate subject, and—optionally—enter some text as an introduction. Click Send a Copy in the toolbar to send the message.

→ For information about addressing a message, **see** "Addressing the Message," **p. 70**.

You can send messages from Excel and PowerPoint in the same way. Access gives you only the ability to send a database as an attachment.

Note

For more detailed information about sending from within Office applications, see such books as *Special Edition Using Microsoft Excel 2002* (ISBN: 0-7897-2511-8) and *Special Edition Using Microsoft Word 2002* (ISBN: 0-7897-2515-0), both published by Que.

USING OUTLOOK TO SEND AND RECEIVE E-MAIL

If you have an Internet e-mail account with an Internet service provider (ISP), you can use Outlook to exchange e-mail messages with anyone who also has an Internet e-mail account. You can also use Outlook to exchange e-mail messages by way of an intranet that uses Internet protocols. Outlook sends messages to your mail server, which routes those messages to recipients' mail servers. Messages addressed to you are delivered to your mail server, from which you can retrieve them.

Outlook saves copies of messages you send in the Sent Items folder. Outlook saves messages you receive in the Inbox folder.

Note

The folders named in the preceding paragraph are the folders Outlook uses by default. You can set up Outlook to save copies of messages you send in folders other than Sent Items and to save messages you receive in folders other than Inbox.

SELECTING A MESSAGE FORMAT AND E-MAIL EDITOR

Outlook lets you choose among three transmission formats for sending messages. By default, Outlook sends all original messages you create in the HTML format. You can change that default, and you can select a different transmission format for individual messages.

→ For information about changing the default transmission format, **see** "Setting the Message Format," **p. 562**.

UNDERSTANDING MESSAGE TRANSMISSION FORMAT CAPABILITIES

You can choose to send messages in HTML, Outlook Rich Text, or Plain Text format. Table 4.1 compares these formats.

Tip from

Don't assume the people to whom you send e-mail messages will be able to receive your messages with all the formatting you create, nor that they will be able to open attachments to your messages. In some cases, you might have to send sample messages to ascertain whether the e-mail programs recipients use are capable of receiving what you send.

TABLE 4.1   MESSAGE FORMATS

Transmission Format	Description
HTML	The *Hypertext Markup Language (HTML)* format offers you the ability to quickly and easily create highly formatted pages that include horizontal lines, pictures, animated graphics, and multimedia files. You can also select a stationery that provides a background design for your messages. Use this format only if you know that the message recipients use e-mail programs that can read HTML.
Outlook Rich Text	Outlook Rich Text is the standard Exchange format, so it's appropriate for Outlook used as a client for Exchange. You can select fonts, font sizes, and font colors, and you can format paragraphs. You can embed objects, including pictures, within the text. Don't use this format to send messages that contain attachments to people who aren't using Outlook or Windows Messaging to receive e-mail. Instead of receiving the attachments you sent, recipients will see attachments called `Winmail.dat` that don't contain any meaningful information.
Plain Text	This format does what you'd expect; you can use it for unformatted text, and you can attach files and Outlook items to Plain Text messages. Despite its limitations, this format is your best choice for general e-mail and messages to newsgroups. Use this format for e-mail you send to people who aren't using Outlook or Windows Messaging as their e-mail programs. You can, of course, use this format for messages to people who do use Outlook or Windows Messaging.

To be on the safe side, use Plain Text for Internet e-mail unless you really need the formatting capabilities of HTML. If you do use HTML, be prepared for the fact that some recipients might not receive your messages as you intend. An advantage of the Plain Text format is that it results in smaller files, something that's important for people who pay for Internet access by the minute, or pay long-distance phone charges.

As described subsequently in this chapter, you can use any of these mail formats to send messages that have attachments.

When you reply to a message you've received, Outlook automatically uses the same message format as the message you received. Similarly, if you want to annotate a message you've received and then forward the message, Outlook uses the same format as the message you received.

SELECTING A MAIL EDITOR

A *mail editor* is a tool you use to create messages. No matter which mail transmission format you select, you can use Outlook's native editor or Word as your editor. Word is Outlook's default message editor if you have Word installed on your computer.

The advantage of using Word is that you can use Word's capabilities, such as justification and creating borders, that aren't available in Outlook's native editor.

One of the disadvantages of using Word is the slight delay incurred in loading Word the first time you start editing in any Outlook session. Another disadvantage of using Word is that recipients of your messages who aren't also using Word often see attachments as meaningless `Winmail.dat` files.

Note

> You'll find many places in this chapter that point out the differences between what you can do while using Word as your mail editor and what you can do while using the native Outlook editor. I apologize if you find this confusing, but all I can say is that's the way Outlook is.

→ For information about changing from Word to the native Outlook editor, **see** "Setting the Message Format," **p. 562**.

CREATING A MESSAGE

The following information assumes you're using the default settings for Outlook: HTML as the message transmission format and Word as your mail editor. You'll notice some differences if you've selected a different transmission format as the default and if you chose to use Outlook's native editor.

OPENING THE MESSAGE FORM

To create a message, start by displaying the Inbox Information viewer. Click New at the left end of the Standard toolbar, or select Actions, New Mail Message. Outlook displays a message form similar to that shown in Figure 4.3 or Figure 4.4, depending on which mail editor you're using.

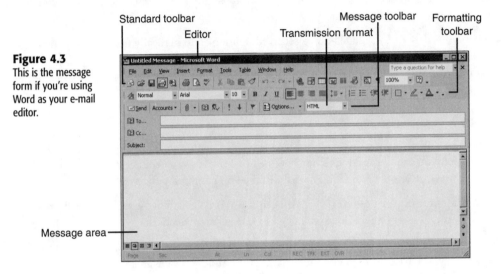

Figure 4.3
This is the message form if you're using Word as your e-mail editor.

The message form is shown in Figure 4.3 with the Standard and Formatting toolbars displayed. These are the same toolbars you see when you're using Word independently. The buttons in the third toolbar are unique to Outlook. All the buttons in the Formatting toolbar and some of the buttons in the Standard toolbar are enabled only when the pointer is in the message area of the form.

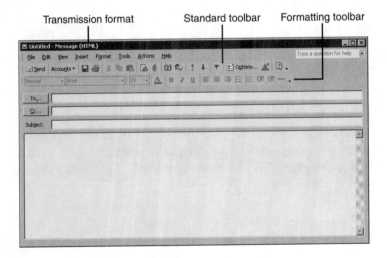

Figure 4.4
This is the message form if you're using the native Outlook editor.

The message form is shown in Figure 4.4 with the Standard and Formatting toolbars displayed. Notice the significant differences between the buttons in the toolbars when using Word as the mail editor compared with using the native Outlook editor.

The menu bar is different depending on whether you're using Word or the native editor. If you're using Word as your editor, the Word menu bar is displayed and each menu contains Word menu items. On the other hand, if you're using the native editor, the available menu items relate only to Outlook.

If you want to use a different transmission format for the message you're about to create, instead of following the first paragraph in this section, select Actions, New Mail Message Using. When you do that, Outlook displays the list shown in Figure 4.5.

Figure 4.5
You can select any item in this list.

The options are

- **More Stationery**—Displays a list of stationeries from which you can select one to use for this message.

- **Microsoft Word (HTML)**—Creates this message employing the HTML transmission format, possibly with the use of a stationery.

- **Microsoft Office**—Creates this message as an Access data page, Excel worksheet, or Word document. Use this option to open Access, Excel, or Word so you can create one of these Office documents directly within Outlook.

- **Plain Text**—Creates this message employing the Plain Text transmission format.

- **Rich Text**—Creates this message employing the Rich Text transmission format.

- **HTML (No Stationery)**—Creates this message employing the HTML transmission format without the use of stationeries.

→ For information about stationeries, **see** "Using Stationery," **p. 77**.

CHANGING THE MESSAGE TRANSMISSION FORMAT

After you've opened the Message form shown previously in Figure 4.3, you can change the transmission format. With Word as your mail editor, open the Message Format drop-down list in the Message toolbar. There, you can select HTML, Rich Text, or Plain Text. Whichever you select applies only to the current message.

If you're using the native Outlook editor, you select a message transmission format differently. In the Message form, shown previously in Figure 4.4, click Format to display a menu that includes Plain Text and HTML—HTML is checked if that's the default message transmission format. You can

- **Switch to Plain Text**—Just select that transmission format.
- **Switch to Rich Text**—Select Plain Text, and then click Format again. Now you can select Rich Text in the Format menu.

ADDRESSING THE MESSAGE

The blank message forms shown previously in Figures 4.3 and 4.4 contain the message header consisting of the To, Cc, and Subject boxes, which is what Outlook always displays if you're using Word as your editor. If you're using Outlook's native editor, you might see only the To box; in that case, select View, Message Header in the form's menu bar to display the complete message header.

Figure 4.6 shows a typical message form (using Word as the editor) with recipient addresses, subject, and message text entered. Apart from the different toolbars and menu bar, the form when you use the native editor is similar.

Figure 4.6
This message is ready
to send.

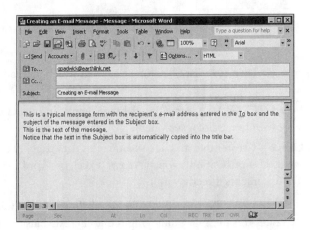

To address the message, enter one or more recipient e-mail addresses in the To box. You can do so in several ways, each of which is convenient in specific circumstances.

→ For more information about addressing a message, **see** "Addressing E-mail and Faxes," **p. 183**.

Note

The following sections make frequent reference to your Contact List. To use the information in these sections, you must already have Contact entries in your Address Book.

MANUALLY ENTERING E-MAIL ADDRESSES

If you know recipients' e-mail addresses, you can enter those addresses in the To box, separating one address from the next with a semicolon. If you're sending the message to just one person, enter something like

```
c_anderson@pumpkin.com
```

in the To box. If you're sending a message to two people, enter something such as

```
c_anderson@pumpkin.com;fgrambo@quickmail.net
```

separating one name from the next with a semicolon. If you're sending mail to all the people in a distribution list, enter the name of the distribution list in the To box.

→ For information about distribution lists, **see** "Working with Distribution Lists," **p. 174**.

After you've finished entering addresses, press Tab to move to the next box. At that time, Outlook attempts to verify the e-mail addresses you entered by comparing them with information in your Address Book, a process referred to as *resolving* addresses.

Tip from

Gordon Crock

After you've entered names in the To box, you can click the Check Names button in the Message toolbar (with Word as the editor) or in the Standard toolbar (with the native editor). When you do that, Outlook looks in your Address Book for the names you entered. Outlook confirms the existence of names by underlining them. If Outlook doesn't find a name, it displays a dialog box in which you can select from a list of similar names or open your Address Book to select a name.

When Outlook finds an address you've entered in the Address Book, Outlook replaces the address with the person's name and underlines that name. If Outlook doesn't find the e-mail address in your Address Book but does recognize the address as being in acceptable Internet format, it simply underlines the address you entered. If Outlook doesn't recognize the address as being in Internet format, Outlook leaves the name as you entered it without underlining it.

If you enter several recipients' e-mail addresses, some of them might be in your Address Book, but others might not. If that's the case, the To box contains a mixture of e-mail addresses and people's names.

ENTERING RECIPIENTS' NAMES INSTEAD OF E-MAIL ADDRESSES

If you're sending a message to recipients whose names and e-mail addresses are in your Address Book, you can enter names instead of e-mail addresses. After you enter one or more names, separating one from the next with a semicolon, press Tab to move to the Cc box. At that time, Outlook looks for the names in your Address Book. If Outlook finds a name, Outlook underlines the name to indicate that it is acceptable.

To be sure the e-mail address is correct, right-click the person's name to display a context menu. Click Properties in the context menu to display the dialog box shown in Figure 4.7.

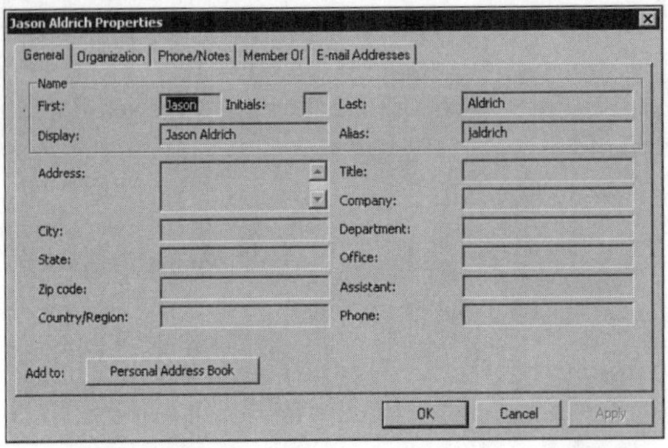

Figure 4.7
The General tab in this
dialog box shows the
person's default
e-mail address in the
Alias box.

> **Caution**
>
> The fact that Outlook underlines a name in the To box on the Message form indicates
> only that the name exists in your Address Book, not that the Address Book contains an
> e-mail address for the contact. That's why you should check a name's Properties to
> make sure an e-mail address is available.

ENTERING PARTIAL RECIPIENT NAMES

Instead of entering the complete names of recipients, you can enter partial names. For
example, you could enter Frank and press Tab. Outlook searches your Address Book and, if
it finds only one Frank, it displays that Frank's full name and underlines it. You should check
the name's properties, as previously described, to ensure Outlook has chosen the correct
e-mail address.

If two or more Franks are in your Address Book and you haven't previously sent e-mail to
either of them, Outlook places a squiggly red line under the name you entered to indicate
that you have to make a decision. Right-click the name you entered and Outlook displays a
list of all the Franks in your Address Book. Select the one to whom you want to send this
message.

If there are two or more Franks in your address book and you have previously sent e-mail to
any of them, Outlook assumes you want to send e-mail to the most recent Frank address
you used and displays that person's name in the To box, underlined in green. To select a different Frank, right-click the name in the To box and then select the name you want to use.

SELECTING NAMES IN YOUR ADDRESS BOOK

Instead of entering recipients' names or e-mail addresses, you can select these names from
your Address Book. In the Message form, click To to display the contacts in your address
book, as shown in Figure 4.8.

Figure 4.8
The Select Names dialog box shows the names in your Address Book. These names are listed at the left side of the dialog box.

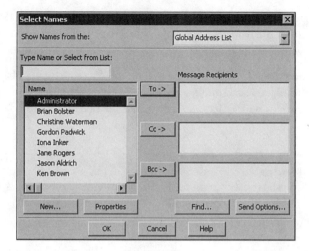

You can use three methods to select recipients from the names in your Address Book.

One method is to scroll down the list of names, select the name of one recipient, and then click To to copy that name into the Message Recipients list at the right side of the dialog box. Click OK to return to the Message form, in which the name you selected is displayed in the To box.

Tip from

To designate more than one recipient, select the first, and then hold down Ctrl while you select others. To select recipient names that are listed consecutively, select the first name and hold Shift while you select the last name.

Alternatively, you can repeatedly click To on the Message form to add names one at a time.

Instead of scrolling through the list, you can enter a person's name in the Type Name or Select from List box. When you do that, Outlook finds the first name in the list that matches what you enter.

A third alternative is to click Find. When you do that, Outlook displays a dialog box in which you can enter a contact's name, e-mail address, address, or phone number, and then click Find. If any of the information is stored in your address book, Outlook matches it to a contact.

After you've selected recipients, click OK to return to the Message dialog box that now shows recipients' names in the To box.

SENDING CARBON COPIES AND BLIND CARBON COPIES OF MESSAGES

A traditional business practice is to send messages to people whom you expect to take some action as a result of the message and to send carbon copies (cc) to people who should know about the message but aren't expected to take any action as a result of it. When you use Outlook, everyone whose name is on the To and Cc lists sees everybody else's name, so all recipients know who sees the message.

Sometimes you might want to send a copy of a message to someone without other recipients knowing. That's when you send a blind carbon copy (bcc). The recipients of blind carbon copies see all the names on the To and Cc lists, but the people on the To and Cc lists don't see the names on the Bcc list.

Tip from

Blind carbon copy is also useful when you want to send a message to a distribution list without revealing the names of everyone on the list to all recipients. In that case, leave the To and Cc boxes empty and enter the name of the distribution list in the Bcc box.

The header of the Outlook Message form contains a Cc box. You can add names and e-mail addresses into it in the same way you add names and addresses to the To box. One minor difference is that if you select names from those listed in your Address Book, you click Cc to copy names into the appropriate Message Recipients list.

Note

The Message form's default header doesn't contain a Bcc box. If you use the Select Names dialog box to copy names into the Bcc list, Outlook automatically expands the Message form's header to show the Bcc box. If you're using Word as your editor, open the Options drop-down list in the Message toolbar and click Bcc to display the Bcc box; if you're using the native Outlook editor, select View, Bcc Field to display the Bcc field.

You might notice that you also can display a From box in a Message form. This box doesn't allow you to send a message so that it appears to come from someone else. The box is used when you're using Outlook as a client for Exchange. In that environment, subject to appropriate permissions, you can send a message on behalf of someone else. Recipients see two names as the source of such a message: the name of the person who actually sent the message and the name of the person on behalf of whom the message was sent.

→ For information about sending a message on behalf of another person, **see** "Sending Mail on Someone Else's Behalf," **p. 447**.

ENTERING A MESSAGE SUBJECT

To enter a subject for a message, move the insertion point into the Subject box, type the text of the subject, and then press Tab to move the insertion point into the message box. As soon as you press Tab, the subject text replaces the original "Untitled" at the left end of the message form's title bar.

You should use succinct and meaningful subjects for your messages. Remember that what you enter in the Subject box is what recipients subsequently see in their inboxes. If the subject doesn't look interesting and relevant, recipients might choose to ignore your message. Busy people often only look at messages they perceive to be important.

Note

Some people deliberately omit entering a subject for their messages, maybe because they're too lazy to do so or because they think curiosity will ensure that recipients open those messages. You should avoid this practice because most people regard it as discourteous.

Although Outlook allows you to enter as many as 256 characters in the Subject box, you should use only four or five well-chosen words.

ENTERING THE MESSAGE TEXT

Say what you have to say briefly and clearly.

Because I'm assuming that you're using the HTML message format, you might expect to find detailed information about HTML here so that you can create beautifully formatted messages. However, this book is about Outlook. If you want to learn all about HTML, consult a book on that subject.

If possible, don't quickly type your message and then send it. Take some time to review what you've typed and make sure it's really what you want to say.

→ To learn about saving a draft of a message that you're not ready to send, **see** "Saving a Message Draft," **p. 91**.

FORMATTING THE MESSAGE TEXT

The Formatting toolbar isn't enabled until you move the insertion point into the message box that occupies the bottom part of the Message form.

Tip from

If the Formatting toolbar isn't displayed, select View on the Message form's menu bar, move the pointer onto Toolbars, and click Formatting.

In the Office style, the first part of the Formatting toolbar is displayed at the right of the Message form's Standard toolbar to provide as much vertical space as possible within the message area. As a result, you don't see all the buttons in the Standard and Formatting toolbars. To see all the buttons in the Formatting toolbar, click the button at the right end of the part that's displayed. Then, you'll see the buttons in a box.

You can drag the vertical bar at the left end of the Formatting toolbar down to display the entire toolbar below the Standard toolbar, or drag it farther to display the toolbar as a floating toolbar on top of the form. When you don't need to see the entire Formatting toolbar, you can drag it back to its original position.

The buttons available in the Formatting toolbar when you're using the HTML or Rich Text message transmission format and Word as the editor are listed in Table 4.2. The same buttons, with the exceptions of those marked with an asterisk, are available when you're using the native editor. In addition to the buttons listed, the native editor has an Insert Horizontal Line button. No text formatting is available when you're using the Plain Text transmission format.

TABLE 4.2 FORMATTING TOOLBAR BUTTONS FOR THE WORD EDITOR

Button	Button Name	Purpose
Normal	Style	Select an HTML format from a list of formats
Arial	Font	Select a font from a list of fonts installed on your computer
10	Font Size	Select a font size from a list
B	Bold	Make selected text bold
I	Italic	Make selected text italic
U	Underline	Underline selected text
	Align Left	Left-align selected paragraphs
	Center	Center selected paragraphs
	Align Right	Right-align selected paragraphs
	Justify*	Align left and right margins
	Line Spacing*	Select from a list of available line spaces
	Numbering	Number selected paragraphs
	Bullets	Add bullets to selected paragraphs
	Decrease Indent	Decrease left indent of selected paragraphs
	Increase Indent	Increase left indent of selected paragraphs
	Outside Border*	Select from available borders

TABLE 4.2   CONTINUED

Button	Button Name	Purpose
	Highlight*	Select from available colors
	Font Color	Select from available colors or open the Colors dialog box to create custom colors

You might be wondering whether you can rely on recipients seeing your messages exactly as you formatted them. If you use Outlook's HTML message format and the people who receive your messages use an e-mail program that's completely compatible with Outlook (such as Outlook or Outlook Express), those people will see your messages exactly as you created them. However, HTML is an evolving standard; it's quite possible that people who receive your messages use an HTML-compatible e-mail program that doesn't interpret HTML in exactly the same way as Outlook. Likewise, you might receive HTML-formatted e-mail messages from other people that Outlook doesn't interpret properly.

If you want to ensure that people see your messages exactly as you create them, use Plain Text format. As mentioned previously, one significant advantage of Plain Text is that it results in significantly smaller messages that are faster to send and receive.

USING STATIONERY

When you're using HTML as your message format, you can choose a stationery to provide a background for your messages.

By default, Outlook creates messages on a plain background using whatever scheme you've selected for Windows Appearance (in the Windows Control Panel). The default Windows Standard scheme provides a white background. You can select a stationery that provides a background appropriate for certain kinds of messages.

Tip from

Using a stationery increases the size of your messages, so they take longer to send and receive. Most people prefer not to receive business messages based on a stationery. I recommend that you use stationeries only for personal messages to your friends.

You can select a default stationery to use in the majority of messages, and you can select a different stationery for individual messages.

→ For information about selecting a default stationery, **see** "Selecting Stationery and Fonts," **p. 565**.

The next time you start to create a message, you'll see the default stationery you selected as a background for your message. After you've chosen a stationery, Outlook uses that stationery for all your messages except those for which you explicitly specify a different stationery or no stationery.

To create a message using a stationery other than the default, select Actions, move the pointer onto New Mail Message Using, and click More Stationery. Outlook displays the Select a Stationery box, which lists the stationeries you have available. Select the stationery you want to use for the current message.

Note

To create a message that doesn't use a stationery, select Blank in the list of stationeries.

SIGNING MESSAGES

You can have Outlook automatically sign the messages you send. First, you must create one or more signatures. Creating and using signatures is significantly different depending on whether you use Word or the native Outlook editor.

CREATING AND USING SIGNATURES WITH WORD AS THE E-MAIL EDITOR

If you use Word as your e-mail editor, you have to create the signature in Word.

To create a signature in Word:

1. Start a new message using Word as your mail editor.
2. In the Message form, select Tools, Options, and select the General tab.
3. Click E-mail Options to display the dialog box shown in Figure 4.9.

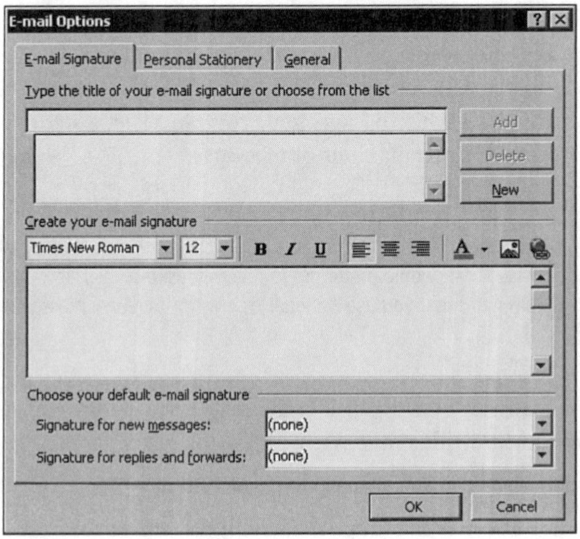

Figure 4.9
This dialog box opens with the E-mail Signature tab selected.

4. Enter a name for the signature in the box at the top of the dialog box.

5. Enter the text for your signature in the Create Your E-mail Signature box. You can use the buttons in the Formatting toolbar above that box to format your signature and to add a picture or a hyperlink.

6. Click Add. The name of the new signature appears in the list of signature names and also in the Signature for New Messages box and the Signature for Replies and Forwards box.

7. Repeat steps 4–6 to create additional signatures.

8. Select the signature you want to have as the default for new messages and the signature you want as the default for replies and forwards.

After creating one or more signatures, you can insert those signatures into any message while you're using Word as your mail editor. To do so, place the insertion point where you want the signature to appear; then select Insert, move the pointer onto AutoText, and click E-mail Signature. Outlook displays a list of your signature names (the names you entered in step 4 of the preceding procedure). Select a name and the corresponding signature appears in the message.

CREATING AND USING SIGNATURES WITH THE NATIVE OUTLOOK EDITOR

With any Outlook Information viewer displayed, select Tools, Options to display the Options dialog box. Select the Mail Format tab. Follow the procedure described in Chapter 27, "Setting Outlook's Options," to create one or more signatures.

→ For information about creating a signature, **see** "Signing Messages," **p. 567**.

After creating one or more signatures, you can insert those signatures into any message while you're using the native Outlook editor as your mail editor. To do so, place the insertion point where you want the signature to appear, and then select Insert, Signature. Outlook displays a list of your signature names. Select a name and the corresponding signature appears in the message.

MESSAGE INSERTIONS

In the early days of e-mail, you could send only standard alphanumeric characters. Now, e-mail messages can contain almost anything, including

- Character sets other than U.S. ASCII
- Images (still and moving)
- Sounds
- Computer files

In Outlook, you can also insert Outlook items within messages.

This capability depends on senders' and recipients' computers having the capability to encode and decode non-ASCII inclusions. Outlook uses the Multipurpose Internet Mail Extensions (MIME) protocol for this purpose.

Note

You can select UUENCODE instead of MIME for encoding and decoding, but only if you're using Plain Text as your message transmission format. To do so, display the Options dialog box's Mail Format tab and click Internet Format to open a dialog box in which you can check the box labeled Encode Attachments in UUENCODE Format when Sending a Plain Text Message.

INSERTING A FILE

You can insert any file into a message from a disk on your computer or from a disk on another networked computer that's available for sharing.

To insert a file:

1. In the Message form's menu bar, select Insert, File to display the dialog box shown in Figure 4.10.

Figure 4.10
The Insert File dialog box initially displays the files and folders in your default folder.

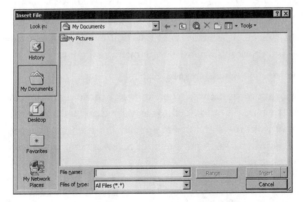

2. You can click any of the buttons in the bar at the left to select specific file locations. After clicking one of those buttons, open the drop-down Look In list to see the relevant folder structure, in which you can select a folder and then select a file within that folder. You can also navigate in the Insert File dialog box in the usual way to select a file.

3. Click Insert. An Attach box appears in the Message form's header containing the name of the inserted file and its size, as shown in Figure 4.11.

Figure 4.11
The names of inserted files are shown in the Attach box in the Message form's header.

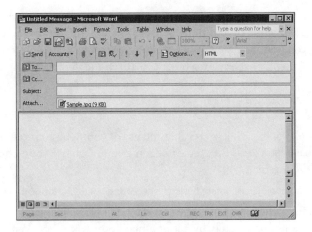

The preceding procedure describes how to insert files into a message. You also can insert a text file as text within a message. In step 3, instead of clicking Insert, click the button marked with a black triangle immediately at the right of the Insert button. When you do so, a menu containing Insert and Insert as Text appears. Click Insert as Text to insert the text file into the message.

Note

To delete an inserted file or item, delete it from the Attach box.

INSERTING AN OUTLOOK ITEM

You can insert any of your Outlook items as text into a message and attach items to a message. This capability, however, is available only if you're using the native Outlook editor.

To attach or insert an Outlook item into a message, select Insert, Item to display the dialog box shown in Figure 4.12.

Figure 4.12
The top pane in the Insert Item dialog box shows your Outlook folders with one folder selected. Items in the selected folder are listed in the bottom pane.

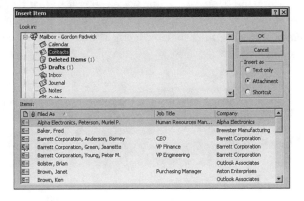

Select the folder that contains the item you want to include in the message. You might have to use the vertical scrollbar to find the folder you want. Scroll down the bottom pane to locate the item you want to attach or insert; then select that item. Select Text Only if you want to insert the item, or select Attachment to attach the item. Click OK.

USING VOTING BUTTONS

Although Outlook's online Help states that the use of voting buttons requires Exchange, several people have found this isn't the case. You can, in fact, use voting buttons in messages sent by way of the Internet.

→ To get detailed information about voting buttons, **see** "Using Voting Buttons," **p. 442**.

You can add voting buttons to a message you send. People who receive a message containing voting buttons can respond simply by clicking one of those buttons. When you receive responses, Outlook automatically tallies those responses and displays a summary of them.

For this to work with Internet messages, you must send the proginal message containing voting buttons using Rich Text Format and recipients must be using Outlook as their e-mail client. Even if you have set Rich Text as the default format in the Options dialog box, you should check that Rich Text is in use. After entering an address in the To box on the Message form, right-click that address and select E-mail Properties. In the E-mail properties box, verify that the Internet Format box contains Send Using Outlook Rich Text Format. If necessary, open the Internet Format drop-down list and select Send Using Outlook Rich Text Format.

INSERTING A HORIZONTAL LINE

If you're using the HTML message transmission format and the native Outlook editor, you can insert a horizontal line in a message. You can use this line to separate parts of a message. To insert a horizontal line, place the insertion point where you want the line to appear and select Insert, Horizontal Line. The horizontal line appears in your message, extending over almost the entire width of the message.

You can adjust the width and depth of the line by selecting it so that handles appear. Drag one of the handles at the left or right end of the line to change its width; drag one of the handles at the center of the line to change its depth. When you increase the depth, the line becomes an empty box.

Note

If you're not using a stationery, you can select a horizontal line in the form, click the Font Color button in the Formatting toolbar, and select a color for the line. After extending the depth of the line to create an empty box, selecting a color results in a solid box. If you use certain stationeries, you can't change the color of a horizontal line.

INSERTING A PICTURE

If you're using the HTML message transmission format, you can insert pictures into a message. An inserted picture appears in the message at the same size it was in its original file. If you want to have a reduced size version of a picture in a message, create a reduced size version before you insert the picture into your message to minimize the size of the message you send.

Note

You can insert pictures saved in the .art, .bmp, .gif, .jpg, .wmf, and .xbf file formats, but not all these formats are compatible with some e-mail clients. You normally should use only .gif and .jpg formats because these are compatible with most e-mail clients, and also because they occupy less space than other formats.

The process of inserting a picture into a message is different according to whether you're using Word or the native Outlook editor as your mail editor.

To insert a picture when using Word as your mail editor, place the insertion point at the position in the message where you want the picture to appear, select Insert in the Message form's menu bar, and move the pointer onto Picture. Outlook displays a menu of picture sources, as shown in Figure 4.13.

PART

II

CH

4

Figure 4.13
Word makes these picture sources available.

Select the picture source you want to use. What happens subsequently depends on the picture source you select. Consult a book such as *Special Edition Using Microsoft Word 2002*, published by Que, for detailed information about this.

To insert a picture when using the native Outlook editor:

1. Place the insertion point where you want the picture to appear in the message.

2. In the Message form's menu bar, select Insert, Picture to display the dialog box shown in Figure 4.14.

3. In the Picture Source box, enter the complete path of the picture. Alternatively, you can click Browse and then navigate to the file.

4. In the Alternate Text box, enter text you want to be displayed if recipients' computers can't display pictures.

5. Open the drop-down Alignment list and select how you want the picture to be aligned in the message.

Figure 4.14
Use this dialog box to identify the picture you want to insert and how you want that picture to appear.

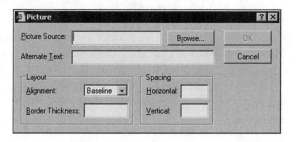

6. If you want the picture to be displayed with a border, enter a number in the Border Thickness box. The number represents the thickness of the border in pixels.

7. In the Spacing section of the dialog box, enter the space (in pixels) you want to have at the sides of the picture in the Horizontal box, and enter the space (in pixels) you want above and below the picture in the Vertical box.

8. Click OK to place the image in the box.

Tip from

After the picture appears in the message, you can drag it to a different position. You can also click the picture to select it, in which case handles appear at the center of its edges and at its corners. You can drag these handles to change the size of the picture. Double-click a picture in a message to open a graphics editor in which you can edit the picture.

INSERTING A HYPERLINK

One way to insert a hyperlink into a message is simply to type the hyperlink. Outlook automatically recognizes anything you type in hyperlink format as a hyperlink. For example, if you type `http://www.quehelp.com` (or just `www.quehelp.com`), Outlook shows it has recognized a hyperlink by changing the color of what you typed to blue and underlining it. This method works for any of the three message transmission formats and with Word or the native Outlook editor as the mail editor.

The other way to enter a hyperlink depends on whether you're using Word or the native Outlook editor as your mail editor.

To insert a hyperlink into a message if you're using the HTML or Rich Text message transmission format and Word as your mail editor:

1. Place the insertion point where you want the hyperlink to appear in the message.

2. Select Insert, Hyperlink to display the dialog box shown in Figure 4.15.

3. Either open the drop-down Address list near the bottom of the dialog box and select a hyperlink or enter a hyperlink in the box.

4. Click OK to close the dialog box. The hyperlink you selected or entered appears in the message.

Figure 4.15
Use this dialog box to enter a hyperlink or to create a hyperlink to an existing location.

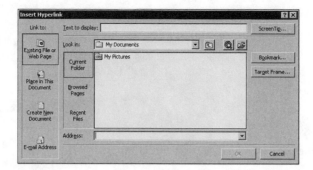

The preceding procedure describes only the simplest way to use the Insert Hyperlink dialog box. For more detailed information, refer to a book such as *Special Edition Using Microsoft Word 2002.*

To insert a hyperlink into a message if you're using the HTML message transmission format and the native Outlook editor as your mail editor:

1. Place the insertion point where you want the hyperlink to be.
2. In the Message form's menu bar, select Insert, Hyperlink to display the dialog box shown in Figure 4.16.

Figure 4.16
This dialog box initially assumes you want to create a hyperlink to a Web site.

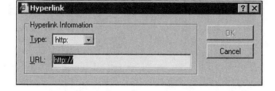

3. Open the drop-down Type list and select the type of hyperlink you want to create. Outlook places the first part of the hyperlink in the URL box, according to the type you select.
4. In the URL box, complete the hyperlink, and then click OK to close the dialog box and insert the hyperlink into the message.

You sometimes might want people to send a message to people and have them send replies to an address other than the one from which you sent the original message. To do that, insert a phrase such as "Please reply to" (usually at the end of the message) and then select Insert, Hyperlink. Click E-mail Address in the bar at the left side of the Insert Hyperlink dialog box, enter the reply address you want people to use in the E-mail Address box, and then click OK. Outlook inserts the reply address as a hyperlink in the original message in this format:

```
mailto:gpadwick@earthlink.net
```

People who receive your message can click that hyperlink to open a Message form already addressed to the address in the hyperlink.

Note

For additional information about inserting hyperlinks in messages and other Outlook items, see the Microsoft Knowledge Base article Q225007, "Using Hyperlinks to Access Outlook Folders and Items." Although this article refers specifically to Outlook 2000, the information seems to apply equally to Outlook 2002.

FLAGGING A MESSAGE

You can flag a message to draw recipients' attention to it. Here's one way to flag a message.

To flag a message:

1. If you're using Word as your mail editor, click the Message Flag button in the Message toolbar. If you're using the native Outlook editor, click the Follow Up button in the Standard toolbar. In either case, Outlook displays the dialog box shown in Figure 4.17.

Figure 4.17
Use this dialog box to select a type of flag.

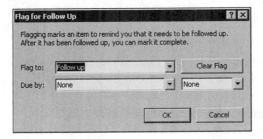

2. Open the drop-down Flag To list to display a list of flag types. Select the type of flag you want to use.

Note

You are not limited to the listed names of flags. You can select any flag so that its name appears in the Flag To box; then replace that name with whatever words are appropriate.

3. By default, the Due By box contains today's date. If you want to change that, click the triangle at the right end of the Due By box to display a one-month calendar. Click the arrows at the ends of the calendar's title bar to display previous or succeeding months. Click a date to close the calendar and display the selected date in the Due By box. If you don't want a date in the reminder, click None at the bottom of the calendar.

→ Instead of selecting a date from the calendar, you can enter descriptive words, such as tomorrow, next week, and so on, and also abbreviations such as "1d" for tomorrow and "1w" for next week, **see** "Describing a Date," **p. 203**.

4. By default, the time box at the right of the Due By box contains the time that corresponds to the end of your workday. You can click the triangle at the right end of the time box to display a list of times from which you can select. Alternatively, you can enter a time into the time box.

→ For information about setting the start and end times for your workday, **see** "Calendar Work Week," **p. 539**.

  5. Click OK. The flag you entered appears in the InfoBar near the top of the Message form, above the To box, as shown in Figure 4.18.

Figure 4.18
This is an example of a flag as it appears in the InfoBar on a Message form.

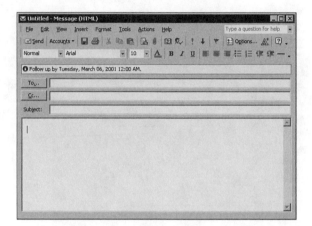

PART

II

CH

4

Flags you attach to messages in the manner just described are flags that are delivered with the message; they are intended for the message recipients. When a person receives a flagged message, that message is normally saved in the person's Inbox. Outlook displays reminders at the appropriate time for flagged messages in the Inbox, but only if those messages remain in the Inbox; Outlook doesn't create reminders if recipients move messages to folders other than the Inbox.

SPELL CHECKING A MESSAGE

With Outlook you can easily check the spelling in the messages you create. Doing so is well worth the few moments it takes. You surely don't want recipients to think less of you because you make spelling errors.

If you're using Word as your mail editor, spell checking works in the same way that it does when you're using Word to create a document. With the option Check Spelling As You Type enabled, Word marks words it considers misspelled with a squiggly red underline while you type. For more information about spell checking in Word, see a book such as *Special Edition Using Microsoft Word 2002*.

The native Outlook editor doesn't have the capability to check spelling while you type. At any time, you can check spelling in a message by selecting Tools, Spelling. After you do so, the editor highlights words that might be misspelled and suggests corrections.

You can enable various options to control how the native editor checks spelling. I particularly recommend you enable Always Check Spelling Before Sending.

→ For information about setting spelling options for the native editor, **see** "Spelling Options," **p. 568**.

SETTING MESSAGE OPTIONS

If you're using Word as your mail editor, click Options in the Message toolbar; if you're using the native editor, click Options in the Standard toolbar. In either case, Outlook displays the dialog box shown in Figure 4.19.

Figure 4.19
Use this dialog box to set various message options.

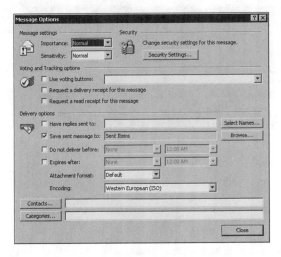

Note

The Security section at the top right is not available unless you have previously obtained a security certificate.

→ To learn how you can obtain a security certificate, **see** "Obtaining a Certificate," **p. 705**.

IMPORTANCE AND SENSITIVITY SETTINGS

In the Message Settings section of the Message Options dialog box, you can select the Importance and Sensitivity of a message. By default, Outlook sets both of these to Normal, but you can change these defaults.

→ For information about changing the default Importance and Sensitivity settings, **see** "Setting Advanced E-mail Options," **p. 535**.

 Open the drop-down Importance list, and select Low, Normal, or High. Instead of making this choice in the Options dialog box, you can click the Importance High button or Importance Low button in the Message form's Message toolbar (when using Word) or Standard toolbar (when using the native editor).

Open the drop-down Sensitivity list, and select Normal, Personal, Private, or Confidential.

SETTING SECURITY

If you've obtained and installed a security certificate on your computer, the two check boxes in the Security section of the Options dialog box are enabled; otherwise, they are disabled.

Use these check boxes to encrypt a message and authenticate a message by adding a digital signature.

→ For detailed information about sending encrypted messages and messages that can be authenticated, **see** "Sending and Receiving Encrypted Messages," **p. 717** and "Sending and Receiving Digitally Signed Messages," **p. 712**.

VOTING AND TRACKING OPTIONS

If you use Outlook to send Internet e-mail, you can use only one of the check boxes in the Voting and Tracking Options section of the Message Options dialog box. That is the Request a Read Receipt for This Message. If you check that box, people who receive your messages are automatically notified that you have requested a read receipt. Those people can choose whether to send a receipt back to you.

→ For more information about read receipts for Internet e-mail, **see** "Responding to a Request for a Read Receipt," **p. 107**.

You can use all three check boxes in this section if you're using Outlook as a client for an Exchange server.

→ For information about voting and tracking options in an Exchange Server environment, **see** "Requesting Receipts," **p. 438** and "Using Voting Buttons," **p. 442**.

By default, the three check boxes in the Voting and Tracking Options section of the Message Options dialog box are unchecked. You can change this so that the Request a Delivery Receipt for This Message and Request a Read Receipt for This Message boxes are checked by default.

→ For information about setting defaults for delivery and read receipts, **see** "Setting Advanced E-mail Options," **p. 535**.

DELIVERY OPTIONS

This section of the Message Options dialog box is where you can specify several aspects of how a message is to be delivered.

When a recipient receives a message and replies to it, the reply normally is sent automatically to your e-mail address. You can, if you like, specify a different e-mail address to which replies should be sent. You might do this if you have an assistant who handles replies, or if you're going to be out of the office for a while.

To have replies automatically sent to an e-mail address other than your own, check the Have Replies Sent To box, and enter the e-mail address in the adjoining box. Instead of entering an e-mail address, you can click Select Names to display your Address Book, and select a name there.

By default, Outlook saves a copy of messages you send in your Sent Items folder. If you don't want to save a copy of a message, uncheck the Save Sent Message To box.

PART
II

CH
4

Note

Instead of saving messages you send in your Sent Items folder, you might prefer to always include yourself in the list of message recipients. In that case, messages you send arrive in your Inbox folder.

If you want to save a copy of the current message in a folder other than your Sent Items folder, leave the Save Sent Message To box checked, click Browse, and select the Outlook folder in which you want to save a copy of the message.

If you check Do Not Deliver Before and then select or enter a date, Outlook keeps the message in your Outbox until the date you specify. The first time you send messages after that date, the message is sent.

Also, if you check Expires After and then select or enter a date, Outlook keeps the message in your Outbox until the specified date, or until (prior to that date) you send messages. The first time you open Outlook after the specified date, the message is automatically deleted from your Outbox.

By default, Outlook encodes message attachments in MIME format. If you use the Plain Text transmission format, you can select UUENCODE as the default encoding.

→ For information about setting the default encoding, **see** "Setting Internet Format," **p. 563**.

You can change the encoding used for attachments for individual messages. To do this, open the Attachment Format drop-down list in the Message Options dialog box. In this list you can select among Default, MIME, UUENCODE, and BINHEX.

Tip from

The default MIME encoding almost always works well. Only if you want to send a message to someone who requests different attachment encoding should you select other than MIME.

The Encoding box refers to the way alphanumeric characters are encoded for transmission. Don't confuse this with the encoding used for attachments. By default, Outlook—as supplied for use in regions that use the roman alphabet—uses Western European (ISO) encoding. If you need to use alternative alphabets, you can open the drop-down Encoding list and select from that list.

ASSIGNING CONTACTS TO A MESSAGE

When you're creating messages (and other Outlook items), keep in mind how you might subsequently want to find those items. You can easily use Outlook to find messages based on the names of the people to whom you sent those messages. Sometimes, though, you might send a message that contains information about one of your contacts, but you don't send a copy to that person.

One possible scenario is that you, as a supervisor, want to send a message to your manager regarding some action you intend to take concerning an employee. In that case, you probably won't send a copy to the employee, but you want to be able to find the message based on that employee's name.

In cases like this, you can enter a person's name in the Contacts box in the Message Options dialog box, or you can select a name from one of your Address Books.

To select a name from one of your Address Books, click Contacts to display a dialog box that lists contacts in your default Contacts folder. You can, if you want, switch to a different Contacts folder. Select one or more contacts, and then click OK to return to the Message Options dialog box with the selected contact or contacts listed in the Contacts box.

ASSIGNING CATEGORIES TO A MESSAGE

As frequently mentioned in this book, assigning categories to Outlook items is key to keeping your Outlook items organized. Click Categories at the bottom of the dialog box to open the Categories dialog box, in which you can assign categories to the message.

→ For detailed information about assigning categories to e-mail messages, **see** "Assigning and Changing Categories in E-mail You Create," **p. 410**.

After making choices in the Message Options dialog box, click Close to return to the Message form.

SAVING A MESSAGE DRAFT

After you've created a message, you don't have to send it immediately; you can save it as a draft to be reviewed or completed later. In fact, while you're creating a message, Outlook automatically saves it periodically as a draft. You can specify the folder in which Outlook saves message drafts and how often it saves those drafts.

→ For information about specifying how Outlook saves drafts, **see** "Setting Advanced E-mail Options," **p. 535**.

<table>
<tr><td>**Tip from**

Gordon Padwick</td><td>To manually save an unsent message, in the Message form's menu bar, select File, Save.</td></tr>
</table>

Subsequently, you can continue working on the message. To do so, select the My Shortcuts group in the Outlook Bar, and click Drafts to see a list of draft messages. Double-click the one you want to work on to display it in the Message form.

<table>
<tr><td>**Note**</td><td>Alternatively, with any Information viewer displayed, you can select View, move the pointer onto Go To, and click Drafts to display a list of draft messages.</td></tr>
</table>

SENDING A MESSAGE

Sending a message is a two-step process. First, Outlook sends a message from the Message form to your Outbox. Then, Outlook sends the message from your Outbox to your mail server, keeping a copy of the message in your Sent Items folder.

PART

II

CH

4

Note

You can set up Outlook so that it attempts to send messages to your mail server immediately after you click Send in the Message form's Standard toolbar. To do this, with any Information viewer displayed, select Tools, Options, and select the Options dialog box's Mail Setup tab. Check Send Messages Immediately When Connected. If Outlook is already connected to the server, it immediately sends the message to the server. Otherwise, Outlook sends the message as soon as a connection to the server becomes available.

SENDING MESSAGES TO YOUR OUTBOX

If you have only one mail account, click Send in the Message form's Message toolbar (using Word as your editor) or Standard toolbar (using the native Outlook editor). Outlook immediately sends the message to your Outbox folder. You can select the My Shortcuts group in the Outlook Bar and then select Outbox to see the messages in your Outbox.

If you have two or more mail accounts and you designated one of these as the default, select Send in the Message form's Standard toolbar to send the message to your Outbox, ready to be sent from the default account. If you want the message to be sent from other than your default mail account, select Accounts in the Message toolbar (Word as mail editor) or in the Standard toolbar (using the native Outlook editor) to display a list of your accounts. Select the account you want to use to send the message.

SENDING MESSAGES FROM YOUR OUTBOX TO THE SERVER

To send messages from your Outbox to your mail server (using any number of accounts on the same server), display any Information viewer, and select Tools. Then move the pointer onto Send/Receive, and select the server you want to use. If necessary, Outlook establishes a connection to the server; then, Outlook starts sending messages.

Instead of selecting Tools, Send, you can select Tools and move the pointer onto Send/Receive to display a list of servers similar to the list shown in Figure 4.20.

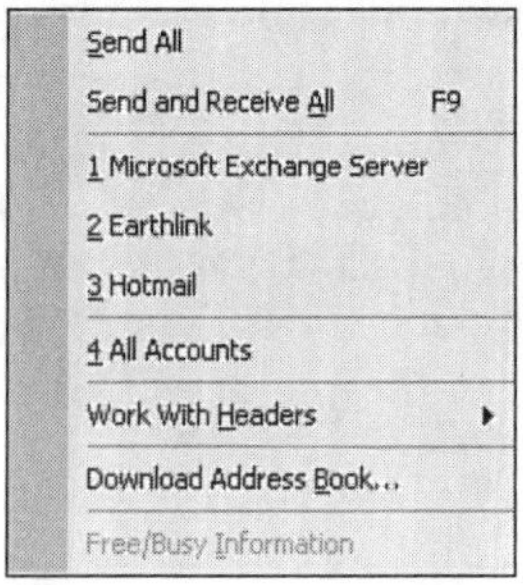

Figure 4.20
This menu contains a typical list of available servers.

Send All
Send and Receive All   F9
1 Microsoft Exchange Server
2 Earthlink
3 Hotmail
4 All Accounts
Work With Headers   ▶
Download Address Book...
Free/Busy Information

RESENDING A MESSAGE

When you send a message to your mail server, Outlook normally moves that message from your Outbox folder to your Sent Items folder. You can select an option that tells Outlook not to save sent items.

→ For information about not saving messages you've sent, **see** "E-mail Options," **p. 533**.

For several reasons, you might need to resend a message you've previously sent. The most likely reason is that you receive a message stating that a message could not be delivered, possibly because you addressed the message incorrectly.

To resend a message, double-click the message in your Sent Items folder to display it in the Message form. Select Actions, Resend This Message to display it in an editable Message form in which you can change any text. For example, if you addressed the original message incorrectly, you can replace the original address with the correct one. After you've made any corrections, click Send to send the message in the normal manner.

SENDING FAXES

Unlike previous Outlook versions, Outlook 2002 doesn't contain any built-in faxing capability. However, you can use various fax transports with Outlook.

At the time Microsoft introduced Outlook 97, faxing was commonly used to transmit information almost instantaneously. Since then, e-mail and instant messaging have largely replaced faxing. Although fax as a communications mechanism is not obsolete, some people would call it obsolescent.

Four years is a short time in the context of many human activities. In the context of electronic communication, though, four years ago is history. In 1997, Microsoft believed that the concept of a universal inbox and outbox was important. That's why Outlook 97 included a faxing capability so that people could save faxes as well as e-mail they received in a single Outlook Inbox folder; Outlook 97 could also send faxes and save those faxes, together with sent e-mail messages, in a single Outlook Sent Items folder. Although the faxing capability provided with Outlook 97 wasn't very sophisticated, it did the job as far as individual faxes were concerned. People who wanted more elaborate faxing capability could use third-party fax software, the most well known of which is Symantec's WinFax Pro.

With Outlook 98 and Outlook 2000, Microsoft continued the tradition of providing basic faxing capability and making it possible to incorporate add-ons such as WinFax Pro if more sophisticated faxing was required.

In Outlook 2002, Microsoft seems to have come to the conclusion that faxing is not something most users need, perhaps inspired by Barry Simon's comment "faxing is e-mail for the computer illiterate." Probably for that reason, Outlook 2002 contains no faxing capability. That doesn't mean you can't use Outlook 2002 to send and receive faxes, however.

PART

II

CH

4

If you really need faxing within Outlook:

- With Outlook 2002 running under Windows 98, install Microsoft Fax, included with Windows 98, as an Outlook E-mail account.
- With Outlook 2002 running under Windows 2000, install the fax transport, included with Windows 2000, as an Outlook E-mail account.

At one time, Microsoft offered Personal Fax for Windows NT, but that's no longer available. Windows Me does not include any faxing capability.

Symantec will probably offer a version of WinFax Pro that can be used with Outlook 2002, but that wasn't available at the time this book was written. Other third-party software suppliers also might offer fax add-ons for Outlook 2002. If and when that happens, the Slipstick site (http://www.slipstick.com) is likely to contain information about such software.

TROUBLESHOOTING

SENDING E-MAIL

In many ways, e-mail is like snail mail: It works almost all the time. When you send a letter by snail mail, the only way you know that the recipient received that message is when you receive a response from the recipient. Similarly, when you send e-mail, the only way you know for certain recipients have received it is when they respond.

Sometimes, messages you send will be undeliverable. This might be because you have addressed them incorrectly or because your server, the recipients' servers, or something in between, is not working. If that happens, you might receive a message in your Inbox from System Administrator. If this happens, check the e-mail address you used and try sending the message again.

Another common reason for messages being undeliverable is your message protocol settings might have become corrupted. If you suspect that might be the case, see Chapter 3, "Managing E-mail Accounts." You can use information in that chapter to correct your account settings.

→ For information about creating e-mail accounts, **see** "Creating E-mail Accounts," **p. 47**.

RECEIVING MESSAGES

In this chapter

Most of the material covered in this chapter applies specifically to receiving Internet, intranet, and Hotmail messages, although much applies also to sending e-mail by way of an Exchange server. A section at the end of the chapter covers using Outlook to receive faxes.

→ For information about receiving faxes, **see** "Receiving Faxes," **p. 111**.

RECEIVING E-MAIL

You can use Outlook to receive e-mail from Internet mail servers that use either the POP3 or IMAP4 protocol as well as from a Hotmail (or other) server that uses the HTTP protocol.

→ To find out more about creating Outlook e-mail accounts, **see** "Creating E-mail Accounts," **p. 47**.

If your computer is always connected to one or more mail servers, messages to you are delivered to your Inbox at intervals you specify. This happens if you have a DSL, an ISDN, or a cable connection to an ISP, or if your computer is currently connected to an Exchange server or a similar messaging system server.

You also can set up Outlook so that, when you initiate exiting from it, it automatically sends all outstanding messages in your Outbox and receives messages waiting for you on servers.

→ For information about specifying how often Outlook connects to mail servers, and whether Outlook does an automatic send and receive before closing, **see** "Selecting Send/Receive Settings," **p. 559**.

If your computer is not always connected to a server, you have to initiate receiving messages. To manually receive e-mail that's waiting for you on a mail server, select Tools, move the pointer onto Send/Receive, and, if you have only one mail account, select that account name. If you have two or more e-mail accounts, you can choose the account you want to use to send and receive messages. Alternatively, if you have several accounts on the same mail server, you can select All Accounts.

Note

Outlook downloads messages in the background while you're working on other tasks.

As incoming messages are received, Outlook displays their headers in the Inbox Information viewer, as described in the next section. Also, if you have the Windows taskbar visible, a box in the taskbar displays the progress of receiving messages.

USING THE INBOX INFORMATION VIEWER

Figure 5.1 shows an example of Outlook's default Inbox Information viewer. Outlook displays message headers in your Outbox, Sent Items, and Drafts folders in similar Information viewers.

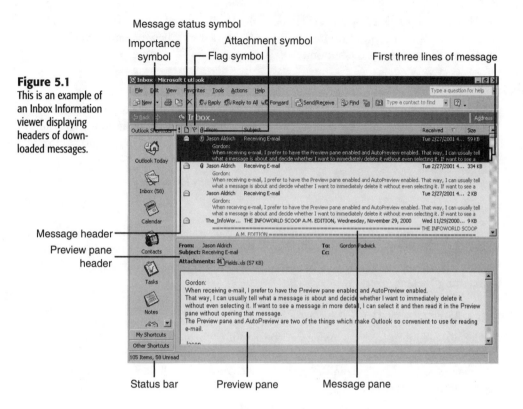

Figure 5.1
This is an example of an Inbox Information viewer displaying headers of down-loaded messages.

If you ever forget what the icons at the top of the Inbox viewer (or any other Table view of Outlook items) represent, move the pointer onto an icon and pause briefly. After a second or so, a ScreenTip appears that contains the icon's name.

The Message pane in the top part of the Information viewer shows message headers and, if AutoPreview is enabled, the first three lines of each message. Four columns at the left of each message contain symbols that provide information about each message.

The Message pane shows messages in a table, although the absence of grid lines might not make that obvious. The four columns at the left are identified by symbols in the row at the top of the table. The other four columns are named.

Initially, the Information viewer lists messages in the order you received them, with the most recent at the top. You can click the symbol or name at the top of each column to reorder messages according to what's in that column. Click the symbol or name at the top of a column again to reverse the order of the messages according to what's in that column. For example, click From in the row at the top of the list of messages to display messages in alphabetical order by sender; click From again to display messages in reverse alphabetical order by sender.

To display messages listed by type, click the symbol at the top of the second column from the left. That lists messages with unread messages at the top. Click the same symbol again to list unread messages at the bottom.

MESSAGE HEADERS

Each message header contains the sender's name, the subject of the message, and the date the message was received by your mail server (not the date Outlook received it). You can customize Outlook to show additional information, such as the message category, in the header. Do that by modifying the message view.

→ To learn how to create custom views, **see** "Creating Custom Views," **p. 679**.

PREVIEWING MESSAGES

AutoPreview, which is turned on by default, is Outlook's capability to display the first three lines of messages below message headers. AutoPreview shows you what messages are about without you having to open them. You can disable AutoPreview (and subsequently enable it) by selecting View, AutoPreview.

VIEWING A MESSAGE IN THE PREVIEW PANE

By default, the Inbox Information viewer consists of two panes, a Message pane and a Preview pane. After you click a message in the Message pane to select that message, the complete message is available in the Preview pane. You can scroll down the Preview pane to see the entire message.

Note

You also can use the Preview pane to view messages in your Sent Items folder. You can't use the Preview pane to view messages in your Outbox folder.

You can remove the Preview pane to enlarge the Message pane so that more message headers are visible. To do so, select View, Preview Pane. After you've removed the Preview pane, select the same command to bring it back.

Tip from

Instead of removing the Preview pane, you can drag the horizontal border between that pane and the Message pane down to increase the size of the Message pane, or up to increase the size of the Preview pane.

The Preview pane has a header in which the sender's name, message subject, message recipients' names, and the names of the people to whom the message is sent as a carbon copy are shown. Also, if the message has attachments, the header lists those attachments as shown previously in Figure 5.1.

CUSTOMIZING THE PREVIEW PANE

To customize the Preview pane, point onto the horizontal line near the top of that pane and right-click. Outlook displays the context menu shown in Figure 5.2.

Figure 5.2
Use this menu to customize the Preview pane.

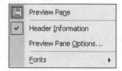

Use the commands in this context menu as follows:

- **Preview Pane**—Removes the Preview pane. To subsequently restore the Preview pane, select View, Preview Pane.
- **Header Information**—Shrinks the Preview pane's header so that only attachments (if any) are shown. To restore the complete header, right-click the top border of the Preview pane to display the same context menu and select Header Information.
- **Preview Pane Options**—Displays the Preview Pane dialog box, shown in Figure 5.3.
- **Fonts**—Displays a list of five font sizes you can select to be used for text in the Preview pane. The sizes are Largest, Larger, Medium, Smaller, and Smallest.

Figure 5.3
Use this dialog box to modify the Information viewer's behavior.

The significance of the check boxes in the dialog box shown in Figure 5.3 is explained subsequently in this chapter.

→ For information about reading messages, **see** "Marking Messages As Read," **p. 101**.

MESSAGE SYMBOLS

The Message pane contains four columns at the left, each column being used for a specific type of symbol.

→ **See** "Outlook's Symbols," **p. 773**, for a list of Outlook's symbols and what each of them means.

The first column is where an Importance symbol might be shown. If a message has Normal importance, no symbol appears. Otherwise, the column contains the Importance High symbol (a red exclamation point) or the Importance Low symbol (a blue down-pointing arrow).

PART

II

CH

5

The second column always contains a symbol. In most cases, that symbol represents an envelope. Unread messages are marked with a closed envelope, and messages you've read are marked with an open envelope. Various other symbols are used: For example, a message you've replied to is marked with an open envelope with a purple arrow. Other symbols appear in this column in the case of mail server messages that warn of a problem with a message you've sent.

The third column contains a symbol that is supposed to look like a flag (most people think it looks like a flower). This symbol is present for messages that are flagged.

The fourth column contains a paper clip symbol in the case of messages that have one or more attachments.

MESSAGE SUMMARIES

The status bar at the bottom of the Information viewer displays the total number of messages in your Inbox and the number of those that are unread.

OPENING MESSAGES

When a message arrives in your Inbox and its header is displayed in your Inbox Information viewer, you can do several things. The following sections describe many of these.

READING A MESSAGE

As explained a couple of pages previously, you can read a message by selecting it in the Message pane so that it's displayed in the Preview pane, and then scroll down the message in that pane.

Alternatively, you can double-click the message to display it in a Message form that's similar to the form you use to create new messages, as shown in Figure 5.4.

Figure 5.4
All the information in the Message form, in which you can see messages you've received, is read-only if it was created using the HTML or Plain Text format. You can directly edit messages that were created in the Rich Text format.

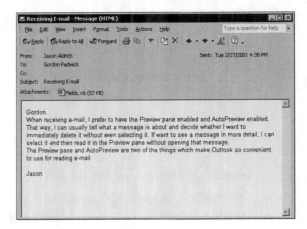

The action of displaying a message in the Message form is referred to as *opening* that message.

You can use the Message form's menus and toolbars to work with the message in various ways.

As the message first appears, you can't edit it (unless it was created in Rich Text). However, you can select Edit, Edit Message to make the received message editable.

 You can click the Follow Up button in the form's Standard toolbar to add a flag to the message—something you might often want to do to remind yourself to do something about the message.

MARKING MESSAGES AS READ

Each message you receive is initially marked with a closed envelope icon in the second column of the Inbox Information viewer. After you open a message to display it in the Message form and then close the Message form, that message is marked by an open envelope symbol in the Inbox Information viewer.

By default, selecting one unread message after another in the Inbox Information viewer's Message pane doesn't change its status from unread to read. However, if, in the Preview Pane dialog box (shown previously in Figure 5.3), you check Mark Messages as Read in Preview Window, Outlook automatically marks messages as read if you display them for more than a certain number of seconds in the Preview pane. Five seconds is the default number of seconds, but you can change that.

You can also set Outlook so that it automatically marks a message as read when, with that message selected, you select a different message. To do that, open the Preview Pane dialog box (shown previously in Figure 5.3) and check Mark Item as Read When Selection Changes.

Note

> The third check box in the Preview Pane dialog box has nothing to do with marking messages as read. If you check Single Key Reading Using Space Bar, you can subsequently select one message after another in the Inbox Information viewer's Message pane by pressing the space bar.

You can use commands in the Inbox Information viewer's Edit menu to control whether individual messages are marked as read or unread. These commands are

- **Mark as Read**—Marks the selected message or messages as read
- **Mark as Unread**—Marks the selected message or messages as unread
- **Mark All as Read**—Marks all messages as read

PART

II

CH

5

DELETING A MESSAGE

If, from the message header, or from the first few lines in the AutoPreview, you quickly decide you don't want to bother with a message, you can immediately delete it. To do so, click the message to select it, and then click the Delete button in the Information viewer's Standard toolbar. In some cases, you might want to take a quick look at the message in the Preview pane before deleting it.

Tip from

If you receive a message you're not expecting, particularly if it's from someone you don't know—and even more particularly if it has one or more attachments—delete the message without opening it. Doing that helps to protect your computer from viruses.

Note

When you delete a message, Outlook moves the message to your Deleted Items folder, from which you can retrieve it if necessary.

→ For more information about deleting messages, **see** "Deleting Messages and Other Outlook Items," **p. 111**.

DISPLAYING A MESSAGE THREAD

Outlook's capability to display related messages in a single list is a very powerful tool, particularly if you send and receive many e-mail messages.

A message *thread*, sometimes referred to as a *conversation*, is a sequence of messages about a specific topic. If you send a message to several people, each of whom replies, you create a thread. The thread is identified by text in the Conversation field in each message. This field initially contains the text in the original message's Subject field. When people reply to the original message, Outlook automatically places the same text in the Conversation field of each reply, even if respondents enter different text in the Subject fields of their replies.

Note

The preceding explanation applies when the sender and respondents all use Outlook as their e-mail programs. If some participants in a conversation use e-mail programs that don't support the Conversation field, their messages won't be automatically identified as part of a thread.

As explained previously, you easily can sort messages in the Inbox and Sent Items Information viewers in several ways. Outlook also provides a way for you to list all items in a thread. To do this, start by selecting any message in a thread to display that message in a Message form. Then, in the Message form, select Actions, move the pointer onto Find All, and click Related Messages. Outlook automatically opens the Advanced Find dialog box with all the messages in the thread listed, as shown in Figure 5.5.

Figure 5.5
Messages in the thread are listed at the bottom of this dialog box. You can double-click any message in this list to open it in a Message form.

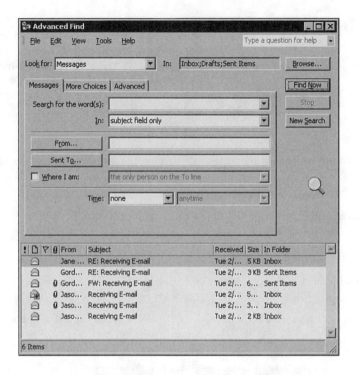

→ For complete information about the Advanced Find dialog box, **see** "Using Advanced Find to Find Words and Phrases," **p. 341**

By default, Outlook searches the Inbox, Drafts, and Sent Items folders in your Personal Folders file for items that have the same text in the Conversation field as the message you originally selected.

Note

If you select the Advanced tab in the Advanced Find dialog box (as shown previously in Figure 5.5), you'll see that Outlook has automatically set the search criterion as the content of the Conversation field, which is exactly the text in the Conversation field of the message you originally selected.

DISPLAYING MESSAGES FROM ONE SENDER

You can use a technique similar to that described in the preceding section to display a list of messages from one sender. Select one message from a particular person to display it in a Message form. Then select Actions, move the pointer onto Find All, and click Messages from Sender. Outlook displays the Advanced Find dialog box, similar to the one previously shown in Figure 5.5, but this time, lists messages from the one person you identified.

Outlook identifies messages by e-mail addresses. When you select a message, as described in the preceding paragraph, you're identifying a person by that person's e-mail address. Subsequently, the Advanced Find dialog box displays all messages from that e-mail address. If the message you select is from a person who uses two or more e-mail addresses, the Advanced Find dialog box doesn't list messages from other e-mail addresses the person uses.

You can double-click any message in the list to open that message in the Message form.

EXAMINING MESSAGE PROPERTIES

You can examine the properties of a message you've received and change a message's importance.

To examine a message's properties:

1. Double-click a message in the Inbox Information viewer to display that message in the Message form.

2. In the form's menu bar, select File, Properties to display a dialog box similar to the one shown in Figure 5.6.

Figure 5.6
This dialog box opens with the General tab selected.

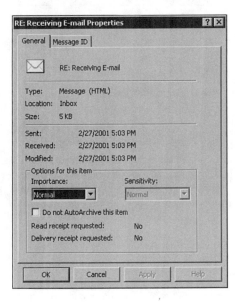

3. If you want to change the importance assigned by the sender, open the drop-down Importance list and select Low, Normal, or High. You can't change the sensitivity of the message, however.

4. If you want to exclude the message from AutoArchiving, check the Do Not AutoArchive This Item box.

→ To understand how Outlook archives items, **see** "AutoArchiving Outlook Items," **p. 392**.

You can select the Message ID tab of the dialog box shown in Figure 5.6. When you do that, you see the unique identification number Outlook assigned to the message.

TRACING THE SOURCE OF A MESSAGE

Although the dialog box shown in Figure 5.6 provides some information about a message, it doesn't provide a means of tracing the source of a message and the route by which it arrived on your computer (something you might want to do if you receive anonymous junk mail).

To trace a message you've received by way of the Internet, right-click the message header in the Inbox Information viewer to display the context menu. Select Options in the context menu to display the dialog box shown in Figure 5.7.

Figure 5.7
Information about the message source and routing is displayed in the Internet Headers box in the lower part of the dialog box.

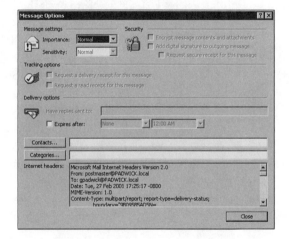

PRINTING A MESSAGE

To print a message you've received, select the message in the Inbox Information viewer's Message pane; then select File, Print. Outlook displays the Print dialog box shown in Figure 5.8.

Tip from

You're not limited to selecting only one message. You can select as many messages as you like in the Message pane.

Figure 5.8
Use this dialog box to
choose how you want
to print the message.

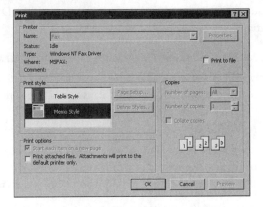

In most cases, the default settings in the Print dialog box are what you want to use. If the message contains attachments, you can check the Print Attached Files box if that's what you want to do; otherwise, leave this box unchecked. Click OK to print the selected message.

HANDLING MESSAGES

You can do several things with a message apart from merely reading it. Some of these are described in the subsequent sections.

REPLYING TO A MESSAGE

To reply to a message, select the message in the Inbox Information viewer, and then click Reply in the viewer's Standard toolbar. Alternatively, if you want to send a reply to everyone to whom the original message was addressed (including those people on the Cc list), click Reply to All. You can't send replies to people the message originator placed on the Bcc list because the message you receive doesn't identify those people.

Note

You can make the same choices when you open a message in the Message form.

Outlook opens a form similar to the form you use to create new messages. In this case, though, the text of the message you're replying to appears in the form with some space above the original message for you to enter your reply. Enter your reply in the space at the top of the form. You also can make comments within the text of the original message (known as *annotating* the message). If the original message is long, you might want to delete all but its first few lines, leaving just enough to remind the originator about the message—there's little point in cluttering up e-mail servers and other people's inboxes with copies of this material.

Note

> The preceding information about replying to a message covers Outlook's default behavior. To modify the default behavior, display any Outlook Information viewer, select Tools, Options, and select the Preferences tab in the Option dialog box. Click E-mail Options. Select the options you want in the On Replies and Forwards section of the dialog box.

When you've finished, send the message in the same way that you send messages you create. If the message you're replying to contained attachments, Outlook doesn't send the attachments with the reply because the person who sent the original message doesn't need another copy of the attachments.

FORWARDING A MESSAGE

You can forward a message to other people. Forwarding a message is similar to replying to a message. Select the message in your Inbox Information viewer, and then select Forward in the viewer's Standard toolbar. Alternatively, open the original message in a Message form, and click Forward.

Enter any introductory comments to the message, annotate the message as you want, and send it. Unlike when you reply to a message, Outlook does send all attachments with forwarded messages. You can select options to modify Outlook's defaults for forwarding messages.

Note

> People have asked how to use Outlook to redirect a message—that is, to send a message you've received to someone else, making it look as though it came directly from the original sender. I suspect Outlook's designers haven't included this capability in an effort to maintain the integrity of e-mail.
>
> Bear in mind that Outlook provides a programming environment. If you want to modify or extend Outlook's performance, you can do that with the help of Visual Basic code. For an introduction to this subject, see a book such as *Programming Microsoft Outlook 2000*, published by Sams.

PART

II

CH

5

RESPONDING TO A REQUEST FOR A READ RECEIPT

Chapter 4, "Sending Messages," describes how you can include a request for a read receipt in messages you send.

→ For information about including a request for a read receipt in messages you send, **see** "Voting and Tracking Options," **p. 89**.

When you receive a message containing a request for a read receipt and double-click that message's header in the Inbox Information viewer, Outlook's default behavior is to display a dialog box such as the one shown in Figure 5.9.

Figure 5.9
This dialog box tells you that the sender has requested a read receipt.

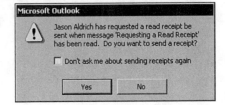

Click Yes if you agree to send a read receipt. Otherwise, click No. If you click Yes, Outlook automatically sends a message to the original sender to confirm you've read the message.

You can change the way Outlook responds when you receive a message containing a request for a read receipt.

→ For information about changing Outlook's default response to receiving a request for a read receipt, **see** "Setting Tracking Options," **p. 537**.

SAVING A MESSAGE AS ANOTHER OUTLOOK ITEM

Buried within Outlook are many capabilities that are not widely known. One of these is the ability to create one type of Outlook item from a different type of Outlook item.

You might, for example, receive an e-mail message that asks you to do something. Being an organized person, you want to add that request to your to-do list. Simple! Just drag the message into your Tasks folder. Here's how.

To convert a message into a task:

1. With your Inbox Information viewer displayed, select the relevant message.
2. Drag the message onto Tasks in the Outlook Bar. When you release the mouse button, Outlook displays the Tasks form with the subject of the message in that form's Subject box and the text of the message in the form's Notes box, as shown in Figure 5.10.
3. Make whatever entries are required in the Tasks form, such as specifying the Due Date.

→ For detailed information about using Outlook to save information about tasks, **see** "Managing Tasks," **p. 251**.

The preceding is just one example of how you can create one type of Outlook item from another, a process Microsoft calls *AutoCreate*. In general, you can drag any type of Outlook item into a folder of a different type to create the type of Outlook item that folder contains.

Figure 5.10
The Tasks form contains information from the message.

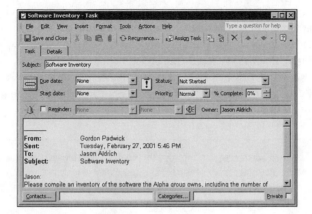

OPENING AND SAVING ATTACHMENTS

Outlook displays the presence of attachments

- By symbols in the Inbox Information viewer's Message pane
- By file names in the header of the Inbox Information viewer's Preview pane
- By file names in the Message form's header

OPENING AN ATTACHMENT

To open an attachment, double-click its file name in the Preview pane's header or in the Message form's header.

Outlook uses the Windows list of associations to find an application installed on your computer that's capable of opening a file, based on the file name extension. If Windows contains an association for the attached type of file, that application is opened and used to open and display the file. If no association exists, you are asked to select the application that should be used to open the file.

SAVING AN ATTACHMENT AS A FILE

You can save an attachment to a message you receive as a file. To do so, in the Inbox Information viewer select one message that has an attachment. Then select File and move the pointer onto Save Attachments. If the selected message has only one attachment, Outlook displays the name of that attachment. If the selected message contains two or more attachments, Outlook displays a menu that lists those attachments and also contains the menu item All Attachments.

To save just one attachment as a file, click that attachment in the menu. Outlook displays the Save Attachment dialog box, where you can navigate to the Windows folder in which you want to save the attachment. By default, Outlook proposes to save the attachment with its original file name. You can accept that name or replace it with a different file name. Click Save to save the attachment.

PART

II

CH

5

To save two or more attachments in the selected message, click All Attachments. Outlook displays a dialog box that lists the attachments. Initially, all attachments are selected. You can deselect any attachments you don't want to save by holding down Ctrl while clicking the names of those attachments. With only the attachments you want to save selected, click OK. Outlook displays a dialog box in which you can navigate to the Windows folder in which you want to save the attachments. Click OK to save the attachments using the original file name for each of them.

Tip from

When you receive any message that contains attachments, and you're not sure that the attachments are virus-free, save those attachments to files before you open them. Then, you can run a virus check on the attachments to ensure they don't contain any viruses that might contaminate your computer.

REMOVING AN ATTACHMENT FROM A MESSAGE

You might want to remove an attachment from a message you've received for several reasons:

- If you've saved an attachment as a file, you might want to remove that attachment from the message in which you received it to conserve storage space—there's no point in saving the same attachment in two places.

- You might want to forward a message to someone without including attachments to the message.

- You might suspect that the attachment contains a virus.

To remove an attachment from a message, double-click the message in the Inbox Information viewer to display that message in a Message form. The Message form lists the attachments in the bottom row of the header.

Right-click the attachment you want to remove to display a context menu. Select Remove in that menu. Outlook immediately removes the attachment.

Note

After you remove an attachment from a message and close the Message form, you'll see the name of the attachment you removed still listed in the header of the Inbox Information viewer's Preview pane. However, if you select another message in the Message pane and then select the message from which you removed the attachment, you'll find that the removed attachment is no longer listed in the Preview pane's header.

DELETING MESSAGES AND OTHER OUTLOOK ITEMS

Unless you choose otherwise, Outlook saves copies of messages you send in your Sent Items folder; it saves messages you receive in your Inbox folder. You can select Sent Items in the Outlook Bar to see the headers of messages you've sent in the Sent Items Information viewer, and you can select Inbox in the Outlook Bar to see headers of messages you've received in the Inbox Information viewer.

 To delete a message from either of these Information viewers, click the message header to select it; then click the Delete button in the Information viewer's Standard toolbar.

Deleting a message doesn't delete the message from your disk; it just moves the message from the Sent Items or Inbox folder to the Deleted Items folder. If you want to recover the deleted message, select Deleted Items in the Outlook Bar to display the Deleted Items Information viewer. In that viewer, locate the deleted item and drag it back to Sent Items or Inbox in the Outlook Bar.

 If you want to completely remove a deleted item from your disk, select Deleted Items in the Outlook Bar. In the Deleted Items Information viewer, select the items you want to delete, and click the Delete button in the Standard toolbar.

If you use a Personal Folders file to store Outlook items, you can't recover items after you delete them from the Deleted Items folder. However, if you save Outlook items in an Exchange store, items deleted from the Deleted Items folder aren't actually deleted; they're just marked as hidden. Those items remain hidden for a period known as the Deleted Item Retention Period, which is set individually for each mailbox by the Exchange administrator. To recover such deleted items, select Deleted Items in the Outlook Bar. Then select Tools, Recover Deleted Items. Select the items you want to recover, and then click Recover Selected Items in the toolbar.

Even though you delete items from your Deleted Items folder, you don't necessarily recover the space those items previously occupied on your hard disk. To recover that space, you have to compact your Personal Folders file, as explained in Chapter 19, "Compacting Folders and Archiving Outlook Items."

→ For information about compacting a Personal Folders file, **see** "Compacting Your Personal Folders File," **p. 390**.

RECEIVING FAXES

Outlook 2002 doesn't include any built-in capability to receive faxes. You can, however, enhance Outlook so that it does have faxing capabilities, as explained in Chapter 4.

→ For information about adding faxing capabilities to Outlook 2002, **see** "Sending Faxes," **p. 93**.

TROUBLESHOOTING

YOUR PERSONAL FOLDERS FILE

Although Outlook usually does a good job of keeping your Personal Folders file in good shape, problems can occur. If you're having problems with a Personal Folders file, the Inbox Repair tool can probably fix them. Although the file's name suggests that it deals only with Inbox folders, the utility actually examines, and attempts to solve problems with, all the folders in a Personal Folders file and the Outlook items saved in those folders.

Note

The Inbox Repair Tool described in this section deals only with Personal Folders files, not with Outlook items saved in an Exchange store. Your Exchange administrator probably has tools to use for fixing problems with the Exchange store.

The Inbox Repair file named `Scanpst.exe` is automatically installed on your computer when you install Windows 98, Windows Me, Windows NT, or Windows 2000. Microsoft supplies a slightly different version of the Inbox Repair Tool with each version of Windows. If you've had various versions of Windows installed on your computer, you'll probably have several versions of the Inbox Repair Tool. Make sure you run the version of the Inbox Repair Tool that's appropriate for the version of Windows you're using.

To use the Inbox Repair tool:

1. Close Outlook, select Start on the Windows taskbar, and move the pointer onto Find or Search, depending on which version of Windows you're using. Click Files and Folders to display the Find or Search Results dialog box.

2. In the Named box, enter **Scanpst.exe** and click Find Now or Search Now. Windows locates `Scanpst.exe` on your computer.

3. Double-click `Scanpst.exe` to display the Inbox Repair Tool dialog box, in which you are asked to enter the name of the file you want to scan. Enter the complete path of your Personal Folders file, or click Browse to navigate to that file; then click Open to select that file.

Note

Your Personal Folders file is probably `C:\Windows\Local Settings\ Application Data\Microsoft\Outlook\outlook.pst,` although it can be located elsewhere and can have a different file name (but it always has .pst as its extension).

4. Select Options and select Replace Log, Append to Log, or No Log according to how you want Scanpst to generate a log of what it finds.

5. Select Start to scan the file and attempt to correct errors in it.

After Scanpst has finished scanning your file, it displays a summary of what it found and what it did. Click OK to close the summary.

If you chose to create a log, that log is named Outlook.log. You can use Notepad (or any other text editor) to display what that file contains. Scanpst creates a log file only if it finds errors in the Personal Folders file it scans.

CHAPTER 6

ACCESSING THE INTERNET

In this chapter

ACCESSING THE INTERNET WORLD

Outlook 2002 is tightly integrated with Windows (including Internet Explorer) and with other Office XP components. Instead of duplicating functionality that's already in Windows, Outlook seamlessly links to Windows. Similarly, Outlook shares functionality with the other components of the Office suite.

Much of this component-sharing goes on behind the scenes and isn't immediately obvious to Outlook users. However, when you use Outlook in the Internet environment, it's apparent that Outlook relies on other Windows and Office components. Specifically, Outlook uses components of Internet Explorer to provide access to the Internet and intranet sites and to provide access to Internet newsgroups.

Note

Unfortunately, Microsoft hasn't taken integration quite far enough. There's no direct way to save information from newsgroups in the data store Outlook uses for messages, contacts, and so on.

The required components of Internet Explorer and Outlook Express are automatically installed on your computer when you install Outlook.

ACCESSING THE INTERNET FROM WITHIN OUTLOOK

From any Outlook Information viewer, you can easily access Web pages and participate in Internet newsgroups.

ACCESSING WEB SITES

With any Outlook Information viewer displayed, select View, move the pointer onto Go To, and click Web Browser. Outlook opens Internet Explorer. You can now use Internet Explorer in the normal way to access Web sites.

Tip from

Gordon Padwick

If you frequently access the Internet from within Outlook, you'll find it handy to add buttons for this purpose to an Outlook toolbar.

→ To learn more about accessing other programs from an Outlook toolbar, **see** "Working with Custom Toolbars," **p. 524**.

Initially, when you select Web Browser, Outlook might tell you This page cannot be displayed. That happens when Internet Explorer isn't configured to connect automatically to the Internet. Select File, Work Offline to continue.

At this stage, you can configure Internet Explorer so that it automatically connects to your Internet service provider (ISP). The following procedure assumes your computer is already set up to connect to the Internet and that you already have an account with an ISP.

To configure Internet Explorer to connect automatically to your ISP:

1. Start Internet Explorer, select Tools, Internet Options, and select the Connections tab to display the dialog box shown in Figure 6.1.

Figure 6.1
The Dial-Up Settings section of this dialog box lists your existing dial-up connections to the Internet.

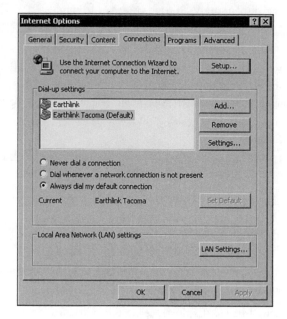

Tip from

If you don't already have an ISP, select Connect. You can then use the Internet Connection Wizard to lead you through the process of finding an ISP and establishing an account.

PART

II

CH

6

2. Select the dial-up setting you want to use, and then click Setup.
3. Make sure either Dial Whenever a Network Connection Is Not Present or Always Dial My Default Connection, whichever is appropriate, is checked.
4. Click OK to close the dialog box.
5. Select File, Close to close Internet Explorer.

The next time you select View, move the pointer onto Go To, and select Web Browser. Internet Explorer opens with your default home page displayed.

This book is primarily about Outlook; it assumes you're familiar with using Internet Explorer. However, here are a few hints about how you can use Internet Explorer and Outlook together.

With any Web page displayed by Internet Explorer, you can send that page, or a link to that page, to other people by e-mail.

To send a Web page by e-mail:

1. In Internet Explorer, display the Web page you want to send.

2. Select File, move the pointer onto Send, and select Page By E-mail to display an Outlook Message form.

3. Address the message in the same way that you address any other Outlook message, as explained in Chapter 4, "Sending Messages."

→ For information about how to address messages, **see** "Addressing the Message," **p. 70**.

4. The Subject box automatically contains the Web page's URL. You can change the contents of this box if you want to.

5. The notes box is empty. You can enter text there to explain why you're sending the Web page.

6. Click Send in the Message form's Standard toolbar to send the message.

But why send the complete page? Instead, just send a link to that page. By doing so, you send a much smaller message.

To send a link to a Web page, use the previous procedure with the exception that, in step 2, select File, move the pointer onto Send, and click Link By E-mail.

After you've finished using Internet Explorer, select File, Close to return to Outlook.

ACCESSING FAVORITE WEB PAGES

If you've been browsing Web pages for a while, you're undoubtedly familiar with making those pages you frequently visit readily accessible by adding them to your list of favorites. In Internet Explorer, you can select a favorite to open it immediately without having to enter its URL.

You can also go directly to a favorite Web page from within Outlook. One way to do this is to open the Other Shortcuts section of the Outlook Bar and select Favorites to see a list of shortcuts to your favorite Web pages. You can select any shortcut to start Internet Explorer and open the page associated with the shortcut. You see the Web page in the Outlook Information viewer.

Alternatively, with any Outlook Information viewer displayed, select Favorites in the menu bar to display a list of favorites. You can select any name from the list to start Internet Explorer and open a Web page.

You can also add a shortcut to a Web page on the Outlook Bar.

→ To learn more about placing shortcuts to a Web page or a local HTML page on the Outlook Bar, **see** "Creating a Shortcut to a Web Page," **p. 501**.

PARTICIPATING IN NEWSGROUPS

You easily can participate in Internet newsgroups from within Outlook. Outlook uses Outlook Express, a component of Internet Explorer, to provide access to newsgroups.

Tip from

Outlook Express, a component of Internet Explorer, which, in turn, is a component of Windows, provides capabilities to send and receive Internet e-mail and to participate in Internet newsgroups. If you're using Outlook, you should be using that to send and receive all your e-mail so all your messages are saved in one place. This chapter deals only with using Outlook Express to participate in newsgroups.

If you already have an Internet account with an ISP and have set up Internet Explorer to use that account, Outlook Express automatically uses the same account. From within Outlook Express, you can select a different Internet account, although it's unlikely you would want to do that.

To participate in Internet newsgroups:

1. With any Outlook Information viewer displayed, select View, move the pointer onto Go To, and select News to display Outlook Express, as shown in Figure 6.2.

Figure 6.2
You can use Outlook Express to connect to various news sites and participate in any number of news-groups at each site.

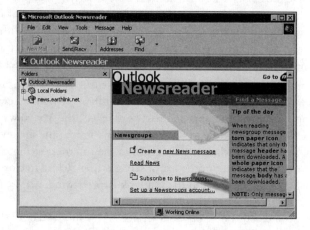

PART

II

CH

6

Note

If your computer is already connected to the Internet, you'll immediately see the window shown in Figure 6.2. If your computer is not connected to the Internet, it will attempt to connect and, after establishing a connection, display that window.

2. Select Tools, Accounts to display the Internet Accounts dialog box and select the News tab. Outlook Express displays a list of your news accounts, such as the one shown in Figure 6.3.

Figure 6.3
If you already have several accounts, one of them is marked as the default.

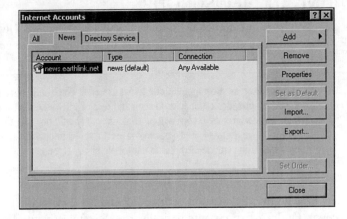

3. To add a news account, select Add, News to open the Internet Connection Wizard, in which the Display Name box contains the name you provided when you installed Office.

4. If you want messages you post on a newsgroup to have a different name, replace the displayed name with that name. Click Next to display the next wizard window in which you can change the displayed e-mail address if necessary. When people read messages you post on a newsgroup, they can reply by way of the newsgroup or by sending you an e-mail message. If you want people to use an e-mail address that's different from the one displayed in this window, enter the address you want people to use. Click Next to display the next wizard window in which you identify the news server.

5. Enter the name of the news server you want to use (such as msnews.microsoft.com) into the News (NNTP) Server box. If you're identifying a private news server that requires people to provide a name and password, check the My News Server Requires Me to Log On box. Click Next to display another window, the final wizard window. Click Finish to close that window and return to the Internet Accounts dialog box that includes the new news server in the list of servers. Click Close to close the Internet Accounts dialog box and return to the Outlook Express window.

Immediately after you create a new news server account, a message box asks whether you want to download newsgroups from that account. Click Yes if you want to do so.

You can use the buttons on the right side of the Internet Accounts dialog box to manage your news server accounts:

- **Add**—Click this button to add a new account.

- **Remove**—Select an account, and then click this button to remove an account from the list.

- **Properties**—Select an account, and then click this button to inspect and possibly change an account's properties.

- **Set as Default**—Select an account, and then click this button to make that account your default account.

- **Import**—Import a news account from a file.

- **Export**—Export a news account to a file.

For more detailed information about setting up and maintaining news accounts, refer to a comprehensive book covering your Windows operating system, such as *Special Edition Using Microsoft Me*, published by Que.

After you've set up news accounts, you can access any of the newsgroups available on those accounts. Some news servers, particularly those provided by ISPs, provide access to thousands of newsgroups. To easily access newsgroups you frequently use, you can subscribe to them. After you subscribe to certain newsgroups, Outlook Express makes it easy to go to those newsgroups.

Tip from

You don't have to subscribe to a newsgroup to have access to it. Subscribing merely makes it easy for you to return to newsgroups; it doesn't mean you'll be billed for accessing that newsgroup.

To subscribe to newsgroups:

1. In Outlook, select View, move the pointer onto Go To, and click News to display the Outlook Express Window.

2. In the left pane, click the name of the news server that provides access to the newsgroups to which you want to subscribe. If you haven't previously accessed that news server, Outlook Express displays a message saying you are not subscribed to any newsgroups and asking whether you want to see a list of newsgroups. Click Yes. Outlook downloads a list of available newsgroups. Depending on the number of newsgroups available on the server, downloading might take several minutes. Eventually, you see the beginning of a list of newsgroups.

Tip from

Instead of downloading the entire list of newsgroups available on a news server, you can download only those whose names contain a certain word. For example, if you want to see which newsgroups have "Outlook" in their names, enter `Outlook` in the Display Newsgroups Which Contain box before you start the download.

3. After you've downloaded a list of newsgroups, scroll down the list until you find the first one to which you want to subscribe. Select that newsgroup; then click Subscribe. An icon at the left of the newsgroup name indicates you've subscribed to it.

PART
II

CH
6

Tip from

Gordon Padwick

To cancel your subscription to a newsgroup, select that newsgroup and then click Unsubscribe.

After you've subscribed to newsgroups, select the Subscribed tab at the bottom of the list of newsgroups to see a list of only those newsgroups to which you've subscribed. Click OK to close the list of available newsgroups and return to the Newsreader window.

To access messages in a newsgroup, select that newsgroup in the Folders pane in the Newsreader window to see a list of message headers in the top pane on the right. Select any message header in that pane. If you've previously downloaded the selected message, the text of that message is displayed in the lower-right pane.

If you've not previously downloaded the selected message, the bottom pane states that the message has not been downloaded. In that case, double-click the message header to see the message in a separate dialog box. After you close that dialog box, the next time you select the message in the upper-right pane, you'll see the message text in the lower-right pane.

Note

The preceding paragraph describes what happens if your computer has a dial-up connection to a newsgroup server. If your computer is connected by way of a LAN to a local server on which newsgroup messages are stored, you might not have to download messages.

With a message selected, you can click these toolbar buttons:

- **New Post**—Creates a new message to send to the newsgroup
- **Reply Group**—Replies to the selected message, making the reply available on the newsgroup
- **Reply**—Replies to the selected message, sending the reply only to the person who posted the original message
- **Forward**—Forwards the selected message as e-mail to someone
- **Print**—Prints the selected message
- **Stop**—Stops sending and receiving messages
- **Send/Receive**—Sends messages waiting to be sent and receives messages waiting for you (this isn't something you would want to do if you're using Outlook Express from within Outlook as a means of accessing newsgroups)

To create your own message to a newsgroup, click New Post in the toolbar. Outlook Express displays a Message form similar to the Outlook Message form. Enter your message, and then click Send in the toolbar to post your message on the newsgroup.

Tip from

Instead of clicking Send/Receive, you can click the small button marked with a triangle at the right of Send/Receive. This displays a menu in which you can select Send and Receive All, Receive All, or Send All.

COMMUNICATING INSTANTLY

Instant communication, otherwise known as *instant messaging* or *chatting*, has recently become widely used and is now available from within Outlook. You can establish a connection with one or more other people by way of the Internet. What you type on your computer is almost instantly displayed to those other people; likewise, what those people type is displayed to you. You can use this to have a private conversation with a friend or a discussion with a group.

ENABLING INSTANT MESSAGING

To enable instant messaging from within Outlook, with any Outlook Information viewer displayed, select Tools, Options, and select the Other tab. In that tab, check Enable Instant Messaging in Microsoft Outlook. You must have a Hotmail or Passport account before you can use instant messaging.

→ For detailed information about installing Instant Messaging within Outlook, **see** "Instant Messaging," **p. 580**. You also can get information at the Web site: http://messenger.msn.com/support/features.asp.

After you've installed instant messaging in Outlook, an MSN Messenger Service icon appears at the right end of the Windows taskbar just to the left of the clock. Double-click that icon to open the MSN Messenger Service dialog box, as shown in Figure 6.4.

Figure 6.4
This is the starting point for your instant messaging activities.

To find out about using instant messaging, select Help, Help Topics in the menu bar. There you'll find topics that describe what you can do.

PARTICIPATING IN ONLINE MEETINGS

Two other Internet facilities available to you are NetMeeting and NetShow. Although you can use NetMeeting and NetShow from within Outlook, these are separate applications that come with Internet Explorer.

USING NETMEETING

NetMeeting enables any number of people to participate in a meeting without being physically present. The meeting participants are connected to each other by way of the Internet or an intranet. During the meeting, participants can exchange information in various ways:

- **Talking with other people**—To use this, each participant's computer must have a sound card installed and a headset with earphones and a microphone.

- **Sending typed messages to other people**—The text each person enters is displayed on all the other participants' screens.

- **Using video to see other people and to let other people see you**—To use this component, each participant's computer must have a video camera installed.

- **Cooperating with other people while working with word processing, spreadsheets, and other documents.**

- **Sharing applications and files with other people**—When you share an application that's installed on your computer, meeting participants can use that application even though they don't have it installed on their computers.

- **Drawing on a shared whiteboard using drawing tools that are similar to those in Microsoft Paint**—Each participant can see what the others draw.

Although all this is possible, it's hardly practical unless all participants have high-speed, bi-directional Internet access such as is available by way of an ISDN, a T1 line, or some other high-speed connection. You can use a modem to get a feel for how NetMeeting works, but not for real-world meetings.

Although you can access NetMeeting from within Outlook, it's really a separate application that's not a part of the Office suite. If you ever need to remove Office from your computer, you have to remove NetMeeting separately.

SETTING UP NETMEETING

The first step in preparing to use NetMeeting is to go through the steps in the NetMeeting Wizard. These steps provide your identification (so that meeting participants can see who you are) and also adjust the audio levels.

Because NetMeeting uses audio, make sure your computer's audio setup is working correctly before you start the NetMeeting Wizard. You should have a headset with earphones and a microphone, rather than speakers and a separate microphone mounted on your monitor.

Note

Windows 98, Windows Me, Windows NT, and Windows 2000 have audio capabilities, but the details are different. The sound card in your computer is controlled by drivers, normally provided by the sound card's manufacturer. There's no way that this book can deal with all the possibilities. For information about setting up your sound card so that it can work with NetMeeting, refer to the information provided with your sound card or available on the manufacturer's Web site. You can also find some information in the Microsoft Knowledge Base and in the Windows 98, Windows Me, Windows NT, and Windows 2000 Resource Kits, published by Microsoft.

Before beginning to set up NetMeeting, close any programs running on your computer that can play or record sounds.

To set up NetMeeting:

1. With any Outlook Information viewer displayed, select View, move the pointer onto Go To, move the pointer onto Internet Call, and click Internet Call to display the first Microsoft NetMeeting Wizard window, shown in Figure 6.5.

Figure 6.5
This window summarizes NetMeeting's capabilities.

Note

The NetMeeting Wizard appears the first time you click Internet Call after installing Office. Follow the steps in the wizard to set up NetMeeting on your computer, as described here. After doing that, subsequently when you click Internet Call, the NetMeeting dialog box, shown in Figure 6.6 later in this chapter, is displayed.

2. Click Next to display a wizard window in which you supply information about yourself.

3. Enter your first name, last name, and e-mail address in the first three boxes and, optionally, enter information about your location in the fourth box. You can also enter comments in the fifth box. Click Next to display the next wizard window.

4. In this window, leave Log on to a Directory Server when NetMeeting Starts checked. By default, the directory server you select lists your name so that other users can select it. If you don't want your name to be listed on the server, check Do Not List My Name in the Directory. Click Next to display the next wizard window.

5. This wizard window wants to know which type of connection you have to the directory server. Select among 14400bps modem; 28800bps or faster modem; Cable, xDSL, or ISDN; or Local Area Network. Click Next to display the next wizard window.

6. Outlook proposes to place a shortcut to NetMeeting on your Windows desktop and in the Quick Launch bar. If you don't want one or both of these shortcuts, uncheck Put a Shortcut to NetMeeting on My Desktop or Put a Shortcut to NetMeeting on My Quick Launch Bar, or both. Click Next to display the next wizard window.

7. This wizard window helps you to adjust your audio settings. As stated at the beginning of this procedure, you must make sure no other programs that can play or record sounds are running at this point; if any are, click Cancel, turn off those programs, and repeat steps 1–5. Click Next to display the next wizard window.

8. Now's the time to put on your headset. Make sure the earphones are positioned directly over your ears and the microphone is about 1 inch (2.5 centimeters) away from your mouth. Click Next to continue.

9. The wizard proposes to use default wave devices for recording and playback. Click Next to accept these defaults.

10. The wizard displays a screen you can use to verify you can hear sounds and adjust the volume level. Click Test to hear the sound in your headphones, and adjust the Volume slider until the sound is at a comfortable level. Click Next to continue.

11. Speak the text displayed in the window at your normal voice level. As you speak, the shallow bar above Record Volume shows green, yellow, and red segments. The wizard automatically adjusts the microphone sensitivity.

Tip from

Gordon Padwick

If, while you speak, you don't see anything in the shallow bar above Record Volume, drag the Record Volume slider all the way to the right (for maximum sensitivity), and try again. If you still don't see anything in the shallow bar, your microphone isn't working. Check that your microphone is plugged into the correct connector on your computer and, if the microphone has an on/off switch, that it's turned on. If that doesn't solve the problem, you probably have trouble with the microphone or with your computer's audio system, a subject that's beyond the scope of this book.

If you drag the Record Volume slider all the way to the right and then start speaking, you'll probably see the shallow bar completely filled. While you continue speaking, the slider automatically moves to the left until it reaches the optimum position.

> The automatic adjustment of the sound level works only from high sensitivity downward. If you set the level too low, the slider doesn't move to the right to increase the level.
>
> Later, while you're using NetMeeting, if people complain about the level of sound they hear, you can return to this window and drag the slider to adjust the level.

12. After you've adjusted the microphone level, click Next to display the final Wizard window. This window confirms you have completed setting up NetMeeting. Click Finish to close the wizard and display the window shown in Figure 6.6.

Tip from

> After you've initially set up NetMeeting, as described in the preceding pages, you can make changes. To do so, display the NetMeeting window shown in Figure 6.6; then select Tools, Options to display the Options dialog box. You can select the six tabs in that dialog box to examine and change NetMeeting's options.

STARTING A MEETING

To start using NetMeeting from within Outlook, display any Outlook Information viewer, select View, move the pointer onto Go To, and click Internet Call to display the window shown in Figure 6.6.

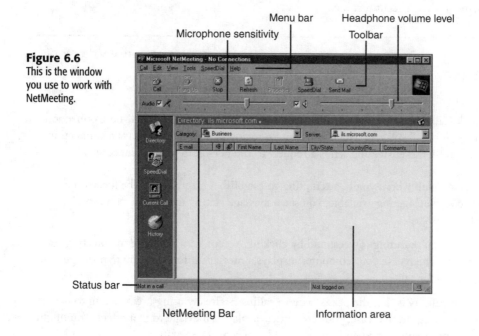

Figure 6.6
This is the window you use to work with NetMeeting.

If you know the e-mail address of the person with whom you want to have a meeting, the easiest way to start the meeting is to call the person. To do so, click Call on the NetMeeting toolbar to display the dialog box shown in Figure 6.7.

Figure 6.7
Use this dialog box to
initiate a meeting.

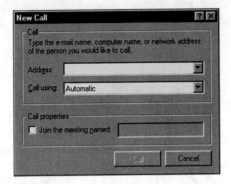

To start a meeting with a specific person:

1. Enter the person's e-mail address into the Address box. Alternatively, if you have previously called the person, open the drop-down Address list and select the person's address.

2. Leave Call Using at the default Automatic selection.

3. If you want to give the meeting a name, check Join the Meeting Named, and enter a name in the adjacent text box.

Tip from

Providing a name for a meeting makes it easy for other people to request to be admitted to the meeting.

4. Click Call. If you are not already logged on to the Internet, the Dial-up Connection dialog box is displayed, which you can use to connect. When you have a connection to the Internet, NetMeeting sends a request to the person to join the meeting.

If the person with whom you're attempting to establish a meeting can't be located or doesn't have NetMeeting available, you see a message stating that the person can't be located.

The person you're calling can respond by clicking Accept, in which case the meeting starts, or Ignore, in which case your computer displays a message informing you that the person has rejected your call.

Another possibility is that the person you're calling is already using NetMeeting to participate in a meeting. In that case, your computer displays a message to that effect. You might be invited into that meeting and can, if you like, accept the invitation.

While you're participating in a meeting, the NetMeeting window contains the Current Call Information viewer, similar to that shown in Figure 6.8.

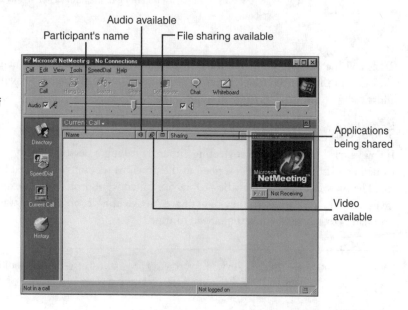

Audio available
Participant's name
File sharing available

Figure 6.8
The Current Call Information viewer displays the names of people participating in the meeting with information about their capabilities.

Applications being shared

Video available

After you have a meeting started, you can use NetMeeting's capabilities to share information. This is fairly intuitive, so this book doesn't go into details about that. You can find detailed information in such books as *Special Edition Using Microsoft Windows Me* and *Special Edition Using Microsoft Windows 2000*, both published by Que.

The preceding information is based on the assumption that you know how to contact the person with whom you want to have a meeting. Another way to use NetMeeting to have an electronic meeting with other people is to use an *Internet Locator Server (ILS)* directory.

Internet Locator Servers are servers maintained by Microsoft and some other organizations that maintain lists of people who allow their names to be available. To see a list of publicly available ILS directories, display NetMeeting's Directories Information viewer. Then, open the drop-down Server list box and select one of the available directories. After a few seconds delay, you'll see the beginning of a list of available names.

A red asterisk superimposed on the computer symbol in the left column of the list indicates that the person is currently participating in a meeting.

Each ILS directory maintains several categories of names. To see the names available in a specific category, open the drop-down Category list box and select a category. After you've selected a category, only names in that category are listed.

PART

II

CH

6

Note

Each time you select a category or an ILS directory, the displayed list of names is regenerated. You can sort the list according to the information in any column by clicking the column title.

To establish a meeting with one of the listed people, select that person's name, and then click Call in the NetMeeting toolbar to display the New Call dialog box with the person's address displayed. Click Call to attempt to start a meeting.

SCHEDULING A NETMEETING

If you've tried to initiate a NetMeeting either by calling a person directly or by selecting a name in an ILS directory, as described in the previous section, you probably weren't successful. The reason for that is that the people you called were probably not expecting to be invited to join a meeting, so they didn't have NetMeeting running. One way around that problem is to schedule a meeting ahead of time.

Tip from

Gordon Padwick

For scheduling to work correctly, it's imperative that all meeting participants have the time and time zone correctly set on their computers.

To schedule a NetMeeting:

1. With Outlook's Calendar Information viewer displayed, select Actions, New Meeting Request to display the Meeting form shown in Figure 6.9.

Figure 6.9
This is the form that's most often used to create an Outlook Appointment item.

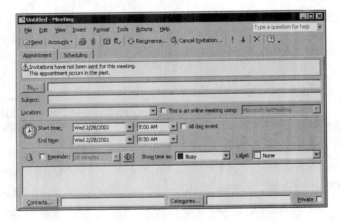

→ For detailed information about entering information in the Meeting form, **see** "Inviting People to Attend a Meeting," **p. 240**.

2. Enter the e-mail addresses of the people with whom you want to have a NetMeeting in the To box.

→ To learn more about entering e-mail addresses in the To box, **see** "Addressing the Message," **p. 70**.

3. Enter a name for the NetMeeting in the Subject box.

4. Check This Is an Online Meeting Using. As soon as you do so, the Meeting form changes to that shown in Figure 6.10.

Figure 6.10
This version of the Meeting form provides boxes for NetMeeting-specific information. By default, the box at the right of This Is an Online Meeting Using contains Microsoft NetMeeting.

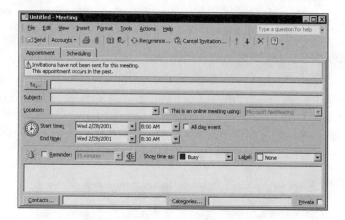

5. Open the drop-down Directory Server list and select the directory server that will host the meeting.

6. If you want a document to be available to participants when the NetMeeting starts, enter the full path name of that document in the Office Document box.

7. Enter a date and time for the meeting to start in the Start Time boxes.

8. Enter a date and time for the meeting to end in the End Time boxes.

9. If you want to be automatically connected to the NetMeeting a few minutes before the meeting is scheduled to start, click Reminder to check that box, open the adjacent drop-down list, select the number of minutes prior to the meeting, and check Automatically Start NetMeeting with Reminder.

10. Click Send in the form's Standard toolbar to send messages to people asking them to participate in the meeting.

The meeting request you create in this way is sent by e-mail to the people you want to participate in the NetMeeting. Those people receive messages in their inboxes, and they can reply to those messages.

→ Asking people to attend a NetMeeting is much the same as asking people to attend a face-to-face meeting. **See** "Inviting People to Attend a Meeting," **p. 240**.

Having sent requests for people to participate in a NetMeeting, and having received responses from them, everyone is ready at the appointed time, so there should be no problem in establishing the necessary connections.

Although you normally will schedule a NetMeeting so participants can prepare for it, you can immediately start a NetMeeting.

STARTING REGULAR NETMEETINGS

If you have regular meetings with the same people, you might find it convenient to add information about setting up a NetMeeting to the other information you have about those people in your Outlook Contacts folder.

To add NetMeeting information for a contact:

1. Select Contacts in the Outlook Bar to display the Contacts Information viewer.
2. Double-click the name of the contact with whom you want to have the NetMeeting to display information about that contact in a Contact form.

→ For information about adding contacts to your Contacts folder, **see** "Creating a Contact Item," **p. 141**.

3. Select the Contact form's Details tab, shown in Figure 6.11.

Figure 6.11
Use the Online NetMeeting Settings section to define how you want a NetMeeting to be configured.

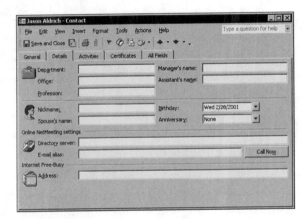

4. Enter the name of the Internet Locator Server you want to use in the Directory Server box.

Tip from

If you intend to use the Internet for your NetMeeting, you'll probably choose a public Internet Locator Server; if you plan to use an intranet, choose a private one.

5. Enter the contact's e-mail address in the E-mail Alias box.
6. Click Save and Close in the form's toolbar to save the information.

Subsequently, to start a NetMeeting with the contact, select the contact, select the Details tab, and click Call Now. Alternatively, with the contact's information displayed in a Contact form, select Actions, Call Using NetMeeting.

USING NETSHOW

NetShow allows one person to give a presentation that other people can see at remote locations. The presentation, which can contain audio and video, is sent from a Web server by way of the Internet to one or more Web clients, such as Internet Explorer.

→ Scheduling a NetShow is very similar to scheduling a NetMeeting. **See** "Scheduling a NetMeeting," **p. 130**.

In the form shown previously in Figure 6.10, check This Is an Online Meeting Using; then open the adjoining drop-down list and select NetShow Services. Complete the remainder of the form in the same way you schedule a NetMeeting, and then send the invitation to receive the NetShow.

When you receive an invitation to view a NetShow and respond by accepting the invitation, Outlook places an item in your calendar. A few minutes before the NetShow is scheduled, double-click the Calendar item to open it in an Appointment form. In that form, select Actions, View NetShow to connect to the server and view the show.

As an alternative to manually joining the NetShow, you can check Reminder in the Appointment form and select a reminder for a few minutes before the show is scheduled to begin. After you've done that, Outlook automatically connects you to the show at the appointed time.

> **Caution**
>
> It's imperative that you and the person who is giving the show have the time set correctly on your computers and also have selected the correct time zone.

GETTING HELP FOR INTERNET EXPLORER

This book is, of course, primarily about Outlook. Although the book includes information about accessing the Internet from within Outlook, by using components of Internet Explorer, there isn't space to cover this subject in detail.

You can also use a text editor, such as Windows Notepad, to open the text file IE.txt, where you'll find information about installing and running Internet Explorer.

TROUBLESHOOTING

INTERNET ACCESS

If you run into problems connecting to the Internet, one likely cause is incorrect settings for connection properties. For example, you might create an account to access newsgroups and then find you can't download names of available newsgroups.

If you're trying to access newsgroups maintained by your ISP, contact the ISP and ask for details about the connection settings required to access newsgroups. Make sure you enter these settings exactly as specified. With the Microsoft Outlook Newsreader dialog box displayed, right-click the name of the news server that's giving you trouble. Then, in the context menu, click Properties to display a Properties dialog box that has four tabs:

- **General**—The News Account Name box contains the name by which you want to identify the account, which can be anything you want. It's not the actual name of the news server. The User Information section of the tab does not affect establishing a connection to a news server.

- **Server**—The Server Name box contains the actual name of the server. This box must contain the name provided by your ISP or, in the case of a public server, that server's actual name. If you're using a server available on your ISP, you probably have to log on using the account name and password you use to access e-mail. Check This Server Requires Me to Log On and enter your account name and password. In the case of a public server, you usually don't have to log on using an account name and a password.

- **Connection**—In most cases, you can ignore this tab. If the news server you're attempting to use requires a specific connection, that server's representatives will provide the information you need to enter in this tab.

- **Advanced**—In most cases, you can ignore this tab. Most news servers use 119 as the server port number, which is the default supplied by Outlook Express, and do not require a secure connection. The server's representatives will provide a different port number if that's necessary and, if necessary, provide you with the information you need to use a secure connection.

By default, Outlook Express automatically terminates attempts to make a connection to a server after one minute if a connection is not completed. In most circumstances, that period is more than adequate. If you're having problems establishing a connection, try increasing the timeout to see if that helps.

USING OUTLOOK AS A PERSONAL INFORMATION MANAGER

CREATING CONTACTS

In this chapter

WHAT ARE CONTACTS?

A *contact* in Outlook is a person or an organization. Outlook can save information about contacts in various places, as described in this chapter. Typically, Outlook saves such information as a contact's name, address, phone and fax number, and e-mail address. But Outlook can save much more information than this, including a contact's photograph.

Outlook uses contacts for various purposes:

- Addressing e-mail messages
- Addressing conventional mail
- Placing phone calls
- Sending faxes
- Arranging meetings
- Assigning tasks

Because so much of what you do with Outlook involves contacts, an understanding of how Outlook deals with contacts is crucial to your efficient use of Outlook.

WHERE OUTLOOK SAVES CONTACT INFORMATION

Outlook saves the information about each contact, a person or an organization, as a Contact item. Each Contact item contains many fields of information, only a few of which you typically use for most contacts.

Outlook saves contact items in the *Outlook Address Book* that provides access to information in the Contacts folder within your Personal Folders (.pst) or, if you're using Outlook as a client for Exchange, in the Contacts folder within your Exchange store. In addition, Outlook can access information about contacts stored in your *Personal Address Book (PAB)*, a *Global Address Book (GAB)*, or another address book maintained by Exchange.

USING A SINGLE CONTACTS FOLDER

A Contacts folder contains any number of Contact items, each of which contains information about one contact. By default, after you install Outlook, you have one Contacts folder that's used in two ways. You can

- Open the Contacts folder to see information about each of your contacts.
- Use your Contacts folder for such purposes as addressing e-mail messages, inviting people to meetings, and assigning tasks to people.

You can always use a Contacts folder for the first of these purposes. If you have just one Contacts folder, simply select that folder in the Outlook Bar or Folder List to see information about contacts. Alternatively, if you have more than one Contacts folder, choose View, Folder List and, in the Folder List, select the folder you want to use. In either case, Outlook displays the Contacts Information viewer with contact information displayed in the Address Cards view, or whichever other view you choose to use.

To use the items in a Contacts folder to address e-mail messages and for similar purposes, that folder must have its properties set so that it acts as an Address Book. After you first install Outlook and have only one Contacts folder, that folder is automatically set to act as an Address Book. You can confirm that by right-clicking Contacts in the Outlook Bar or right-clicking the name of the Contacts folder in the Folder List to display a context menu; in the context menu, click Properties to display the Contacts Properties dialog box. Select the Outlook Address Book tab to display the dialog box shown in Figure 7.1.

Figure 7.1
This tab of the Contacts Properties dialog box is used to set the properties of a Contacts folder so that it can be used as an Address Book.

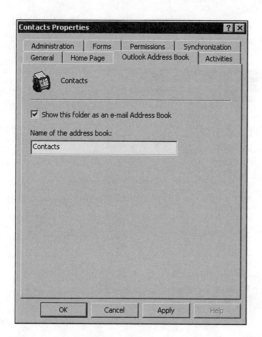

As you see in Figure 7.1, Show This Folder as an E-mail Address Book is checked, indicating that the items in the folder can be used for addressing e-mail messages.

USING MULTIPLE CONTACTS FOLDERS

Most people use just one Contacts folder to hold all their contact items. You can, if you want, create additional Contacts folders. You might, for example, want to have one Contacts folder for your business contacts and another for your personal contacts. I don't advise that, though, due to the problem that arises when a person is both a business and a personal contact.

PART
III

CH
7

Note

You can create additional Contacts folders within an existing Personal Folders, as described here. You also can create one or more additional Personal Folders and place new Contacts folders in them. See Chapter 33, "Enhancing Outlook's Capabilities," for information about creating Personal Folders.

→ To learn more about creating Outlook folders and subfolders, **see** "Creating Folders and Subfolders," **p. 631**.

To create an additional Contacts folder within a Personal Folders:

1. Select View, Folder List and select the folder under which you want the new folder to be created.

2. Select File, move the pointer onto Folder, and then click New Folder to display the dialog box shown in Figure 7.2.

Figure 7.2
The large box lists your current folders.

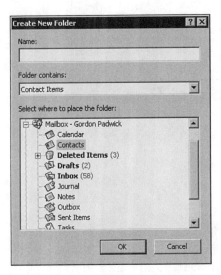

3. Enter a name for the new folder in the Name box. The name you enter must not be the same as that of a folder that already exists at the level in the folder tree structure where you intend to place the new folder. If you do enter the name of a folder that already exists, Outlook refuses to create the new folder.

4. Open the Folder Contains drop-down list and select the type of Outlook item the new folder will contain.

5. In the Select Where to Place the Folder box, select where you want to place the new folder in your folder tree structure. If you want the new folder to be at the same level in the structure as the default Outlook folders, select the root folder. If you want the new folder to be a subfolder under an existing folder, select that folder.

6. Click OK. Outlook asks whether you want to create a shortcut to the new folder in the Outlook Bar. Click Yes or No as you prefer.

After completing these steps, you can select View, Folder List to see the new folder in your folder list. After you've created a new folder, you can choose whether the new folder can be used as an Address Book. To do so, right-click the folder in the Folder List to display the folder's properties and select the Outlook Address Book tab. By default, the Show This Folder as an E-mail Address Book box is checked. Uncheck the box if you don't want the folder to be used as an e-mail address book.

→ You can use any number of Contacts folders as Address Books for addressing e-mail and similar purposes. You must, however, designate one Contacts folder as the default in which Outlook saves information about new contacts. **See** "Designating a Default Store," **p. 629**.

CREATING A CONTACT ITEM

You can use Outlook to save as much or as little information about your contacts (people and organizations) as you like.

SELECTING CONTACT OPTIONS

Outlook offers several ways in which you can name Contact items; Outlook also provides various ways to display Contact items in lists.

When you open a list of Contact items for such purposes as addressing e-mail, Outlook lists those items in alphabetical order by each contact's first name, middle name, and last name. You can change that so that contacts are listed by last name and then first name. After you've changed the listing order, that change affects only new contact items you subsequently create; it doesn't affect the way existing items are listed.

Tip from

Gordon Podoll

The effect of choosing the option that lists contacts by last name and then first name is to control what happens when you create a new contact item. The contact's first name is placed in the Lastname field, and the contact's last name is placed in the Firstname field. I don't recommend selecting this option.

When you create Contact items, you can choose a File As name by which Outlook lists items in the Contacts Information viewer when a Card view is selected. Outlook constructs the File As name for a person from various combinations of that person's name and company. You can choose a default combination and then, when you create a new Contact item, Outlook proposes to use that combination but, on an item-by-item basis, you can choose an alternative combination. File As names are covered in more detail subsequently in this chapter.

→ For more detailed information about File As names, **see** "Selecting a File As Name," **p. 145**.

PART
III

CH
7

To control how Outlook names and lists contact items:

1. With any Outlook Information viewer displayed, select Tools, Options and, with the Preferences tab selected, choose Contact Options to display the dialog box shown in Figure 7.3.

Figure 7.3
Use this dialog box to select how you want contact items to be named and filed.

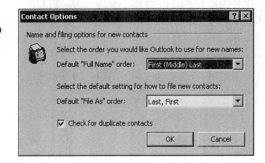

2. Open the Default "Full Name" Order drop-down list and select the order you want to use.

3. Open the Default "File As" Order drop-down list and select the order you want to use.

STARTING TO CREATE A CONTACT ITEM

Start by displaying the contact form in which you enter information about a contact. To do this, click Contacts in the Outlook Bar or Folder List, and then select New in the Standard toolbar (or select Actions, New) to display the Contact form shown in Figure 7.4.

Figure 7.4
The form opens with the General tab selected. The form is shown here with typical information entered.

The General tab is where you enter most of the information about a contact.

Note
> In addition to the General tab, the other tabs are sometimes used when creating a Contact item.

ENTERING A CONTACT'S NAME, JOB TITLE, AND COMPANY

Note
> An apology from the author: The information in this section (and throughout the book) is based on English usage. I've not had the opportunity to work with the versions of Windows and Outlook available from Microsoft for other languages. If some of the information I provide is not accurate for the language version of the product you're using, please accept my apologies.

If the contact is a person, enter that person's name in the Full Name box. If the contact is an organization, leave this box empty.

Note
> Some contact-related Outlook functions, such as phone call logging, aren't available if a contact name isn't provided.

Here are some examples of how you might enter a person's name:

- Jean Morrows
- Bonnie Y. Carter
- C. Jason Smith
- Dr. Brian Humphrey
- Stephanie Green, PhD

In addition to entering a person's name in first, middle, last order, you can enter the last name, a comma, and then the first and middle names. For example, instead of Bonnie Y. Carter, you could enter Carter, Bonnie Y.

If a contact has a hyphenated last name, such as Ron Smith-Caruthers, Outlook parses the name correctly. But, what if a contact has two last names that are not hyphenated? You can deal with this situation in two ways:

- Use the Check Full Name dialog box (described subsequently) and enter the two last names in the Last box.
- Enter the name as Smith Caruthers, Ron.

After you enter a name in any of these ways, Outlook parses the name into its components. To see these components, choose Full Name to display the Check Full Name dialog box shown in Figure 7.5. This dialog box shows how Outlook saves the name you entered.

PART

III

CH

7

Figure 7.5
Outlook saves the
name you enter using
five separate fields.

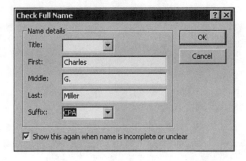

You don't have to check the name you enter in this way. Outlook almost always correctly parses the name into its components. However, if you have any doubt, you can do this to confirm that Outlook correctly understands the name you entered. With the Check Full Name dialog box displayed, you can edit the five individual components of a name.

Note

If Outlook doesn't understand the format of a name you enter into the Full Name box, it usually displays the Check Full Name dialog box automatically so you can make any necessary changes. You can't rely on this happening all the time, though. Make sure Show This Again When Name Is Incomplete or Unclear is checked in the Check Full Name dialog box.

After you enter a name in the Full Name box, or leave that box empty if the contact is an organization, press Tab to move the insertion point into the Job Title box. If you entered a name in the Full Name box, that name replaces "Untitled" in the form's title bar. Also, the name appears a little lower on the form in the File As box with the family name first (if you enter Peter Smith in the Full Name box, the name appears as Smith, Peter in the File As box), unless you have changed the Save As default, as described previously in this chapter.

→ To find out how you can control the way Outlook proposes to list a contact in the File As box, **see** "Selecting Contact Options," **p. 141**.

You don't have to enter anything into the Job Title box. If the contact is a person, enter that person's job title if appropriate; otherwise, leave the box empty. Press Tab to move the insertion point into the Company box.

If the contact is an organization, and you left the Full Name box empty, you must provide an organization name. However, if the contact is a person, you can leave this box empty. If appropriate, enter the name of the contact company or organization in this box; then press Tab. If you've left the Full Name box empty, the name you enter in the Company box replaces "Untitled" in the form's title bar and also appears in the File As box.

Note

Outlook ignores "The" at the beginning of a company name when File As names are listed alphabetically by company. For example, if the company name is "The XYZ Company," Outlook lists that company in alphabetical order as "XYZ Company, The."

SELECTING A FILE AS NAME

The File As name for a contact is the name by which contacts are normally alphabetized in the Contacts Information viewer.

As mentioned previously, Outlook suggests one File As name as soon as you enter a person's name in the Full Name box or an organization's name in the Company box. If you enter a person's name and an organization's name, Outlook creates several File As names from which you can select one.

After you enter a person's name and an organization name, Outlook proposes a File As name based on the selection you made in the Contact Options dialog box, as described previously in this chapter.

→ For information about how you can control the way Outlook proposes to list a contact in the File As box, **see** "Selecting Contact Options," **p. 141**.

If you want to use a different File As name, open the drop-down File As list to see the File As names Outlook suggests, as shown in Figure 7.6.

Figure 7.6
You can select any of the File As names Outlook proposes.

Miller, Charles G.
Charles G. Miller CPA
Miller Associates
Miller, Charles G. (Miller Associates
Miller Associates (Miller, Charles G

Instead of selecting one of the File As names Outlook proposes, you can enter any name you want (a nickname, for example) in the File As box.

Tip from

Be consistent in your choice of File As names to make it easy to find contacts in the Contacts Information viewer. I suggest you choose the first format in the File As drop-down list for personal friends and the last format in the list for business contacts.

ENTERING PHONE AND FAX NUMBERS

Although the Contact form has only four boxes for phone and fax numbers (Business, Home, Business Fax, and Mobile), you can enter as many as 19 numbers for each contact. To see the available numbers, click one of the buttons marked with a triangle between one of the phone labels and that label's text box. Outlook displays a list of types of phone and fax numbers, as shown in Figure 7.7.

PART

III

CH

7

Figure 7.7
These are the available phone and fax number types. Those for which you have previously entered numbers are checked.

You can select any name in the list. After you do so, that name replaces the label displayed on the form. Although the form displays only four numbers at any one time, Outlook can save all 19 numbers.

Note

You can't change the labels Outlook provides for phone and fax numbers. Although you will rarely want to enter as many as 19 numbers for a contact, you might sometimes want to enter a number with a different label—for example, if a contact has three home phone numbers. In cases such as that, you must use one of the existing labels, such as Other for the third home phone.

To enter a phone or fax number, select one of the phone number types, and then enter the number. See the following section, "Formatting Phone and Fax Numbers."

Use the same steps to enter additional phone or fax numbers.

FORMATTING PHONE AND FAX NUMBERS

Here are some facts you need to know about phone and fax number formats. These facts are based on the assumption that you've set Regional Settings to English (United States) in the Windows Control Panel. Some differences might exist if you're using a different Regional Setting:

- *When entering a phone number, it's optional whether you group numbers by using spaces, hyphens, or parentheses.* When you press Tab to signify you've finished entering the number, Outlook automatically formats the number according to the conventions of the Regional Settings you've selected in the Windows Control Panel.

- *Always enter the complete phone number including, in North America, the area code (even if it's a local area code that you don't need to dial).* If Dial-up Networking is set up correctly in Windows, the local area code is ignored if it's not needed. By including the area code with the phone number, however, you can use your contact information when you're traveling or after your area code changes. If you omit an area code, Outlook automatically inserts your local area code.

■ *Don't enter a 1 before the area code.* Dial-up Networking automatically inserts the 1 before area codes. However, if you do enter the 1, Outlook ignores it.

■ *Enter international phone numbers in the format*

+021(982)494-4321

where 021 is the country code. The parentheses and the hyphen are optional.

■ *Outlook saves any text you enter after the phone number, but doesn't use that text when placing phone calls.* You can, for example, append a contact's extension number after the phone number. When you place a call, the extension number is there for you to refer to. If you precede the extension number with an alphabetical character, such as *x*, the following numbers aren't dialed. Without the alphabetical characters, the numbers are dialed, but most telephone systems ignore them.

When you enter a phone or fax number and press Tab, Outlook might, in North America, insert +1 in front of the number. As explained below, you can choose whether Outlook does this. Microsoft claims that preceding a phone number with +1 provides

■ Better handling of 10-digit phone numbers

■ Better parsing of international phone numbers

■ Automatic validation of fax numbers

After you enter a phone or fax number and press Tab, you can double-click that number to display the dialog box shown in Figure 7.8. You can correct the number in that dialog box if necessary.

Figure 7.8
This dialog box shows how Outlook parses a telephone number you've entered.

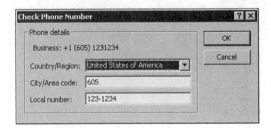

You can edit the boxes in the Check Phone Number dialog box if you need to.

If Outlook does insert +1 before phone numbers and this seems to be giving you trouble, you can disable this functionality.

PART

III

CH

7

To disable the insertion of +1:

1. Display the Contacts Information viewer and select any contact.

2. Choose the Dial button in the Standard toolbar to display the dialog box shown in Figure 7.9.

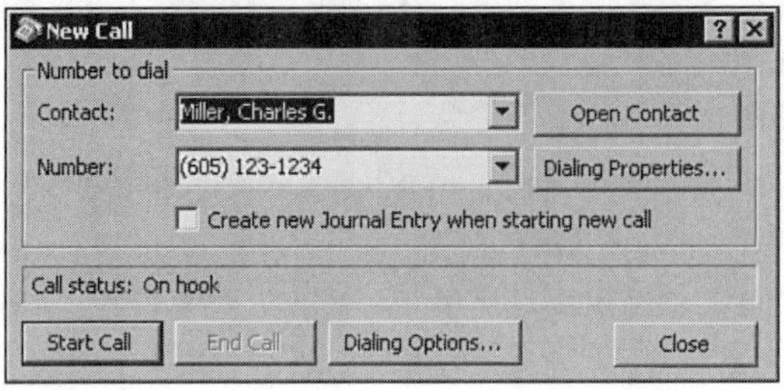

Figure 7.9
The New Call dialog box displays the name of the selected contact and one of that contact's phone numbers.

3. Click the Dialing Options button (be careful not to click Dialing Properties) to display the dialog box shown in Figure 7.10.

Figure 7.10
You can use this dialog box to set up speed dialing.

4. If it's checked, uncheck the Automatically Add Country Code to Local Phone Numbers box. Click OK and then Close to return to the Information viewer.

If you run into problems with phone numbers, the "Troubleshooting" section at the end of this chapter provides information about what to do.

ENTERING POSTAL ADDRESSES

Outlook can save three postal addresses for each contact: Business, Home, and Other. These address labels are built into Outlook; you can't change them.

By default, Outlook expects you to enter a Business address. If you want to enter a different address, click the button with the triangle icon just below Address to display the three address labels; then select the one you want to use.

Entering a postal address is similar to entering a contact's name:

- You can enter the complete address in the large text box at the right of Address.
- You can choose Address to display the Check Address dialog box that contains separate boxes for each element of an address, as shown in Figure 7.11.

For straightforward home addresses, you should normally enter the complete address in the large text box. For more complex business addresses, you sometimes need to enter an address in the Check Address dialog box.

To enter a postal address:

1. Select Business, Home, or Other as appropriate.
2. Enter the street address on the first line and press Enter.
3. Enter the city name, a comma, the state or province abbreviation, and a space, and then enter the postal (ZIP) code. Press Enter.
4. If the address is for a country or region other than your own, enter the country or region name and press Enter.
5. Press Tab to signify that you've finished entering the address.
6. Repeat steps 1–5 to enter a second or third address.

Tip from

If you need to save more than three postal addresses for a contact, you must create two or more Contact items for that contact.

When you press Tab, Outlook attempts to parse the address into its components. If a problem occurs, Outlook automatically displays the Check Address dialog box shown in Figure 7.11. If you want to confirm that Outlook has parsed the address correctly, choose Address to display the Check Address dialog box.

Figure 7.11
This dialog box displays the individual components of the address in separate boxes.

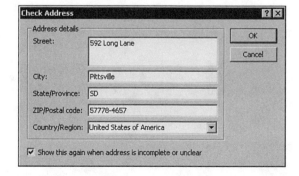

Notice that Outlook automatically provides the name of your own country or region, unless you entered a different one. The country or region name is derived from the Regional Setting in the Windows Control Panel.

If the text in any of the boxes is incorrect, you can make corrections using normal editing techniques. Click OK when you're satisfied with the address.

Tip from

Leave the Show This Again When Address Is Incomplete or Unclear box checked. If you uncheck this box, Outlook won't display the Check Address dialog box when you enter what Outlook considers to be incomplete or unclear addresses.

To enter complex addresses, such as many business addresses, you're usually better off choosing Address and then entering the individual components of the address in the individual text boxes in the Check Address dialog box. You can enter as many lines of information as necessary in the Street box, but only one line of information in each of the other four boxes. You can open the Country/Region drop-down list and select a country or region; alternatively, you can enter a country or region name (either one that's in the drop-down list or one that isn't). After you've entered an address in this way, click OK to close the Check Address dialog box.

When you start entering the first address for a contact, Outlook automatically checks the This Is the Mailing Address box. If you don't want to mark that address as the mailing address, uncheck the box. Only one of the three postal addresses for each contact can be marked as the mailing address.

Note

The address marked as the mailing address is the one Outlook uses when you use contact items to address letters. It's also the address that's displayed in the Contacts Information viewer and printed with the default Address Cards view selected.

ENTERING E-MAIL ADDRESSES

Outlook can save three e-mail addresses for each contact—identified as E-mail, E-mail 2, and E-mail 3. These labels are built into Outlook; you can't change them.

To enter the first e-mail address, place the insertion point in the E-mail box and then enter the address in the normal manner.

The Display As box under the E-mail box is new in Outlook 2002. The text you enter in this box is what's displayed when you select the contact from elsewhere in Outlook. For example, when you're addressing an e-mail message and select an addressee from one of your Address Books, the To box in the Message form contains the Display As text instead of the contact's e-mail address.

→ For information about addressing e-mail messages, **see** "Addressing the Message," **p. 70**.

If you already have an e-mail address in an Outlook address book, you can copy the address from there.

To copy an e-mail address from an Address Book:

1. Click the button that is a book icon at the right of the E-mail box to display the dialog box shown in Figure 7.12.

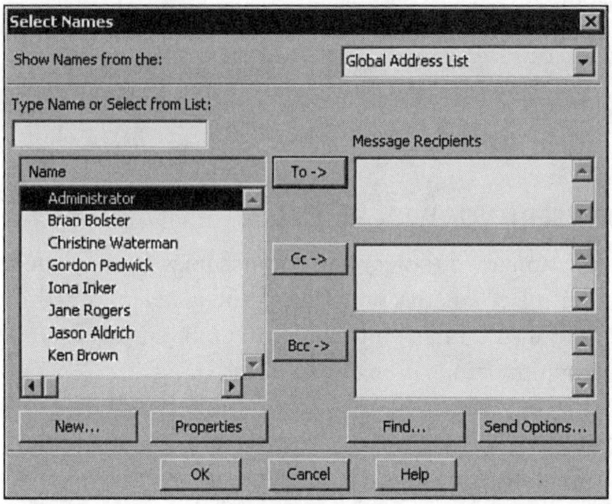

Figure 7.12
This dialog box displays the names in an address book.

2. Open the drop-down Show Names from the list and select the address book you want to use.

3. Select a name from the list and click OK to close the Select Name dialog box. The E-mail box in the contact form now contains the name you selected, underlined to indicate the name is a valid e-mail address.

After you've entered one e-mail address, you can click the button with the triangle icon (at the left of the E-mail box) to open a drop-down list, choose E-mail 2 or E-mail 3, and enter one or two other e-mail addresses.

Tip from

Gordon Padwick

If you need to save more than three e-mail addresses for a contact, you must create two or more Contact items for that contact.

ENTERING WEB PAGE AND INSTANT MESSAGING ADDRESSES

To enter a contact's Web page address, place the insertion point in the Web Page Address box and enter the address, normally in the following format:

```
http://www.company.com
```

PART

III

CH

7

Note

You don't have to enter `http://`. If you omit those characters, Outlook provides them automatically when you press Tab to leave the box. You also can drag URLs from your Favorites folder into the Web Page Address box.

To enter a contact's Instant Messaging address, place the insertion point in the IM Address box and enter the address.

Note

The capability to support Instant Messaging is new in Outlook 2002.

ADDING NOTES AND INSERTING ATTACHMENTS

You can use the large, unnamed (notes) box that occupies most of the lower part of the Contact form to enter miscellaneous notes about the contact. You also can choose Insert in the form's menu bar to insert a file, an Outlook Item, or an object. Inserting attachments is quite similar to making insertions in mail messages.

Note

You can drag (or copy and paste) such things as graphics files—a photograph of a person (someone you see only occasionally but want to be able to recognize), for example—and Outlook items into the notes box. After you do that, the notes box contains a reference to the file. You can subsequently open that reference to see the image the file contains.

➔ For information about inserting files into Outlook items, **see** "Message Insertions," **p. 79**.

ASSOCIATING A CONTACT WITH OTHER CONTACTS

The ability to associate a contact with other contacts was new in Outlook 2000 and is retained in Outlook 2002. You'll find this very useful in several circumstances:

- When you're creating contact items for friends, you can associate each contact with others in the same family.
- When you're creating contact items for business associates, you can associate each person with that person's supervisor and colleagues.

After you've saved a new Contact item, you can associate other contacts with it. To associate a previously saved contact with other contacts, start by opening the Contact item. Then, proceed as follows:

1. In the Contacts form, click Contacts to display the dialog box shown in Figure 7.13.
2. If you have more than one Contacts folder, you can select one of them in the upper pane to see a list of the contacts that folder contains in the lower pane.

Figure 7.13
The Select Contacts dialog box lists contact items in your default Contacts folder.

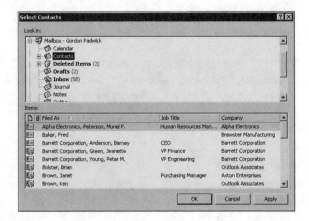

3. Select one or more contacts, and then click OK. The dialog box closes and the selected contacts are listed in the contact form's Contacts box.

ASSIGNING CATEGORIES TO A CONTACT

You should get into the habit of assigning one or more categories to every Outlook item, including contact items. By doing so, you can easily display all the items that have the same category, as well as group and filter items by category. If you're involved in a particular project, you can create a category for that project and assign that category name to all Outlook items related to that project. Subsequently, you easily can access items (messages, contacts, tasks, meetings, and so on) related to that project.

To assign categories to a contact:

1. Choose Categories to display the Categories dialog box shown in Figure 7.14.

Figure 7.14
The Categories dialog box lists your categories. If you have already assigned categories to the current contact item, those categories are listed in the Item(s) Belong to These Categories box.

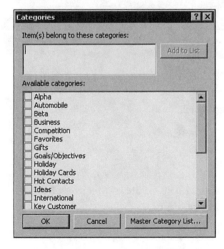

PART

III

CH

7

2. Select one or more categories for the contact item; then click OK to close the dialog box. The contact form now shows the selected categories in the Categories box.

Note

To remove a category already assigned to an item, scroll down the Available Categories list in the Categories dialog box to display the checked category name. Click the name to uncheck it.

MARKING A CONTACT AS PRIVATE

If you intend to share the contents of your Contacts folder with other people, but you don't want other people to see information about some contacts, check the Private box at the bottom-right of the contact form for those contacts you want to keep private.

➔ For information about sharing contact items with other people, **see** "Sharing Contacts with Other Outlook Users," **p. 188**.

If you're using Outlook as a client for Exchange, you can allow specific people with whom you share your folders to see private items.

➔ For information about making your private items available to certain other people, **see** "Giving Permission to Access Your Folders," **p. 470**.

ENTERING MORE CONTACT DETAILS

In many cases, you can enter all the information you need to save about a contact in the contact form's General tab. However, you can add more information in the Details tab shown in Figure 7.15.

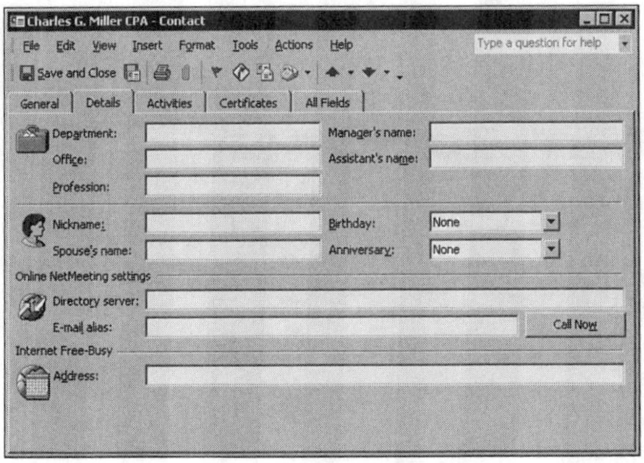

Figure 7.15
Use the Details tab to enter more information about a contact.

To enter information into any of the boxes in the top section of the tab, place the insertion point in that box and enter the information.

Tip from

Gordon Prod

Instead of entering the names of the contact's manager and assistant, it's usually better to create separate contact items for those people and associate those items with the current one (using Contacts on the General tab). By doing so, you can save other information about the manager and assistant, such as their e-mail addresses.

You also can enter a contact's nickname and spouse's name in the second section of the tab. If you want to save more information than just a name for the spouse, create a separate contact item and create an association with it.

→ For information about associating one contact with another, **see** "Associating a Contact with Other Contacts," **p. 152**.

You can enter the contact's birthday and anniversary either by typing dates or by clicking the button at the right end of the Birthday or Anniversary box to display a calendar and selecting a date from the calendar. One problem with entering birthdays and anniversaries is that Outlook insists on including a year, and you frequently don't know the year. My workaround for this problem is to use the year 1900 when I don't know the correct year (none of my contacts was born or married in 1900).

Note

If you enter a date without a year (such as 11/14), Outlook automatically provides the current year.

If you include a contact's birthday or anniversary, when you save the contact item, Outlook automatically creates a recurring event in the Calendar folder. Also, the next time you open the contact item, you'll see links to the Calendar items in the notes section of the contact form.

→ For information about the way Outlook handles dates, **see** "Creating a One-Time Appointment in the Calendar Information Viewer," **p. 196**, and "Creating Recurring Appointments and Events," **p. 209**.

The next section of the Details tab contains NetMeeting-related information. If the contact is someone with whom you have NetMeetings, and that contact is listed in a directory server, enter the name of that server in the Directory Server box. You also can enter the contact's e-mail address in the E-mail Alias box. After you've provided this information, you can initiate a NetMeeting by choosing Call Now.

Note

Outlook uses Internet Explorer to provide NetMeeting functionality.

→ To read about online meetings, **see** "Participating in Online Meetings," **p. 124**.

The Internet Free-Busy section at the bottom of the Details tab contains the Address box. Use this box for the address of the Internet server that contains the contact's free/busy information.

→ For information about sharing free/busy information, **see** "Setting Up Calendar Sharing," **p. 235**.

USING OTHER CONTACT FIELDS

Outlook saves each piece of information you provide about a contact in a separate storage location known as a field. Separate fields exist for each of the five components of a full name: Title, First, Middle, Last, and Suffix. Likewise, separate fields exist for each component of an address, as well for all the other elements of information you can save for each contact.

You can enter information into the fields you use most often in the contact form's General tab. In addition, you can access a few more fields in the Details tab. To access other fields, use the All Fields tab. When you first open this tab, you'll probably see no fields listed. That's because, by default, the tab lists User-Defined Fields in This Item. Unless you've created one or more user-defined fields, no fields are available to be listed.

To see some of the predefined fields, select the All Fields tab of the Contact dialog box, open the Select From drop-down list, and select Frequently-Used Fields, as shown in Figure 7.16.

Figure 7.16
The Frequently-Used Fields list contains fields listed in alphabetical order.

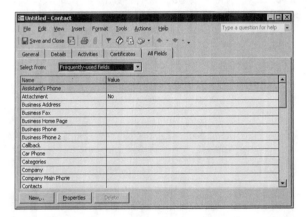

Field names are displayed in the left column. The content (if any) of each field for the selected contact is displayed in the right column. You can scroll down the list to see those fields not initially visible.

Outlook has two kinds of fields: those you can edit and those you can't. The Assistant's Phone field at the top of the list shown in Figure 7.16 is an example of a field you can edit. Notice that this is a field that isn't accessible from the General or Details tabs. To enter a phone number for the Assistant, select the row and type the number. The characters you type appear in the Value column.

Tip from

Instead of entering a value for a field that's not displayed on any of the tabs of the contact form, you can create a custom form that contains that field.

The second field in the list is Attachment, a field whose value you can't change. This field reports the presence or absence of one or more attachments to the currently selected contact item. The Value column shows Yes if the contact item has an attachment, or No if the item doesn't have an attachment. If you click the Attachment field, the entire row becomes blue; no insertion point exists because you can't change the value of this field in this tab.

Note

The only way to change No to Yes is to open the General tab and insert an attachment into the item. Likewise, the only way to change Yes to No is to remove all attachments.

The third field in the list of frequently used fields is Business Address. If you have entered a business address for the selected contact, this field contains that address. Because this is information you entered, you might expect to be able to change it, but you can't. The reason is that Business Address contains information that Outlook has constructed from other fields, specifically from the Business Address City, Business Address Country, Business Address Postal Code, Business Address State, and Business Address Street fields (you can see these fields if you open the list of Address Fields). You can edit the information in these individual fields and, after you do, the changes in those fields appear in the Business Address field.

Now that you understand that some fields are editable and others are not, you can go ahead and use this tab to enter contact information you can't enter from the General and Details tabs.

The only reason for entering information about a contact is so that you can subsequently see that information. Outlook displays information in various Information viewers, but viewers supplied with Outlook display only a few of the available fields. To display information you've entered in the All Fields tab, you have to either modify a standard view or create a custom view.

→ For information about creating custom Information viewers, **see** "Creating Custom Views," **p. 679**.

FLAGGING A CONTACT ITEM

You can flag a contact item at the time you create it or anytime thereafter. You might want to flag a specific contact so that Outlook gives you an automatic reminder related to that contact on a certain date. To flag a contact, select a contact in one of the Contact Information viewers and choose the Follow Up button on the contact form's Standard toolbar to display the Flag for Follow Up dialog box, shown in Figure 7.17.

Figure 7.17
Use this dialog box to select a flag and, if appropriate, a due by date.

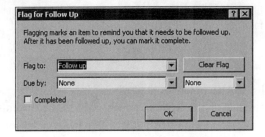

Flag a contact item in the same way that you flag an e-mail message.

Tip from

As explained in Chapter 4, "Sending Messages," you can replace the flag names available in Outlook with any appropriate words. If you select a Due By date, Outlook displays that date together with a time—the end of your workday. You can change that time to any other time.

→ To refresh your memory about flagging messages, **see** "Flagging a Message," **p. 86**.

SAVING A CONTACT ITEM

After you've finished entering information for a contact item in a contact form, you can save that item in your default Contacts folder by choosing Save and Close in the contact form's Standard toolbar. Alternatively, you can open the form's File menu and choose:

- **Save**—This saves the item in the default Contacts folder and leaves the form open. Information about the current item is displayed in the form.
- **Save and New**—This saves the item in the default Contacts folder and leaves the form open with all fields empty, ready for you to enter information about another contact.
- **Save As**—This saves the item in a specific format, as described in the following paragraphs.
- **Save Attachments**—This saves attachments to the item as subsequently described.

If you choose Save and Close in the form's toolbar or choose File, Save or File, Save and New, Outlook saves the new item in the default Contacts folder, which is the Contacts folder in the current e-mail account. To save the new item in a different Contacts folder, select File in the form's menu bar and click Copy to Folder to open the Copy Item To dialog box, where you can select the folder in which you want to save the item.

When you choose Save As, Outlook opens the Save As dialog box, in which you can choose where you want to save the item and in what format you want to save it, as shown in Figure 7.18.

Figure 7.18
Outlook initially proposes to save the contact information in Rich Text Format.

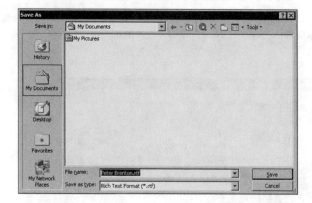

Navigate in the Save As dialog box to locate the Windows folder where you want to save the item. Then, open the drop-down Save as Type list to display a list of types. The available types are:

- **Text Only**—Use this if you want to use the contact information in an application that accepts text files.
- **Rich Text Format**—Use this if you want to use the contact information in an application that accepts files in Rich Text Format.
- **Outlook Template**—Use this if you want to save the item as an Outlook template from which you can create other Outlook items.
- **Message Format**—Use this if you want to save the item so that it's compatible with clients such as Exchange client.
- **vCard Files**—Use this to save the contact in the industry-standard vCard format so that you can share it with people who use Outlook or various other clients.

Outlook proposes to save the file with the contact's full name as the file name and an extension appropriate for the file type. You can choose a different file name, but you normally won't want to. Click Save to save the file.

If the currently displayed contact item doesn't have any attachments, nothing happens when you click Save Attachments. However, if the item does have attachments, Outlook displays the Save Attachment dialog box, in which you can navigate to a Windows folder, give the new file a name, and click Save to save the attachments.

CREATING DUPLICATE CONTACT ITEMS

If you create a contact item for a person who has the same name as an existing contact, Outlook alerts you when you save the new item by displaying the dialog box shown in Figure 7.19.

The capability to detect possible duplicate contacts and to merge information from one contact item into another is known as AutoMerge Contact.

Figure 7.19
This dialog box alerts you to the fact that you're about to save a duplicate contact.

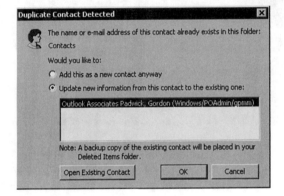

You can

- Choose Add This as a New Contact Anyway to create the duplicate contact item.
- Choose Update New Information from This Contact to the Existing One to merge information from the new contact item into the existing contact item.

To examine the existing contact, click Open Existing Contact.

CREATING SIMILAR CONTACT ITEMS

Outlook keeps information about each contact as a separate contact item. Although each contact item has a Spouse field, you can save only the spouse's name—no fields are available for the spouse's birthday or other personal information. Similarly, each contact item has a Children field (this field is available in the contact form's All Fields tab). You can use the Children field to list children's names, but no fields exist for other information about a contact's children. For your family contacts, therefore, you'll usually want to create a separate contact item for each family member.

In the case of contact items for organizations, one set of fields exists for a person's name. If you have several contacts within an organization, you'll need to have separate contact items for each member of the organization.

One way to create several similar contact items is to create and use an Outlook template.

➜ For more information about using templates to create similar contact items, **see** "Creating Similar Contact Items," **p. 333**.

CREATING CONTACT ITEMS FOR MEMBERS OF A FAMILY

You probably have better things to do with your time than to create separate contact items from scratch for each family member. And the good news is you don't have to. Instead, you can create a contact item for one member of the family; copy that item as many times as necessary; and then edit the individual items so that each has the correct name, birthday, and other personal information.

To create multiple contact items for family members:

1. Create a complete contact item for one family member. Save that contact item.

2. Locate the contact item you just created in the Contacts Information viewer.

3. Create a copy of that contact item by holding down Ctrl while you drag the item onto Contacts in the Outlook Bar.

4. Repeat step 3 as many times as necessary to create additional copies of the contact item.

5. Double-click each of the new contact items to open them one at a time in the Contact form. Edit each contact item as necessary; then choose Save and Close in the form's Standard toolbar to save the changes.

This procedure saves time by eliminating the need to enter such information as the postal address and phone numbers separately for each family member.

CREATING CONTACT ITEMS FOR MEMBERS OF AN ORGANIZATION

You can use the method described in the previous section to create contact items for members of an organization. However, Outlook offers a more convenient method.

To create contact items for organization members:

1. Create a contact item for one member of the organization. Save that contact item.

2. Select the contact item you just created in the Contact Information viewer.

3. Choose Actions, New Contact from Same Company. Outlook creates a new contact item and displays that item in the Contact form with the organization's name, postal address, business phone, and business fax numbers already entered. All other phone and fax numbers are not copied into the new contact item.

4. Complete the new contact item by entering the person's name and whatever other information is appropriate.

VIEWING AND PRINTING CONTACT ITEMS

After you've entered several contact items, you can use an Information viewer to display those items. After you install Outlook, you have several Contact Information viewers at your disposal. You can use any of these viewers, modify them, or create custom views.

PART

III

CH

7

→ For detailed information about displaying and printing contact items, **see** "Creating Views and Print Styles," **p. 651**.

DISPLAYING CONTACT ITEMS IN THE ADDRESS CARDS VIEW

The Address Cards view of contact items, as supplied with Outlook, shows contact items in a manner similar to how information about contacts is often written on index cards.

Outlook also can show information about contacts in the Detailed Address Cards view. This view is similar to the Address Cards view, but contains additional information. The next section explains how to select alternative views.

To display contact items in the Address Cards view, select Contacts in the Outlook Bar; then select View, move the pointer onto Current View, and click Address Cards. Now you see your contacts in the Address Cards view, as shown in Figure 7.20.

Figure 7.20
The Address Cards view shows basic information about each contact. Cards are listed in alphabetical order by File As name.

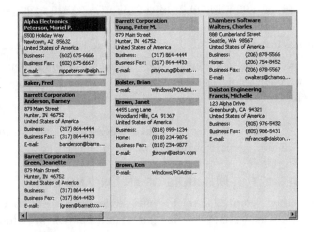

You can find information about a specific contact in several ways:

- Use the horizontal scrollbar at the bottom of the Information viewer to scroll through the cards.
- Click one of the index buttons at the right side of the viewer to locate a card according to the first letter of its File As name.
- Press an alphanumeric key on your keyboard to find cards that have File As names starting with a specific character.

You can double-click any contact to display the information about that contact in a contact form. Then, in the Contact form, you can edit any information field and add new information.

VIEWING CONTACTS IN OTHER INFORMATION VIEWERS

You can view contacts in ways other than the default Address Card view. To choose a different view of contact items, choose View and move the pointer onto Current View. Then, select one of the listed views.

The Address Cards and Detailed Address Cards views show contacts in index-card format. The remaining views show contact items in table format.

→ For information about view formats, **see** "Using Default Views," **p. 652**.

In addition to using the information viewers supplied with Outlook, you can create custom views.

→ For information about creating custom views, **see** "Creating Custom Views," **p. 679**.

CONTROLLING THE SORT ORDER FOR CONTACTS

By default, contacts are listed in alphabetical order by their File As names. However, you can change this sort order, using any other field as the basis for sorting. For detailed information about this, see Chapter 31, "Creating Views and Print Styles."

→ For information about contolling the sort order for contacts and other Outlook items, **see** "Sorting Items," **p. 672**.

PRINTING CONTACT ITEMS

Outlook offers several formats for printing contact items. With the Address Cards or Detailed Address Cards view of contact items selected, choose File, and move the pointer onto Page Setup to choose from this list of print styles:

- Card Style
- Small Booklet Style
- Medium Booklet Style
- Memo Style
- Phone Directory Style

With a Table view of contact items selected, you can choose either Table Style or Memo Style.

→ To find out about modifying the standard print styles and creating your own, **see** "Using Print Styles," **p. 682**.

When you choose a print style, Outlook displays the Page Setup dialog box, in which you can refine the page layout. After you've done that, click Print.

ORGANIZING CONTACT ITEMS

Many people start using Outlook quite casually and don't think through all the implications before they start creating Outlook items, contact items among them. People are busy; they grab onto what they need and start charging ahead. New users often ignore Outlook's categories but later wish they hadn't. By that time, they might have several hundred Outlook items—too many to go back and individually assign categories to.

Here's a way to simplify assigning categories to existing contact items. After you've done this, you can easily assign colors to each category.

ASSIGNING CATEGORIES TO EXISTING CONTACT ITEMS

You can use Outlook's Organizer to assign categories to existing Outlook items. This is much easier than opening each contact item separately in the contact form and assigning categories to it.

To assign categories to existing contact items:

1. Display any view of the Contacts Information viewer. In this case, a table view is likely to be more convenient than a card view.
2. Click Organize in the Information viewer's Standard toolbar.
3. In the Organizer pane, select Using Categories.
4. Open the drop-down Add Contacts Selected Below To list, and then select the category you want to assign to contact items.
5. While holding down Ctrl, select the items you want to assign to that category.
6. After you've selected all the items to which you want to assign the category, choose Add. Outlook assigns the category to the selected items.

You can repeat these steps as often as necessary to assign other categories to items.

APPLYING COLORS TO ITEMS ACCORDING TO THEIR CATEGORIES

After you've assigned categories to items, you can display items in colors according to their categories. The procedure described here applies only to a specific view of an item; to display certain contact items in a specific color in a card view, you must have that view selected.

This procedure assumes you have assigned a category named Alpha to certain contact items and that you want to display those contact items in red in the Address Cards view.

To assign colors to contact items:

1. Display the view of the Contacts Information viewer in which you want certain contact items to be colored.
2. Click Organize in the Information viewer's Standard toolbar.
3. In the Organizer pane, select Using Views. At this point, Outlook gives you the opportunity to select a different view.
4. Click Customize Current View near the upper-right of the Organizer pane to display the View Summary dialog box.
5. Choose Automatic Formatting to display the dialog box shown in Figure 7.21.

Figure 7.21
This dialog box lists the rules that already exist for the currently selected view. The checked rules are enabled.

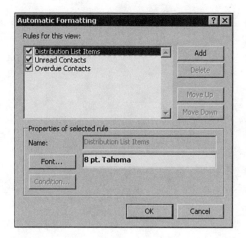

Note

Rules control how Outlook automatically processes items, such as placing certain items in specific folders or, in this case, automatically coloring items.

→ For detailed information about rules, **see** Chapter 28 "Creating and Using Rules," **p. 583**.

6. Click the Add button to add a new rule provisionally named Untitled. Outlook creates a new rule and automatically enables that rule as shown by the checked box adjacent to its name. The steps that follow create a new rule that displays all contact items to which the category Alpha is assigned in red.

7. Replace the name of the new rule in the Name box with a name such as Make Alpha Red.

8. Click Font to display the standard Windows Font dialog box.

9. Open the Color drop-down list, select a color (red in this case), and then click OK to return to the Automatic Formatting dialog box.

10. Click Condition to display the Filter dialog box. Select the More Choices tab shown in Figure 7.22.

11. Click Categories and enter the name of the category for which you want to color items (Alpha in this case).

12. Click OK three times to close the dialog boxes. Close the Organizer pane. Now the items with the specified category are colored red.

The new rule applies to all existing items and to any new contact items you create.

If you want to disable a rule, open the Automatic Formatting dialog box, previously shown in Figure 7.21, and remove the check mark from the box adjacent to its name. To delete a rule, open the Automatic Formatting dialog box, select the rule you want to delete, and choose Delete.

PART

III

CH

7

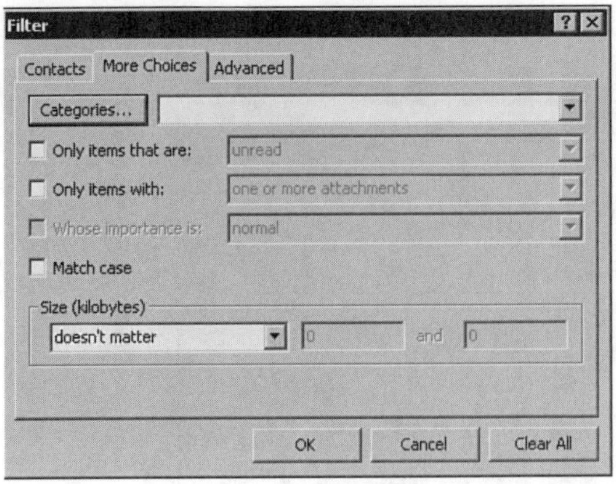

Figure 7.22
The More Choices tab opens with the Categories box empty.

USING OTHER METHODS TO CREATE CONTACT ITEMS

So far in this chapter, we've considered only one way to create contact items—by opening the contact form and entering information. Outlook provides several other methods in which you can create new contact items.

SAVING AN E-MAIL SENDER AS A CONTACT ITEM

When you receive an e-mail message, that message normally contains the sender's e-mail address. If you want to keep a record of that sender's e-mail address, you can easily create a new contact item.

After you've received an e-mail message, the header of that message is listed in your Inbox Information viewer. Follow these steps to create a contact item for the message sender:

1. Double-click the message header in the Inbox Information viewer to display it in the Message form.
2. Right-click the sender's name at the top of the message to display a context menu.
3. Click Add to Contacts to display a Contact form with the sender's name and e-mail address in the appropriate boxes.
4. Enter information in any other boxes on the form (at least enter a category), and then click Save and Close in the form's Standard toolbar.

Here's another way to create a contact item for a person who has sent you a message:

1. Drag the message header from the Inbox Information viewer onto the Contacts icon in the Outlook Bar. The sender's name and e-mail address are displayed in their appropriate boxes on a Contact form.
2. Enter information in any other boxes on the form; then click Save and Close in the form's Standard toolbar.

Using either of these methods, you might accidentally attempt to duplicate an existing contact item. If this happens, Outlook displays the Duplicate Contact Detected dialog box, previously shown in Figure 7.19. You can use this dialog box to decide whether you want to add the duplicate contact or update information in the existing item, as described previously in this chapter.

→ For information about dealing with duplicate contact items, **see** "Creating Duplicate Contact Items," **p. 160**.

IMPORTING CONTACTS FROM A MAIL MERGE DATA FILE

You can create contact items from an existing Word Mail Merge data source file. The data source file must be in the comma-delimited format.

Word creates a data source file in table format. You must convert that file to comma-delimited format before you can import the data into Outlook.

To convert a data source file in table format to comma-delimited format:

1. In Word, open the data source file.
2. Click anywhere within the data source file in table format.
3. Select Table, move the pointer onto Convert, and click Table to Text. Word displays a list of separators.
4. Click Commas, and then click OK. Word redisplays the data source file in comma-delimited format.
5. Select File, Save As to display the Save As dialog box.
6. Open the Save As Type drop-down list and select Plain Text. Word displays the File Conversion dialog box.
7. In the File Conversion dialog box, accept the defaults, and click OK to save the file.
8. Close Word.

After completing these steps, you have a text file that contains your data source in comma-delimited format. You can proceed to import the contact items in your data source into an Outlook address book.

To import a data source file into an Outlook address book:

1. In Outlook, select File, Import and Export to display the first Import and Export Wizard window.
2. Select Import from Another Program or File; then click Next to display the second wizard window.
3. Select Comma Separated Values (Windows), and then click Next to display the third wizard window.

PART

III

CH

7

Note

At this point, Outlook might display a message stating "Microsoft Outlook cannot start the required translator." With the Office XP CD installed in your drive, click Yes to install the translator.

4. Navigate to the folder that contains the comma-delimited data source you created in the preceding procedure; then click Next to display the fourth wizard window.

5. Select the Contacts folder into which you want to import the new contacts; then click Next to display the fifth wizard window.

6. This window displays the name of the file from which you intend to import and the name of the Outlook folder into which you intend to import. Click Map Custom Fields to display the dialog box shown in Figure 7.23.

Figure 7.23
Use this dialog box to relate the fields in the data source file to the fields in the Outlook Address Book.

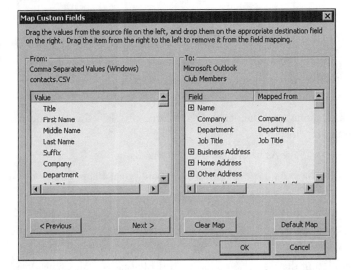

7. Drag fields from the data source in the From list into the To list.

8. Click OK to finish importing the files into the Outlook Address Book.

SHARING CONTACT INFORMATION WITH VCARDS

vCards are electronic business cards that use an industry-standard format recognized by Outlook and several other e-mail clients. You can find detailed information about vCards on the Internet Mail Consortium's Web page:

http://www.imc.org/pdi/vcardwhite.html

Each vCard is a file that has .vcf as its file name extension. You can

- Save a contact item as a vCard file.
- Attach a vCard to an e-mail message.

- Import information from a vCard file as an Outlook item.
- Receive a vCard in an e-mail message and save its contents as a contact item.

The following procedures explain each of these in detail.

To save a contact item as a vCard file:

1. With any Contacts Information viewer displayed, select the contact you want to save as a vCard.
2. Select File, Save As to open the Save As dialog box. Navigate to the folder in which you want to save the file.
3. Open the Save As Type drop-down list and select vCard Files.
4. The File Name box contains the name of the contact you selected in step 1 extension. You can change the file name if you want to.
5. Click Save to save the vCard.

Note

As an alternative to step 1, you can display a contact item in a Contact form and then select File, Save As in the form's menu bar.

After you've created a vCard containing information about yourself, you can send that vCard to other people via e-mail. You shouldn't send a vCard with every message you send because that unnecessarily increases the size of your messages. Each person needs to receive your vCard only once.

Here's how to send a vCard by e-mail:

1. With any Contacts Information viewer displayed, select the contact item you want to send as a vCard.
2. Select Actions, Forward as vCard. Outlook opens a message form with a vCard shown as an attachment.
3. Complete and send the message in the normal manner.

Tip from

As an alternative to step 1, you can display a contact item in a contact form and then select Actions, Forward as vCard in the form's menu bar.

To import information from a vCard file as a contact item:

1. With any Outlook Information viewer displayed, select File, Import and Export to display the first Import and Export Wizard window.
2. Select Import a vCard file (.vcf), and then click Next to display the vCard File dialog box. Navigate to the Windows folder that contains the vCard file you want to import.

3. Select the vCard file, and then click Open. Outlook imports the vCard into your Contacts folder.

Outlook doesn't detect duplicates when you import in this way from a vCard.

To save a vCard you've received by e-mail as a contact item:

1. In the Inbox Information viewer, double-click the header of the message to which a vCard is attached to display that message in a Message form. The attachment is displayed as an icon at the bottom of the form.

2. Double-click the vCard icon. Outlook displays the information from the vCard in a contact form.

3. Click Save and Close in the form's Standard toolbar to save the item.

IMPORTING CONTACT INFORMATION FROM OTHER APPLICATIONS

Outlook can import contact information from various other applications. See Chapter 18, "Importing and Exporting Outlook Items," for detailed information about this.

→ For information about importing information about contacts from other applications, **see** "Exporting Items to, and Importing Items from, Other Applications," **p. 378**.

Various add-ins are available from other companies for sharing contact (and other) Outlook items with other applications.

FINDING A CONTACT

Chapter 17, "Finding and Organizing Outlook Items," deals with finding Outlook items in general. You can use the information in that chapter to find Outlook items.

→ For detailed information about finding Outlook items, **see** "Finding Outlook Items," **p. 340**.

In addition to the general methods available, Outlook has a QuickFind Contact tool for finding contact items.

With any Outlook Information viewer displayed, the Standard toolbar contains the Find a Contact box. To find a contact, place the insertion point in the Find a Contact box, type all or part of the contact's name you want to find, and press Enter.

If what you type is sufficient to uniquely identify one (and only one) of the contacts in your Contacts folder, Outlook displays information about that contact in a Contact form. If two or more contacts match what you type, Outlook displays the Choose Contact dialog box, which lists the matching contacts. Select a contact and click OK to display information about that contact in a Contact form.

Outlook remembers each entry you make in the Find a Contact box. After you've made entries, you can click the small button marked with a black triangle at the right end of the Find a Contact box to display a list of your previous entries. Select a previous entry to find that contact again.

Note

If you have two or more Contacts folders, Outlook looks in all of them.

TROUBLESHOOTING

CONTACT INFORMATION

When you select Contacts in the Outlook Bar or Folder List, you might see the message There are no items to show in this view. That might puzzle you if you know your Contacts folder does, indeed, contain Contact items. The reason for not being able to display information about contacts is probably because your Contacts folder isn't enabled for use as an Outlook Address Book.

To solve the problem, right-click Contacts in the Outlook Bar or Address List to display a context menu, and click Properties in that menu. Select the Outlook Address Book tab in the Properties dialog box. You'll probably see that the Show This Folder as an E-mail Address Book box is not checked. Check the box, and then click OK to close the dialog box. Now, the Contacts Information viewer should show information about your contacts.

The information in this chapter covered most of what you need to know about phone numbers. In some cases, though, there's more to take care of. Microsoft has published several Knowledge Base articles that explain how to deal with some of these problems. You can probably also get help from your local telephone company.

Some regional phone companies in North America employ area code overlays that use two or more area codes for the same geographic area. If you live or work in such an area, you might have to dial an area code even if it's the same as your own. The Microsoft Knowledge Base article Q129049, "How to Perform 10-Digit Dialing in Windows 95 and Windows NT," describes three ways in which you can solve this problem. For specific information about Outlook, see the Microsoft Knowledge Base article Q197637, "Dialing 10-Digit Local Calls." Although these articles refer specifically to Outlook 2000, they apply also to Outlook 2002.

Windows keeps a list of international telephone access codes in a file named Telephon.ini. From time to time, some countries change their access codes. When this happens, if you rely on Telephon.ini, you can add a CountryOverrides section to that file. The Microsoft Knowledge Base article Q142328, "How to Change International Dialing Access Codes," explains how to update the file and also contains an updated list of international access codes.

The best resource I've found for detailed information about how Outlook handles phone numbers is the article "Microsoft Outlook Phone Numbers," which is available on the Slipstick Web site. Go to

```
http://www.slipstick.com/config/olphone.htm
```

CHAPTER 8

MANAGING AND USING CONTACTS

In this chapter

Chapter 7, "Creating Contacts," focused on creating contact items. This chapter describes some of the ways you can use those items.

WORKING WITH DISTRIBUTION LISTS

After saving contact items in a contacts folder as described in Chapter 7, you can use those items for many purposes, one of which is to create e-mail distribution lists, otherwise known as mailing lists. After you've created a distribution list, you can use that list as an address for e-mail messages to send a message to everyone on the list.

Note

This capability was new in Outlook 2000 and continues in Outlook 2002. In Outlook 97 and Corporate or Workgroup (C/W) Outlook 98, you had to use a personal address book if you wanted to create a distribution list. Internet Mail Only (IMO) Outlook 98 had a different way of creating distribution lists.

→ Instead of using a distribution list to send messages to a group of people, you can create and use a template, as described in Chapter 16, "Using Outlook Templates." **See** "Using Templates for Distributing Messages," **p. 332**.

CREATING A DISTRIBUTION LIST

To create an e-mail distribution list:

1. With a Contacts Information viewer displayed, select Actions, New Distribution List to display the dialog box shown in Figure 8.1.

Figure 8.1
The Distribution List dialog box opens, initially displaying an empty list.

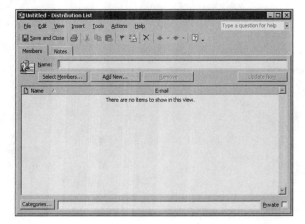

2. To add contacts to the distribution list, click Select Members. Outlook displays the dialog box shown in Figure 8.2.

Figure 8.2
This dialog box shows the contact items in your default contacts folder.

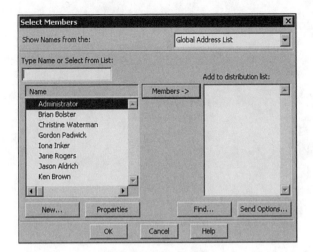

3. If you want the distribution list to contain a name that's in a contacts folder other than the default, open the Show Names From The drop-down list and select an Address Book.

Note

If you're using Outlook as a client for an Exchange server, the Select Members dialog box previously shown in Figure 8.2 initially displays contacts in the server's Global Address List. You can select contacts in that list or use a different Address Book.

4. Scroll down the list of contacts and select the contacts you want to have in the distribution list. Then, click Members to move those contacts into the Add to Distribution List box. Next, click OK to return to the Distribution List dialog box, as shown in Figure 8.3.

Note

If you have a long list of contacts, instead of scrolling to find those you want in your distribution list, you can click Find to locate contacts.

5. If you want to add names and e-mail addresses that aren't in your contacts folder, select Add New to display the dialog box shown in Figure 8.4.

6. Enter the new contact's name in the Display Name box and the contact's e-mail address in the E-mail Address box.

7. By default, Outlook assumes the contacts receive Internet mail in Simple Mail Transport Protocol (SMTP) format. If that's not the case, select Custom Type to select any other e-mail available protocol.

Figure 8.3
The selected contact names and their e-mail addresses are listed.

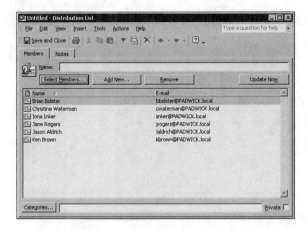

Figure 8.4
Use this dialog box to add a new contact to the distribution list and, optionally, to your contacts folder.

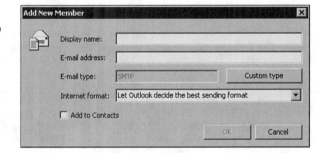

8. If you want to add the new contact to your contacts folder, check the Add to Contacts box.

9. Click OK to return to the Distribution List dialog box with the new contact listed.

10. Enter a name for the distribution list in the Name box.

11. Click Categories and assign one or more categories to the distribution list.

12. If you intend to share your contacts folder but want to keep the distribution list private, check the Private box.

13. Click Save and Close in the Standard toolbar to save the distribution list in your contacts folder.

The distribution list appears in Contacts Information viewers with the name of the distribution list as a File As name. A distribution list is identified in a card view by a pair of heads near the right end of a card's title. It's identified in a table view by a pair of heads superimposed on the contact item symbol in the Icon column.

MODIFYING A DISTRIBUTION LIST

To examine or modify a distribution list, double-click the list's name in a Contact Information viewer. Outlook opens the distribution list in the Distribution List dialog box.

At this point, you can:

- **Add more people to the distribution list**—Choose Select Members to add people from one of your Address Books. Click Add New to enter a new name and e-mail address that isn't in an Address Book.

- **Remove people from the distribution list**—Select the names you want to remove, and then click Remove.

- **Update the distribution list**—If you've made changes to items in your contacts folder (or other folders you used to add names into the distribution list) since you created the list, click Update Now to update the distribution list with those changes.

After you've made changes to the distribution list, click Save and Close to save the changed list.

USING A PERSONAL ADDRESS BOOK

You can have a personal address book in addition to a contacts folder. In Outlook 97 and Outlook 98, it was necessary to have a personal address book if you wanted to create distribution lists. However, now that you can create distribution lists based on contact items, it's no longer necessary to have a personal address book for that reason.

The main benefit of having a personal address book is that it gives you one place in which to keep information about contacts you frequently use. In a networked situation, you might have to look in several places for various contacts. If you have a personal address book, you can copy contact information from those various places into your personal address book to make that information readily available.

SETTING UP A PERSONAL ADDRESS BOOK

Here's how to set up a personal address book. Outlook allows you to create only one personal address book. If you already have a personal address book and attempt to create a second one, Outlook displays an error message.

To create a personal address book:

1. With any Information viewer display, select Tools, E-mail Accounts to display the dialog box shown in Figure 8.5.

2. Select Add a New Directory or Address Book, and then click Next to display the dialog box shown in Figure 8.6.

Figure 8.5
Use this dialog box to manage your e-mail accounts and directories.

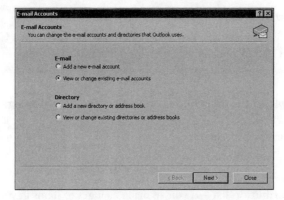

Figure 8.6
This is where you can choose whether to add a directory or address book.

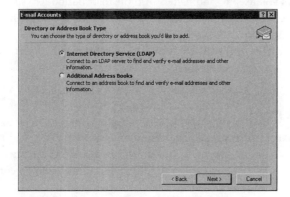

3. Select Additional Address Books, and then click Next to display the dialog box shown in Figure 8.7.

Figure 8.7
This is where you can choose which type of address book you want to create.

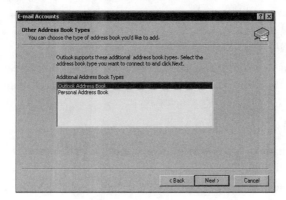

4. Select Personal Address Book and then click Next to display the dialog box shown in Figure 8.8.

Figure 8.8
Outlook proposes a name and path for the new address book.

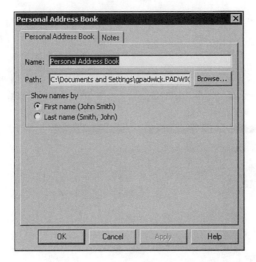

> **Note**
>
> The name "Personal Address Book" is the name used within Outlook. The path includes the file name used within the Windows environment.

5. You can change the name in the Name box to something more descriptive.

6. You can change the path (including the file name) in the Path box if you want. Click Browse if you want to search your Windows folder structure to locate a suitable path.

7. By default, people's names in a personal address book are shown in first-name, last-name order. It's usually preferable to list names in last-name, first-name order so names are listed alphabetically by last name. Click Last Name if you want to do that.

> **Note**
>
> If you want to add descriptive information about the new personal address book, select the Notes tab.

8. Click OK to complete creating the new personal address book. Outlook warns you that the new account (the personal address book) will not be available until you exit from Outlook and then restart Outlook. Click OK to continue.

9. Select File, Exit to close Outlook; then restart Outlook to start working with your new personal address book.

After restarting Outlook, you can verify that you have created a personal address book.

To verify the existence of a personal address book:

1. Select Tools, E-mail Accounts to display the E-mail Accounts dialog box previously shown in Figure 8.5.

2. Select View or Change Existing Directories or Address Books; then click Next to display a dialog box similar to the one shown in Figure 8.9.

Figure 8.9
This dialog box lists all your address books.

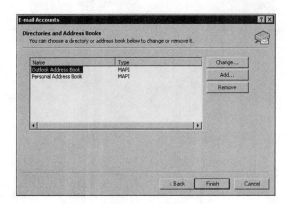

You might see more address books listed than are shown in Figure 8.9. If you've created a personal address book, as described in the preceding section, you should have Personal Address Book listed. Step 5 of the procedure in the preceding section described how to change the name of your personal address book. If you didn't change the name, the address book is listed simply as "Personal Address Book"; if you did change the name, the address book is listed as "Personal Address Book" followed by the name you entered enclosed within parentheses.

You can make changes to your address books in the dialog box shown in Figure 8.9. Click:

- **Change**—To make changes to the selected address book
- **Add**—To add an Internet Directory Service or another address book
- **Remove**—To remove the selected address book

ENTERING INFORMATION MANUALLY INTO A PERSONAL ADDRESS BOOK

This section describes how to enter information into your personal address book manually. You also can copy information into your personal address book, as explained in the next section.

To open your personal address book, display the Inbox Information viewer and click the Address Book icon in the Standard toolbar. Outlook displays the Address Book dialog box with one of your contacts folders selected in the Show Name From The box. Open the Show Names From The drop-down list and select Personal Address Book (or the name you gave your personal address book), as shown in Figure 8.10.

Figure 8.10
The Address Book dialog box initially opens with no contacts displayed.

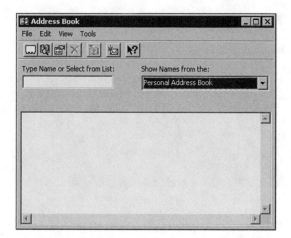

To create a new entry in your personal address book:

1. Click New Entry in the Address Book's toolbar. Outlook displays the dialog box shown in Figure 8.11.

Figure 8.11
Use this dialog box to specify whether you want to create a new contact or a new distribution list and where you want to save it.

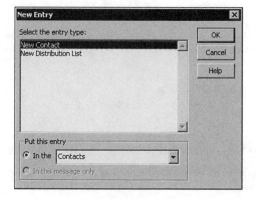

2. Select New Contact in the Select the Entry Type list.

3. Open the drop-down In The list and select Personal Address Book (or the name you gave your personal address book); then click OK. Outlook displays a dialog box that lists various entry types. Select Internet Address, and then click OK to display the dialog box shown in Figure 8.12.

4. Enter a contact's name in the Display Name box and enter the contact's e-mail address in the E-mail Address box.

5. Leave the Always Send to This Recipient in Microsoft Outlook Rich-Text Format box unchecked if appropriate, or check the box.

Figure 8.12
This dialog box opens
with the SMTP -
General tab selected.

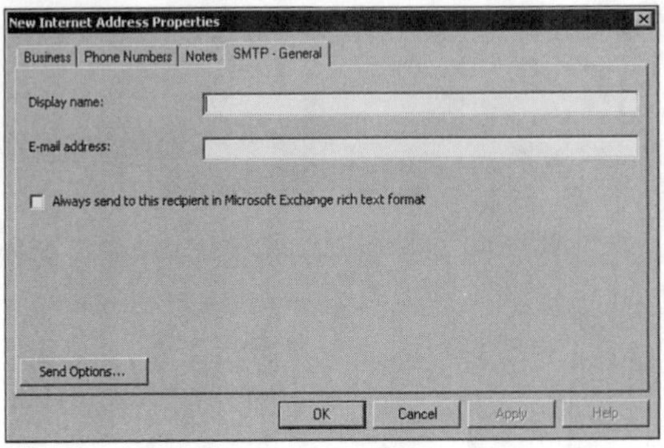

6. At this stage, you can select the other tabs to enter a business address and other business information, various phone numbers, and miscellaneous notes.

7. Click OK to save the new contact. Outlook displays the new contact's name in the Address Book dialog box previously shown in Figure 8.10.

You can use the Address Book menus and toolbar to do such things as

- Enter and edit contact information
- Find a contact
- Display and change a contact's properties
- Delete contacts
- Create a message to a contact
- Access help

COPYING CONTACT INFORMATION INTO THE PERSONAL ADDRESS BOOK

You can selectively copy contact information from other address books into your personal address book.

To copy contact information into your personal address book:

1. Click Inbox in the Outlook Bar to display the Inbox Information viewer.

2. Click Address Book in the standard toolbar to display the Address Book dialog box, similar to the one previously shown in Figure 8.10.

3. Open the Show Names From The drop-down list to display a list of available address books.

4. Select the address book from which you want to copy contact items. The Address Book dialog box displays a list of contact items in the selected address book.

5. Select those contacts you want to copy into your personal address book.

6. Click Add to Personal Address Book in the Address Book toolbar.

USING CONTACT ITEMS

You can use contact items in many ways, some of which are described in the following sections.

ADDRESSING E-MAIL AND FAXES

You can use contacts' e-mail addresses to address e-mail messages and contacts' fax numbers to send faxes.

→ For information about addressing an e-mail message, **see** "Addressing the Message," **p. 70**.

You also can autocreate a message by dragging a contact item onto the Inbox icon in the Outlook Bar. When you do so, Outlook creates a message form with the contact's e-mail address already in the To box.

USING CONTACTS FOR MASS E-MAILING

One way to use contacts for mass e-mailing is to create a distribution list and insert the name of that distribution list into the Message form's To box.

→ For information about distribution lists, **see** "Working with Distribution Lists," **p. 174**.

Another way to use contacts for mass e-mailing is to assign a category to all the contacts to whom you want to send the mailing. Then, display contact items in the By Category view. Drag the Category header onto the Inbox icon in the Outlook Bar. Outlook uses AutoCreate to open the Message form with the e-mail addresses of the contacts to which the category is assigned in the To box.

→ To find information about assigning categories to items, **see** "Assigning and Changing Categories for Other Items, " **p. 411**.

PLACING A PHONE CALL

> **Note**
>
> To place a phone call, your computer must have a modem with direct access to a phone line.

To place a phone call, select a contact in one of the Contact Information viewers and click the Autodialer button in the Standard toolbar to display the dialog box shown in Figure 8.13.

If the number you want to call is displayed in the Number box, click Start Call to place the call. You can open the Number drop-down list to select one of the contact's other phone numbers.

Figure 8.13
The dialog box opens with the contact's name in the Contact box and one of the contact's phone numbers in the Number box.

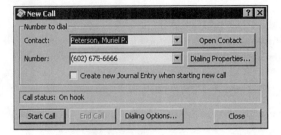

WRITING A LETTER TO A CONTACT

Select a contact in one of the Contact Information viewers, and then select Actions, New Letter to Contact to open Word with the first Letter Wizard window displayed, as shown in Figure 8.14.

Figure 8.14
Use the Letter Wizard to complete your letter.

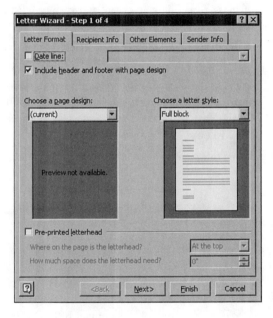

Follow the steps of the Letter Wizard to address and write the letter. The wizard uses the postal address you designated as the mailing address on the Contact form.

CREATING A FORM LETTER

You can use Outlook contacts as a data source for Mail Merge documents you create in Word. In Word, create a form letter as you normally do. You can use an Outlook distribution list as a data source for addressing form letters. Refer to a book about Word, such as *Special Edition Using Microsoft Word 2002*, published by Que, for information about this.

Setting Up a Meeting with a Contact

Select a contact in one of the Contact Information viewers; then select Actions, New Meeting Request to Contact to display the Meeting form shown in Figure 8.15.

Figure 8.15
The Meeting form opens with the contact's e-mail address in the To box.

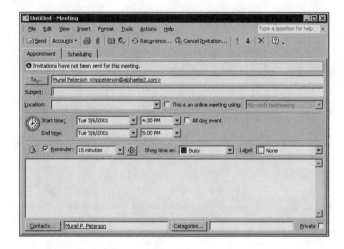

Complete the form, and then send it as an e-mail message.

→ To learn about creating one-time appointments, **see** "Creating a One-Time Appointment in the Appointment Form," **p. 200**.

Making a Note of an Appointment with a Contact

Select a contact in one of the Contact Information viewers. Then select Actions, New Appointment with Contact to display the Appointment form shown in Figure 8.16.

Figure 8.16
The Appointment form opens with the contact's name in the Contacts box at the bottom of the form.

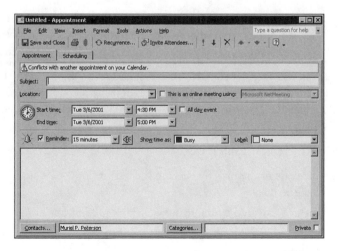

Complete the form, and then save it as a calendar item in your Calendar folder.

SENDING A TASK TO A CONTACT

Select a contact in one of the Contact Information viewers, and then select Actions, New Task for Contact to display the Task form shown in Figure 8.17.

Figure 8.17
The Task form opens with the contact's name in the Contacts box at the bottom of the form.

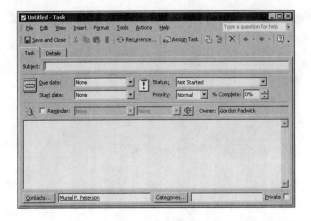

Complete the form, and then click the Assign Task button in the form's Standard toolbar to send the task assignment as an e-mail message.

→   For information about assigning tasks, **see** "Asking Someone to Accept an Existing Task," **p. 269**.

CREATING A MAP SHOWING A CONTACT'S LOCATION

You can display and print a map showing any contact's location in the United States and some other countries. To do so, you must have an e-mail account within Outlook that provides access to an Internet service provider and you must, of course, have an account with that service provider.

Double-click a contact item in one of the Contact Information viewers to display the details of that contact in a Contact form. If you have entered more than one postal address for the contact, make sure the one you want to see on the map is displayed on the form.

To display a map showing the contact's location, click the Display Map of Address button in the Contact form's Standard toolbar. Outlook establishes a connection to your Internet service provider, finds the Microsoft Expedia Maps site, and displays a map of your contact's location as shown in Figure 8.18.

You can do several things at this stage:

- Change the scale of the map by clicking the buttons in the Zoom Level box on the right side of the map.
- Change the area covered by the map by clicking the buttons in the Map Mover box on the right side of the map.
- Print the map.

- Save the map.
- Send an e-mail message containing the map.

Figure 8.18
The contact's location is marked with a push-pin on the map.

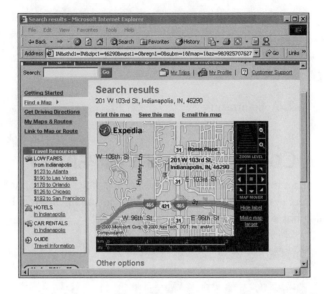

Notice, also, the Travel Resources box at the left, in which you can find information about airlines, hotels, car rentals, and more. By scrolling down below the map, you can get driving directions to the location.

TRACKING A CONTACT'S ACTIVITIES

You can use Outlook to track various activities of a contact, such as appointments, documents, e-mail, notes, and tasks. To display a contact's activities, double-click that contact in any Contact Information viewer to display details of that contact in the contact form. Select the Activities tab, as shown in Figure 8.19.

Figure 8.19
The Activities tab initially lists a summary of the contact's activities.

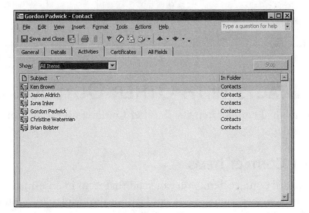

The Activities tab opens with a list of all activities relating to the selected contact. You can open the drop-down Show list to select various types of activities:

- All Items
- Contacts
- E-mail
- Journal
- Notes
- Upcoming Tasks/Appointments

EXAMINING A CONTACT ITEM'S PROPERTIES

To examine a contact item's properties, double-click a contact item in one of the Contacts Information viewers to display that item in a Contact form. Then select File, Properties to display the dialog box shown in Figure 8.20.

Figure 8.20
The Properties dialog box shows information about the selected contact item.

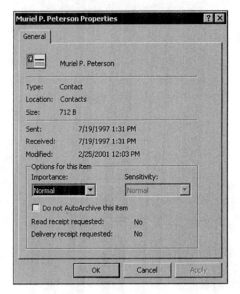

SHARING CONTACTS WITH OTHER OUTLOOK USERS

You can share individual contact items with other Outlook users, and you can share an entire Contacts folder.

SHARING INDIVIDUAL CONTACT ITEMS

To share an individual contact item, you can send that item in an e-mail message. In any Contact Information viewer, right-click a contact item to display its context menu. Click Forward to display a Message form with the selected contact item as an attachment.

You can drag additional contact items from the Contact Information viewer in the message.

Send the e-mail message in the normal manner. When a recipient receives the message, that recipient can drag the attached contact item from the message onto the Contacts icon in the Outlook Bar. Outlook adds the contact into the recipient's Contacts folder.

→ You also can save or forward contact information as a vCard. For detailed information about vCards, **see** "Sharing Contact Information with vCards," **p. 168**.

SHARING YOUR CONTACTS FOLDER

Several ways exist to share folders, including Contacts folders, between Outlook users.

One way to share a folder with someone else is to export the folder to a file from one computer, and then import it into the other computer. You can use this method for networked computers. You also can use it for computers that aren't connected to a network. Be aware, though, that Outlook folders often contain much more information than can be saved on an ordinary floppy disk. You will probably have to use high capacity disks (such as Iomega's Zip disks) or use a utility such as WinZip to compress the file and save it on several—perhaps many—floppy disks.

→ For information on importing and exporting Outlook items, **see** "Importing and Exporting Outlook Items," **p. 369**.

If you're using Outlook as a client for Exchange and have your Contacts folder in the Exchange store, you can make that folder sharable and allow specific users to have access to it.

→ To understand how you can share a contacts folder in your Exchange store, **see** "Delegating Access to Your E-mail," **p. 446**.

SETTING UP AND USING DIRECTORY SERVICES

Outlook supports the *Lightweight Directory Access Protocol (LDAP)* that provides access to Internet directories. An *Internet directory* is similar to one of your own address books, but provides access to worldwide Internet addresses. You can set up Outlook to have access to various Internet directories and subsequently use those directories in much the same way as you use your own address books. Table 8.1 lists some widely available directory services.

TABLE 8.1 GENERALLY AVAILABLE INTERNET DIRECTORY SERVICES	
Name	**Server**
Bigfoot	`ldap.bigfoot.com`
InfoSpace	`ldap.infospace.com` and `ldapbiz.infospace.com`
Switchboard	`ldap.switchboard.com`
Verisign	`directory.verisign.com`
WhoWhere	`ldap.verisign.com`
Yahoo! People Search	`ldap.yahoo.com`

You might find that your Internet service provider doesn't support all these services.

ACCESSING DIRECTORY SERVICES

To access LDAP directory services, you must add directory services to your accounts. You can access those directory services that are available from your Internet service provider.

To add LDAP directory services to your accounts:

1. With any Outlook Information viewer displayed, select Tools, E-mail Accounts to display the E-mail Accounts dialog box shown previously in Figure 8.5.

2. Select Add a New Directory or Address Book and click Next to display the dialog box shown previously in Figure 8.6.

3. Select Internet Directory Service (LDAP) and click Next to display the dialog box shown in Figure 8.21.

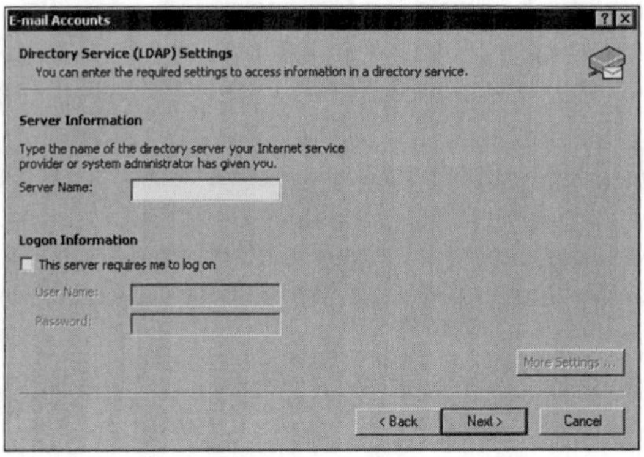

Figure 8.21
Use this dialog box to identify one of the Internet directory servers available from your ISP.

4. Enter the name of an available directory server (such as ldap.whowhere.com) in the Server Name box.

5. In most cases, you're not required to log on to the server, so leave This Server Requires Me to Log On unchecked.

6. Click More Settings. Outlook displays a message stating that the service won't be available until you exit from Outlook and then restart it. Click OK to display the dialog box shown in Figure 8.22.

7. Change the default name Outlook proposes for the directory service to a more meaningful name. For example, change the name to WhoWhere.

8. Unless you've been instructed otherwise by your Internet service provider, accept the port number Outlook proposes. Then, click OK to return to the dialog box previously shown in Figure 8.21. Click Next to move to the dialog box that states you have finished setting up the account. Click Finish to close that dialog box.

After you've added a directory service you can, if you want, confirm its presence.

Figure 8.22
Use this dialog box to provide a display name for the directory service and, if necessary, to specify a port setting.

Here's how you confirm the availability of a directory service:

1. With any Information viewer displayed, select Tools, E-mail Accounts to display the E-mail Accounts dialog box.

2. Select View or Change Existing Directories or Address Books; then click Next to display the second E-mail Accounts dialog box. This dialog box lists your e-mail accounts, including the directory service you just added.

USING DIRECTORY SERVICES

After you've set up Outlook to use Directory Services, you can access an Internet directory service in much the same way that you access one of your Outlook address books. After installing a directory service, you must have exited from Outlook and then restarted Outlook before you can use that directory service. Also, you must have a connection to the Internet established.

To find a person listed in a directory service:

1. With the Inbox Information viewer displayed, click Address Book in the Standard toolbar to display a dialog box that lists contacts in one of your address books.

2. Open the drop-down Show Names From The list and select the directory service you want to use.

Tip from

At this point, you might see a message stating `Can't contact LDAP Directory server`. This happens if the directory server is too busy to accept your connection. You might have to try several times to establish a connection to the directory server.

3. Click Find People in the Address Book dialog box's toolbar to display the Find dialog box.

4. Enter the full or partial name of the person you want to find in the Find Names Containing box; then click OK. After a few seconds delay, the directory service returns a list of names that match what you're looking for.

5. Double-click any name on the list returned by the directory service to see detailed information about that person.

Outlook can display up to 100 names returned by a directory service. Unfortunately, there's no simple way to see more than 100 names. The Microsoft Knowledge Base article Q262848, "How to Change the Query Limit for an LDAP Client," explains how you can edit the Windows registry to change the maximum number of names displayed by a directory service.

→ For information about editing the Windows registry, **see** "Changing the Data in a Key or Subkey Value," **p. 806**.

TROUBLESHOOTING

CONTACT FOLDERS

On the whole, I've found that creating and using contact items in Outlook works smoothly and reliably. The main problems with contact items are caused by incorrect entries and not keeping entries up to date.

Rather than being about solving problems after they occur, this section is principally about steering clear of problems. Some of the most common problems people have are caused by using too many address books.

In Outlook you initially have one Contacts folder, although you can create more. It might be tempting to have several Contacts folders: one for business contacts, one for friends, another for members of a society to which you belong, and so on. But what if some people move to a different address or change their phone numbers? Do you want to go to the trouble of making changes in several folders, and will you always remember to do so? It's far better, in my opinion, to keep information about everyone in a single folder. You can use Outlook's categories to group people as you want, assigning more than one category to a contact where that's appropriate. You also can create distribution lists based on contacts in a folder; Outlook can automatically update information in those lists if you change any information in your contacts folder.

So, before you create more than one Contacts folder, think carefully about why you want to, and look for a way to achieve your objective while using only one Contacts folder.

In a business situation, you might be using Outlook as a client for Exchange or other servers. If you're using Outlook as a client for Exchange server and are deskbound, you can keep your Contacts folder—and other Outlook folders—on your local computer or on the server. Each approach has advantages and disadvantages. To get the best of both worlds, you can keep information on both and regularly synchronize the two sets of folders. That way, you have access to your folders when the server goes down or a LAN problem occurs. In addition, you can easily share information with other people.

Until the arrival of Outlook 2000, the only way to conveniently create distribution lists was to add a personal address book to your C/W Outlook profile. In Outlook 2000 and Outlook 2002, however, you can create distribution lists based on your Contacts folder; therefore, that reason for having a personal address book has disappeared. However, if you're using Outlook with access to a mail server, particularly if you have access to several mail servers, you still have a good reason for using a personal address book. You can copy information about the people with whom you regularly communicate into your personal address book so that you have them all in one place and don't have to hunt around on various servers to find them.

The bottom line in working with contacts is to use as few address books as possible, be very careful to enter information correctly, be meticulous about keeping your contact items up to date, and—as I repeatedly say—always assign a category to every Outlook item.

CREATING CALENDARS

In this chapter

WHAT IS OUTLOOK'S CALENDAR?

You can use Outlook's Calendar to plan your future activities and also to refer back to previously planned activities.

The Calendar deals with three principal types of activities:

- **Appointments**—Activities that occur at specific times on specific days. Some appointments are with another person; others might be times you set aside to work by yourself.
- **Meetings**—Times when you meet with other people, usually a group. You can use Outlook to schedule meetings at times when other people are available. Similar to appointments, meetings occur on specific days at specific times.
- **Events**—Occasions, such as birthdays and holidays, that occur on specific days, but not at particular times on those days.

Any of these activities can be one-time or recurring. Recurring activities can be daily, weekly, monthly, or yearly.

These activities are created as Calendar items, saved in your Calendar folder, and displayed in a Calendar Information viewer.

Tasks are strongly related to your calendar, but Outlook deals with them separately because tasks don't (in the Outlook context) occur on a specific date and time.

→ For information about using Outlook to save information about tasks, **see** "Managing Tasks," **p. 251**.

CREATING A ONE-TIME APPOINTMENT IN THE CALENDAR INFORMATION VIEWER

We'll use the example of a one-time appointment to explain most of what you need to know about creating any kind of Calendar item.

Two ways exist to create an appointment: You can do so in the Calendar Information viewer or in the Appointment form.

Begin by clicking Calendar in the Outlook Bar to display whichever Calendar Information viewer was most recently displayed. Click View, move the pointer over Current View, and inspect the list of views shown in Figure 9.1.

Select Day/Week/Month to close the list and display the calendar in that view.

Click Day in the Information viewer's Standard toolbar to display a daily calendar, as shown in Figure 9.2.

The principal parts of the calendar's Day view are

- **Appointment Area**—Displays appointments for the current day
- **Event Area**—Displays events for the current day

- **Date Navigator**—Displays calendars for the current and next months
- **TaskPad**—Displays a list of current tasks

Figure 9.1
The checked view is the one that's currently displayed.

PART

III

CH

9

Appointment Area   Event Area   Date Navigator

Figure 9.2
The default Day view looks like this.

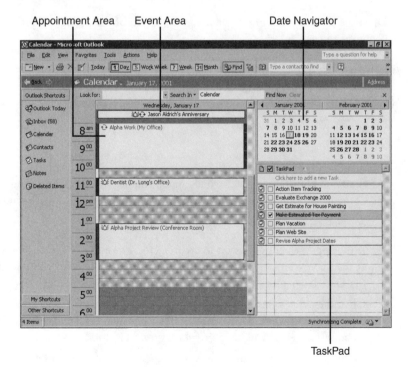

TaskPad

By default, the Appointment Area that occupies most of the left half of the viewer divides the day into half-hour segments. To change the scale, right-click anywhere in the

Appointment Area to display a context menu. Select Other Settings in that menu to display the dialog box shown in Figure 9.3.

Figure 9.3
You can use this dialog box to change the appearance of the calendar.

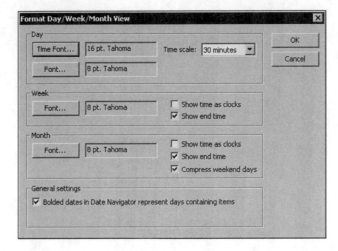

Open the drop-down Time Scale list near the top of the dialog box and select the time scale you want to use.

You can select from the displayed list of times, but you can't enter other times. The time increment you select for the time scale is also the default duration Outlook uses for meetings.

By default, the Date Navigator displays two months. The current day number is outlined in red. The number of the day for which appointments are displayed in the Appointment Area has a gray background. Day numbers for which appointments are scheduled are bold.

To create an appointment:

1. If the appointment you want to create is for a month not shown in the Date Navigator at the upper-right of the Information viewer, click the black triangle at the right end of the Date Navigator's banner until the correct month is displayed.

2. Click the date of the appointment in the Date Navigator. The Appointment Area now shows the hours in the selected day. That day's date is displayed at the top of the Appointment Area and has a gray background in the Date Navigator.

3. Point onto the time segment at which the appointment is to start, press and hold down the mouse button, drag down to select the period of the appointment, and then release

the mouse button. The period of the appointment is shown in dark blue. You can use the vertical scroll bar at the right edge of the Appointment Area to display times not initially shown.

Tip from

You can create appointments that start and end only on the time increments marked in the Appointment Area. If necessary, you can adjust start and end times in the Appointment form, as described subsequently.

4. Press Enter to signify you've finished defining the period for the appointment. The selected appointment period changes to white with colored top, left, and bottom borders. The insertion point is at the upper-left of the white area.

5. Enter a few words to describe the appointment, and then press Enter. The new appointment is displayed, as shown in Figure 9.4.

Figure 9.4
You now have an appointment entered in your calendar.

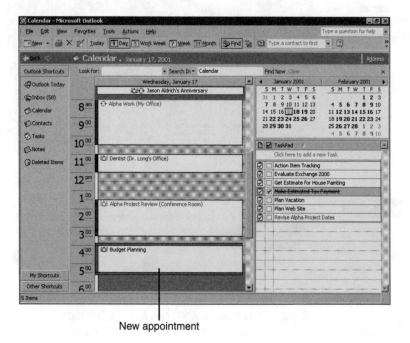

New appointment

Although these five steps provide a quick and easy way to enter appointments, they don't give you access to Outlook's capabilities to include additional information with Appointment items. To see more about the additional information you could include, double-click the appointment you just created to show it in the Appointment form, shown subsequently in Figure 9.5.

CREATING A ONE-TIME APPOINTMENT IN THE APPOINTMENT FORM

You can begin creating an Appointment item in the Calendar Information viewer, as described in the preceding section, and then fill in more details in the Appointment form. Alternatively, you can enter all the information for the Appointment item in the Appointment form, as described here.

To begin creating an Appointment item, display a Calendar Information viewer; then click New in the viewer's Standard toolbar to display the Appointment form shown in Figure 9.5.

Figure 9.5
This Appointment form is shown here with the Appointment tab selected and with typical information entered, ready to be saved.

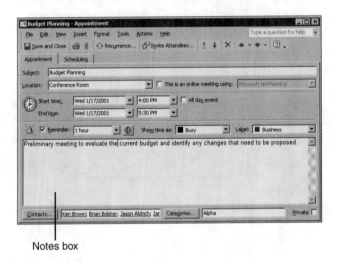

Notes box

Only the Appointment tab of the Appointment form is considered in this chapter. The Scheduling tab is principally used for planning meetings, as described in Chapter 10, "Managing Calendars."

When you open the Appointment form, it assumes you want to create an appointment for the day selected in the Date Navigator. If you haven't created an appointment during your current Outlook session, the Start Time box contains 8:00 a.m.; the End Time box contains 8:30 a.m. If you have created an appointment during your current Outlook session, the Start Time and End Time boxes contain the same times as in the most recent appointment you created.

The Appointment form defaults to the current date and a 30-minute appointment. The default appointment duration is the setting you select for the Appointment Area's time scale, as described previously in this section. You can change the default start time by displaying an Information viewer and choosing Tools, Options, Calendar Options to display the Calendar Options dialog box. In that dialog box, you can change the Start Time to a time other than 8:00 a.m.

If you open the Appointment form after the default start time, the InfoBar near the top of the form tells you This appointment occurs in the past. The InfoBar goes away when you change the start time to a later time in the current day or to a subsequent day.

Note

Outlook is pretty smart about telling you when the appointments and other activities you create might cause problems. In addition to alerting you when you try to create an appointment in the past, the InfoBar also warns you if you attempt to create an appointment that conflicts with an existing appointment.

ENTERING THE SUBJECT AND LOCATION FOR AN APPOINTMENT

When the Appointment form opens, the insertion point is in the Subject box. Enter a few words to describe the appointment. Try to place key words at the beginning of what you enter so that the nature of the appointment is obvious in the limited space available in the Calendar Information viewers.

Tip from

Even though Outlook shows you all the text in the subject of an appointment when you point onto it in a Calendar view, you should name appointments so that the first one or two words indicate the nature of each appointment.

After you've entered a subject for the appointment, press Tab to move the insertion point into the Location box.

Outlook remembers all previous locations you've entered. If the location for the appointment you're creating is the same as the location for previous appointments (such as My Office, Conference Room, or Home), click the button at the right end of the Location box to display a drop-down list of existing locations and select the appropriate one. Alternatively, enter a brief description of the location.

Note

If the appointment is for an online meeting, click the check box at the left of This Is an Online Meeting Using; otherwise, leave that check box unchecked. If you do check that box, several things happen: The adjoining drop-down list is enabled—you can open that list to select the type of online meeting, according to what's installed on your computer; also the Appointment form expands so that you can provide additional information.

→ For detailed information about online meetings, **see** "Participating in Online Meetings," **p. 124**.

After you've selected or entered a location, you can specify the start and end times for the appointment.

SPECIFYING START AND END TIMES

Start and end times are specified as a date and a time. Although most appointments are for a specific date, you can specify an appointment that starts on one day and ends on another.

Leave the All Day Event box unchecked. If you check this box, the appointment becomes an event.

→ For information about creating events, **see** "Creating a One-Time Event," **p. 207**.

ENTERING A DATE

What follows describes how you specify a start date. When you specify a start date, Outlook automatically uses the same date as the end date. You can use the information in this section to specify a different end date for appointments that extend from one day into the next.

When you open the Appointment form, the Start Time date box contains the current date. You can replace the displayed date by entering a different date. When you do so, you must use a date format that's compatible with your Windows Regional Settings. For example, if you want to create an appointment for July 5, 2001, and you've set your Windows Regional Settings for English (United States), you must enter 7/5/01; however, if you've set your Windows Regional Settings to English (United Kingdom), you must enter 5/7/01.

SELECTING A DATE

Instead of entering a date, you can select it from a calendar. To select a date, click the button at the right end of the Start Time date box to display a calendar that shows the current month, as shown in Figure 9.6.

Figure 9.6
Outlook displays a calendar for the current month.

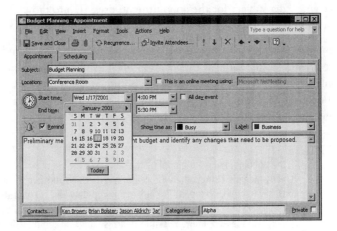

If you want to create an appointment within the current month, click the day within the month. To create an appointment for a subsequent month, click the right-pointing triangle in the month's banner to display subsequent months. With the appropriate month displayed, click the day for the appointment to return to the Appointment form with the selected day shown in the Start Time date box.

DESCRIBING A DATE

You can avoid the problem of defining dates in a way that's compatible with your Windows Regional Settings by describing dates instead of defining them.

Instead of entering a date in the Start Time or End Time date boxes, you can enter words or phrases, such as

- **Tomorrow**—Outlook displays the date of the day after today.
- **Next Week**—Outlook displays the date of the day one week after today.
- **Next Month**—Outlook displays the date of the day one month after today.
- **Three Days from Now**—Outlook displays the date three days after today.
- **First Day of Next Week**—Outlook displays the date of the first day of next week.
- **Third Day of Next Week**—Outlook displays the third day of next week.

PART
III
CH
9

Tip from

In addition to describing dates in words, you can use abbreviations. For example, "10d" means ten days from now, "3w" means three weeks from now, "2mo" means two months from now, and "5y" means five years from now. In each case, "now" is the date shown in the Start Time box, not the current date as indicated by your computer's internal clock.

You can combine these abbreviations. For example, "1mo 3d" means one month and three days from now.

These are just some examples of descriptive phrases I found Outlook understands. I also tried "Third day of month after next" and was rewarded with the You must specify a valid month message. There are some limitations to Outlook's intelligence.

ENTERING A TIME

You can enter a time in the box at the right of the Start Time date box using the 12-hour or 24-hour format. Here are some typical entries: 7:15, 7:15 AM, 7:15 PM, 19:15.

Tip from

If you enter a time without appending AM or PM, Outlook always assumes PM. To enter a time in the morning, you must append AM (or just A) to that time.

The advantage of entering a time in this manner is that you are not limited to times in a list. You can enter whatever times are appropriate. Such times as 3:17 or 18:21 are quite acceptable.

Note   Midnight is 12:00 AM. Noon is 12:00 PM.

SELECTING A TIME

To select a time, click the button at the right end of the Time box to display a list of times. These times are always at half-hour intervals; you can't change that. Select a time from the list.

DESCRIBING A TIME

You can describe a time in words, just as you can describe dates in words. Some of the words you can use are Noon, Midnight, Three PM, and Ten AM.

When you specify a start time, Outlook automatically changes the end time so that the duration of the appointment remains unchanged. You can separately change the end time without affecting the start time.

SETTING A REMINDER

By default, Outlook doesn't provide reminders for appointments. If you want to be reminded about an appointment, check Reminder on the Appointment form. After you've done that, Outlook pops up a reminder on your screen 15 minutes before a meeting starts. You can change the default reminder time in the Options dialog box.

→ To learn how you can change the default reminder time, **see** "Calendar Options," **p. 539**.

To change the time ahead of the start of the appointment when the reminder appears, you can enter any number of minutes, hours, or days. Alternatively, you can click the button at the right end of the Reminder box to open a drop-down list and select from it.

Tip from

When you enter a time (instead of selecting it from a list), you can enter any number of minutes, hours, weeks, months, or years. You can use "m" as an abbreviation for minutes, "h" as an abbreviation for hours, "d" as an abbreviation for days, and "w" as an abbreviation for weeks. Outlook also accepts decimal numbers, such as 1.5h, 2.3d, and so on.

You can choose to have an audible reminder. To do that, click the button that has a loudspeaker icon at the right side of the Reminder box. Outlook displays a dialog box in which you can select any .wav sound file installed on your computer.

Tip from

To see reminders on your screen, or to hear them, Outlook must be running. That's why it's a good idea to have Outlook running (probably minimized) while you're not using it.

If Outlook isn't running when a reminder is due, you see or hear that reminder the next time you start Outlook. Unfortunately, that is often too late!

CLASSIFYING AN APPOINTMENT

By default, Outlook classifies the time for your appointments as Busy. You can open the drop-down Show Time As box and select among Free, Tentative, Busy, and Out of Office.

When you subsequently display an appointment in the Day/Week/Month view of the Calendar Information viewer, each appointment has a colored border that identifies the appointment's classification. The colors are

- **Busy**—Blue
- **Free**—White
- **Out of Office**—Purple
- **Tentative**—Blue with white stripes

COLORING AN APPOINTMENT ITEM

One of the improvements in Outlook 2002 is the ability to use colors to identify appointment items. To use this capability, open the drop-down Label list to display this list of colors and their corresponding labels:

- **White**—None
- **Red**—Important
- **Blue**—Business
- **Green**—Personal
- **Gray**—Vacation
- **Orange**—Must Attend
- **Light blue**—Travel Required
- **Olive**—Needs Preparation
- **Purple**—Birthday
- **Dark Green**—Anniversary
- **Yellow**—Phone Call

Click one of the colors to identify an appointment item. Subsequently, when you display a calendar, the item has the selected color as its background.

You can't change the colors available for coloring appointment items, but you can change the labels associated with each color. To change one or more labels, right-click an Appointment item in the Calendar Information viewer and, in the context menu, move the pointer onto Label to see a list of colors with their current labels. At the bottom of that list, click Edit Labels to display the Edit Calendar Labels dialog box, in which you can change the text associated with each color.

ADDING NOTES TO AN APPOINTMENT ITEM

You can add notes to an Appointment item in the unnamed notes box that occupies most of the lower part of the Appointment form. It's often useful to enter notes here at the time you create the Appointment to provide information about what the appointment is about and what you intend to accomplish. During the appointment or after, you can add notes about what happened during the appointment.

To add notes, place the insertion point in the notes box and begin typing.

While the insertion point is in the notes box, you can select Insert in the form's menu bar and then select File to attach a file to the Appointment item. You also can select Item to attach an Outlook item to the Appointment item, or Object to attach a Windows object.

→ For general information about insertions, **see** "Message Insertions," **p. 79**.

ASSOCIATING CONTACTS WITH AN APPOINTMENT ITEM

If the appointment is with people who are listed in one of your address books, you can associate the Appointment item with those people. After doing that, when you subsequently open the Appointment item you can double-click a name in the Contacts box to find information about that person.

Click Contacts to open the Select Contacts dialog box, select the appropriate contacts, and click OK to list those contacts in the Contacts box.

→ For more information about associating contacts, **see** "Associating a Contact with Other Contacts," **p. 152**.

ASSIGNING CATEGORIES TO AN APPOINTMENT ITEM

As for all Outlook items, you should make a habit of assigning at least one category to every Appointment item so that you can quickly find items in the future.

Click Categories to open the Categories dialog box, select the appropriate categories, and click OK to return to the Appointments form in which the selected categories are listed.

→ Outlook's categories are described in Chapter 20, "Using Categories and Entry Types," **p. 403**.

MAKING AN APPOINTMENT PRIVATE

If you sometimes share calendar information with other people, you might want to keep details about some of your appointments private. To do so, check the Private box at the bottom-right of the Appointment form. After doing that, people with whom you share your calendar will see that you have an appointment at that time, but won't see any information about the appointment.

→ For information about sharing your calendar, **see** "Sharing a Calendar," **p. 234**.

SAVING THE APPOINTMENT ITEM

Click Save and Close in the Appointment form's Standard toolbar to save the Appointment item in your Calendar folder. Alternatively, you can select File, Save or File, Save As to save the item in other formats.

→ If you need help with saving Outlook items, **see** "Saving a Contact Item," **p. 158**.

To see the Appointment item, select the Day/Week/Month view of the Calendar Information viewer. Select Day, Work Week, Week, or Month in the Standard toolbar. Navigate to the period that contains the new appointment in the Date Navigator to see the new appointment in your calendar.

→ For information about viewing appointments, **see** "Viewing Appointments and Events," **p. 220**.

Note

Notice that the Day/Week/Month view with Day selected now shows the appointment location in parentheses next to the subject of the appointment.

CREATING A ONE-TIME EVENT

As mentioned previously in this chapter, Outlook's events are very similar to appointments. The only difference is that events occur on a day or days without any times being specified, whereas appointments have start and end times. Birthdays, anniversaries, and holidays are typical events.

You can create Event items in the Day/Week/Month view of the Calendar Information viewer or in the Event form.

CREATING A ONE-TIME EVENT IN THE INFORMATION VIEWER

Display the Day/Week/Month view of the Calendar Information viewer; then click Day in the Standard toolbar to display the Information viewer shown previously in Figure 9.2.

Use the Date Navigator to display the day of the event. Point into the Event Area above the Appointment Area and click the mouse button. The Event Area becomes white to show it's ready for you to enter the name of an event. Type the name of the event and press Enter. Click in an unoccupied part of the Appointment Area. Now the event appears in a white box within the Event Area, as shown in Figure 9.7.

To create another event for the same day, point onto the gray area below the first event and click the mouse button. The dark gray area becomes white. Type the name of the second event. The words you type appear above the first event. Press Enter after you've finished typing the name of the second event, and then click an unoccupied part of the Appointment Area. Now two white event boxes are in the Event Area.

Figure 9.7
The bell symbol at the left of the event name indicates that Outlook has created a reminder for the event.

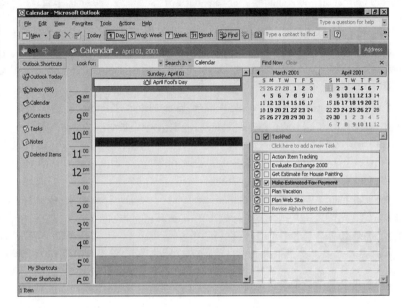

After you've created one or more events in this way, you can double-click an event to display that event in the Event form shown in Figure 9.8.

CREATING A ONE-TIME EVENT IN THE EVENT FORM

You can use the Event form to provide more information about an event you created in the Calendar information viewer, or you can create an Event item from scratch in the Event form, as described in the following paragraphs.

To create an Event item in the Event form, display the Calendar Information viewer and select Actions, New All Day Event to display the Event form shown in Figure 9.8.

→ Enter dates in this form in the same way that you enter dates in the Appointment form. **See** "Creating a One-Time Appointment in the Appointment Form," **p. 200**.

CHANGING AN APPOINTMENT INTO AN EVENT AND VICE VERSA

Because appointments and events are so similar, changing one into the other is easy.

To change an appointment into an event, display the appointment in the Appointment form; then check the All Day Event box. As soon as you do this, the times for the appointment disappear and the name of the form changes to Event. Click Save and Close in the form's Standard toolbar to return to the Calendar Information viewer. Now, what was previously shown as an appointment is shown in the Event Area above the Appointment Area.

Figure 9.8
The Event form is almost identical to the Appointment form. The important difference is that the Start Time and End Time boxes show only dates (not times).

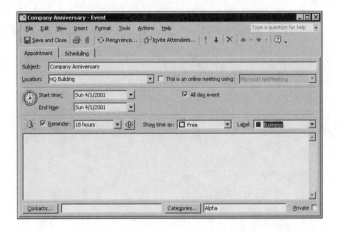

PART

III

CH

9

To change an event into an appointment, display the event in the Event form, and then uncheck the All Day Event box. As soon as you do that, the time boxes for the appointment appear and the name of the form changes to Appointment. Enter appropriate start and end times; then click Save and Close in the form's Standard toolbar to return to the Calendar Information viewer.

CREATING RECURRING APPOINTMENTS AND EVENTS

Recurring appointments and events are those that occur regularly. A weekly appointment with your supervisor is an example of a recurring appointment. A person's birthday is an example of an annual recurring event.

The easiest way to create a recurring appointment or event is to start by creating a one-time appointment or event, and then convert that into a recurring one. The following example applies specifically to an appointment. You can use almost exactly the same technique for an event.

Create a one-time appointment and display that appointment in the Day/Week/Month view of the Calendar Information viewer. Double-click the appointment to show it in the Appointment form. Click the Recurrence button in the form's Standard toolbar to display the Appointment Recurrence dialog box, shown in Figure 9.9.

MODIFYING THE APPOINTMENT TIME

The Appointment Time section at the top of the dialog box shows the start and end times of the appointment and its duration. You can change either of these times:

- If you change the Start time, the End time changes automatically to keep the duration the same.

- If you change the End time, the Duration changes to show the new duration.
- If you change the Duration, the End time changes to show the correct period between the Start and End times.

Figure 9.9
Use this dialog box to specify a weekly recurrence pattern.

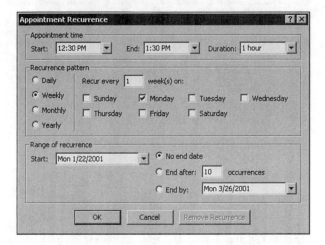

If you click OK after making changes in the Appointment Time section to go back to the Appointment form, that form shows the changed times.

SETTING THE RECURRENCE PATTERN

The Recurrence Pattern section of the dialog box is where you can select Daily, Weekly, Monthly, and Yearly recurrence. The dialog box opens with Weekly recurrence selected, as shown previously in Figure 9.9.

WEEKLY RECURRENCE

You can define the weekly interval. By default, the dialog box shows 1 in the Recur Every box. You can change this to another number. For example, if the appointment occurs every other week, you would change the number to 2.

You can define the days of the week on which the recurring meeting occurs. Check the appropriate days. If the meeting occurs on Mondays, check Monday and make sure no other day is checked. You can check as many days as necessary.

DAILY RECURRENCE

For a daily recurrence, select Daily. The pattern options change to those shown in Figure 9.10.

The default daily option is Every 1 Day(s). Select this if you have an appointment on all seven days of the week. If you have an appointment on all weekdays, select Every Weekday.

Figure 9.10
Use the Daily option to define a daily recurrence pattern.

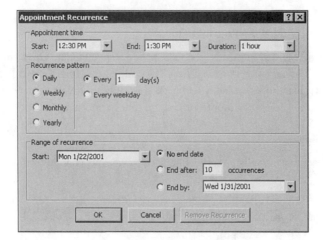

MONTHLY RECURRENCE

For a monthly recurrence, select Monthly. The pattern options change to those shown in Figure 9.11.

Figure 9.11
Use the Monthly option to define a monthly recurrence pattern.

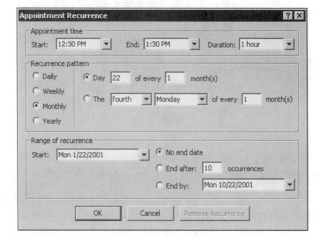

The default recurrence pattern is for one day every month. Outlook initially chooses the day number specified for the original appointment date. You can change that day number to any number in the range 1–31.

Note

If you enter 29, 30, or 31 as the day number, Outlook creates the appointment for the last day of the month for those months that don't have a corresponding day.

The number 1 (for months) indicates every month. You can change this to 2 for every other month, 3 for every third month, and so on.

Instead of specifying day numbers, you can specify a specific day. Open the drop-down list to the right of The and select among First, Second, Third, Fourth, and Last. Open the second drop-down list and select a day name. As described in the previous paragraph, you can accept the default 1 for every month or change that to another number.

YEARLY RECURRENCE

For a yearly recurrence, select Yearly. The pattern options change to those shown in Figure 9.12.

Figure 9.12
Use the Yearly option to define a yearly recurrence pattern.

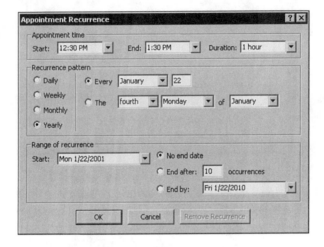

The default yearly recurrence pattern is for every year on the date specified for the original one-time appointment. You can open the drop-down list of months and select a month. You also can replace the default day number with any number in the range 1–31.

Instead of specifying a specific date, you can define a date descriptively by selecting the second option button. Open the first drop-down list at the right of The and select among First, Second, Third, Fourth, and Last. Open the second drop-down list and select a day name. Then open the third drop-down list and select a month.

Note

Although Outlook provides a considerable amount of flexibility for recurrence patterns, it has some limitations. For example, United States residents are required to pay their income taxes by April 15 unless that is a Saturday or Sunday, in which case taxes are due on the next Monday. Outlook can't create recurrence patterns with exceptions like this.

SETTING THE RECURRENCE RANGE

Use the Range of Recurrence section of the Appointment Recurrence dialog box to specify when the recurring appointment starts and stops.

By default, the recurrence starts on the date of the original one-time appointment. You can click the button at the right end of the Start box to display a drop-down calendar in which you can select a different start date. Alternatively, you can enter a date in the Start box.

Also by default, Outlook selects No End Date. You can choose to end the recurrence pattern after a certain number of occurrences or at a certain date. To stop the recurrence pattern after a certain number of occurrences, click the End After option button and replace the default 10 with the appropriate number. To stop the recurrence pattern at a certain date, click the End By option button and then click the button at the right end of the End By box to open a drop-down calendar in which you can select a date. Alternatively, you can enter a date in the End By box.

DISPLAYING RECURRING APPOINTMENTS AND EVENTS

After you've finished defining the recurrence pattern, click OK to display the Recurring Appointment form shown in Figure 9.13, which is similar to the Appointment form.

Figure 9.13
This form describes the recurring appointment instead of showing its start time and end time in boxes.

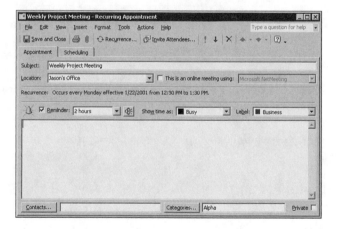

Click Save and Close in the form's Standard toolbar. Now you can use the Calendar's Day/Week/Month view to display the recurring appointment.

To display recurring appointments:

1. If necessary, select View, move the pointer onto Current view, and select Day/Week/Month.

2. Select Day in the Information viewer's Standard toolbar.

3. Use the Calendar Navigator to display the day calendar for the first occurrence of the recurring appointment. Figure 9.14 shows how this appointment is displayed in the calendar.

Figure 9.14
An occurrence of a recurring appointment is displayed in almost the same manner as a one-time appointment.

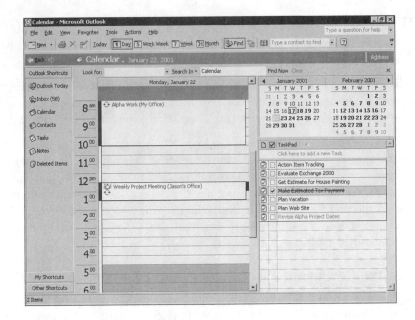

Note

The two curved arrows within the appointment indicate that you're seeing one occurrence of a recurring appointment.

4. Use the Date Navigator to select the next occurrence of the recurring appointment. This occurrence is displayed just like the first.

You can use the same technique to display subsequent occurrences of the recurring appointment.

CREATING RECURRING APPOINTMENTS IN ANOTHER WAY

Instead of starting from a one-time appointment, you can create a recurring appointment by using the method described in this section. Outlook doesn't offer a similar method to create recurring events.

To create a recurring appointment or event:

1. With any Calendar Information viewer displayed, select Actions, New Recurring Appointment to display the Appointment Recurrence dialog box shown previously in Figure 9.9.

2. In the Appointment Time section of the dialog box, enter or select the start time in the Start box. Then enter either the end time in the End box or the duration in the Duration box.

3. In the Recurrence Pattern section of the dialog box, select a recurrence pattern.

4. In the Range of Recurrence section of the dialog box, enter or select a start date in the Start box; then select No End Date, End After, or End By.

5. Click OK to display the Appointment Recurrence form shown previously in Figure 9.13. Enter whatever additional information is appropriate.

6. Click Save and Close in the form's Standard toolbar to save the recurring appointment.

ENTERING HOLIDAYS AND OTHER SPECIAL DAYS

Holidays and other special days are common examples of yearly recurring events. You can create these recurring events in two ways:

- Automatically, by using Outlook's built-in lists of holidays for various countries and cultures

- Manually, by creating individual recurring events

I usually prefer to do things automatically rather than manually—I'm all for saving time and effort—but, in this case, I recommend the manual method. I don't recommend you use Outlook's automatic method for these reasons:

- *The automatic method adds holidays only over the period from January 1, 2000 to December 31, 2005.* That's a problem if you want to find out the day on which a holiday occurred a few years ago, or when it will occur several years ahead.

- *The automatic method creates all holidays as individual one-time events, rather than as recurring events.* This means that holidays occupy much more disk space than necessary.

- *If you choose two or more countries or cultures that have the same holidays, the automatic method duplicates those holidays in your calendar.*

- *The automatic method assigns the Holiday category to all the one-time events it creates.* I prefer to reserve that category for events that really are holidays. Groundhog Day and Valentine's Day aren't holidays for me!

One advantage of using Outlook's automatic holidays is that you have ready access to holidays for countries and cultures other than your own. Another advantage is that it provides holidays that do not have a regular recurrence pattern.

CREATING HOLIDAYS AUTOMATICALLY

Here's how you can create Calendar items for holidays automatically.

To create holidays automatically:

1. With any Information viewer displayed, select Tools, Options to display the Options dialog box. Make sure the Preferences tab is selected.

2. Click Calendar Options to display the Calendar Options dialog box in which you can set several Calendar options.

3. Click Add Holidays to display the dialog box shown in Figure 9.15.

Figure 9.15
Use this dialog box to select the countries and cultures for which you want to add holidays.

Add Holidays to Calendar

Select the locations whose holidays you would like copied to your Outlook Calendar:

☐ Thailand
☐ Tunisia
☐ Turkey
☐ United Arab Emirates
☐ United Kingdom
☑ United States
☐ Uruguay
☐ Venezuela
☐ Yemen

OK   Cancel

4. Check those countries and cultures for which you want to add holidays; then click OK.

After following these steps, you can examine your calendar to see the holidays that have been added.

Tip from

The holidays Outlook can add to your calendar automatically are listed in the text file Outlook.hol. You can use Windows Notepad or another text editor to examine this file. You can edit this file to delete holidays and insert more holidays.

CREATING HOLIDAYS AND SPECIAL DAYS MANUALLY

You can use the method described previously in this chapter to enter most holidays and special days manually as recurring events. Some holidays and special days, though, have a recurrence pattern that's beyond Outlook's capabilities to cope with—you must enter these as one-time events for each year. Some examples of these are

- In the United States, income tax filings are due on April 15 unless that is a Saturday or Sunday, in which case the filings are due on the following Monday.
- In the United States, election day is the Tuesday after the first Monday in November.
- The Christian Easter Sunday is the first Sunday after the first full moon after the vernal equinox; other Christian holy days are a certain number of days before or after Easter Sunday.

When you create Calendar events for holidays and special days, I suggest you assign Holiday as a category for items that really are holidays for you, such as Christmas Day and Thanksgiving Day if you live in the United States. Assign another category, such as Special Day, for such special days as Valentine's Day, which aren't really holidays.

Everyone in a group doesn't necessarily have to individually enter holidays and other days into a calendar. One person can create a master calendar and export it to a file. Other people can then import that file into their Outlook calendars.

→ For information about sharing Outlook items with other users, **see** "Sharing a Calendar," **p. 234**.

MAKING CHANGES TO APPOINTMENTS AND EVENTS

You can make changes to

- One-time appointments and events
- All the appointments and events in a recurring series
- Individual appointments and events in a recurring series

CHANGING A ONE-TIME APPOINTMENT OR EVENT

You can change any of the information about an appointment or event by opening the item in the form in which it was created, editing information in that form, and then saving the changes.

To make changes in a form:

1. Display a Calendar Information viewer and locate the appointment or event you want to change.
2. Double-click the appointment to display it in the Appointment form, or double-click the event to display it in the Event form.
3. Change any of the information on the form.
4. Click Save and Close in the form's Standard toolbar to save the changes and close the form.

You also can make changes to an appointment or event displayed in the Day/Week/Month view of the Calendar Information viewer.

You can change the subject of an appointment or event.

To change the subject of the appointment or event:

1. Display the Day/Week/Month view of the Calendar Information viewer.
2. Use the Date Navigator to locate the appointment or event whose subject you want to change.
3. Click the appointment or event to select it. Place the insertion point where you want to make the change in the subject text; then use normal editing techniques to delete and insert characters. Press Enter when you've finished.

If you make a change to the subject of a recurring appointment or recurring event in this way, the change applies only to the single occurrence you edited. Outlook indicates this by adding a slanted line through the curved arrows that mark recurrence.

You can also change the date of an appointment or event.

To change the date of an appointment or event:

1. Display the Day/Week/Month view of the Calendar Information viewer.

2. Use the Date Navigator to locate the appointment or event you want to move.

3. Drag the appointment or event to another day in the Date Navigator.

You can change the time of an appointment.

To change the time of an appointment:

1. Display the Day/Week/Month view of the Calendar Information viewer.

2. Click Day in the Information viewer's Standard toolbar.

3. Use the Date Navigator to locate the appointment.

4. To change the time at which the appointment starts without changing its duration, point onto the appointment and drag up or down. To change the start time without changing the end time, point onto the top border of the appointment and drag up or down. To change the end time without changing the start time, point onto the bottom border of the appointment and drag up or down.

CHANGING RECURRING APPOINTMENTS AND EVENTS

When you're dealing with recurring appointments and events, you can make changes to all the events in a series, or you can make changes to individual items within the series. You might, for example, want to change a regularly scheduled Monday appointment to Tuesday; in that case, you would change the series. However, if you have a regular Monday appointment, you might want to change the appointment to Tuesday if a particular Monday is a holiday. In that case, you would change only an individual appointment to Tuesday.

If you drag one occurrence of a recurring appointment or event to another date in the Date Navigator, Outlook displays a message telling you that only that one occurrence will be changed. Click OK if that's what you want to do. Likewise, if you change the time of one occurrence of an appointment, Outlook tells you that only that one occurrence will be changed.

To change the time of one or all appointments or events in a recurring series, double-click the appointment or event to display a dialog box in which you can select whether you want to make changes to the selected occurrence or to the complete series. Then, proceed to make the changes.

DELETING APPOINTMENTS AND EVENTS

You can delete a one-time appointment or event just as you delete any other Outlook item. Select that appointment or event in an Information viewer and click the Delete button in the Standard toolbar. Outlook moves the selected item into the Deleted Items folder.

You can delete individual appointments and events from a recurring series, or you can delete the entire series.

To delete appointments and events in a recurring series:

1. Display the Day/Week/Month view of the Calendar Information viewer and use the Date Navigator to locate the item to be deleted.

2. Click an item in a recurring series of appointments or events to select that item.

3. Click the Delete button in the Standard toolbar. Outlook displays the Confirm Delete dialog box that asks you whether you want to delete all occurrences or just this one.

4. Select Delete All Occurrences or Delete This One, according to what you want to do. Then click OK.

PART

III

CH

9

EXAMINING APPOINTMENT AND EVENT PROPERTIES

Each Appointment and Event item has properties that are set by default. You can examine and change these properties to suit your preferences.

To examine appointment and event properties, double-click that appointment or event in the Calendar Information viewer to display it in the Appointment or Event form. In that form, select File, Properties to display the dialog box shown in Figure 9.16.

Figure 9.16
The Properties dialog box opens with the General tab selected and displays information about the selected appointment or event.

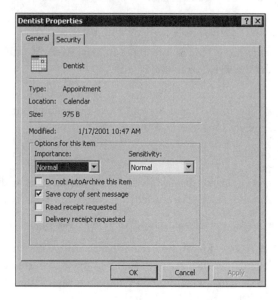

By default, appointments and events have Normal importance and Normal sensitivity. You can change the importance by opening the drop-down Importance list and selecting a different importance; you can change the sensitivity by opening the drop-down Sensitivity list and choosing a different sensitivity.

If you want to exclude the selected item from AutoArchiving, check the Do Not AutoArchive This Item box.

If the Calendar item is one you use to send a message (such as a Meeting Request), check or uncheck the Save Copy of Sent Message, Read Receipt Requested, and Delivery Receipt Requested boxes as appropriate.

Select the Security tab to display a dialog box that contains various settings related to message security. These settings aren't generally applicable to Calendar items.

→ To learn more about backing up your Outlook items, **see** "AutoArchiving Outlook Items," **p. 392**.

→ For information about message security settings, **see** "Setting Security," **p. 88**.

VIEWING APPOINTMENTS AND EVENTS

The preceding pages of this chapter have focused on creating appointments and events as Calendar items. When it has been necessary to talk about viewing appointments and events you've created, I've referred mostly to the Day/Week/Month view of the Calendar Information viewer with Day selected. Now it's time to take a broader view of how you can view appointments and events. You can view appointments and events in an Information viewer that displays those items in calendars, or you can view them in tables.

VIEWING APPOINTMENTS AND EVENTS IN CALENDAR VIEWS

You can view appointments and events in four types of Day/Week/Month calendars: by the day, by the work week, by the week, or by the month.

To select your view of a calendar, click Calendar in the Outlook Bar to display the current default view. Then click View in the menu bar and move the pointer onto Current View to display a menu of views. Select Day/Week/Month.

USING THE DAY VIEW

In the Standard toolbar, click Day to display a view of the current day, with your planned activities shown in the Appointments Area (refer to Figure 9.2).

The Day view has three panes: the Appointment Area, Date Navigator, and TaskPad.

USING THE APPOINTMENT AREA   The Appointment Area shows your activities for the current day. The current day's date is displayed at the top of the Appointment Area. By default, the current day starts at 8:00 a.m. and ends at 5:00 p.m. You can change the times at which your current day starts and stops in Outlook's Options.

→ For detailed information about setting Outlook's Calendar options, **see** "Calendar Options," **p. 539**.

Note

Use the vertical scroll bar at the right side of the Appointment Area to scroll to hours that aren't initially visible within the currently displayed day.

Each appointment is shown within a box in the Appointment Area that shows the duration of that appointment. If the subject of an appointment contains more text than can be displayed within the box, the subject is truncated. However, if you point onto the appointment, Outlook automatically enlarges the box to show all the text of the appointment's subject.

Tip from

The capability to show hidden text in this way is not limited to the Calendar Information viewer. You can use the same technique in other Information viewers.

Use the vertical scroll bar at the right side of the Appointment Area to see times that are not initially shown in the Appointment Area.

Each event for the day is shown in a box above the Appointment Area.

As explained previously in this chapter, you can use the Appointment Area to create appointments. You also can double-click an existing appointment to display its details in the Appointments form.

USING THE DATE NAVIGATOR   By default, the Date Navigator shows a calendar for the current month and the next month. You can drag the left border and the bottom border of the Date Navigator to display more months.

By default, each row in the Date Navigator shows a week from Sunday to Saturday. To select a day other than Sunday to start each row, open the Options dialog box, select the Preferences tab, and click Calendar Options. In the same Options dialog box, you can choose to display week numbers in the Date Navigator.

→ For more information about controlling how the Date Navigator displays dates, **see** "Calendar Options," **p. 539**.

The current day, as determined by your computer's internal clock, is shown with a gray background enclosed in a red border. To display a day other than the current day, click the day you want to see in the Date Navigator.

The banner across the top of the Date Navigator has a triangle icon at the left and another triangle icon at the right. Click the triangle icon at the left to display previous months; click the triangle icon at the right to display subsequent months.

To display planned activities for a day other than the current day, click that day in the Date Navigator. After you do that, the planned activities for the selected day are shown in the Appointment Area (with that day's date above the Event Area), and the selected day is shown with a gray background in the Date Navigator.

You can show the activities for more than one day. To do so, click one day in the Date Navigator. Then, hold down Ctrl while you select one or more other days to select additional days in the Appointment Area, as shown in Figure 9.17.

Figure 9.17
Here is the Appointment Area with two days displayed.

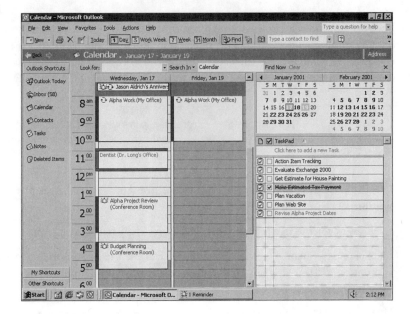

To go back to displaying just one day in the Appointment Area, click that day in the Date Navigator.

USING THE TASKPAD   The TaskPad displays your current tasks. See Chapter 11, "Managing Tasks," for information about tasks.

USING THE WORK WEEK VIEW

With the Day/Week/Month view of the Calendar Information viewer selected, click Work Week in the Standard toolbar to display the Work Week view. By default, this shows a calendar with activities for Monday through Friday of the current week displayed, as shown in Figure 9.18.

The space available to display the subject of appointments and events is very limited in this view, so the text is truncated. You can display the entire text for an appointment or event by resting the pointer on that appointment or event.

USING THE WEEK VIEW

With the Day/Week/Month view of the Calendar Information viewer selected, click Week in the Standard toolbar to display the Week view. By default, this shows a calendar with activities for an entire week, as shown in Figure 9.19.

Figure 9.18
The default work week is Monday through Friday. The days displayed have a gray background in the Date Navigator.

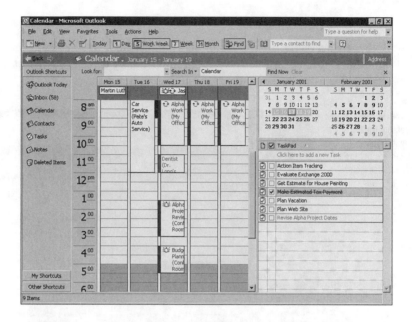

Figure 9.19
The selected week has a gray background in the Date Navigator.

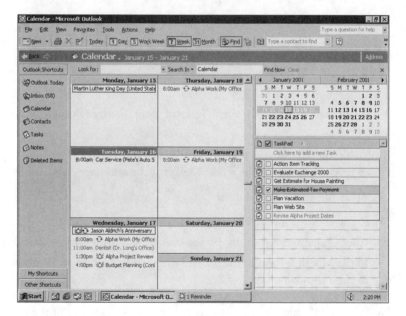

Initially, Outlook displays the week that includes the current day. To display the calendar for a different week, click at the left of the week you want to see in the Date Navigator.

To display more than one week, hold down Ctrl while you click at the left of the weeks you want to display in the Date Navigator.

USING THE MONTH VIEW

With the Day/Week/Month view of the Calendar Information viewer selected, click Month in the Standard toolbar to display the Month view. By default, this shows a calendar with activities for a complete month, as shown in Figure 9.20.

Figure 9.20
By default, the Date Navigator and TaskPad are not displayed in the Month view.

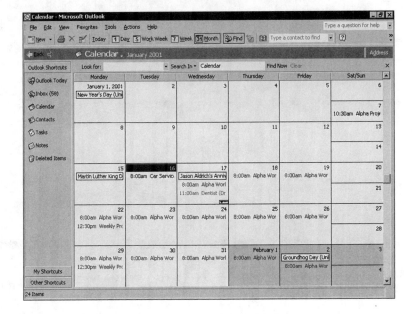

To display the Date Navigator and TaskPad, drag the right border of the Calendar to the left.

By default, the Month view shows Saturday and Sunday at half the size of the other days. However, you can display the weekend days at the same size as the other days.

To display full-size weekend days:

1. Right-click within the Calendar to display its context menu.
2. Click Other Settings to display the dialog box shown previously in Figure 9.3.
3. In the Month section of the dialog box, uncheck Compress Weekend Days. Click OK to close the dialog box.

Now the Month calendar has seven columns, one for each day of the week.

MODIFYING THE DAY/WEEK/MONTH VIEW

The default Day/Week/Month view doesn't show any information you've provided for appointments and events in the Notes box on the Appointment or Event form. You can modify this view so that information in the Notes box is displayed.

One way to do this is to use the Day/Week/Month view with AutoPreview view. To display this view, with any Calendar view displayed, select View, move the pointer onto Current View, and select Day/Week/Month View with AutoPreview. After you do this, Outlook displays the text you entered in the Notes box for each appointment.

As an alternative, with the Day/Week/Month view displayed, select View, Preview Pane. Then select an appointment to display the view shown in Figure 9.21.

Figure 9.21
With Preview Pane selected, the Day/Week/Month view displays a pane that contains detailed information about a selected appointment or event.

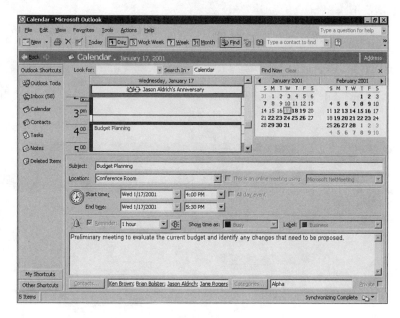

VIEWING APPOINTMENTS AND EVENTS IN TABLE VIEWS

Although the Day/Week/Month views are what you will often use to see an instant picture of your plans and commitments, Outlook's table views of Calendar items provide useful insight into those items.

The standard table views of Calendar items are

- **Active Appointments**—Shows appointments and events for today and subsequent days listed in chronological order, grouped by recurrence

- **Events**—Shows only events grouped according to recurrence

- **Annual Events**—Shows only events that have annual recurrence

- **Recurring Appointments**—Shows recurring appointments and events, grouped by recurrence

- **By Category**—Shows all appointments and events, grouped by category

You can modify any of these standard views, and you can create your own custom views.

→ For information about creating custom views of Outlook items, **see** "Creating Views and Print Styles," **p. 651**.

PRINTING APPOINTMENTS AND EVENTS

You can print appointments and events in a calendar format or in a table format.

PRINTING IN CALENDAR FORMAT

To print your calendar in a calendar format, start by choosing the Day/Week/Month view of your calendar.

To print a calendar:

1. Click File and move the pointer onto Page Setup. Outlook displays a list of available print styles, as shown in Figure 9.22.

Figure 9.22
You can select one of the predefined print styles, or you can define your own custom styles.

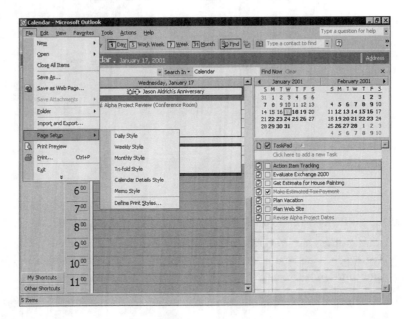

2. Select the print style you want to use, such as Monthly Style. Outlook displays the Page Setup dialog box, shown in Figure 9.23.

3. After defining how you want the calendar to be printed, click Print Preview to see what your setup looks like, as shown in Figure 9.24.

4. If you're satisfied with the preview, click Print to print the calendar. Otherwise, click Page Setup to go back to the Page Setup dialog box to make changes to the setup.

Figure 9.23
Use the three tabs in this dialog box to specify how you want the calendar to be printed.

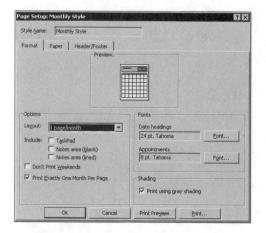

Figure 9.24
This is a preview of how your calendar will be printed.

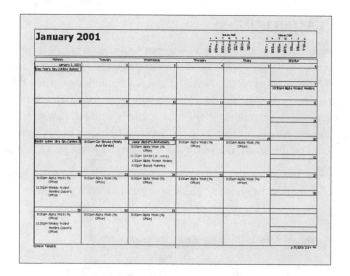

PRINTING IN TABLE OR MEMO FORMAT

If you want to print a calendar in table or memo format, select one of the table views.

To print a table view of a calendar:

1. Click File and move the pointer onto Page Setup. Outlook offers Table Style or Memo Style.

2. Select the style you want to use to display the Page Setup dialog box.

3. Use the three tabs of this dialog box to specify how you want Outlook items to be printed.

4. Click Print Preview to see what your setup looks like.

5. If you're satisfied with the preview, click Print to print the Calendar items. Otherwise, click Page Setup to return to the Page Setup dialog box.

PRINTING CALENDARS IN OTHER WAYS

You are not limited to Outlook's built-in ways of printing calendars. Instead you can

- Create your own Print Styles
- Use Word templates
- Use another application, such as Seagate's Crystal Reports

→ For information about printing Outlook items, **see** "Using Other Applications and Utilities to Print Outlook Items," **p. 693**.

VIEWING REMINDERS

When you create an appointment or meeting in Outlook, you can choose to be given a reminder a certain time before the appointment or meeting is due to begin. Also, if you create a task in Outlook, you can choose to be given a reminder a certain time before that task is due for completion. If you ask to be given a reminder for an appointment, a meeting, or a task, Outlook displays a reminder at the appropriate time. For this to happen, Outlook must be running, either visible onscreen or minimized. If Outlook isn't running at the time a reminder should be displayed, the reminder is displayed when you next start Outlook.

Previous versions of Outlook displayed only one reminder at a time. Outlook 2002 improves the display of reminders by showing all current reminders in a single dialog box, as shown in Figure 9.25.

Figure 9.25
The Reminders dialog box lists current reminders.

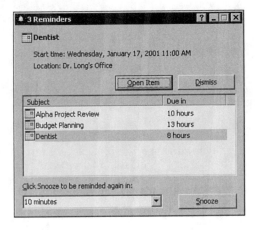

Each item in the reminder list is in a separate row that contains three columns:

- The first column contains a symbol that indicates the type of the reminder. Reminders can be for calendar or task items.
- The second column contains the subject of the item.
- The third column shows when items are due.

You can select any of the listed reminders to see information about it. You also can select one of the reminder items and then click Open Item to see that item in a form, or you can click Dismiss to permanently delete the item from the list of reminders.

If you want to temporarily remove a reminder from the current list and be reminded later, select that reminder, open the drop-down Click Snooze to Be Reminded Again In list and select a reminder time; then click Snooze.

TROUBLESHOOTING

CALENDARS

On the whole, I've not found many problems with Outlook's calendars, nor have I received many requests for help in this area. Nevertheless, you might have difficulty with some areas.

Perhaps you don't see the TaskPad when you display your calendar. By default, Outlook displays the TaskPad when you select the Day, Work Week, or Week view of a calendar, but only if a Tasks folder is available. If you don't see a TaskPad, that might be because you don't have a Tasks folder. Check your Folder List and, if necessary, create a Tasks folder. Outlook doesn't display the TaskPad in the Month view.

If you've been experimenting with Outlook's capability to automatically display holidays, you might have many national and cultural holidays in your calendar. If you want to remove some of these, select View, point onto Current View, and click Events to see your Calendar items in a Table view. Click the Location column title to sort events by location. Select all the events associated with the location you want to remove, and then click Delete in the toolbar to remove those events.

CHAPTER 10

MANAGING CALENDARS

In this chapter

USING TIME ZONES

If there's one universal standard, it's that days consist of 24 hours. However, those 24 hours are not the same around the world. The world is divided into 24 latitudinal regions, each of which sets its times so that midnight occurs at 0:00 and midday occurs at 12:00. That results in 5:00 in one region being 6:00, 7:00, 8:00, or whatever in other regions. The time within each latitudinal region of the world is known as a *time zone*.

In the days when people were concerned with only their immediate vicinity, that wasn't a problem. Now, though, many of us communicate with people throughout the world, so time zones are something we have to be concerned about.

Your computer has an internal clock that keeps track of times and dates. Using your computer's Setup utility, you can set this clock to your local time and date. In Windows, you can select Date/Time in the Windows Control Panel and, with the Date & Time tab selected, set the date and time. You also can select the Time Zone tab, in which you can select your personal time zone.

Note

Your computer's internal clock is not as accurate as a Rolex watch. You should reset your computer's clock at least once a month.

Several programs are available on Internet sites that you can use to synchronize your computer's internal clock with time references available from the National Institute of Standards and Technology (NIST) or the United States Naval Observatory (USNO). One of these is ClockRack, which you can download from

```
http://www.zdnet.com
```

For additional information, visit

```
http://www.time.gov
```

After you've done that, Windows applications—including Outlook—use your computer's internal clock to time-stamp your activities. However, a couple of points do need clarification:

- The time and date you send an e-mail message is the time and date you sent it from your Outbox to the mail server, not the time and date the message was sent from the Message form to your Outbox.

- The time and date you receive a message is the time and date the message arrived in your mail server, not the time and date the message arrived in your Inbox.

If you're using Outlook within one physical location, time zones are not a major issue. However, if you use Outlook to communicate with people in other time zones, particularly if you want to be able to plan time-critical events, such as net meetings, it's very important that you and the people with whom you communicate set up time zones properly.

SETTING THE TIME ZONE

Fundamentally, Windows saves all times as *Universal Coordinated Time (UCT)*, previously known as Greenwich Mean Time (GMT). Outlook uses the Windows time zone setting to convert UCT times into local times. You can use Outlook's options to set your local time zone.

→ For information about setting the time zone, **see** "Time Zone," **p. 546**.

For information about setting the time zone, **see** "Time Zone," **p. 546**.

Note

The time zone you select in Outlook affects Windows and all applications running under Windows.

PART
III

CH
10

When you change from one time zone to another, Outlook automatically changes the times displayed for all Calendar items. For example, suppose your computer is set for the Eastern Time (U.S. and Canada) time zone and you have an appointment for 9:00 a.m. After you change the time zone to Pacific Time (U.S. and Canada), Outlook shows the appointment at 6:00 a.m., which is sometimes appropriate and sometimes inappropriate.

Suppose you're in the eastern United States and arrange to make a telephone to someone in the same time zone at 2:00 p.m. on Wednesday. By Wednesday you are on the West Coast and have changed the time zone in Outlook accordingly. As a result, Outlook reminds you to make the call at 11:00 a.m., which is exactly what you need.

Let's look at another scenario. Anticipating your trip to the West Coast, you arrange to meet a friend there at 6:00 p.m. on Wednesday and enter that appointment into Outlook while you're still in the east. When you arrive in the west, you change the time zone in Outlook. As a result, Outlook reminds you about your 3:00 p.m. appointment. That's not what you need.

One way to solve this problem is to set up Outlook to work in two time zones, as described subsequently in this chapter. That doesn't help, though, if you travel a lot and schedule appointments in more than two time zones.

Tip from

Gordon Padwick

The important point is to understand how time zones work in Outlook and other applications. With that understanding and some mental effort, you can keep things straight. My preference when I'm traveling is to keep Outlook and my watch set to my home time and to make mental adjustments.

⚠ *If you start using Outlook and subsequently find the time zone is incorrect, **see** "Time Zones and Meeting Invitations" in the "Troubleshooting" section at the end of this chapter to adjust your time zone while keeping your entered work.*

WORKING WITH TWO TIME ZONES

In the Day/Week/Month view of the Calendar Information viewer, with Day selected, the Appointment Area normally shows the hours of the day for the time zone you've selected. Outlook can display hours of the day for two time zones. This is useful, for example, if you have frequent contact with people in a different time zone.

→ For information about setting up two time zones, **see** "Time Zone," **p. XXX**. (ch 27)

After you've set up two time zones, the Day view of a calendar shows both sets of time, as shown in Figure 10.1.

East and West time zones

Figure 10.1
The names at the top of the two time columns are the names you entered in the Time Zone dialog box.

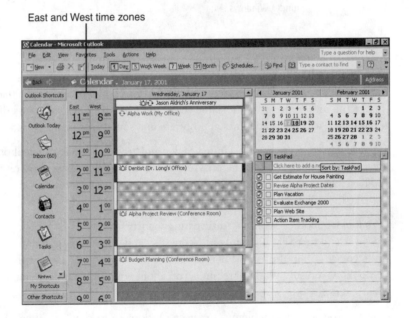

Times in the primary time zone are shown in the right column; times in the secondary time zone are shown in the left column. You can swap these two columns by clicking Swap Time Zones in the Time Zone dialog box.

SHARING A CALENDAR

You can share your Calendar folder or individual Calendar items with other people. The principal purpose of sharing calendars is to simplify the process of scheduling meetings. If other people make their calendars available to you, you can schedule meetings when the people you want to invite are free. Likewise, if you share your own calendar, other people can invite you to meetings at times when you're not busy with other activities.

SETTING UP CALENDAR SHARING

If you're using Outlook as a client for an Exchange server, sharing calendar information is automatic. All you have to do is open the Free/Busy Options dialog box, shown in Figure 10.2, and set the number of future months of your calendar you want to publish and how often you want your published calendar to be updated.

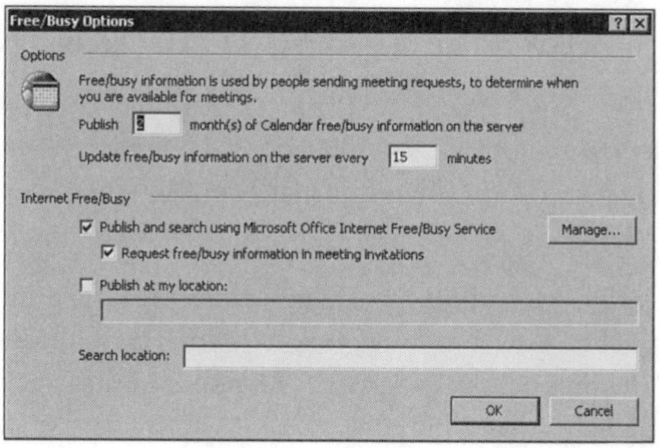

Figure 10.2
By default, Outlook proposes to publish your calendar for the next two months and to update it every 15 minutes.

→ For information about the Free/Busy Options dialog box, **see** "Free/Busy Options," **p. 544**.

If you're not using Outlook as a client for an Exchange server, or you want to share your calendar with people who don't have an Exchange account, you can

- Use the Internet or an intranet
- Use a folder on your network

You also can make your calendar folder available as a Public Folder that specific other people can access.

→ For additional information about public folders, **see** "Using Public Folders," **p. 454**.

To share your calendar by way of the Internet:

1. Select Tools, Options to display the Options dialog box. In the Preferences tab, select Calendar Options, and then select Free/Busy Options to display the dialog box shown previously in Figure 10.2.

2. Change the number of months to be published if you want to do so. You can publish up to 12 months of your calendar.

3. Change the frequency for updating your published calendar. The maximum interval you can specify is 60 minutes. Outlook updates your published calendar only if you've made changes since the last update.

Tip from

The default of updating your calendar every 15 minutes might be reasonable if you have a high-speed, always-on connection to the Internet. You'll probably want to increase that time considerably if you have a dial-up connection.

PART III
CH
10

4. Check Publish and Search Using Microsoft Office Internet Free/Busy Service or Publish at My Location, or both, depending on how you want to publish your calendar. See the subsequent paragraphs for more information about this.

If, later, you want to stop sending your free/busy information to a server, return to the Free/Busy Options dialog box and uncheck the appropriate Publish check box.

PUBLISHING CALENDAR INFORMATION ON THE MICROSOFT OFFICE INTERNET FREE/BUSY SERVICE

Microsoft maintains a server you can use to publish your calendar. To use this service, check Publish and Search Using Microsoft Office Internet Free/Busy Service in the Free/Busy Options dialog box.

The first time you check Publish and Search Using Microsoft Office Internet Free/Busy Service and subsequently click OK, a message box tells you that Outlook needs to install some files. Click Yes in the message box to install the required files.

Note

If you're using Windows 2000, you must have Administrator privileges to install the files. Outlook prompts you to insert the Office XP CD into your drive and then installs the required files.

After installing the files, you must connect to the Internet. Depending on how you've set up Outlook, this connection might occur automatically, or you might see a dialog box you can use to make the connection.

The first time you attempt to connect to the Microsoft Office Internet Free/Busy Service, you see a dialog box that states you must sign up for the service. Click Sign Up to see a Welcome screen.

After you've digested the information on the Welcome screen, click Continue to display a screen that describes the terms of use for service. This screen tells you that your free/busy information is hosted on Microsoft servers located in the United States and assures you that the information will not be used for any purpose other than supporting the Microsoft Office Internet Free/Busy Service. To continue, you must click Yes I Agree to signify your acceptance of the conditions.

You next see a screen that tells you how to enable Outlook to work with the service. That screen seems to be redundant because you must have followed the steps in the preceding procedure to get this far.

Click Continue to see the window shown in Figure 10.3.

Figure 10.3
Follow instructions here to authorize people to see your free/busy information and to send a message to people who are not members of the service.

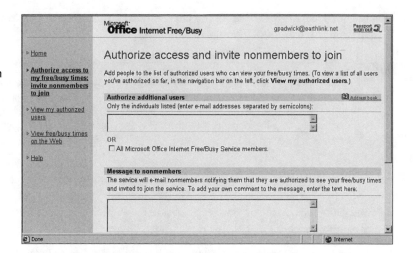

Tip from

Click Address Book at the right side of the window to display your address books so that you easily can select the people you want to authorize. If you follow this process, you'll see a warning message about another program trying to access e-mail addresses you have stored in Outlook. That is, of course, what is happening, so click the check box to allow access; then click Yes to continue.

After you have entered information in this window, click OK to display the final window, which is similar to the one shown in Figure 10.4.

Figure 10.4
This window lists the people you have authorized to see your free/busy information.

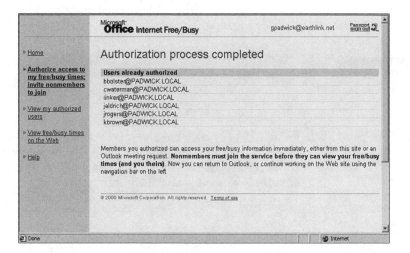

Finally, click Passport Sign Out. If you later want to return to setting up the service, click Passport Sign In. Close the Internet Explorer window.

Note

> A short time after you sign on to the Microsoft Office Internet Free/Busy Service for the first time, you'll receive an e-mail message congratulating you on joining the service. This message contains the URL of the Web page you can access when you want to change the list of people authorized to see your free/busy information.

Subsequently, providing you have a connection to the Internet, your calendar information is automatically sent to the server and updated at the interval specified in the Free/Busy Options dialog box. Also you have access to other people's calendar information when you're planning meetings.

In addition, you can send your free/busy information to the server manually. To do so, open the Calendar Information viewer, select Tools, move the pointer onto Send/Receive, and select Free/Busy Information. If necessary, Outlook asks you to establish an Internet connection. When the Internet connection is available, your free/busy information is sent.

→ For information about using free/busy information for planning meetings, **see** "Planning a Meeting Around People's Commitments," **p. 246**.

PUBLISHING CALENDAR INFORMATION ON A SPECIFIC WEB SITE

You also can publish your calendar on any Web site to which you have access. After checking Publish at My Location in the Free/Busy Options dialog box, enter the fully qualified path to the Web site. You can use any valid URL format (including http, file, and ftp). An example is

```
ftp://MyServer/Freebusy/roger.vfp
```

Note

> Free/busy files have .vfp as their file name extensions.

Tip from

Gordon Padwick

> If you don't already have a Web site to use for sharing your calendar, you can easily create one. Your ISP probably offers the capability for creating a small Web site suitable for personal use; alternatively, consider using the free Web hosting services offered by Lycos, Yahoo!, and others. For business purposes, you should seek the help of a professional hosting service for which you will have to pay a monthly fee.

In addition to sharing your own calendar information, you probably want to be able to access calendar information other people share. To do so, enter the address of the location in the Search Location box, using the %NAME% environment string to represent the name of the contact whose calendar information you want to see, as in

```
ftp://MyServer/Freebusy/%NAME%.vfp
```

When you search for a contact's calendar information, Outlook replaces %NAME% with the name of the actual contact.

After you've saved your free/busy information on a server, you can send the information from that server to other people.

PUBLISHING CALENDAR INFORMATION LOCALLY

You can use a technique very similar to that described in the preceding section to share calendar information within a local workgroup. In that case, instead of using a Web site, you can use a folder that's accessible to everyone in the workgroup to store the shared information.

The first step is to create a folder to which everyone has access. Suppose that folder is on the computer named Arletta, is on the C: drive, and is named FreeBusy.

Each Outlook user should open the Free/Busy Options dialog box, shown previously in Figure 10.2, check Publish at My Location, and enter the location address as:

```
File://Arletta/c/freebusy/gpadwick.vfb
```

replacing, of course, gpadwick with that user's own e-mail account name.

Also, each Outlook user who wants to be able to access other people's calendar information should make an entry such as

```
File://Arletta/c/freebusy/%NAME%.vfb
```

in the Search Location box. Outlook will replace %NAME% with the name of the actual contact. The previous section contains an explanation of %NAME%.

SENDING YOUR CALENDAR INFORMATION TO SOMEONE

Instead of sharing your calendar in the ways described previously in this chapter, you can send that information to one or more people.

To send free/busy information to someone:

1. In the Contact Information viewer, select the name of a person to whom you want to send your free/busy information to display information about that person in a Contact form.
2. In the Internet Free-Busy section at the bottom of the Details tab, enter the name of the server on which your free/busy information is stored.
3. Select File, Save As and select vCard Files in the Save as Type box.
4. Create an e-mail message and insert the vCard file into that message.
5. Send the message.

ARRANGING MEETINGS

Outlook provides two ways for you to invite people to a meeting:

- You can decide when you want the meeting to occur and send e-mail messages inviting people to attend.
- If you have access to other people's calendars, you can choose a time for the meeting when other people are free and then send e-mail messages inviting people to attend.

Note

Meetings involve resources as well as people. Resources are such things as:
- A room in which to hold the meeting
- Audio-visual equipment
- Remote conferencing facilities

You can set up an account for each of the meeting resources available in your organization. Then, when you arrange a meeting, you can "invite" the necessary resources.

INVITING PEOPLE TO ATTEND A MEETING

If you have decided on a time for a meeting, you can invite people to attend and reserve the resources you need. Outlook sends invitations by automatically generating e-mail messages.

To request people to attend a meeting:

1. With any Calendar Information viewer displayed, select Actions, New Meeting Request. Outlook displays the Meeting form shown in Figure 10.5.

Figure 10.5
Use this form to create an e-mail message that invites people to attend a meeting. The form is shown here with the invitation ready to send.

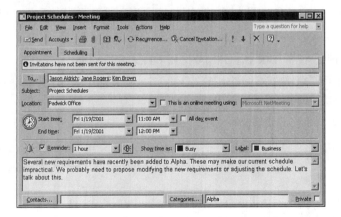

Note

The InfoBar in the form shown in Figure 10.5 tells you that invitations haven't been sent (which is obvious because you've only just begun creating the invitation). When you first open the form, it probably also tells you `The appointment occurs in the past`. That's because the form initially assumes a meeting at the beginning of the current day.

2. Click the To button to display the Select Attendees and Resources dialog box, in which you can select people from one or more of your address books. Select attendees and resources; then click OK to return to the Meeting form.

Note

You can address attendees as Required, Optional, or Resources.

3. Enter the subject of the meeting in the Subject box and the location in the Location box.
4. Specify the Start Time and End Time in the same way that you specify start and end times for appointments.

Note

If you specify a time for the meeting that conflicts with appointments in your calendar, the InfoBar displays `Conflicts with another appointment in your calendar`.

5. If you want a reminder before the meeting, check the Reminder box and then enter or select the time before the start of the meeting when you want to be reminded.
6. If the date and time of the meeting aren't firm, open the drop-down Show Time As list and select Tentative.
7. Open the drop-down Label list and select an appropriate label for the meeting.
8. Use the unnamed notes box to provide information about the meeting. This might be an agenda or a statement of the purpose of the meeting. You should always let people know as much as possible about a proposed meeting so that they can come prepared.
9. You probably won't want to use the Contacts box in this form because the contacts are those people to whom you're sending the meeting invitation.
10. Click Categories and then select the appropriate categories.
11. Click Send in the form's Standard toolbar to send the message. The proposed meeting is added to your calendar with a meeting icon to identify it. Outlook places the meeting invitation in your Outbox and sends it as an e-mail message in the normal way.

After you've sent the message, you can look in your Sent Items folder to confirm it has been sent.

RECEIVING A REQUEST TO ATTEND A MEETING

When you receive a request to attend a meeting, that message appears in your Inbox Information viewer, as shown in Figure 10.6. If you have the Preview pane enabled (as it is in this figure), you can see the details of the message when you select the message in the Message pane.

Meeting invitation

Figure 10.6
The symbol at the left end of the message header identifies the message as a meeting request.

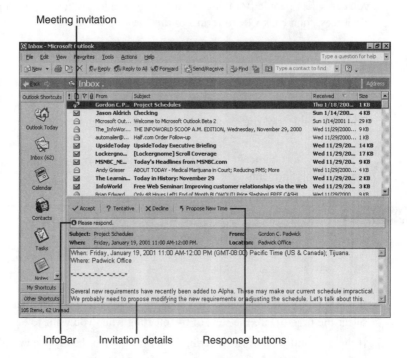

InfoBar   Invitation details   Response buttons

An InfoBar automatically alerts you to any conflict with existing appointments. You can reply to the invitation by choosing one of the response buttons. Most likely, though, you want to see the complete message before responding.

To see the complete message, double-click the message in the Inbox Information viewer's Message pane. Outlook displays the message in the form shown in Figure 10.7.

Before replying to the meeting invitation, you can select Calendar in the form's toolbar to display your calendar with the proposed meeting in place. That's a quick way to see whether you can fit the meeting into your day.

In replying to the request, you can click one of these buttons in the form's toolbar:

- **Accept**—Outlook creates an item on your calendar and marks the time as busy.
- **Tentative**—Outlook creates an item on your calendar and marks the time as tentative.
- **Decline**—Outlook creates an item in your Deleted Items folder.

■ **Propose New Time**—Outlook displays a dialog box (as explained subsequently), in which you can propose a new time, and creates an item on your calendar with the time marked as tentative.

Figure 10.7
The InfoBar asks you to respond and alerts you to any conflicts with items in your calendar.

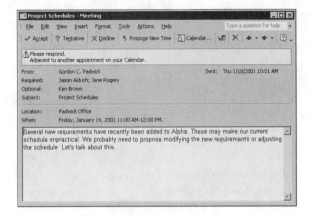

Note

The ability to propose a new time isn't available in previous versions of Outlook.

If you click Accept, Tentative, or Decline, you can then select:

■ Edit the Response Before Sending

■ Send the Response Now

■ Don't Send a Response

After you accept the request, the meeting is displayed in your calendar with a dark blue border. After you tentatively accept a meeting, it appears in your calendar with a light blue border.

When you send a response to a request to attend a meeting, that response is sent as an e-mail message to the original sender. You can confirm that the response has been sent by looking in your Sent Items folder.

Note

Many possible scenarios exist for the sequence of messages that Outlook can send between the person who initiates a meeting and the people invited to that meeting. The next few paragraphs describe only one of these scenarios, but should be sufficient to give you a good idea of how Outlook can help you set up meetings.

If you select Propose New Time in the Meeting form, Outlook displays a dialog box similar to the one in Figure 10.8.

Figure 10.8
This dialog box displays the schedules of all the people invited to the meeting.

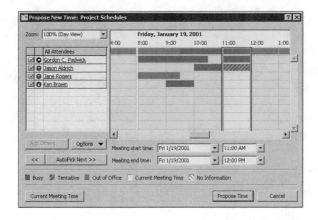

Each row in this dialog box shows a person's commitments with colored bars indicating times when people already have commitments. The vertical bar shows the time proposed for the meeting. If, as in Figure 10.8, the proposed meeting time conflicts with your (or another person's) schedule, you can drag the proposed meeting time to a period that doesn't conflict with anyone's schedule. After you've done that, click Propose Time.

→ For more detailed information about the dialog box shown in Figure 10.8, **see** "Planning a Meeting Around People's Commitments," **p. 246**.

After you've inserted whatever text is appropriate in the Notes box, click Send in the form's toolbar to send your response back to the person who invited you to the meeting. At this time, the proposed meeting is shown in your calendar as tentative for the original proposed time. It remains in your calendar like this until the person who proposed the meeting accepts your proposed change. Also, when you send a response, Outlook deletes the original proposal message from your Inbox folder because the meeting exists as an item in your Calendar folder. You can find your response to the meeting request in your Sent Items folder.

RECEIVING A RESPONSE TO A REQUEST TO ATTEND A MEETING

A response to a request to attend a meeting appears as a message in your Inbox Information viewer, as shown in Figure 10.9. Any comments the respondent has included with the response are shown in the Preview pane.

The message shown in Figure 10.10 is what you see when one of the people you have invited to a meeting tentatively accepts the response, but suggests a time change. Notice that the InfoBar summarizes the purpose of the message. You receive a similar message if a person accepts or tentatively accepts your invitation without asking for a time change, or if a person rejects your invitation.

Double-click the response to see its details in the Meeting Response form, similar to that shown in Figure 10.10.

Figure 10.9
The icon (two heads) at the left of the message header in the Message pane identifies the message as a response to a meeting request.

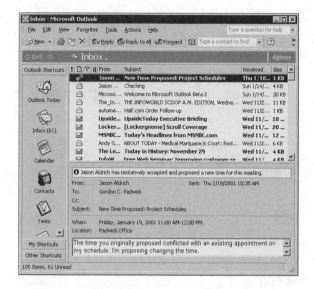

Figure 10.10
The Meeting Response form shows the message from the respondent and also contains a summary of who has accepted, tentatively accepted, and declined your request.

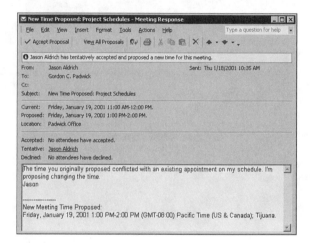

To accept the proposed change, select Accept Proposal. Outlook displays the form shown in Figure 10.11.

The important things to notice in this form are

- *The time for the meeting is now what the respondent suggested.*

- *The form's toolbar contains a Send Update button.* You can click this button to send updated meeting request messages to all the people you originally invited to the meeting.

- *The form contains two additional tabs: Scheduling and Tracking.*

If you click the Scheduling tab, you see a dialog box similar to the one shown previously in Figure 10.8, in which you see the schedules for all the people invited to the meeting. If you click the Tracking tab, you see a dialog box similar to the one shown in Figure 10.12.

Figure 10.11
This form is similar to the form in which you originally proposed the meeting, but has some significant differences.

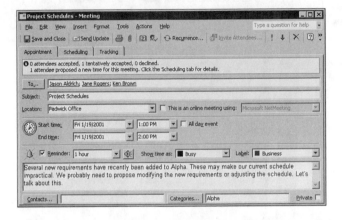

Figure 10.12
This dialog box summarizes the responses you've so far received to the invitations you originally sent.

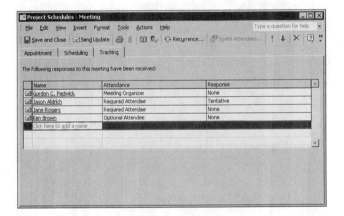

After reading this far, you should have a good idea about how you can use Outlook to send meeting invitations and keep track of the responses you receive.

PLANNING A MEETING AROUND PEOPLE'S COMMITMENTS

In Outlook's terminology, *planning a meeting* is the process by which you find a time for a meeting when the people you want to attend and the resources you need are available. This is in contrast to setting a time for a meeting and then asking other people to attend, as described in the "Inviting People to Attend a Meeting" section, previously in this chapter.

FINDING A TIME FOR A MEETING

Outlook's tool for planning meetings can be used in several ways. The following paragraphs suggest one way you can use this tool.

Start by selecting the earliest time you want to have the meeting in the Day/Week/Month Calendar Information viewer with Day selected. Then select Actions, Plan a Meeting to display the dialog box shown in Figure 10.13.

Figure 10.13
The Plan a Meeting dialog box opens with the time you marked in the Calendar Information viewer shown as a white column.

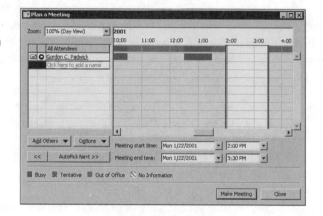

Initially, the dialog box shows only your own schedule. You need to add the schedules of the people you want to attend the meeting and also for any resources you need.

To add schedules for people and resources:

1. Click Add Others and then select Add from Address Book to display the Select Attendees and Resources dialog box, in which you can select people's names from any of your address books.

2. Select the people and resources, and then select Required, Optional, or Resources to move the selected names into the boxes at the right side of the dialog box.

3. Click OK to return to the Plan a Meeting dialog box that shows schedules for the selected people and resources, as shown in Figure 10.14.

Figure 10.14
The free/busy information for the people and resources you selected is displayed in this dialog box.

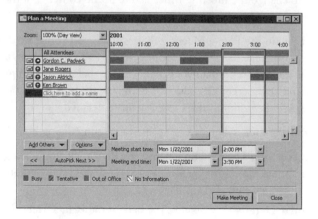

Note

If the schedule for a person or resource isn't available, the corresponding row is hatched.

4. If you're lucky, the date and time you originally proposed for the meeting won't conflict with the schedule of any of the people or resources. However, some conflicts are likely to exist, in which case you must change the date or time of the meeting, as subsequently explained.

Tip from

Gordon Cook

The row above the top person's schedule contains the combined schedule for all the people and resources listed. The information in this row is particularly useful if you have more schedules than can be seen at one time.

One way to change the time for the meeting is to let Outlook automatically find a period when people and resources are available. Click AutoPick Next to find the first available period after the date you originally proposed, or click << to find the first available period prior to the original date. In either case, Outlook redisplays the Plan a Meeting dialog box, showing the first available period for the meeting (refer to Figure 10.14). At this point, you can click Make Meeting to create invitation messages.

Another way to change the proposed meeting date and time is by dragging in the Plan a Meeting dialog box. In that box, the beginning of the proposed meeting is shown by a green vertical line and the end is shown by a red vertical line. You can point to either of these lines and drag them to the right or left to change the meeting times. After you drag these lines, the contents of the Meeting Start Time and Meeting End Time boxes change to show the new meeting times.

Yet another way to change the meeting times is to edit the contents of the Meeting Start Time and Meeting End Time boxes.

The period displayed in the Plan a Meeting dialog box is controlled by the content of the Zoom box at the upper-left. By default, Zoom is set to 100% (Day View), in which the dialog box shows the hours of a normal working day if the dialog box occupies the full width of your monitor and your screen resolution is 800×600 pixels. You can open the drop-down Zoom list and select other Zoom values to get a more detailed view or show more hours.

Click Options to make some changes to the Plan a Meeting dialog box. The options are

- **Show Only Working Hours**—By default, the Plan a Meeting dialog box shows only your working hours. Click this option to switch between showing only working hours and showing 24-hour days.

- **Show Calendar Details**—By default, the bars in the Plan a Meeting dialog box aren't identified. Click this option to switch between showing the subjects of appointments represented by each of the bars in your own calendar.

- **AutoPick**—Move the pointer onto AutoPick to display a list of options that control how AutoPick works. You can choose among All People and Resources, All People and One Resource, Required People, or Required People and One Resource.

- **Refresh Free/Busy**—Select this to refresh the free/busy information for the people listed in the Plan a Meeting dialog box.

NOTIFYING ATTENDEES

After you've established what appears to be a time when all the people and resources are available, you still must notify those people and resources. By default, Outlook can send e-mail messages to all the people and resources. This default is signified by the envelope icons at the left of people and resource names in the dialog box. If, for any reason, you don't want to send an e-mail notification to a specific person or resource, click the icon and select Don't Send Meeting to This Attendee.

To prepare e-mail to send, click Make Meeting. Outlook displays the Meeting form with the attendees' names in the To box and the resources' names in the Location box. You can enter appropriate information about the meeting in the Notes box.

Click Send in the form's toolbar to send the messages.

Attendees receive the message and can reply to it in the manner described previously in this chapter.

→ For information about inviting people to meetings, **see** "Inviting People to Attend a Meeting," **p. 240**.

SENDING UPDATES TO ATTENDEES

After you've invited people to attend a meeting, you might want to send updated information. To do so, double-click the meeting on your calendar to open the original meeting request in the Meeting form.

Make any changes to the information on that form, and then click Send Update on the form's Standard toolbar. Outlook sends an updated message to the attendees.

TROUBLESHOOTING

TIME ZONES AND MEETING INVITATIONS

Outlook saves the times for appointments in Universal Coordinated Time (UCT) and converts those times according to the Windows time-zone setting to your local time. If you start out by using the wrong time-zone setting and subsequently switch to the correct time zone, you'll find that all your existing appointment times have changed. You can, however, make a change to the time-zone setting without changing the displayed appointment times.

To make this change, export the items in your Calendar folder to a file, change your Windows time zone, and then import the Calendar items back into Outlook. The Microsoft

Knowledge Base article Q181170, "Changing the Time Zone Without Changing Appointment," describes this process in detail.

→ For information about importing and exporting Outlook items, **see** "Importing and Exporting Outlook Items," **p. 369**.

When you attempt to plan a meeting, you might not be able to see free/busy times for some of the people you want to invite, or you might see some people's free/busy times for only a limited period.

If you can't see a person's free/busy times, that's probably because that person hasn't made those times available. The solution is to ask that person to make free/busy time available.

→ For information about making free/busy times available, **see** "Sharing a Calendar," **p. 234**.

When you're planning a meeting for a few months ahead, you might find you can see people's free/busy times for only the next two months. That's because, by default, Outlook proposes to publish free/busy information for the next two months (refer to Figure 10.2). If you need to see people's free/busy time further ahead than two months, you must ask those people to increase the number of months. Outlook enables people to publish free/busy information for up to the next 12 months.

CHAPTER 11

MANAGING TASKS

In this chapter

UNDERSTANDING TASKS

Tasks are activities planned for the future, but not things you must do on a specific day or at a specific time, although they might have a start date and a due date. This is in contrast to appointments, which always have a specific date and time, and events that always occur on a specific day or days.

Here are a couple of examples to clarify the distinction between tasks and appointments. When you arrange a visit to the dentist, you create an appointment for a specific date and time. On the other hand, when your boss says, "It's time we had a Web page. I'd like to have it up and running by the end of next month," that's a task. No specific date and time are set when you must work on the project, but you must have it done by a certain date.

Tasks can be categorized in several ways, one of which is if they have a start date or due date, or both:

- Unscheduled tasks are those that don't have to be done by a certain date—the "when I get around to it" type of thing.
- Tasks that must be completed by a certain date.
- Tasks you plan to start working on by a certain date.
- Tasks you plan to start working on by a certain date and must have completed by a certain date.

Similar to appointments and events, tasks can be either one-time or recurring.

You can

- Create a task for yourself.
- Create a task for someone else.
- Receive a task someone created for you.

Outlook can display tasks in the TaskPad in the Day/Week/Month view of the Calendar Information viewer. It also can display tasks in various views of the Tasks Information viewer.

You can work with tasks in four places:

- In Outlook Today
- In the TaskPad
- In the Tasks Information viewer
- In a Task form

In the order listed, these four places give you progressively more control over the information Outlook stores and displays about tasks.

WORKING WITH TASKS IN OUTLOOK TODAY

The Outlook Today window, shown in Figure 11.1, contains a summary of your uncompleted tasks:

- Those that don't have a start or due date (shown in black)
- Those that have a start date on or after today (shown in black)
- Those you marked today as completed (shown in gray with the text struck through)
- Those that are overdue (shown in red)

Tip from

You can change the colors of overdue and completed tasks. To do so, select Tools, Options; select the Preferences tab; and select Task Options. The colors you choose also apply to tasks displayed in the TaskPad.

MARKING A TASK AS COMPLETE

Each task in the Outlook Today window has a small, empty box at the left of the subject, as shown in Figure 11.1.

Figure 11.1
The Outlook Today window shows your current tasks with their due dates in the center column.

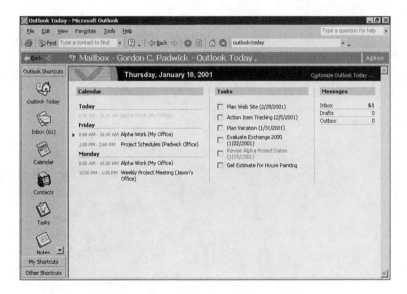

→ If you haven't created any tasks in Outlook, the Outlook Today window won't, of course, display any tasks. For information about creating a few basic tasks, **see** "Creating a Task," **p. 255**.

You can mark a task as complete in this window by clicking in the small box. When you do so, a check mark appears within the box and the subject is displayed in gray with strikethrough marks.

Note

If you mark a task as complete by mistake, click the small box again to restore the task to its original status. The check mark disappears from the small box, and the task subject is again displayed in black without the strikethrough.

DISPLAYING DETAILED TASK INFORMATION

To display details about a task, click the task subject. Outlook displays information about the task in a Task form.

→ For detailed information about using the Task form, **see** "Examining and Creating Tasks in the Task Form," **p. 258**.

You can't create new tasks in Outlook Today.

WORKING WITH TASKS IN THE TASKPAD

As described in Chapter 9, "Creating Calendars," the TaskPad is usually displayed in the Day/Week/Month Calendar Information viewer with the Day or Week view selected.

You can use the TaskPad, shown in Figure 11.2, to examine your to-do list, create tasks for yourself, and mark tasks as completed.

Figure 11.2
The TaskPad is at the bottom-right of the Day/Week/Month Calendar Information viewer. It contains a list of your current tasks.

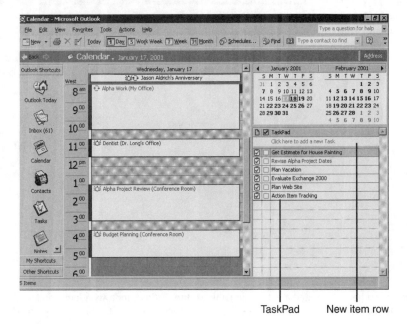

TaskPad   New item row

Note

The TaskPad isn't normally shown in the Month view. However, you can drag the right border of the Month view to the left to reveal the TaskPad.

The TaskPad is similar to a miniature table view of an Information viewer. The default TaskPad contains three columns. From left to right, these are

- **Item Type**—This column contains the Task symbol (a checked clipboard) in every row. Recurring tasks are marked with two curved arrows.

- **Completion**—For uncompleted tasks, this column contains an empty box. For completed tasks, this column contains a checked box.

- **Subject**—This column contains the subject of the task.

→ You can customize the TaskPad in much the same way that you can customize table views of Information viewers; **see** "Modifying a View," **p. 658**.

CREATING A TASK

Although limited in scope, the default TaskPad offers a quick and easy way to create new tasks.

To create a new task in the TaskPad:

1. Display the Day/Week/Month view of the Calendar Information viewer, as shown previously in Figure 11.2.

2. Click the New Item row of the TaskPad in the place that initially contains the words "Click here to add a new Task." When you click, those words disappear.

3. Enter the subject for a new task and press Enter. The subject of the new task moves into the list of current tasks.

Tip from

Put the keywords of the subject at the beginning. Then, if you list tasks in alphabetical order (as subsequently described), related tasks are listed in consecutive rows.

Also, try to use only a few words as the subject of each task—there's not much space in the TaskPad.

A task you create in this way has no start date and no due date. As explained subsequently in this chapter, you can add start and due dates, as well as other information.

PART

III

CH

11

EXAMINING TASKS IN THE TASKPAD

The TaskPad initially shows tasks in the order you created them, with the most recently created task at the top. Completed tasks are indicated by a checked box in the Completed column and by the subject of the task being struck through. Overdue tasks are shown in red.

Note

> If you don't remember what a column in the TaskPad is for, point onto the heading of that column and pause. Outlook displays a ScreenTip that identifies the column.

You can change the order of tasks by clicking in the title row. Click once in the title of the Subject column to arrange tasks in alphabetical order; click again to arrange tasks in reverse alphabetical order. Click once in the title of the Completed column to sort tasks so that uncompleted tasks are listed above completed tasks; click again to list completed tasks at the top.

→ You also can rearrange the order of columns by dragging column titles to the right or left, just as you can rearrange columns in a table view of an Information viewer. **See** "Changing the Order of Fields in a View," **p. 661**.

→ To examine a task in detail, double-click that task's subject in the TaskPad. Outlook displays information about the task in a Task form. **See** "Creating a Task," **p. 255**.

MARKING A TASK AS COMPLETE

To mark a task as complete, click the empty box in the Completed column (the second column from the left). You also can change a task that's marked completed to uncompleted by clicking the checked box in the Completed column.

DELETING A TASK

To delete a task, select that task in the TaskPad; then click the Delete button in the Calendar Information viewer's Standard toolbar.

CUSTOMIZING THE TASKPAD

Several ways exist to customize the TaskPad. You can add columns to the TaskPad in the same way you can add columns to a Table view of an Information viewer.

→ Customizing the TaskPad is a straightforward process; **see** "Adding a Field to a View," **p. 663**.

Tip from

Gordon Padwick

> I find it useful to add a Due Date column to the TaskPad. After doing that, I display tasks in due-date or reverse due-date order by clicking the title of the Due Date column.

By default, the TaskPad contains your current tasks. These are

- All tasks that don't have a due date
- All uncompleted tasks that do not have a start date or have a start date on or after today

→ Tasks in the TaskPad are displayed in the same colors as tasks in Outlook Today. For information about this, **see** "Working with Tasks in Outlook Today," **p. 253**.

You can change the tasks listed in the TaskPad by selecting View and moving the pointer onto TaskPad View to display the menu shown in Figure 11.3.

Figure 11.3
You can use this menu to select various groups of tasks.

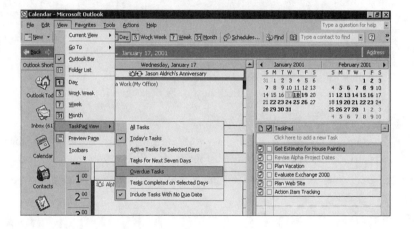

You also can change the tasks displayed in the TaskPad by setting a filter for it.

To set a filter for the TaskPad:

1. Right-click anywhere in the title row of the TaskPad to display the context menu shown in Figure 11.4.

Figure 11.4
You can use this context menu to customize the TaskPad.

2. Select Customize Current View to display the dialog box shown in Figure 11.5.

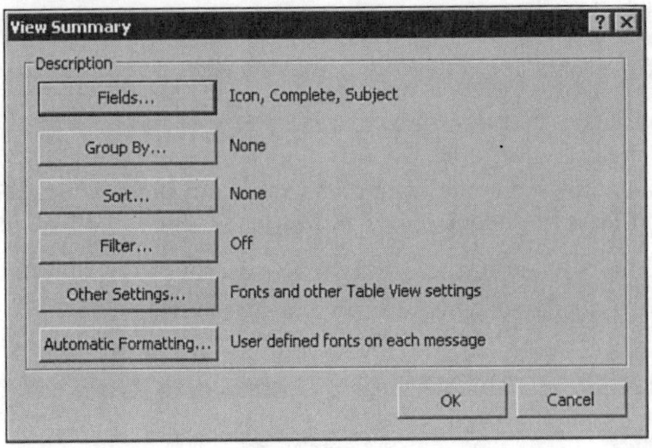

Figure 11.5
You can use this dialog box to change the properties of the TaskPad.

3. Click Filter to set a filter. Proceed from there in the same way that you set a filter for a Table view of an Information viewer, as described in Chapter 31, "Creating Views and Print Styles."

You can use the context menu (refer to Figure 11.4) and the View Summary dialog box (refer to Figure 11.5) to further customize the TaskPad.

→ You can customize the TaskPad using the context menu; **see** "Modifying a View," **p. 658**.

EXAMINING AND CREATING TASKS IN THE TASK FORM

Although you can use the TaskPad to create tasks, as described previously in this chapter, that method is more appropriate for creating a personal to-do list. You should use the Task form to create Outlook items that contain detailed information about tasks. You can use the Task form to examine and modify existing tasks as well as to create new tasks.

EXAMINING AND MODIFYING EXISTING TASKS

You can display information about any task in the Task form and then add information to that task or modify existing information.

To display an existing task in the form, click that task in Outlook Today, or double-click it in the TaskPad or any Tasks Information viewer.

The Task form displays information about the selected task, as shown in Figure 11.6.

The Task form shows only the information you previously entered for the task. When you create a task in the TaskPad, the only information you supply is the subject of the task, so only the Subject box in the Task form contains information you entered in the TaskPad; all other boxes on the form are either empty or contain default values. You can enter information into empty boxes on this form and edit information in other boxes.

Figure 11.6
This Task form displays information about a task created in the TaskPad.

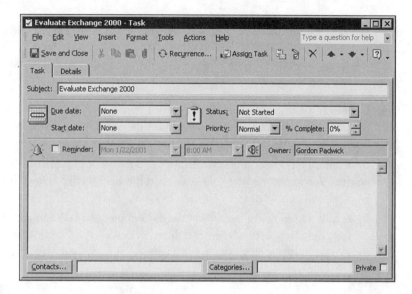

CREATING A NEW TASK IN THE TASK FORM

You can use the Task form to create a task for yourself or a task you want someone else to work on. In either case, start by defining the task.

To define a task:

1. Select Tasks in the Outlook Bar to display a Tasks Information viewer.

2. Click New in the Standard toolbar to display a form similar to the one in Figure 11.6, but with all fields empty or containing default values.

3. Enter the subject of the task in the Subject box. Remember the suggestions earlier in this chapter to enter key words at the beginning of the subject and to use only a few words.

4. By default, the Due Date is shown as None. If you want to specify a due date, open the drop-down Due Date list to display a calendar and select the due date in that calendar. Alternatively, enter the due date using a date format that's compatible with your Windows Regional Settings.

5. By default, the Start Date is shown as None. If you want to specify a start date, open the drop-down Start Date list to display a calendar and select the start date in that calendar. Alternatively, enter the start date using a date format that's compatible with your Windows Regional Settings. If you specify a start date that's later than the due date, Outlook changes the due date to the same as the start date.

If you select or enter a Start Date without having entered a Due Date, Outlook automatically makes the Due Date the same as the Start Date. Also, if you attempt to set a

Start Date while the Due Date is set to None, Outlook automatically sets the Due Date to the same as the Start Date. Outlook doesn't allow you to set a Start Date without also setting a due date.

6. By default, Outlook displays the Status of a new task as Not Started. When you create a new task (or sometime later), you can open the Status drop-down list and select Not Started, In Progress, Completed, Waiting on Someone Else, or Deferred.

7. By default, Outlook displays the Priority of a new task as Normal. When you create a new task (or sometime later), you can open the Priority drop-down list and select Low, Normal, or High.

8. By default, Outlook displays 0% in the % Complete box. When you create a new task (or sometime later), you can enter a different percentage (or click the spin button at the right of the box to change the percentage).

Note

When you set the percentage to 0, Outlook automatically sets the Status to Not Started; when you set the Status to 100, Outlook sets the Status to Completed; when you set the status to any other value, Outlook sets the Status to In Progress.

Also, when you select Not Started as the Status, Outlook sets the percentage to 0; when you select Completed, Outlook sets the percentage to 100. When you set the Status to Waiting on Someone Else, or to Deferred, changing the percentage to anything other than 100% has no effect on the Status; changing the percentage to 100 changes the Status to Completed.

9. Initially, the Reminder box is unchecked. However, as soon as you enter a Due Date, Outlook automatically checks the Reminder box and sets the reminder date to the same as the Due Date, with the reminder time set to the beginning of your work day. When working with reminders, you should keep several points in mind:

■ *If you haven't entered a Due Date, you can check the Reminder box.* When you do so, Outlook sets the reminder date to the current day and the reminder time to the beginning of your work day.

■ *You can change the reminder date in the same way that you set the Due Date and the Start Date (see steps 4 and 5).*

■ *You can change the reminder time by opening the drop-down list of times and selecting a reminder time (this provides only half-hour time increments).* Alternatively, you can enter a reminder time (in which case you aren't limited to half-hour increments).

Note

The default reminder time is always the beginning of your work day. You can change the beginning of your work day in the Preferences tab of the Options dialog box.

10. If you've chosen to be reminded about a task, Outlook displays a message at the time the reminder becomes due (providing Outlook is running). To have Outlook play a sound when a reminder is due, click the button at the right of the time box to display a dialog box in which you can select a sound to be played when the reminder becomes due.

11. You can insert whatever notes are appropriate in the unnamed Notes box that occupies most of the lower part of the form. You also can insert Windows files and Outlook items in this box, just as you can for Calendar items.

→ Use the Notes box to help you keep track of Calendar items; **see** "Adding Notes to an Appointment Item," **p. 206**.

12. To associate one or more contacts with the task, click Contacts to display the Select Contacts dialog box, in which you can select contacts.

13. To assign one or more categories to the task, click Categories to display the Categories dialog box, in which you can select categories.

14. If you intend to share your Tasks folder with other people but want to keep this task private, check the Private box.

15. Unless you want to enter more details about the task, click Save and Close in the form's Standard toolbar.

OWNING A TASK

Every task is owned by someone. Only the person who owns a task can change any information about that task.

Initially, the person who creates a task owns it. In Figure 11.6, the Owner box contains the name of the person who created the task. That name has a gray background to indicate that you can't change it.

Note

Each Task item has an Owner field that is normally read-only. If you create a Table view of tasks, you can display the content of the Owner field. Outlook allows you to change the name in the Owner field in the Table view, but when you move out of that field, Outlook displays a message stating `You must be in a public folder to change the Owner field of a task. The original owner name will be restored.` Sure enough, when you close the Outlook message, the original owner name reappears.

If you create a task, offer it to someone else, and that person accepts the task, Outlook automatically transfers ownership of the task to that person. After that, you can't make changes to the task; only the new owner can do that.

→ If you're a manager, assigning tasks is something you'll do frequently; **see** "Assigning Tasks to Other People," **p. 268**.

PART

III

CH

11

ENTERING MORE INFORMATION ABOUT A TASK

Although you can use the preceding procedure to enter all the information you'll normally need about a task, you can enter more information in the Task form's Details tab, shown in Figure 11.7. This tab is particularly useful in the case of tasks for which you need to keep billing records.

Figure 11.7
Use this tab to enter more information about a task.

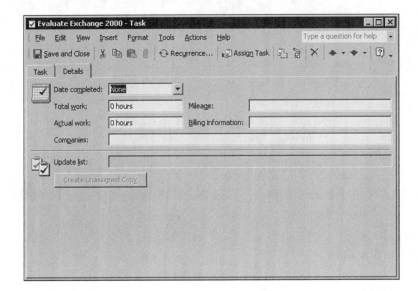

Use the boxes in this tab as follows:

- **Date Completed**—This box initially contains None. When the task is completed, open the drop-down calendar and select the completion date (or enter the completion date). When you do so, Outlook automatically sets the Status box in the Task tab to Completed and the % Complete box to 100. If you change the Status in the Task tab to Completed, the Date Completed box in the Details tab contains the date on which you marked the task as completed. Likewise, if you open the drop-down Date Completed calendar on the Details tab and click None, the Status on the Task tab changes to In Progress and the % Complete changes to 75.

- **Total Work**—Use this box for your estimate of the total amount of time required to complete the task.

- **Actual Work**—Use this box to keep track of the time you actually spend on the task.

- **Mileage**—Use this box to keep track of the number of miles you travel in connection with the task.

- **Billing Information**—Use this box for any information related to billing, such as the hourly rate to be charged.

- **Companies**—Enter the names of organizations associated with the task, such as the name of the client for whom the task is being performed.

The Update List box and Create Unassigned Copy button are used when you assign a task to someone else.

→ After you've been assigned a task, you have the option of accepting or rejecting it. **See** "Accepting a Task," **p. 271**.

WORKING WITH THE TASKS INFORMATION VIEWER

Even though the TaskPad provides a useful way for you to keep up to date with your current tasks, it doesn't provide all the information you need to see or enter about tasks. The Tasks Information viewer displays more detailed information.

Click the Tasks shortcut in the Outlook Bar to display the Tasks Information viewer, shown in Figure 11.8.

New item row

Figure 11.8
Outlook initially displays the Simple Task view of the Tasks Information viewer, in which the subject and due date of all tasks are listed.

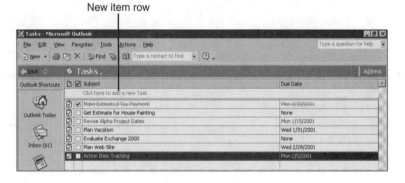

If you see a different view on your computer, select View, move the pointer onto Current View, and select Simple List.

The Simple List view is similar to the TaskPad described previously in this chapter. You can use it in the same way as the TaskPad.

With the Simple List, or another, view of tasks displayed, you can select View, Preview Pane so that you can see more information about a selected task, as shown in Figure 11.9.

In the case of recurring tasks, the Preview pane contains an InfoBar that describes the recurrence pattern.

→ For more information about the Preview pane, **see** "Previewing Messages," **p. 98**.

Note

You can't create a Preview pane in the TaskPad.

In addition to the Simple List view shown here, you can select various other Table views and one Timeline view.

Figure 11.9
The Preview pane header shows the Subject, Status, Due Date, and Owner of a task selected in the list. The pane also shows any information about the task you entered in the Notes box on the Task form.

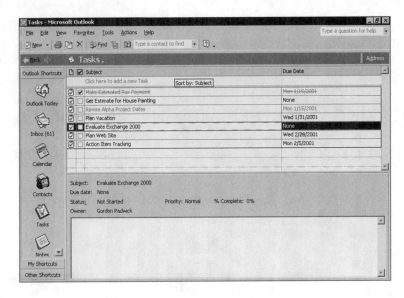

→ If none of the existing views suits your needs, **see** "Creating Views and Print Styles," **p. 651**.

USING THE TASKS INFORMATION VIEWER TO CREATE TASKS

You can use the Simple List view of the Tasks Information viewer, shown previously in Figure 11.8, to create a new task in much the same way that you can use the TaskPad.

→ If you need to create a new task, **see** "Creating a Task," **p. 255**.

If you don't see the New Item row on your computer screen, follow these steps.

To display the New Item row:

1. With the Simple List view of the Tasks Information viewer displayed, select View, move the pointer onto Current View, and select Customize Current View to Display the View Summary dialog box shown previously in Figure 11.5.
2. Click Other Settings to display the dialog box shown in Figure 11.10.
3. Check the Show "New Item" Row box; then click OK twice to close the dialog boxes. Now you should see the New Item row at the top of the Simple List view of tasks.

To create a new task in the Simple List view of the Tasks Information viewer, click within the words `Click here to add a new task`. The New Item row changes to show two cells, one for the subject of the new task and one for the due date. Enter the subject, optionally enter the due date, and press Enter. Outlook moves the new task into the list of tasks.

You're not limited to entering only the subject and due date for a new task in this way. You can, for example, use the Detailed List view of the Tasks Information viewer to enter more information for a new task.

To display the Detailed List view, select View, move the pointer onto Current View, and select Detailed List. A Detailed List view is shown in Figure 11.11.

Figure 11.10
You can use this dialog box to change the appearance of a view.

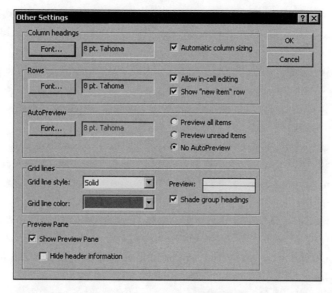

Figure 11.11
You can use this view to see and enter additional information about tasks.

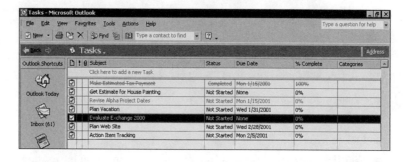

Tip from

If you enable the Preview pane for the Simple List view and then switch to the Detailed List view, you'll probably notice that the Preview pane isn't there. That's because Outlook keeps information about each view separately. If you want to have the Preview pane displayed for the Detailed List view, you must select View, Preview Pane while the Detailed view is displayed.

USING THE TASKS INFORMATION VIEWER TO VIEW TASKS

You can use the Tasks Information viewer to see tasks in various Table views and in one Timeline view:

- **Simple List**—Contains all tasks and displays only the Subject and Due Date fields.
- **Detailed List**—Contains all tasks and displays the Subject, Status, Due Date, % Complete, and Categories fields.

- **Active Tasks**—A filtered list containing tasks that have a status of Not Started, In Progress, or Waiting On Someone Else; it also displays the same fields as the Detailed List.

- **Next Seven Days**—A filtered list containing tasks due in the next seven days; it also displays the same fields as the Detailed List.

- **Overdue Tasks**—A filtered list containing tasks due before today; it also displays the same fields as the Detailed List.

- **By Category**—Contains all tasks grouped by category and contains the same fields as the Detailed List.

- **Assignment**—Contains tasks offered to you and accepted by you and displays the Subject, Owner, Due Date, and Status fields.

- **By Person Responsible**—Contains all tasks grouped by Owner and displays the Subject, Requested By, Owner, Due Date, and Status fields.

- **Completed Tasks**—A filtered list containing only completed tasks; it also displays the Subject, Due Date, Date Completed, and Categories fields.

- **Task Timeline**—Contains all tasks arranged chronologically.

→ You can modify these standard views and create custom views. **See** "Creating Views and Print Styles," **p. 651**.

In any of the Table views you can use the techniques described in the section "Working with Tasks in the TaskPad" previously in this chapter to

- Change the order in which tasks are listed

- Mark tasks as completed

- Delete tasks

- Edit the contents of the displayed fields (providing you have Allow In-cell Editing enabled)

- Double-click a task to display it in a Task form

→ If you prefer to use the TaskPad, **see** "Working with Tasks in the TaskPad," **p. 254**.

CREATING RECURRING TASKS

The preceding pages of this chapter have described only one-time tasks. You can create recurring tasks just as you can create recurring appointments. You might want to create such recurring tasks as submitting a monthly report, due on a specific day of the month, or having your hair cut, due every four weeks.

→ To learn more about recurrence, **see** "Creating Recurring Appointments and Events," **p. 209**.

Whereas you can create a recurring appointment from scratch or create one based on an existing one-time appointment, you can create a recurring task based only on an existing one-time task.

Note

Recurring tasks have a distinct difference from recurring appointments and events. Whereas the Calendar Day/Week/Month Information viewer shows every instance of recurring appointments and events, Task Information viewers show only one future instance of a recurring task.

Outlook creates recurring tasks one instance at a time. When you mark one instance of a recurring task as complete, Outlook creates the next instance. Notice, though, that if you mark one instance of a recurring task as complete so that the next instance is created and then remove the completion mark, the next instance is not deleted.

Outlook creates two types of recurring tasks, which are best illustrated by examples:

- **Regularly recurring tasks**—One type of recurring task occurs regularly; an example of this is a monthly report required on the last day of every month. If you are late submitting the report for one month, the next month's report is still due on the last day of the next month.

- **Dependent recurring tasks**—Another type of recurring task is one in which the next instance occurs a specific period after the last instance; an example of this is having your hair cut. If you create a recurring task to have your hair cut every four weeks and are sometimes late, the next occurrence Outlook creates is always four weeks after you mark the previous instance as complete.

To create a regularly recurring task:

1. With a Tasks Information viewer displayed, double-click a task to display that task in a Task form.
2. Click Recurrence in the form's Standard toolbar to display the dialog box shown in Figure 11.12.

PART

III

CH

11

Figure 11.12
Use this dialog box to define the task's recurrence pattern. A monthly recurrence is shown here.

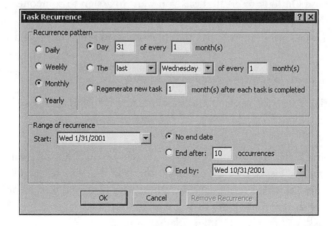

3. In the Recurrence Pattern section of the dialog box, select Daily, Weekly, Monthly, or Yearly and select the appropriate recurrence pattern. Make sure you don't click the Regenerate New Task option button.

4. In the Range of Recurrence section of the dialog box, specify the start and end of the recurrence pattern.

5. Click OK to return to the Task form, in which the InfoBar summarizes the recurrence pattern.

6. Click Save and Close in the form's Standard toolbar to save the recurring task.

To create the Dependent type of recurrence pattern in which Outlook generates the next instance of a task a specific interval after the previous instance is completed, follow the preceding steps with the exception of step 3. In that step, click Regenerate New Task and change the number in the box to whatever is appropriate. For example, to set up a task to have your hair cut four weeks after it was last cut, click Weekly recurrence, click Regenerate New Task, and change the number to 4.

Recurring tasks are indicated in the TaskPad and in Table views of the Tasks Information viewer by the symbol in the Icon column. Instead of the checked clipboard icon, recurring tasks are indicated by the checked clipboard icon on which a pair of curved arrows is superimposed.

Note

The Outlook Today window doesn't indicate that a task is recurring. It shows only the next occurrence of a recurring task.

ASSIGNING TASKS TO OTHER PEOPLE

So far, this chapter has described how you can use Outlook to keep track of your own tasks. You also can use Outlook to create tasks you want to assign to someone else. Although Outlook uses the word "assign," you can't actually assign a task to someone else. Instead, you can offer a task to someone, with that person having the option of accepting or declining the task.

You can offer a task to someone else in two ways:

- By creating a task for yourself and then offering it to someone else
- By creating a task request

When you offer a task to someone else, you can choose whether you want to keep a copy of the task in your task list. If you choose to do that and the person accepts the task, any changes that person makes to the task are automatically copied to the copy of the task you keep (assuming the computers the two of you use can communicate). If you don't keep a copy of the task, you relinquish all knowledge of it.

Also, when you offer a task to someone, you can request a report when the task is complete. If you do that, and the person accepts the task, an automatic report is sent to you when that person marks the task as complete.

If the person to whom you offer a task declines to accept it, the task remains as one of your personal tasks.

ASKING SOMEONE TO ACCEPT AN EXISTING TASK

After creating a task for yourself, you can offer that task to someone else by sending an e-mail message.

To offer an existing task to someone else:

1. With any view of the Tasks Information viewer displayed, double-click a task to display it in a Task form.

2. Click Assign Task in the form's Standard toolbar. Outlook modifies the Task form to resemble a Message form, as shown in Figure 11.13.

Figure 11.13
The InfoBar near the top of the form indicates that the message has not been sent.

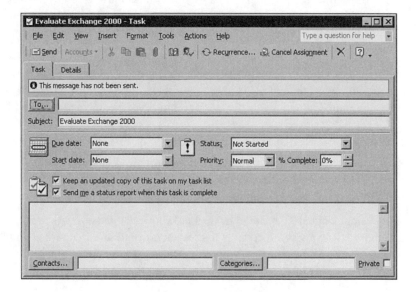

PART

III

CH

11

3. Click To to display a dialog box in which you can select a person from one of your address books.

4. Select the name of the person to whom you want to offer the task from the list at the left, click To to copy that name into the list on the right, and click OK to return to the Task form. The selected person's name is now in the To box on the Task form.

5. If you want to retain the task and be updated about the progress of the task (should the person accept it), leave the Keep an Updated Copy of This Task on My Task List box checked; otherwise, uncheck the box.

6. If you want to receive a status report when the task is marked complete (should the person accept the task), leave the Send Me a Status Report When This Task Is Complete box checked; otherwise, uncheck the box.

7. Enter whatever information is appropriate in the Notes box and, if necessary, select Insert to append files and Outlook items to the message.

8. Click Send in the form's Standard toolbar to send the message that offers the task. If you had previously asked to be reminded when the task becomes due, Outlook displays a message saying you are no longer the owner of the task so the task reminder has been turned off.

After you offer a task to someone else, Outlook changes the symbol representing the task. In the TaskPad and Table views of tasks, the symbol becomes a checked clipboard held in a hand, as if the task is being offered.

If you uncheck the Keep an Updated Copy of This Task on My Task List box (step 5 in the preceding procedure), the task disappears from your task list when you send the message that offers the task, but reappears if that person declines to accept the task. If you leave that box checked, the message remains in your task list; the task symbol in the TaskPad and Tasks Information viewer has a sending hand supporting it to indicate the task has been offered.

As is the case for other messages, when you click Send, Outlook moves the task message to your Outbox folder and the message stays there until Outlook has access to your mail server. At that time, Outlook sends the message and keeps a copy in your Sent Items folder.

CREATING A TASK REQUEST FOR A GROUP

So far, the method of asking someone to accept a task that has been described assumes that you are asking only one person to accept the task. But, what if you want to ask several people to accept a task, or a similar task?

You could, of course, create individual tasks for each person, in the manner just described. A more efficient way, however, is to create a task and save that task as an Outlook template. Having created the template, you can now easily create identical tasks to send to several people or create modified task requests to send to individual people.

Tip from

Gordon Padwick

If you only want to send identical tasks to several people, you can create a distribution list in your Contacts folder and send the task to the distribution list.

If you send a task to more than one person, Outlook can't update you with each person's progress on the task.

→ You're stretching Outlook beyond what it's really intended to do when you try to use it to assign tasks to several people. If that's what you need to do, though, consider using the Outlook Team Folders Add-in or integrating Outlook with Microsoft Team Manager. **See** "Going Further with Task Management," **p. 273**.

SENDING A TASK REQUEST

Instead of creating a task and then offering it to someone else, you can create a task request.

To create and send a task request:

1. With any Tasks Information viewer displayed, select Actions, New Task Request to display the Task form previously shown in Figure 11.7.

2. Use this dialog box to create a new task, as described previously in this chapter.

3. Follow steps 3–7 in the previous procedure to send the task request.

→ If you want to offer an existing task to another person, **see** "Asking Someone to Accept an Existing Task," **p. 269**.

After you've sent a task to someone else, you can send an unassigned copy of that task to another person by clicking Create Unassigned Copy in the Details tab of the Task form. You can use this to send a "for your information" copy of the task. When you click this button, Outlook issues the following warning: If you create an unassigned copy of this task, you will own the copy, and you will no longer receive updates for the task you assigned.

PART

III

CH

11

RESPONDING TO A TASK REQUEST

The process of offering a task to someone and that person responding is similar to inviting people to a meeting and those people responding.

→ For information about inviting people to meetings, **see** "Inviting People to Attend a Meeting," **p. 240**.

When you receive a task request, you see a message header in your Inbox Information viewer that contains the subject of the task being offered to you, the task's status, and the percent complete. The symbol at the left indicates the message is offering you a task.

You can double-click the message header in the Inbox Information viewer to see details of the task in a Task form.

The Task form's Standard toolbar contains Accept and Decline buttons.

ACCEPTING A TASK

Click the Accept button if you agree to accept the task. When you do so, Outlook displays a dialog box you can use to send an acceptance message. You can add your comments to the message before you send it.

Enter your comments in the unnamed Notes box in the lower part of the form; then click Send in the form's Standard toolbar to send your response. To send your acceptance without any comments, click the Send Immediately button. Outlook immediately sends your response to the person who offered you the task.

In addition to sending your acceptance to the person who offered the task to you, Outlook

- Adds the task to your Tasks folder
- Makes you the new owner of the task, as you can see if you double-click the task in your Tasks Information viewer to see that task in a Task form

You now can double-click the task you've accepted in your Tasks Information viewer to see its details in a Task form. Because you now own the task, you have full access to the information about the task, and you can use the Task and Details tabs to keep that information updated. If the person who offered you the task chose to keep a copy of that task, Outlook automatically updates that person's copy each time you make a change to the information about the task (subject, of course, to your computer being capable of communicating with the computer used by the person who offered you the task).

Note

If the person who offered the task kept a copy of the task, that person's name appears in the Update List box in the Details tab of the Task form on your computer.

DECLINING A TASK

To decline an offered task, click the Decline button in the Task forms Standard toolbar. Outlook displays the Declining Task dialog box that's the same, except for the title, as the Accepting Task dialog box.

You can send a message declining the task with or without comments, just as you can for an acceptance message. In this case, Outlook doesn't add the task to your task list.

RECEIVING A RESPONSE TO A TASK REQUEST

When you receive a response from someone to whom you offered a task, your Inbox Information viewer displays the message, just like any other message you receive. You can double-click the message header to see any comments the person might have sent with the message.

When you offer a task to someone and don't choose to keep a copy of that task in your Tasks folder, Outlook temporarily removes that task from your Tasks folder. If the person declines the task, Outlook restores that task into your Tasks folder.

When someone accepts the task you offered, Outlook permanently removes that task from your Tasks folder unless you chose to keep a copy of the task. In this case, the InfoBar reminds you that the task has been accepted and also indicates that the task is now owned by the person who accepted it.

GOING FURTHER WITH TASK MANAGEMENT

You can use the Outlook Team Folders add-in and Microsoft's Team Manager to extend Outlook's capabilities for working with tasks.

The Outlook Team Folders add-in to Outlook 2000 and Outlook 2002 works in conjunction with an Exchange server to enable team members to work together on projects. You must be using Outlook as a client for an Exchange server to take advantage of Team Folders.

Team Manager is another Microsoft application that gives you the ability to delegate tasks to a team and monitor the work of that team. To quote from Microsoft's Design Goals for Team Manager, "Microsoft Team Manager is a new workgroup tool that helps everyone on the team stay in sync by consolidating, coordinating, and tracking team activities." Team Manager can be integrated with Outlook.

You can find detailed information about Team Manager on the Web site:

```
http://www.microsoft.com/office/teammanager/default.htm
```

Note

Although Microsoft no longer actively promotes Team Manager and hasn't offered upgrades since 1997, the product is (at the time of writing this chapter) still available. The URL contains information about ordering Team Manager.

Team Manager integrates with Outlook by synchronizing task lists. Synchronization occurs when you open or close Team Manager and when you accept a team member's settings messages or a team task update message from the team manager.

Team members can create and track their own tasks using Team Manager, Outlook, or Schedule+; Team Manager keeps those tasks synchronized.

Team Manager has many capabilities, some of which are similar to those in Outlook. Other Team Manager capabilities not available in Outlook are

- **Actual Work**—Actual work tracking is available in several project-management applications. It keeps track of and displays work hours, overtime work hours, costs, work completed, and changes in the number of hours worked.

- **Best Fit Scheduling**—Best fit scheduling analyzes workloads to determine whether team members can complete their tasks within the available time, based on priorities and deadlines. It also can suggest schedule adjustments.

- **Consolidated Status Reporting**—This capability combines individual team members' reports into a consolidated report.

- **Work Calendar Views**—This view provides information about what members are working on by day, week, or month.

- **Workload Graph**—This graph provides a visual summary of team members' workloads.

- **Vacation Tracking**—This capability allows scheduled vacations to be taken into account when planning projects.

If you find Outlook doesn't provide all you need as far as task management is concerned, consider integrating Team Manager into Outlook.

TROUBLESHOOTING

TASKS

When you use the Task form to create a task, you can enter a date and time for a Reminder. If you set a Due Date for the task, Outlook automatically enters the same date and time in the Reminder box. If you want to be reminded about the task some time ahead of the Due Date, you can change the date and time in the Reminder box.

Outlook provides reminders only for tasks in the default Tasks folder. If you save tasks in folders other than the default Tasks folder, Outlook doesn't display reminders for those tasks.

You might think it would be a good idea to organize your tasks by keeping tasks related to individual projects in separate folders. If you do that, though, you sacrifice receiving task reminders and your tasks won't be displayed in Outlook Today. Rather than saving tasks in separate project folders, I strongly recommend you keep all tasks in the default Tasks folder and allocate a specific category, or perhaps more than one category, to each task. You can subsequently display tasks by category. If a particular task relates to more than one project, you can allocate as many categories as necessary to that task; that's much more convenient than entering the same task in two or more folders.

CHAPTER 12

KEEPING A JOURNAL

In this chapter

WHAT IS OUTLOOK'S JOURNAL?

If you have a perfect memory, you probably don't need Outlook's Journal. However, if you sometimes forget things you've done or when you did them, the Journal can be a very useful memory supplement.

Note

> Outlook 2000 and Outlook 2002 retain the journaling capability that is also in Outlook 97 and Outlook 98. However, Outlook 2000 and Outlook 2002 have Contact Activity Tracking, which is, in some ways, more convenient than journaling. Contact Activity Tracking, though, doesn't completely replace journaling.

→ For information about tracking contacts' activities, **see** "Tracking a Contact's Activities," **p. 187**.

Outlook's Journal is a place where you can keep records of your daily activities. The Journal can automatically record such activities as

- E-mail messages you send to, and receive from, specific contacts, including messages that request appointments or attendance at meetings and those about accepting task assignments
- Faxes you send and receive by way of Outlook
- Telephone calls you make
- Each time you work with an Office application and certain Office-compatible applications

In addition, you can use the Journal to manually record activities such as

- Letters, memos, and other paper documents you receive
- Telephone calls you receive
- Conversations you have
- Items you purchase
- Anything else you do or experience

Outlook saves a record of each activity as a Journal item in the Journal folder in your Personal Folders file on your computer's hard disk or, if you're using Outlook as a client for Exchange, in your Journal folder in the Exchange store. You don't need to have Outlook running for file activities to be automatically saved as Journal items.

You choose what you want Outlook to save as Journal items. You can see the items Outlook has saved in your Journal folder by opening the Journal Information viewer.

Tip from

In Outlook 97 and Outlook 98, the Journal icon is in the Outlook Shortcuts section of the Outlook Bar. In Outlook 2000 and Outlook 2002, that icon is in the My Shortcuts section. If you're a frequent Journal user, you might find moving the Journal icon into the Outlook Shortcuts section of the Outlook Bar more convenient.

→ For information about moving icons between sections of the Outlook Bar, **see** "Changing the Order of Icons," **p. 493**.

Much of this chapter is about the Timeline view of Journal items because Journal items are most often displayed in a timeline. I'd like to remind you that, although Outlook doesn't offer a built-in Timeline view for other types of items, you can display any Outlook items in a timeline. You might find it convenient, for example, to create a Timeline view for items in your Inbox and Sent Items folders so that you can easily search for messages by date.

→ All the information about timelines in this chapter applies equally to timelines used to display any type of Outlook item. **See** "Creating Custom Views," **p. 679**.

SETTING UP AUTOMATIC JOURNALING

Journaling is initially disabled after you install Outlook. The first time you select Journal in the Outlook Bar, Outlook displays a message box that says ...the Activities tab on the contact item is the best way to track e-mail and does not require the Journal. If you're principally interested in tracking only e-mail, and don't intend to use the Journal, click No in this box so that the Journal is not activated. If you do want to use the Journal, click Yes to activate the Journal. The remainder of this chapter assumes you have clicked Yes.

When you click Yes, Outlook displays the Journal Options dialog box, shown in Figure 12.1.

PART

III

CH

12

Figure 12.1
This is where you select the activities you want the Journal to record.

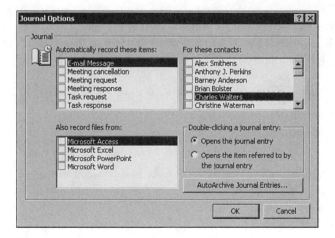

Note

You also can open the Journal Options dialog box from any Outlook Information viewer. Select Tools, Options. In the Preferences tab, select Journal Options.

Use this dialog box to specify the types of activities you want the Journal to record, as described in Chapter 27, "Setting Outlook's Options."

→ For information about selecting the activities you want the Journal to record, **see** "Journal Options," **p. 550**.

After you've set up the Journal in this way, Outlook creates separate journal items when any of the activities you specify occur.

Note

The process of setting up Journaling, as described in the first paragraph of this section, creates a value in a specific key of the Windows registry. If you subsequently don't want to have Journaling available, you must remove that value from the registry.

After setting up Journaling, close Outlook; then open the Registry Editor and search for a value named `EnableJournal`. To disable Journaling, delete that value. When you restart Outlook and click Journal in the Outlook Bar, you'll see the message referred to in the first paragraph. Click No to continue without Journaling enabled.

As always, I caution you to save a copy of the registry before making any changes to it.

→ For information about working with the Windows registry, **see** "Working with the Windows Registry," **p. 799**.

EXTENDING JOURNALING CAPABILITIES

By default, Outlook can create Journal items corresponding to e-mail messages (including those involved with scheduling meetings and assigning tasks), and it also can create Journal items each time you work with Access, Excel, PowerPoint, and Word documents. You can extend the Journaling capabilities in several ways, as described in the next few sections.

JOURNALING PHONE CALLS

Outlook can automatically create Journal items for phone calls you make, providing you use Outlook to place those calls.

→ For information about using Outlook to make phone calls, **see** "Placing a Phone Call," **p. 183**.

You can set up Outlook to automatically create Journal items for phone calls you make to specific people. Unfortunately, before you do that, you must make some changes to the Windows registry. By default, the Automatically Record These Items list in the upper-left box of the Journal Options dialog box (previously shown in Figure 12.1) doesn't contain a Phone Call item. After you make the registry change described in the next few paragraphs, the box does contain a Phone Call item.

> **Caution**
>
> Information in the registry controls how Windows and applications running under Windows run. Incorrect changes to the contents of the registry can affect Windows or an application, and can even make your computer unusable. Always make a backup copy of the registry before making any changes to it.

→ For information about backing up the registry, **see** "Backing Up and Restoring the Registry," **p. 800**. For information about changing the contents of the registry, **see** "Adding and Deleting Subkeys," **p. 806**; "Changing the Data in a Key or Subkey Value," **p. 806**; and "Managing Values in a Subkey," **p. 807**.

Before following these steps, close Outlook if it's running.

To modify the Windows registry so that you can create Journal items for phone calls you make:

1. In the Windows desktop, select Start, Run to display the Run dialog box.

2. In the Open box, enter `Regedit` and click OK to start the Registry Editor.

3. Navigate to the registry key `HKEY_CURRENT_USER\Software\Microsoft\Shared Tools\Outlook\Journaling\Phone Call`.

4. Select the Phone Call key to display the values it contains in the Registry Editor's right pane.

5. Select the AutoJournaled value (which is `0` by default); then select Edit, Modify to display the Edit DWORD Value dialog box.

6. Replace the default value of `0` (zero) in the Value Data box with `1` (one); then click OK.

7. Select Registry, Exit to close the Registry Editor.

After modifying the registry in this way, start Outlook and select Tools, Options, and in the Preferences tab select Journal Options. Now you should see Phone Call listed in the Automatically Record These Items box. Check that item to enable creating Journal items for phone calls. In the For These Contacts box, check the names of the contacts for whom Journal items are to be created.

Now, Outlook is set up to automatically create Journal items whenever you make phone calls to specific people.

JOURNALING FAXES

You also can use Outlook to send and receive faxes, as explained in the section "Sending and Receiving Faxes" in Chapter 5, "Receiving Messages." The Journal handles faxes in much the same way as it handles e-mail messages.

If you've listed a fax number for a contact, enabled that contact in the Journal Options dialog box, and addressed a message to the contact's fax number, Outlook creates a Journal item when you send the fax. Likewise, when you receive a fax from that person, Outlook creates a Journal item.

PART

III

CH

12

CREATING JOURNAL ITEMS FOR MORE APPLICATIONS

As explained previously in this chapter, you can set up the Journal to create a Journal item each time you use one of the major Office applications to work with a document. You can extend this to include applications other than the predefined Office applications. However, this applies only to applications that contain the capability to interact with Outlook. Microsoft makes information about doing this available to application developers, but it is up to those developers to incorporate the capability. Even some major Microsoft applications, such as FrontPage, don't have it.

Visio (now a Microsoft product) is one example of an application that can create Journal items. To enable this capability, open Visio 2000, select Tools, Options, and select the Advanced tab. In that tab, check Record Actions in Microsoft Outlook Journal. After doing that, return to the Outlook Journal Options dialog box, select the Preferences tab, and select Journal Options. Now, you'll see Microsoft Visio listed in the Also Record Files From box. Check that item to enable creating Journal items for Visio.

CLASSIFYING JOURNAL ITEMS

Outlook saves Journal items in the Journal folder, classifying each item according to what's called an *entry type*. For example, an e-mail message is automatically classified with the entry type E-mail Message, and the use of a Word file is automatically classified with the entry type Microsoft Word.

When you create Journal items manually, it's up to you which entry type you assign to each item.

The principal purpose of entry types is to provide a way to organize how Outlook displays Journal items, as you'll see in subsequent sections of this chapter.

→   To learn more about entry types later in this chapter, **see** "Creating Journal Items Manually," **p. 283**.

DISPLAYING JOURNAL ITEMS

By default, Outlook displays Journal items in a Timeline view, as shown in Figure 12.2.

To display a Timeline view of Journal items:

1. Select Journal in the My Shortcuts section of the Outlook Bar to display the Journal items in the Journal Information viewer.
2. If a Timeline view isn't displayed, select View, move the pointer onto Current View, and select By Type to display a view similar to that shown in Figure 12.2.

Note

If you have only just specified items to be journaled, you won't see anything in the Journal at this time because Outlook hasn't recorded anything in the Journal yet.

Figure 12.2
The Timeline view initially shows only headers for the entry types for which Outlook has saved Journal items. The timeline shown here displays Journal items for one day.

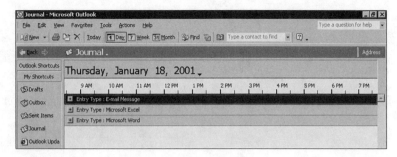

To expand an entry type, click the button marked with a plus sign at the left end of the appropriate entry-type header. After you do so, the space under that header expands to show details about the Journal items of that entry type, as shown in Figure 12.3.

Figure 12.3
The E-mail, Microsoft Excel, and Microsoft Word entry types are expanded here to show each Journal item.

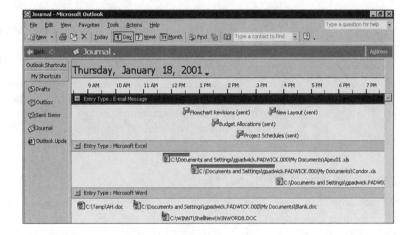

You can click the Day, Week, or Month button in the Journal Information viewer's Standard toolbar to vary the scale of the timeline. You can use various ways to scroll backward and forward in time, one of which is to use the horizontal scroll bar near the bottom of the viewer. The status bar at the bottom of the viewer shows the total number of items in your Journal folder.

When Day is selected, as in Figure 12.3, or Week is selected, text adjacent to each icon provides detailed information about what that icon represents. However, with Month selected, only icons are displayed; in that case, you can move the pointer onto an icon and pause briefly to see a ScreenTip that describes that icon.

To see the details of any Journal item, double-click that item to display it in a Journal Entry form, as shown in Figure 12.4.

PART

III

CH

12

Figure 12.4
This Journal item is for an e-mail message. You can double-click the message icon in the Notes box to open the message.

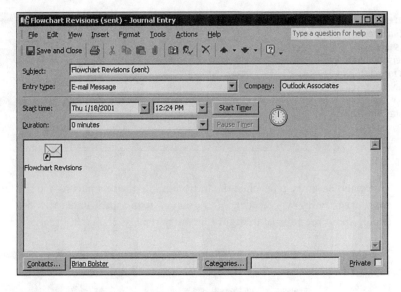

Tip from

Gordon Padwick

In the Journal Options dialog box shown previously in Figure 12.1, you can select Opens the Item Referred to by the Journal Entry (in the "Double-clicking a Journal Entry" section). Subsequently, when you double-click an item in the Timeline view, Outlook displays the item itself instead of an icon representing the item.

MOVING AROUND IN A TIMELINE

As mentioned previously, you can move backward and forward in time by using the horizontal scroll bar. That's adequate when you want to move only a short distance. Other ways of moving around are often more convenient. The following two sections separately describe how to move by date and time, and how to move from one item to another.

MOVING BY DATE AND TIME

Notice there are two time scales at the top of the timeline:

- The top time scale shows the currently displayed date in Day view, or the currently displayed month in Week and Month views.
- The lower time scale shows hours in Day view, or days in Week and Month views.

When you first open a timeline, the lower time scale is active. With the lower time scale active, you can press the right-arrow and left-arrow keys to move a blue marker by the hour or day increment in that scale.

To activate the upper time scale, press Shift+Tab. Now pressing the right-arrow key or left-arrow key moves the displayed time one day at a time with Day view selected, one week at a time with Week view selected, or one month at a time with Month view selected.

To return to having the lower time scale active, press Tab.

Whether the upper or lower time scale is active, you can click the triangle at the right of the date or month in the upper time scale to display a calendar, as shown in Figure 12.5.

Figure 12.5
The calendar shows the days of the month corresponding to the date or month adjacent to the trian- gle you clicked.

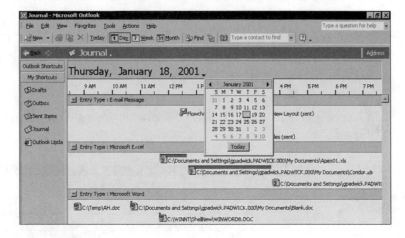

With a calendar displayed, you can

- Select any day in the calendar to view the part of the timeline that covers that day
- Click one of the arrows in the calendar's banner to move from month to month
- Click Today to view the part of the calendar that covers the current day

In the Journal Information viewer's menu bar, you can select View, move the pointer onto Go To, and select Go to Today (to display the current day's part of the timeline) or Go to Date (to display a dialog box in which you can enter a date or open a calendar).

Wherever you are in the timeline, you can select Go to Today in the Information viewer's Standard toolbar to return to the current day.

MOVING BY ITEM

When you click an item on a timeline, that item is selected. With an item selected, you can press the left-arrow key to select the previous item within a group or press the right-arrow key to select the next item within a group. For example, if you have a message item selected, pressing an arrow key selects the previous or next message item.

You also can press Home to select the first item within a group or End to select the last item within a group.

CREATING JOURNAL ITEMS MANUALLY

In addition to letting Outlook create Journal items automatically, you can use Outlook to create items manually.

PART
III

CH
12

SAVING JOURNAL ITEMS FOR THINGS YOU DO

You might want to use Outlook to chronicle the significant events in your life. I find it particularly useful, for example, to record when I install new hardware and software on my computer and make changes to its configuration. I also use Outlook to record when I have work done on my car. If you're a gardener, you might want to record various jobs you do in your garden, such as planting and fertilizing.

To manually create a Journal item:

1. Select Journal in the My Shortcuts section of the Outlook Bar to display any Journal Information viewer.

2. Click New in the Standard toolbar to display the Journal Entry form shown in Figure 12.6.

Figure 12.6

The Journal Entry form initially displays the current date and time in the Start Time boxes. This figure shows a typical completed form.

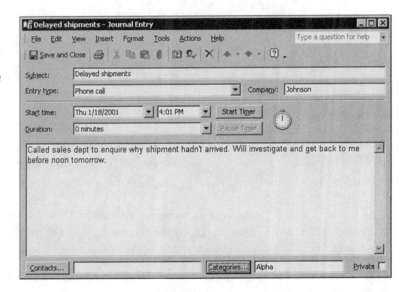

3. Enter a subject for the Journal item in the Subject box. After you've entered a subject and moved the pointer out of the Subject box, the text of the subject replaces Untitled in the form's title bar.

4. Open the drop-down Entry Type list and select one of the available entry types.

Note

You must select one of the entry types in the list. Outlook doesn't let you enter other entry types in the Entry Type box. Subsequently in this chapter, you'll learn how to create your own entry types.

5. If the Journal item has something to do with one or more of your contacts, click Contacts to open the Select Contacts dialog box, in which you can select contacts from

your Address Book. When you click OK in that dialog box, the selected contacts' names appear in the Contacts box. If the Journal item has something to do with people whose names aren't in your Address Book, enter their names in the Contacts box. You can leave this box empty.

6. If the Journal item has something to do with an organization, enter that organization's name in the Company box. You can leave this box empty.

7. By default, the Start Time boxes contain the date and time you opened the Journal Entry form. You can open a drop-down calendar from the date box and select a different date. You also can open a drop-down list of times from the time box and select a different time. Additionally, you can enter a date and time instead of selecting them (be careful to use standard Windows formats for dates and times you enter). You can't, however, leave the date and time boxes empty.

8. If a duration is associated with the Journal item, you can enter that duration in the Duration box. You can't leave this box empty. Use the default 0 minutes to mean that the duration is not relevant.

Tip from

If you're recording an event, such as an incoming phone call, while it's happening, you can use Outlook's built-in timer to keep track of the duration of the event. See "Journaling Outgoing Phone Calls," in the next section.

9. Enter whatever text is appropriate in the unnamed Notes box that occupies most of the lower part of the form. With the insertion point in the Notes box, you can (using the form's menu bar) select Insert, Item to insert an icon representing an Outlook item into the Notes box, or select Insert, Object to insert a Windows object (such as a picture) into the Notes box. You also can leave the Notes box empty.

10. Click Categories to open the Categories dialog box and select one or more categories to assign to the Journal item. You can, but shouldn't, leave the Categories box empty.

11. Click Save and Close in the Standard toolbar to save the item.

CREATING CUSTOM ENTRY TYPES

The drop-down Entry Type list on the Journal Entry form contains entry types that relate to Outlook items and Office applications. You can add your own entry types to the list, but to do this, you must edit the Windows registry, as explained in Chapter 20, "Using Categories and Entry Types."

→ For detailed information about adding entry types, **see** "Creating New Entry Types," **p. 413**.

JOURNALING OUTGOING PHONE CALLS

You can use Outlook to create Journal items for outgoing and incoming phone calls. These Journal items record the fact that you made the phone calls and, optionally, the duration of the calls; they don't record your phone conversation. Outlook's capability to record the duration of phone calls (and other activities) is particularly useful to people who bill clients based on time.

The easiest way to create a Journal item for an outgoing call is to use your computer's modem to dial the call. To use this method, your computer's modem must be connected to the same phone line as your telephone.

Note

If you don't have a modem that's connected to the same phone line as your telephone, you must record phone calls manually, as described in the next section, "Journaling Incoming Phone Calls."

To place a phone call, follow the procedure described in Chapter 8, "Managing and Using Contacts." Make sure Create New Journal Entry When Starting New Call is checked.

→ For information about placing a phone call to a contact, **see** "Placing a Phone Call," **p. 183**.

JOURNALING INCOMING PHONE CALLS

You must create Journal items manually for incoming phone calls because Outlook can't tell when one begins and ends.

Tip from

You can use the method described here to create a Journal item for a face-to-face conversation.

To create a Journal item for an incoming phone call:

1. Select Journal in the My Shortcuts section of the Outlook Bar to display any Journal Information viewer.
2. Click New in the Standard toolbar to display the Journal Entry form shown previously in Figure 12.6.
3. When the call starts, click Start Timer. As soon as you do that, the hand in the clock icon starts moving around the clock to indicate that Outlook is timing the call.
4. Either while the call is in progress or after it has finished, enter information into the various boxes on the form. Don't forget to select the Phone Call entry type.
5. At the completion of the call, click Pause Timer to stop the clock.
6. Click Save and Close in the Standard toolbar to save the item and close the form.

If you're using this method to create an Outlook item for a face-to-face conversation, interruptions, such as when a phone call arrives, might occur. In that case, click the Pause Timer button to stop the clock. When the conversation resumes, click Start Timer to continue timing.

WING AND PRINTING JOURNAL ITEMS

By default, Outlook displays the Journal Information viewer using the By Type Timeline view, in which items are grouped by entry type, as shown previously in Figure 12.2. Outlook also can display Timeline views with Journal items grouped by contact or by category.

If, with a Journal Information viewer displayed and a Journal item selected, you select View, Preview Pane, Outlook displays a preview pane below the timeline (see Figure 12.7). The Journal displays an icon representing the selected item in the Preview pane. You can double-click the icon to see the item's details.

Figure 12.7
With Preview pane enabled, you can select any item in the timeline to see the details of that item in the Preview pane.

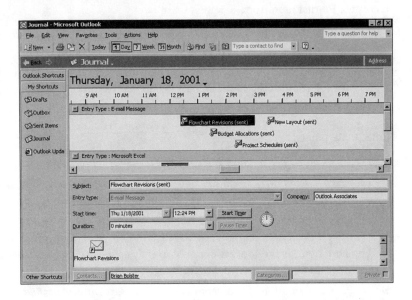

Note

The Preview pane always displays an icon. The selection you make in the Double-clicking a Journal Entry section of the Journal Options dialog box doesn't affect this.

In addition to Timeline views, Outlook can display Journal items in these Table views:

- **Entry List**—A tabular view of all Journal items
- **Last Seven Days**—A tabular view of Journal items created or modified during the last seven days
- **Phone Calls**—A tabular view that includes only Phone Call entry type items

To select a view:

1. Start with any Journal Information viewer displayed.
2. Select View and move the pointer onto Current View to see a list of available views.
3. Select the view you want to use.

ADDING APPOINTMENTS AND TASKS TO YOUR JOURNAL

Appointment items show when appointments are supposed to happ...
whether or not they actually did. Likewise, Task items show when tas...
you actually worked on them. You might find it useful to create Journa...
Appointments that happened and for Task items on which you spent son...

Here's one way you can create a Journal item from a Calendar item. You ca...
method to create a Journal item from a Task item. Outlook's capability to cre...
item from another is known as *AutoCreate*.

To create a Journal item from an appointment:

1. Select Calendar in the Outlook Bar to display the Calendar Information viewer.
   view in which you can conveniently see the Calendar item you want to use.

2. While holding down Ctrl, drag the Calendar item onto the Journal icon in the My
   Shortcuts section of the Outlook Bar. When you release the mouse button, the Journ...
   Entry form is displayed with information from the Calendar item.

Notice these points:

- *The subject of the Journal item is the same as the subject of the appointment.*
- *The Journal item's entry type is Meeting, which is often appropriate.* If it isn't appropriate,
  you can select a different entry type. You might have to create one or more custom
  entry types, as suggested previously in this chapter.
- *The Start Time for the Journal item is the same as the Start Time of the Appointment item.*
  The Duration for the Journal item is correctly calculated as the difference between the
  Calendar item's End Time and Start Time.
- *The Journal form's notes box contains an icon that represents the original Calendar item.* You
  can double-click it to display the Calendar item.

Step 2 in the preceding procedure describes what happens when you drag in the usual manner with the left mouse button pressed. If, instead, you drag with the right mouse button
pressed, Outlook offers several choices when you release the mouse button:

- **Copy Here as Journal Entry with Shortcut**—Outlook creates a new Journal item
  with a shortcut to the Calendar item in the Notes box.
- **Copy Here as Journal Entry with Attachment**—Outlook creates a new Journal item
  with a copy of the Calendar item attached (represented by an icon in the Notes box).
- **Move Here as Journal Entry with Attachment**—Outlook creates a new Journal item
  with the Calendar item moved into that item's Notes box. The Calendar item no longer
  exists in the Calendar folder.
- **Cancel**—Cancels creating the new Journal item.

→ You can modify the views supplied with Outlook and you can create your own. **See** "Creating Views and Print Styles," **p. 651**.

You can print Journal items based on a Table view, but not based on a Timeline view. You can, however, print individual items selected in a Timeline view.

To print Journal items based on a Table view:

1. Select a Table view of Journal items, as described in the previous section.
2. Select File, Print to display the Print dialog box.
3. With Table Style selected, click OK to print the table.

To print Journal items selected in a Timeline view:

1. Select a Timeline view of Journal items.
2. Select one or more items in the view.
3. Select File, Print to display the Print dialog box. Memo Style is the only print style available.
4. Click OK to print the selected Journal items.

→ For more detailed information about printing Outlook items, **see** "Printing Contact Items," **p. 163**.

VIEWING JOURNAL ITEMS FOR A CONTACT

You easily can display the Journal items related to a specific contact.

To see a contact's Journal items:

1. Select Contacts in the Outlook Bar to display any Contacts Information viewer.
2. Double-click a contact to display information about that contact in a Contact form.
3. Select the Activities tab.
4. Open the drop-down Show list and select Journal to see all the Journal items related to the selected contact.

TROUBLESHOOTING

JOURNALING

As explained earlier in this chapter, you can set up the Journal so that it records file activities associated with some Office and Office-compatible applications. You do this by checking application names in the Journal Options dialog box's Also Record Files From section.

Normally, when you install Office XP, all the principal Office applications are available to be checked. If you install Office-compatible applications, such as Microsoft's Project and Team Manager, after you've installed Outlook, the names of these applications should automatically be added to the list in the Outlook Options dialog box. If that does happen, try the method suggested earlier in this chapter for adding applications to the list.

→ For information about adding applications to be journaled, **see** "Setting Up Automatic Journaling," **p. 277**.

If that method doesn't work, an alternative is to add applications to the list by editing the Windows registry.

Using the method described in Appendix F, access this registry key:

```
My Computer\HKEY_CURRENT_USER\Software\Microsoft\Shared Tools\Outlook\Journaling
```

Within that key, add a registry key corresponding to a missing application, using the same format as the existing keys.

→ For information about working with registry keys, **see** "Working with the Windows Registry," **p. 799**.

In addition to some Windows applications available from Microsoft, you can make some applications from other companies accessible to the Journal. This capability depends on the required functionality being present within each application.

CHAPTER 13

USING OUTLOOK TO KEEP NOTES

In this chapter

WHAT ARE NOTES?

Think of Notes in Outlook as the computer equivalent of the sticky yellow paper notes decorating your computer monitor and desk in your office, and your refrigerator door at home. Outlook Notes have an advantage over the sticky notes you buy at the stationery store—they're free!

You can use Outlook's Notes to jot down reminders, ideas, phone numbers, and suggestions—all those pieces of information you mustn't forget, but can't immediately take the time to file in their proper places. Later, you can review your notes, act on them, or move the information they contain into appropriate Outlook folders or other folders on your computer.

Many people who use Outlook either ignore Notes or use Notes when they should be using a different Outlook facility. After reading this chapter, you'll understand the value of Notes and, I hope, start giving Notes the opportunity to help you work more efficiently.

SETTING UP NOTES

After installing Outlook on your computer, Notes is set up and ready to use.

You can make some minor changes to how Outlook displays Notes by making choices in the Options dialog box. By default, notes have a yellow background, are of medium size, and use the 10-point Comic Sans MS font. You can change any of these defaults.

→ For information about changing the default appearance of notes, **see** "Note Options," **p. 552**.

CREATING A NOTE

In this book, I've previously recommended that you always keep Outlook running, probably minimized, while you're working with other applications. If you do so, Outlook is always ready for you to make a note.

Note

Another advantage of keeping Outlook running is that Reminders you create for appointments, tasks, and so on always pop up on your screen at the appropriate times.

To create a note:

1. If Outlook is minimized, click the Outlook button in the Windows taskbar to display an Information viewer.

2. Select Notes in the Outlook Bar to display the Notes Information viewer.

3. Click New on the Standard toolbar to display the Notes form shown in Figure 13.1.

Figure 13.1
The Notes form pops up on top of the Information viewer with the current date and time at the bottom.

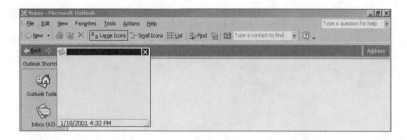

Note

If you have any Outlook Information viewer displayed, you can click the black triangle at the right of New to display a menu. Select Note in the menu to display the Notes form. Another way to display the Notes form is to press Ctrl+Shift+N from just about anywhere within Outlook.

4. Type your note, and then click the X at the upper-right of the Notes form to save and close the note; after you do so, the Notes Information viewer contains an icon representing that note. Alternatively, you can click outside the note to save it, hide it behind whatever else is displayed, display a button representing the note in the Windows taskbar, and display an icon representing that note in the Notes Information viewer.

As you type a note, the text automatically wraps within the width of the Notes form. If you enter more text than will fit within the height of the form, the text automatically scrolls vertically.

You can change the size of the Notes form by dragging its borders or by dragging the shaded bottom-right corner.

After you save or hide a note, Outlook displays that note as an icon with the first few words of the text in the Notes Information viewer. You can see the entire note by double-clicking the icon.

If you select View, Preview Pane, Outlook displays a preview pane in the bottom part of the Notes Information viewer. Then, when you select any note, the text of that note appears in the Preview pane.

PART

III

CH

13

WORKING WITH NOTES

To work with a note, right-click the note's icon in the Notes Information viewer to display its context menu, as shown in Figure 13.2. You can use this menu to open or print the note, forward the note to someone, change the color of the note, assign categories to it, delete it, or move it to a folder.

Figure 13.2
A note's context menu contains several commands you can use in addition to the Print command.

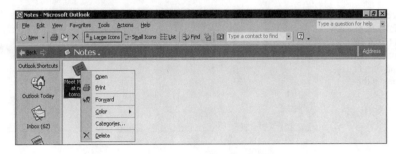

OPENING AND PRINTING A NOTE

To open a note displayed as an icon in the Notes Information viewer, either double-click the note or right-click it and select Open on the context menu.

To print all the notes in your Notes folder, select File, Print to display the Print dialog box. Click OK to start printing.

To print an individual note, right-click that note's icon in the Notes Information viewer to display its context menu, shown previously in Figure 13.2, and then select Print. The selected note is immediately printed.

Note

You can select as many notes as you want. If you select two or more notes (by holding down the Ctrl key while you select them), the Print dialog box gives you the option of starting each note on a new page or printing notes one after the other on pages.

FORWARDING A NOTE

Notes are an easy way to send information to other people. You might, for example, come across someone's phone number. Jot down that phone number in a note. Then open the note's context menu and select Forward. Outlook displays a Message form with the note inserted as an attachment. Complete the Message form in the normal way and send the message.

CHANGING A NOTE'S BACKGROUND COLOR

Open the note's context menu and move the pointer onto Color to display a list of five colors. Select the background color you want. You might find it useful to use a different color for various kinds of notes.

ASSIGNING CATEGORIES TO A NOTE

Because notes are usually temporary items, you usually don't have to assign categories to them. However, you can assign categories to notes if you want to do so.

Tip from

If you're in the habit of creating a lot of notes, you might find it convenient to assign categories to each of them. Subsequently, you can view your notes grouped in categories.

Open a note's context menu and select Categories to display the Categories dialog box. Select the categories you want to assign to the note and click OK.

DELETING A NOTE

Click the note in the Notes Information viewer to select it; then click the Delete button in the Standard toolbar. Alternatively, open the note's context menu and select Delete. Outlook moves the note from the Notes folder to the Deleted Items folder.

MOVING AND COPYING A NOTE TO ANOTHER FOLDER

To move or copy a note to another folder, drag the note icon in the Notes Information viewer onto the other folder's icon in the Outlook Bar. Hold down Shift while you drag to move the note; hold down Ctrl to copy the note.

Tip from

You also can select View, Folder List to display your folder list, and then move or copy the note into any folder in the list.

When you move or copy a note to another Outlook folder, the note appears in that folder's form with the text of the note in the form's Notes box.

VIEWING NOTES

Outlook provides several built-in views of notes, the default being the Icons view. You can click buttons in the Standard toolbar to modify the appearance of this view:

- **Large Icons**—Each note is represented by a large icon with the first few words of its text beneath it. Icons are displayed side by side in rows in the Information viewer.
- **Small Icons**—Each note is represented by a small icon with the first few words of the note's text at the icon's right. Notes that contain only a few words of text are shown side by side.
- **List**—Each note is represented by a small icon with the first few words of the note and text at the icon's right. Each note starts a new row in the Information viewer.

To choose other views, select View and move the pointer onto Current View to see a list of views. Select the view you want to use from

- **Icons**—Notes represented by icons arranged in the date order
- **Notes List**—Table view of all notes sorted by the date they were created or last modified
- **Last Seven Days**—Table view of notes created or modified during the last seven days
- **By Category**—Table view of notes grouped by categories and sorted within each category by order of creation or modification dates
- **By Color**—Table view of notes grouped by color and sorted within each color by order of creation or modification dates

→ You can modify the standard Notes views and create your own views. **See** "Creating Views and Print Styles," **p. 651**.

Note

You can easily copy a note into an Office document. To copy a note into a Word document, display the Outlook Notes Information viewer and the Word document side by side on your monitor. Locate the place in the Word document where you want to insert the note. Hold down the Ctrl key while you drag the note into the Word document.

Alternatively, you can copy the note into the Windows Clipboard, and then paste it into the document.

COPYING A NOTE ONTO THE DESKTOP

You can copy a note to the Windows desktop by dragging in the normal way. If you drag with the right mouse button pressed, you can choose whether you want to copy or move the note to the desktop.

When you close or minimize Outlook, notes you've dragged onto the desktop remain there. You can right-click a note icon on the desktop to see the context menu shown in Figure 13.3, even if Outlook isn't running.

Tip from

If you open notes by double-clicking them within Outlook and then close Outlook, the open notes remain displayed on the desktop. You can close notes displayed on the desktop by clicking the Close button at the right end of the note's title bar.

Figure 13.3
Among other things, you can use this context menu to send a note as a mail message or save it on a disk.

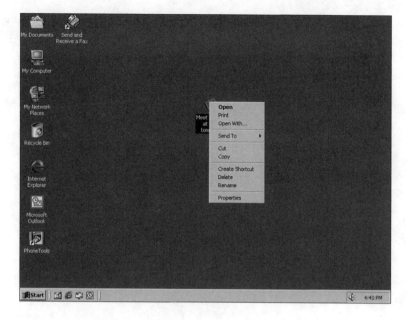

USING NOTES IN THE REAL WORLD

Here are some hints that might help you to use Outlook's Notes productively:

- *Use Notes only as a temporary place to keep information.* Remove each note as soon as you've done what the note is intended to remind you of, or when you've copied the information it contains to an appropriate folder. At the end of each day, move any outstanding notes into the appropriate Outlook folder, such as your Calendar, Contacts, or Tasks folder.

- *Don't bother to assign categories to notes that are there to remind you to do something before the end of the current day.* Do be meticulous about assigning categories to notes you will convert into permanent Outlook items. The categories you assign to notes stay with those notes when you convert them into other types of Outlook items.

- *Use colors to identify various types of notes.* You have five colors from which to choose.

- *If an idea for an e-mail message flashes into your mind, but you haven't time to deal with it immediately, write the gist of it as a note.* Subsequently, choose Forward in the note's context menu to create an e-mail message based on the note.

- *Use only a few key words in the first line of a note so that you easily can identify a note in the Notes Information viewer.*

- *With the Preview pane enabled, you can select the text in a note, copy that text to the Windows Clipboard, and paste that text into another Outlook item or Windows application.*

- *If you save a URL in a note and have the Preview pane enabled, you can select that URL to activate it.*

PART

III

CH

13

- *By default, Outlook provides only one Notes folder.* You can create as many other Notes folders as necessary so that you can save various kinds of notes in appropriate folders.

- *Don't use notes as a substitute for inserting comments in individual items' Notes boxes.* For example, if you want to create a note about a contact, open the information about that contact in a Contact form, and insert the note in that form's Notes box.

CHAPTER 14

MANAGING OUTLOOK FOLDERS

In this chapter

HOW OUTLOOK SAVES INFORMATION

Outlook saves items of information you create and receive in what are called *folders*. These aren't the type of folders you see on your disks when you use Windows Explorer. Rather, they are information containers that are either within a Personal Folders file on your computer's hard disk or, if you're using Outlook as a client for Exchange, in your Exchange store.

In addition to items of information, Outlook saves setup and reference information in several other files, some of which contain the Windows registry database. For example, the categories you can assign to items are saved within the registry. In various places in this book are references to information in the registry, along with a description of how you can access that information if you need to change it.

If several people have individual Windows profiles on a computer, the information that Outlook saves in the registry is saved separately for each person. As a result, each person can have a separate set of categories and other Outlook settings.

ACCESSING FOLDER LISTS

When you click an icon in the Outlook Bar, Outlook opens the folder associated with that icon and displays the items contained in the folder in an Information viewer.

You also can select a folder and see its contents by selecting View, Folder List, and then selecting the name of a folder. Another way to display the Folder List if you have the Advanced toolbar displayed is to click the Folder List button in that toolbar.

Yet another way to display the Folder List is to click the name of the currently displayed Information viewer in that viewer's banner. When you do this, the Folder List pops up on top of the Information viewer. If you subsequently click anywhere outside the Folder List, the list disappears. To convert this pop-up Folder List into the normal one that's displayed by the other methods, click the yellow pushpin at the upper-right of the list.

To hide the normal Folder List, click the X at the upper-right, select View, Folder List, or click the Folder List button in the Advanced toolbar.

Whichever way you choose to open the Folder List you'll probably see one similar to that shown in Figure 14.1.

Note

If you see only the heading, click the small box that contains a plus sign at the left of the heading to expand the list so that the names of all the folders are shown.

Figure 14.1
This typical Folder List contains Outlook's standard folders under the heading Outlook Today – [Mailbox – Gordon C. Padwick].

The Folder List shown in Figure 14.1 is typical when you're using Outlook as a client for an Exchange server. The list contains Outlook's standard folders, which are

- Calendar
- Contacts
- Deleted Items
- Drafts
- Inbox
- Journal
- Notes
- Outbox
- Sent Items
- Tasks

At the right of some folder names might be some numbers in parentheses. These numbers indicate how many items are waiting for your attention:

- The number adjacent to the Drafts folder indicates how many message drafts are in that folder.
- The number adjacent to the Inbox folder indicates how many received messages are waiting to be read.
- The number adjacent to the Outbox folder indicates how many messages are waiting to be sent to your mail server.

PART

III

CH

14

You're not limited to having only one Personal Folders file and one set of folders. As you'll see in this chapter, you can create additional Personal Folders files. After you do so, you'll see them all in the Folder List. However, you must designate one Personal Folders file as the default file, the one in which Outlook normally saves items.

If you're using Outlook as a client for Exchange and use the Exchange store to save Outlook items, the Folder List shows the folders within your Exchange store. However, you can have a Personal Folders file on your local hard disk and save your Outlook items there. If you do have a Personal Folders file on your hard disk, you must choose whether you want to save Outlook items there or in your Exchange store.

If you're using Outlook as a client for another messaging system, you might see a set of folders relating to that system in the Folder List.

WORKING WITH FOLDERS

With the Folder List displayed, you can access the contents of a folder by clicking the name of the folder. You also can right-click the name of a folder to display a context menu, such as the one shown in Figure 14.2. The following sections describe some of what you can do from the context menu.

Note
Some of the menu items in the context menu are available only for folders you create, not for Outlook's standard folders. You can't move, delete, or rename a standard folder.

Figure 14.2
This is the context menu for Outlook's standard Calendar folder.

OPENING A FOLDER

In the context menu, select Open to display the contents of the folder. This command is somewhat redundant because you can do the same just by clicking the name of the folder.

OPENING A FOLDER IN A NEW WINDOW

In the context menu, select Open in New Window to open the selected folder in its own Outlook window. By doing this, you can have two or more Outlook folders visible at the same time, as shown in Figure 14.3. This can be useful when you want to refer to information in one Outlook folder while you're working with information in another. It's also convenient when you want to move or copy items from one folder into another.

Figure 14.3
In this case, the contents of the Calendar and Tasks folders are shown side by side on the screen.

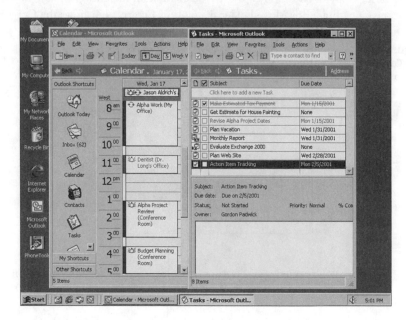

Tip from

You'll ordinarily work with Outlook maximized. When you display two or more Outlook windows simultaneously, you should click the Restore button near the right end of the Windows' title bar and arrange the individual windows on your monitor so that you can see what you need. Alternatively, you can tile two or more windows by right-clicking an empty place in the Windows taskbar and selecting Tile Windows Horizontally, Tile Windows Vertically, or Cascade Windows.

FINDING ITEMS IN A FOLDER

To find items in a folder, open that folder's context menu and select Advanced Find to display the Advanced Find dialog box.

→ For information about Advanced Find, **see** "Using Advanced Find to Find Words and Phrases," **p. 341**.

PART

III

CH

14

COPYING AND MOVING FOLDERS

You can copy any folder, including its contents, to another location within your Folder List. You can move only those folders you've created, not the standard Outlook folders, to a new location. With only that difference, copying and moving are quite similar.

Open the folder's context menu from the Folder List (not from the Outlook Bar) and select either Copy or Move (in each case the menu item includes the name of the folder) to open the Copy Folder or Move Folder dialog box. Figure 14.4 shows the Copy Folder dialog box.

Figure 14.4
The Copy Folder dialog box shows your Folder List. The Move Folder dialog box does the same.

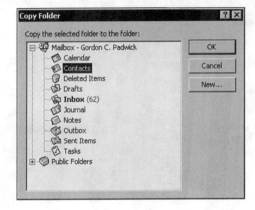

Whether you're moving or copying the folder, select the name of the folder under which you want the folder to be and click OK.

Note

You can move a folder you've created (but not a standard Outlook folder) by dragging it to a new location within the Folder List. You can, however, create a copy of a standard folder, in which case the copy is a folder you've created. You can move the copy.

Yet another way to copy or move a folder is to point onto a folder name in the Folder List, press the right mouse button, and drag to the new location. When you release the mouse button, a menu containing Move, Copy, and Cancel appears. Select Move to move the folder, Copy to copy the folder, or Cancel to do neither.

Instead of selecting a folder in the Copy Folder dialog box, you can click New Folder to open the Create New Folder dialog box (see Figure 14.5) in which you can enter a name, select which type of item the folder will contain, and specify a location in the folder structure for the new folder. When you click OK, Outlook redisplays the Folder List, which now contains the name of the new folder.

DELETING A FOLDER

You can delete a folder you've created, but not one of Outlook's standard folders.

To delete a folder, open its context menu from the Folder List and select Delete (Delete is followed by the folder name). Outlook displays a message asking you to confirm that you want to delete the folder by moving the folder and its contents into the Deleted Items folder. Click Yes if you want to delete the folder and its contents.

If you subsequently look at the Deleted Items folder, you'll see the folder you deleted as a folder within the Deleted Items folder. To permanently delete the folder, display its context menu and select Delete. Outlook asks whether you want to permanently delete the folder. Click Yes.

RENAMING A FOLDER

You can rename a folder you've created, but not one of Outlook's standard folders.

To rename a folder, open its context menu from the Folder List and select Rename (Rename is followed by the folder name). Outlook makes the folder name available for editing. Replace the original folder name with a new name, and then press Enter.

CREATING A NEW FOLDER

You can create a new folder within your Personal Folders file or, if you're using Outlook as a client for Exchange, within your Exchange store. The new folder can be

- A top-level folder at the same level as the standard Outlook folders
- A subfolder under a top-level folder (either one of the standard Outlook folders or a top-level folder you've created)
- A subfolder under a subfolder

To create a new folder, right-click your Personal Folders file in the Folder List or right-click your Exchange store, if you want the new folder to be a top-level folder. Alternatively, right-click the existing folder under which you want to create a new subfolder. Whichever you do, Outlook displays a context menu. In that context menu, select New Folder to display the dialog box shown in Figure 14.5. Another way to display this dialog box is to select File, move the pointer onto Folder, and select New Folder.

You can use the Create New Folder dialog box to create a folder for any of the standard types of Outlook items.

To create a new folder:

1. Enter a name for the new folder in the Name box. The name should be different from the name of any folder that already exists at the same level as the new folder.

2. Open the drop-down Folder Contains list and select the type of item the new folder will contain.

PART

III

CH

14

3. In the Select Where to Place the Folder box, select a position in the Folder List for the new folder.

4. Click OK to create the folder. Outlook asks whether you want to have a shortcut to the new folder in the Outlook Bar. Click Yes or No according to your preference.

After you've completed these steps, the new folder appears in the Folder List.

Figure 14.5
Use this dialog box to define the new folder.

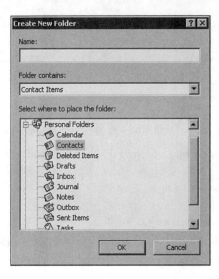

ADDING A FOLDER ICON TO THE OUTLOOK BAR

The Outlook Shortcuts and My Shortcuts groups in the Outlook Bar initially contain icons representing the standard Outlook folders. If you create folders you will access frequently, adding icons representing those folders to the Outlook Bar is convenient. You can add icons to the standard groups of the Outlook Bar, or you can create one or more custom groups in the Outlook Bar for these icons.

→ To find out how to add groups to the Outlook Bar, **see** "Renaming, Adding, and Removing Outlook Bar Groups," **p. 495**.

To create an Outlook Bar icon for a folder:

1. Select the Outlook Bar group in which you want to place the folder icon.

2. In the Folder List, right-click the folder for which you want to create an Outlook Bar icon to display its context menu.

3. In the context menu, select Add to Outlook Bar.

The icon appears in the Outlook Bar group.

Note

You also can drag a folder name into an Outlook Bar group.

If you subsequently want to remove the icon from the Outlook Bar, right-click the icon in the Outlook Bar and select Remove from Outlook Bar. Outlook asks you to confirm that you want to remove the icon. Click Yes.

Note

People sometimes ask whether replacing the icons in the Outlook Bar with others is possible. Outlook provides no way to replace icons in the Outlook Bar.

COPYING AND MOVING OUTLOOK ITEMS

You can copy and move Outlook items from one folder to another. However, each folder can hold only one type of Outlook item. If you copy or move an item from one folder to another folder of the same type, the item is unchanged. In contrast, when you copy or move an item to a folder of a different type, Outlook changes the item to the type of the new folder. For example, if you copy or move an item from a Calendar folder to a Task folder, the item becomes a Task item.

Note

Microsoft calls the process of creating one type of Outlook item from another *AutoCreate*.

When you copy an item, Outlook creates a new item in another folder, leaving the original item in its folder. When you move an item, Outlook places the item in another folder, deleting it from the original folder.

The methods of copying and moving described in this section are used primarily when you want to handle individual items. To move several items at a time, using Outlook's Organize capability is more convenient.

→ For information about organizing items, **see** "Organizing Outlook Items," **p. 365**.

COPYING AND MOVING ITEMS BETWEEN SIMILAR FOLDERS

Although a specific example is used here to illustrate copying and moving items, the methods described can be used with all types of items.

Suppose you are involved with several projects. In that case, you might find it convenient to create several Tasks folders, one for each project, and keep the tasks for each project in the appropriate folder. If you presently have all your tasks in the standard Tasks folder, you easily can move individual tasks into separate folders. The first step is to create the new folders, as explained previously in this chapter.

Figure 14.6 shows an example of a Folder List with two subfolders for tasks.

PART

III

CH

14

Figure 14.6
This Folder List shows Tasks subfolders named Alpha and Beta under the standard Tasks folder.

Tip from

To avoid the possible confusion that's likely to occur if you have two versions of each item, you should move items from the standard Tasks folder to the new subfolders, instead of copying them.

With the Folder List displayed, as shown in Figure 14.6, drag items from the Tasks Information viewer onto the appropriate subfolder name in the Folder List. Outlook assumes you want to move items, so you don't need to hold down the Shift key while you drag. When you release the mouse button, the item you dragged disappears from the list of tasks in the Tasks Information viewer. To confirm that the task is in the subfolder, you can click the subfolder name in the Folder List to show its contents in that task's Information viewer.

Note

If, for some reason, you want to copy an item instead of move it, hold down Ctrl while you drag.

You can select several items and drag them all in one operation. To select consecutive items, select the first item, and then hold down Shift while you select the last item. To select non-consecutive items, select the first item, and then hold down Ctrl while you select additional items. After you've selected all the items you want to move, drag one of them onto the subfolder name. All the selected items move.

If you have an icon on the Outlook Bar corresponding to the target folder, you can drag items onto that icon instead of onto the folder name in the Folder List.

COPYING ITEMS INTO A DIFFERENT TYPE OF FOLDER

One of Outlook's most useful capabilities is being able to change one type of Outlook item into another type, which is known as AutoCreating an item. Suppose you receive an e-mail message asking you to get something done by a certain date. To ensure you don't forget, you can add that request to your to-do list. One way to do so is to create a new Task item from scratch. An easier way, though, is to copy the e-mail message into your Tasks folder to automatically create a Task item; you might have to make a few adjustments to it, but that's less work than creating a new Task item from scratch.

To use AutoCreate to create a new item, display the Information viewer that includes the item you want to start with. If you want to start with an e-mail message you've received, display the Inbox Information viewer.

You probably want to leave the original item in its folder, so you'll copy the item, not move it. Drag the item either onto an icon in the Outlook Bar or onto a folder name in the Folder List. For example, if you want to create a new task in the standard Outlook Tasks folder, drag the item onto the Tasks icon in the Outlook Bar. When you release the mouse button, Outlook displays the Task form with the subject of the original message in the Subject box and the text of the message in the form's Notes box, as shown in Figure 14.7. All you have to do is enter the appropriate due date (if one exists) in the Due Date box; then click Save and Close in the form's Standard toolbar to save the item in your Tasks folder.

Figure 14.7
This is a Task form with a new task created from an e-mail message by AutoCreate.

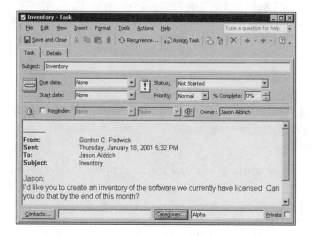

The preceding paragraph describes what happens when you drag in the normal way by holding down the primary (left) mouse button. If you drag holding down the secondary (right) mouse button, Outlook gives you a choice when you release the mouse button. The options are

- **Copy Here as Task with Text**—This has the same effect as dragging with the left mouse button pressed. The original message remains in your Inbox folder.

PART
III

CH

14

- **Copy Here as Task with Shortcut**—Instead of copying the text of the message into the task's Notes box, a shortcut to the message is copied into the task's Notes box. The original message remains in your Inbox folder. You can double-click the shortcut in the task's Notes box to see the original message.

- **Copy Here as Task with Attachment**—Instead of copying the text of the message into the task's Notes box, the message is attached to the task and an icon representing the attachment is displayed in the task's Notes box. The original message remains in your Inbox folder. You can double-click the attachment in the task's Notes box to see the original message.

- **Move Here as Task with Attachment**—The only difference between this and the previous option is that the original message is deleted from your Inbox folder.

- **Cancel**—The operation is canceled. Nothing is added to your Tasks folder and the original message remains in your Inbox folder.

Tip from

Gordon Padwick

You'll save yourself a lot of time and avoid forgetting tasks and appointments if you make a habit of using AutoCreate to create Task and Calendar items based on e-mail messages you receive.

In most case, dragging with the left mouse button pressed is a good choice. However, if you're creating an item from an item in another folder, and you have permanent access to the other folder, you might consider copying the item as a shortcut to minimize the disk space occupied.

If you're copying an item other than incoming e-mail, copying as a shortcut is sometimes useful. If you do that, you see any change to the original item when you open the shortcut. This is not useful, however, if you've copied an incoming e-mail because you can't change a message you've received. However, it could be useful if you copy a Calendar item to a Task item, or something similar.

Copying as an attachment can be useful if you need to copy many items. You might, for example, have many e-mail messages you want to use to create a new task. You can select all those items in your Inbox Information viewer and then, with the right mouse button pressed, drag to your Tasks folder. Select Copy Here as Task with Attachment; you then see icons representing each of the e-mail messages in the Task item's Notes box. You can then readily see which attachments you have and double-click any of them to display their details.

You'll probably rarely use the Move Here as Task with Attachment option. It's available if you want to move an Outlook item out of one folder into another.

If you want to add a shortcut to another Outlook item or add an attachment to an existing item, open the existing item. Then select Insert, Item.

USING MORE THAN ONE PERSONAL FOLDERS FILE

Outlook doesn't limit you to having only one Personal Folders file, although—in most cases—you don't need more than one. If you do have more than one, you must designate which one you want Outlook to use as the default for items you create and receive.

One possible purpose of having a second Personal Folders file is to have a place where you can experiment with Outlook and learn how to use it. Use the primary Personal Folders file for your normal work; have a second Personal Folders file in which you can work without the risk of damage to your work items.

The Folder List shows all the available storage locations. The storage location Outlook currently uses as the default to store all new items is indicated by an image of a house superimposed over the storage location's icon in the Folder List. Only one storage location can be designated as the default.

CREATING A PERSONAL FOLDERS FILE

When you install Outlook on a computer that hasn't previously had Outlook or Windows Messaging installed, it automatically creates a Personal Folders file in your `C:\Windows\Local Settings\Application Data\Microsoft\Outlook` folder.

If you install Outlook on a computer on which a previous version of Outlook or Windows Messaging has been installed, Outlook usually detects and uses your previous Personal Folders file, in whichever Windows folder it exists.

The process of creating a Personal Folders file has changed since Outlook 2000 and is now somewhat less than intuitive.

To create a new Personal Folders file:

1. Select Tools, E-mail Accounts, to display the dialog box shown in Figure 14.8.
2. Accept the default View or Change Existing E-mail Accounts, and then click Next.
3. Click New Outlook Data File to display a dialog box that lists only Personal Folders File as the type of file you can create. Select Personal Folders, and then click OK. Outlook displays the Create or Open Outlook Data File dialog box shown in Figure 14.9.

4. If you want to save the new file in a folder other than the one proposed in the dialog box, navigate to that folder. In the File Name box, enter a name for the new Personal Folders file; then click OK to display the Create Microsoft Personal Folders dialog box.

Figure 14.8
You can use this dialog box to work with e-mail accounts and directories.

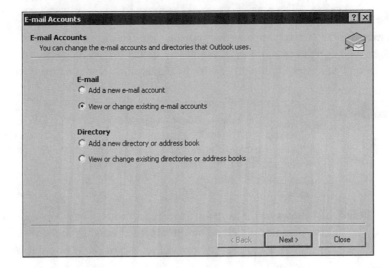

Figure 14.9
This dialog box partially displays the full path of the new file.

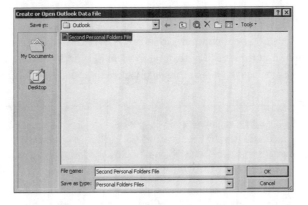

Note

Each Personal Folders file has two names. One name is the file name you see in Windows Explorer. The other is the name you see in the Outlook Folder List. The name in the Name box of this dialog box is the name that appears in the Folder List.

5. In the Create Microsoft Personal Folders dialog box, change the proposed name of Personal Folders in the Name box to a name that identifies the purpose of the new Personal Folders file.

6. In the Encryption Setting section of the dialog box, select the level of encryption you want to use.

Note

The only time you can set the encryption setting for a Personal Folders file is when you create the file. After you've created the file, you can't subsequently change its encryption setting.

7. If you want to password-protect the new file, enter a password in the Password box and again in the Verify Password box.

Note

You can password-protect a Personal Folders file that you didn't password-protect at the time you created it. You also can change the password for a Personal Folders file.

8. Leave the Save This Password in Your Password List box unchecked.
9. Click OK to finish creating the file. Outlook returns to the Outlook Data Files dialog box, in which the new data file is listed. Click Close to return to the E-mail Accounts dialog box. Click Finish.

You'll see the new Personal Folders file listed in the Folder List. Initially, this file contains only the Deleted Items folder.

Outlook shows the default file that is currently being used to save items by the small house superimposed on the file's icon in the Folder List.

ACTIVATING A NEW PERSONAL FOLDERS FILE

You can activate a new Personal Folders file, that is, make it the default file in which Outlook saves items.

Start by selecting View, Folder list to display the Folder List.

To activate a Personal Folders file:

1. With any Information viewer displayed, select Tools, E-mail Accounts to display the E-mail Accounts dialog box previously shown in Figure 14.8.
2. Accept the default View or Change Existing E-mail Accounts, and then click Next to display the E-mail Accounts dialog box previously shown in Figure 14.9.
3. Open the drop-down Deliver New E-mail to the Following Location list and select the location into which you want Outlook to deliver e-mail and all other newly created items.
4. Click Finish. Outlook displays a message stating that the new location will take effect after you close and reopen Outlook.
5. Close and reopen Outlook.

After you've made a new Personal Folders file the default storage location, you see that file in the Folder List marked with the image of a house superimposed over its icon in the Folder List. Also, instead of containing only a Deleted Items folder, as it did immediately after you created it, the folder now contains a full complement of standard Outlook folders.

REMOVING A PERSONAL FOLDERS FILE

If you no longer need a certain Personal Folders file, you can detach it from Outlook so that it no longer appears in the Folder List. You can't detach a currently activated Personal Folders file, though. If you want to detach the currently activated Personal Folders file, you must first activate a different Personal Folders file or other storage location.

After you've detached a Personal Folders file, that file still exists on your hard drive; it just isn't available to Outlook. If you've really finished with the file, you can delete it from your hard drive under Windows in the same way that you delete any other file.

Caution

Don't delete a Personal Folders file from your hard drive without first detaching it from Outlook. If you do, Outlook will complain that it can't find the file.

After making sure the storage location you want to detach isn't the current default, follow these steps to detach the file.

To detach a Personal Folders file from Outlook:

1. Select View, Folder List to display the Folder List.
2. Right-click the name of the Personal Folders file you want to detach to display its context menu.
3. Click Close. The name of that Personal Folders file disappears from the Folder List.

Now, you can safely use Windows Explorer to delete the unwanted Personal Folders file from your Windows file environment.

To reattach a Personal Folders file (a file that you've detached but haven't deleted from your hard drive) to Outlook, use the procedure described in the preceding section "Creating a Personal Folders File." In step 5, instead of entering a name for a new file, select the existing file you want to reattach.

USING FOLDER PROPERTIES

Your Personal Folders file and the folders it contains all have properties you can inspect and, in most cases, change.

UNDERSTANDING PROPERTIES OF A PERSONAL FOLDERS FILE

Right-click the name of a Personal Folders file in the Folder List to display the file's context menu. In that menu, select Properties to display a dialog box such as that shown in Figure 14.10.

Figure 14.10
The Properties dialog box contains three or more tabs.

The icon at the upper-left of the General tab has a house superimposed if the Personal Folders file you're currently accessing is the one Outlook uses to save items; the icon represents a file drawer if you're accessing any other Personal Folders file. The name of the folder appears at the right of the icon. Although it looks as though you can change the name, in fact you can't do so in this dialog box. To change the name, click the Advanced button, as described later in this section.

You can use the Description box to enter information about the Personal Folders file.

The When Posting to This Folder, Use box contains the name of the default form used to enter and display information in the selected folder. You can open the drop-down list to select other available forms.

Leave the Automatically Generate Microsoft Exchange Views checked if you intend to share this folder with other people who use Exchange Client (Windows Messaging) as their e-mail client. Otherwise, uncheck this box.

Click the Folder Size button to open a dialog box similar to the one shown in Figure 14.11.

Figure 14.11
The Folder Size dialog box shows the size of the file and also the size of all the folders and subfolders it contains.

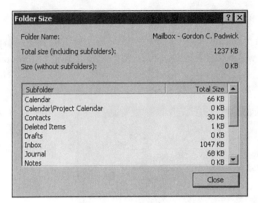

Note

The folder size shown here is considerably less than the space occupied by the file on your hard drive. What is shown here is the size in terms of the number of bytes within your Personal Folders file. It does not take account of any overhead, nor does it take account of information such as settings, views, and links that are saved in a Personal Folders file.

Close the Folder Size dialog box, and then click Advanced to open the dialog box shown in Figure 14.12.

Figure 14.12
You can use the tabs in this dialog box to set various properties of the folder.

→ For information about displaying Web views, **see** "Using Page Views," **p. 318**.

UNDERSTANDING FOLDER PROPERTIES

Right-click the name of an individual folder in the Folder List to display its context menu. Select Properties in the context menu to display the dialog box shown in Figure 14.13.

Figure 14.13
The Properties dialog box for most folders is similar to the Properties dialog box for a Personal Folders file.

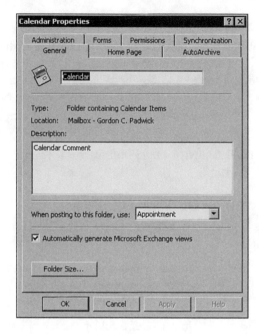

The Properties dialog boxes for folders have the same General and Home Page tabs as those for Personal Folders file. In addition, most of these dialog boxes contain AutoArchive, Administration, and Forms tabs.

The AutoArchive tab is used to define how Outlook archives items within a folder.

→ For information about AutoArchiving, **see** "Managing AutoArchiving," **p. 396**.

The Administration tab is used principally when you're using Outlook as a client for an Exchange server. The Forms tab is useful if you have custom forms available.

The Properties dialog box for the Contacts folder doesn't have an AutoArchive tab because Outlook doesn't automatically archive Contact items. This dialog box does have two other tabs, though: Outlook Address Book and Activities.

The Outlook Address Book tab is where you can choose to have Outlook use the contents of a Contacts folder as an e-mail address book.

→ For information about using your Contacts folder as an address book, **see** "Using a Single Contacts Folder," **p. 138**.

PART

III

CH

14

The Activities tab is where you can define the activities Outlook associates with contacts.

→ For information about how you can track a contact's activities, **see** "Tracking a Contact's Activities," **p. 187**.

USING PAGE VIEWS

In Outlook 97 and Outlook 98, the Information viewers can be used to display the contents of Outlook folders and, if the Integrated File Management component of Outlook is installed, the contents of folders and files within the Windows environment. In addition to these capabilities, Outlook 2000 and Outlook 2002 Information viewers can be used to display Web pages.

Briefly, it works like this: You can associate a Web page with any Outlook folder. The Web page can be designated as the default view Outlook displays when you select the folder, or it can be available as an optional view.

ASSOCIATING A WEB PAGE WITH AN OUTLOOK FOLDER

Here's a practical example of how you might want to use Web views. You easily can adapt the example for other purposes.

You can set up Outlook so that you can easily access one of the Web sites that provides information about people. The site used in this example—www.whowhere.com—is just one of several sites of this type.

To associate a Web page with the Outlook Contacts folder:

1. With a Contacts Information viewer displayed, select View, Folder List; right-click the new folder to display its context menu; and click Properties. Select the Home Page tab in the Properties dialog box, as shown in Figure 14.14.

2. Enter the address (URL) of the Web page you want to associate with the folder in the Address box near the top of the dialog box.

3. If you want to display the home page whenever you open the folder, check Show Home Page by Default for This Folder. Leave the box unchecked if you want to display the contents of your Outlook folder.

Note

In step 2, you can click Browse to open the Find Web Files dialog box. You can navigate to any file to which you have access, or select Favorites, and then select a Web page from your favorites.

If you subsequently want to remove the association, click Restore Defaults.

Figure 14.14
The Home Page tab is
shown here with a
Web page address
entered.

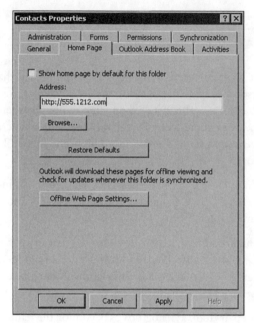

VIEWING A FOLDER THAT HAS AN ASSOCIATED WEB PAGE

To view a Web page, open the Outlook folder to which you've associated a Web page. Outlook displays a message stating that the folder has a Web page associated with it. Click OK to close the message box. At this point, the folder's Information viewer contains a list of Outlook items in the folder.

To display the Web page associated with the folder, open the View menu. The menu contains an item that wasn't there before you associated a Web page with the folder—Show Folder Home Page. Select Show Folder Home Page to display the Web page in the Information viewer.

To switch back to the normal view of the folder's contents, select View, Show Folder Home Page.

You can associate a Web page (only one) with any Outlook folder, the standard folders, and folders you create. Here's an example of how you might associate a Web page with Outlook's Calendar folder. Suppose someone in your organization maintains a corporate calendar and posts that calendar on a Web page. You could associate that Web page with the Calendar folder on your computer. Then you easily can switch between viewing your personal calendar and the corporate calendar.

Troubleshooting

Folders

Sometimes Outlook's folders get corrupted and can't be opened. When that happens, you often can restore your Personal Folders file by using the Inbox Repair Tool—the file's name is Scanpst.exe. The tool is automatically installed on your computer when you install Office XP. Despite the tool's name, it examines your Personal Folders file's structure and item headers and attempts to recover all folders and items. The Inbox Repair Tool doesn't repair folders in the Exchange store.

To run the Inbox Repair Tool, close Outlook. Then click Start in the Windows taskbar, move the pointer onto Programs, move the pointer onto Accessories, move the pointer onto System Tools, and select Inbox Repair Tool.

Alternatively, if you don't find the Inbox Repair Tool listed, you can click Start in the Windows taskbar, move the pointer onto Find, and select Files and Folders to display the Find dialog box; in that dialog box, enter **Scanpst.exe** in the Named box and click Find Now. Double-click Scanpst.exe to run the file.

When you run the Inbox Repair Tool, a dialog box asks you for the name of the file you want to repair; alternatively, you can click Browse to locate files that have .pst as their file name extensions and select the file.

After naming the file, click Start. A progress bar keeps you informed as the tool runs through eight phases. The process takes only a few seconds if no problems are found. However, if the tool does find problems, the process can take quite a while, particularly if you have a large Personal Folders file.

At the end of the process, the tool displays an information box that contains a list of recovered folders and items.

Some people want to have several folders for incoming e-mail so that they can keep different types of messages in separate folders. You can do that by creating rules, as described in Chapter 28, "Creating and Using Rules." You can create several rules, each of which examines incoming messages for some characteristic, such as the name of the sender or a specific word or phrase in the subject. Those messages that satisfy the condition in a rule can be automatically moved or copied to a specific folder.

CHAPTER 15

USING OUTLOOK TO MANAGE YOUR WINDOWS FILES

In this chapter

Integrated File Management is an Outlook component that gives you access to files on your computer's local hard drives as well as network hard drives from within Outlook.

This chapter describes some of the facilities available when you have Integrated File Management installed.

USING OTHER SHORTCUTS IN THE OUTLOOK BAR

You can use the shortcut icons in the Other Shortcut section of the Outlook Bar as an alternative to Windows Explorer.

USING MY COMPUTER

Select My Computer in the Other Shortcuts section of the Outlook Bar to display the Desktop Information viewer, as shown in Figure 15.1.

Figure 15.1
The viewer opens, displaying information about your Windows desktop.

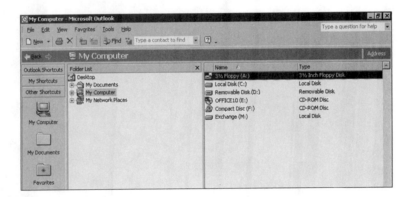

The Information viewer initially shows icons representing your disks. You can expand any of the desktop icons, select View, move the pointer onto Current View, and select Details to display a list of disk names. You also can select View, Folder List, as shown in Figure 15.2.

The menu bar in the Outlook Information viewer is the same as the menu bar in Windows Explorer. However, if you open the individual menus, you'll find the Outlook Information viewer's menus contain more items than the corresponding Windows Explorer menus. Also, notice that the toolbars in the two windows are different. The menu and toolbar differences make the Outlook Information viewer more powerful than Windows Explorer.

In particular, notice that the Outlook Information viewer has a Print button in the toolbar and also a Print command in the File menu. You can use this button or command to print what's displayed in the right pane, something you can't easily do in Windows Explorer.

You can expand any of the desktop components, just as you can in Windows Explorer. As in Windows Explorer, you can click any of the column titles to display a folder's contents listed alphabetically by name or type, numerically by size, or by date. If you select a folder that contains documents, you can click the Author column to display documents sorted by author.

Figure 15.2
With the Folder List displayed, this Window is quite similar to the Windows Explorer window.

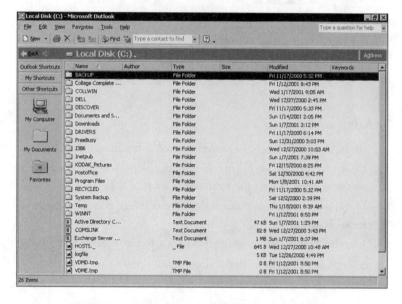

Note

Dates are listed with the abbreviation of day names preceding the date. Consequently, if you click the Modified column, the folder's contents are listed in alphabetical order by day name, instead of by date.

You can click a column title a second time to reverse the sort order.

The Information viewer can show various views of a folder's contents in addition to the Icon view shown in Figure 15.1. To select a different view, select View and move the pointer onto Current View to display the available views: Icons, Details, By Author, By File Type, Document Timeline, and Programs.

You also can select Customize Current View to customize the standard views, Define Views to define a new view, or Format Columns to display the Format Columns dialog box in which you can define how you want the columns in the viewer to appear.

→ For information about customizing views, **see** "Creating Views and Print Styles," **p. 651**.

You can select View, move the pointer onto Current View, and select Format Columns to display the dialog box shown in Figure 15.3.

Figure 15.3
You can use this dialog box to format the individual columns of the My Computer Information viewer.

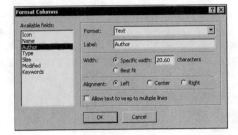

To format a column:

1. In the Available Fields list, select the column you want to format.

2. Open the drop-down Format list. If alternative formats are available for the column you've selected, select the format you want to use.

3. If you want to change the name for the column, edit the default name displayed in the Label box.

4. Use the Width section of the dialog box to select (or specify) the width of the column.

5. Select Left, Center, or Right alignment.

6. Check Allow Text to Wrap to Multiple Lines if you prefer that layout.

7. Repeat steps 1–6 to format other columns.

Note

The ability to wrap text (step 6 in the preceding procedure), new in Outlook 2002, simplifies reading such things as long file names.

If you select View, Folder List, the left pane disappears and the right pane is enlarged. Select the same command again to restore the left pane.

You can select View and move the pointer onto Toolbars to see a list of available toolbars. In addition to the Standard toolbar, which is displayed by default, you can display the Advanced toolbar, the Web toolbar, and the Private toolbar. You also can select Customize to customize menus and toolbars.

→ For information about customizing toolbars, **see** "Customizing Command Bars," **p. 505**.

USING THE MY DOCUMENTS OR PERSONAL BUTTON

If you're running Outlook under Windows 98 or Windows 2000, the Other Shortcuts section of the Outlook Bar contains a My Documents button. Click My Documents to display an Information viewer that's similar to the one displayed when you select My Computer. In this case, the viewer opens displaying the contents of your My Documents folder.

If you're running Outlook under Windows NT, the Other Shortcuts section of the Outlook Bar contains a Personal button. Click Personal to display an Information viewer that's similar to the one displayed when you select My Computer. In this case, the viewer opens displaying the contents of your Personal folder.

USING THE FAVORITES BUTTON

Click the Favorites button in the Other Shortcuts section of the Outlook Bar to display an Information viewer that's similar to the one displayed when you select My Computer. In this case, the viewer opens displaying the contents of your Favorites folder.

You can add folders, files, and URLs to your Favorites folder in several ways. Two of these are

- In Internet Explorer, open a Web page and select Favorites, Add to Favorites. After choosing how you want to save the page, click OK.

- Click My Computer in the Outlook Bar and navigate through the folder tree to display the folder or file you want to add to your Favorites folder in the right pane. Drag the file or folder onto the Favorites icon in the Outlook Bar.

Any changes you make to your Favorites in either of these ways affects what you see in Internet Explorer and Outlook.

If you want to organize your favorites, you'll probably find that it's more convenient to do so in Outlook, rather than in Internet Explorer.

CREATING AN OUTLOOK BAR SHORTCUT FOR A FOLDER

You can add shortcut buttons into any group in the Outlook Bar to provide shortcuts to folders. The following steps describe how to add such a shortcut to a group in the Outlook Bar.

To add a shortcut to the Outlook Bar:

1. Select a group in the Outlook Bar, such as the Other Shortcuts group.

2. Right-click the background of the Outlook Bar to display its context menu.

3. Select Outlook Bar Shortcut to display the dialog box shown in Figure 15.4.

Figure 15.4
You can use this dialog box to find Outlook folders and folders in the Windows file system.

4. If necessary, open the Look In drop-down list and select File System.

5. Navigate to the Windows folder for which you want to create a shortcut.

6. Select the folder and click OK. A shortcut to the folder appears in the Outlook Bar.

→ For more detailed information about customizing the Outlook Bar, **see** "Adding Shortcut Icons to an Outlook Bar Group," **p. 497**.

To delete a shortcut from the Outlook Bar, right-click the shortcut icon in the Outlook Bar to display its context menu. Select Remove from the Outlook Bar.

SEARCHING THE FILE SYSTEM FOR A FILE

You can search the Windows file system from within Outlook to find a file.

To find a file:

1. With any Outlook Information viewer displayed, select Tools, Advanced Find to display the Advanced Find dialog box shown in Figure 15.5.

Figure 15.5
The Advanced Find dialog box opens, expecting you to want to find Outlook items in whichever Outlook folder you previously had selected.

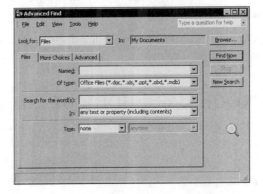

2. Open the Look For drop-down list and select Files.

Note

Make sure you select Files, not Files (Outlook/Exchange).

3. Enter the name of the file you want to find in the Named box. If the file doesn't have a standard Office extension to its file name, you must include the extension with the file name.

4. Click Find Now to initiate the search.

→ For detailed information about using Advanced Find, **see** "Finding Files," **p. 361**.

Organizing Outlook Items

CHAPTER 16

USING OUTLOOK TEMPLATES

In this chapter

WHAT ARE TEMPLATES?

A *template* is a foundation on which you can build Outlook items that have similar character-istics. Instead of creating every Outlook item from scratch, you can create templates from items, and then create other Outlook items based on those templates.

For example, you might have to create a monthly report of your activities in a standard for-mat. That report might well have standard text that changes very little from month to month; it also might contain standard sections, and perhaps even tables that contain budget and expense information that's in the same format each month. Instead of creating all this from scratch every month, you can create and save a *template*. Subsequently, all you have to do each month is fill in the blanks. This can be a great timesaver. With the help of templates you might even get your monthly reports in on time!

Outlook saves templates as files in the Windows file system. Each template is a separate file with .oft as its file name extension.

CREATING AN E-MAIL TEMPLATE

You create a template for an e-mail message in the same way that you create any other e-mail message. In this case, though, instead of creating the complete message, just create a skeleton containing any standard text, section headings, and tables. To create a message template, you must use Outlook's built-in editor, not Word.

Note

To select Outlook's built-in editor, select Tools, Options, and display the Mail Format tab. Make sure Use Microsoft Word to Edit E-mail Messages is not checked.

→ If you usually assign the same categories to certain types of messages, you can save yourself some time by creating templates that have those categories assigned to them. **See** "Creating a Message with Predefined Categories," **p. 411**.

After you've created the template, instead of clicking Send in the toolbar to send it, click File in the form's menu bar, and then click Save As to open the dialog box shown in Figure 16.1.

The dialog box opens with the subject of the message as the proposed file name and with the same file type in which you created the template—Text Only in this case.

Open the drop-down Save as Type list to see the list of available file formats, as shown in Figure 16.1.

Figure 16.1
These are the avail-able file types for a message created using Outlook's built-in editor.

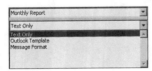

Select Outlook Template. Outlook proposes to save the message as a template in your Templates folder with a file name (the subject of the message) that has .oft as its extension. You can change this to another name, but leave the file name extension as .oft.

> **Caution**
>
> Don't be tempted to choose a folder other than the default Templates folder for saving templates. If you do, Outlook won't be capable of finding your templates.

Click Save to save the template. Close the Message form. When Outlook asks whether you want to save changes to the form, you could click No because you've already saved the form as a template. However, you should click Yes to save the form as an Outlook item. The reason for this is to provide a way to recover your work if, for some reason, the template isn't saved properly. You can find more about this in the "Troubleshooting" section at the end of this chapter. After you're satisfied that the template has been saved properly and is available for your use, you can safely delete the Outlook item.

→ For information about possible problems with templates, **see** "Troubleshooting," **p. 334**.

USING AN E-MAIL TEMPLATE

When it comes time to write a monthly report, or whatever other message you created the template for, follow these steps to open the template.

To open a template to create a message:

1. In the Outlook Bar, click Inbox.

2. Select Tools, move the pointer onto Forms, and select Choose Form to display the dialog box shown in Figure 16.2.

Figure 16.2
The Choose Form dialog box opens, expecting you to select a form in the Standard Forms Library.

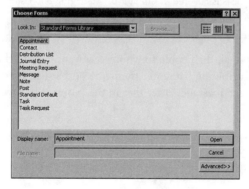

3. Open the drop-down Look In list and select User Templates in File System to display the dialog box shown in Figure 16.3.

Figure 16.3
This dialog box shows the templates available in your templates folder.

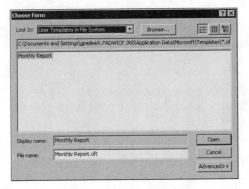

4. Select the template you want to use and click Open to display the form (a Message form in this case) with the information in the template displayed.

5. Use this template to finish creating your message.

6. When you've finished, click Send in the form's toolbar to send the message.

> **Note**
>
> You can use the techniques described in the previous two sections to create templates based on other types of Outlook items and to create new items based on those templates.

USING TEMPLATES FOR DISTRIBUTING MESSAGES

If you frequently send messages to a group of people, you can create a distribution list and send each message to the distribution list.

→ Creating and using distribution lists is covered in Chapter 8, "Managing and Using Contacts." For information about distribution lists, **see** "Working with Distribution Lists," **p. 174**.

Create a prototype message, as described previously in this chapter.

Enter the e-mail addresses of all the people to whom you want to send the message in the To box, or, if you have a distribution list, enter the name of that list. If you have any boilerplate text that's usually in each message, enter that in the Notes box. Save the prototype message as a template.

When you want to send a message to the group, open the template, enter the text, and send the message in the normal way.

USING TEMPLATES FOR OTHER TYPES OF OUTLOOK ITEMS

You can use a similar method to create templates for other types of Outlook items. Here are some examples.

SENDING REGULAR MEETING REQUESTS

If you regularly send meeting requests to people, you can create a template of a meeting request. Then, instead of creating the meeting request from scratch, you can open the template, fill in the specific details, and send it.

→ To find out about using Outlook to invite people to meetings, **see** "Inviting People to Attend a Meeting," **p. 240**.

CREATING SIMILAR CONTACT ITEMS

Perhaps you want to create many contact items for people in the same organization. Although you can use Outlook's Create Contact from Same Company option, you might find this doesn't do exactly what you want. In that case, you can create and save a prototype Contact item as a template. Then, you can use that template to create individual Contact items.

→ For information about creating similar Contact items, **see** "Creating Similar Contact Items," **p. 160**.

ASSIGNING TASKS TO A TEAM

As a manager of a team, you might need to assign a similar task to several team members. The Task items you need to create for each member probably contain some text that's the same for everyone and some text that's specific to each person. In that case, create a Task item that contains all the information that goes to everybody and save that as a template. Using the template, you can then customize the Task item for each team member without having to retype everything.

→ To learn about using Outlook to assign tasks, **see** "Assigning Tasks to Other People," **p. 268**.

MODIFYING A TEMPLATE

After you've created a template, you'll probably want to modify it from time to time. That's easy to do.

To modify an existing template:

1. In the Outlook Bar, click the type of icon you would normally choose if you were creating an Outlook item from scratch. For an e-mail message, select Inbox in the Outlook Bar.

2. Select Tools, move the pointer onto Forms, and select Choose Form to display the dialog box shown previously in Figure 16.2.

3. Open the drop-down Look In list and select User Templates in File System to display the dialog box previously shown in Figure 16.3.

4. Double-click the name of the template you want to modify to open the template in a Template form, which is similar to a Message form.

5. Make any changes to the template, such as changing e-mail addresses in the To box, text in the Subject box, and boilerplate text in the Notes box.

6. Select File, Save to save the modified template; then close the template.

PART

IV

CH

16

Note

If you want to save the original template and the modified template, in step 6, select File, Save As to display the Save As dialog box. Here, you must give the modified template a name that's different from that of the original template. Make sure you select Outlook Template in the Save as Type drop-down list; if you don't, you won't be able to use the modified template.

SHARING TEMPLATES

Each template is a separate file in your Windows file system, so copying a file to another computer either by way of a network or by way of a floppy disk is easy. In Windows Explorer, locate the folder that contains templates—usually `C:\Windows\Application Data\Microsoft\Templates`—and copy the file either directly to the other computer by way of a network or onto a floppy disk.

Make sure you copy the template into the folder on the other computer that Windows uses for templates. That might not be the same folder as on your computer.

Tip from

Gordon Padwick

To locate the folder in which Windows stores templates, click Start in the Windows taskbar, move the pointer onto Find (or Search if you're using Windows Me or Windows 2000), and select Files or Folders. In the Find dialog box, enter `*.oft` in the Named box and select Find Now. After a few seconds, a list of template files is displayed; the list shows the folder that's used for template files.

But what if no templates are already saved? In that case, you must create a simple template on that computer and save it. Then you can use the method explained in the preceding paragraph to locate where templates are saved.

Another possible problem is that you'll see templates saved in several folders. That can occur if a previous version of Office has been used on that computer. The folder you need is most likely the folder in which the most recently created template is saved. If you have any doubt, create a simple template and look to see where it's saved.

Outlook and other Office applications automatically recognize template files and make them available as long as they are in the correct folder and have `.oft` as their file name extensions.

TROUBLESHOOTING

TEMPLATES

You're unlikely to have much trouble with templates. The only problem I recall people having is when Outlook can't find a template. The most likely reasons for this are if you forget to save a template you've created as an Outlook template, or if you save it in the wrong folder. When you have finished creating an Outlook item that you want to use as a template, select File, Save As to display the Save As dialog box. There, you must open the drop-down Save as Type list and select Outlook Template. If you don't, the file will be saved as a text file. Outlook won't subsequently display the file in the list of templates, so you won't be able to use it.

As far as I know, no way exists to convert the file you saved as a text file to a template file. That's why, previously in this chapter, I recommended that you save a new template as an Outlook item until you're certain the template has been properly saved and is available to be used.

If you save a template in the wrong folder, use Windows Explorer to move it to the correct folder. The tip in the previous section explains how to find the folder in which template files should be saved.

CHAPTER 17

FINDING AND ORGANIZING OUTLOOK ITEMS

In this chapter

SEARCHING FOR INFORMATION

After you've used Outlook for several months, you're likely to have a lot of information stashed away in your folders; some of it is easy to find, but finding other Outlook items isn't always so easy.

It's easy to find the e-mail you sent to a certain person. Just open your Sent Items folder and click To at the top of the table view of items you've sent to see all the items listed alphabetically by the name of the person to whom you sent mail. Similarly, you can click Sent to see items listed in date order, or Subject to see items listed alphabetically by subject.

Note

In either case, click the column heading a second time to reverse the sort order.

Finding an item by subject, though, presents problems because, quite often, the first word of an item's subject doesn't define what a message is really about. Outlook's Find capability offers a solution to this problem. This chapter describes how to simplify finding items by using Outlook's QuickFind Contact, Find, and Advanced Find capabilities.

USING THE QUICKFIND CONTACT TOOL

Before we get deeply into finding items, let's take a quick look at the QuickFind Contact tool that was new in Outlook 2000 and is continued in Outlook 2002.

Apparently, Microsoft found that the most frequent information Outlook users wanted to find was information about contacts. Microsoft's answer to that need is the QuickFind Contact tool that's available near the right end of each Information viewer's Standard toolbar, as shown in Figure 17.1.

No matter which Information viewer is displayed, you can use the QuickFind Contact tool to get information about one of your contacts.

To display information about a contact:

1. Place an insertion point in the QuickFind Contact tool.
2. Enter a name or partial name and press Enter. If only one name matches, Outlook displays a Contact form containing information about that contact, such as that shown in Figure 17.3. If two or more names match, Outlook displays a dialog box, such as that shown in Figure 17.2, which lists matching contacts.

Note

The characters you enter into the QuickFind Contact box can be any one character or group of consecutive characters at the beginning contacts' first, middle, or last names.

QuickFind Contact tool

Figure 17.1
The empty box near the right end of an Information viewer's Standard toolbar provides access to the QuickFind Contact tool.

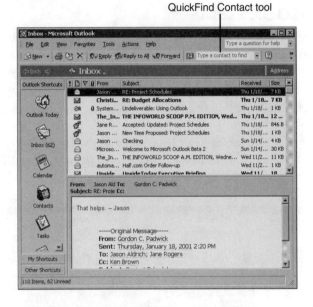

Figure 17.2
This dialog box lists all contacts that match your entry.

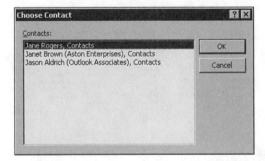

3. Select the contact for whom you want to see information; then click OK to see information about that contact in a form such as that shown in Figure 17.3.

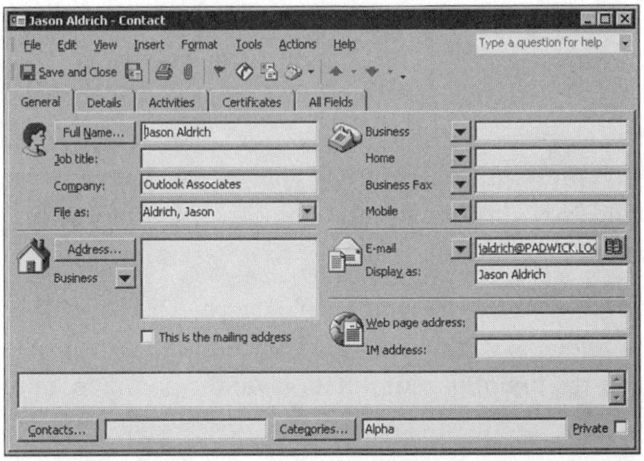

Figure 17.3
Outlook displays information about the contact in a Contact form.

FINDING OUTLOOK ITEMS

As an introduction to using Outlook's Find capability, we'll look specifically at how you can find contacts. You can use the same technique to find other types of Outlook items, such as messages. This section describes only Outlook's basic Find capability. If you don't see what you need here, look subsequently in this chapter for information about Advanced Find.

→ To learn more about using the Outlook Advanced Find capabilities, **see** "Using Advanced Find to Find Words and Phrases," **p. 341**.

To find all the items in a folder that contain certain text, display the Information viewer for that folder. Click Find in the Standard toolbar (alternatively, select Tools, Find). When you do so, a row appears near the top of the Information viewer, as shown in Figure 17.4.

Figure 17.4
The new row at the top of the Information viewer contains the Look For and Search In boxes in which you enter the text you want to find and the folder in which you want to search.

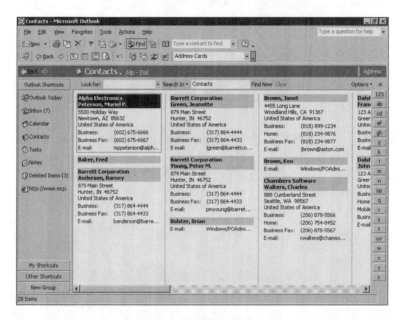

Tip from

If you don't see Find in the Standard toolbar, either maximize Outlook or stretch it horizontally so that it occupies almost the entire screen width.

Enter the text you want to find in the Look For box. Alternatively, open the Look For drop-down list to find previous text for which you've searched and select from that list. When you select Find Now or press Enter, Outlook searches for items that match the text and displays those items.

By default, Outlook searches for the word or phrase you specify in only the headers of the items in the current folder. If you want to search within the complete text of items, select Options in the row at the top of the Information viewer, and then, in the drop-down list, select Search All Text in Each Message. Select the same item again to revert to just searching in item headers.

The Search In box initially displays the name of the folder in which the items displayed in the current Information viewer are saved. You can open the drop-down Search In list and select among

- The name of the folder that contains items displayed in the current Information viewer
- All Mail Folders
- Mail I Received
- Mail I Sent
- Choose Folders

If you select Other Folders, Outlook displays the Select Folders dialog box, in which you can select one or more of your Outlook folders.

PART

IV

CH

17

Initially, Clear (immediately to the right of Find Now) is dimmed. After you search for items, Clear becomes available. Click Clear to clear the results of the search so you can perform another search. Click X at the extreme right to restore the Information viewer to its original appearance.

USING ADVANCED FIND TO FIND WORDS AND PHRASES

Although the Find command described in the preceding section provides an easy way to find certain types of information, it won't always provide what you need. You can't use Find to find Outlook items that contain specific text in certain fields. For example, you can't find contacts who have a specific telephone area code in this way. Advanced Find can perform these types of searches and much more.

ACCESSING ADVANCED FIND

Outlook's Advanced Find provides many ways to find Outlook items, as well as Windows files. You can access Advanced Find in three ways:

- With any Information viewer displayed, select Tools, Advanced Find.
- With the Inbox or Sent Items Information viewer displayed, select a message, select Actions, move the pointer onto Find All, and select Related Messages or Messages from Sender.
- After selecting Find so that the extra row is displayed at the top of an Information viewer, click Options to display a drop-down list. In that list, select Advanced Find.

Whichever method you use, Outlook displays a dialog box similar to the one in Figure 17.5.

Note

Related messages are messages in a single conversation. A *conversation* consists of an original message, replies to that message, replies to those replies, and so on.

Figure 17.5
The Advanced Find dialog box opens with the first tab in the subform selected.

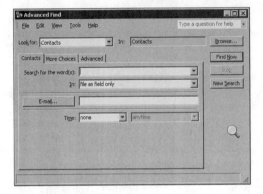

The Advanced Find dialog box contains a three- or four-tabbed subform. The name of the first tab corresponds to the name of the Information viewer that was displayed when you opened the Find pane. Figure 17.5 shows this tab as Contacts because the Contacts Information viewer was displayed when Advanced Find was chosen in this example. The other tabs are always named More Choices, Advanced, and SQL. The latter tab is available only if you have access to a SQL server.

SPECIFYING THE TYPE OF ITEM TO FIND

Outlook assumes you want to find items of the type contained in the currently open folder and displayed in the current Information viewer. If the Contacts Information viewer is displayed when you start Advanced Find, the first tab within the dialog box is named Contacts, the Look For box contains Contacts, and the In text box also contains Contacts (the name of the folder in which Outlook proposes to search).

If you want to look for a different type of item, open the Look For drop-down list, in which you can select

- Any Type of Outlook Item
- Appointments and Meetings
- Contacts
- Files
- Files (Outlook/Exchange)
- Journal Entries
- Messages
- Notes
- Tasks

Tip from

Selecting Any Type of Outlook Item is particularly useful if you want to find all the Outlook items that relate to a particular subject, such as a person or project.

Select a type of item in the Look For drop-down list. After you do so, the name of the item type you select appears as the name for the first tab in the Advanced Find dialog box's sub-form.

DECIDING WHERE TO LOOK FOR THE ITEM

Outlook items can be in various places, usually in one of two places:

- In the folders within your Personal Folders file if you're not using Outlook as a client for an Exchange server, or if you are using Outlook as a client for an Exchange server but save items in your Personal Folders file
- In the folders within your Exchange store (if you are using Outlook as a client for an Exchange server)

PART

IV

CH

17

When you first open the Advanced Find dialog box, the In text box (near the upper-right) is gray and contains the name of an Outlook or Exchange folder (sometimes more than one), Personal Folders, or Mailbox. This means Outlook is ready to search for items in those places. After you open the Look For drop-down list and select a type of item, Outlook replaces the initial folder name with the name of the folder in which the type of item you've selected is normally kept. For example, if you select Tasks, Outlook expects to find Task items in the Tasks folder.

If the name in the In text box isn't where you want to search, click Browse to open the Select Folders dialog box. In this dialog box, expand the appropriate top-level folder if necessary, deselect any folders you don't want to search, select the folder or folders in which you want Outlook to search, and then click OK. The names of the folders you select appear in the In text box.

Note

You can select any number of folders in this way, but only folders within a single store. If you select two or more folders, one folder name is separated from the next in the In text box by a semicolon.

→ To learn more about working with Outlook folders, **see** "Working with Folders," **p. 302**.

STARTING YOUR SEARCH

Suppose you want to search for a contact. You've selected Contacts to look for and you've accepted Outlook's proposal to search in the Contacts folder. Now select the subform's Contacts tab if it isn't already selected.

Tip from

Advanced Find searches for items that satisfy criteria specified in all four tabs of the Advanced Find dialog box. Before you start specifying a new search, click New Search to remove all existing search criteria. This ensures that any criteria in tabs you're not using won't interfere with the search. This isn't strictly necessary when you first open Advanced Find because all search criteria are initially cleared. However, it is necessary if you use Advanced Find two or more times while it is open.

To set up your search:

1. Enter the word or phrase you want to search for in the Search for the Word(s) box.

Tip from

If you've previously searched for the same word or phrase, you can open the Search for the Word(s) drop-down list and select a word or phrase.

2. If you don't want to search in the field proposed in the In text box (the one in the Contacts tab, not the In text box at the top of the dialog box), open the In drop-down list and select the fields in which you want to search. The selections available vary according to the type of item you're looking for. If you're searching for contacts, you can select among

   - File As Field Only (the default)
   - Name Fields Only
   - Company Field Only
   - Address Fields Only
   - E-mail Fields Only
   - Phone Number Fields Only
   - Frequently-Used Text Fields

3. In many cases, the information you've entered and selected so far is all that's necessary. Click Find Now to initiate the search. Outlook displays the results of the search in a table at the bottom of the Advanced Find box, as shown in Figure 17.6.

You can double-click any item in the search results table to open that item in the Outlook form in which that item was originally created. You can also use the horizontal scroll bar at the bottom of the table to see more information fields.

Note

As is the case for other tables, you can click the name of a field to sort the table in alphabetical, numerical, or date order based on that field.

Figure 17.6
Outlook displays the result of the search in a table.

By default, Outlook displays the results table in Phone List view.

→ For more information about the results table, **see** "Viewing Find Results," **p. 352**.

When you're finished with the results table, click New Search to close the table and clear all search criteria.

UNDERSTANDING HOW OUTLOOK SEARCHES

In the preceding pages of this section, you've been told to enter the word or phrase you want Advanced Find to search for. There's more to know than you might expect about how Outlook interprets a word or phrase.

LOOKING FOR SEVERAL WORDS

When you enter several words, Outlook searches for those words as a phrase. The entire phrase must exist for Outlook to find it.

Outlook can also search for items that contain one word or another—this is sometimes referred to as a *Boolean* search. For example, if you want to search for an item that contains the word "apple" or the word "orange", you enter these words in the Search for the Word(s) box with a comma or semicolon separating one word from the next (a space after the comma or semicolon is optional). If you enter

```
apple orange
```

Outlook searches for items that contain the phrase "apple orange". If you enter

```
apple,orange
```

or

```
apple;orange
```

Outlook searches for items that contain either "apple" or "orange" or both words.

Instead of single words, you can use phrases. For example, if you enter

```
sweet apples,bitter oranges
```

Outlook searches for items that contain either the phrase "sweet apples" or the phrase "bitter oranges" or both phrases.

PUNCTUATION MARKS

If you want to search for a phrase that contains punctuation marks, you must enclose the entire phrase within double quotation marks. For example, if you want to search for items that contain the phrase "apple, orange, or banana", enter

```
"apple, orange, or banana"
```

If you omit the quotation marks, Outlook will search for items that contains either "apple", "orange", "banana", or any combination of those words.

PLURALS AND VERB FORMS

If you ask Outlook to search for "apple", it finds items that contain "apple" and also items that contain "apples". However, if you ask Outlook to search for "apples", it finds only items that contain "apples"—not items that contain "apple".

Outlook's capability to find plurals when you specify a singular noun extends to nouns that have slightly irregular plural forms. For example, if you specify "box", Outlook finds items that contain "box" or "boxes". Outlook isn't smart enough, however, to find "mice" when you specify "mouse". If you want to find "mouse" or "mice", you have to enter

```
mouse,mice
```

Tip from

Gordon Padwick

To be on the safe side, if you want Outlook to find singular and plural forms of nouns that have irregular plurals, specify both forms (separated by a comma or semicolon) in the search text.

The same principle applies to verb forms. For example, if you search for "play", Outlook will also find "plays" and "played". Don't expect Outlook to find various forms of irregular verbs. For example, if you search for "is", Outlook won't find such words as "are" and "were".

FINDING SPECIFIC OUTLOOK ITEMS

You can use Advanced Find to find words and phrases in any type of item. You can also look for items based on something other than words or phrases. What you can search for depends on the type of item for which you're searching.

FINDING CALENDAR ITEMS

When you select Appointments and Meetings in the Look For drop-down list, Outlook assumes you want to search for items in your Calendar folder. The first tab in the subform is named Appointments and Meetings and contains the three sections shown in Figure 17.7.

Figure 17.7
You can search for words, meeting organizers, meeting attendees, and times in Calendar items.

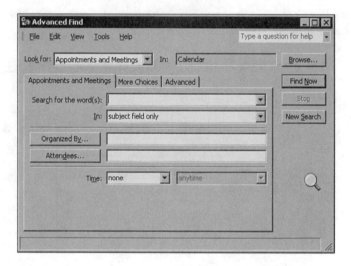

You can enter search criteria in any one or more of the sections in the Advanced Find dialog box's Appointments and Meetings tab. It's important to understand that all the criteria you enter must be satisfied for Outlook to find an item. Suppose, for example, you enter the word "Alpha" in the Search for the Word(s) box, and you enter the name of an attendee (such as Jane Rogers) in the Attendees box. Outlook then finds those appointments and meetings for which the subject contains the word "Alpha" and the people with whom you had the appointment or attended the meeting include Jane Rogers.

The top section of the Appointments and Meetings tab is where you can enter a word or phrase to search for, as already described.

The second section applies to Calendar items that represent meetings. In this section, you can specify one or more people who organized meetings and one or more people who were invited to attend meetings. Click Organized By to display the Select Names dialog box in which you can select organizers' names from your address books. Click Attendees to select attendees' names from your address books. Alternatively, you can type the names of people.

The third section applies to all types of Calendar items. By default, none appears in the Time box—time is not used as a criterion for finding items. Open the Time drop-down list and select from the following: None, Starts, Ends, Created, and Modified. After you select any of these except None, the adjacent drop-down list is enabled with Anytime selected. Open this drop-down list and select from the 12 timeframes. For example, you can direct Outlook to search for items received or created today, tomorrow, in the last seven days, and so on. This feature narrows your search, thus helping you find items quickly.

Enter the appropriate search criteria in all three sections of this tab.

→ For more information about making the most of Outlook searches, **see** "Creating Precise Searches," **p. 353**.

FINDING CONTACT ITEMS

After you select Contacts in the Look For drop-down list, Outlook assumes you want to search in your Contacts folder; the Contacts tab contains three sections, as shown in Figure 17.8.

Figure 17.8
You can search for words, e-mail addresses, and times in Contacts items.

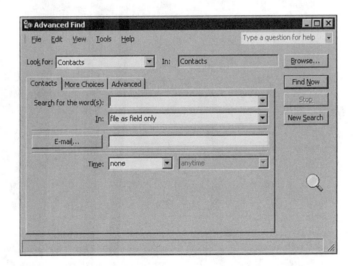

Use the top section of this tab to enter words and phrases to search for, as previously described.

In the second section, you can enter a complete or partial e-mail address. You can use this to find all your contacts who have e-mail addresses on a certain server by entering the name of the server. For example, enter the name of that server (such as hotnet.net) in the E-mail box. Outlook will subsequently find all your contacts who have an e-mail account on that server.

The third section is similar to the third section of the Appointments and Meetings tab (described previously in this chapter), but with fewer selections. You can choose among

- None
- Created (the period during which the item was originally created)
- Modified (the most recent period during which the item was modified)

FINDING JOURNAL ITEMS

After you select Journal Entries in the Look For drop-down list, Outlook assumes you want to search in your Journal folder. The Journal Entries tab contains three sections, as shown in Figure 17.9.

Figure 17.9
You can search for text, specific Journal entry types, contacts, and times in Journal items.

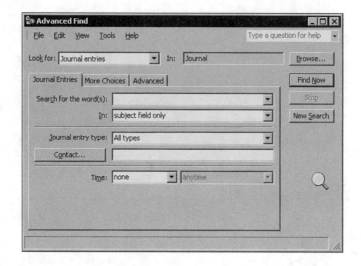

PART

IV

CH

17

By now, you should be getting the picture. You can search each type of Outlook item for words and also define periods of time. In addition, special search criteria are available for each type of item.

For Journal items, you can open the Journal Entry Type drop-down list and select all entry types or a specific type of Journal entry. You can also click Contact to open the Select Names dialog box, in which you can select a contact's name (or several contacts' names).

➔ To learn more about Outlook's advanced searching capabilities, **see** "Using Advanced Find to Find Words and Phrases," **p. 341**.

FINDING MESSAGE ITEMS

After you select Messages in the Look For drop-down list, Outlook assumes you want to search in your Inbox folder. The Messages tab contains three sections, as shown in Figure 17.10.

As always, you can enter a word or words to search for in the Search for the Word(s) box, or open the drop-down list and select previous words you've searched for. You can open the drop-down In list and select Subject Field Only, Subject Field and Message Body, or Frequently-Used Text Fields.

You can click From or Sent To (or both) to open the Select Names dialog box to select the name or names of people to whom you've sent messages or from whom you've received messages, but that doesn't necessarily do what you want, as explained in the subsequent tip. Instead of selecting names, you should type names in either or both text boxes.

Figure 17.10
You can search for words in a message, for names of message senders and recipients, for your involvement with the message, and for times in Messages items.

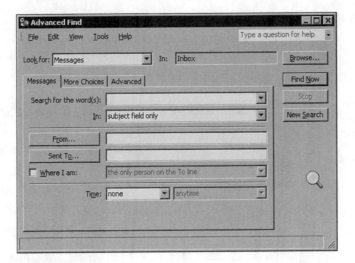

The names you enter in the From or Sent To boxes must be the exact names in the messages stored in your folders. These might be people's e-mail addresses or people's real names. Suppose you have a contact named Eduardo Mendoza, whose e-mail address is eduardom@mailnet.com. If your Contacts folder doesn't contain an item that relates the person's name to the e-mail address, messages you receive from, or sent to, that person are saved in your Inbox or Sent Items folders with the name as eduardom@mailnet.com. If you have that person in your Contacts folder and select his name, Outlook enters the name Eduardo Mendoza in the From or Sent To box. Then, when you click Find Now, Outlook finds no messages because all the messages from or to that person contain eduardom@mailnet.com in the From or Sent to fields, not the person's actual name.

Instead of selecting a name from your Address Books, you must enter a name as it appears in your Inbox or Sent Items folder. In this example, you should enter eduardom—it's usually not necessary to enter any more than that.

If you want to have your involvement in the message as one of the search criteria, check the Where I Am box to activate the drop-down list at its right. Open the drop-down list and select from

- The Only Person on the To Line
- On the To Line with Other People
- In the CC Line with Other People

You can open the drop-down Time list and select among

- None
- Received
- Sent
- Due
- Expires
- Created
- Modified

After you select anything other than None, the box on the right becomes enabled with Anytime initially displayed. If you select Received in the Time drop-down list, you are asking Outlook to find messages you've received on any date or time.

Instead of accepting the default Anytime, you can open the drop-down list and select one of AnyTime, Yesterday, Today, In the Last 7 Days, Last Week, This Week, Last Month, This Month.

To specify dates and times more precisely than is possible by making selections here, you can use the Advanced tab, as explained subsequently in this chapter.

→ To learn more about effectively narrowing your Outlook searches, **see** "Defining Advanced Find Criteria," **p. 356**.

FINDING NOTES ITEMS

After you select Notes in the Look For drop-down list, the Notes tab contains two sections, as shown in Figure 17.11. Outlook gives you the option to search Notes for words in the subject field or in the contents of notes. You can also search based on dates notes were created or modified.

Figure 17.11
You can use text and times as search criterion in Notes items.

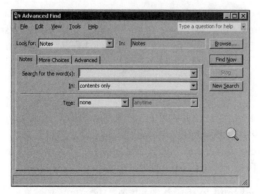

> **Note**
>
> The Subject field of a note contains the first paragraph of that note. The Contents field of a note contains the entire text, including the first paragraph.

The drop-down Time lists contain the selections available when you're specifying criteria for finding messages, as described in the preceding section.

FINDING TASK ITEMS

After you select Tasks in the Look For drop-down list, the Tasks tab contains three sections, as shown in Figure 17.12.

Figure 17.12
You can search for words, task status, from whom you received tasks, to whom you sent tasks, and times.

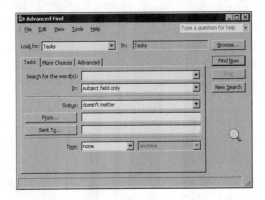

Open the Status drop-down list and select one of Doesn't Matter, Not Started, In Progress, Completed, Waiting on Someone Else, or Deferred.

Click From or Sent To (or both) to open the Select Names dialog box to select the name or names of people to whom you've sent tasks or from whom you've received tasks. Alternatively, you can type names in these boxes.

Open the drop-down Time list and select one of None, Due, Starts, Completed, Created, or Modified.

If you select any of these other than None, the adjacent box becomes enabled with Anytime inside it. You can open the drop-down list and select one of Anytime, Yesterday, Today, Tomorrow, In the Last 7 Days, In the Next 7 Days, Last Week, This Week, Next Week, Last Month, This Month, or Next Month.

VIEWING FIND RESULTS

Outlook displays the results of a search—whether you start from the Find command or the Advanced Find dialog box—as a table in a default view. The default view Outlook uses depends on the type of item you're finding. If you're using Advanced Find, you can easily choose a different view of the results of the search.

After you've used Advanced Find to search for items, the items that match your search criteria are displayed in a table at the bottom of the Advanced Find dialog box, as shown previously in Figure 17.6. To see the items in a different view, click View in the Advanced Find menu bar, move the pointer onto Current View, and select the view in which you want to see the search results. In the case of messages, you can also click AutoPreview in the Advanced Find's View menu to display the first three lines of message texts.

Note

The AutoPreview menu item isn't available until the results of a search are displayed.

→ For additional information about Outlook views, **see** "Modifying a View," **p. 658** and "Creating Custom Views," **p. 679**.

SAVING AND REUSING SEARCH CRITERIA

After you've constructed a set of search criteria (and confirmed that it satisfies your needs), you can save it so it's immediately available to be used again.

To save your search criteria:

1. Select File in the Advanced Find menu bar and select Save Search to display the Save Search dialog box.

2. Navigate through your folder structure to find the folder in which you want to save the search or, alternatively, create a new folder.

3. Enter a name for the search file. Outlook provides .oss as the file name extension; this is the same file name extension used for saved searches in other Office applications.

4. Click OK to save the search.

To reuse saved search criteria:

1. Open the Advanced Find dialog box.

2. Select File in the Advanced Find menu bar and select Open Search. If you already have search criteria defined in the Advanced Find dialog box, Outlook warns you that your current search will be cleared if you proceed. Click OK.

3. Navigate to the folder in which you previously saved searches and select the search you want to use.

4. Click OK to run the search.

MODIFYING A SAVED SEARCH

You can make changes to an existing saved search and then resave it. Save it with its existing file name if you want to replace the original saved search; save it with a different name if you want to save it in addition to the existing saved search.

Use the two procedures in the preceding section. Start by using the first four steps of the second procedure to open the existing saved search, make your changes, and then use the first procedure to save those changes.

CREATING PRECISE SEARCHES

What you've learned about searching for items with Advanced Find so far in this chapter might be all you'll ever need. Chances are, however, that there will be times when you need

PART
IV

CH
17

more. That's when you'll use the subform's More Choices, Advanced, and SQL tabs within the Advanced Find dialog box.

Before going any further, you need to understand one thing clearly. You can specify search criteria in any or all four tabs of the Advanced Find dialog box. When you click Find Now, Outlook looks for items that satisfy all the criteria specified in all the tabs. Although you can see only one tab at a time, Outlook sees all four. If you're not getting the search results you expect, a likely cause is that there are search criteria in one of the tabs you haven't looked at.

Tip from

I strongly recommend that, before you start creating a set of criteria, you click New Search. When you do that, all search criteria in all the tabs are cleared. That way you know you're starting from scratch. Now, any criteria set in the tabs you're not looking at can't affect your search.

REFINING YOUR SEARCH

Select the More Choices tab in the Advanced Find dialog box's subform, shown in Figure 17.13, to see the additional criteria you can use to narrow your search.

Figure 17.13
The More Choices tab offers additional search criteria.

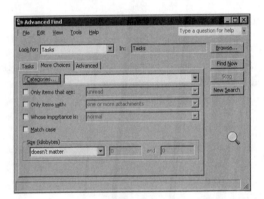

The most useful part of this tab is the Categories button. I can't stress too strongly the benefits of assigning categories to all your Outlook items. If you want to take advantage of Outlook's capability to give you control over your personal and business activities, you must assign one or more categories to every Outlook item (with the exception of Note items that you'll deal with before the end of the day).

→ To learn more about assigning categories to your Outlook items, **see** "Using Categories and Entry Types," **p. 403**.

Suppose you are involved in a project called Alpha and you create a category named Alpha. Each time you create an appointment or a meeting item related to the project, you should assign the category Alpha to that Calendar item; the same goes for every Alpha-related message you send and receive, contacts involved with the project, and tasks. Every Outlook item having to do with project Alpha should have the Alpha category assigned to it.

Now, you can easily find every Outlook item that relates to project Alpha by using the steps in the following procedure.

To find Outlook Items to which specific categories are assigned:

1. Open Advanced Find and click New Search to make sure no search criteria exist.
2. In the Look For list, select Any Type of Outlook Item.
3. If the In text box doesn't correctly identify where you want to look for items, click Browse to select the appropriate locations.
4. Open the More Choices tab and click Categories to display the Categories dialog box, which lists the categories in your personal Master Category List.
5. In the Available Categories list, check Alpha for the categories you want to search for. You can select more than one category. After selecting one or more categories, click OK. Outlook displays the Advanced Find dialog box with the selected categories in the Categories box.
6. Click Find Now to display a list of all Outlook items to which the categories you speci-fied are assigned. The list shows the Outlook folder that contains each item found by the search.

Note

Instead of selecting categories, you can type category names. If you enter more than one category, separate one category from the next with a comma or semicolon. Outlook finds all the items to which at least one of the categories is assigned.

Being able to search by category is a powerful capability, but only if you're meticulous about assigning categories to all Outlook items.

The five other choices you can make in the More Choices tab are:

- **Only Items that Are**—Check this, and then select either Unread or Read.
- **Only Items With**—Check this, and then select One or More Attachments or No Attachments.
- **Whose Importance Is**—Check this, and then select Normal, High, or Low.
- **Match Case**—Check this if you want the search for text specified in the first tab to be matched for case (uppercase or lowercase).
- **Size (Kilobytes)**—By default, Doesn't Matter is selected. You can open the drop-down list and then select from among Doesn't Matter, Equals (Approximately), Between, Less Than, and Greater Than. After you select any of these options other than Doesn't Matter, one or both of the boxes on the right become enabled so you can enter the size (or range of sizes) in kilobytes.

Tip from

Each type of Outlook item contains a Size field that contains the item's size in kilobytes. This field isn't displayed in any standard view. However, you can add the Size field to a Table view so the sizes of items are displayed in an Information viewer. You can also examine the size of individual items.

→ For information about adding fields to a view, **see** "Adding a Field to a View," **p. 663**.

→ For more information about examining the size of individual Outlooks, **see** "Displaying the Size of Outlook Items," **p. 386**.

DEFINING ADVANCED FIND CRITERIA

Select the Advanced tab in the Advanced Find dialog box if you want to get serious about your searches. In this tab, you can define conditions and values for one or more fields in an item. You can create search criteria above and beyond what's available in the other two tabs. You can, for example, use a date field as a criterion to search for items that contain a specific date, or range of dates, in a date field.

The top part of this tab contains the Find Items that Match These Criteria box. Initially, this box is empty except for text that says Add Criteria from Below to This List, as shown in Figure 17.14.

Figure 17.14
You can use this tab to be creative in defining searches.

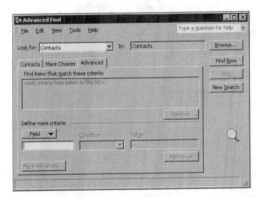

The following example illustrates how to create Advanced Find criteria.

Suppose you want to search for contacts whose home phone numbers are within a certain area code. If you already have search criteria in any of the three tabs, click New Search to remove all those criteria.

To search for Contacts who have a specific telephone area code:

1. Open the Look For drop-down list at the top of the dialog box and click Contacts.

2. In the Advanced Find dialog box's Advanced tab, click Field to display a list of field types, and move the pointer onto Phone Number Fields. Outlook displays the list of phone number fields shown in Figure 17.15.

Figure 17.15
Outlook displays a list of all phone number fields.

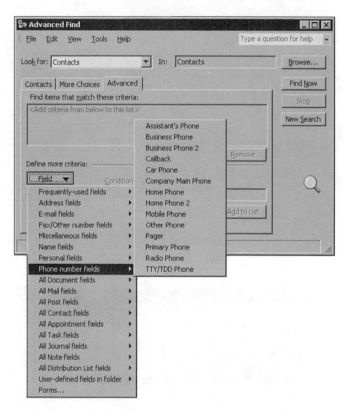

3. Select a type of phone number, such as Home Phone. The field you select appears in the Field box. Now the Condition box is enabled, as shown in Figure 17.16.

Figure 17.16
The Condition box initially contains the word "contains."

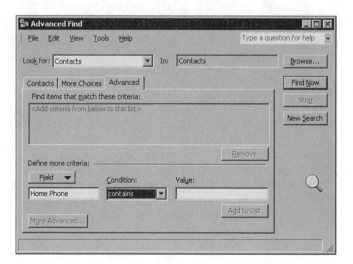

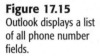

PART

IV

CH

17

4. You can open the Condition drop-down list to select one of these conditions: Contains, Is (Exactly), Doesn't Contain, Is Empty, and Is Not Empty. In this case, Contains is what you want.

5. In the Value box, enter the area code you want to find, such as (818). Be sure you enclose the number within parentheses.

Note

Outlook automatically formats phone numbers you enter for contacts according to regional conventions. If you're running Outlook under Windows in which Regional Settings is set to English (United States), Outlook automatically encloses telephone area codes within parentheses.

6. Click Add to List to add the criterion into the Find Items That Match These Criteria box, as shown in Figure 17.17.

Figure 17.17
The Find Items That Match These Criteria list contains a summary of the criteria you've defined.

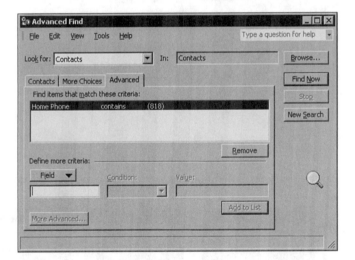

7. Click Find Now to start the search.

Outlook searches your Contacts folder and displays all items in which the Home Phone field contains the area code you specified.

The preceding example showed only one criterion specified. You can make your search more specific by adding more criteria. For example, you could add a criterion that specifies a certain last name. The following steps show how to add a second criterion to the one you just created.

To search for items by multiple criteria:

1. With the Advanced tab of the Advanced Find dialog box already containing one search criteria, such as that described in the preceding steps, click Field, select a group of fields such as Name Fields, and then select a specific name field such as Last Name.

2. As previously, Contains in the Condition box is what you want. Enter a value, such as a person's last name, in the Value box.

3. Click Add to List to add the second criterion into the Find Items That Match These Criteria box. The Advanced tab now contains two search criteria, as shown in Figure 17.18.

Figure 17.18
This is an example of a search based on two criteria.

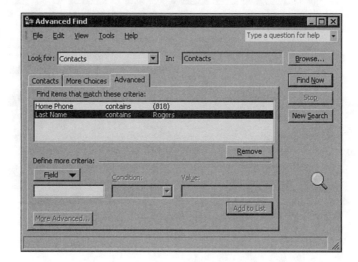

4. Click Find Now to initiate the search.

Both criteria in the Find Items That Match These Criteria box must be satisfied for Outlook to find an item. This search finds only those contacts who have the specified area code and the specified last name.

Microsoft doesn't specify any limit to the number of criteria you can specify in this way. If, after creating a criterion, you want to remove it from the list, select that criterion and click Remove.

FINDING ITEMS BASED ON DATES AND TIMES

When you're using Advanced Find to look for messages, items in your calendar, or task-related items, you'll probably want to search by date and, perhaps, by time. Recall that the first tab provides some capability to search by time, but only in certain broad categories, such as last week or next month. You can use Advanced criteria to specify exact dates and also exact times (with a one-minute resolution).

Suppose you want to look for messages that arrived this morning before 11:00 a.m.

To search for messages received within a certain period:

1. With Messages selected in the Advanced Find dialog box's Look For box, select the Advanced tab.

2. Click Field to display the list of field groups and move the pointer onto Date/Time Fields. Outlook displays the available date/time fields, as shown in Figure 17.19.

Figure 17.19
These are the available Date/Time fields.

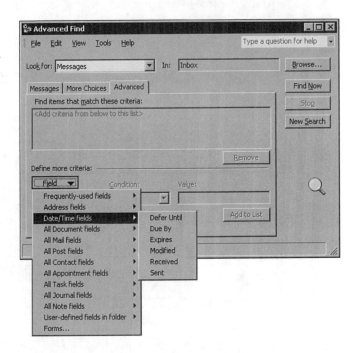

3. Because you're looking for messages you've received, select Received in the list of available fields. The Condition box becomes enabled with Anytime inside it.

4. Open the drop-down Condition list. You can select from quite a long list of conditions, including Between, which is the one to select.

5. In the value box, enter a range of dates, such as
   `5/26/2001 0:00 AM and 5/26/2001 11:00 AM`

6. Click Add to List to display the criterion in the Find Items That Match These Criteria box, as shown in Figure 17.20.

Tip from

If you display Outlook in a small window, you won't see the entire criterion in the Advanced tab. Either stretch the window to make it wider, or maximize the window so you can see the entire criterion.

Figure 17.20
Make sure the search
criterion, as it appears
here, is correct.

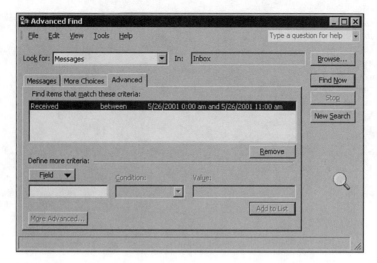

7. Click Find Now to start the search.

PART

IV

CH

17

Note

The examples given here are meant to get you started. It's worth taking time to explore what's available in the Advanced tab and practice creating searches.

FINDING FILES

So far in this chapter, you've looked only at finding Outlook items. You can also use Advanced Find to find files on any disk accessible to your computer.

SPECIFYING FOLDERS TO FIND

To find files within the Windows folder structure:

1. Start with any Outlook Information viewer displayed. Select Tools, Advanced Find to open the Advanced Find dialog box.

2. Open the Look For drop-down list and select Files to display the dialog box shown in Figure 17.21. Notice that the first tab is named Files.

Tip from

If you select File (Outlook/Exchange), Outlook will look for Office files within an Outlook folder, such as a Word document that's an attachment to a message in the Inbox folder. Make sure you select Files (not Files (Outlook/Exchange)) if you want to find files within the Windows folder structure.

Figure 17.21
Outlook proposes to search for files in your My Documents folder if you're working under Windows 98 or Windows 2000, or in your Personal folder if you're working under Windows NT.

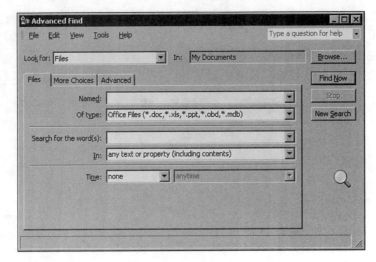

3. If you want to search in a folder other than My Documents or Personal, click Browse to open the Select Folders dialog box and navigate to the folder in which you want to search. Click OK to close the dialog box.

Note

Outlook looks for files in the folder you specify and in all that folder's subfolders.

SPECIFYING FILE NAMES AND TYPES

You can specify the file you want to search for by file name and extension.

Outlook initially assumes you want to search for an Office file, so the Of Type box contains the standard file name extensions for Office files. You can open the drop-down list of types and select from

- All Files (*.*)
- Office Files (*.doc, *.xls, *.ppt, *.obd, *.mdb)
- Documents (*.doc)
- Workbooks (*.xls)
- Presentations (*.ppt)
- Binders (*.odb)
- Databases (*.mdb)
- Templates (*.dot, *.xlt, *.oft, *.pot, *.obt)

Note

You can't enter any other file name extension; you can only select from the list. Don't worry about this if you want to search for a different type of file. A little later in this chapter, you learn an easy way to accomplish this.

After selecting the appropriate file name extension, enter the name of the file or files you want to search for in the Named box. If you want to search for just one file and you know its exact name, enter that name without the extension. If you want to search for several files, enter the file names, separating one from the next by a semicolon.

If you don't know exact file names, or you want to search for several files with similar names, you can use these wildcard characters:

- Use * to represent any number of characters.
- Use ? to represent a single character.

Note

As the following examples show, the * wildcard character behaves a little differently than it does within the DOS environment.

For example, if you enter catfish*, Outlook will find files with such names as catfish, catfish01, catfish02, catfish23, catfishfood, and so on. If you enter *fish, Outlook will find files with such names as fish, catfish, dogfish, and so on. If you enter catfish0?, Outlook will find files with such names as catfish01, catfish02, but not catfish23 or catfishfood. One more example: If you enter *fish*, Outlook will find such names as fish, catfish, fish01, and so on.

What if you want to find a file with a name that doesn't have one of the standard Office extensions, such as Readme.txt? In that case, enter the complete file name and extension in the Named box. When you enter a file name with an extension, Outlook ignores whatever extensions are in the Of Type box.

After you've specified one or more file names, click Find Now. Outlook searches in the folder you specified in the In box and in all its subfolders and displays a list of all the files that match the file name and extension you specified. You can double-click any name in the list to open the file.

Narrowing the Search for Files

You can narrow the search for files by entering a word or phrase in the Search for the Word(s) box. The method described here significantly increases the time it takes Outlook to find files because it has to search within files.

To specify where Outlook should search for the words or phrases you've specified, open the In list within the Files tab to select one of

- Any text or property (including contents)
- Contents only

By default, the Time box contains None, meaning that Outlook doesn't consider times and dates when it searches for files. You can open the Time drop-down list and select Modified, in which case the adjacent drop-down list is available. Open that list, and select one of Anytime, Yesterday, Today, In the Last 7 Days, Last Week, This Week, Last Month, or This Month.

MAKING MORE CHOICES WHEN FINDING FILES

The More Choices tab contains two check boxes and a drop-down list when you're searching for files, as shown in Figure 17.22.

Figure 17.22
You can refine your search by making selections in the More Choices tab.

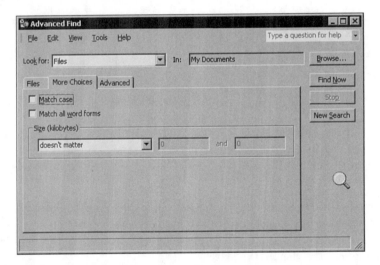

Outlook normally searches for the file contents you specify in Search for the Word(s) (in the Files tab) without regard for text being in uppercase or lowercase. Check Match Case if you want the search to be case sensitive.

Outlook normally searches for files that contain exactly the word you specify in Search for the Word(s). If you check Match All Word Forms, Outlook locates files that contain variations of the words you specify. For example, if you enter write, Outlook finds files that contain variations of write, such as writes, wrote, and written.

You can also specify the size of files you want Outlook to find by opening the Size drop-down list and selecting one of Doesn't Matter, Equals (Approximately), Between, Less Than, or Greater Than.

After you select anything other than Doesn't Matter, enter the file size or range of sizes in the two adjacent boxes.

Using the Advanced Criteria for Finding Files

The Advanced tab contains the same elements as the Advanced tab described earlier in this chapter you use when finding Outlook items. One difference, however, is that the Fields drop-down list contains fields associated with files instead of those in Outlook items. You can select either Frequently-Used Fields (which contains Created, Modified, and Size) or All File Fields (which contains a long list of fields, only some of which are associated with any particular type of file). You can select specific fields in documents and create criteria based on the values in those fields.

Using Find from the Windows Desktop

You can use Outlook's Find capabilities from the Windows desktop without starting Outlook.

To use Outlook's Find feature from the Windows desktop:

1. Select Start on the Windows taskbar to open the Start menu.
2. Move the pointer onto Find in Windows 98 or Windows NT, or Search in Windows Me or Windows 2000.
3. Select Using Microsoft Outlook. The Advanced Find dialog box is displayed with Files in the Look For box.
4. Use Find to locate files, as described previously in this chapter.

→ For more information about using Outlook's Find capabilities, **see** "Finding Files," **p. 361**.

To look for Outlook items, open the Look For drop-down list and select a type of Outlook item. Outlook opens so you can proceed.

Organizing Outlook Items

Finding items, as described in the preceding pages of this chapter, temporarily organizes items into a table based on criteria you enter. You can also organize Outlook items permanently by moving selected items into specific folders.

Outlook offers two ways for you to organize items: One is by using the Organize capability described here. The other is to create rules that automatically place e-mail messages you receive and copies of e-mail messages you send in specific folders.

The following pages refer specifically to organizing e-mail messages you've received, but they also apply to all types of Outlook items.

ORGANIZING E-MAIL MESSAGES

Instead of keeping all the e-mail messages you receive in your Inbox folder, you can create folders for specific types of messages and move appropriate messages into those folders. For example, you can create a folder for all messages relating to a specific project so you can keep those messages in one place.

Tip from

I'm describing this capability here because it's available in Outlook and some people like to use it. My preference is to keep almost all items in Outlook's standard folders for two principal reasons. First, saving all Outlook items in the standard folders makes finding items easy—I don't have to search in several folders. Second, it avoids the problem of deciding which folder to use for items that could logically be placed in more than one folder.

Rather than saving items in separate folders, I prefer to allocate categories to items.

CREATING A FOLDER FOR SPECIFIC MESSAGES

The first step in organizing your e-mail messages into folders is to create these folders. See Chapter 14 for information about creating new folders.

→ For information on creating Outlook folders, **see** "Creating a New Folder," **p. 305**.

MOVING SELECTED MESSAGES INTO A NEW FOLDER

Having created new folders, you can organize your mail by moving specific messages into them. Use the steps that follow if you want to move only one or two messages into a new folder.

To organize e-mail messages you've received:

1. With the Inbox Information viewer displayed, select one message you want to move into a new folder. Then hold down the Ctrl key while you select additional messages.

2. Click Organize in the Standard toolbar to display the Ways to Organize Inbox pane shown in Figure 17.23.

Note

The Organize pane has four buttons at the left. Make sure the Using Folders button is selected if you want to move selected messages into a specific folder.

3. If the folder Outlook proposes to move the selected messages to isn't correct, open the drop-down list, select Other Folder, and then select the folder you want to use.

4. Click Move to move the selected messages into the new folder.

You probably noticed that the Organize pane invites you to create a rule that will automatically move messages you receive in the future into the new folder. We'll postpone dealing with that subject until Chapter 28.

Figure 17.23
The Organize pane initially proposes to move the selected message.

→ To learn more about Outlook organizing your e-mail automatically, **see** "Creating a Rule," **p. 585**.

USING FIND TO LOCATE MESSAGES TO MOVE

The method described in the preceding steps is fine if you have only a few messages to move. But, if you want to move many messages, finding all those messages in the Inbox Information viewer can be time-consuming and tedious. You can simplify the process by using Outlook's Find capability to find specific messages.

If you're moving messages relating to a specific project into a new folder, you should have assigned the project name as a category to all those messages. If you haven't been meticulous about assigning categories, many of the messages likely contain the project name in the Subject box. You can use Find, as described previously in this chapter, to find all the messages that have a specific category assigned or have the project name in the subject box. After you've found messages in this way, select those messages in the Results table, and then use Organize to copy the messages into the new folder. You should look carefully through the messages in the Results table to make sure that all the messages there really do relate to the project. If some don't, be sure those messages are not selected before you use Organize.

To select all the messages in the Results table, select Edit, Select All (or press Ctrl+A). To select or deselect specific messages, hold down the Ctrl key while you click those messages.

You might have to use Find several times to ensure you find all the projected related messages. For example, you could look for messages from specific people who are involved in the project.

ORGANIZING MESSAGES BY COLOR

You can also use the Organize pane to display selected messages in a specific color.

PART

IV

CH

17

Select the messages you want to color either manually or by using Find to identify messages to which specific categories are assigned or which contain some other identifying characteristic. Then, select Using Colors at the left of the Organize pane. The Organize pane changes to that shown in Figure 17.24.

Figure 17.24
The Organize pane proposes to color the messages you selected in red.

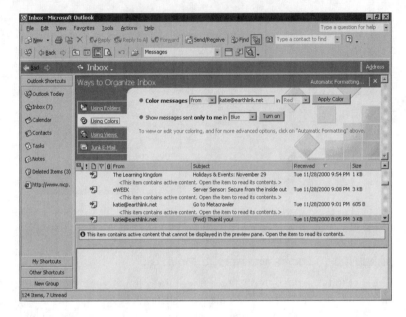

At this stage, you can

- Open the drop-down list at the right of Color Messages, and select Sent To instead of From
- Replace the name in the text box
- Open the drop-down list of colors and select a color other than red

Click Apply Color to color the selected messages. Outlook colors all the messages from the selected person in the new color so you can easily identify them.

TROUBLESHOOTING

FIND

You're not likely to find problems with the QuickFind tool; it works as described. Just enter one or more letters in a contact's name and you'll see a list of contacts whose File As names contain those characters.

When you use Advanced Find, remember that Outlook searches based on all four panes of the Advanced Find dialog box. If you don't find what you're looking for, click New Search to clear out all search criteria; then go back into each of the panes and carefully set up criteria in each of them.

CHAPTER 18

IMPORTING AND EXPORTING OUTLOOK ITEMS

In this chapter

WORKING WITH DATA FROM OTHER APPLICATIONS

Although Outlook is a very powerful application, it doesn't exist in a world of its own. Most Outlook users work with several other applications and receive files created in other applications from other people.

If you've previously used another application, such as Access, Excel, Word, or a Personal Information Manager, to keep your personal records, you'll probably want to bring these records into Outlook's integrated environment. When you receive information from other sources, you'll want to combine that information with information you already have in Outlook folders.

This chapter contains information about several techniques you can use to bring information into Outlook's folders and also how you can export information from Outlook into other applications.

IMPORTING WHEN YOU FIRST RUN OUTLOOK

The first time you run Outlook, it examines your computer environment to see whether you have other applications installed that you might have used to save such things as appointments and information about contacts. If it finds such applications, it displays a list of them and asks you whether you want to import information from them. You can select any or all of the listed applications or, if you don't want to import from any of them, select None. If you select any existing applications, Outlook imports information from them into the appropriate Outlook folders.

Note

> Outlook can import calendar and contact information from various Personal Information Managers from companies other than Microsoft. It's possible, though, that you have been using a PIM that Outlook doesn't recognize.

If you choose not to import your existing calendar and contact information the first time you run Outlook, you can import that information later, as described in the next section.

IMPORTING FROM OUTLOOK EXPRESS

If you've previously used Outlook Express or another messaging application to send and receive e-mail, you can import messages and your address book from that application into Outlook. The following steps refer specifically to Outlook Express. You can, however, use the same technique to import messages and your address book from some other applications.

To import Outlook Express messages:

1. With any Outlook Information viewer displayed, select File, Import and Export to display the first Import and Export Wizard window, shown in Figure 18.1.

Figure 18.1
The first wizard window asks you want you want to do. After you've selected an action, the Description section provides information about that action.

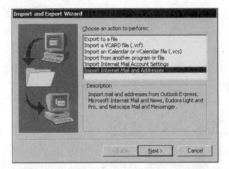

2. In the first wizard window, select Import Internet Mail and Addresses; then click Next to display the second wizard window, shown in Figure 18.2.

Figure 18.2
The second wizard window asks you which e-mail application you want to import messages from.

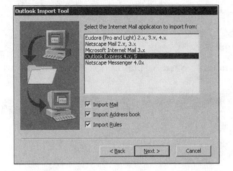

3. Select Outlook Express or whichever other e-mail application you want to import from.

4. If you select Outlook Express, the wizard proposes to import your Outlook Express mail, address book, and rules. If you select any of the other sources, the option to import rules is not available. Uncheck Import Mail if you don't want to import messages; uncheck Import Address Book if you don't want to import the address book; uncheck Import Rules if you don't want to import rules. Click Next to display the third wizard window, shown in Figure 18.3.

Figure 18.3
Use this wizard window to specify where you want addresses to be imported into and what to do about duplicates.

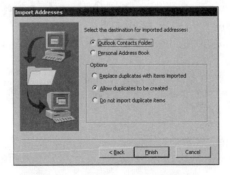

5. In most cases, accept the defaults in this dialog box; then click Finish to import the data.

As an alternative to importing into Outlook from Outlook Express, you can export from Outlook Express into Outlook.

SAVING OUTLOOK ITEMS AS FILES

You can save any Outlook item as a file so you can work with that item in other applications. Outlook can save items in several formats. The following example refers specifically to a message item, but you can use the same technique for other types of Outlook items.

To save a message as a file:

1. Select Inbox in the Outlook Bar to display the Inbox Information viewer if you want to save a message in your Inbox folder. Select Sent Items in the Outlook Bar if you want to save a message in your Sent Items folder.

2. Select the message you want to save.

3. Select File, Save As to display the Save As dialog box shown in Figure 18.4.

Figure 18.4
By default, Outlook proposes to save the message in the mail format (HTML, RTF, or TXT) in which you received or created it.

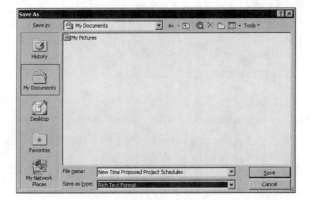

4. Open the drop-down Save as Type list to display a list of available file types. If you're saving a Message item, you can select Text Only, Outlook Template, Message Format, or HTML. Select the format you want to use.

5. By default, Outlook proposes to use the subject of the message as the name of the file. You can replace this name.

6. If you want to save the file in a folder other than the one Outlook proposes, navigate to that folder.

7. Click Save to save the message.

Note

The preceding procedure refers to saving one mail item at a time. You also can select several items and save them all in a single file. In that case, Outlook doesn't propose a file name for the saved items; you must provide a name for the file in which the group of items are saved.

Table 18.1 lists the file formats available for various Outlook items.

TABLE 18.1   AVAILABLE FILE FORMATS

Item	Text Only	Rich Text	Outlook Template	Message	iCalendar	vCalendar	vCard
Message	Yes	Yes	Yes	Yes	No	No	No
Calendar	Yes	Yes	Yes	Yes	Yes	Yes	No
Contact	Yes	Yes	Yes	Yes	No	No	Yes
Journal	Yes	Yes	Yes	Yes	No	No	No
Task	Yes	Yes	Yes	Yes	No	No	No

Note

An alternative way to save an item as a file is to drag that item into a folder using Windows Explorer. The created file is in Message format with .msg as its file name extension.

You also can drag an item onto the Windows desktop to create an icon on the desktop that represents a file in Message format.

PART

IV

CH

18

Text Only and Rich Text Format are general-purpose formats you can use when you want to access Outlook items in various applications.

Use the Outlook Template format when you want to create a template based on one item that you can use as the basis for similar items, as explained in Chapter 16, "Using Outlook Templates." Use the iCalendar format to exchange calendar information, and use the vCard format to exchange contact information in industry-standard formats with other people, including those who use applications other than Outlook that support these formats.

Note

iCalendar supercedes vCalendar as the original industry standard for exchanging calendar information. Outlook 2000 and Outlook 2002 support both formats. You should use vCalendar only when you need compatibility with older applications that don't support iCalendar.

Use the Message format to move individual Outlook items from one computer to another when you don't have e-mail connectivity.

→ To learn more about generating Outlook items from templates, **see** "Using Outlook Templates," **p. 329**.

→ For additional information about sharing your calendar and contact information with other Outlook users, **see** "Sharing a Calendar," **p. 234** and "Sharing Individual Contact Items," **p. 188**.

SHARING ITEMS WITH OTHER OUTLOOK USERS

One way to share Outlook items with other Outlook users is to export items to a Personal Folders file so that other people can import items from that folder into their own Personal Folders files or Exchange stores. This is particularly convenient when you want to share items by way of a LAN.

It's less convenient, though, if you can't share the file by way of a LAN because the Personal Folders file is likely to be too large to copy to a standard floppy disk and probably larger than you want to send by e-mail. In that case, you must resort to using a utility such as WinZip to copy the file onto several floppy disks, using high-capacity disks such as Iomega's Zip disks, or copying onto a CD-R or CD-RW disc.

EXPORTING ITEMS TO A PERSONAL FOLDERS FILE

You can use Outlook's Import and Export Wizard to copy Outlook items to a Personal Folders file, as well as to other file formats.

To export Outlook items to a Personal Folders file:

1. With any Outlook Information viewer displayed, select File, Import and Export to display the first Import and Export Wizard window, shown previously in Figure 18.1.

2. Select Export to a File, and then click Next to display the second wizard window, shown in Figure 18.5.

Figure 18.5
The second wizard window asks you what sort of file you want to create.

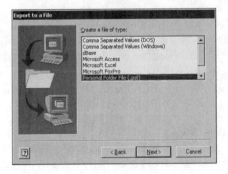

3. Select Personal Folder File (.pst), and then click Next to display the third wizard window, shown in Figure 18.6.

Figure 18.6
The third wizard window asks which Outlook folder you want to export from.

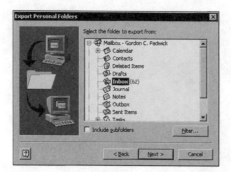

4. By default, Outlook selects the folder that was displayed in an Information viewer when you started using the wizard. If you want to export from a different folder, select that folder. If you want to export items from all your folders, select Personal Folders if you're using a Personal Folders file to store Outlook items or Mailbox if you store those items in an Exchange store.

5. If your folder structure contains subfolders and you want to export items from the selected folder and all its subfolders, make sure Include Subfolders is checked. If you don't want to export from subfolders, make sure that box is unchecked.

PART

IV

CH

18

> **Note**
>
> If you want to export items in all folders in a store (your Personal Folder file or your Exchange store), select that store and check Include Subfolders.

6. If you want to export all items from the selected folder, go to step 8. If you want to export only certain items, click Filter to display the Filter dialog box shown in Figure 18.7.

Figure 18.7
The Filter dialog box has four tabs in which you can define how you want to filter items.

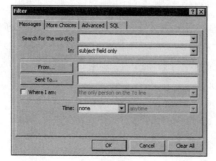

7. Set up filter conditions in the same way that you set up an Advanced Find, as explained in Chapter 17, "Finding and Organizing Outlook Items." After you've set up the filter conditions, click OK to return to the third wizard window. Click Next to display the fourth wizard window, shown in Figure 18.8.

→ To learn more about Outlook's Advanced Find capabilities, **see** "Using Advanced Find to Find Words and Phrases," **p. 341**.

Figure 18.8
The fourth wizard window asks you to provide a path and name for the file that will be created.

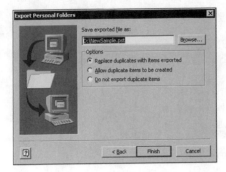

8. Either enter a full path for the new file in the Save Exported File As box or click Browse, navigate to the folder in which you want to create the file, and enter a file name.

9. It doesn't usually matter which option button you select in the Options section of the dialog box because you probably want to create a new file that doesn't already contain any Outlook items. Click Finish. Outlook creates the new file.

> **Note**
>
> If you want to copy Outlook items to a file that already contains items, follow the steps in the preceding procedure. In that case, though, it's important to make the appropriate selection in the Options section of the dialog box shown in Figure 18.8.

IMPORTING ITEMS FROM A PERSONAL FOLDERS FILE

The process of importing items from a Personal Folders file into your existing store is very similar to the process of exporting items, which is described in the preceding section.

To import Outlook items from a Personal Folders file:

1. With any Outlook Information viewer displayed, select File, Import and Export to display the first Import and Export Wizard window, shown previously in Figure 18.1.

2. Select Import from Another Program or File, and then click Next to display the second wizard window, shown in Figure 18.9.

Figure 18.9
The second wizard window asks you what type of file you want to import from.

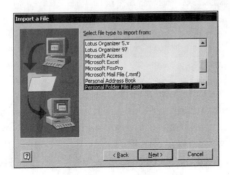

3. Scroll down the list and select Personal Folder File (.pst). Then click Next to display the third wizard window, which is similar to the one previously shown in Figure 18.8.

4. Enter the full path of the file you want to import into the File to Import box; otherwise, click Browse, navigate to the file, select the file, and click Open.

5. In the Options section of the dialog box, select an option button according to how you want Outlook to deal with duplicate items. Either the first or third option is usually appropriate. Click Next to display the fourth wizard window, shown in Figure 18.10.

Figure 18.10
The fourth wizard window lists the folders in the Personal Folders file that's to be imported.

6. If you want to import all the items in all the folders in the Personal Folders file, select Personal Folders and check the Include Subfolders box. If you want to import the items in only one folder, select that folder (Outlook lets you select only one folder). If you want to import all items, click Finish and proceed to step 8. To select certain items to import, click Filter to display the Filter dialog box shown previously in Figure 18.7.

7. Set up filter conditions in the same way that you set up an Advanced Find, as explained in Chapter 17. After you've set up the filter conditions, click OK to return to the fourth wizard window.

→ To learn more about setting up filter conditions, **see** "Using Advanced Find to Find Words and Phrases," **p. 341.**

8. Select whichever of the two options buttons is appropriate. If you select Import Items into the Current Folder, Outlook imports items into whichever folder you had open when you started using the Import and Export Wizard. If you select Import Items into the Same Folder In, Outlook imports items into a folder of the same type as the one from which items are being imported; the name of the folder into which items will be imported is shown in the box below the second check box. If you have more than one Personal Folders file or Exchange store, you can open the drop-down list and select the one into which items will be imported.

9. Click Finish. Outlook copies items into the specified folders.

PART

IV

CH

18

EXPORTING ITEMS TO, AND IMPORTING ITEMS FROM, OTHER APPLICATIONS

Outlook can export items directly to and import items directly from various other applications.

IMPORTING INFORMATION FROM PERSONAL INFORMATION MANAGERS

If you've previously been using a Personal Information Management (PIM) to maintain your calendar, contact information, and so on, you probably can use Outlook's Import and Export Wizard to import information directly into Outlook. To do so, open the wizard (as explained in the previous two sections) and, in the first wizard window, select Import from Another Program or File. Click Next to open the second wizard window. In that window, you can select these PIMs:

- ACT! 2.0, 3.X, 4.0 Contact Manager for Windows
- ECCO 2.0, 3.0, and 4.0
- Lotus Organizer 4.x, 5.x, 97
- Schedule Plus Interchange
- Schedule+ 1.0, 7.0

Note   Although Outlook can import from these applications, it can't export to them.

If the PIM you've been using isn't listed, you might be able to export from that PIM into one of the file formats from which Outlook can import.

→ For information about compatible file formats, **see** "Importing from, and Exporting to, More Applications," **p. 379**.

IMPORTING FROM, AND EXPORTING TO, WINDOWS APPLICATIONS

Outlook can directly import information from, and export information to, dBASE, Microsoft Access, Excel, and FoxPro.

Use the Outlook Import and Export Wizard to import from files created by these applications and to export to files that can be read by these applications. The methods for doing this are quite similar to those described previously for importing from and exporting to a Personal Folders file. Some specific points relating to this are covered subsequently in this chapter.

→ For more information about using database information with Outlook, **see** "Importing Data from a Database," **p. 380**.
→ To learn more about using Excel data with Outlook, **see** "Importing Information from an Excel Worksheet," **p. 382**.

Importing from, and Exporting to, More Applications

Outlook can directly import information from dBASE and export information to dBASE and other applications that create files in the .dbf format.

If you want to import information created in an application that's not listed in the Import and Export dialog boxes, you can solve this problem in two ways. You can use similar methods to export information created in Outlook to make it possible for an application not listed in the Import and Export dialog boxes to be able to work with that information.

One way is to use an intermediate file format. Suppose, for example, you have been keeping your contact information in a Paradox database and want to import that information into an Outlook Contacts folder. Unfortunately, Outlook can't directly import from Paradox. What you can do, though, is use Access to convert the Paradox files into Access format. After you've done that, you can import the information in Access format into Outlook.

Note

The preceding paragraph contains just one example of how you can use an intermediate application. Various Microsoft applications can import information from other applications; also, some other applications can export information in a format that's compatible with Microsoft applications.

Part IV
Ch
18

Another way to import information from and export information to other applications is to use industry-standard formats. Outlook and many other applications support

- Comma Separated Values (otherwise known as comma-delimited values) for DOS
- Comma Separated Values (otherwise known as comma-delimited values) for Windows
- Tab Separated Values (otherwise known as tab-delimited values) for DOS
- Tab Separated Values (otherwise known as tab-delimited values) for Windows

You can use these formats to transport information between Outlook and other applications.

These four formats are all text file formats. In the case of comma separated values, one field of information is separated from the next by a comma. In tab separated values, one field of information is separated from the next by a tab character.

Tip from

If the application you're importing from encloses the information in text fields within quotation marks, Outlook doesn't regard commas or tabs within fields as field-separation characters. However, if you're importing text that's not enclosed within quotation marks and that text includes commas or tab characters, you can expect problems. You'll have to edit the text file before you can import it into Outlook.

In these formats, one record is separated from the next by a sequence of two characters: a carriage return and a line feed.

Note

For more information about using these formats, see the Microsoft Knowledge Base article Q243476, "How to Import and Export Text Data with Outlook."

IMPORTING DATA FROM A DATABASE

Importing information from a database involves copying data from specific database fields into specific Outlook fields. Outlook fields have specific names, as listed in Appendix B, "Outlook's Files, Folders, Fields, and Registry Keys." The database you're importing from often has fields with different names, usually names assigned by the person who created the database. There's no automatic way by which Outlook can know the name of the fields in the database that should be imported into Outlook's fields. For that reason, you must use a process known as Field Mapping to define the relationships between Outlook fields and database fields. The process of field mapping is described in the following procedure, which uses importing contact information from an Access database as an example.

To import contact information from an Access database:

1. Select File, Import and Export to display the first Import and Export Wizard window, previously shown in Figure 18.1.

2. Select Import from Another Program or File and click Next to display the wizard window previously shown in Figure 18.9.

3. Select Microsoft Access, and then click Next. If you haven't previously imported from Access, Outlook displays a message box telling you that it can't start the Import/Export engine because the feature is not currently installed and asking whether you would like to install it now. Click Yes. Outlook attempts to install the Import/Export Engine from the Office XP CD-ROM (if the CD-ROM isn't in your drive, a message tells you to insert it). After you do so, the wizard window in which you specify the database file to be imported is displayed.

4. Either enter the path of the file you want to import or click Browse to locate the file.

5. In the Options section, select how you want Outlook to handle duplicates. Outlook isn't likely to recognize any items in your Access database as duplicates, so accept the default Allow Duplicates to Be Created. Click Next to display the wizard window that shows your Outlook folder structure.

6. Select the Outlook folder into which you want to import information from the database; then click Next to display a dialog box similar to the one shown in Figure 18.11.

Figure 18.11
This dialog box lists the tables in the database. In this case, the database contains two tables.

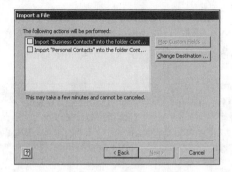

7. Check the table you want to import. When you do that, the Map Custom Fields button becomes enabled.

8. Click Map Custom Fields to display the dialog box shown in Figure 18.12.

Figure 18.12
Use this dialog box to establish relationships between fields in the source database and Outlook fields.

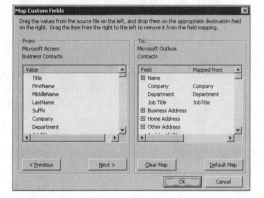

> **Note**
>
> The Map Custom Fields dialog box contains two lists. The list on the left displays the names of fields in the database from which you want to import. The list on the right contains the names of Outlook fields and groups of fields; group names are indicated by a box at the left of the name containing a plus sign. To see individual field names within a group, click the +.
>
> The list of Outlook fields has two columns: the left field, which contains field names, and the right field, which contains the names of database fields to be copied into each Outlook field.
>
> You can select which fields in the database you want to import into Outlook and which Outlook field to use for each database field.

9. Point onto a field in the list of database fields. Press the mouse button, and drag to the corresponding field in the list of Outlook fields. The name of the database field appears in the right column of the Outlook list of fields, indicating that you want the information from that database field to be copied to the Outlook field.

10. Repeat step 9 for each field of the database you want to import into Outlook. When you've finished, click OK to return to the Import a File dialog box.

11. Click Finish to begin importing data from the database into Outlook.

Note

You can use the Previous and Next buttons in the Map Custom Fields dialog box to display data in specific database fields. Click the Clear Map button to remove all relationships between database and Outlook fields. Click the Default Map button to automatically create relationships between database and Outlook fields that have the same name.

IMPORTING INFORMATION FROM AN EXCEL WORKSHEET

To import information from an Excel worksheet into Outlook, the information must be in a named range. Also, the top row of the named range must contain field names that correspond to Outlook field names.

To create a named range in an Excel worksheet, select the block of cells you want to have in the range, select Insert, move the pointer onto Name, and select Define to open the Define Name dialog box. Enter a name for the range into the Names in Workbook box, and then click OK. Select File, Save to save the workbook with the named range.

Caution

The name you give the range must not be the same as any of the field names in the top row of the named range. Also, range names cannot contain spaces.

TROUBLESHOOTING

IMPORTING AND EXPORTING ITEMS

Importing into and exporting from Outlook folders seems to go fairly smoothly as long as you stay within the applications and file formats Outlook directly supports. You sometimes might run into some problems that require some ingenuity to solve when you work with other applications.

The most likely problem you might run into when importing into or exporting from Outlook is that you run out of disk space because of the size of the information. If that happens, the operation aborts without losing any data. Your only loss is the time wasted.

To avoid this problem, you should find out the size of the information you're going to import or export before you begin and compare that with the space available. You can, of course, use My Computer or Windows Explorer to find out the size of complete files and how much space is available on a disk.

→ You can use the methods previously described in this chapter to find out the size of Outlook folders and individual Outlook items. **See** "Managing Outlook Folders," **p. 299**.

Ross Payne, a reader of my previous book *Special Edition Using Microsoft Outlook 2000*, was generous enough to share this experience with me. Ross had previously been using Corel InfoCentral to store information about his contacts, and he wanted to import that information into an Outlook Contacts folder. He exported from InfoCentral into a CSV file and then imported that file into Outlook. The process went smoothly with the exception that Outlook displayed all phone numbers with a 1 in front of every area code.

The problem was that InfoCentral appends the 1 when it creates a CSV file. Ross's solution was to import the CSV file into WordPerfect and use WordPerfect's find and replace capability to automatically remove the appended 1s. Then he saved the file (being careful to save it as text only) and imported that file into Outlook. That solved the problem. Although Ross used WordPerfect, he could just as well have used Word to perform the find and replace.

The important lesson to learn from this story is not to automatically blame Outlook if importing doesn't work out quite right. If you export a file from another application and Outlook doesn't import that file as you expect, use another application to examine the file and, if necessary, modify it before importing it into Outlook.

CHAPTER 19

COMPACTING FOLDERS AND ARCHIVING OUTLOOK ITEMS

In this chapter

UNDERSTANDING ARCHIVING AND BACKING UP

Two reasons exist for backing up or archiving Outlook:

- To avoid keeping unnecessarily large files on your hard disk. Archiving is intended for this purpose.
- To be able to restore Outlook after a disk crash, or move your Outlook configuration to another disk. Backing up is used for this purpose.

Outlook saves two types of information. The most obvious type of information is your Outlook items—e-mail messages, information about contacts, your calendar, and so on. The other type of information is what can collectively be called Outlook's *settings*.

If you're using Outlook as a client for Exchange, you can keep your Outlook items in an Exchange store on the server, or you can save those items in a Personal Folders file on a hard drive. If you're using Outlook not as a client for Exchange, you have no choice but to save Outlook items in a Personal Folders file on a hard drive. Wherever you save Outlook items, Outlook's settings are saved in various files on your hard drive.

This brings us back to the two reasons for archiving and backing up Outlook. You can use three techniques to minimize the space occupied by Outlook items:

- Deleting Outlook items you don't need to keep
- Compacting folders so they occupy as little space on your hard drive as possible
- Archiving items by moving them from your hard drive to another storage medium

Backing up Outlook involves copying all the Outlook items you need to keep (and also the files that contain Outlook's settings) onto another storage medium.

This chapter is principally about deleting Outlook items, compacting folders, and archiving items.

DISPLAYING THE SIZE OF OUTLOOK ITEMS

If you use Outlook regularly, your Personal Folders file (or Exchange store) can grow very rapidly. You easily can find out the size of individual items.

To determine the size of an Outlook item:

1. Click one of the shortcut icons on the Outlook Bar to display an Information viewer.

Note

You can also select View, Folder List to display a list of Outlook folders in which you can select a folder. This method provides a way to open folders for which no corresponding icon exists in the Outlook Bar.

2. Double-click an item to display that item in a form.

3. In the form's menu bar, select File, Properties, to display a Properties dialog box such as that shown in Figure 19.1.

Figure 19.1
This dialog box shows the properties of an e-mail item.

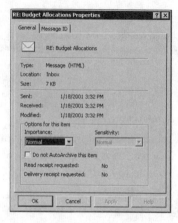

The fourth row in the dialog box shows the size (in bytes) of the selected item. If the item contains attachments, the indicated size includes those attachments. Message items, particularly those that have attachments, can occupy much more space than Contact items.

Another way to keep track of the size of Outlook items is to add the Size field to one of the standard Outlook views or create a custom view that contains the Size field. You can use a view that contains the Size field to display the size of all Outlook items of a specific type.

→ For information about modifying and creating views, **see** "Adding a Field to a View," **p. 663**.

It's a little-known fact that the message format has a significant effect on message size; this applies to messages you create and save in your Sent Items folder as well as to messages you receive and save in your Inbox folder. Messages in Plain Text format are much smaller than messages in HTML or Rich Text format. For example, one particular 50-line message in Plain Text format (with no attachments) occupies 1KB. The same message in HTML or Rich Text format occupies 8KB.

The much smaller size of Plain Text messages is a good reason for preferring this format unless you really need the formatting capabilities of HTML or Rich Text.

→ For information about selecting a message format, **see** "Selecting a Message Format and E-mail Editor," **p. 66**.

Tip from

One way to minimize the space occupied by mail is to take advantage of Outlook's capability to automatically reject junk e-mail. Note, though, that this places junk mail in your Deleted Items folder; you have to delete items from that folder to recover the disk space they occupy.

→ For information about automatically deleting junk e-mail, **see** "Dealing with Junk Mail," **p. 606**.

DELETING OUTLOOK ITEMS

After understanding how much space individual items occupy, you won't be surprised to learn that a frequent user's Outlook items easily can occupy several tens of megabytes of disk space.

Note

> The remaining part of this section describes how you can manually delete items. Archiving, which you can set up to automatically delete items, is described later in this chapter.

→ To learn about AutoArchiving, **see** "Managing AutoArchiving," **p. 396**.

You can delete an item from an Outlook folder in several ways. When you delete an item from any Outlook folder other than the Deleted Items folder, Outlook moves the item into the Deleted Items folder. After selecting an item to be deleted, do one of the following:

- On the Standard toolbar, click the Delete button.
- Select Edit, Delete.
- Press Ctrl+D.
- Press Delete.
- Drag the item onto the Deleted Items icon on the Outlook Bar.
- Drag the item onto the Deleted Items folder in the Outlook folder list.
- Drag the item onto the Windows Recycle Bin (even though you drag to the Recycle Bin, the item moves into the Outlook Deleted Items folder).
- Right-click an item and click Delete in the context menu.

You can use the same methods to delete an Outlook folder you've created, but not one of Outlook's standard folders. When you delete a folder, Outlook moves that folder (and all the items it contains, including any subfolders) into the Deleted Items folder, creating a new subfolder within the Deleted Items folder.

MOVING ITEMS INTO THE DELETED ITEMS FOLDER

Your first line of defense in keeping the amount of disk space Outlook uses under control is to make a regular habit of deleting all items you don't need to keep. Each time you download e-mail, for example, immediately delete items you don't want to keep.

Note

> Some employers have specific policies about saving e-mail. Government agencies and law firms, for example, usually require employees to keep all business-related messages. On the other hand, some companies require employees to delete all e-mail messages older than a certain number of days.
>
> If you're working on a contract, the terms of that contract might require you to keep all related messages.

To delete Outlook items:

1. Open the Information viewer that displays items you want to delete. For example, to delete unwanted mail items you've received, open the Inbox Information viewer.

2. Select one item you want to delete. To select additional items, hold down Ctrl while you select those items.

 3. Click the Delete button in the Standard toolbar. Outlook immediately removes the selected items from the Information viewer.

These steps don't actually delete items from your hard drive. All they do is move items from their original folder (the Inbox folder in the case of mail items you've received) into the Deleted Items folder. As you'll see in a moment, you can easily move any items you deleted accidentally back into their original folders.

Note

Because you can easily restore deleted items to their original folders, Outlook doesn't ask you to confirm that you really want to delete items.

RESTORING ITEMS TO THEIR ORIGINAL FOLDERS

You easily can restore items in the Deleted Items folder back into their original folders.

To restore deleted items:

1. Select Deleted Items in the Outlook Bar to display the Deleted Items Information viewer.

2. Select one or more items in the Deleted Items Information viewer. All the items you select must be intended to be restored to the same folder.

3. Drag the selected items onto the Outlook Bar shortcut icon that represents the folder into which you want to restore the items. If you've selected several items in the Deleted Items Information viewer, all items are restored when you drag one of them.

   If you want an alternative to dragging, after you've selected items in the Deleted Items Information viewer, select Edit, Move to Folder. The Move to Folder dialog box then appears. Select the folder to which you want to move the items and click OK.

Tip from

Gordon Padwick

If you want to restore a deleted item into a folder for which a corresponding icon doesn't exist on the Outlook Bar, open the folder list and drag the item onto the folder name there.

DELETING ITEMS FROM THE DELETED ITEMS FOLDER

To completely delete items from your hard drive, you must delete items from your Deleted Items folder. You can delete all items or delete only specific items. You can delete items from the Deleted Items folder manually or set an Option so that Outlook automatically deletes everything in that folder when you close Outlook, as described subsequently in this section.

To delete all items from the Deleted Items folder, right-click the Deleted Items icon in the Outlook Bar to display its context menu. Then select Empty "Deleted Items" Folder. Outlook asks you to confirm that you want to permanently delete all the items and folders in the Deleted Items folder. Click Yes.

Instead of deleting everything in the Deleted Items folder, you can delete specific items or folders.

To delete specific items or folders from the Deleted Items folder:

1. Select Deleted Items in the Outlook Bar to display the Deleted Items Information viewer.

2. Select the items you want to delete.

 3. Click the Delete button in the Standard toolbar. Outlook displays a message asking you to confirm that you really want to delete the items. Click Yes if you do want to delete the items; click No if you don't. If you click Yes, Outlook permanently deletes the items.

→ For information about automatically emptying the Deleted Items folder when Outlook closes, **see** "Setting General Options," **p. 573**.

→ For additional information about deleting items and recovering deleted items, **see** "Deleting Messages and Other Outlook Items," **p. 111**.

COMPACTING YOUR PERSONAL FOLDERS FILE

After you've deleted items from the Deleted Items folder in your Personal Folders file, Outlook doesn't release the space those items previously occupied. To get the space back, you must compact your Personal Folders file.

To see how much space is recovered by compacting your Personal Folders file, you can find out its size before and after compacting. You don't have to do that, but doing so gives you a useful insight into the disk space Outlook uses.

To see the size of your Personal Folders file:

1. With any Outlook Information viewer displayed, select View, Folder List to display your list of folders.

2. Right-click the name of your Personal Folders file, not one of the individual folders within that file, to display its context menu.

3. Select Properties to display the Personal Folders Properties dialog box, which opens with the General tab selected.

4. Click Folder Size to display the dialog box shown in Figure 19.2.

Figure 19.2
This dialog box shows the size of the file and the sizes of the individual folders within it.

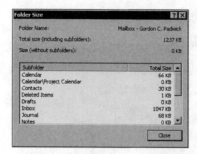

Note

The sizes shown apparently represent the space occupied by Outlook items. A Personal Folders file is considerably bigger than the size indicated in this dialog box due to the overhead in the file. In one case in which the dialog box shows a size of 775KB, Windows Explorer shows the size of the file to be 1,008KB.

The top section of this dialog box contains three rows:

- The name of the Personal Folders file
- The total size of data within the file
- The size of data within the file but excluding data in subfolders

The bottom section contains a table that lists the size of individual folders and subfolders. You might want to make a note of the size of your file and subsequently compare that size with the size after you've compacted the file.

To compact your Personal Folders file:

1. With any Outlook Information viewer displayed, select View, Folder List to display your list of folders.
2. Right-click the name of your Personal Folders file, not one of the individual folders within that file, to display its context menu.
3. Select Properties to display the Personal Folders Properties dialog box, which opens with the General tab selected.
4. Click Advanced to display the dialog box shown in Figure 19.3.

Figure 19.3
You can use this dialog box to change your password and to compact your Personal Folders file.

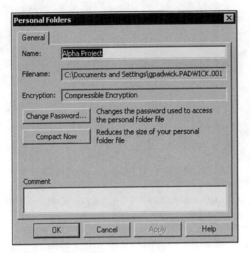

5. Click Compact Now to recover unused space within your Personal Folders file.

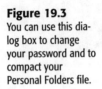

Note

Compacting a file just once doesn't necessarily make the file as small as possible. You might have to compact it two or three times.

Some people recommend compacting from the Windows Control Panel instead of from within Outlook. In the Control Panel, double-click Mail to display a Properties dialog box, select the Personal Folders file, and click Properties. Click Compact Now to compact the file.

After you've compacted your file, you might want to repeat the procedure shown at the beginning of this section to ascertain how much disk space you've recovered.

AUTOARCHIVING OUTLOOK ITEMS

AutoArchiving is the process by which Outlook either copies or deletes items from your Outlook folders periodically. Outlook can AutoArchive items in all folders except your Contacts folder.

→ As explained subsequently in this chapter, you can archive items manually. **See** "Archiving Items Manually," **p. 397**.

The items Outlook AutoArchives are those that are expired. You can specify the expiration period for items in each folder, and you can specify the interval at which Outlook performs AutoArchiving.

DEFINING EXPIRATION PERIODS

Each folder has a default expiration period for the items it contains, as listed in Table 19.1. AutoArchiving occurs by default for some folders, as indicated by Yes in the Default column of Table 19.1. AutoArchiving doesn't occur by default for some other folders, as indicated by No in the Default column, even though those folders have a default expiration period.

TABLE 19.1 DEFAULT EXPIRATION PERIODS

Folder	Period	Default	Basis
Calendar	6 months	Yes	Item start date or date of last item modification.
Contacts	None	N/A	Not archived.
Deleted Items	2 months	Yes	Date item moved into folder.
Drafts	3 months	No	Date item created or last modified.
Inbox	3 months	No	Date message received or last modified.
Journal	6 months	Yes	Entry date or date of last modification.
Notes	3 months	No	Entry date or date of last modification.
Outbox	3 months	No	Creation date or date of last modification.
Sent Items	2 months	Yes	Date item was sent.
Tasks	6 months	Yes	Completion date or date of last modification. Uncompleted tasks are not archived.

Note

The Period and Default for *custom* folders depends on the type of item each folder contains. If you create a custom folder to hold Task items, for example, that folder has the same Period and Default as the standard Outlook Tasks folder.

→ For information about custom folders and subfolders, **see** "Creating Folders and Subfolders," **p. 631**.

Although each folder has a default AutoArchive period, AutoArchiving is initially activated only for those folders marked Yes in the Default column in Table 19.1.

ENABLING AND DISABLING AUTOARCHIVING

As Table 19.1 shows, some folders have AutoArchiving turned on by default, and others do not. You can change these defaults.

To turn AutoArchiving on or off for a folder:

1. Right-click the shortcut icon in the Outlook Bar (or the folder name in the Folder List) corresponding to the folder for which you want to turn AutoArchiving on or off to display the folder's context menu.

2. Select Properties in the context menu to display the folder's Properties dialog box.

3. Select the AutoArchive tab (available for all folders except the Contacts folder), as shown in Figure 19.4.

Figure 19.4
This dialog box shows whether AutoArchiving is turned on and the period between AutoArchiving.

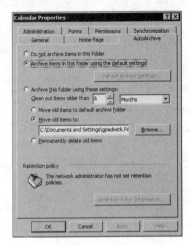

4. Check Archive This Folder Using These Settings to enable AutoArchiving. Uncheck it to disable AutoArchiving.

CHANGING AUTOARCHIVING PERIODS

You can change the intervals between which Outlook performs AutoArchiving.

To change the AutoArchive period:

1. Follow steps 1–3 in the preceding procedure.

2. In the box at the right of Clean Out Items Older Than, change the number. Open the adjacent drop-down list and select Months, Weeks, or Days.

CONTROLLING WHAT AUTOARCHIVING DOES

By default, AutoArchiving moves Outlook items from your Personal Folders file into an archive file. You can determine, separately for each folder, the location of the archive file. You also can choose whether AutoArchiving should permanently delete items or move them to an archive folder. If you choose to move items into an archive folder, those items are added to items already in that folder.

→ Although what follows applies to all items in a folder, you can separately mark individual items to be excluded from AutoArchiving. **See** "Excluding Individual Items from AutoArchiving," **p. 395.**

To control what AutoArchiving does:

1. Follow steps 1–3 in the procedure in the "Enabling and Disabling AutoArchiving" section previously in this chapter.

2. If you want to move eligible items to another folder, enter the full path name of the folder into the Move Old Items To box; alternatively, click Browse and navigate to the file in which you want to save the archived items.

3. If you want to delete, instead of move, eligible items, click the Permanently Delete Old Items option button.

Caution

If you click Permanently Delete Old Items, items are not moved to your Outlook Deleted Items folder; they are permanently deleted.

EXCLUDING INDIVIDUAL ITEMS FROM AUTOARCHIVING

By default, the AutoArchiving properties you define for a folder apply to all items in that folder. You can, however, mark specific items to be excluded from AutoArchiving. Suppose, for example, a specific Calendar item exists that you want to retain in your Calendar folder, even though that item is eligible for being AutoArchived.

To exclude a Calendar item from AutoArchiving:

1. Open the Calendar Information viewer and double-click the item you want to exclude from AutoArchiving to display the item in the form in which it was created.

2. In the form's menu bar, select File, Properties to display the item's Properties dialog box, such as that shown in Figure 19.5.

Figure 19.5
This dialog box shows the properties of the selected item.

3. Check the Do Not AutoArchive This Item box to exclude the item from AutoArchiving and from manual archiving.

Note

You can use this procedure to exclude any type of item from AutoArchiving. Although Outlook never AutoArchives Contact items, you can archive these items manually. If you check the Do Not AutoArchive This Item box for a Contact item, that item is excluded from manual archiving.

MANAGING AUTOARCHIVING

Now that you understand how Outlook AutoArchives items, you need to see what control you have over the entire AutoArchiving process. To control AutoArchiving, display any Information viewer, select Tools, Options, select the Other tab, and click AutoArchive to display the dialog box shown in Figure 19.6.

Figure 19.6
Use this dialog box to define how you want AutoArchive to work.

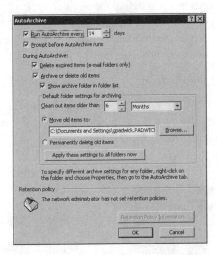

→ For information about making choices in the AutoArchive dialog box, **see** "AutoArchiving Options," **p. 578**.

Tip from

When you open Outlook, it checks to see whether it should AutoArchive items. If you leave your computer on with Outlook running all the time, Outlook never checks whether AutoArchive is due. If you do leave your computer on all the time, close down Outlook each evening and open it again each morning for Outlook to check whether AutoArchive is due.

Windows 98 and Windows Me have a Scheduled Task Wizard you can use to automatically start and stop Outlook (or any other application) on a regular basis. From the Windows taskbar, select Start, move the pointer onto Programs, move the pointer onto Accessories, move the pointer onto System Tools, and select Scheduled Tasks to display the Scheduled Tasks dialog box. Double-click Add Scheduled Task to display the first Scheduled Task Wizard; then follow the instructions in the wizard.

Caution

By default Outlook deletes, rather than archives, e-mail items. Organizations might want to make it corporate policy that everyone uses this default.

The reason is that e-mail tends to be a free-wheeling environment in which people say things that could be used to their disadvantage. Recent legal proceedings have involved subpoenas for e-mail records that have had a significantly adverse effect on a corporation's standing.

For this reason, it's usually advisable to keep only those e-mail records that you specifically need.

Note, though, that any contract you might have with a government agency may require you to keep records of all communications.

Whether you choose to have AutoArchiving move items to another folder or delete items, items are deleted from your Personal Folders file. As previously stated in this chapter, Outlook doesn't necessarily recover the space previously occupied by items that have been deleted.

→ You should regularly compact your Personal Folders file. **See** "Compacting Your Personal Folders File," **p. 390**.

ARCHIVING ITEMS MANUALLY

If you have not turned on AutoArchiving, or if you have turned on AutoArchiving and you want to archive items before AutoArchiving is due, you can use manual archiving. Although AutoArchiving never archives Contact items, you can manually archive these items.

To manually archive items:

1. With any Outlook Information viewer displayed, select File, Archive to display the dialog box shown in Figure 19.7.

PART
IV

CH
19

Figure 19.7
The Archive dialog box opens with the folder corresponding to the Information viewer you started from selected.

2. Leave the Archive This Folder and All Subfolders option button selected if that's what you want to do. Alternatively, select the Archive All Folders According to Their AutoArchive Settings option button.

3. If you selected Archive This Folder…, select the folder you want to archive.

4. If you selected Archive This Folder…, open the Archive Items Older Than drop-down calendar and select the age of the items you want to archive. You can, alternatively, enter a date in the box.

5. Also, if you selected Archive This Folder…, check Include Items with "Do Not AutoArchive" Checked if that's what you want to do. Otherwise, leave this box unchecked.

6. If you selected Archive This Folder…, enter the full path and file name of the file into which you want to archive items in the Archive File box. Alternatively, click Browse and navigate to the file.

7. Click OK to proceed with archiving.

If you select Archive All Folders According to Their AutoArchive Settings, Outlook does exactly the same as it does when AutoArchiving occurs; it AutoArchives now, rather than waiting for the appointed AutoArchive time. This option either moves items into the file that AutoArchiving uses, adding items to those already in the file or, if you've so specified, deletes items.

→ For a full description of AutoArchiving, **see** "Managing AutoArchiving," **p. 396**.

By selecting Archive This Folder and All Subfolders, you can control which folders are archived, the age of the items in those folders that are archived, and the file into which the archived items are moved. If you specify a file that doesn't already exist, Outlook creates that file. Each time you manually archive, Outlook adds items to the items already in the archive file.

MANAGING ARCHIVE FILES

The purpose of archiving is to avoid filling your hard drive with Outlook items. It makes no sense, therefore, to use a folder on your hard drive for your archive; you need to choose another medium.

When considering which medium to use for your archive, you also should consider how you will retrieve archived items when you need them. After all, you archive items because you might want to access them at some future time. You must be sure you can conveniently retrieve archived items.

CHOOSING AN ARCHIVE MEDIUM

Here are some suggestions for archive media:

■ If your computer is connected to a network, create an archive file on the server and let the network administrator worry about space on the server disks. Remember, though, that the network administrator might copy old files to tape. When you want old Outlook items, you might need to ask the administrator to mount old tapes to access your items.

- If you want to maintain your own archive files, use such media as Iomega Zip or Jaz disks (or other high-capacity disks, writable CD-ROMs, or the like).

Don't let your archive file get too large. If you want to access archived items, you might have to copy the archive file back onto your hard drive. Rather than have one enormous archive file, it's usually better to create new archive files periodically. Depending on your Outlook usage, you should create a new archive file every month, quarter, or year. To be on the safe side, don't let your archive files grow to a size that's larger than you can copy back to your hard drive.

Tip from 	Keeping all Outlook items related to a project in a separate archive makes retrieving those items convenient if you subsequently need to do so. When you've finished a project, move items relating to that project to individual folders, and then archive those folders.

RETRIEVING ARCHIVED ITEMS

You can use three ways to retrieve archived items:

- Import archived items into the file in which they were created.
- Select File, move the pointer onto Open, and select Personal Folders File (.pst) to display the Open Personal Folders dialog box. In that dialog box, navigate to the archive file, select it, and click OK.

Tip from 	If you intend to use this method, don't save your archive on a CD-ROM of the CD-R kind. That's because Outlook requires read/write access to a Personal Folders file.

- Create a new Personal Folders file and import the archived items into that.

IMPORTING ARCHIVED ITEMS INTO THE ORIGINAL FOLDER

You can choose to retrieve all items from an archive file or a folder within that file, or only items from a folder within that file.

To import all items:

1. With any Information viewer displayed, select File, Import and Export to display the first Import and Export Wizard window.
2. Select Import from Another Program or File and click Next.
3. Select Personal Folder File and click Next.

4. In the File to Import box, enter the full path and file name of the archive file, or click Browse and then navigate to the file.

5. Select one of the options in the Options section of the dialog box. To avoid the possibility of overwriting existing items, the best choice is usually Allow Duplicates to Be Created. Click Next.

6. In this wizard window, select either the entire file or a folder within the file. Outlook lets you select either the entire file or just one folder within it. By default, Outlook proposes to import subfolders. You can uncheck the Include Subfolders box.

7. If you want to import only items that satisfy certain criteria, you can click Filter and then define criteria for the files to be imported. Click Finish to import the files from your archive.

IMPORTING ARCHIVED ITEMS INTO A NEW FOLDER

Instead of importing archived items into their original folders, you might want to import them into a separate folder. To do so, you have to create a new Personal Folders file.

→ For information about creating a new Personal Folders file, **see** "Creating a Personal Folders File," **p. 311**.

Now you have a new Personal Folders file into which you can import items from your archive. Don't forget to use the Filter capability to selectively import only the items you need.

→ For information about importing items, **see** "Importing Items from a Personal Folders File," **p. 376**.

BACKING UP OUTLOOK

Backing up your Outlook configuration so that you can install it on another disk or another computer involves saving all your Outlook items and saving Outlook's settings.

The preceding sections of this chapter explain how you can save the Outlook items you've created or received. To completely back up Outlook, you also have to save all the files that contain all of Outlook's settings.

Many of Outlook's settings are saved within the Windows registry, so one thing you must do is to save the registry.

→ For detailed information about backing up the registry, **see** "Backing Up and Restoring the Registry," **p. 800**.

Microsoft hasn't published a complete list of all the files that contain information that Outlook uses. However, some of these files are

■ **Personal Folders**—These are files that have .pst as their file name extensions and contain Outlook items you've saved in a Personal Folders file.

■ **Offline Folders**—These are files that have .ost as their file name extensions and contain Outlook items you've saved for offline use. You have these files only if you're using Outlook as a client for Exchange.

- **Personal Address Book**—These are files that have .pab as their file name extensions and contain contact information you have in your Personal Address Book.

- **Outlook Configuration Files**—Some of the other files that Outlook uses have .dat (Outlook forms, menus, toolbars, and views); .fav (Outlook Bar shortcuts); .inf (default settings); .nick (Outlook nicknames); .rwz (rules); and .rtf, .txt, and .htm (AutoSignatures) as their file name extensions.

→ For more information about Outlook files, **see** "Outlook Files," **p. 746**.

MANAGING YOUR OUTLOOK STORE

The preceding sections of this chapter contain information about what Outlook 2002 inherited from previous Outlook versions. New in Outlook 2002 is the Tools menu command Mailbox Cleanup.

The Microsoft people responsible for Outlook don't always, in my opinion, pay sufficient attention to the terminology they use. If you're an experienced Exchange user, you're probably familiar with thinking of your mailbox as the store within Exchange Server that contains, not only your mail items but also all the items you create and access by way of Outlook— items in your Calendar, Contacts, Tasks, Notes, and Deleted Items folders. If you're a person who uses Outlook as a personal information manager and also to send and receive Internet e-mail, you might not immediately realize that Microsoft uses the term Mailbox to refer to your entire Personal Folders file.

With any Information viewer displayed, select Tools, Mailbox Cleanup to display the dialog box shown in Figure 19.8, in which you can manage your mailbox, whether that mailbox is an Exchange store or a Personal Folders file.

PART

IV

CH

19

Figure 19.8
This dialog box conveniently brings together some of the capabilities that are available elsewhere in Outlook.

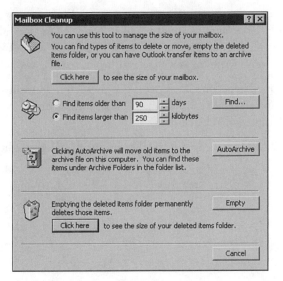

The Mailbox Cleanup dialog box provides shortcut ways to do what you can do elsewhere in Outlook.

In the top section of the Mailbox Cleanup dialog box, you can click Click Here to display the Folder Size dialog box that shows the total size of your mailbox together with the sizes of the individual folders it contains. This is the same information as that displayed when you display the properties of a mailbox and, in the General tab, select Folder Size.

You can use the second section of the Mailbox Cleanup dialog box. You can specify either a maximum item age or a maximum item size, and then click Find to display a list of items that satisfy that condition. This displays information also available by using Advanced Find.

By clicking AutoArchive in the third section of the Mailbox Cleanup dialog box, you initiate AutoArchiving according to the AutoArchive conditions for each folder. What happens is the same as when you select File, Archive, select Archive All Folders According to Their AutoArchive Settings, and then click OK.

In the fourth section of the Mailbox Cleanup dialog box, you can click Click Here to see the size of your Deleted Items folder. You also can click Empty to delete all items in your Deleted Items folder. If you use a Personal Folders file to save Outlook items, you can't subsequently recover items deleted from your Deleted Items folder. If you use an Exchange store, items deleted from your Deleted Items folder are, in fact, temporarily hidden rather than deleted.

→ For additional information about deleting items and recovering deleted items, **see** "Deleting Messages and Other Outlook Items," **p. 111**.

TROUBLESHOOTING

ARCHIVING MEDIA

You might want to use CD-R discs as archive media because those discs are inexpensive. If you do that, though, you can't directly display the archive data in Outlook. That's because Outlook needs to be able to write to, as well as read from, archive media.

If you do archive Outlook items on CD-R discs, you must copy an archive file from a CD-R drive to a hard drive and remember to remove the read-only attribute from the file. After you do that, Outlook can read archived items.

When archiving to CD-R discs, keep the archive files small enough so they can be copied to a hard drive.

CHAPTER **20**

USING CATEGORIES AND ENTRY TYPES

In this chapter

WHAT ARE CATEGORIES?

A *category* is a word or phrase you can assign to any Outlook item so that you can easily group like items together. For example, you can create a category for each project on which you work. After you've created a category for a project, you can assign that category to all messages, contacts, appointments, tasks, and notes that have anything to do with the project. Subsequently, you easily can find all Outlook items related to the project.

Categories are key to keeping your information organized and easy to find. If you discipline yourself to assign categories to all your Outlook items, you'll be amazed at how organized you are. On the other hand, if you ignore categories, you'll have the electronic equivalent of piles of paper on your desk.

Some of your items might relate to several projects. No problem! You can assign as many categories as you like to any Outlook item. Using categories to keep your information organized is much easier and more efficient than attempting to place each type of information in a separate folder.

Outlook considers every piece of information to be an item. Each mail message, calendar activity, task, and so on is an item. You can assign one or more categories to each item by

- Entering the category in a form's Categories box
- Selecting from a master list of categories, as explained in the next section.

Tip from

> You should normally select from a Master Category List to ensure that you use consistent category names. If the built-in Master Category List supplied with Outlook doesn't contain the categories you need, you can remove any of the categories you don't need and add more categories.

→ For information about adding categories to, and deleting categories from your Master Category List, **see** "Customizing Your Personal Master Category List," **p. 405**.

The action of assigning categories to items results in text being inserted into the Categories field for those items. That text is not linked in any way to the categories in the Master Category List. If, after assigning categories from the Master Category List to items, you make changes to the categories in the Master Category List, those changes have no effect on the categories you previously assigned to items.

USING A MASTER CATEGORY LIST

Outlook has a built-in Master Category List. You can see this list in two ways:

- Open an Information viewer that displays items in one of Outlook's folders (such as the Inbox Information viewer) and select Edit, Categories to display the Categories dialog box (the Categories menu item is dimmed and not available if no items are in the selected Information viewer). Click Master Category List to display the dialog box shown in Figure 20.1.

■ Open one of the forms in which you create a new item (such as the Appointment form), click Categories to display the Categories dialog box, and then click Master Category List to display the dialog box shown in Figure 20.1.

Tip from

The Message form doesn't have a Categories button. In this form, click Options in the Standard toolbar to display the Message Options dialog box that contains a Categories button at the bottom. Click that button to display the Categories dialog box.

Figure 20.1
Outlook's built-in Master Category List contains a variety of predefined categories listed in alphabetical order.

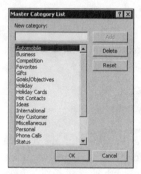

HOW OUTLOOK SAVES CATEGORY LISTS

When Outlook is initially installed, each user can use the built-in Master Category List. Each user can create a personal Master Category List by modifying the built-in Master Category List. When a user does that, Outlook automatically creates an entry in the Windows registry—a database that contains information about the settings for Windows itself, applications that run under Windows, and computer users. This entry contains a list of the categories in a user's personal Master Category List. Each user can have an independent personal Master Category List because a separate registry entry exists for each user.

→ Appendix D contains information about books you can consult for detailed information about the Windows registry. **See** "Outlook Resources," **p. 779**.

Each Outlook user can restore the categories in that user's personal Master Category List by clicking Master Category List in the Categories dialog box and then clicking Reset in the Master Category List dialog box. This deletes all the categories in that user's personal Master Category List and then copies the built-in categories into it.

CUSTOMIZING YOUR PERSONAL MASTER CATEGORY LIST

When you begin to use Outlook, the categories initially available to you are those in the built-in Master Category List. More than likely, those categories won't suit your personal needs. You can easily delete some of those categories and add categories that you will use so you have a personal Master Category List.

PLANNING YOUR MASTER CATEGORY LIST

It's worth taking the time to give some serious thought to planning categories, just as you would before setting up a file system for paper documents. You'll probably want to have categories for business and personal items. Categories you might need for business items include

- Separate categories for each project you're involved with
- Separate categories for each type of business contact
- Separate categories for each of your organization's departments

Categories you might need for personal items include

- Separate categories for each type of personal contact (family, friend, medical, finance, legal, and so on)
- Separate categories for each of your interests and hobbies
- Separate categories for each type of family activity

These are just suggestions to start you thinking. While planning your categories, remember that you can assign several categories to each item. When you assign several categories to one item, Outlook saves each item only once, but when you display items sorted by category you'll see those items listed several times, once under each category assigned to the items.

Tip from

Try to make your list of categories fairly complete. Although you can add categories at any time, doing so might make it necessary to change the categories you've already assigned to items—a time-consuming process.

DELETING AND ADDING CATEGORIES

After you have a reasonably complete list of the categories you want in your personal list, display the Categories dialog box. Then click Master Category List to display the dialog box previously shown in Figure 20.1.

To delete categories from your personal Master Category List, display the Master Category List, select one or more categories you want to delete, and click Delete.

To add categories to your personal Master Category List:

1. In the Master Category List dialog box, shown previously in Figure 20.1, place the insertion point in the New Category box.
2. Type a word or short phrase to name the new category. As soon as you type the first character, the Add button becomes enabled.
3. Click Add. The new category immediately appears in your Master Category List in its correct alphabetical position.

Note

If the word or phrase you type already exists in the category list, Outlook doesn't add a duplicate when you click Add.

4. Repeat the preceding three steps to add as many new categories as you need.

5. When you've finished deleting and adding categories, click OK to close the Master Category List dialog box. Now you can use your new Master Category List to assign categories to items.

ADDING CATEGORIES ON-THE-FLY

Sometimes you won't be able to find the category you want to assign to an item in your personal Master Category List. You can, of course, use the method described in the previous section to add a new category to your Master Category List, but there's an even faster way to add a new category.

To add a category on-the-fly, follow these steps:

1. Double-click an Outlook item to which you want to assign a category. Outlook displays that item in a form, which, except for Message items, contains a Categories button.

2. Click Categories to display the Categories dialog box shown in Figure 20.2. In the case of Message items, you have to click Options in the Standard toolbar to display the Message Options dialog box and then click Categories.

Figure 20.2
This is the dialog box you use to assign categories to items.

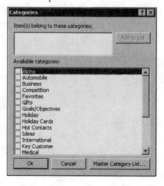

3. Enter the name of the new category in the Item(s) Belong to These Categories box, as shown in Figure 20.3. As soon as you enter the first character, the Add to List button becomes enabled.

4. Click Add to List to add the new category to your personal Master Category List. The new category immediately appears in the list of Available Categories. It's automatically checked to indicate it will be assigned to the Outlook item you're creating.

5. Click OK to assign the category to the Outlook item.

Figure 20.3
Enter a new category
directly into the
Categories dialog box.

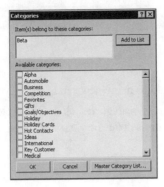

The next time you open your Master Category List (as described earlier in this chapter), you'll find the new category is listed.

HOW CATEGORIES ARE ASSIGNED TO ITEMS

Each Outlook item consists of many predefined fields, including a Category field. When you assign a category to an item, the name of the category is copied into the item's Category field. Like many Outlook fields, the Category field can contain as many as 256 characters, so you can assign many categories to an item. When two or more categories are assigned to an item, a comma separates one category from the next. You normally won't assign more than two or three categories to an item.

After you've assigned categories to an item, it doesn't matter whether those categories still exist in your personal Master Category List. When you delete a category from your personal Master Category List, Outlook doesn't delete that category from the items to which you previously assigned it. However, when you open an item to which a category that's not in your personal Master Category List is assigned and open the Categories dialog box, you'll see that the category is marked as "not in Master Category List."

I recommend that you assign categories to items by choosing categories from your Category List, not by typing category names into a form's Categories box. If you insist on doing so, however, nothing prevents you from just entering category names into the Categories box on a form.

The problem that arises when you enter, rather than select, categories is that you probably won't always enter category names consistently. If you use the singular form of a category name one time and the plural form another time, Outlook sees two category names. Even the slightest difference between the text in one category name and another results in separate categories. This will likely cause you problems when you sort items by category. Avoid these potential problems by always selecting categories from your personal Master Category List.

Category names are not case sensitive. Suppose your Master Category List contains a category name Alpha. If you create a new Outlook item and manually enter the category name `alpha` and subsequently view items sorted by category, Outlook includes that item in the Alpha section of the view.

Items in Outlook folders have categories assigned to them in yet another way when you receive Outlook items from other people. If someone creates an e-mail message, assigns categories to it, and sends it to you, the item in your Inbox folder has those categories assigned to it, whether those categories are in your personal Master Category List.

→ Within a single organization, people should be encouraged to use the same Master Category List. **See** "Sharing Your Personal Category List," **p. 412**.

Of course, you have no control over the categories assigned to Outlook items by people outside your own organization. When you receive those messages, however, you can change the assigned categories to those in your own Master Category List. By doing so, Outlook items you receive are organized in a way that is consistent with the organization of items you create.

DETERMINING AND CHANGING CATEGORIES

You can find out which categories are assigned to any item and, if necessary, change those categories. In this section, you'll find out how you can look at categories assigned to a message you've received. Remember, of course, that categories can be assigned to any Outlook item, including e-mail messages, calendar items, and so on.

CHANGING A MAIL ITEM'S CATEGORIES

You can use the method described here to determine and change categories in mail items in your Sent Items folder as well as items in your Inbox folder.

Categories you add to, or change in, items in your Sent Items folder affect only the items in that folder. Those category changes have no effect on the categories of the corresponding items in message recipients' Inbox folders.

To display, and possibly change, the categories assigned to an e-mail item you've received:

1. Open the Inbox Information viewer and select the message.

2. Select Edit, Categories to display the Categories dialog box shown previously in Figure 20.2. The Item(s) Belong to These Categories box contains the names of the categories already assigned to the item. Also, the individual categories assigned to the message are checked in the Available categories box. Any categories assigned to the message that don't exist in your personal Master Category List are marked in the list as "not in Master Category List."

Note

If the message is open in a message form, select View, Options to display the Message Options dialog box and then click Categories to display the Categories dialog box.

3. If you want to change the categories assigned to the message to be consistent with the way you assign categories, remove the check marks from categories you don't want to use and check those categories you do want to use. Click OK to close the Categories dialog box.

Tip from

To make assigning categories to messages easier and faster, you can add a Categories button to one of the toolbars. **See** "Adding Tools to a Toolbar," in Chapter 26 (**p. 512**) for detailed information about doing this.

ASSIGNING AND CHANGING CATEGORIES IN E-MAIL YOU CREATE

To assign or change categories in a message you're creating, click Options in the Message form's Message toolbar (if you're using Word as your editor) or Standard toolbar (if you're using Outlook's native editor) to display the Message Options form shown in Figure 20.4.

To assign or change the categories assigned to the message:

1. Click the Categories button in the Message Options dialog box to display the Categories dialog box.

2. Check the categories you want to assign to the message. If necessary, uncheck already-assigned categories you don't want to assign to the message.

3. Click OK to return to the Message Options form, in which the assigned categories are displayed in the Categories box.

4. Click Close to return to the Message form.

Note

As suggested in the preceding section, you can add a Categories button to one of the toolbars to simplify the process of assigning categories to e-mail items.

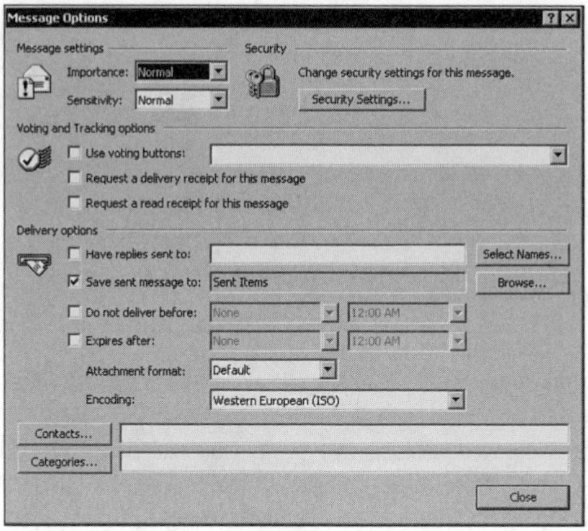

Figure 20.4
The Message Options form contains a Categories box near the bottom.

CREATING A MESSAGE WITH PREDEFINED CATEGORIES

Instead of individually assigning categories to every message you create, you can create any number of message templates—each with specific categories assigned—as explained in Chapter 16, "Using Outlook Templates."

→ For information about creating a message template, **see** "Creating an E-mail Template," **p. 330**.

After creating these templates, you can use any of them as the basis for messages. This method has several advantages:

- It saves you the time and trouble of separately assigning categories to each message.
- It avoids the possibility of forgetting to assign categories to messages.
- It helps you assign the same categories to every message of each type.

ASSIGNING AND CHANGING CATEGORIES FOR OTHER ITEMS

The forms you use to create Outlook items other than messages and notes all contain a Categories box similar to that in the Appointment form shown in Figure 20.5. Click Categories and then follow the four steps described in the preceding section to assign or change categories.

Figure 20.5
The Appointment
form contains a
Categories box at
the bottom-right.

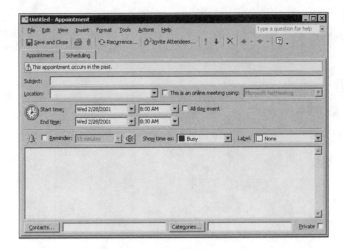

> **Note**
>
> You can create templates for all types of Outlook items, except notes, with each template containing predefined categories. Refer to the previous section in which this concept is explained in the context of e-mail messages.

SHARING YOUR PERSONAL CATEGORY LIST

The "How Outlook Saves Category Lists" section earlier in this chapter explained that Outlook keeps your personal Master Category List in the Windows registry.

If you want to share your Master Category List with someone else, you must export part of the registry from one computer into a file and then import that file into the registry of the other computer (as described later in this section). This also works well if you want to copy the personal Master Category List you use at home onto the computer you use in your office.

After customizing your personal Master Category List, close or minimize Outlook; then proceed as follows.

> **Caution**
>
> Before working with your registry, you should back up the registry file. That way, if you make mistakes, you can restore the registry to its original state with your backup copy.

→ For information about backing up the Windows registry, **see** "Working with the Windows Registry," **p. 799**.

Appendix F, "Working with the Windows Registry," contains a detailed description of the method you can use to export any registry key to a file and then import that file into another computer's registry. The registry key that contains your personal Master Category List is

`HKEY_CURRENT_USER\Software\Microsoft\Office\10.0\Outlook\Categories`

Note

In previous versions of Outlook, this key's value—the list of categories—is stored and displayed in text format and is easily read. In Outlook 2002, the list of categories is stored Unicode and is displayed in hexadecimal. This is only a minor inconvenience because you rarely, if ever, need to use the Registry Editor to read the list of categories.

If you administer a workgroup or LAN, consider using this procedure to copy a standard Master Category List to everyone's computers.

UNDERSTANDING ENTRY TYPES

When you manually create entries in Outlook's Journal, you can assign categories to each Journal item. In addition, you must assign an entry type to each item.

→ For information about creating Journal items, **see** "Creating Journal Items Manually," **p. 283**.

Outlook contains a built-in list of entry types. These are

Conversation	Microsoft Excel
Document	Microsoft PowerPoint
E-mail message	Microsoft Word
Fax	Note
Letter	Phone call
Meeting	Remote session
Meeting cancellation	Task
Meeting request	Task request
Meeting response	Task response
Microsoft Access	

As you see, all the entry types in this built-in list relate to Outlook items and Office applications. What if you want to record in your journal items such as adding hardware or software to your computer, buying something, having your car serviced, and so on? None of the entry types is suitable for these activities. Outlook solves this problem by enabling you to create new entry types.

CREATING NEW ENTRY TYPES

Whereas you can easily tailor Outlook's categories, as explained in the first part of this chapter, there's no simple way to modify Outlook's list of entry types. Similar to categories,

Outlook's list of entry types is in the Windows registry. To modify that list, you must resort to editing the registry.

> **Caution**
>
> As always, be aware that information in the registry controls how Windows and the applications under Windows run. Any incorrect change you make to the registry could affect Windows or an application, or even make your computer unusable. Always make a backup copy of the registry before making any changes to it. See Appendix F for detailed information about this subject.

Suppose you want to add a new entry type, such as Computer, to the list.

To add an entry type:

1. Select Start, Run on the Windows taskbar to display the Run dialog box.

2. In the Open box, enter **Regedit** and click OK to start the Registry Editor.

3. Navigate to the registry key

   `HKEY_CURRENT_USER\Software\Microsoft\Shared Tools\Outlook\Journaling`

   You can expand this key to display subkeys representing each of the default entry types.

4. Right-click the Journaling key to display its context menu.

5. Move the pointer onto New in the context menu, and click Key. New Key #1 appears at the bottom of the Registry Editor's Key pane.

6. Replace New Key #1 with the name of the new entry type, such as Computer, and press Enter.

7. Right-click the new key to display its context menu, move the pointer onto New, and select String Value. New Value #1 appears in the registry's Value pane.

8. Replace New Value #1 with the word `Description` and press Enter. Double-click the word `Description` to display the Edit String dialog box, in which the Value Name box contains `Description`.

9. In the Value Data box, enter the name of the new entry type, such as Computer, and click OK. The registry's Value pane now contains a value named `Description` with its data shown as `Computer`.

10. Select Registry, Exit to close the Registry Editor.

You can add as many new item types as you like in this manner.

After you've followed these steps, the next time you create a new Journal item and open the drop-down Entry Type list, you'll find the new entry types in the list.

→ For information about creating Journal items, **see** "Creating Journal Items Manually," **p. 283**.

→ For more information about working with the registry, **see** "Working with the Windows Registry," **p. 799**.

SELECTING AN ENTRY TYPE

The next time you create a new Journal item, you can assign one of the built-in entry types or an entry type you've created to that item.

To create a journal item having a custom entry type:

1. Start Outlook and select Journal in the Outlook Bar.
2. Click New in the Standard toolbar to display the Journal Entry form.
3. Open the drop-down Entry Type list that contains the standard Outlook entry types together with the custom entry types you created all arranged in alphabetical order.
4. Select an entry type from the drop-down list.

TROUBLESHOOTING

MASTER CATEGORY LIST

Your personal Master Category List is saved in keys in the Windows registry, as explained previously in this chapter. You therefore can run into trouble with categories if your registry becomes corrupted, you accidentally remove keys, or you enter data in the wrong format.

In anticipation that this might happen, you should regularly make a backup copy of your registry using the methods described in Appendix F. Then you can restore your registry if problems occur.

→ For information about backing up the registry, **see** "Backing Up and Restoring the Registry," **p. 800**.

Note

The advice about making regular backups of the registry doesn't apply only to solving possible problems with Outlook's categories. It's good advice that applies to using Windows and all applications that run under Windows.

Using Outlook As a Client for Exchange Server and Other Information Systems

CHAPTER 21

EXCHANGE SERVER OVERVIEW

In this chapter

OUTLOOK AS A CLIENT FOR EXCHANGE

Outlook is Microsoft's premier client for Exchange Server. Although Outlook can be used as a client for other e-mail servers, it is as an Exchange client that Outlook offers its full capabilities.

> **Note**
>
> You don't have to use Outlook to access e-mail and other information in Exchange. You can use various applications available from Microsoft and other companies.

The next four chapters provide detailed information about using Outlook as a client for Exchange. This chapter briefly explains what Exchange is and what it can do. This chapter doesn't provide detailed information about administering Exchange. Refer to a book such as *Special Edition Using Microsoft Exchange Server 2000*, published by Que, for that information.

If you're already familiar with Exchange Server, you should probably skip this chapter.

WHAT IS EXCHANGE?

Before going any further, I should point out that Microsoft has used the name Exchange for two completely different products. Windows 95 contained an application known as Exchange that was a mail client intended for use with Microsoft Mail, Internet e-mail, and a few other e-mail systems. It was, in fact, the precursor of Outlook, which became available in Office 97. This Exchange is now known as Windows Messaging.

The other Exchange, the one that's the subject of this chapter, is a mail server that first became available in 1996.

> **Note**
>
> References to Exchange Server in the remainder of this chapter apply specifically to version 2000 and, for the most part, to version 5.5. They don't necessarily apply to earlier versions of Exchange Server.

Exchange is the heart of corporate messaging and collaboration systems. It includes facilities for

- Transmitting e-mail messages between computer users
- Connecting to other e-mail systems, including the Internet, Lotus Notes, Lotus cc:Mail, Microsoft Mail, and IBM PROFS
- Automatically responding to messages according to user-defined rules
- Recalling and replacing messages you've previously sent but haven't been read by recipients

- Providing a way for people to vote on issues and for the results of those votes to be tallied
- Allowing individual users to assign delegates
- Allowing users to work offline and from time to time to synchronize their information with that maintained on an Exchange server
- Acting as an information store that can be used to publish information
- Acting as an electronic bulletin board, either unmoderated or moderated
- Organizing Web pages for a group to share
- Scheduling group activities, such as meetings
- Hosting online meetings
- Creating and distributing electronic forms

The preceding list is intended to give you an idea of the scope of Exchange's capabilities, and it is by no means comprehensive.

Exchange can be used as a messaging and collaboration system by groups of almost any size. It's available as part of Microsoft's Small Business Server package with licenses for only five people. At the other end of the spectrum, Exchange can be used by international enterprises with hundreds of thousands of employees.

Exchange 2000, the latest version of Exchange, runs under Windows 2000 Server and is, in many ways, integrated with Windows 2000 Server. For example, Exchange can be installed in such a way that each user can have a single password to log on to the server network and on to Exchange. Exchange can be set up to share user account information with Windows 2000, thus simplifying an administrator's tasks.

Note

You must have the Windows 2000 Service Pack 1 or later installed before you can install Exchange Server 2000.

STORING INFORMATION

Exchange saves information in what's known as *information stores*, of which there are three: Public, Private, and Directory. Prior to Exchange version 5.5, each of these stores had a maximum capacity of 16GB. Although this is more than sufficient for small organizations, it is not adequate for large enterprises. In versions 5.5 and 2000, the maximum capacity of each store has been increased to 16,000GB.

Each user keeps e-mail and other personal information in the Private store, and an Exchange administrator can limit the amount of space available to each user. Shared information is kept in the Public store.

PART

V

CH

21

Note

> If you use Outlook as a client for Exchange, you can choose whether you want to save e-mail messages and other information in the Exchange store or in a Personal Folders file on your computer's hard drive.

When a person sends a message to a number of people, Exchange saves that message only once, a technique known as *single-instance message storage*. The message remains in the store until the last recipient deletes it.

SENDING AND RECEIVING E-MAIL

You can send and receive e-mail within the Exchange environment. You can also use Exchange to connect to other e-mail environments.

WORKING IN THE EXCHANGE ENVIRONMENT

With Outlook as your mail client, you can create messages and click Send. As long as your computer is connected to Exchange Server, your messages are immediately sent to the Exchange information store and, from there, to the recipients' inboxes. Similarly, messages sent to you arrive from the Exchange information store in your Inbox.

SENDING AND RECEIVING INTERNET MESSAGES

You can use Exchange to send and receive e-mail messages and other information by way of the Internet or an intranet. Exchange supports many Internet protocols, including these:

- **Simple Mail Transfer Protocol (SMTP)**—Used to send e-mail messages to an Internet or intranet e-mail server
- **Post Office Protocol 3 (POP3)**—The most common protocol used to retrieve messages from an Internet or intranet e-mail server
- **Internet Mail Access Protocol 4 (IMAP4)**—Another protocol used to retrieve messages from an Internet or intranet e-mail server
- **Network News Transfer Protocol (NNTP)**—Used to send and receive newsgroup messages
- **Lightweight Directory Access Protocol (LDAP)**—Used to read and write information to Internet or intranet directories
- **Hypertext Transport Protocol (HTTP)**—Used for sending hypertext documents on the Internet or an intranet
- **Hypertext Markup Language (HTML)**—A language used to create hypertext documents
- **Simple Security Layer (SSL)**—Used to protect data traveling on the Internet
- **Secure Multipurpose Internet Mail Extensions (S/MIME)**—Used to secure attachments to e-mail messages

The preceding list contains only the major Internet protocols Exchange supports.

Because Exchange supports all the major Internet protocols, you can use Outlook and any other Internet e-mail client to send and receive messages from your Exchange information store.

COMMUNICATING WITH OTHER MESSAGING SYSTEMS

You can interchange e-mail messages with users who use other messaging systems.

Quite often, organizations that have been using earlier messaging systems, such as cc:Mail, want to upgrade to Exchange but can only do so in phases. That's not a significant problem because Exchange includes a cc:Mail connector that makes it possible to send messages to, and receive messages from, cc:Mail users.

IBM's Lotus Notes and Microsoft Exchange are today's major contenders for enterprise e-mail and collaboration systems. It doesn't have to be one or the other, though. With the recent acquisition of Linkage Software, Microsoft has been able to enhance and integrate Linkage technology into Exchange to provide reliable connectivity with Lotus Notes.

Note

You could use Outlook 2000 as a client for Lotus Notes by installing the MAPI Service Provider (a .dll file) provided by Lotus. After doing this, you could send and receive Lotus Notes e-mail but not access other Notes databases. For a description of this capability, see
`http://www.slipstick.com/addins/services/lotusnotes.htm`.

For additional information about using Outlook as a client for Lotus Notes, see `http://www.lotus.com/home.nsf/welcome/inotes` and, in that page, click iNotes Access for Microsoft Outlook.

I assume Lotus will provide updated support for Outlook 2002, but information about that wasn't available at the time this book was written.

I offer my thanks to David Wade for providing information about using Outlook as a client for Lotus Notes.

Many large organizations have invested substantial resources into creating messaging systems based on IBM's PROFS OfficeVision and SNADS messaging systems running on mainframe computers and minicomputers. Exchange includes Linkage technology that can link Exchange to these systems.

AUTOMATING MESSAGING

You can create rules to automate how Exchange deals with e-mail. For example, you can use a rule, known as the Out of Office Assistant, to deal with e-mail that arrives while you're not logged on to Exchange. You can use this rule to send an automatic response to the sender saying that you're out of the office until a certain date and will respond to the message when you return. Or, you can use the rule to automatically route the message to someone else.

You can use Exchange rules in many other ways. For example, you could create a rule that redirects a message in which a certain word or phrase is mentioned to another person.

Delegating Your Work

You can give one or more people delegate access to any of your Outlook folders. These people must, of course, have Exchange accounts. For each delegate, you can provide access to one or more of your Outlook folders. You can assign three levels of access for each person to each folder:

- **Reviewer Access**—This allows the delegate only to read items in a folder.
- **Author Access**—This allows the delegate to read items and create new items in a folder.
- **Editor Access**—In addition to being able to read items and create new items, this allows the delegate to modify existing items.

Although you grant a delegate access to read items in your folders, by default, Outlook doesn't allow delegates to read items you've marked as private. However, you have the option of granting specific delegates permission to see your private items.

→ To learn more about granting access to your private Outlook items, **see** "Giving Permission to Access Your Folders," **p. 470**.

If you have delegate access to someone else's Exchange account, you can send e-mail messages on behalf of that person. Recipients see messages sent in this way with the actual sender's name and the name of the person on behalf of whom the message was sent.

Sharing Your Folders

You can share the Outlook folders you keep in the Exchange store with specific other people, giving each person one or more of these following permissions:

- Read items
- Create items
- Delete items
- Create subfolders

A person with whom you have shared your folders can open those folders to see your Outlook items and, subject to the permissions you give, create and delete items.

USING PUBLIC FOLDERS

Sharing folders, as described in the preceding section, is appropriate when you want to share information with one other person, or perhaps a small group. When you want to share information with many people, it's better to use Exchange's public folders.

Any Outlook user to whom the Exchange administrator has granted the appropriate permission can create a public folder that resides within the Exchange store. The person who creates the folder owns it and can allow specific people or groups to access it. As with shared folders, the public folder owner decides which permissions each person has.

Public folders are typically used to make information available to many people. For example, an organization might place its employee policy manual in a public folder, something that has advantages over printing and distributing paper copies: It's a lot less expensive and much easier to update. This is an example of a public folder to which everyone has read access, but only one person has permission to edit.

You can use public folders as an electronic bulletin board people can use to exchange ideas. Used in this way, a public folder is similar to an Internet newsgroup. The bulletin board can be unmoderated, in which case anyone can post whatever they like on it. Alternatively, it can be moderated, in which case people submit their contributions to a moderator, who decides whether to publish each contribution in the public folder.

WORKING REMOTELY

Using Exchange as an e-mail system is particularly useful for people who travel. You can create an offline Outlook folder on your laptop's hard disk. After doing so, you can copy information from your folders in the Exchange store into the offline folder so you can work with Outlook while you're not connected to Exchange.

While you're away from the office, you can connect to Exchange using a dial-up connection to receive information from, and send information to, Exchange. While connected, you can synchronize the information on your remote computer with that in your Exchange store so your folders in both locations have the latest information. Similarly, when you return to your office, you can again synchronize so you can continue to work with the latest information while your computer is connected to Exchange.

→ For more information on synchronizing folders, **see** "Synchronizing Folders," **p. 478**.

PLANNING MEETINGS

As explained in Chapter 10, "Managing Calendars," with Exchange as your server, you can plan meetings at times when other people and the resources you need are available.

→ To learn more about scheduling meetings and resources using Outlook, **see** "Arranging Meetings," **p. 240**.

PART

V

CH

21

SYNCHRONIZING EXCHANGE FOLDERS

The subject of synchronizing folders was mentioned in the "Working Remotely" section of this chapter. That was in the context of updating your offline folders and your folders in the Exchange store so that both sets of folders contained the latest (and the same) information. Exchange also uses synchronization when an organization has two or more separate Exchange installations.

Many large enterprises have business units in various locations. In these circumstances, it's common for each business unit to have its own Exchange server. The various Exchange installations are interconnected and, at times chosen by the administrators, synchronize the information in their stores.

GETTING MORE INFORMATION ABOUT EXCHANGE SERVER

This chapter gives you a brief overview of what you can do with Exchange. You can find more information in two books: *Introducing Exchange* and *Exchange in Business*, both published by Microsoft Press.

Refer to *Special Edition Using Microsoft Exchange Server 2000*, published by Que, for detailed information about administering Exchange Server.

CHAPTER 22

USING EXCHANGE SERVER FOR E-MAIL

In this chapter

USING OUTLOOK AS A CLIENT FOR EXCHANGE

This chapter is about sending and receiving e-mail messages between people who use Outlook as clients for an Exchange server. The subjects covered here are relevant only to people who have an e-mail account on an Exchange server.

Note

This chapter describes a typical Exchange Server environment. The server administrator can modify the way Exchange works in many ways, so you might find some of what's described in this chapter isn't exactly what you see on your computer.

SETTING UP OUTLOOK AS AN EXCHANGE CLIENT

To use Outlook as an Exchange client, you must have a connection to a server on which Exchange Server is installed, have a mailbox on that Exchange Server, and have a Microsoft Exchange Server account set up in Outlook. The subjects of establishing a connection to a server and setting up a mailbox on that server are beyond the scope of this book. Consult the server administrator if you need help with these matters.

VERIFYING THE EXISTENCE OF AN EXCHANGE SERVER E-MAIL ACCOUNT

To check whether you have a Microsoft Exchange Server account in Outlook, with any Information viewer displayed, select Tools, E-mail Accounts to display the E-mail Accounts dialog box. Click View or Change Existing E-mail Accounts, and then click Next to display a dialog box similar to the one shown in Figure 22.1.

Figure 22.1
The list of e-mail accounts should include Microsoft Exchange Server. That account does not necessarily have to be marked as the default as it is here.

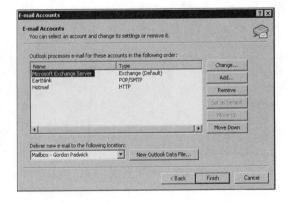

If Microsoft Exchange Server isn't listed as one of your e-mail accounts, you'll have to create that account.

→ For basic information about creating a Microsoft Exchange Server account in Outlook, **see** "Creating a Microsoft Exchange Server Account," **p. 48**.

Tip from

If you need to set up mailboxes in Exchange Server, refer to such books as *Special Edition Using Microsoft Exchange Server 5.5* or *Special Edition Using Microsoft Exchange Server 2000*, both published by Que.

REFINING AN EXCHANGE SERVER E-MAIL ACCOUNT IN OUTLOOK

Chapter 3, "Managing E-mail Accounts," explains how you can set up a basic Microsoft Exchange Server e-mail account in Outlook so you have access to a mailbox that an administrator has created for you within Exchange Server. That might be all you have to do, but you might want to, or need to, refine your basic account.

To refine your account, with any Information viewer displayed, select Tool, E-mail Accounts to display the dialog box shown in Figure 22.2.

Figure 22.2
This dialog box opens with View or Change Existing E-mail Accounts selected.

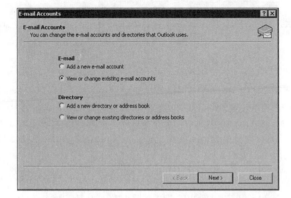

Click Next to display the dialog box previously shown in Figure 22.1.

Select Microsoft Exchange Server, and then click Change to display a dialog box similar to the one shown in Figure 22.3.

Figure 22.3
Make sure your Exchange Server and Exchange mailbox are correctly named.

Click More Settings to display the dialog box shown in Figure 22.4.

Figure 22.4
This dialog box opens with the General tab selected.

GENERAL SETTINGS

In many cases, the settings in the General tab are satisfactory. The Exchange Account box near the top contains the name by which you can subsequently refer to the Exchange Server—by default this is Microsoft Exchange Server. You can replace the default words with anything else. The text you enter is the name displayed in the E-mail Accounts dialog box previously shown in Figure 22.1.

By default, Automatically Detect Connection State is selected. With this setting, Outlook automatically detects whether your computer is connected to the Exchange server so you can work online. If your computer is not connected to the Exchange Server, you can work offline.

If you prefer, select Manually Control Connection State. After doing that, each time you start Outlook you're given the choice of working online or offline (online is available only if your computer is connected to the Exchange server). You can also select Connect with the Network, or you can select Work Offline and Use Dial-up Networking.

By default, Outlook attempts to make a connection to the Exchange server for 30 seconds. If no connection is available after that time, a message states that a connection is not available. You can change the default period to another number of seconds.

ADVANCED SETTINGS

Select the Advanced tab to work with advanced settings, as shown in Figure 22.5.

When you connect to Exchange Server, you normally have access only to your own mailbox. If the owners of other mailboxes have given you the appropriate permissions, you can gain access to those other mailboxes. To do so, click Add to display the Add Mailbox dialog box, enter a mailbox name there, and click OK. The Mailboxes list then includes the name you entered.

Figure 22.5
The settings in this tab enable you to access other people's mail-boxes and use enhanced security.

Check the boxes in the Encrypt Information section of the dialog box if you want to employ encryption.

Exchange Server protects your mailbox with a password. The Logon Network Security section near the bottom of the tab provides a choice of how password security works. Open the drop-down list and select among

- **Password Authentication**—Exchange Server uses the same password as the one you use to log on to the server computer.

- **Distributed Password Authentication**—Select this if the server under which Exchange Server runs employs Microsoft Membership Directory Services.

- **None**—If you select this, you'll be asked for your password whenever you attempt to make a connection to Exchange Server.

Unless your server administrator tells you otherwise, select Password Authentication.

Ignore the Offline Folder File Settings button at the bottom of the tab unless you plan to work with offline folders.

→ For information about working with offline folders, **see** "Working with Exchange Server Remotely," **p. 473**.

CONNECTION SETTINGS

Select the Connection tab, shown in Figure 22.6, to work with connection settings.

By default, Outlook expects you to connect to the Exchange server by way of a LAN. You can select

- Connect Using My Local Area Network (LAN), which is the default
- Connect Using My Phone Line
- Connect Using Internet Explorer's or a Third-Party Dialer

Figure 22.6
Use this tab to select your method of connection to the server.

If you select Connect Using My Phone Line, the Modem section in the lower part of the tab becomes available. You can use that to select a dial-up connection, change the properties of a dial-up connection, and add a dial-up connection.

REMOTE MAIL SETTINGS

To work with remote mail settings, select the Remote Mail tab, shown in Figure 22.7.

Figure 22.7
Use remote mail when your computer doesn't have a local connection to the Exchange server.

→ For information about remote connections to an Exchange server, **see** "Working with Exchange Server Remotely," **p. 473**.

SELECTING A STORAGE LOCATION

If you use Outlook as a client for Exchange Server, you can select one of three places to store your e-mail and other Outlook items:

- A Personal Folders file on your local hard drive
- The Exchange Server information store
- An Offline Folders file on your local hard drive

This chapter assumes you're using a computer that's permanently connected to Exchange Server, so the chapter considers only the first two places where you can save Outlook items.

→ If you need to work with offline folders, **see** "Understanding Offline Folders," **p. 474**.

It's usually best to keep your Outlook items in the Exchange Server information store to take advantage of Exchange Server's capabilities. If you and other Outlook users do that, you easily can share such information as Calendar and Contact items and replicate your offline folders with the information store. The downside of doing this is that each time you work with Outlook items, you create traffic on the LAN. If you have a reliable, high-performance LAN, you should keep your Outlook items in the Exchange Server information store. Only if you experience LAN problems should you consider saving Outlook items locally.

> **Note**
>
> The decision about where you save Outlook items is usually made by the Exchange administrator.

SPECIFYING WHERE OUTLOOK SAVES ITEMS

The Deliver New Mail to the Following Locations box at the bottom of the E-mail Accounts dialog box previously shown in Figure 22.1 indicates where Outlook saves items. If that box contains the word Mailbox followed by the name of a mailbox owner, as it does in Figure 22.1, Outlook currently saves items in an Exchange store. If that box contains the phrase Personal Folders, Outlook currently saves items in a Personal Folders file.

CHANGING WHERE OUTLOOK ITEMS ARE STORED

Use these steps to change where Outlook saves items. The following example assumes Outlook currently saves items in the Exchange store and you want to change to saving items in a Personal Folders file. The example also assumes you have previously created a Personal Folders file.

→ For information about creating a Personal Folders file, **see** "Creating a Personal Folders File," **p. 311**.

To change where Outlook saves items:

1. With any Outlook Information viewer displayed, select Tools, E-mail Accounts to display the E-mail Accounts dialog box. Click View or Change Existing E-mail Accounts, and then click Next to display the dialog box previously shown in Figure 22.1. The Deliver New Mail to the Following Location box shows where Outlook currently saves items.

> **Note**
>
> Although the name of the box refers specifically to mail, the named location is where Outlook saves all items.

2. Open the drop-down Deliver New E-mail to the Following Location list to display a list of available locations.

3. Select the location in which you want to save Outlook items. Select a location that has a name starting with "Mailbox" to save Outlook items in the Exchange store; select the name of a Personal Folders file to save Outlook items on your hard drive.

4. Click Finish to close the dialog box. A message reminds you that the new delivery location doesn't take effect until you close and subsequently restart Outlook.

When you restart Outlook, a message reminds you that The location messages are delivered to has been changed.... The message also states that Outlook must re-create the standard shortcuts on the Outlook Bar, but you'll have to re-create any shortcuts you previously created. Click Yes to close the message box; then wait a few seconds while Outlook re-creates the Outlook Bar. Select View, Folder List to see a folder list similar to the one in Figure 22.8.

Figure 22.8
The image of a house superimposed over the icon at the left of a folder name indicates the folder in which Outlook currently saves items.

The remainder of this chapter assumes that you're using the Exchange store to save Outlook items.

COPYING ITEMS TO THE MAILBOX FOLDER

If you've previously been using a Personal Folders file to save Outlook items, you might want to copy those items to the Exchange store. To do this, display the items to be copied in a table-type view. Mail items in your Inbox and Sent Items folder and Task items in your Tasks folder are normally displayed in Table views, so you usually don't have to change the view of these items. You might, however, need to change the views used for Calendar and Contact items.

→ For information about selecting views, **see** "Creating Views and Print Styles," **p. 651**.

To copy Outlook items from a Personal Folders file to an Exchange store:

1. With any table-type Outlook Information viewer displayed, select View, Folder List.

2. If necessary, expand your Personal Folders file to display the names of the folders it contains. Also, if necessary, expand your Exchange store to display the folders it contains.

3. In the folder list, select the folder in your Personal Folders file from which you want to copy items.

4. Select one or more items. If you want to select all items in the folder, select Edit, Select All.

5. Hold down Ctrl while you drag the selected item or items onto the folder in your Mailbox into which you want to copy items. If you want to move items from one folder to the other instead of copying them, hold down Shift while you drag.

SENDING AND RECEIVING E-MAIL

Sending and receiving e-mail messages using Exchange Server as the mail server is almost the same as sending and receiving Internet e-mail messages. One difference is that, because your computer is permanently connected to the server, you don't have to do anything to send messages from your Outbox to the server, nor do you have to do anything to receive messages waiting for you on the server. Outlook automatically sends messages you create to the server and saves copies of them in your Sent Items folder. Outlook also automatically receives messages waiting for you on the server and places them in your Inbox folder.

→ For information about sending Internet e-mail messages, **see** "Sending a Message," **p. 91**.

→ For information about receiving Internet e-mail messages, **see** "Receiving E-mail," **p. 96**.

Note

The preceding paragraph describes what happens if, in the Mail Setup tab of the Options dialog box, the Send Immediately When Connected check box is checked. If that box isn't checked, Outlook places messages you send in the Outbox folder. Those messages stay in the Outbox folder until you select Tools, move the pointer onto Send/Receive, and select Microsoft Exchange Server. At that time, Outlook sends messages to the server and moves those messages from the Outbox folder to the Sent Items folder.

In addition to sending messages on your own behalf, you can send messages on behalf of another person.

When you create messages to be sent to other people who have accounts on an Exchange server, you normally should use the Microsoft Outlook Rich Text mail format because that's the native format used by Exchange. By using this format, you can be sure recipients will see your messages exactly as you created them. However, for messages that go to people outside your Exchange environment who might not be using message clients that accept Rich Text Format, you should use Plain Text.

Note

You might, under some circumstances, run into formatting problems if you send messages using the HTML transmission format. Refer to the Microsoft Knowledge Base article Q195595, "HTML Formatting Not Retained on Exchange 5.5," for detailed information about this.

The remainder of this chapter describes messaging capabilities provided by Exchange Server that are in addition to the basic processes of sending and receiving messages.

CHANGING DELIVERY OPTIONS FOR MESSAGES

You can set several delivery options for messages you send by way of Exchange Server.

REDIRECTING REPLIES

Normally, when you send messages and recipients reply to them, the replies are automatically sent to you. You can, however, request that replies to specific messages be automatically sent to someone else.

To redirect replies:

1. At any time while you're creating a message in the Message form, click Options in the form's Message toolbar (if you're using Word as your editor) or Standard toolbar (if you're using the native editor) to display the Message Options dialog box, shown in Figure 22.9.

Figure 22.9
Use this dialog box to change the delivery options for a message.

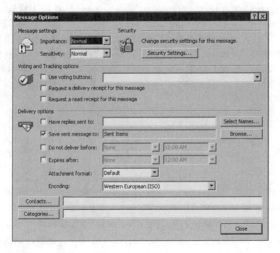

2. In the Delivery Options section of the dialog box, check Have Replies Sent To. When you do so, your own name appears in the adjacent text box. The name is underlined to indicate the name is an alias for an e-mail address.

3. If you know the e-mail address of the person to whom you want replies to be sent, you can replace your own name with the e-mail address of the person to whom you want replies to be sent. Otherwise, click Select Names to display the Have Replies Sent To dialog box, in which you can display names in any of your Address Books and select the name of the person to whom you want replies sent.

Note

This dialog box might be a little confusing. The box labeled Message Recipients is actually where the name of the person who should receive replies to your message appears, not a list of the people who receive your messages.

4. The Have Replies Sent To dialog box opens with your name already in the Message Recipients list. Delete your name from that list unless you want replies sent to you in addition to another person.

5. In the list of names on the left, select the name of the person to whom you want replies to be directed. Then, click Reply To to copy that name into the Message Recipients list.

6. Click OK to return to the Message Options dialog box that now shows the name of the person you selected in the Have Replies Sent To box.

The name you select in this manner applies only to the message you're currently creating.

Note

If the person who receives messages has created a rule that generates automatic replies to messages, that automatic reply is sent to you, not to the person you designate to receive replies.

→ For information about creating rules, **see** "Creating and Using Rules," **p. 583**.

When recipients receive a message in which replies have been redirected, they won't see anything unusual about the message. The message header contains the name of the sender as usual. However, when recipients reply to those messages, the replies will be addressed to the person designated in the Have Replies Sent To box in the original messages.

SCHEDULING A MESSAGE FOR LATER DELIVERY

In the Exchange messaging environment, you can create a message and mark it not to be delivered until a certain time and date.

To schedule a message for later delivery:

1. At any time while you're creating a message in the Message form, click Options in the form's toolbar to display the Message Options dialog box, shown previously in Figure 22.9.

2. In the Delivery Options section of the dialog box, check Do Not Deliver Before. Outlook proposes today's date and the time of the end of your workday (5 p.m., by default).

3. You can edit the proposed date and time. Alternatively, click the button at the right end of the date box to display a calendar in which you can select a date. You can also click the button at the right end of the time box and then select a time.

> **Note**
>
> Outlook doesn't let you change the delivery times in the list. If you want to set a delivery time that's not in the list, you must enter that time in the time box.

Outlook saves messages scheduled for later delivery in the Outbox folder. At the scheduled time, those messages become available to be sent but stay in the Outbox folder until the next time Outlook sends messages. You can send the delayed messages to the server manually or automatically. To send messages available to be sent:

- **Manually**—Select Tools, move the pointer onto Send/Receive, and select Microsoft Exchange Server. Outlook sends messages that are available to be sent to the server.

- **Automatically**—In the Mail Setup tab of the Options dialog box, click Send/Receive to display the Send/Receive Groups dialog box. In that dialog box, check the Schedule an Automatic Send/Receive Every box and specify the time between automatic sends and receives. At each scheduled time, Outlook examines messages in the Outbox and sends those messages that are available to be sent to the server.

In either case, Outlook moves the messages that have been sent from the Outbox folder to the Sent Items folder.

SETTING AN EXPIRATION DATE AND TIME

You can set an expiration date and time for a message. After you do so, Exchange automatically deletes the message if the recipient hasn't opened it by the date and time you specify. If recipients open messages before the expiration date and time, those messages are handled in the same manner as messages that don't have an expiration date and time. The procedure for setting an expiration time and date is the same as that described in the preceding section. Instead of checking the Do Not Deliver Before box, however, check the Expires After box.

You can see the headers of messages you've sent that have an expiration date in your Sent Items Information viewer. You also can double-click a message header to display it in a Message form. The InfoBar near the top of the form contains the expiration information.

REQUESTING RECEIPTS

You can request two types of receipts for messages you send within an Exchange Server environment:

- **Delivery Receipts**—Receipts generated when messages you send arrive on recipients' servers

- **Read Receipts**—Receipts generated when recipients open messages you send

Note

The ability to generate delivery and read receipts depends on the type of mail servers and mail clients recipients use. The information in this section is based on the assumption that you and your message recipients use Exchange as a server and Outlook as a client. If you send messages by way of the Internet, only read receipts are generated.

You can set Outlook's options so that one or both types of receipts are automatically requested for all messages you send. By default, Outlook doesn't request either type of receipt. The options you set apply to all types of messages you send, including meeting requests and requests to accept tasks.

→ For information about setting Outlook's options to request receipts, **see** "Setting Tracking Options," **p. 537**.

To control requesting delivery and read receipts for individual messages, click Options in the Message form's Message toolbar (if you're using Word as your editor) or in the Standard toolbar (if you're using the native editor). In either case, Outlook displays the Message Options dialog box, shown previously in Figure 22.9.

If you haven't changed Outlook's defaults, the Request a Delivery Receipt for This Message and Request a Read Receipt for This Message boxes are unchecked. Check one or both of these boxes if you want to request receipts for the current message.

If you have changed Outlook's defaults, one or both of the check boxes might be checked. Check or uncheck the boxes according to whether you want receipts to be requested for the current message.

After you send messages for which you request one or both receipts, Exchange automatically sends receipt messages to your Inbox.

Tip from

When you receive a read receipt, all you know is that a recipient opened the message, or marked it as read. You have no guarantee the recipient actually read it. If you really want to know that a recipient has read the message, you should request the recipient to send an acknowledgment to you.

TRACKING MESSAGE RECEIPTS

If you send a message in which you have requested a delivery receipt, a read receipt, or both to several people, you can easily see a tally that shows which people have read your message.

To see a tally of people who have read your message:

1. With any Outlook Information viewer displayed, select the My Shortcuts section of the Outlook Bar and select Sent Items to display the Sent Items Information viewer.

2. In the Sent Items Information viewer, double-click the message for which you want to see the tally. Outlook displays a message form that now has two tabs. The Message tab is selected—it contains your original message.

3. Select the Tracking tab shown in Figure 22.10.

Figure 22.10
The Tracking tab contains a table that lists the message recipients to whom you sent the original message and shows which of those recipients have read it. Notice the status totals at the top of the table.

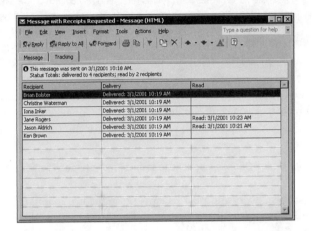

4. If you want to print a copy of the response tally, open the form's File menu and select Print.

Tip from

You can arrange the list of recipients in alphabetical order by clicking the title at the top of the Recipient column. To send a copy of some or all rows in the list to someone else, select the rows you want to send, press Ctrl+C to copy the list into the Clipboard, create a new message, and press Ctrl+V to paste the selected rows into that message.

RECALLING MESSAGES

Subject to certain conditions, you can recall a message that you've previously sent by way of an Exchange server. For a message recall to be successful

■ The recipient must have Outlook running.

■ The recipient must be logged on to Exchange.

■ The recipient must not have opened the message.

■ The recipient must not have moved the message from the Inbox folder to another folder.

As mentioned in various places in this book, it should be normal practice for all users to keep Outlook running (probably minimized) while their computers are turned on. If that happens, the first of these conditions is satisfied.

Normally, when a user logs on to Windows NT Server or Windows 2000 Server, that user is automatically logged on to Exchange Server. That satisfies the second condition.

The third condition is common sense. A recipient who has opened a message has probably read it, or at least knows it's waiting to be read. You wouldn't want to open a message and subsequently find that somebody else has deleted it from your Inbox.

The last condition is the one that's likely to give you the most trouble. That's because many users employ Rules in Outlook or Exchange to place messages in specific folders other than their Inbox folders. Because of that, many of the messages you send are likely to be in folders other than Inbox folders on users' computers or in their Exchange stores.

Here's another point to be aware of. For Outlook on your computer to know whether a recipient has opened a message, you must have sent the message with a read receipt requested. If you sent the message you're trying to recall without requesting a read receipt, Outlook won't receive a read receipt even though the recipient has opened the message. As a result, Outlook will report No recipients have reported reading the message even though some might have done so. This will make you think that you can successfully recall the message when in fact you can't. For this reason, you should consider requesting a read receipt for all messages you send by way of Exchange.

Note

The disadvantages of requesting receipts are that it increases network traffic and also increases each Outlook user's storage requirements.

Caution

Because there's a strong possibility that you won't be able to recall messages, be careful what you send. Check each message carefully before your send it. Don't rely on being able to recall a message you subsequently wish you hadn't sent.

Being aware that message recall works only some of the time, here's how you attempt to recall a message.

To recall a message:

1. With any Outlook Information viewer displayed, select the My Shortcuts section of the Outlook Bar and click Sent Items to display the Sent Items Information viewer.

2. Double-click the message you want to recall to display that message in the Message form.

3. Select Actions, Recall This Message to display the dialog box shown in Figure 22.11.

4. Click the Delete Unread Copies of This Message button and go to step 6. Alternatively, click the Delete Unread Copies and Replace with a New message option button and go to step 5.

5. Edit the original message that Outlook automatically displays in a Message form. Then, click Send in the form's toolbar to send the revised message. If the recall is successful, the revised message replaces the original message in recipients' Inboxes.

Figure 22.11
This dialog box warns you that you might not be able to recall the message from some recipients.

6. Normally, leave the Tell Me if Recall Succeeds or Fails for Each Recipient box checked.

Within a short time, you should have messages in your Inbox telling you whether your recalls have succeeded or failed.

USING VOTING BUTTONS

Using Exchange Server, you can send a message that asks a question to which you want people to reply with one of a set of possible answers. The message can include Outlook's built-in voting buttons or voting buttons you define. When people receive your message, they can select one of the voting buttons to send you a reply. At your end, Outlook keeps track of recipients' responses so you easily can display a tally of those responses.

Outlook offers three sets of predefined voting buttons you can include in a message. These buttons are labeled

- Approve; Reject
- Yes; No
- Yes; No; Maybe

You can select one of these sets of voting buttons or define your own voting buttons with as many choices as you like. Each message you send can contain only one set of voting buttons, though.

CREATING A MESSAGE THAT CONTAINS VOTING BUTTONS

Start by creating a message in the normal way. At any time while you're creating the message, click Options in the Message form's Message toolbar (if you're using Word as your editor) or Standard toolbar (if you're using the native editor) to display the Message Options dialog box, shown in Figure 22.12. Then proceed as follows.

To create a message containing voting buttons:

1. Check the Use Voting Buttons box. Outlook displays the first built-in choice of voting buttons: Approve; Reject, as shown in Figure 22.12.

Figure 22.12
Outlook initially suggests Approve; Reject as the names of the voting buttons.

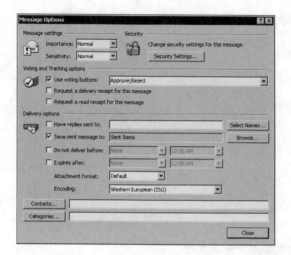

2. If you want to use a different set of built-in voting buttons, click the button at the right end of the Use Voting Buttons box to display a list and select from that list. If you want to define your own voting buttons, enter the names of these buttons in the Use Voting Buttons box, separating one button name from the next with a semicolon.

3. Click Close to close the Message Options dialog box and return to the Message form.

4. Complete the message and send it in the normal manner.

REPLYING TO A MESSAGE THAT CONTAINS VOTING BUTTONS

When you receive a message that contains voting buttons, you don't see the voting buttons in your Inbox Information viewer, even if AutoPreview is enabled. However, if you have the Preview pane enabled, when you select a message in the Message pane, the Preview pane's header contains an InfoBar that states Please respond by opening this message and using the voting buttons at the top.

Note

The InfoBar that alerts you to the fact that a message contains voting buttons is new in Outlook 2002.

Double-click the message header in the Inbox Information viewer to display the message in a Message form, as shown in Figure 22.13.

Notice that the InfoBar draws your attention to the voting buttons with the words Please respond using the buttons above at the top of the message header. As usual, the InfoBar has a bright yellow background, so it's immediately obvious.

To reply to the message, click one of the voting buttons. Outlook displays the dialog box shown in Figure 22.14.

Figure 22.13
The Message form shows the voting buttons immediately below the toolbar.

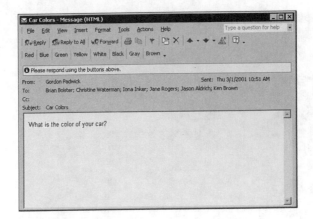

Figure 22.14
This dialog box confirms which voting button you chose.

If you click Send the Response Now and then click OK, Outlook immediately sends your response back to the sender. The InfoBar in the Message form changes to show which voting button you chose as well as the date and time you sent the response.

If you click Edit the Response Before Sending and then click OK, Outlook displays a Message form that's addressed to the sender of the original message with the name of the voting button you selected in the Subject box. You can enter a message to the original sender, and then click Send in the form's toolbar to send your message back to the original sender.

Note

As is the case with any message you receive, you can reply to it more than once. If you reply more than once to a message that asks you to respond by clicking a voting button, only your first response counts in the tally subsequently seen by the person who sent the original message.

RECEIVING VOTING RESPONSES

When you receive responses to a message you sent that contained voting buttons, those responses appear as usual in your Inbox Information viewer. The message header there contains the name of the respondent in the From column and the name of the voting button that respondent selected in the Subject column. You can double-click the message header to see the message in a Message form.

You can click the InfoBar to see a summary of the responses you've received to the original message, as explained in more detail in the next section. If the respondent sent a message with the response, that message is displayed in the notes box.

DISPLAYING A TALLY OF VOTING RESPONSES

One way to display a summary of responses to a message containing voting buttons that you sent is to click the InfoBar in one person's response, as explained in the preceding section.

Another way to display a summary of responses is to follow these steps.

To see a tally of responses to a message containing voting buttons:

1. With any Outlook Information viewer displayed, select the My Shortcuts section of the Outlook Bar and click Sent Items to display the Sent Items Information viewer.
2. Double-click the original message containing voting buttons that you sent to display that message in a Message form, which now has two tabs. The Message tab showing the original message is initially selected.
3. Select the Tracking tab, shown in Figure 22.15.

Figure 22.15
The InfoBar near the top of the Tracking tab contains a summary of the responses you've received. The table shows the voting button chosen by each respondent who has replied.

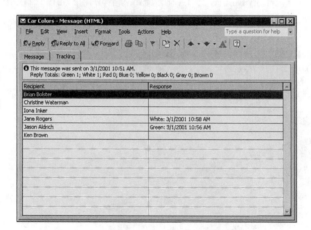

As described previously in this chapter, you can sort the table that contains details of responses, print it, and copy it into another message.

DELEGATING ACCESS TO YOUR FOLDERS

When using Exchange as your messaging system, you can let other people act as delegates on your behalf.

If you have a trusted administrative assistant, you can give that assistant full delegate access to any or all of your Outlook folders. That's quite different from allowing your assistant to log on as you because you can control which of your Outlook folders your assistant can access.

If you're going to be out of the office for a while, you can give one of your colleagues delegate access to your mail folders so that person can respond to mail on your behalf while you're away.

DELEGATING ACCESS TO YOUR E-MAIL

Here's how you give another person delegate access to your e-mail. Although Outlook allows you to select more than one delegate, it's usually best to select only one.

Note

The procedure described here is based on the assumption that you save your Outlook items in the Exchange store. If you save your Outlook items in a Personal Folders file or an Offline Folders file, a delegate can only send mail on your behalf, not access your folders.

Proceed as follows to give delegate access to your mail. With any Outlook Information viewer displayed, select Tools, Options to display the Options dialog box, and then select the Delegates tab shown in Figure 22.16 (this tab is available only if you have a Microsoft Exchange Server e-mail account).

Figure 22.16
The tab is shown here with a delegate already added.

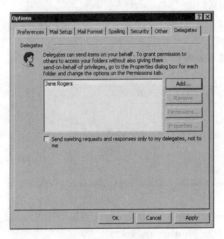

You can use the dialog box shown in Figure 22.16 to add and remove delegates, and also to specify which permissions each delegate has.

→ For information about adding and removing delegates, **see** "Delegates Options," **p. 581**.

Note

You can reopen the Delegates tab in the Options dialog box at any time to change a delegate's permissions. To do so, select the delegate, and then click Permissions. To remove a delegate, select that delegate's name in the Delegates tab of the Options dialog box, and then click Remove.

ACCESSING FOLDERS FOR WHICH YOU HAVE DELEGATE ACCESS

After you've been granted delegate access to someone else's folders, you can open that person's folders as well as your own.

When you click a shortcut icon in the Outlook Bar, Outlook opens your own Outlook folders in the normal manner.

To open someone's folders for which you have delegate permission:

1. With any Outlook Information viewer displayed, select File, move the pointer onto Open, and click Other User's Folder. Outlook displays the dialog box shown in Figure 22.17.

Figure 22.17
Use this dialog box to specify the folder you want to open.

2. In the Name box, enter the name of a person who has given you delegate access. Alternatively, click Name to display the Select Name dialog box in which you can select a person's name.

3. Open the Folder drop-down list and select the folder you want to open. Click OK. If the person you named has not given you delegate permission at all, or if the folder you select is not a folder for which you've been given delegate permission, Outlook displays a message stating `Unable to display folder`. If the person you named has given you delegate permission for the selected folder, Outlook displays that folder in an Information viewer superimposed over your Information viewer.

With the other person's folder displayed in an Information viewer, you can work with the information in that viewer in the same way you work with information in your own folders. You are, of course, subject to the permissions the folder's owner granted to you. For example, if you have only permission to read information, you won't be able to create new items or edit existing ones.

After you've finished working with the other person's folder, you can close that Information viewer by clicking the X at the right end of the viewer's banner.

The next time you select File and move the pointer onto Open, you'll see a list of folders you recently opened. You can select any folder from the list to open that folder again.

SENDING MESSAGES ON SOMEONE ELSE'S BEHALF

You need delegate permission to send messages on another person's behalf.

To send a message on behalf of someone else:

1. With any Information viewer displayed, click New in the Standard toolbar to display the Message form.

2. If you're using Word as your e-mail editor, open the drop-down Options list in the Message toolbar and click From to add the From box near the top of the Message form's header. If you're using the native editor, select View, From Field.

3. Enter the name of the person on behalf of whom you're sending into the From box. Alternatively, click From to display the Choose Sender dialog box, and then select the person's name in that dialog box.

4. Complete the remaining parts of the form as you normally do. Then, click Send in the form's Standard toolbar to send the message.

As usual, Outlook saves a copy of the message you sent in your Sent Items folder. If you open that copy, you'll see something similar to the message shown in Figure 22.18.

Figure 22.18
Notice that the From line shows the message from you on behalf of someone else.

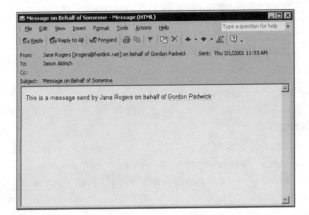

Note

If you attempt to send a message on behalf of someone who hasn't given you delegate permissions, it might initially appear that you have been able to do so. However, soon after you send the message, Exchange will send you a message that will appear in your Inbox Information viewer: The originator does not have permission to submit the message. The person to whom you sent the message will not receive it.

RECEIVING A MESSAGE SENT ON BEHALF OF ANOTHER PERSON

When you receive a message that was sent on behalf of someone other than the actual sender, the message header appears in your Inbox Information viewer. The message appears to be from the person on behalf of whom it was sent, not from the actual sender. You find out that the message was sent on behalf of the person it appears to be from when you view the message in the Preview pane or double-click the message header to display the message in a Message form, just like the one previously shown in Figure 22.18. If you reply to a message that was sent to you on behalf of someone else, Outlook sends the reply to the person on behalf of whom the original message was sent.

USING SERVER-BASED RULES

Chapter 28, "Creating and Using Rules," introduces you to rules that can process incoming and outgoing messages automatically. That chapter focuses on rules that run on your computer and are active only when your computer is turned on and Outlook is running.

If you use Outlook as a client for Exchange, you can also set up rules that run on the server—rules that operate whether your computer is turned on, provided, of course, the server is up and running.

One of the examples in Chapter 28 is a rule that automatically sends a reply to messages you receive. As stated in that chapter, you must leave your computer turned on with Outlook running for the rule to work. If you're using Outlook as a client for Exchange, a better solution exists—it's called the Out of Office Assistant.

→ For information about creating a rule running on your computer that automatically replies to messages, **see** "Automatically Replying to Messages," **p. 599**.

USING THE OUT OF OFFICE ASSISTANT

Using Outlook as a client for Exchange, you can use the Out of Office Assistant running on Exchange to process your e-mail automatically, even when your computer is turned off. After you turn on the Out of Office Assistant, it automatically sends whatever reply you choose to senders. You also can set up the Out of Office Assistant to process rules you create. Of course, the Out of Office Assistant deals only with e-mail you receive by way of Exchange. It doesn't, for example, know anything about Internet e-mail that arrives directly to your computer.

To turn on the Out of Office Assistant:

1. With the Inbox Information viewer displayed, select Tools, Out of Office Assistant to display the dialog box shown in Figure 22.19.

Note

The Out of Office Assistant item is present in the Tools menu only if you have a Microsoft Exchange Server e-mail account set up in Outlook.

Figure 22.19
This dialog box opens with I Am Currently In the Office selected.

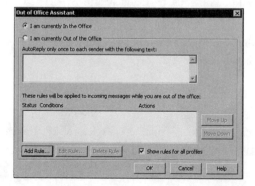

2. Select I Am Currently Out of the Office.

3. In the box labeled AutoReply Only Once to Each Sender with the Following Text box, enter the message you want to be sent. Click OK.

From now on, the message you entered in step 3 will be automatically sent whenever the first message from each sender arrives in your Exchange store.

When you return to the office and are ready to respond to messages, open the Out of Office Assistant dialog box again and select I Am Currently in the Office.

You can use the Out of Office Assistant to do much more than just send an automatic reply. With the Out of Office Assistant dialog box open, click Add Rule to display the dialog box shown in Figure 22.20. You can use this dialog box to create several rules.

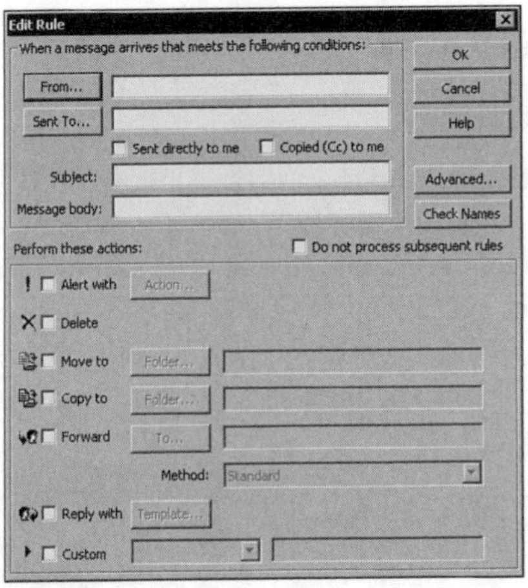

Figure 22.20
Use this dialog box to define a rule that runs on the server when a message arrives in your mailbox in the Exchange store.

The top section of the dialog box contains boxes in which you can define certain aspects of incoming messages. The rule is applied only if it satisfies all the criteria you define in these boxes.

The bottom section of the dialog box is where you can define what the rule does. The choices you make here should be obvious, particularly after you read Chapter 28, so they're not covered in detail here.

You can make more precise definitions of the message to be acted on by clicking Advanced to display the dialog box shown in Figure 22.21.

RUNNING OUTLOOK RULES ON EXCHANGE

As an alternative to creating rules as described in the preceding sections, you can use the Outlook Rules Wizard to create rules, as explained in Chapter 28. You can then ask Outlook to move rules that can be processed by the server into Exchange.

Figure 22.21
Use this dialog box to specify additional criteria about messages for which you want Exchange Server to respond automatically.

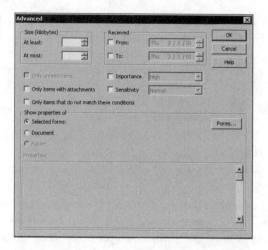

When you've finished designing a rule using the Outlook Rules Wizard, click Finish to save that rule. At that time, Outlook examines the rule to see whether it can run on Exchange without access to your computer. If for some reason that's not possible—for example, if the rule involves saving a message in a folder on your computer's hard drive—Outlook displays a message stating This rule is a client-only rule, and will process only if Outlook is running. When you see that message, you have no alternative but to click OK. Outlook saves the rule, and the wizard window lists the rule with the words "client only" after the rule's name.

→ For information about the Rules Wizard, **see** "Using the Rules Wizard to Manage Incoming Messages," **p. 589**.

If you create a rule that can be run on the server and doesn't need access to your computer, by default Outlook automatically saves that rule on the server instead of on your computer's hard disk. In that case, the rule's name is displayed in the wizard window without the words "client only" being added.

You know, therefore, that rule names displayed in the wizard window with the words "client only" appended refer to rules that operate only when Outlook is running on your computer; rule names without those words appended run on the server whether or not Outlook is running on your computer.

USING WEB SERVICES

If your Exchange Server administrator has set up and enabled Outlook Web Access on Exchange, you can create and access forms in HTML format from within Outlook. In this situation, the new command Web Form appears on Outlook's Actions menu. When you select this command, you can select a form that your default Web browser opens automatically.

For detailed information about Outlook Web Access, refer to the Microsoft publication *Exchange 2000 Outlook Web Access*, which is available on the Web site `http://www.microsoft.com/exchange/outlook/OWA2000.htm`. You can find additional information in various white papers available at `http://www.microsoft.com/exchange/outlook/default.htm` and in books about Exchange, such as *Special Edition Using Microsoft Exchange Server 2000*, published by Que.

TROUBLESHOOTING

EXCHANGE E-MAIL

Everyone has trouble, from time to time, with e-mail. Finding out the cause of those problems is difficult; correcting them is even more difficult. That's because e-mail is a very complex process that involves hardware and software on your computer, the physical connection between your computer and your e-mail servers, the paths between your servers and your recipients' servers, and the hardware and software your recipients use. You can only be responsible for your own hardware and software.

If you have trouble sending and receiving e-mail, you can try to isolate the problem by sending a message to yourself. By doing that, you're limiting the problem to what happens on your local computer and your account on the local Exchange server. If that works okay, you know that what you've set up is satisfactory. If that doesn't work, you need to ask for help from your local network or Exchange administrator.

After you've been able to send a message to yourself, you know that your end of Outlook is fine. Now try sending messages to a colleague who has an account on the same Exchange server. Gradually expand your horizon until you find out where the difficulty arises. After you've identified the problem, the only thing you can do is talk (yes, plain old telephone) to the person responsible for the system where the problem occurs to get help in resolving it.

CHAPTER 23

Using Exchange Server to Share Information

In this chapter

SHARING INFORMATION

When you're using Outlook as a client for an Exchange server, you can choose among three ways to share information with other people who have Exchange accounts:

- **Delegate Access**—To give someone permission to access your Outlook folders and act on your behalf. For example, designating delegate access is useful if you are a manager and need an assistant to act on your behalf while you are away.

- **Public Folders**—To make information available throughout a group or organization.

- **Shared Folders**—To share information in your folders with several or many people in a workgroup.

→ If you want to designate another person to have delegate access to your folders, **see** "Delegating Access to Your Folders," **p. 445**.

This chapter focuses on public and shared folders.

USING PUBLIC FOLDERS

Public folders on the server are used to make information available to members of a group of any size. A common use of public folders is to publish companywide information, such as employee policy manuals and corporate calendars.

Note

The process of putting information into a public folder is known as *posting*.

You can use public folders for such purposes as:

- **Posting information for many people to see**—Normally, one person has permission to post, edit, and delete information in a public folder of this type, whereas everyone has permission to read that information.

- **Maintaining an unmoderated electronic bulletin board**—Used in this way, a public folder is very similar to an Internet newsgroup. Everyone has permission to post and read information. Normally, though, only one person has permission to delete information.

- **Maintaining a moderated bulletin board**—People offer items to a moderator who decides which items to post on the bulletin board. Only the moderator has post and delete permissions; everyone has read permission.

- **Sharing Outlook items with other people**—The people who own the items copy those items to a public folder and give specific people permission to read them.

- **Sharing files created in other applications, such as documents created in Word, worksheets created in Excel, and databases created in Access**—The people who own the files copy them to a public folder and give specific other people whichever permissions are appropriate.

CREATING A PUBLIC FOLDER

Public folders are created within an existing public folder in the Exchange store. Exchange Server provides up to 16GB of space for public folders; the Exchange administrator can limit the size of individual public folders. You must have permission to create a folder to create a folder within an existing public folder.

> **Note**
>
> The Exchange Server administrator uses Exchange Server Administrator to control permissions for creating folders on the server. This subject is beyond the scope of this book. For information about this, I recommend reading *Special Edition Using Microsoft Exchange Server 5.5* or *Special Edition Using Microsoft Exchange Server 2000*, both published by Que.

This chapter assumes you have the permission required to create public folders. If that's not the case, ask your Exchange Server administrator to grant you the necessary permission.

To create a public folder:

1. With any Outlook Information viewer displayed, select View, Folder List to display your folder list, such as the one shown in Figure 23.1.

Figure 23.1
If you have a Microsoft Exchange Server e-mail account set up in Outlook, your folder list should contain a folder named Public Folders.

2. Expand the Public Folders folder and then expand the All Public Folders folder, as shown in Figure 23.2.

Figure 23.2
The Public Folders folder contains a Favorites folder and an All Public Folders folder.

The All Public Folders folder in Figure 23.2 contains just one folder. Your Public Folders folder might be empty or might contain a long list of folders. The icon at the left of each folder name indicates the type of item that folder contains.

3. Right-click All Public Folders to display its context menu (be careful to right-click All Public Folders, not Public Folders). Select New Folder in the context menu to display the dialog box shown in Figure 23.3.

Figure 23.3
Use this dialog box to create a public folder.

4. Unless you specifically intend to use the new folder for a particular type of Outlook item, leave Mail and Post Items selected in the Folder Contains box. Otherwise, open the Folder Contains drop-down list and select the type of items the new folder will contain.

> **Note**
>
> Select Mail and Post Items if you're setting up a public folder to use for general information or as a bulletin board.

5. Enter a name for the new public folder in the Name box.

6. Because you started creating the new folder with All Public Folders selected in the Folder list, Outlook proposes to save the new folder as a subfolder of All Public Folders. Don't change that, unless you want the new folder to be a subfolder under an existing folder.

7. Click OK to finish creating the new folder.

8. Outlook asks whether you want to add a shortcut to the new folder on the Outlook Bar. Click Yes if you expect to access the public folder frequently; otherwise, click No. The dialog box closes and the new folder is shown in the Folder list as a subfolder of All Public Folders.

The name of the new public folder appears in your folder list in its correct alphabetical position.

GIVING PEOPLE ACCESS TO A PUBLIC FOLDER

After you create a public folder, you own it and control who has access to it. The only other person who can control access is the Exchange administrator. You can give access to individual people or to groups. Outlook provides two ways to do this. You can give specific permissions to people or groups, or you can assign permission levels to people or groups. The available permissions are listed in Table 23.1; predefined permission levels are listed in Table 23.2. Table 23.2 lists permission levels in order of decreasing power, with the exception of Custom, which can have any combination of permissions.

> **Note**
>
> Prior to Outlook 2002, permission levels were known as *roles*.

TABLE 23.1   AVAILABLE PERMISSIONS

Permission Type	Individual Permissions
Access	Create items, Read items, Edit own items, Edit all items, Create subfolders, Folder visible
Ownership	Folder owner, Folder contact
Delete	Delete own items, Delete all items

TABLE 23.2 OUTLOOK'S PREDEFINED PERMISSION LEVELS

Permission Level	Permissions
Custom	Any combination of permissions
Owner	Create, read, edit, and delete all items and files; Create subfolders; Set permissions for other people to access the folder
Publishing Editor	Create, read, edit, and delete all items and files; Create subfolders
Editor	Create, read, edit, and delete all items and files
Author	Create, read, edit, and delete own items and files
Publishing Author	Create and read items; Edit and delete own items; Create subfolders
Nonediting Author	Create and read items, Delete own items
Contributor	Read items, Submit items and files
Reviewer	Read items

EXAMINING THE DEFAULT PERMISSIONS

With a public folder (one that you own) for which you want to assign permissions visible in the Folder list, right-click the name of that folder to display its context menu. In the context menu, select Properties to display the folder's properties dialog box. Select the Permissions tab to display the dialog box shown in Figure 23.4. The Properties dialog box has a Permissions tab only for the public folders you own.

Figure 23.4
The dialog box opens with some names listed, each with a specific permission level.

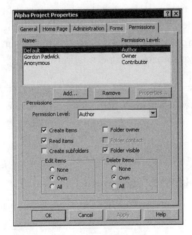

Note

After you right-click the name of a public folder that someone else created and, therefore, owns, the dialog box has a Summary tab instead of a Permissions tab. Select the Summary tab to see, but not change, the permissions you have for that folder.

Outlook defines default permissions to three names: Default, Anonymous, and your own name:

- **Default**—Defines the permissions everyone who has an Exchange Server account gets unless you specifically give a person different permissions. Outlook assigns Author permissions to default users.

- **Anonymous**—Defines the permissions given to people who don't have an Exchange Server account but, if the server administrator allows, log on to Exchange Server as Anonymous. The same permissions apply to people who log on as Anonymous by way of Outlook Web Access or an Active Server Page. Outlook assigns Contributor permissions to anonymous users.

Note

For information about Outlook Web Access, see *Special Edition Using Microsoft Exchange Server 5.5* or *Special Edition Using Microsoft Exchange Server 2000*, both published by Que. For more information about Active Server Pages (ASP), see *Special Edition Using Microsoft FrontPage 2002*, also published by Que.

- **Your own name**—Defines the permissions you have as the owner of the public folder. Outlook assigns Owner permissions to the folder owner.

When the dialog box first appears, the first name in the list—Default—is selected. The permissions section in the bottom part of the dialog box shows the permissions given to default users. You can select the other two names to see the permissions given to them.

For each name in the list of users, the Permissions section of the dialog box shows permissions in two ways. The Permission Level box shows permissions in terms of a predefined permission level. Below that are check boxes and option buttons that show the individual permissions associated with the permission level.

CHANGING PEOPLE'S PERMISSIONS

You don't have to accept the default permissions Outlook assigns. For example, you might want to change the permissions for Default to None, so that only those people to whom you specifically assign permissions can access the public folder. If the public folder is intended to contain information available for everyone on the LAN to read but not change, you should change the permissions for Anonymous to Read Items.

To change a person's or group's permission level:

1. Select the person or group in the list in the upper part of the Properties dialog box.
2. Open the drop-down Permission Level list, and select the level you want to assign. The permission level in the second column of the list of users changes to the level you select. Also, the check boxes and option buttons below Permission Level change to show the individual permissions associated with the new level.

To assign specific permissions to a person or group:

1. Select the person or group in the list in the upper part of the dialog box.

2. Check the check boxes and select the option buttons in the lower part of the dialog box to assign specific permissions. If you select a combination of check boxes and option buttons that correspond to a predefined permission level, the name of that level appears in the Permission Level box. Otherwise, the Permission Level box contains the word Custom.

Note

If you don't want a group, such as Anonymous, to see the public folder, remove the check mark from the Folder Visible box.

ADDING PERMISSIONS FOR MORE PEOPLE

You can add people and groups to the permissions list.

To add permissions for a person or group:

1. In the Permissions tab of the public folder's Properties dialog box, click Add to display the dialog box shown in Figure 23.5.

Figure 23.5
This dialog box opens showing a list of people who have accounts on the Exchange server.

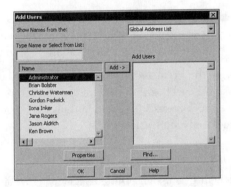

2. Select the name of a person (or of several people) for whom you want to assign permissions.

3. Click Add to move the selected names into the Add Users list; then click OK to return to the dialog box that shows the names you selected with the permissions you previously assigned to Default users.

4. Select the new users (you can select them individually or select any combination of them).

5. Either assign a permission level to the new user (or users) or select the individual permissions you want them to have.

WITHDRAWING A USER'S PERMISSIONS

To withdraw the permissions you've previously given for a user to access the public folder, select that user's name in the Permissions tab, and then click Remove. Outlook immediately removes the user's name from the list of users.

> **Note**
>
> If a person is accessing a public folder at the time permission to do so is withdrawn, that person can continue the present activity but will not subsequently be able to access the folder.

GETTING INFORMATION ABOUT A USER

To see information about a user, select that user's name in the list of users in the Permissions tab. Then, click Properties. Outlook displays the selected user's Properties dialog box, such as the one shown in Figure 23.6.

Figure 23.6
Individually select the five tabs in this dialog box to see information about the selected user.

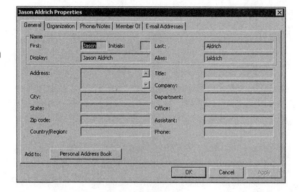

POSTING INFORMATION ON A PUBLIC FOLDER

You can post Outlook items or files on a public folder for which you have Create Items permission. After you post an item in a public folder, other people who have permission to create items can respond to it. The chain of responses is known as a *conversation* or *thread*. A conversation has a name that's the same as the subject of the message that started the conversation.

POSTING A MESSAGE

Posting information in a public folder is similar to sending an e-mail message.

To post information in a public folder:

1. Select the public folder into which you want to post information. If you have a shortcut icon for the public folder in your Outlook Bar, click it. Otherwise, open your folder list and select the public folder. Either way, Outlook displays an Information viewer that shows items already in the public folder.

2. Click New at the left end of the viewer's Standard toolbar to display the Discussion form, shown in Figure 23.7.

Figure 23.7
The Discussion form opens with the name of the public folder near the top. The form shown here is ready to post.

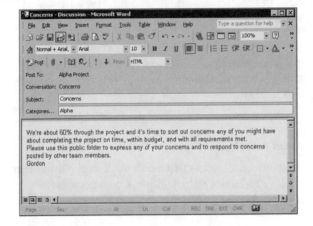

3. Enter a subject for the item in the Subject box and press Enter or Tab to move the insertion point into the large text box. The subject text appears as the name of the conversation in the header.

4. Click Categories to display your list of categories. Select a category for the new conversation.

5. Enter the text for the new post into the large box that occupies most of the form.

6. Click Post in the form's Standard toolbar to post your item into the public folder.

You can insert files and other types of objects into a post in the same way you make insertions into e-mail messages.

An item posted in this way appears in the public folder's Information viewer in the same way as received e-mail appears in the Inbox Information viewer. You, or anyone else who has access to the public folder, can double-click the posted items header in the viewer to see the item in the Discussion form.

Note

A public folder's Information viewer can be displayed with or without a Preview pane. Select View, Preview Pane to display or hide the Preview pane.

RESPONDING TO A POST

When you read something another person has posted in a public folder, you might want to ask a question or add information, something you can do if you have permission to create items. Instead of creating a new post, you should reply to the existing one. In that way, you create a conversation in which your reply is linked to the original message, as subsequently described in this chapter.

→ You can use Public Folders as a conversation forum. **See** "Using a Public Folder As an Unmoderated Bulletin Board," in the next section.

POSTING A FILE

You can post a file created in an Office, or Office-compatible, application into a public folder.

To post an Office file into a public folder:

1. Open the file you want to post using the Office application in which the file was created.

2. Select File, move the pointer onto Send To, and click Exchange Folder. After a few moments delay, a dialog box that lists your top-level Outlook folders is displayed.

3. Expand Public Folders, expand All Public Folders, and select the public folder into which you want to post the file.

4. Click OK to post the file in the selected public folder.

After following these steps, you'll find the file available in the public folder's Information viewer. Double-click the item's name to display the Opening Mail Attachment dialog box, in which you can choose to open the item or save it to disk.

USING A PUBLIC FOLDER AS AN UNMODERATED BULLETIN BOARD

You can use a public folder as a bulletin board, a community resource people can use to discuss whatever is on their minds. Anyone who has Create Items permission for the public folder can post items on the bulletin board and respond to items already posted there.

To use a public folder you've created in this way, you should probably set the Default permission level to Author. Having done that, anyone who has an Exchange account can post items in the folder, read whatever anyone else has posted, and respond to posted items. You might consider, though, whether you want to allow users to edit and delete items they've previously posted, both of which are permissions included in the Author permission level.

In the Permissions tab of the public folder's dialog box, you can change the Default permissions to include only Create and Read items. After you've done that, users can't change or delete items after they've posted them—more in the spirit of a bulletin board.

When a public folder is used as a bulletin board, users can post items onto that board. Other users see those items when they open the bulletin board public folder, and they can double-click the item header to see the item in full in the Discussion form.

Note

> Author permissions allow a user to read items, create new items, and edit only items that user has created.

To respond to an item, after double-clicking the item header in the public folder's Information viewer to display the item in a Discussion form, click Post Reply in the form's Standard toolbar. Now you see the original post with space above it for your response, as shown in Figure 23.8.

Figure 23.8
The form you use for a response already has the original post's subject as the name of the conversation, but the Subject box is empty. You should provide a subject for your response.

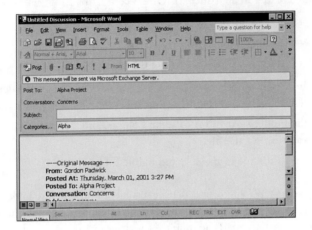

Responding to a post is similar to replying to an e-mail message. After completing your response, click Post in the Discussion form's Standard toolbar to post the reply. After you've posted your response, you're left with the original post displayed in the Discussion form. Close that form when you've finished reading what it contains.

VIEWING A CONVERSATION

A public folder used as a bulletin board might contain many conversations, each started by the person who posted the message that started the conversation. Any number of people can respond to the original message; other people can respond to those responses. Before long, the bulletin board contains many conversations, each with several (perhaps many) responses.

You can group messages by conversation so you can easily follow through a thread of messages. To do so, display the public folder's Information viewer, select View, move the pointer onto Current View, and click By Conversation Topic. Outlook displays conversation topics, initially with all of them collapsed so you can't see the items within each conversation. Click the + at the left of a conversation topic to expand that topic.

In this view, double-click any message to display it in the Discussion form.

SENDING AN E-MAIL RESPONSE TO A CONVERSATION ITEM

People normally should respond to bulletin board messages on the bulletin board so that everyone can benefit from those responses. Sometimes, though, you might want to send a private response to a person who posted a message. You can do so by sending e-mail directly to that person.

Also, you might want to send a copy of a bulletin board message to someone who doesn't have access to the bulletin board. You can do so by using e-mail.

To e-mail a conversation item or send e-mail to someone who posted an item:

1. Display the public folder's Information viewer.

2. Select the conversation item you want to send by e-mail.

3. Click Reply in the viewer's toolbar if you want to send a reply to the person who posted the conversation item; alternatively, click Forward if you want to send the item to someone. In either case, Outlook displays a Message form that contains the conversation item.

4. Proceed in the normal way to send the message.

USING A PUBLIC FOLDER AS A MODERATED BULLETIN BOARD

A moderated bulletin board is one for which people can submit items for posting on the bulletin board to a moderator. The moderator decides whether to post those items.

To designate a public folder as a moderated bulletin board, you must be the owner of that public folder. Proceed as follows.

To create a moderated bulletin board:

1. In the Folder list, right-click the name of a public folder for which you have Owner permission to display the folder's context menu.

2. Click Properties to display the folder's Properties dialog box. Select the Administration tab to display the dialog box shown in Figure 23.9.

Figure 23.9
Click Help at the bottom of this dialog box if you want to see information about what it contains.

3. Click Moderated Folder to display the dialog box shown in Figure 23.10.

Figure 23.10
Read the text at the top of this dialog box to get a brief description of how moderated folders work.

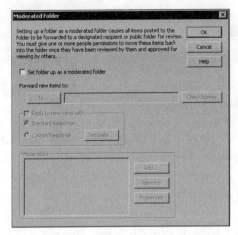

4. Check Set Folder Up As a Moderated Folder. When you do so, some of the boxes and buttons in the lower part of the dialog box become available.

5. Click To to display a dialog box in which you can select the name of a moderator to whom items submitted to the moderated folder will be forwarded for consideration.

> **Note**
>
> The person you select here is the person to whom Outlook automatically sends submissions, not necessarily the person who accepts or rejects submissions. The people who actually accept or reject submissions are selected in step 7. Instead of naming a person, you can name another public folder where submitted messages are to be saved for review by the moderators.

6. If you want Outlook to automatically reply to all submissions, check Reply to New Items With. To use Outlook's automatic response, accept the default Standard Response; otherwise, select Custom Response (in which case you must have a response previously saved as an Outlook template; click Template to select that template).

→ To save a response as a template, **see** "Using Outlook Templates," **p. 329**.

7. Click Add to open the Select Additional Moderators dialog box. Select one or more moderators and then click OK. The names of the moderators you select are displayed in the Moderators box at the bottom of the Moderated Folder dialog box.

After you've selected one or more moderators, all items submitted to the public folder are automatically forwarded to those moderators. Those moderators need to have Create Items permission to the public folder so that, if they approve items, they can post them in the folder.

USING CUSTOM FORMS WITHIN PUBLIC FOLDERS

By default, public folders offer the Discussion form, such as the one previously shown in Figure 23.7, for people to use when posting items. However, you can create public folders for many specialized purposes that require the use of a custom form.

After you've created a custom form, you can associate that form with a public folder. You must have Owner permission to do so.

To associate a custom form with a public folder:

1. Display your folder list and right-click the name of the public folder to which you want to associate a form.

2. Click Properties in the public folder's context menu and select the General tab, shown in Figure 23.11.

Figure 23.11
By default, Outlook proposes the Post form for use when posting to the folder.

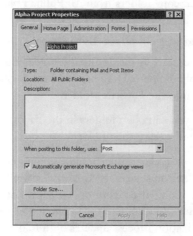

3. Open the When Posting to This Folder, Use drop-down list. Most likely, you'll see only Post and Forms listed. Click Forms to display the dialog box shown in Figure 23.12.

Figure 23.12
This dialog box opens showing a list of forms in the Outlook Standard Forms Library.

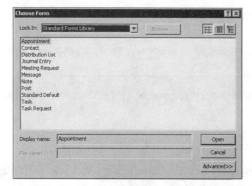

4. Open the drop-down Look In list and select the forms library in which you have saved the custom form (probably Personal Forms Library).

5. Select the form you want to associate with the public folder and click Open to return to the Properties dialog box, in which the name of the form you chose is displayed in the When Posting to This Folder, Use box.

Subsequently, when a person clicks New in the public folder's Information viewer toolbar, Outlook displays the form you specified.

MAKING A PUBLIC FOLDER AVAILABLE OFFLINE

Normally, public folders are available when your computer is connected to Exchange Server. When you're working offline (without a connection to Exchange Server), you can't access folders listed under All Public Folders in the Folder List because those folders are stored on the Exchange server. You can, however, copy folders from All Public Folders into your computer. While working offline, you can access those local copies.

→ For information about setting up Outlook to work offline, **see** "Using Outlook Offline," **p. 478**.

To make public folders available offline, start by displaying the Folder List and expand Public Folders, Favorites, and All Public Folders. Drag copies of the public folders you want to use offline from All Public Folders into the Favorites folder.

Subsequently, when you work offline, you can open folders in the Favorites list. You'll find, though, that you can't access folders in the All Public Folders list.

When you work offline, any changes you make to the contents of your copy of the public folder don't affect the actual public folder on the server. Likewise, any changes other people make to the public folder on the server don't affect your offline copy. Later, when you're again online, you can synchronize your offline copy of the public folder with the actual public folder on the server. The synchronization process updates both folders so that each of them contains the most recent information.

→ For information about synchronizing folders, **see** "Synchronizing Folders," **p. 478**.

CREATING RULES FOR A PUBLIC FOLDER

You can create rules for a public folder in a similar manner to creating other Exchange Server rules.

→ For information about Exchange Server rules, **see** "Using Server-Based Rules," **p. 449**.

Note   You must have Owner permission for a public folder to create rules for it.

To create rules for a public folder:

1. Display the Folder List, right-click the name of a public folder to display its context menu, and click Properties. Select the Administration tab previously shown in Figure 23.9.

2. Click Folder Assistant to display the dialog box shown in Figure 23.13.

Figure 23.13
Initially, this dialog box contains no rules.

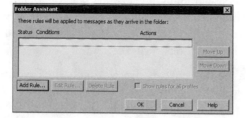

3. Click Add Rule to display the dialog box shown in Figure 23.14, in which you can enter and select information to define a rule.

Figure 23.14
This dialog box provides facilities for you to specify the details of a rule for a public folder.

4. After you've defined the rule, click OK to return to the Folder Assistant dialog box that lists the rule you created.

Note

Chapter 28, "Creating and Using Rules," contains detailed information about creating rules for e-mail messages. Much of the information there applies to creating rules for public folders.

USING THE FAVORITES FOLDER

The word "favorites" in the Outlook environment has two completely different meanings:

- The Favorites shortcut in the Other Shortcuts section of the Outlook Bar provides access to files, folders, and shortcuts (including URL shortcuts) in the Windows Favorites folder.

- Favorites in the Folder list is an Outlook folder that contains copies of the public folders available in the Exchange store.

This section deals with the second meaning of the word.

The Exchange store in a large organization might contain hundreds, if not thousands, of public folders, only a few of which each person accesses regularly. To simplify access to frequently used public folders, each person can copy those public folders from the All Public Folders section of the folder list into the Favorites section.

To copy a public folder from the All Public Folders section to the Favorites section, simply drag the name of the public folder from one section to the other. After you've done that, you can access a public folder by selecting from the few folders listed in the Favorites section instead of from the many folders listed in the All Public Folders section.

As explained previously in this chapter, you can make public folders listed in the Favorites section of Public Folders available for offline use, something you can't do for public folders listed only in the All Public Folders section.

SHARING YOUR FOLDERS

If you're using Outlook as a client for Exchange Server and you save your Outlook items in the Exchange store, you can give other people access to your folders. You can't use the method described in this section to share folders in a Personal Folders file, however.

Note

You can, of course, share your entire Personal Folders file within the Windows environment. When you do that, you have no control over sharing individual folders within the file.

GIVING PERMISSION TO ACCESS YOUR FOLDERS

Sharing your own folders has much in common with sharing public folders. Most organizations use public folders to create a long-term resource available throughout a large group or even the entire enterprise. Individual people who want to share information with a few colleagues often prefer to share information in their own existing folders instead of taking the time to create a public folder. Whereas you need to have the appropriate permission from the Exchange Server administrator to create a public folder, you don't require any such permission to share your own folders.

To share a single Outlook folder:

1. Display the Folder List, right-click the name of a folder you want to share to display its context menu, and click Properties to display the Properties dialog box. Select the Permissions tab, which is similar to the tab previously shown in Figure 23.4.

Note

The Permissions tab initially shows that Default users have None as their permission level, meaning that nobody other than yourself has access to the folder.

2. To give someone access to the folder, click Add to display the Add Users dialog box, shown previously in Figure 23.5, in which you can select the names of people who have accounts on Exchange to whom you want to grant access permission.

3. Select the names of one or more people to whom you want to give access to the folder. Click Add, and then click OK to return to the folder's Properties dialog box, which now shows the people's names you just selected. Each has the same permission level (None) as the Default.

4. Select one or more of the names you selected in the previous step.

5. To assign a permission level to the selected names, open the Permission Level drop-down list and select a permission level. Alternatively, check individual permissions and select option buttons. This is similar to granting permissions for a public folder, described previously in this chapter.

→ If others in your workgroup need to access your public folders, **see** "Giving People Access to a Public Folder," **p. 457**.

Now, the people you selected have the permissions you assigned to access your folders. At any time you can return to this dialog box to change these permissions:

- You can select a person's name and then click Remove to remove all the permissions you gave that person.

- You can select a person's name and then change the permission level or individual permissions you gave that person.

ACCESSING ANOTHER PERSON'S FOLDERS

After other people have granted you access to their folders in the Exchange store, you can open those folders. You do this in the same way that you open folders for which you have delegate access, as described in Chapter 22, "Using Exchange Server for E-mail."

→ For information about opening other people's folders, **see** "Accessing Folders for Which You Have Delegate Access," **p. 447**.

TROUBLESHOOTING

PUBLIC FOLDERS

Public folders are quite simple at the Outlook level; the types of problems you'll run into there mainly have to do with permissions. However, public folders are maintained on your Exchange server, so you might run into all sorts of connectivity problems, just as you might do when using your network for other purposes. Fortunately for you, connectivity problems are the province of the network administrator; they're not for you to solve (unless you have the misfortune to be that person).

One of the key concepts of public folders is ownership. Depending on the permissions the Exchange administrator gives to you, you can create public folders. You own those folders and can grant permissions to other people to access your folders. The only other person who can change permissions is the Exchange administrator. You can delete your own public folders; the Exchange administrator can, too, but only after granting himself ownership permissions to your public folders.

If the owner of a public folder hasn't granted you specific permissions to access that folder, you get only default permissions, which usually means you have no access to the folder. If you can't access a public folder, or can't do what you think you ought to be able to do within the folder, your only recourse is to contact the folder's owner and ask that person to change your permissions.

But what if the owner has left the organization? In that case, you can contact the Exchange administrator. That person can grant ownership permissions to himself or herself (or to someone else), so that changes can be made to your permissions.

You might find that access to public folders is slow. Apart from the obvious problem of a slow network, the speed problem might be caused by the way Exchange handles views. Whenever you or another person creates a new view or sort order for a public folder, Exchange creates a new index and stores that index in a temporary cache. The process of creating the new index can take a considerable amount of time if the folder is large. By default, Exchange keeps indexes for eight days and then deletes them (the Exchange administrator can change this default).

As a result of this mechanism, your access to a public folder might be slow the first time you create a new view. Also, if you haven't accessed a public folder for eight days, or whatever other aging period the Exchange administrator has set, you'll have to wait while Exchange creates a new index. To minimize this problem, create new views only when you really need them; also, make a habit of opening public folders to which you want fast access once a week.

CHAPTER 24

WORKING WITH EXCHANGE SERVER REMOTELY

In this chapter

WHEN YOU'RE OUT OF THE OFFICE

Quite a lot of people use Outlook in more than one place. If you're like many people who work in an office, you probably do most of your Outlook work there; sometimes, perhaps often, you use Outlook at home.

If you travel on business, you probably take a laptop computer with you. You might use the same laptop with a connection to your server while you're in the office, or you might use a desktop computer that stays on your desk. You don't have a permanent connection to the server while you're traveling with your laptop.

In these and other circumstances, you need a way to use Outlook while you're not connected to the server, and you need a way to keep your Outlook data on two or more computers synchronized, to ensure that the same and most recent data is on all the computers.

Outlook offers two ways for you to work while you're out of the office:

- Taking your files with you by using Offline Folders
- Making a remote connection to your Exchange store

Note

Let me be honest with you. Setting up a computer to work remotely in the Exchange environment isn't always simple. That's because Outlook has to deal with various configuration matters, not because Outlook is inherently difficult to use. If you work for a large enterprise, you will probably be issued a laptop for your remote work, all set up and ready to go. Lucky you! If you have to set up a laptop by yourself for remote use, and you've never done it before, be prepared for some headaches.

TAKING YOUR FILES WITH YOU

The scenario considered here is that of a corporate environment in which desktop computers are connected by way of a LAN to a server on which Exchange Server is used as an e-mail system. To take advantage of the collaboration facilities available in Exchange, people save their Outlook items in the Exchange store.

People who work away from the office use an Offline Folders file to save Outlook items while their computers aren't connected to the server.

UNDERSTANDING OFFLINE FOLDERS

An Offline Folders file is similar to a Personal Folders file. The file contains folders that are used to save Outlook items.

Note

Although a Personal Folders file and an Offline Folders file are similar in that they both contain folders used to store Outlook items, there is a significant difference between the two. A Personal Folders file contains a set of Outlook folders that are independent of any other Outlook folders.

In contrast, an Offline Folders file contains Outlook folders that are closely related to Outlook folders in the Exchange store. When you create an Offline Folders file, that file contains a copy of the Outlook folders you have in your Exchange store. You can synchronize the Outlook folders in your Offline Folders file with your Outlook folders in the Exchange store so both contain the most recent data.

Personal Folders files have .pst as their file name extensions; Offline Folders files have .ost as their file name extensions.

When your laptop computer is connected to a LAN, you can synchronize the information in your Offline Folders file with information from your Exchange store. Then you can disconnect the computer from the LAN and work with Outlook while you're traveling or in a different location. Sometime later, when your computer is again connected to the LAN, you can again synchronize your Offline Folders file with your Exchange store.

Note

Synchronization is the process by which two sets of folders are compared and updated so that the most recent items are saved in both sets of folders.

ENABLING E-MAIL ACCOUNTS FOR OFFLINE USE

If you want to use Outlook offline to send and receive e-mail, you must make sure the e-mail accounts you will use are available for offline use. Chapter 27, "Setting Outlook's Options," explains how e-mail accounts can be grouped and how each group of accounts has specific settings. One of these settings enables a group of accounts to be used for sending and receiving e-mail when Outlook is offline. Make sure this setting is enabled.

→ For information about enabling a group of accounts to be used to send and receive e-mail when Outlook is offline, **see** "Selecting Send/Receive Settings," **p. 559**.

CREATING AN OFFLINE FOLDERS FILE

To create and use an Offline Folders file, you must have a Microsoft Exchange Server e-mail account set up on your computer.

→ For information about creating a Microsoft Exchange Server e-mail account, **see** "Setting Up Outlook As an Exchange Client," **p. 428**.

To create an Offline Folders file:

1. With any Information viewer displayed, select Tools, E-mail Accounts and, with View or Change Existing E-mail Accounts selected in the E-mail Accounts dialog box, click Next.

2. In the second E-mail Accounts dialog box, select Microsoft Exchange Server (or the name you previously gave to that account); then click Change.

3. In the third E-mail Accounts dialog box, click More Settings to display the Microsoft Exchange Server dialog box with the General tab selected, as shown in Figure 24.1.

Figure 24.1
Use the When Starting section of this dialog box to specify how you want Outlook to start.

Note

It's important to make the appropriate selection in the When Starting section of the General tab. Automatically Detect Connection State, selected by default, is probably what you want to use if you have a laptop computer that's sometimes connected to the server and sometimes not connected. In that case, Outlook automatically connects to the server and gives you access to your folders in the Exchange store if a connection is available; if a connection is not available, Outlook accesses folders in your Offline Folders file.

If you want to be able to access your Offline Folders file while your computer is connected to the server, select Manually Control Connection State and check Choose the Connection Type When Starting. After you've done that, each time you start Outlook you can click one of these buttons:

- **Connect**—Connects to the server so you have access to folders in the Exchange store
- **Work Offline**—Enables you to have access to folders in your Offline Folders file
- **Cancel**—Prevents Outlook from starting

4. Select the Advanced tab, as shown in Figure 24.2.

Figure 24.2
This dialog box contains the settings you established when you created the Microsoft Exchange Server e-mail account.

5. Click Offline Folder File Settings to display the dialog box shown in Figure 24.3.

Figure 24.3
Outlook proposes to create an Offline Folders file named `outlook.ost`.

6. You can accept the proposed location and name for the new Offline Folders file. Alternatively, click Browse to navigate to a folder and enter a file name.

Tip from

It's a good idea to replace the default file name with your own name or e-mail account name. For example, if your e-mail account name is `kbrown`, use `kbrown.ost` as the name for the Offline Folders file. After doing that, you'll be able to readily locate the file in your Windows file structure if you need to do so.

7. Select the encryption setting you want to use.

Note

You must select an encryption setting at the time you create an Offline Folders file. You can't subsequently change the encryption setting.

8. Click OK. Outlook displays a message stating that the file couldn't be found and asking whether you want to create it. Click Yes to continue and return to the Microsoft Exchange Server dialog box. Click OK to close the Microsoft Exchange dialog box and return to the E-mail Accounts dialog box. Click Next, and then click Finish.

After completing these steps, you have on your computer an Offline Folders file that contains a duplicate of the folders in your Exchange store.

Tip from

After you've created an Offline Folders file, you might want to confirm its existence by using Search in Windows 2000 or Windows Me, or Find in Windows NT or Windows 98, to locate the file. You can also use Windows Explorer to locate the file.

If you're using Windows 2000, you must set the Folder Options to Show Hidden Files and Folders. If you set the Folder Options to Do Not Show Hidden Files and Folders (the default), Search won't locate, and Windows Explorer won't display, Offline Folders files, Personal Folders files, and certain other files that are hidden by default.

> To set Folder Options in Windows 2000, from the Windows desktop, select Start, move the pointer onto Search, and select For Files or Folders. In the Search dialog box, select Tools, Folder Options, and select the View tab. In the Advanced Settings box, click Show Hidden Files and Folders.

USING OUTLOOK OFFLINE

After completing the steps described in the preceding two sections, you can unplug your computer from the network and use Outlook offline. When you do so, Outlook automatically accesses folders in your Offline Folders file instead of those in the Exchange store.

The note following step 3 in the preceding section describes how you can control whether Outlook is connected to the server or is used offline. If you have set up Outlook so that you manually control the connection type and click Work Offline when Outlook starts, you have access to folders in your Offline Folders file, whether your computer is connected to the server or not.

Note

> In previous Outlook versions, you could tell whether Outlook was accessing folders in the Exchange store or in your Offline Folders file by displaying the Folder List. In that list, folders in an Offline Folders file were marked with a small white page with a down-pointing arrow adjacent to the folder icons. Folders in the Offline Folders file are not marked in any way in Outlook 2002.

SYNCHRONIZING FOLDERS

Before you disconnect your computer from the Exchange Server, use synchronization to copy items from your Exchange store to folders in your Offline Folders file so the two places contain the same information.

If you subsequently use your computer offline, any changes you make to the contents of your folders affect only the Offline Folders file. While that's happening, other people might send messages to you, which are saved in the Exchange store. Also, while you're offline, the contents of public folders in the Exchange store might change. All this results in differences between what you have in your Offline Folders file and what's in the Exchange store.

When you return online, you can again use synchronization to update information in your Offline Folders file and in the Exchange store. Synchronization results in the most recent information being in both places. You can use manual or automatic synchronization.

Note

> During synchronization, an item that has been deleted from an Offline Folder is deleted from the corresponding server folder. Likewise, any item that has been deleted from the server folder is deleted from the corresponding Offline Folder.

SYNCHRONIZING MANUALLY

To synchronize folders, Outlook must be connected to the Exchange store. You can synchronize individual folders or all folders.

To synchronize an individual folder manually, select that folder. Then select Tools, move the pointer onto Send/Receive, and click This Folder (Microsoft Exchange Server). To synchronize all folders manually, select Tools, move the pointer onto Send/Receive, and then click Send and Receive All. The Outlook Send/Receive Progress dialog box appears while synchronization takes place.

> **Note**
>
> In addition to synchronizing folders, Outlook also sends all messages waiting in the Outbox and downloads messages from the server into the Inbox folder.

SYNCHRONIZING AUTOMATICALLY

To set up automatic synchronization, select Tools, point onto Send/Receive Settings, and then click Define Send/Receive Groups to display the dialog box shown in Figure 24.4.

Figure 24.4
Use this dialog box to specify how automatic synchronization should occur.

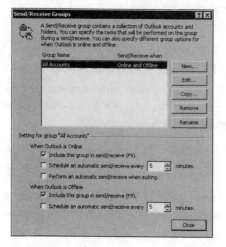

Use the When Outlook Is Online section of the dialog box to specify automatic synchronization when Outlook is connected to the server. Check the Schedule an Automatic Send/Receive Every box, and set an interval in the range from 1 to 1440 minutes. You can also check the Perform an Automatic Send/Receive When Exiting box so that synchronization occurs automatically whenever you exit from Outlook.

Use the When Outlook Is Offline section of the dialog box to specify automatic synchronization when Outlook is not connected to the server. Check the Schedule an Automatic Send/Receive Every box, and set an interval in the range from 1 to 1440 minutes. For this to work, Outlook must be set up to automatically connect to the server as needed.

VERIFYING SYNCHRONIZATION STATUS

After you've synchronized a folder, you can verify the synchronization status. Right-click a folder name in the Outlook Bar or Folder List to display the context menu. Select Properties in the context menu, and then select the Synchronization tab in the Properties dialog box, as shown in Figure 24.5.

Figure 24.5
The Statistics for This Folder section confirms the date of the most recent synchronization and the number of items in the Server and Offline folders.

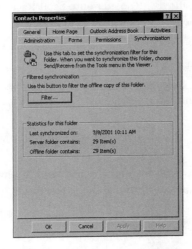

COPYING AN ADDRESS BOOK INTO YOUR REMOTE COMPUTER

If you intend to send e-mail while you're working remotely, you need to have a list of e-mail addresses available. One way you can do this is to copy the Global Address Book from your Exchange server into your remote computer.

With your remote computer connected to the LAN, proceed as follows.

To copy the Global Address Book:

1. With any Outlook Information viewer displayed, select Tools, move the pointer onto Send/Receive, and select Download Address Book. Outlook displays the dialog box shown in Figure 24.6.

Figure 24.6
Use this dialog box to specify what you want to download.

2. The first time you copy the Global Address Book, uncheck Download Changes Since Last Send/Receive. When you subsequently copy the Global Address Book, check this box.

3. In the Information to Download section of the dialog box, you'll normally want to leave the default Full Details selected.

4. Click OK to start downloading.

MAKING CUSTOM FOLDERS AVAILABLE OFFLINE

The Offline Folders file always contains the standard Outlook folders: Calendar, Contacts, Deleted Items, Drafts, Inbox, Journal, Notes, Outbox, Sent Items, and Tasks. If you have created custom folders in your Outlook store, you can choose whether you want to have these folders available when you're working offline.

To make a custom folder available in your Offline Folders file, select that folder, select Tools, move the pointer onto Send/Receive Settings, and then select Make This Folder Available Offline. Repeat that for any other custom folder you want to make available offline.

USING PUBLIC FOLDERS REMOTELY

When you're working offline, you can't access Exchange public folders directly. You can, however, access copies of public folders that have been created in Exchange's public folders Favorites folder.

As explained in Chapter 23, "Using Exchange Server to Share Information," the person who owns a public folder can create a copy of that folder in the public folders Favorites folder. Subsequently, when you synchronize, items in the Favorites folder are copied into a Favorites folder in your Offline Folders file.

While you're working offline, you can access the Favorites folder that contains the information that existed the last time you synchronized. Any offline changes you make are copied to your Favorites folder in the Exchange store the next time you synchronize.

USING REMOTE MAIL

Remote Mail is an alternative way to send and receive e-mail. You can use Remote Mail for such purposes as receiving e-mail from, and sending e-mail to, an e-mail server

- From your desktop computer
- From a computer you use at another location, such as a laptop computer you have with you while you're traveling

With Remote Mail, you can access e-mail in

- A Personal Folders file on another computer
- An e-mail server such as your Internet server

You're probably wondering why you would want to use Remote Mail to send and receive e-mail when Outlook already provides other ways to do so. The answer to that question is that, although Remote Mail is somewhat less convenient, it has the advantage that you can use it to download only message headers and subsequently download only the complete messages you want to see.

The primary purpose of Remote Mail is to provide a way for you to receive important e-mail messages from a remote location without incurring the expense of high long-distance phone charges for messages you don't need. However, Remote Mail also provides a way for you to save time when you're working at your desk by not downloading unnecessary messages.

SETTING UP REMOTE MAIL

Start by creating an Offline Folders file, as described previously in this chapter.

→ For information about creating an Offline Folders file, **see** "Creating an Offline Folders File," **p. 475**.

Although having an address book available if you're working with a remote computer isn't essential, it is very convenient. You can copy the server's Global Address Book to your remote computer using the method described previously in this chapter.

→ If your address book isn't copied onto your remote computer, **see** "Copying an Address Book into Your Remote Computer," **p. 480**.

RECEIVING MESSAGE HEADERS

To receive message headers, select Tools, Send/Receive, move the pointer onto Work with Headers, and then move the pointer onto Download Headers from, as shown in Figure 24.7.

Figure 24.7
At this point, you can select the server from which you want to download headers.

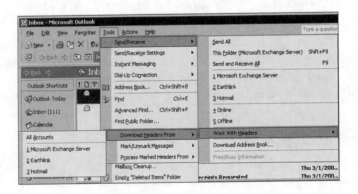

Select a server to download message headers from it. When downloading is complete, you'll see the headers as shown in Figure 24.8.

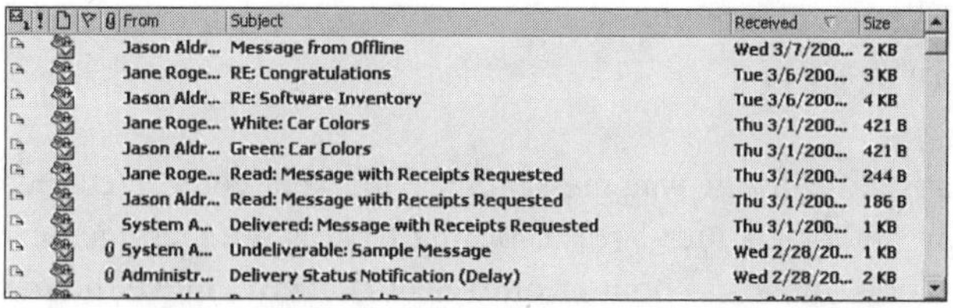

Figure 24.8
Symbols at the left of each header show that only the header has been downloaded.

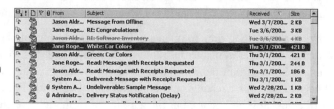

You can decide what you want to do with each downloaded header. You can

- **Mark the headers of messages you want to download from the server**—Right-click a header; then click Mark to Download Messages(s). When you subsequently download those messages, they are deleted from the server.

- **Mark the headers of messages you want to copy from the server**—Right-click a header; then click Mark to Download Message Copy. When you subsequently copy the messages, they are left on the server.

- **Mark the headers of messages you want to delete from your computer**—Right-click a header; then click Delete. When you subsequently copy the headers, the corresponding messages are deleted from the server.

Figure 24.9 shows three messages that have been marked in this way. If you look carefully at the symbols in the left column, you'll see that the symbols for the first two messages contain a small down-pointing arrow (blue on your screen); these messages are marked to be downloaded. The symbol for the third message is marked with an X (red on your screen), and the text in that message header is gray and struck through; this message is marked to be deleted from the server without being downloaded.

Figure 24.9
The top two messages have been marked for downloading and the third message has been marked for deletion.

If you change your mind about what you want to do with message headers you marked, you can change how any of them are marked. To change how specific message headers are marked, select those message headers, select Tools, move the pointer onto Send/Receive, move the pointer onto Work with Headers, and move the pointer onto Mark/Unmark Messages to display a menu in which you can select

- Mark to Download Message(s)
- Mark to Download Message Copy
- Delete

- Unmark Selected Headers
- Unmark All Headers

After you're satisfied with the way messages are marked, you can connect to the server and download, copy, and delete messages according to how the message headers are marked. To do this, select Tools, move the pointer onto Send/Receive, move the pointer onto Work with Headers, and select Process Marked Headers.

TROUBLESHOOTING

REMOTE CONNECTIONS

Outlook's capabilities to work remotely usually work smoothly. However, that's not always the case. Problems can cause headaches.

If you're at a remote location and find that you can't send or receive e-mail messages, the most likely reason is that your server is down or some interconnection problem has occurred. To be prepared for this type of problem, set up and test Remote Mail while you're at home base. That way, you can get assistance from your local administrator before you travel. After getting Remote Mail working locally, try it from your home computer before you travel. Again, if you have problems, you have a local resource to help you solve your problems.

You might find that folders you've previously had access to are no longer available to you. That could be because the people who own those folders have changed the access permissions. If you can't access a folder you think should be shared, contact the owner of that folder to verify that you have access.

Perhaps you can access a folder but can't see all the items in it. That might be because the view you're using applies a filter. Examine your view and, if necessary, remove the filter.

Do you find that it takes a long time to open a public folder? That could be because you're using a view that is no longer available on the server and the server has to rebuild it. Make a habit of opening your important public folders regularly so that Exchange doesn't delete your views. You'll have to ask your Exchange administrator how frequently Exchange discards unused views (the default is eight days, but the administrator might have changed that).

OFFLINE FOLDERS INTEGRITY

You can use the Inbox Repair Tool (scanpst.exe), described in the Troubleshooting section at the end of Chapter 5, "Receiving Messages," and the OST Integrity Check Tool (scanost.exe) to diagnose and repair problems in an Offline Folders file. Both these tools automatically are installed on your computer when you perform a standard Outlook installation.

Use the Inbox Repair Tool to scan an Offline Folders file to verify the integrity of the file structure and to attempt to repair that file. That tool examines only an Offline Folders file on your computer.

Use the OST Integrity Check Tool if you run into problems when synchronizing an Offline Folders file with an Exchange store. This tool scans an Offline Folders file and the equivalent Exchange store and, if it finds any discrepancies between the two sets of information, attempts to reconcile them.

For more information about the OST Integrity Check Tool, see the file Scanost.txt that's installed on your computer when you perform a standard Outlook installation.

PART VI

CUSTOMIZING OUTLOOK

CHAPTER 25

CUSTOMIZING THE OUTLOOK BAR

In this chapter

OUTLOOK BAR OVERVIEW

The Outlook Bar, displayed at the left edge of Outlook's Information viewers, contains shortcut icons you can click to gain immediate access to the standard Outlook folders and your Windows folder structure.

The default Outlook Bar has three groups of shortcut icons:

- **Outlook Shortcuts group**—This group contains shortcut icons that provide access to most of the standard Outlook folders.

- **My Shortcuts group**—This group contains shortcut icons that provide access to folders containing e-mail messages you're preparing to send or have sent to your Outlook Journal folder, and to the Outlook Update Web page.

- **Other Shortcuts group**—This group contains shortcut icons that access your Windows folder structure.

Note

The Outlook Update Web page contains information about updates to Outlook and other Office XP applications available from Microsoft. The Web page URL is `http://officeupdate.microsoft.com/welcome/outlook.asp`.

The default Outlook Bar gives only basic access to your Outlook and Windows folders. You can add more shortcut icons to any group, and you can add more groups to the Outlook Bar to provide fast access to your entire information environment.

In this chapter, you learn how to add shortcuts to existing Outlook Bar groups and add more groups to the Outlook Bar. You also learn how to add shortcuts to your Windows folders and files and to Web pages.

SELECTING AN OUTLOOK BAR GROUP

By default, Outlook displays the Outlook Shortcuts group of shortcut icons, as shown in Figure 25.1.

Figure 25.1
The Outlook Bar, as you first see it, displays most of the shortcut icons in the Outlook Shortcuts group.

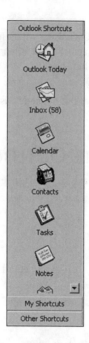

Tip from

To see hidden shortcut icons, click the triangle button near the bottom of the Outlook Shortcuts group. After you've done that, you can click the triangle button near the top to see hidden icons above those you can see.

With the Outlook Shortcuts group displayed, you can click the My Shortcuts or Other Shortcuts button to display those Outlook Bar groups. With either of those groups displayed, you can click the Outlook Shortcuts button to display that group again.

DISPLAYING AND HIDING THE OUTLOOK BAR

By default, Outlook displays the Outlook Bar at the left edge of all Information viewers, but it doesn't have to be displayed. Chapter 1, "How Outlook Works," contains information about modifying the Outlook startup so that an Information viewer is displayed without the Outlook Bar. This has the advantage that Information viewers are enlarged so you can see more of what's in them.

→ To get tips on altering your Information viewers' startup appearance, **see** "Outlook and Outlook Today," **p. 15**.

With any Outlook Information viewer displayed, you can select View, Outlook Bar to hide or unhide the Outlook Bar.

Tip from

If you frequently hide and then redisplay the Outlook Bar, it's useful to create a button on one of the toolbars for this purpose. Clicking that button is more convenient than selecting View, Outlook Bar—one click instead of two.

→ For more information on creating a toolbar button, **see** "Customizing a Toolbar," **p. 510**.

CHANGING THE APPEARANCE OF THE OUTLOOK BAR

You can make the Outlook Bar narrower or wider by dragging the border between the Outlook Bar and an Information viewer. The following sections describe how you can make other changes to the Outlook Bar's appearance.

CHOOSING SMALL ICONS

When you have the Outlook Shortcuts group displayed, you can't see all its shortcuts (unless you have a big monitor that displays a large number of pixels). After you use the techniques described in this chapter to add more shortcut icons to a group on the Outlook Bar, you'll probably wish that more could be seen at one time.

You can choose to have small icons, instead of the default large icons, displayed in the Outlook Bar. This choice is available separately for each Outlook Bar group.

To have small icons in an Outlook Bar group, select that group, and then right-click within the Outlook Bar group (not on an icon) to display the Outlook Bar's context menu, shown in Figure 25.2.

Figure 25.2
This is the menu you use to customize the Outlook Bar.

Select Small Icons. Instead of the large icons previously displayed in the Outlook Bar, you now have small icons, as shown in Figure 25.3.

Figure 25.3
Here is the Outlook
Bar with small icons.

You'll probably prefer to use Outlook with small icons in the Outlook Bar, unless you're displaying Outlook on a small screen. You can, of course, go back to large icons by again displaying the Outlook Bar context menu and selecting Large Icons.

CHANGING THE ORDER OF ICONS

You can change the order of icons in a group so those you use most often are close together. You can also move icons from one group to another.

To move a shortcut icon within a group, simply drag it up or down.

You can use a similar method to move a shortcut icon from one group to another. For example, you can move the Deleted Items shortcut icon from the Outlook Shortcuts group to the My Shortcuts group. With the Outlook Shortcuts group displayed, drag the Deleted Items icon down onto the My Shortcuts group button. The My Shortcuts group opens with a black bar representing the icon you're dragging below the last icon in that group. Drag up to place the Deleted Items icon where you want it to be within the My Shortcuts group.

Tip from

Whether you're dragging a shortcut icon within a group, or from one group to another, if you drag onto a group name and then release the mouse button, Outlook displays a message stating that you can't do that. If that happens, click OK to close the message. Try the process again, this time making sure you don't release the mouse button while you're pointing onto a group name.

PART

VI

CH

25

USING A SHORTCUT ICON'S CONTEXT MENU

Right-click a shortcut icon to see its context menu, as shown in Figure 25.4.

Figure 25.4
This is a shortcut
icon's context menu.

Select an item on the context menu, according to what you want to do:

- **Open**—Opens the Outlook folder represented by the shortcut icon to display its contents in an Information viewer. This is the same thing that happens when you click a shortcut icon.

- **Open in New Window**—Opens the Outlook folder represented by the shortcut icon in a separate window on your screen. This enables you to have two or more windows visible, each showing the contents of a separate folder.

- **Send Link to This Folder**—This is a mystery item that's always dimmed. Perhaps Microsoft has something in mind for this in a subsequent release of Outlook.

- **Advanced Find**—Opens the Advanced Find dialog box. The Advanced Find dialog box opens ready to search in the folder corresponding to the Outlook Bar shortcut with which you're working.

→ For information about working with Advanced Find, **see** "Using Advanced Find to Find Words and Phrases," **p. 341**.

- **Remove from Outlook Bar**—Removes the icon from the Outlook Bar.

- **Rename Shortcut**—Renames the shortcut icon.

- **Properties**—Displays the shortcut icon's properties. Properties are explained in the next section.

UNDERSTANDING A SHORTCUT ICON'S PROPERTIES

When you select Properties in a shortcut icon's context menu, you have access to the properties of the folder to which the icon is a shortcut. For example, if you right-click the Contacts shortcut icon and then select Properties, you see the dialog box shown in Figure 25.5.

Figure 25.5
This is the Contacts
Properties dialog box.

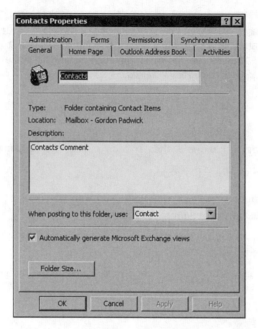

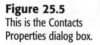
The Properties dialog box tabs vary according to the Outlook Bar shortcut you're look-
ing at and according to which types of e-mail accounts you have available.

You can use this dialog box to examine and, if necessary, change the properties of the
Contacts folder, as explained in Chapter 8, "Managing and Using Contacts."

→ To learn more about adjusting the settings for Contacts, **see** "Examining a Contact Item's Properties,"
p. 188.

For information about the properties of other folders, refer to the chapters in which specific
types of Outlook items are described.

RENAMING, ADDING, AND REMOVING OUTLOOK BAR GROUPS

If you're like me, you don't particularly like the names Microsoft has given to two of the
default Outlook Bar groups. Outlook Shortcuts might be okay, but My Shortcuts and Other
Shortcuts? You can change the names of the Outlook Bar shortcuts to whatever seems more
appropriate. You can also add groups to, and delete groups from, the Outlook Bar.

Note

Outlook saves your Outlook Bar configuration in a file named Outlook.FAV. After you've customized the Outlook Bar, you can restore it to its default. Close Outlook and delete the Outlook.FAV file. When you restart Outlook, a new file based on the default settings is automatically created.

RENAMING AN OUTLOOK BAR GROUP

Suppose you want to change the name of the My Shortcuts group to E-mail Shortcuts.

To change the name of an Outlook Bar group:

1. In the Outlook Bar, right-click the group name you want to change to display the group's context menu, shown previously in Figure 25.2.
2. Select Rename Group in the context menu. The group name button changes to white with the name selected.
3. Edit the group name in the normal way; then press Enter. Now the group has the new name.

ADDING A GROUP

The default Outlook Bar has three groups of shortcut icons. The maximum number of groups allowed is 12, so you can add up to 9 more.

To add a group to the Outlook Bar:

1. Right-click any group name to display that group's context menu, shown previously in Figure 25.2.
2. Click Add New Group. A button appears at the bottom of the Outlook Bar with the temporary name "New Group" selected.
3. Change the temporary name to the name you want the new group to have, and then press Enter.

Tip from

Gordon Padwick

Each new group you create always appears below the existing group buttons in the Outlook Bar. There appears to be no straightforward way to change the order of group buttons in the Outlook Bar.

→ If you must change the group order, one possible workaround is suggested at the end of this chapter. **See** "Outlook Bar," **p. 503**.

REMOVING A GROUP

You can remove any group from the Outlook Bar, including the default groups.

To remove an Outlook Bar group:

1. Right-click the name of the group you want to remove to display its context menu.

2. Select Remove Group in the context menu. Outlook asks you to confirm that you want to remove the group.

Caution

When Outlook asks you to confirm that you want to remove the group, it doesn't name the group you've selected. Be sure, in step 1, that the group you select is really the one you intend to remove. After you've removed a group, you can't undo the remove. You can, however, re-create the group, but that's a considerable amount of work.

3. Click Yes to remove the group.

ADDING SHORTCUT ICONS TO AN OUTLOOK BAR GROUP

Whenever you create a new Outlook folder, Outlook asks whether you want to create a shortcut to that folder in the Outlook Bar. If you choose not to create a shortcut at that time, you can do so later.

In addition to creating Outlook Bar shortcuts to Outlook items, you can also create shortcuts to Windows folders and files, Web pages, and items on the Windows desktop.

PART
VI

CH
25

CREATING A SHORTCUT ICON WHEN YOU CREATE AN OUTLOOK FOLDER

Chapter 14, "Managing Outlook Folders," explains how to create a new Outlook folder and how you can add a shortcut icon to the Outlook Bar to access that folder.

→ To gain fast access to a new folder by creating a shortcut to it on the Outlook Bar, **see** "Adding a Folder Icon to the Outlook Bar," **p. 306**.

CREATING A SHORTCUT TO AN EXISTING OUTLOOK FOLDER

You can add a shortcut to any Outlook Bar group to provide easy access to that folder.

To add an Outlook folder shortcut icon to an Outlook Bar group:

1. Select the Outlook Bar group into which you want to add a shortcut icon.

2. Select View, Folder List to display the Outlook folder list.

3. If necessary, expand the folder list so that the name of the folder for which you want to create a shortcut icon is visible.

4. Drag the folder name into the Outlook Bar group.

Note

If you subsequently change your mind about which Outlook Bar group you want the new shortcut to be in, you can drag it to another group.

→   You can make your Outlook Bar more convenient to use by placing those icons you use most often at the top of a group. To learn more, **see** "Changing the Order of Icons," **p. 493**.

If you're using Outlook as a client for Exchange, you can create Outlook Bar shortcut icons for public folders in the Exchange store. Expand your folder list to display the names of public folders; then drag a folder name into the Outlook Bar.

CREATING A SHORTCUT TO A WINDOWS FOLDER OR FILE

You can create a shortcut to any folder or file in your Windows folder structure, including folders and files on other network computers to which you've been granted access. You can use the first method described in this section to create a shortcut only to a folder; you can use the second method to create a shortcut to a folder or file.

To add a Windows folder shortcut icon to an Outlook Bar group:

1. Select the Outlook Bar group into which you want to add a shortcut icon.

2. Right-click that Outlook Bar group (not an icon in the group) to display its context menu.

3. Click Outlook Bar Shortcut to display the dialog box shown in Figure 25.6.

Figure 25.6
Use this dialog box to add shortcuts to Outlook folders as well as to Windows folders.

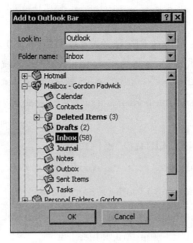

4. Open the drop-down Look In list and select File System. The list now shows you the Windows desktop structure, as shown in Figure 25.7.

Figure 25.7
You can expand this
list to show any part
of your Windows
folder structure.

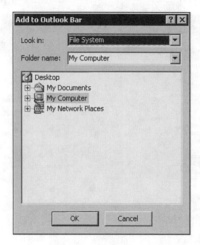

Tip from

Notice that the folder structure includes Network Neighborhood or My Network Places
(depending on the operating system). You can expand that to see folders on other
computers to which you have access and create shortcut icons on the Outlook Bar to
those folders.

5. Expand the list to display the folder for which you want to create a shortcut.

6. Select that folder and click OK. The shortcut icon appears in the Outlook Bar.

Here's a way to add shortcuts representing Windows folders or files into an Outlook Bar
group.

To add a shortcut to a Windows folder or file into the Outlook Bar:

1. Display Outlook and Windows Explorer together on your screen, as shown in
   Figure 25.8.

PART
VI

CH

25

Figure 25.8
Adjust the size of the windows so that the Outlook Bar is visible and you can see as much as you need in the Windows Explorer window, as shown here.

Outlook window ─────

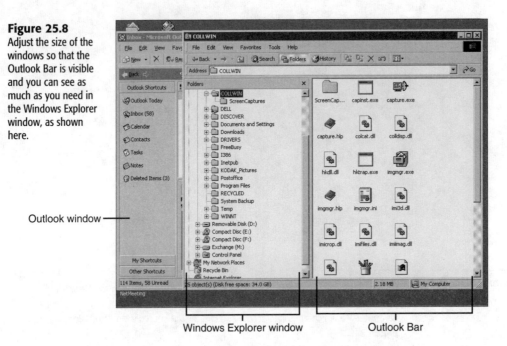

Windows Explorer window   Outlook Bar

2. Drag whichever folder or file you want from the left or right panes of the Windows Explorer window into the Outlook Bar.

After adding a shortcut representing a Windows folder or file to the Outlook Bar, you can click the icon in the Outlook Bar to access that folder or file.

What happens when you click an icon in the Outlook Bar depends on what that icon represents:

- If the icon represents a Windows folder, the Information viewer displays a list of files and folders in that folder.
- If the icon represents a document, Windows opens the application associated with that type of document and displays that document.
- If the icon represents an executable file, Windows runs the file.

CREATING A SHORTCUT TO THE WINDOWS DESKTOP

You already know that you can create icons on your Windows desktop to provide fast access to applications. For example, while writing this book, I often need to use the Collage Complete Screen Capture and Image Manager applications. By having shortcuts to those applications on my desktop, I can quickly open them.

However, if I have Outlook maximized, I can't see shortcuts on my desktop. Here's where Outlook simplifies my life. I can drag shortcuts from my Windows desktop into the Outlook Bar. Now I have shortcuts in the Outlook Bar that are copies of the shortcuts on my desktop.

Here's another example of the versatility and usefulness of creating shortcuts in the Outlook Bar. Do you often want to take a look at something in the Windows Control Panel? If so, you can create a shortcut to it in the Outlook Bar. First, create a shortcut to the Control Panel on the Windows desktop. Then, drag that shortcut into the Outlook Bar. Here are the details.

To create a shortcut to the Control Panel in the Outlook Bar:

1. Open Windows Explorer and select your Windows folder.
2. Scroll down the list of files in the Windows folder to find Control.exe.
3. Drag Control.exe onto the Windows desktop. Now you have a shortcut to the Control Panel on your Windows desktop.
4. Open Outlook, restore it so that it occupies only a part of your screen, and select the Outlook Bar group in which you want to have the Control Panel shortcut.
5. Drag the Control Panel shortcut from your Windows desktop to the Outlook Bar.

Now, from within Outlook, you can instantly bring up the Windows Control Panel.

CREATING A SHORTCUT TO A WEB PAGE

You can create shortcuts in your Outlook Bar to get direct access to specific Web pages.

Note

The Outlook Update shortcut in the default My Shortcuts Outlook Bar group is a shortcut to a Web page.

To create a shortcut in the Outlook Bar to a Web page:

1. Use Internet Explorer to access an Internet Web page.
2. Display the Web page for which you want to create a shortcut on an Outlook Bar.
3. Open Outlook and arrange the Internet Explorer and the Outlook windows on your screen, as shown in Figure 25.9.

PART

VI

CH

25

Web page icon   Outlook Bar

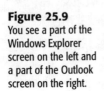

Figure 25.9
You see a part of the
Windows Explorer
screen on the left and
a part of the Outlook
screen on the right.

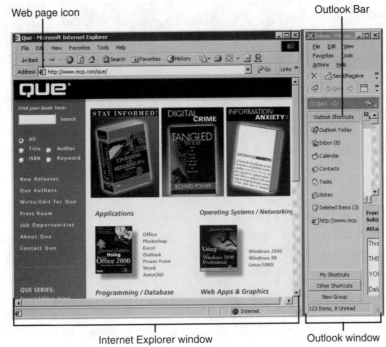

Internet Explorer window   Outlook window

4. Drag the Web page icon shown in Figure 25.9 into the Outlook Bar in the Outlook window.

After you've done that, you can click the new shortcut in the Outlook Bar to access whatever Web site you specified.

Note

You also can drag existing shortcuts in the Favorites Information viewer into the Outlook Bar.

After you've created a shortcut to a Web page, you simply click the shortcut in the Outlook Bar to display that Web page.

→ For more detailed information about opening a Web page from within Outlook, **see** "Accessing Web Sites," **p. 116**.

REMOVING SHORTCUT ICONS FROM THE OUTLOOK BAR

You can remove any shortcut icon from the Outlook Bar.

To remove a shortcut icon:

1. Right-click the shortcut icon you want to remove to display its context menu.
2. Select Remove from Outlook Bar. Outlook asks you to confirm that you want to remove the selected shortcut icon.
3. Click Yes.

TROUBLESHOOTING

OUTLOOK BAR

As mentioned previously in this chapter, although you can easily change the order of shortcut items within a group, you can't change the order of groups within the Outlook Bar. Suppose, for example, you create a new group and you want to have that group at the top of the Outlook Bar so that it's the one displayed when you open Outlook. Here's a workaround you can use.

To create a new Outlook Bar group at the top of the Outlook Bar:

1. Add a new group to the Outlook Bar.

→ For details on how to add new groups to the Outlook Bar, **see** "Adding a Group," **p. 496**.

2. Drag the existing shortcuts from the Outlook Shortcuts group into the new group.

→ To learn more about reordering icons on your Outlook Bar, **see** "Changing the Order of Icons," **p. 493**.

3. Insert new shortcuts into the group you just emptied.

→ For additional information about shortcuts and the Outlook Bar, **see** "Adding Shortcut Icons to an Outlook Bar Group," **p. 497**.

4. Rename the two Outlook Bar groups.

→ To learn the steps for changing group names, **see** "Renaming an Outlook Bar Group," **p. 496**.

CHAPTER 26

CUSTOMIZING COMMAND BARS

In this chapter

WHAT ARE COMMAND BARS?

You might be used to thinking of the menu bar and toolbars as separate components of an application's user interface. Even though they're visually separate in Outlook, they have a lot in common, so much so that Microsoft now uses the term Command Bars for both.

Note

The similarity between the menus and toolbars extends to what's in them. Toolbars can contain menus, and menus can contain tools.

Like other Office applications, Outlook has predefined command bars. You can customize these command bars and create your own so that Outlook is convenient for you to use.

In common with the other Office XP applications, Outlook 2002 offers adaptive menus and toolbars that use Microsoft IntelliSense technology to adapt automatically to how people work. By default, Outlook's menus and toolbars group together the menu items and tools you use frequently and temporarily hide others.

Tip from

The illustrations in this book were saved with adaptive menus and toolbars turned off (that is, with menus and toolbars always completely shown) to make the book easier to follow. To turn adaptive menus and toolbars on or off, select Tools, Customize to display the Customize dialog box. Select the Options tab. By default, Always Show Full Menus is unchecked, meaning that adaptive menus and toolbars are enabled; check this box if you want to display complete menus and toolbars. The setting you choose applies to all Office XP applications.

COMMAND BARS IN THE DEFAULT USER INTERFACE

The default Outlook user interface when Information viewers are displayed has a menu bar at the top and a single toolbar under the menu bar, as shown in Figure 26.1.

Menu bar   Standard toolbar

Figure 26.1
This is the Outlook menu bar and Standard toolbar (with the Inbox Information viewer displayed).

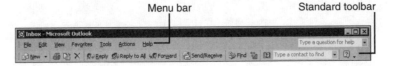

The menu bar contains the same menus for all the Information viewers that display Outlook items—with only one slight difference when an Information viewer that displays

Windows folders is open. Many of the items in the menus are also the same. Some of the tools in the toolbars, however, are different for each Information viewer because the tools provide quick access to the types of Outlook items shown in each viewer. If you move the pointer onto a tool and pause for a moment, a ScreenTip containing the name of the tool appears.

DISPLAYING AND HIDING TOOLBARS

The Standard toolbar, initially displayed by Outlook, contains the tools most frequently used when you're working with Information viewers. You can also display the Advanced toolbar by selecting View, moving the pointer onto Toolbars, and selecting Advanced. The Advanced toolbar, which contains additional tools, appears under the Standard toolbar.

Tip from

You can also right-click any button in a displayed toolbar to display a list of available toolbars, and then select from that list to display a hidden toolbar or hide a displayed toolbar.

Instead of displaying the two toolbars in this way, you can drag one of them so that it's in the same row as the other. For example, point onto the Advanced toolbar's handle (the column of dashes at the extreme left end of the toolbar) and drag to the right and up. When you display the toolbars like this, only some of the buttons in each toolbar are visible. You can click the Toolbar Options button at the right end of each toolbar, shown in Figure 26.2, to see the hidden buttons.

Standard toolbar   Advanced toolbar

Figure 26.2
The Standard and
Advanced toolbars
are shown in one row
here.

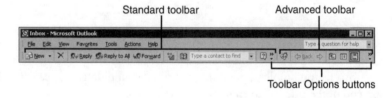

Toolbar Options buttons

Note

To change the number of visible tools in each toolbar, drag the Advanced toolbar's handle to the left or right.

You can also select View, move the pointer onto Toolbars, and click Web to display the Web toolbar, which you might find useful for accessing Web sites.

To hide a toolbar, select View, move the pointer onto Toolbars, and click the name of the toolbar you want to hide.

MOVING A TOOLBAR

The Standard and Advanced toolbars are initially displayed in the docked position at the top of an Outlook window.

You can drag a docked toolbar to another docked position. For example, if you have the Standard and Advanced toolbars displayed in one row, as previously shown in Figure 26.2, you can drag the Advanced toolbar down and to the left so it's immediately below the Standard toolbar. To do so, point onto the Advanced toolbar's handle (the vertical bar near its left edge). When you're pointing onto the correct position, the pointer changes to a four-headed arrow. Now, drag down and to the left until the Advanced toolbar is in the correct position.

You also can drag a toolbar that's docked at the top of the window to a docked position at the left, right, or bottom of the Outlook window. Point onto a docked toolbar's handle and drag to a different edge of the window.

You can convert a docked toolbar to a floating toolbar. To do so, point onto the toolbar's handle and drag the toolbar away from the window border, as shown in Figure 26.3.

Toolbar name   Title bar   Toolbar Options   Close

Figure 26.3
Here is the Standard
toolbar in a floating
position.

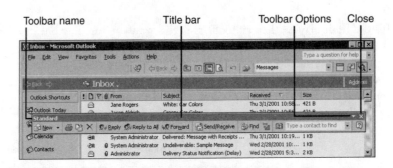

As Figure 26.3 shows, a floating toolbar has a title bar that contains the name of the toolbar. To move a floating toolbar, point into the title bar and drag. You can also click the X at the right end of the title bar to close the toolbar. You can click the Toolbar Options button to customize the toolbar, as described subsequently in this chapter.

Whereas a docked toolbar always consists of a single row or column of tools, that isn't so for a floating toolbar. To change a floating toolbar to an array with several rows and columns of tools, point onto one of the toolbar's borders. If you point onto the left or right border, you can drag to the right or left; if you point onto the top or bottom border, you can drag up or down. Figure 26.4 shows the result of doing this.

To return a floating toolbar to the docked position, point onto the toolbar's title bar and drag to one of the borders of the window.

Figure 26.4
Here is the Standard toolbar as an array of tools.

SAVING AND RESTORING TOOLBARS

Outlook automatically saves the status of toolbars in a file named Outcmd.dat. Status indicates

- Which toolbars are displayed
- Whether each toolbar is docked or floating
- The position of each toolbar
- In the case of a floating toolbar, the size of the array
- Any changes you've made to the contents of the default toolbars
- Complete information about any custom toolbars you've created

Note

Any changes you make to the menu bar and the individual menus are also saved in Outcmd.dat, a file that can't be edited. This is one of the files you should save if you want to move Outlook from one computer to another.

PART
VI

CH

26

Outlook saves this file separately in each user's Windows profile. As a result, if several people have separate Windows accounts on one computer, each person can have separate customized toolbars and menus.

Outlook refers to Outcmd.dat on startup so that toolbars and menus appear as they were when you previously closed Outlook.

After you've made changes to Outlook's toolbars, menu bar, or individual menus, you can restore the defaults. This process removes any custom toolbars you've created.

Note

If you inherit a computer from someone who has customized Outlook's toolbars and menus, you might want to restore the default toolbars and menus.

To restore Outlook's default toolbars, menu bar, and individual menus, exit Outlook and use Search (in Windows 2000 or Windows Me) or Find (in Windows NT or Windows 98) to locate Outcmd.dat. Rename Outcmd.dat to something such as Outcmd.old; then restart Outlook. On startup, Outlook looks in your Windows profile for Outcmd.dat and, if it's not available, creates a new one based on the built-in defaults.

Note

By default, Windows 2000 and Windows Me hide .dat files. To be able to find .dat files, you must set Folder Options to show hidden files and folders.

CUSTOMIZING A TOOLBAR

Having described what you can do with Outlook's default toolbars, it's time now to think about how you can modify the existing toolbars and create new ones. A word of warning is appropriate before getting started with this. This warning applies to modifying menus as well as to modifying toolbars.

By changing toolbars and menus, you're changing Outlook's user interface. If you work by yourself with Outlook and never ask anyone for help, change the toolbars and menus as much as you like. You've made the changes, you know what they are, and you have to solve any problems that arise.

However, if you work in a group and rely on other people for support, you're heading for problems if you make more than minor changes to toolbars and menus. This is particularly the case if you rely on support by telephone from a help desk. A support person can't guide you through a process if your Outlook installation doesn't have the standard toolbar buttons and menu items (or, perhaps, customized toolbars and menus that match a group standard).

Groups of users should either not make changes to toolbars and menus or, if changes are necessary, every member of the group should have the same customized toolbars and menus. Think about that before making changes.

The remainder of this chapter describes how you can customize toolbars and the menu bar.

You can change the size of toolbar buttons, delete buttons from a toolbar, and add buttons to a toolbar. You can also create custom toolbars.

Tip from

Gordon Padwick

Before you start making changes to toolbars, the menu bar, and individual menus, you should save a copy of the original Outcmd.dat file. Then, if things go wrong, you can restore the saved file to return to your configuration before you started making changes.

CHANGING THE SIZE OF TOOLBAR BUTTONS

By default, all toolbar buttons are small. You can, however, choose to have large buttons displayed.

With any Outlook Information viewer displayed, select Tools, Customize to display the Customize dialog box. Select the Options tab shown in Figure 26.5.

Figure 26.5
Use this dialog box to select options that apply to all Office XP applications installed on your computer.

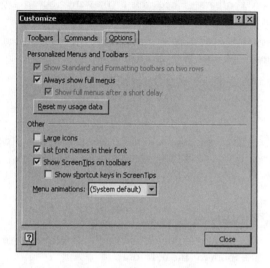

Check Large Icons, and then click Close. The Outlook window now has large icons.

Tip from

In most cases, you won't want to use large icons. However, if you're using a laptop with a small screen, have poor vision, or work in difficult lighting conditions, large icons might be preferable to the standard small icons.

Unless you want to keep large icons, return to the Customize dialog box, previously shown in Figure 26.5, and uncheck Large Icons.

While you have the Options tab open, notice the other choices it offers:

■ **Show Standard and Formatting Toolbars on Two Rows**—This option applies to forms such as Outlook's Message form, in which Standard and Formatting toolbars are available.

■ **Always Show Full Menus**—Uncheck this to enable Office XP's adaptive menus and toolbars capability, described at the beginning of this chapter. What you select here affects all Office XP applications.

■ **Reset My Usage Data**—Click this button to restore the default menus and toolbars in Outlook (and other Office XP applications) when you have unchecked Always Show Full Menus.

■ **Large Icons**—Check this to display large icons in toolbars and menus. Uncheck it to display small icons.

- **List Font Names in Their Font**—Check this if you want Office XP applications to show lists of fonts with each font's name displayed in that font.

- **Show ScreenTips on Toolbars**—Check this if you want a ScreenTip to display a tool's name when you move the pointer onto a tool.

- **Show Shortcut Keys in ScreenTips**—Check this if you want ScreenTips to display shortcut keys for those tools that have shortcut keys.

- **Menu Animations**—Open the drop-down list and select among None, Random, Unfold, and Slide.

Note

Instead of attempting to describe menu animations, I'll leave it to you to experiment with them and decide if there's an animation you'd like to use.

DELETING TOOLS FROM A TOOLBAR

If you want to add your own tools to a toolbar, you might want to remove some standard tools you rarely use to make room for the new tools.

To delete a toolbar button, point onto the button you want to delete. Hold down the Alt key while you drag the button off the toolbar. When you release the Alt key, the button disappears from the toolbar.

ADDING TOOLS TO A TOOLBAR

You can add a new tool to a toolbar, or replace a tool you previously removed from a toolbar.

To add a tool to a toolbar:

1. Display the toolbar to which you want to add a tool.
2. Select Tools, Customize to display the Customize dialog box.

Tip from

Alternatively, right-click any tool in a toolbar to display the context menu, and select Customize in that menu.

3. Select the Commands tab to display the dialog box shown in Figure 26.6.
4. In the Categories list on the left side of the dialog box, select the category of the command you want to add. For example, if you want to add an Outlook Today tool to a toolbar, select the View category. The right side of the dialog box now lists the commands in that category, as shown in Figure 26.7.

Figure 26.6
This dialog box displays the commands available to be added as tools to a toolbar.

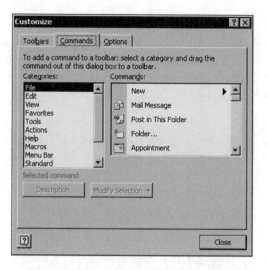

Figure 26.7
With the View category selected, the Commands list contains the commands available in that category.

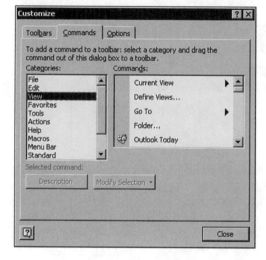

5. Move the pointer onto the command you want to add, press the mouse button, and drag the command to the position where you want it on the toolbar. When you release the mouse button, the new command appears within a black-bordered box on the toolbar.

6. Click Close in the Customize dialog box. The black-bordered box in the toolbar disappears, leaving the new button displayed in the normal manner.

Tip from

In the Customize dialog box, with the Commands tab selected, you can select a command in the list on the right and then click Description to see a description of the selected command.

ADDING A CUSTOM MENU TO A TOOLBAR BUTTON

Toolbars can contain tools that display menus as well as conventional tools. For an example of a tool that displays a menu, click the black triangle near the right edge of the New button in the Inbox Information viewer's Standard toolbar to see a menu. You can add tools that display menus to Outlook's toolbars.

Note	Outlook identifies each menu tool in toolbars with a black triangle near its right edge.

To add a tool that displays a menu into a toolbar:

1. Display the toolbar into which you want to insert the tool.

2. Select Tools, Customize and select the Commands tab shown previously in Figure 26.6.

3. Scroll down in the Categories list and select New Menu. When you do so, New Menu appears in the Commands list, as shown in Figure 26.8.

Figure 26.8
With New Menu selected in the Categories list, the Commands list contains only New Menu.

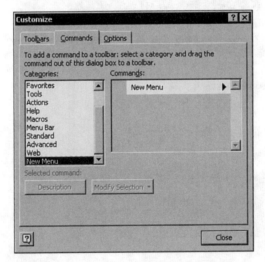

4. Drag New Menu from the Commands list into the toolbar in which you want to have the new tool. While the mouse button is pressed, you see only a black vertical bar in the toolbar. Drag the black bar horizontally to the position where you want to have the tool; then release the mouse button. The new tool appears in the menu, as shown in Figure 26.9.

5. Right-click the new tool to display its context menu, as shown in Figure 26.10.

Inserted menu tool

Figure 26.9
In this case, the new tool has been added near the right end of the Advanced toolbar.

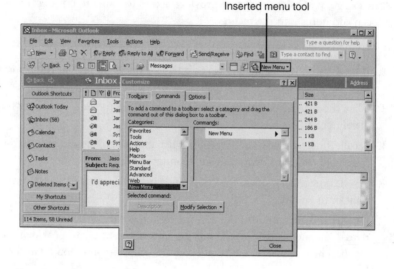

Figure 26.10
The third item in the context menu contains the temporary name New Menu.

6. Change the temporary name to an appropriate name for the tool, and then press Enter. You can either close the Customize dialog box at this stage or continue on to the procedure to add items into the menu.

Note

When entering a name for the tool, place an ampersand immediately before the character to be underlined in the menu name. That character becomes a hot key. Subsequently, hold down Alt and type that character to open the menu. Be careful not to select a hot-key character that is already used in the menu bar or any other displayed toolbar.

At this stage, you have a tool that provides access to a menu, but that menu is empty. Now you can add items into the menu.

To add items into a menu:

1. If the Customize dialog box isn't displayed, select Tools, Customize to display it. Make sure the Commands tab is selected.

2. Click the menu tool you previously placed in the toolbar. An empty box appears immediately below the button.

3. Scroll, if necessary, in the Categories list and select a command category to display commands in that category in the Commands list.

4. Scroll, if necessary, down the commands in the Commands list to find a command you want in the menu.

5. Drag that command into the empty box below the tool in the toolbar. When you release the mouse button, the box expands horizontally to provide space for the command. The command's name and its icon—if available—appear in the box, as shown in Figure 26.11.

Figure 26.11
Here's how the menu appears after you've added one item to the menu.

6. Repeat steps 3–5 to add more commands to the menu.

7. Close the Customize dialog box.

You can click the new tool in the toolbar to display the menu you've just created and then select any item in that menu.

CHANGING THE POSITION OF A TOOL IN A TOOLBAR

To change the position of a tool, point onto that tool, hold down the Alt key, and drag the tool to a new position. You can use this method to move a tool within a toolbar and also to move a tool from one toolbar to another.

INSERTING AND DELETING SEPARATORS BETWEEN TOOLS

If you look closely at one of Outlook's Standard toolbars, you'll notice vertical gray lines that divide tools into groups; these lines are known as *separators*. You can insert separators into toolbars and remove separators from toolbars.

To insert a separator at the left of a tool, hold down the Alt key while you drag the tool a short distance to the right. The separator appears when you release the Alt key.

To delete a separator at the left of a tool, hold down the Alt key while you drag the tool a short distance to the left. The separator disappears when you release the Alt key.

MODIFYING A TOOL

You can make changes to an existing tool, but only if the Customize dialog box is displayed. With the Customize dialog box displayed, right-click a tool to display the context menu shown in Figure 26.12.

Figure 26.12
These are the items available in a tool's context menu.

Use a tool's context menu as follows:

- **Reset**—Resets all aspects of a tool to what it was before you made changes to it by using any other command in this menu. Selecting this doesn't restore the tool to its original default condition.

- **Delete**—Deletes the selected tool.

- **Name**—Changes a tool's name. The tool's current name, if any, is displayed in the menu with an ampersand (&) preceding the underlined character as it appears (or could appear) on the tool. You can change the displayed name and change the position of the ampersand so that a different character becomes underlined and acts as the hot key. When you change a tool's name, make sure the ampersand precedes a character that's not underlined in any other tool on the toolbar. The changed name also appears as a ScreenTip when you point onto a tool and pause briefly.

- **Copy Button Image**—Copies the tool's image (not the tool's text) to the Clipboard.

- **Paste Button Image**—Replaces the image (not the text) on the selected tool with an image previously copied to the Clipboard.

- **Reset Button Image**—Resets the tool's image (not its text) to what it was before you made changes to it.

- **Edit Button Image**—Opens the Button Editor dialog box to display the image's individual pixels, as shown in Figure 26.13.

Figure 26.13
You can use this dialog box to make changes to a tool's image or to create an image for a tool that previously didn't have one.

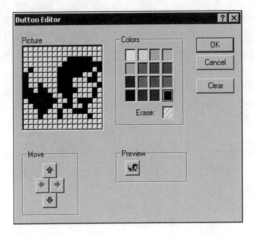

Tip from

Although functional, this image editor is somewhat limited. If you make more than occasional small changes to images, consider using a graphics editor, such as Windows Paint, or a specialized image editor, saving the image to the Clipboard, and pasting it from there.

- **Change Button Image**—Selects an icon from an available set of icons.
- **Default Style**—Displays only the default icon in the selected tool (no text). If no default icon exists, the tool is displayed as an empty box.
- **Text Only (Always)**—Displays only text in the tool.
- **Text Only (in Menus)**—With a tool selected, this command has the same effect as Default Style. With a menu item selected, it displays only text.
- **Image and Text**—Displays an icon and text in the selected tool.
- **Begin a Group**—Inserts a separator at the left of the selected tool.
- **Assign Hyperlink**—Creates a tool that accesses a file on your computer, a file on another computer to which you have network access, or a Web page. You can also use this to prepare pre-addressed Message forms.

Note

The items in this menu use the word *image* to refer to what, in other places, is called an *icon*. The text in this book refers to images as icons.

By using these commands, you can customize a toolbar to satisfy your personal taste and requirements. For example, you can add text to a tool that, by default, contains only an icon; you might consider doing this for people who have difficulty remembering what some tools are for. You also can remove text from tools to make them smaller; this can be useful if you want to make room for several custom tools.

→ For detailed information about adding tools to a toolbar, **see** "Adding Tools to a Toolbar," **p. 512**.

The capability to create tools that enable hyperlinks is very powerful, although you might need some practice to become fully comfortable with it. The next four sections provide an introduction to this subject. All four sections assume you have selected the Assign Hyperlink command in a tool's context menu, as described in this section.

AUTOMATICALLY ADDRESSING AN E-MAIL MESSAGE

You can create toolbar tools that automatically address e-mail messages to specific people. First, create a new tool on a toolbar, as previously explained. The new tool must represent a command, not a menu or list. It doesn't matter which command the tool represents because you'll subsequently replace the command.

→ For an explanation of how to create a new tool, **see** "Adding Tools to a Toolbar," **p. 512**.

If the Customize dialog box isn't already displayed with the Commands tab selected, select Tools, Customize and select the Commands tab. You must have this dialog box open before proceeding. Right-click the new tool in the toolbar to display its context menu, move the pointer onto Assign Hyperlink, click Open to display the Assign Hyperlink dialog box, and select E-mail Address in the Link To column on the left, as shown in Figure 26.14.

Figure 26.14
You can use this dialog box to assign an e-mail address to a toolbar button.

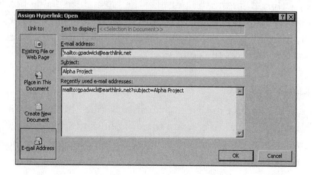

Enter an e-mail address in the E-mail Address box and, optionally, a message subject in the Subject box. If the e-mail address you want to use already appears in the Recently Used E-mail Addresses box, you can click that address to place it in the E-mail Address box.

Click OK to close the Assign Hyperlink dialog box, and click Close to close the Customize dialog box. At this stage, the new tool contains the icon representing the command you chose when you created that tool. However, if you point onto the tool, a ScreenTip displays the e-mail address the tool now represents. When you click the tool, Outlook displays the Message form with the e-mail address in the To box and the message subject, if any, in the Subject box. Complete the message in the normal manner.

You can make the tool easier to use by replacing the icon displayed in the tool with the name of the person whose e-mail address the tool represents. To do this, select Tools, Customize, right-click the tool, and click Text Only (Always) in the context menu. Now, instead of an icon, the tool contains the name of the command the tool originally represented.

Right-click the tool again and, this time, in the context menu, click Name. When you click Name, the text of the original tool's name becomes highlighted. Edit that name to replace the text with the name of the person the tool now represents and press Enter. The new name immediately appears in the tool. Click Close to close the Customize dialog box.

EDITING AND REMOVING A HYPERLINK

After you've changed a tool so that it represents a hyperlink, as described in the preceding section, you can change that hyperlink or remove that hyperlink from the tool.

To edit the hyperlink, select Tools, Customize to display the Customize dialog box. With that dialog box open, right-click the tool and, in its context menu, move the pointer onto Edit Hyperlink, and click Open to open the dialog box previously displayed in Figure 26.14. Instead of containing Assign Hyperlink in its title bar, the dialog box is now appropriately named Edit Hyperlink. You can change the address in the E-mail Address box and change the text in the Subject box. Click OK to save the changed hyperlink.

To remove the hyperlink from the tool, display the Customize dialog box, right-click the tool, move the pointer onto Edit Hyperlink in the context menu, and click Remove Link. After you do that, the tool behaves in the manner it did when you first created it. When you click the tool, Outlook executes the command the tool originally represented.

LINKING TO A FILE OR WEB PAGE

You can use the method similar to that previously described in the section "Automatically Addressing an E-mail Message" to create a tool that links to a file or Web page. This is useful, for example, when you want to make referring to specific information while you're working with Outlook easy.

Create a new tool representing a command, and then, with the Customize dialog box open, right-click the new tool, move the pointer onto Assign Hyperlink, and click Open. Outlook displays the dialog box previously shown in Figure 26.14.

Click Existing File or Web Page in the column on the left to display a dialog box similar to the one in Figure 26.15.

In the second-from-the-left column you can click

- **Current Folder**—Use the large pane to navigate to the folder that contains the file to which you want to create a link; then select the file. The path of that file appears in the Address box.

- **Browsed Pages**—The large pane contains a list of pages you've used your browser to access. Select the page to which you want to create a link. The address of that page appears in the Address box.

- **Recent Files**—The large pane contains a list of files you've recently opened. Select the file to which you want to create a link. The path of that page appears in the Address box.

Figure 26.15
This dialog box offers a wide range of places to which you can create a link.

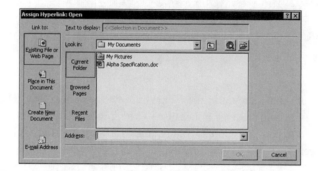

After selecting a file or page in this manner, click OK; then click Close to close the Customize dialog box. When you subsequently click the tool, the file or page the tool represents is displayed. You can modify the appearance of the tool so that its purpose is identified, as described previously in this chapter.

→ For information about changing the appearance of a tool, **see** "Automatically Addressing an E-mail Message," **p. 519**.

LINKING TO DOCUMENTS

The column at the left side of the Open Hyperlink dialog box, shown previously in Figure 26.14, contains two buttons that refer to documents:

- **Place in This Document**—When you click this button, Outlook displays the message Internal hyperlinks are disabled in this mode. This button serves no function within Outlook. You can use this button to creates links within a document if you're working with Word.

- **Create New Document**—You can click this button to create a new document or open an existing document, as described in this section.

To create a tool that creates or opens a document, start by creating a new tool on a toolbar, as previously described in this chapter.

→ For information about creating a new tool, **see** "Adding Tools to a Toolbar," **p. 512**.

With the Customize dialog box displayed, right-click the new tool, point onto Assign Hyperlink in the context menu, and click Open to display the Assign Hyperlink dialog box previously shown in Figure 26.14. Click Create New Document in the column at the left to display the dialog box shown in Figure 26.16.

PART

VI

CH

26

Figure 26.16
Use this dialog box to name the document you want to create or open.

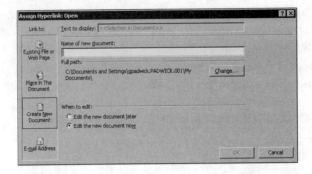

Enter the name of the document in the Name of New Document box. The name you enter must include the file name extension because Outlook uses the extension to identify the type of document. If you don't supply a file name extension, Outlook subsequently displays an error message.

Outlook proposes to save the file in your default documents folder, the path of which is listed under Full Path. If you want to save the document in a different folder, click Change and navigate to that folder.

The two option buttons in the When to Edit section of the dialog box control when the new document opens for editing. If you retain the default Edit the New Document Now and subsequently click OK to save the hyperlink, the new document immediately opens. However, if you select Edit the New Document Later and subsequently click OK, Outlook saves the new hyperlink without opening the document.

Click OK to create the new hyperlink. If the new document opens for editing, edit as necessary and then close the document. Click Close to close the Customize dialog box. Subsequently, when you click the tool in the toolbar, the document opens, running under the application with which it's associated.

CHANGING THE WIDTH OF A DROP-DOWN LIST

Some toolbars contain drop-down lists. For example, the Inbox Information viewer's Standard toolbar contains a drop-down Find a Contact list. The box from which this list drops down is quite wide to provide enough space for contacts' names. To conserve space in the toolbar, you might want to make the box somewhat narrower.

To change the width of a drop-down list:

1. Display the toolbar that contains the drop-down list.
2. Select Tools, Customize to display the Customize dialog box shown previously in Figure 26.5. It doesn't matter which tab is selected.

Note

The only purpose of displaying the Customize dialog box is to enable toolbar customization. You don't actually use the dialog box in this procedure.

3. In the toolbar, click the box from which the list drops down. The border of the box changes from gray to black.

4. Point onto the left or right border of the box, press the mouse button, and drag to change the width of the box.

5. Close the Customize dialog box.

RESETTING INDIVIDUAL BUILT-IN TOOLBARS

After you've made changes to one of Outlook's built-in toolbars, you can reset that toolbar to its original condition—so that it has the original buttons in their original positions.

→ For information about resetting all toolbars, the menu bar, and individual menu items to their default states, **see** "Saving and Restoring Toolbars," **p. 509**.

To reset an individual toolbar, select Tools, Customize to display the Customize dialog box; then select the Toolbars tab, which displays a list of available toolbars. Select the toolbar you want to reset, and then click Reset to reset the selected toolbar to its original condition.

Note

You can't rename or delete Outlook's built-in toolbars.

The Toolbars box in the Toolbars tab lists the Menu Bar and the available toolbars with a check box adjacent to each. You can check an item in the list to display it or uncheck an item to hide it.

You can also reset individual toolbars in another way. The method is slightly different depending on whether the toolbar is docked or floating:

- For a docked toolbar, click the black triangle at its right end.
- For a floating toolbar, click the arrow at the left of the toolbar name in the title bar.

In either case, this opens a menu that contains only one item—Add or Remove Buttons. Select that menu item to display a menu. Select Reset Toolbar near the bottom of that menu.

Notice that the Add or Remove Buttons menu contains a list of the default tools in the selected toolbar. Each name in the list has a check box that's checked if the current toolbar contains that tool. You can uncheck these boxes to remove individual tools from the toolbar and subsequently check these boxes to restore individual tools.

Each Add or Remove Buttons menu also contains Customize—yet another way to open the Customize dialog box.

WORKING WITH CUSTOM TOOLBARS

There are at least two reasons why you might want to create custom toolbars:

- You might want to have more tools than there's space for on existing toolbars.
- You might want to create a set of tools useful for a specific task.

CREATING A CUSTOM TOOLBAR

Each Outlook Information viewer and form has its own set of toolbars and its own menu bar. You must customize existing toolbars and the menu bar separately for each viewer and form. Similarly, you have to create custom toolbars separately for each viewer and form.

To create a custom toolbar:

1. Open the Information viewer or form for which you want to create a custom toolbar.
2. Select Tools, Customize to display the Customize dialog box. Select the Toolbars tab.
3. Click New to display the dialog box shown in Figure 26.17.

Figure 26.17
Outlook proposes to create a new toolbar named Custom 1.

4. Replace the proposed name with something more descriptive; then click OK to return to the Customize dialog box, which now lists the name of the new toolbar. In addition, a prototype of the new toolbar is displayed, as shown in Figure 26.18.

Figure 26.18
The prototype of the new toolbar has room for only one button.

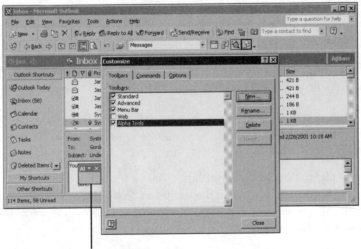

Prototype of new toolbar

5. Select the Customize dialog box's Commands tab; select a Category for the first tool you want to have in the new toolbar; select a command, menu, or list in that category; and drag it into the new toolbar.

6. Repeat step 5 as many times as necessary to place more tools in the new toolbar. The width of the new toolbar automatically increases each time you drag a command, menu, or list into it.

7. Click Close to close the Customize dialog box.

8. Drag the new toolbar to a docked position or wherever you want it to be displayed.

ADDING TOOLS TO A CUSTOM TOOLBAR

After you've created a custom toolbar, you can add more tools to it and remove tools from it in the same way you can with the built-in Outlook toolbars (described previously in this chapter).

→ For detailed information about adding a button to a toolbar, **see** "Adding Tools to a Toolbar," **p. 512**.

Another way to add tools to a toolbar (custom or built-in) is to drag tools from one toolbar to another. To do this, you first must enable toolbar editing by opening the Customize dialog box; select Tools, Customize.

Select the tool you want to move by pointing onto it and pressing the mouse button. When you do so, the tool's border becomes black. Drag the selected tool into another toolbar and release the mouse button. Close the Customize dialog box.

RENAMING AND DELETING A CUSTOM TOOLBAR

You can rename or delete custom toolbars. However, you can't rename or delete Outlook's built-in toolbars.

To rename or delete a custom toolbar:

1. Display the Information viewer that contains the custom toolbar.

2. Select Tools, Customize to display the Customize dialog box. Select the Toolbars tab.

3. Select the custom toolbar you want to rename or delete.

4. Click Rename if you want to rename the toolbar; Outlook displays a dialog box in which you can edit the toolbar's name. Click Delete if you want to delete the toolbar; Outlook asks you to confirm that you want to delete it.

PART
VI

CH
26

Note

You can't reset a custom toolbar because there's no default to go back to.

CUSTOMIZING THE MENU BAR

Outlook handles the menu bar in much the same way as a toolbar. You can add menus to the menu bar and delete menus from the menu bar; you can add menu items to, and delete menu items from, each menu; you can also change the order of menu items in a menu.

One thing you can't do is create a custom menu bar. Outlook can have only one menu bar.

REMOVING A MENU ITEM FROM A MENU

To remove a menu item from a menu, start by displaying the Customize dialog box, even though you don't actually use that dialog box. You can't edit menus without having the Customize dialog box displayed.

To remove a menu item from a menu:

1. With the Outlook Information viewer or form from which you want to remove a menu item displayed, select Tools, Customize. It doesn't matter which tab of the Customize dialog box is selected.

2. In the viewer's or form's menu bar (not in the Customize dialog box), select the menu item you want to remove, as shown in Figure 26.19.

Figure 26.19
The selected menu item name is enclosed in a black box. The black box signifies that the menu is available for editing.

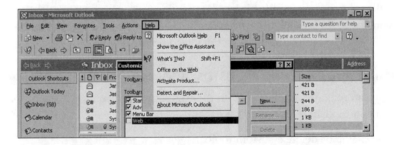

3. Drag the selected menu item out of the menu.

4. Close the Customize dialog box.

ADDING MENU ITEMS TO A MENU

Outlook's menus contain menu items the application's designers expected to be useful. You easily can add menu items to Outlook's menus to suit your own needs.

To add a command to a menu:

1. Display the Information viewer or form to which you want to add a menu command.

2. Select Tools, Customize to display the Customize dialog box.

3. Select the Commands tab to display the dialog box previously shown in Figure 26.6.

4. In the Categories list at the left side of the dialog box, select the category of the command you want to add. The right side of the dialog box now lists the commands in that category, as previously shown in Figure 26.7.

5. Drag the command onto the name of the menu into which you want to add the command. The menu opens. Keeping the mouse button pressed, drag down to the position where you want the command to be in the menu. When you release the mouse button, the new command appears in the menu enclosed within a black border.

6. Close the Customize dialog box. The black border disappears, leaving the new command as a normal-looking command.

Tip from

You can use the procedure just described to add commands to submenus.

CHANGING THE POSITION OF A MENU ITEM IN A MENU

You can change the position of a menu item in a menu.

To change the position of a menu item in a menu:

1. With the Information viewer or form in which you want to change the position of a menu item displayed, select Tools, Customize to display the Customize dialog box.

2. In the viewer's or form's menu bar (not in the Customize dialog box), select the menu that contains the menu item you want to move.

3. Point onto the menu item and drag it up or down.

4. Release the mouse button when the item is in the position where you want it.

5. Close the Customize dialog box.

Note

You can use this procedure to change the position of items in submenus.

ADDING AND DELETING SEPARATORS IN A MENU

Outlook's menus contain horizontal, gray separator bars that divide menu items into related groups. You can add more separators and delete separators.

To insert or delete separators:

1. With the Information viewer or form in which you want to insert or delete menu separators, select Tools, Customize to display the Customize dialog box.

2. In the viewer's or form's menu (not in the Customize dialog box), point onto the menu item above which you want to add or remove a separator.

3. Press the mouse button and drag down slightly to insert a separator, or press the mouse button and drag up slightly to remove a separator.

4. Close the Customize dialog box.

DELETING A MENU

You can delete Outlook's default menus as well as custom menus.

To delete a menu and all the menu items it contains, move the pointer onto the menu item; then press and hold down Alt while you drag the menu out of the menu bar.

Caution

As you see, removing a menu from the menu bar is very easy, probably too easy, to do. One simple drag, and the menu's gone. There's no Undo for this action. While you can easily reset the menu bar to its default state, you can't easily reset the menu bar to what it was before you dragged the menu out of it. See the section "Troubleshooting Command Bars" at the end of this chapter for more information about this.

ADDING A NEW MENU TO THE MENU BAR

Instead of adding menu items to existing menus, you can create new menus. The procedure that follows is not necessarily intuitively obvious, so pay close attention.

To add a new menu to the menu bar:

1. With the Information viewer or form to which you want to add a new menu displayed, select Tools, Customize to display the Customize dialog box; then select the Commands tab.

2. Scroll to the bottom of the Categories list and select New Menu. The Commands list at the right shows New Menu.

3. Drag New Menu from the Commands list into the position you want to have the new menu in the menu bar. This step is the one people sometimes miss; make sure you do it. The new menu appears in the menu bar with the name "New Menu" in a box with a black border.

4. In the Customize dialog box, click Modify Selection to display a context menu in which the proposed name "New Menu" is selected. Click the Name item in the context menu so that "New Menu" becomes highlighted. Replace the suggested menu name "New Menu" with an appropriate name and press Enter. The menu name in the menu bar changes to the new name.

Note

Alternatively, with the Customize dialog box displayed, you can right-click the new menu name in the menu bar to display the context menu.

5. Close the Customize dialog box.

Tip from

Just as you can add menus to toolbars, you can add buttons to menus. You also can add hyperlinks to menus, just as you can add hyperlinks to toolbars, as described previously in this chapter.

At this stage you have a new menu, but it contains no menu items and no separators. Use the methods previously described in this chapter to add menu items and separators into the new menu.

→ For detailed information about adding menu items and separators to a menu, **see** "Adding Menu Items to a Menu," **p. 526** and "Adding and Deleting Separators in a Menu," **p. 527**.

CREATING SEPARATORS IN THE MENU BAR

The default menu bar contains no separators. You can insert vertical lines that separate the menus in the menu bar into groups.

To insert a separator at the left of a menu name:

1. Select Tools, Customize to display the Customize dialog box. Select the Commands tab.
2. In the Outlook menu bar, select the menu to the left of which you want to add a vertical separator. Outlook creates a black border around the menu name.
3. Click Modify Selection in the Customize dialog box to display a context menu.
4. Click Begin a Group. Now a vertical separator appears at the left of the menu you chose. Click Close in the Customize dialog box.

REMOVING A SEPARATOR FROM THE MENU BAR

To remove a separator from the menu bar, select Tools, Customize to display the Customize dialog box. Then, drag the menu name to the right of the separator you want to remove to the left until the separator disappears.

RESETTING THE MENU BAR

After you've made changes to the menu bar or to the contents of individual menus, you can reset the entire Outlook menu structure to its default condition.

To reset the menu structure and contents:

1. Select Tools, Customize to display the Customize dialog box.

2. Select the Toolbars tab.

3. In the Toolbars list, select Menu Bar.

4. Click Reset. Outlook asks you to confirm that you want to reset the menu bar. Click OK.

5. Close the Customize dialog box.

TROUBLESHOOTING

COMMAND BARS

As is so often the case, the best way to solve problems is to anticipate them before they happen and have a strategy prepared. It's too late to buy earthquake insurance when your house is rocking and rolling!

Outlook's insurance policy for toolbar and menu bar problems is the Outcmd.dat file, which was described earlier in this chapter. This file contains complete information about all changes you have made to the default toolbars, the menu bar, and individual menus. If several people have separate Windows accounts on the same computer, a separate Outcmd.dat file exists in each person's Windows profile.

→ For detailed information about saving and restoring toolbars, **see** "Saving and Restoring Toolbars," **p. 509**.

I strongly recommend that you make a copy of your Outcmd.dat file before you make any significant changes to your toolbars or menu bar. Then, if something goes wrong, you can restore the file you saved to get Outlook back to the condition it was in before you started making changes.

If you don't save your Outcmd.dat file, you can still reset Outlook's toolbars and menu bar to their default conditions, but in doing so, you lose any previous toolbar and menu bar customizations you've made. To do so, in Windows find and then delete or rename the Outcmd.dat file. The next time you start Outlook, it automatically creates the default menu bar and toolbars and also creates a new Outcmd.dat file.

CHAPTER 27

SETTING OUTLOOK'S OPTIONS

In this chapter

OUTLOOK'S OPTIONAL SETTINGS

Outlook has many optional settings. If you install Outlook from the Office XP CD-ROM, you'll start off with certain default settings. However, if you install Outlook from your organization's LAN, you'll have default settings determined by your LAN administrator.

Note

The optional settings described in this chapter are those you can change after Outlook is installed. See Appendix A, "Installing and Maintaining Outlook 2002," for information about installation options.

This chapter covers the options available after a standard Outlook installation. Additional options might be available if you've installed add-ins. Although many of the options in Outlook 2002 are the same as those in Outlook 2000, you'll notice some changes and additional options.

Tip from

A good way to gain information about many of the new capabilities in Outlook 2002 is to take a careful look through all the tabs of the Options dialog box. Of particular significance is the Mail Setup Options tab that provides much greater control of how Outlook 2002 sends and receives messages than was available in previous versions.

ACCESSING OUTLOOK'S OPTIONAL SETTINGS

With any Information viewer displayed, select Tools, Options to display the Options dialog box, which has several tabs.

Note

You'll most likely be concerned with only a few of Outlook's options. If you're using Outlook on a standalone computer, most of the options set when you install Outlook are probably what you need. If you're using Outlook as a network client, your network administrator has probably set the options appropriate for the network.

When you select Tools, Options, Outlook displays the Options dialog box with the Preferences tab selected, as shown in Figure 27.1.

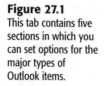

Figure 27.1
This tab contains five sections in which you can set options for the major types of Outlook items.

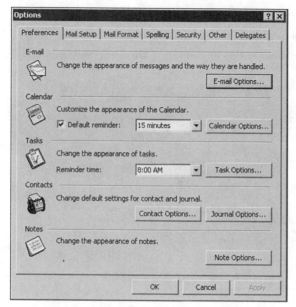

PREFERENCES OPTIONS

Separate sections in the Preferences enable you to set options for each major type of Outlook item.

E-MAIL OPTIONS

In the E-mail section near the top of the Preferences tab, click E-mail Options to display the dialog box shown in Figure 27.2.

HANDLING MESSAGES

Open the After Moving or Deleting an Open Item drop-down list to specify what happens after you move or delete an open item in the Input, Outbox, Sent Items, and Drafts Information viewers. Choose among

- Open the Previous Item (the default)
- Open the Next Item
- Return to the Inbox

Check or uncheck the five check boxes according to your preferences:

- Close Original Message on Reply or Forward (unchecked by default)
- Save Copies of Messages in Sent Items Folder (checked by default)

PART

VI

CH

27

- Display a Notification Message when New Mail Arrives (unchecked by default)
- Automatically Save Unsent Messages (checked by default)
- Remove Extra Line Breaks in Plain Text Messages (checked by default)

Figure 27.2
Use this dialog box to specify how you want Outlook to handle messages.

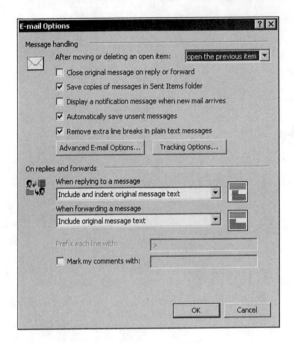

Note The last of these check boxes is new in Outlook 2002.

The On Replies and Forwards section in the lower half of the E-mail Options dialog box deals with how you want to use Outlook to reply to incoming messages and to forward messages to other people. Open the When Replying to a Message drop-down list and choose among

- Do Not Include Original Message
- Attach Original Message
- Include Original Message Text
- Include and Indent Original Message Text (the default)
- Prefix Each Line of the Original Message

Open the When Forwarding a Message drop-down list and choose among

- Attach Original Message
- Include Original Message Text

- Include and Indent Original Message Text (the default)
- Prefix Each Line of the Original Message

If you select the last possibility in either or both drop-down lists, the text box at the right of Prefix Each Line With becomes active and contains > as the default prefix character. You can change the default to a different character.

The Mark My Comments With check box near the bottom of the dialog box is unchecked by default. After you check that box, the adjoining text box becomes active. By default, that box contains your name or whatever name was entered during the Office installation process. You can replace that name with any other text.

SETTING ADVANCED E-MAIL OPTIONS

Click Advanced E-mail Options to display the dialog box shown in Figure 27.3.

Figure 27.3
Use this dialog box to further customize how Outlook handles messages.

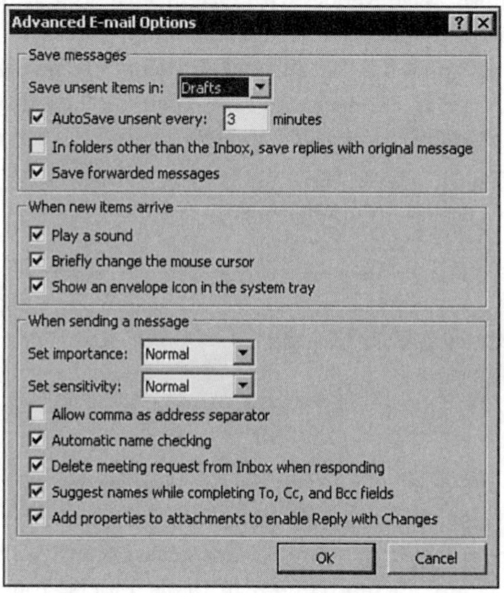

Open the Save Unsent Items In drop-down list to specify the folder in which you want unsent messages to be sent. You can choose among

- Drafts (the default)
- Inbox
- Sent Mail
- Outbox

I strongly recommend you use the default Drafts folder so that you don't confuse unsent messages with messages you've received, messages you've sent, or those in your Outbox.

PART
VI

CH
27

By default, Outlook saves unsent messages every three minutes. You can uncheck the AutoSave Unsent Every check box if you don't want Outlook to automatically save unsent messages—something I don't advise—and you can change the interval for saving unsent messages.

Note

If you have AutoSave enabled, you'll notice that while you're typing, Outlook hesitates momentarily from time to time while saving occurs. If you reduce the AutoSave time too much, this can become irritating. On the other hand, if you make the AutoSave period too long, you might lose a lot of your work in the event of a power failure or other disaster.

By default, Outlook saves your replies to messages you've received in the Sent Items folder. For received messages you've saved in a folder other than the Inbox, you can check In Folders Other Than the Inbox, Save Replies with Original Message to save your replies with received messages. My preference is to save all incoming messages in my Inbox folder and all outgoing messages (original messages I send and replies to incoming messages) in my Sent Items folder. However, if you decide to save incoming messages in separate folders according to their subject or source, you might want to save replies to those messages in the same folders as the incoming messages. Replies are saved with the incoming message, but not with any attachments to the incoming message.

Tip from

Gordon Padwick

Rather than save each type of message in a separate folder, I prefer to use categories to organize messages. By doing that, I don't have to search through many folders to find specific messages.

By default, Outlook saves messages you forward in the same folder as other messages you send. The advantage of this is that you have a record of all the messages you forward. The disadvantage, though, is the increase in occupied disk space because each message and its attachments are saved twice, in your Inbox and Sent Items folders. You can uncheck Save Forwarded Messages if you want.

Outlook normally plays a sound and very briefly changes the mouse pointer each time a message arrives in your Inbox. You can uncheck either or both of Play a Sound and Briefly Change the Mouse Cursor if that's what you want to do.

Also, Outlook displays an envelope icon in the System Tray (at the right end of the Taskbar) when a message arrives. If you don't want that icon to be displayed, uncheck Show an Envelope Icon in the System Tray.

You can use the bottom section of the Advanced E-mail Options dialog box to change the default Normal importance and Normal sensitivity settings for message you send. Unless your ego is so inflated that you want every message you send to be marked High importance and Personal sensitivity, you probably should stay with the default Normal settings. You can open the Set Importance drop-down list and select among Low, Normal, and High; you can open the Set Sensitivity drop-down list and select among Normal, Personal, Private, and Confidential.

The bottom section of the Advanced E-mail Options dialog box contains these five check boxes, all of which are checked by default:

- **Allow Comma as Address Separator**—With this box checked, multiple names in the To, Cc, and Bcc boxes in a Message form can be separated by a comma or a semicolon. If this box is unchecked, names can be separated only by a semicolon.

- **Automatic Name Checking**—With this box checked, names you enter in the To, Cc, and Bcc boxes in the Message form are automatically checked against entries in your address books (a process known as resolving) so that the corresponding e-mail addresses are used. If this box is unchecked, you must enter e-mail addresses in the To, Cc, and Bcc boxes.

- **Delete Meeting Request from Inbox when Responding**—With this box checked, Outlook automatically deletes a meeting request from your Inbox when you reply to that request. If this box is unchecked, meeting requests remain in your Inbox.

- **Suggest Names While Completing To, Cc, and Bcc Fields**—With this box checked, Outlook automatically completes partial names you enter in the To, Cc, and Bcc boxes, based on names you have previously entered into those boxes.

- **Add Properties to Attachments to Enable Reply with Changes**—With this box checked, you can make changes to message attachments and send those changes back to the person who sent the original message.

You can uncheck any of these boxes.

SETTING TRACKING OPTIONS

After returning to the E-mail Options dialog box, click Tracking Options to display the dialog box shown in Figure 27.4.

> **Note**
>
> The availability of tracking depends on recipients' software and their e-mail servers. Just because these options are available in Outlook doesn't necessarily mean they'll work in all e-mail environments. Refer to chapters in this book about specific e-mail environments for some additional information.

→ For more information about delivery options, **see** "Delivery Options," **p. 89** and "Changing Delivery Options for Messages," **p. 436**. For more information about voting, **see** "Using Voting Buttons," **p. 442**. For more information about tracking options, **see** "Tracking Message Receipts," **p. 439**.

PART

VI

CH

27

Figure 27.4
In addition to tracking options, this dialog box provides options about how voting responses and read receipts are handled.

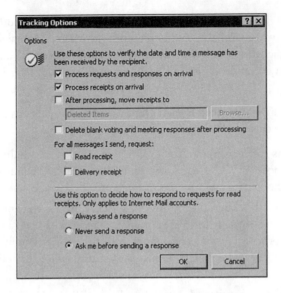

The first group of four check boxes deals with delivery receipts and blank voting and meeting responses:

- **Process Requests and Responses on Arrival**—With this checked, as it is by default, Outlook immediately processes all message responses and requests.

- **Process Receipts on Arrival**—With this checked, as it is by default, Outlook immediately sends a receipt as soon as a message requesting a receipt is received.

- **After Processing, Move Receipts To**—With this unchecked, as it is by default, the Browse button in the next line is dimmed and Outlook saves incoming receipts in the same folder as other messages. If you check this box, the Browse button becomes available and you can click it to display a list of folders; then select the folder in which you want to save receipts.

- **Delete Blank Voting and Meeting Responses After Processing**—With this unchecked, as it is by default, Outlook saves all voting and meeting response messages in the same folder as other incoming messages. In addition, responses to meeting requests are automatically placed on your calendar and the status of each voting and meeting response is placed in the Tracking tab of the original message in the Sent Items folder. If you check this box, responses are saved with other incoming messages only if they contain comments; otherwise, those messages are automatically deleted after your calendar is updated and the status is recorded in the Sent Items Tracking tab.

The next two check boxes enable you to automatically request read and delivery receipts for every message you send. With these boxes unchecked, as they are by default, you can request read and delivery receipts for individual messages:

- **Read Receipt**—Check this box if you want to be notified when recipients read your messages. Remember that the act of opening a message is taken to mean that a recipient has read that message, something that is not necessarily true.

- **Delivery Receipt**—Check this box if you want to be notified when your messages are delivered to recipients' mail boxes. As the dialog box reminds you, delivery receipts are not available for messages sent to Internet e-mail accounts. The availability of delivery receipts from accounts on other e-mail systems depends on the functionality of recipients' e-mail servers.

The next three check boxes enable you to specify how Outlook handles requests for read receipts. You can choose

- Always Send a Response
- Never Send a Response
- Ask Me Before Sending a Response (the default)

If you accept the default, Outlook displays a message asking you whether to send a read response when you open a message containing a request for a read receipt.

Calendar Options

In the Calendar section of the Preferences tab of the Options dialog box (shown previously in Figure 27.1) you can choose whether you want Outlook to create reminders automatically and specify the default interval before a calendar event when a reminder is to appear.

The Default Reminder check box is checked by default. Uncheck that box if you don't want Outlook to create reminders automatically. With the box checked, the adjoining text box contains the reminder interval, which is 15 minutes by default. You can open the reminder drop-down list and select one of the preset reminder intervals.

Instead of selecting one of the preset reminder intervals, you can enter a time in terms of minutes, hours, or days. When entering a time, you can use these abbreviations: "m" for minutes, "h" for hours, and "d" for days.

> **Note**
>
> If you don't choose automatic reminders, you can select reminders for individual calendar items. If you do choose automatic reminders, you can change the reminder interval for individual items.

Click Calendar Options to display the dialog box shown in Figure 27.5.

Calendar Work Week

The top section of the Calendar Options dialog box is where you define your work week.

By default, Outlook considers Monday through Friday to be the work week, as shown by the checked boxes at the top of Figure 27.5. With this default, when you display the Calendar Information viewer with the Day/Week/Month view selected and select Work Week, Outlook displays your calendar for Monday through Friday.

Figure 27.5
The Calendar Options dialog box is organized somewhat differently from what it was in Outlook 2000.

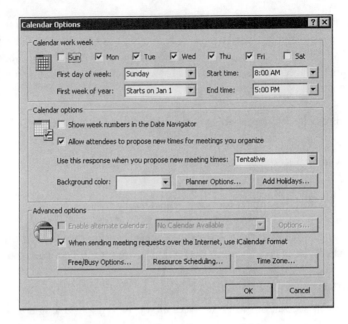

If your work week is other than the default, such as Tuesday through Saturday, you can uncheck Mon and check Sat. Then, the Work Display in the Calendar Information viewer displays your calendar for Tuesday through Saturday.

Previous versions of Outlook insisted that your work week consisted of consecutive days. Outlook 2002 removes this limitation. As an example, now you can check Mon, Tue, Wed, Thu, and Sat, leaving Sun and Fri unchecked. After doing that, the work week displayed in the Calendar Information viewer correctly shows Monday, Tuesday, Wednesday, Thursday, and Saturday.

You can open the First Day of Week drop-down list to select the first day of your week, which, by default, is Sunday. As a result, the day check boxes in the row above start with Sun. Also, the Date Navigator in the Calendar Information viewer, with the Day/Week/Month view selected, shows weeks starting with Sunday. After you select a day other than Sunday as the first day of the week, the day check boxes and weeks in the Date Navigator start with that day.

You can open the First Week of Year drop-down list and select the first week of the year from

- Starts on January 1 (the default)
- First 4-day Week
- First Full Week

The choice you make affects only how Outlook allocates numbers to weeks, as described in the next section, "More Calendar Options."

The Start Time and End Time boxes affect the Calendar Information viewer with Day/Week/Month selected and Day chosen. That view shows a single day with activities listed hour by hour. With the default start time of 8:00 a.m. and the default end time of 5:00 p.m., each day's schedule is shown in a bright color between 8:00 a.m. and 5:00 p.m.; the hours before 8:00 a.m. and after 5:00 p.m. are shown in a dark color.

You can open the Start Time and End Time drop-down lists and select times other than the defaults. Alternatively, you can enter times into the Start Time and End Time boxes to specify times other than those in the drop-down lists. When you do so, you can use the abbreviations "a" for a.m. and "p" for p.m.

Note

Although you can enter any times you want in the Start Time and End Time boxes, the Calendar Information viewer approximates start and end times to the nearest time increment selected for that view.

MORE CALENDAR OPTIONS

The second section of the Calendar Options dialog box is named Calendar Options. This section offers various calendar-related options.

The first check box in this section is labeled Show Week Numbers in the Date Navigator. By default, this box is unchecked so that the Date Navigator in the Day/Week/Month Calendar Information viewer doesn't display week numbers. If you check this box, the Date Navigator shows week numbers in small digits at the left of each week.

The selection made in the First Week of Year drop-down list, referred to in the previous section, determines which week is numbered as the first of the year. For example, if the Date Navigator is displaying January of the year 2004 and you have selected First Four-day Week as the first week of the year, the week starting on January 4 is labeled as week number 1; that's because the week that contains January 1 contains only three days. In contrast, in the same year, if you selected Starts on Jan 1 as the first week of the year, the week starting on December 28, 2003 is labeled as week number 1.

Tip from

Gordon Padwick

If you're in an organization that schedules by week numbers, make sure that everyone in the organization has set Outlook to use the same setting for the First Week of Year.

The second check box in this section, labeled Allow Attendees to Propose New Times for Meetings You Organize, is new in Outlook 2002 and is checked by default. If you leave this box checked, people to whom you send invitations to meetings can respond by suggesting a date and time different from what you proposed. If you don't want people to be able to do that, uncheck this box.

The third line in this section, also new in Outlook 2002, affects responses you make to invitations to attend meetings. You can open the drop-down list and select among

- Tentative (the default)
- Accept
- Decline

By default, the background color in the Day and Work Week view of the calendar is yellow so that appointments, shown in white, stand out clearly on the background. You can open the drop-down Background Color list to select a different color for the background.

This section of the Calendar Options dialog box contains the Planner Options and Add Holidays command buttons, the use of which is described later in this chapter.

ADVANCED CALENDAR OPTIONS

The first row in the Advanced Options section of the Calendar Options dialog box enables you to use an alternative calendar if you've installed a version of Outlook 2002 for a region that uses a calendar other than the standard Roman calendar. If that's the case, check the Enable Alternate Calendar box; then open the adjoining drop-down list to display a list of available calendars. Select the calendar you want to use.

By default, Outlook sends meeting requests over the Internet in iCalendar format so that those requests can be understood by people who use any iCalendar-compatible messaging system. If you don't want meeting requests to be sent in this format, uncheck the When Sending Meeting Requests Over the Internet, Use iCalendar Format check box.

SETTING PLANNER OPTIONS

In the Calendar Options dialog box, click the Planner Options button to display the dialog box shown in Figure 27.6. This dialog box is new in Outlook 2002.

Figure 27.6
This dialog box enables you to control how the planner works.

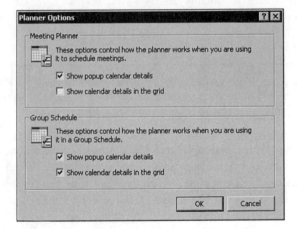

In this dialog box, you can enable or disable

- Show Popup Calendar Details (checked by default). With this box checked, a pop-up calendar displays details of meeting schedules. If the box is unchecked, the pop-up calendar isn't available.

- Show Calendar Details in the Grid (unchecked by default). With this box checked, Show Calendar Details is available when you're planning a meeting. If the box is unchecked, Show Calendar Details is not available.

The second section of the Planner Options dialog box enables you to control how the planner works when you are creating a schedule for a group. You can enable or disable

- Show Popup Calendar Details (checked by default). With this box checked, a pop-up calendar displays details of group schedules. If the box is unchecked, the pop-up calendar isn't available.

- Show Calendar Details in the Grid (checked by default). With this box checked, Show Calendar Details is available when you're planning a group schedule. If the box is unchecked, Show Calendar Details is not available.

ADDING HOLIDAYS

In the Calendar Options dialog box, click the Add Holidays button to display the dialog box shown in Figure 27.7.

Figure 27.7
You can use this dialog box to select one or more locations or cultures for which you want to add holidays to your calendar.

You can select one or more locations in the Add Holidays to Calendar dialog box and then click OK. Before you do that, you should understand these limitations:

- Outlook adds holidays as one-time events, not as recurring events.

- Outlook adds holidays for only the years starting from 2001 through 2005.

- If you choose two or more locations or cultures and the same holidays are listed for more than one of them, you'll have some holidays duplicated in your calendar.

- Outlook assigns the category Holiday to all items, whether or not they really are holidays.

Note

Outlook's list of holidays is in the text file `Outlook.txt`. You can use a text editor to modify this file.

Instead of using Add Holidays, I suggest you consider adding holidays manually as recurring events and associate appropriate categories to each of them.

→ For more information about adding holidays to your calendar, **see** "Entering Holidays and Other Special Days," **p. 215**.

FREE/BUSY OPTIONS

Free/Busy options enable you to control how your calendar is made available to other people who want to invite you to attend meetings. You can make this information available by way of the Internet or by way of a messaging server.

In the Calendar Options dialog box, click Free/Busy Options to display the dialog box shown in Figure 27.8.

Figure 27.8
You can use this dialog box to specify how many months ahead you want to publish your calendar and to identify the server on which it is to be published.

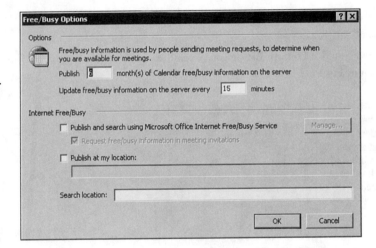

→ For more information about scheduling meetings, **see** "Inviting People to Attend a Meeting," **p. 240** and "Planning a Meeting Around People's Commitments," **p. 246**.

By default, Outlook proposes to publish your calendar for the next two months and update your published calendar every 15 minutes. You can change the number of months for which you want to publish information, and you can change how often the published information is updated.

You can choose to publish your calendar information on the Microsoft Office Internet Free/Busy Service, on an Exchange server, or both. Your calendar information is published only if you check one or both of the check boxes in the lower half of the Free/Busy Options dialog box.

Check Publish and Search Using Microsoft Office Internet Free/Busy Service if you want your free/busy information to be published there.

Check Publish at My Location if you want your free busy information to be published on an Exchange server. When this box is checked, the text box below it becomes enabled. You can enter the Web address at which the free/busy information is available in this box. Use the Search Location box to specify the Exchange server in which the free/busy information is available.

RESOURCE SCHEDULING

The section "Inviting People to Meetings" in Chapter 10, "Managing Calendars," explains how you can use Outlook to arrange meetings, a process that involves inviting people and reserving such resources as meeting rooms and equipment. If you're responsible for coordinating the use of resources such as meeting rooms and audiovisual equipment, Outlook offers you assistance.

In the Calendar Options dialog box, click Resource Scheduling to display the dialog box shown in Figure 27.9.

Figure 27.9
You can use choose how Outlook automatically responds to requests for resources.

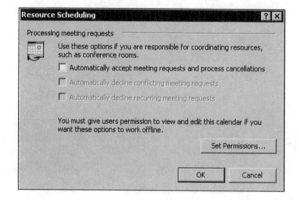

By default, Outlook doesn't automatically respond to requests for resources. If you want Outlook to respond to these requests, check Automatically Accept Meeting Requests and Process Cancellations. When you do so, the next two check boxes become available:

■ Automatically Decline Conflicting Meeting Requests

■ Automatically Decline Recurring Meeting Requests

Both of these are unchecked by default. Check either or both boxes according to your preferences.

The Set Permissions button is available if you're using an Exchange Server account but is unavailable if you're using an Internet account. If you're using an Exchange Server account and want users to be able to create resource requests while working offline, you must give these people access to your Calendar folder. Click Set Permissions to display the Calendar

PART

VI

CH

27

Properties dialog box. In that box, select the Permissions tab shown in Figure 27.10 to give people access to your calendar.

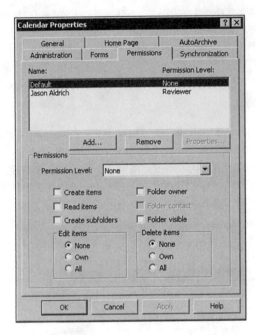

Figure 27.10
You can give specific people or groups access to your calendar in this dialog box.

TIME ZONE

Outlook relies on the underlying Windows operating system to keep track of time. Fundamentally, Windows maintains time in terms of Universal Coordinated Time (UCT), previously known as Greenwich Mean Time (GMT). You can use Date/Time in the Windows Control Panel to select a time zone that is used in all your Windows applications, including Outlook. After doing that, even though Windows is keeping track of UCT, Windows—and the applications running under it—display your local time.

You can select your time zone from within Outlook. By doing that, you select the time zone for Windows and all the applications running under it. In the Calendar Options dialog box, click Time Zone to display the dialog box shown in Figure 27.11.

Open the Time Zone drop-down list and select the time zone you want to use as your local time zone. Ignore the Label box above the Time Zone box unless you intend to designate an additional time zone. If you do intend to designate an additional time zone, give the current time zone a name, such as Current or Local. Make sure Adjust for Daylight Saving Time is checked so that Outlook will show the correct time throughout the year.

The Day view in Outlook's calendar normally shows each day's activities according to your current time zone. You can, if you want, specify an additional time zone, in which case the calendar's Day view shows activities according to the current and the additional time zones.

Figure 27.11
You can use the Time Zone dialog box to specify your local time zone and, optionally, a secondary time zone.

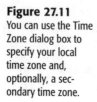

→ For more information about using time zones, **see** "Using Time Zones," **p. 232**.

To activate an additional time zone, check Show an Additional Time Zone. After you do that, open the Time Zone drop-down list and select the additional time zone. Give the additional time zone a name in the Label box. Also, check Adjust for Daylight Saving Time if you want to do that.

After you've established an additional time zone, Outlook's Day view shows the current time and the additional time, with the names of the times above each list of times.

You can click Swap Time Zones to make the additional time zone the current time zone and the current time zone the additional time zone.

TASK OPTIONS

The third section of the Options dialog box, previously shown in Figure 27.1, enables you to specify the Reminder Time you want to appear in Task items. By default, this time is 8:00 AM. You can open the drop-down list and select a different time. You're not limited to the times in the list; you can enter any other time in the Reminder Time box.

→ For more information about task reminders, **see** "Entering More Information About a Task," **p. 262**.

To set other options for Task items, click Task Options to display the dialog box shown in Figure 27.12.

Figure 27.12
This dialog box contains three check boxes that weren't available in previous versions of Outlook.

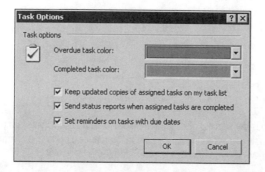

Outlook displays the names of tasks that are not overdue and not completed in black characters. By default, Outlook displays overdue tasks in red characters and completed tasks in gray characters that are struck through with a horizontal line.

You can open the drop-down Overdue Task Color list and select a different color for overdue tasks. You also can open the drop-down Completed Task Color list and select a different color for completed tasks.

The three check boxes in the lower part of the dialog box are new in Outlook 2002. The Keep Updated Copies of Assigned Tasks on My Task List box is checked by default. In this case, if you assign a task to someone else and that person accepts the task, the task remains on your task list and is updated when the person performing the task updates the status of the task. If you uncheck this box, all tasks you assign to other people that are accepted by those people are automatically removed from your task list.

→ For more information about assigning tasks to people, **see** "Asking Someone to Accept an Existing Task," **p. 269**.

The Send Status Reports When Assigned Tasks Are Completed box is also checked by default. This check box affects tasks you have accepted from someone else. With this box checked, Outlook automatically sends a status report to the person who assigned the task to you when you mark the task completed. If you uncheck this box, no report is sent.

The third check box, Set Reminders on Tasks with Due Dates, is also checked by default. With this box checked, all new tasks you create with a due date automatically generate a reminder on the due date. If you uncheck this box, reminders are not automatically generated, although you can manually add a reminder to each task.

CONTACT OPTIONS

The fourth section of the Options dialog box, shown previously in Figure 27.1, contains Contact Options and Journal Options buttons. Click Contact Options to display the dialog box shown in Figure 27.13.

Figure 27.13
The choices you make in this dialog box determine how Outlook parses people's names you enter in the Contact form and how Contact items are filed.

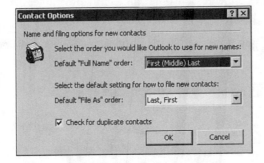

Note

Parsing is the process of dividing a phrase or sentence into its components. In this context, parsing refers to dividing a person's name into up to five components: Title, First (name), Middle (name), Last (name), and Suffix.

The choice you make in the Default "Full Name" Order drop-down list affects how Outlook places names in the First Name, Middle Name, and Last Name fields. Open the drop-down list and select among

- **First (Middle) Last (the default)**—If you enter three names, Outlook places the first in the First Name field, the second in the Middle Name field, and the third in the Last Name field. If you enter two names, Outlook places the first in the First Name field and the second in the Last Name field. If you enter only one name, Outlook places that in the First Name field and displays the Check Full Name dialog box to prompt you to supply other names.

- **Last First**—If you enter three names, Outlook places the first in the Last Name field and the other two in the First Name field. If you enter two names, Outlook places the first in the Last Name field and the second in the First Name field. If you enter only one name, Outlook places that in the Last Name field and displays the Check Full Name dialog box to prompt you to supply other names.

- **First Last1 Last2**—If you enter two or more names, Outlook places the first in the First Name field and all other names in the Last Name field. If you enter only one name, Outlook places that in the First Name field and displays the Check Full Names dialog box to prompt you to supply other names.

→ For more information about entering contacts' names, **see** "Entering a Contact's Name, Job Title, and Company," **p. 143**.

The second drop-down list enables you to specify how you want Outlook to initially propose File As names for your contacts. Open the drop-down Default "File As" Order list and select among

- Last, First (the default)
- First Last
- Company
- Last, First (Company)
- Company (Last, First)

Note

The terms in parentheses are included in the File As name only if text exists for those fields.

You can select one of these ways of constructing File As names as your personal default. Whichever you choose is unlikely to be suitable for all contacts, so you can select a different style of File As name each time you enter a new contact.

→ For more information about entering contacts' names, **see** "Selecting a File As Name," **p. 145**.

By default, the Check for Duplicate Contacts box is checked so Outlook automatically warns you if you have what appear to be duplicate items in your Contacts folder. If you uncheck this box, Outlook doesn't provide such warnings.

PART

VI

CH

27

JOURNAL OPTIONS

In the Contacts section of the Preferences tab of the Options dialog box, shown previously in Figure 27.1, click Journal Options to display the dialog box shown in Figure 27.14.

Figure 27.14
Use this dialog box to select the activities you want Outlook to record in the Journal.

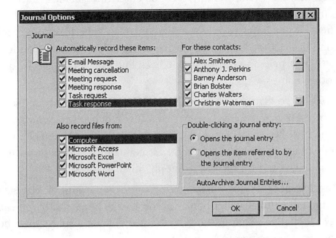

This dialog box is unchanged from Outlook 2000.

Note

Outlook's Journal is not activated when you install Outlook. The first time you attempt to display the Journal Information viewer, Outlook asks whether you want to activate the Journal. If you choose to do so, the dialog box shown in Figure 27.14 is displayed.

The top-left section of the Journal Options dialog box contains a list of the six types of Outlook message items:

- E-mail Message
- Meeting Cancellation
- Meeting Request
- Meeting Response
- Task Request
- Task Response

By default, none of these types of message items is checked. Check those types of message items you want Outlook to record in the Journal.

Tip from

> In addition to the six types of message items listed in the Journal Options dialog box, Outlook also can automatically record the time and duration of outgoing telephone calls initiated from within Outlook. This capability can't be set up from within the Journal Options dialog box—it requires editing the Windows registry.

→ For information about recording phone calls, **see** "Journaling Phone Calls," **p. 278**.

Even though you select certain types of messages to be recorded in the Journal, Outlook doesn't record any messages until you specify the name of the person to whom the messages are sent or from whom the messages are received. The upper-right section of the Journal Options dialog box lists the names of people in your default Contacts folder. By default, all the names in this list are unchecked. Check the names of people for whom you want the Journal to record messages.

Tip from

> When you add a new contact to your Contacts folder, that contact is added to the list of contacts in the Journal Options dialog box and is unchecked. If you want messages to or from the new contact to be recorded in the Journal, you must return to the Journal Options dialog box and check the new name.

In addition to automatically creating a Journal item based on messages you send and receive, Outlook also can create a Journal item each time you work with Office applications or certain Office-compatible applications. The lower-left section of the Journal Options dialog box lists the applications for which this capability is available, all of which are unchecked by default. Check those applications for which you want Outlook to create Journal items.

As with other Outlook items displayed in an Information viewer, you can double-click an item to display it in detail. The Journal Options dialog box lets you choose how a Journal item referring to an Office document is displayed in the Journal Entry form. Choose among

- **Opens the Journal Entry**—Outlook displays the Journal Entry form with an icon representing the Office document in the Notes box.
- **Opens the Item Referred to by the Journal Entry**—Outlook displays a dialog box in which you can choose whether you want to open the Office file referred to by the Journal item or want to save the file. If you choose to open the file, Windows displays the file in the associated application. For example, if a Journal item refers to a Word file, Word opens to display the file.

AutoArchive Journal Entries at the bottom right of the Journal Options dialog box gives you the opportunity to control how Outlook AutoArchives Journal items. Click this button to display the dialog box shown in Figure 27.15.

PART
VI

CH
27

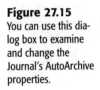

Figure 27.15
You can use this dialog box to examine and change the Journal's AutoArchive properties.

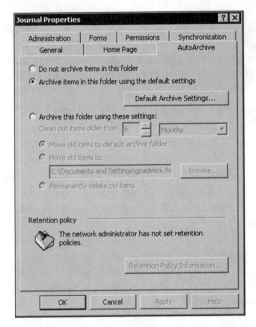

By default, Outlook AutoArchives Journal items using the default settings. You can examine and, if you want, change the default settings by clicking Default Archive Settings.

→ For more information about AutoArchiving, **see** "AutoArchiving Outlook Items," **p. 392**.

Instead of accepting the default Outlook proposes, you can choose not to archive items in the Journal folder, or you can specify how you want items in the Journal folder to be archived.

The Retention Policy section at the bottom of the Journal Properties dialog box is relevant only if you save Outlook items in an Exchange store. The Exchange administrator can establish a retention policy to define how long items you delete from your Deleted Items folder are retained as hidden, rather than finally deleted. You can click Retention Policy Information to find out what, if any, retention policy the administrator has established.

NOTE OPTIONS

To select your preferences for the appearance of Note items, click Note Options in the Preferences tab of the Options dialog box. Outlook displays the dialog box shown in Figure 27.16.

This dialog box is unchanged from Outlook 2000. To change the background color of notes from the default yellow, open the drop-down Color list and select one of the available colors. To change the default size of notes, open the drop-down Size list and choose among Small, Medium (the default), and Large.

Figure 27.16
You can use this dialog box to change the appearance of notes.

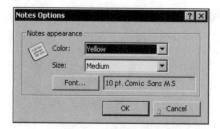

By default, notes are displayed using the 10-point Comic Sans font. If you prefer to use a different font, click Font to display the standard Windows Font dialog box and select a font, font style, and size. You also can select Strikeout and Underline effects and a font color.

MAIL SETUP OPTIONS

The second tab in the Options dialog box enables you to set up and modify e-mail accounts. The choices available in this tab are significantly different from those in preceding versions of Outlook. This tab replaces the Mail Services tab in a Corporate/Workgroup installation of Outlook 2000 and the Mail Delivery tab in an Internet Mail Only installation of Outlook 2000.

One of the first things you'll notice in Outlook 2002 if you've previously used Outlook 98 or Outlook 2000 is that you no longer have to choose between an Internet Mail Only (IMO) or Corporate/Workgroup (C/W) installation. Now, you simply install Outlook and set up accounts for Internet, Exchange, or other e-mail systems, or some combination of these, according to your needs.

When you install Outlook 2002 on a computer that has previously used an earlier version of Outlook, whichever e-mail system you used is automatically set up in Outlook 2002. For example, if you previously used an IMO installation of Outlook 2000 with a connection to an Internet mailbox, your new Outlook 2002 installation gives you access to the same Internet mailbox. Likewise, if your previous Outlook 2000 installation provided access to an Exchange mailbox, your new Outlook 2002 installation gives you access to the same mailbox. If you install Outlook 2002 on a computer that didn't previously have Outlook installed, the Setup Wizard leads you through the process of creating an e-mail account.

You can use the Mail Setup tab of the Options dialog box to set up e-mail accounts that don't already exist and to modify existing e-mail accounts. Figure 27.17 shows the Mail Setup tab.

SETTING UP E-MAIL ACCOUNTS AND DIRECTORIES

The top section of this dialog box is where you set up e-mail accounts. Click E-mail Accounts to display the dialog box shown in Figure 27.18.

Figure 27.17
This dialog box is new in Outlook 2002. You can use it to set up and modify e-mail accounts and directories.

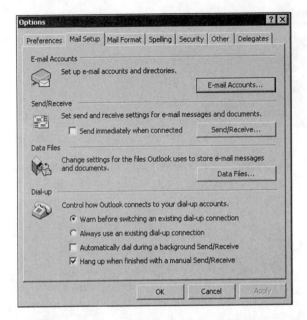

Figure 27.18
You can use this dialog box to define e-mail accounts and directories.

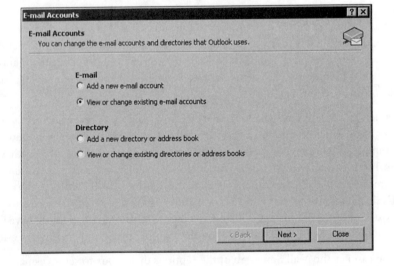

In this dialog box, you can choose

■ Add a New E-mail Account

■ View or Change Existing E-mail Accounts

■ Add a New Directory or Address Book

■ View or Change Existing Directories or Address Books

These options are not described here because they are covered in previous chapters of this book.

→ For information about setting up e-mail accounts, **see** "Creating E-mail Accounts, **p. 47**. For information about directories, **see** "Using Directory Services," **p. 191**.

SENDING AND RECEIVING MESSAGES

The second section of the Mail Setup tab of the Options dialog box deals with sending and receiving messages. If you want Outlook to immediately send and receive messages when it is connected to a server, leave the Send Immediately When Connected box checked. You can uncheck this box if you don't want Outlook to automatically send and receive messages.

Click Send/Receive to display the dialog box shown in Figure 27.19.

Figure 27.19
You can use this dialog box to create groups of e-mail accounts and to define properties for each group.

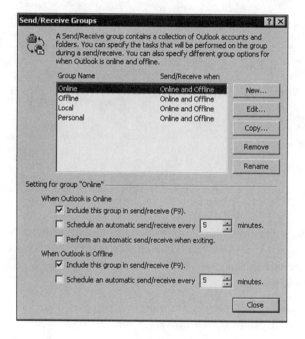

In Outlook 2002, but not in earlier Outlook versions, you can create groups of e-mail accounts and set properties for all the accounts in each group.

The large box in the upper part of the dialog box contains a list of all your e-mail account groups. By default, the only group that exists contains all your e-mail accounts and is named All Accounts.

The five buttons at the right of the large box enable you to work with account groups. These buttons are described in the next five sections.

CREATING A NEW E-MAIL ACCOUNT GROUP

Click New to create a new e-mail account group. When you do so, a dialog box asks you to provide a name for the new group. Enter the name and click OK. Outlook displays the dialog box shown in Figure 27.20.

Figure 27.20
You can use this dialog box to select which e-mail accounts to include in the new group and to set properties for the group.

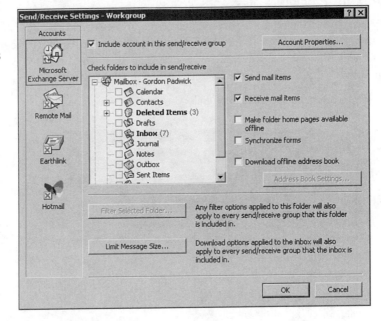

The column at the left of the dialog box lists available e-mail accounts. Select each account you want to have in the group and check Include Account in This Send/Receive Group. For each account, make sure the appropriate folders are checked in the Check Folders to Include in Send/Receive box.

With an account selected, you can check the appropriate check boxes near the right edge of the dialog box. The check boxes available vary according to the type of account selected. For example, with an Internet e-mail account selected, the available buttons are

- Send Mail Items (checked by default)
- Receive Mail Items (checked by default)

With an Exchange Server account selected, the available check boxes are

- Send Mail Items (checked by default)
- Receive Mail Items (checked by default)
- Make Folder Home Pages Available Offline (unchecked by default)
- Synchronize Forms (unchecked by default)
- Download Offline Address Book (unchecked by default)

With an account selected, you also can click Account Properties to display that account's Properties dialog box to inspect and, if necessary, change that account's properties.

In the case of an Exchange Server account, you can click Address Book Settings to display the Offline Address Book dialog box, in which you can set properties that determine whether an address book is to be automatically downloaded from the server and, if it is, which address book is to be downloaded and whether full details or no details are to be downloaded.

The lower part of the Send/Receive Settings dialog box contains options that vary according to the type of e-mail account selected. The options available for an Internet e-mail account are

- Download Item Description Only option button (not selected by default)
- Download Complete Item Including Attachments (selected by default)

With the second option selected, the Download Only Item Description for Items Larger Than check box is available and is unchecked. If you check this box, you can accept the default of 50KB as the limit for item size or enter a different limit.

The options available for an Exchange Server account are of two types, the first of which applies to individual folders. Select the folder in the Check Folders to Include in Send/Receive box and then choose Filter Selected Folder to display a dialog box in which you can set filter options. Take note that, as the dialog box says, "any filter options applied to this folder will also apply to every send/receive group that this folder is included in."

The second option enables you to limit the size of downloaded messages. Click Limit Message Size to display a dialog box in the same way that you can for Internet e-mail accounts, as described previously in this section.

EDITING AN E-MAIL ACCOUNT GROUP

In the Send/Receive Groups dialog box, select a group and then click Edit to display the Send/Receive Settings dialog box shown in Figure 27.21.

The column at the left lists the available accounts. Accounts not currently included in the group are marked with a red X. To include an account in the group, select that account and then check the Include Account in This Send/Receive Group box. To exclude an account from the group, select that account and then uncheck the Include Account in This Send/Receive Group box.

The large box in the Send/Receive Settings dialog box displays the current folder structure. Make sure the correct folder is checked for the selected account.

Use the check boxes at the right to designate whether the selected account is to be used for sending mail items, for receiving mail items, or for both purposes.

By default, Outlook downloads complete messages as indicated by the Download Complete Item Including Attachments box being selected. If you prefer to download only item descriptions, select Download Item Description Only. If you do allow Outlook to download complete items, you can limit this to items not exceeding a specific size. To do that, check Download Only Item Description for Items Larger Than and then enter the size limit (the default is 50KB).

Figure 27.21
The dialog box is shown here with an Internet account selected.

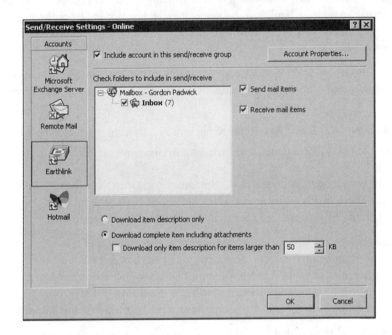

For accounts you use to download messages from the Internet or from other sources that might contain viruses and other rogue messages, I recommend selecting the option to download only message descriptions. By doing that, you can avoid the risk of getting files that can cause damage to your system. After downloading a message description, you can delete that message if you're uncertain about its source, or you can choose to download the complete message.

For accounts you use to download messages from controlled environments, such as your Exchange server, downloading complete messages is usually safe.

COPYING AN E-MAIL ACCOUNT GROUP

You might often want to create an e-mail account group that's similar to an existing account group. In this case, rather than creating the new group from scratch, copying the existing group and then making a few changes to the copy is easier.

To copy an e-mail account group, select that group in the Send/Receive Groups dialog box and click Copy. Outlook displays a dialog box and asks you to provide a name for the new group. After entering the name, click OK to return to the Send/Receive Groups dialog box. Now, you can select the new group and click Edit to make changes to it.

REMOVING AN E-MAIL ACCOUNT GROUP

To remove an e-mail account group, select that group in the Send/Receive Groups dialog box, and then click Remove. This removes the group from the list shown in the dialog box.

RENAMING AN E-MAIL ACCOUNT GROUP

To change the name of an e-mail account group, select that group in the Send/Receive Groups dialog box, and then click Rename. Outlook displays a dialog box in which you can edit the group's name. Make whatever changes are necessary to the group's name; then click OK to return to the Send/Receive Groups dialog box, which now lists the group with the new name.

SELECTING SEND/RECEIVE SETTINGS

The lower part of the Send/Receive Groups dialog box contains five check boxes that enable you to control how Outlook sends and receives messages. Each of these settings applies to the group selected in the Group Name list in the upper part of the dialog box. You can select different settings for each group. The first three check boxes affect what happens when Outlook is online. These are

- **Include This Group in Send/Receive (F9)**—This is checked by default.
- **Schedule an Automatic Send/Receive Every 5 Minutes**—This is unchecked by default. You can change the default of 5 minutes to a different interval.
- **Perform an Automatic Send/Receive when Exiting**—This is unchecked by default.

The remaining two check boxes affect what happens when Outlook is offline. These are the same as the first two check boxes for online behavior.

The Account Properties button at the top right of the Send/Receive Settings dialog box gives you access to the properties of the selected account. These properties are described in Chapter 3, "Managing E-mail Accounts."

→ For information about account properties, **see** "Creating E-mail Accounts," **p. 47**.

DATA FILES OPTIONS

In the Mail Setup tab of the Options dialog box, click Data Files to display the dialog box such as the one shown in Figure 27.22.

Note

The Outlook Data Files dialog box lists only Personal Folders files used as data stores.

The text at the top of the dialog box provides introductory information about data stores. Click Tell Me More at the top right to display an Outlook Help topic that provides additional information about data stores.

PART

VI

CH

27

Figure 27.22
Use this dialog box to display and, if necessary, modify information about your data stores.

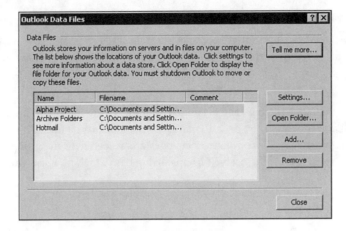

The large box at the center of the dialog box lists the available data stores and names the folders used by them. One of these data stores is the default store in which new items are stored.

DATA STORE SETTINGS

Select one of the data stores and click Settings at the right side of the Outlook Data Files dialog box to display a dialog box similar to the one shown in Figure 27.23.

Figure 27.23
This dialog box shows information about a Personal Folders file.

If you had selected a Personal Folders information store, the dialog box displayed is named Personal Folders and provides information about that store.

In addition to displaying basic information about the selected store, the dialog box has a Compact Now button.

OPENING A FOLDER

Select one of the data stores and click Open Folder to display a dialog box which displays the contents of the Windows folder that contains information store files. You can double-click one of the displayed file names to open it.

ADDING A NEW FOLDER

When you install Outlook, one data store is automatically created. You can create additional data stores by clicking Add in the Outlook Data Files dialog box to display the dialog box shown in Figure 27.24.

Figure 27.24
You can create addi-tional data stores by using this dialog box.

REMOVING A DATA STORE

Outlook always has one default data store, the place where all new items are stored. You can remove any store except the one that's the default.

To remove a data store, select it in the Outlook Data Files dialog box and then click Remove. Outlook displays a message asking you to confirm that you want to remove the store.

If you attempt to remove the default data store, Outlook displays a message telling you that you can't remove it and describes how to make a different store the default so that you can remove the one you selected.

DIAL-UP OPTIONS

The Dial-up section at the bottom of the Mail Setup tab in the Options dialog box contains options you can use to control how Outlook connects to dial-up accounts.

The text at the right of the two option buttons and two check boxes provides an explanation of what each of them does.

PART

VI

CH

27

MAIL FORMAT OPTIONS

The choices available in this Options dialog box tab, shown in Figure 27.25, enable you to specify your preferences for message format and related subjects.

Figure 27.25
The contents of this tab are very similar to those of the Mail Format tab in Outlook 2000 and Outlook 98.

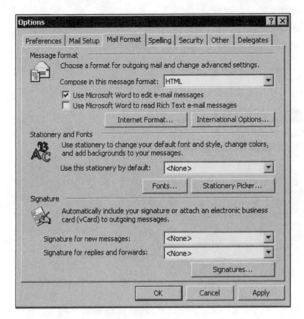

SETTING THE MESSAGE FORMAT

The top section of the Mail Format tab enables you to select a message format and an e-mail editor. Open the drop-down Compose in This Message Format list and select among the formats listed in Table 27.1.

TABLE 27.1   AVAILABLE MESSAGE FORMATS

Message Format	Use For
HTML	Messages to recipients who use an e-mail application that can accept HTML if you want your messages to incorporate formatting that's available in HTML.
Rich Text	Messages to recipients who use an e-mail application that can accept Rich Text if you want your messages to incorporate formatting that's available in Rich Text. If you want to take advantage of voting buttons in Internet e-mail messages, you must send those messages in Rich Text format.
Plain Text	Messages to recipients who use a text-based e-mail application, or if you want to minimize the size of your messages.

Outlook uses HTML format by default. However, HTML is not always the best choice, particularly if you send messages to a lot of people and you don't know that all those people use e-mail applications that can interpret HTML. Plain text is often the best choice because its use means your messages can be read by all recipients and the size of your messages is minimized.

The message format you select here is the default Outlook uses when you create messages. You can select a message format other than the default for individual messages.

> **Note**
>
> When you reply to messages, Outlook automatically uses the same message format as the message to which you're replying.

By default, Outlook uses Word to edit e-mail messages. If you don't have Word installed on your computer or if you prefer not to use Word, uncheck Use Microsoft Word to Edit E-mail Messages, in which case Outlook uses its built-in editor, which lacks many of Word's capabilities.

By default, Outlook uses its built-in editor to read incoming messages in Rich Text format. If you prefer to use Word for this purpose, check Use Microsoft Word to Read Rich Text E-mail Messages.

SETTING INTERNET FORMAT

Click Internet Format to display the dialog box shown in Figure 27.26.

Figure 27.26
This dialog box, which you can use to control certain aspects of Internet messages, is new in Outlook 2002.

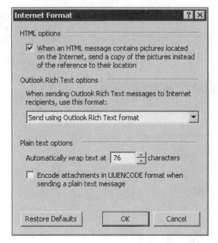

PART
VI

CH
27

By default, when you send an Internet e-mail message that contains pictures located on the Internet, Outlook sends a copy of these messages so that your recipients don't have to go the Internet site to retrieve the pictures. This means, of course, that your messages of this type are much larger than necessary. You can uncheck the box at the top of this dialog box so that your messages contain only references to the locations of pictures, thereby reducing the size of your messages.

When you send messages to Internet recipients and have the Rich Text message format selected, Outlook converts the format to HTML by default. If you don't want this to happen, open the drop-down list near the center of the dialog box and choose among

- Convert to HTML (the default)
- Convert to Plain Text Format
- Send Using Outlook Rich Text Format

The bottom section of the Internet Format dialog box deals with plain text options. By default, Outlook automatically wraps the text you send in plain text format at 76 characters. In some cases, this results in unwanted line breaks in messages recipients see. You can usually cure this problem by changing the value to 72.

Most modern messaging systems—Outlook included—use the MIME protocol to allow binary data, such as graphics and sound, to be transmitted. If you send messages to people who don't have a MIME-compatible e-mail application, you might be able to send binary information to those people by switching to the UUENCODE protocol. You can do this by checking Encode Attachments in UUENCODE Format when Sending a Plain Text Message at the bottom of the dialog box.

You can restore the defaults in this dialog box by clicking Restore Defaults.

SETTING INTERNATIONAL OPTIONS

If you're using a non-English version of Outlook, you can send English versions of message headers even though the text of the message is in a different language. Click International Options to display the dialog box shown in Figure 27.27.

Figure 27.27
You can use this dialog box to specify English headers in messages that use a different language.

You can check

- Use English for Message Flags
- Use English for Message Headers on Replies and Forwards

Outlook's preferred encoding for outgoing messages is Western European (ISO). You can select an alternative coding by opening the drop-down Preferred Encoding for Outgoing Messages list and selecting one of the many codings available.

SELECTING STATIONERY AND FONTS

The stationery settings you select in the center section of the Mail Format tab are applicable only if you're sending messages in HTML format and using Outlook's built-in editor. The fonts setting applies to all the e-mail messages you create.

> **Note**
>
> *Stationery* refers to the overall design of your messages, including a background pattern. Stationeries are HTML files that, if you accepted the default file locations when you installed Outlook, are in the `C:\Program Files\Common Files\ Microsoft Shared\Stationery` folder. In addition, graphics used in stationeries are in the same folder.

Open the Use This Stationery by Default drop-down list and select the stationery you want to use—the default is None. The use of stationery might be appropriate for messages to family members and friends, but it is generally inappropriate for business and professional communications.

Click Fonts to display the dialog box shown in Figure 27.28.

You can use this dialog box to specify a font for three purposes. In each case, click Choose Font to open the standard Windows Font dialog box, in which you can select a font, a font style, a font size, font effects, and a font color.

> **Tip from**
>
> *[signature]*
>
> Because you have no control over the fonts installed on recipients' computers, it's usually best to use only the standard Windows fonts because you can be reasonably sure recipients have those and can therefore see your messages as you intend.

Automatically Display Rich Text in Draft Font when Using High Contrast is checked by default in an attempt to make messages as easy to read as possible on small monitors. You can uncheck this if you want.

Click International Fonts to display the dialog box shown in Figure 27.29.

PART

VI

CH

27

Figure 27.28
You can use this dialog box to select the default fonts you want to use in your messages.

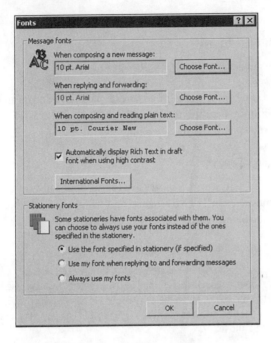

Figure 27.29
You can use this dialog box to create default fonts for various languages.

For each language you use, select that language and then assign default fonts for it.

Some stationeries specify certain fonts. You can choose to use the specified fonts or override with your own fonts. You can choose among

- Use the Font Specified in Stationery (if Specified)
- Use My Font when Replying to and Forwarding Messages
- Always Use My Fonts

You can click Stationery Picker in the Mail Setup tab to open the dialog box shown in Figure 27.30.

Figure 27.30
You can use this dialog box to select existing stationeries, edit stationeries, and create new ones.

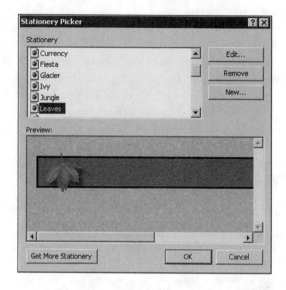

To select an existing stationery, scroll down the Stationery list and select one. The large box in the lower part of the dialog box shows what the selected stationery looks like. If you can't find a suitable stationery, click Get More Stationery. If your computer can connect to the Internet, your Web browser opens a Microsoft Web page where more stationeries are available. Check one or more stationeries you want to download, and then click Go to Basket to download those stationeries you've selected.

In the Stationery Picker dialog box, you can select a stationery and then click

- **Edit**—Used to make changes to the selected stationery
- **Remove**—Used to remove the selected stationery from the list
- **New**—Used to create a new stationery

Tip from

Gordon Padwick

You easily can create a new stationery that contains only text. If you want to create a stationery that includes graphics, you must already have the graphics available in JPG, JPEG, GIF, or BMP format.

SIGNING MESSAGES

Signatures are available only if you've selected Outlook's built-in editor as your e-mail editor instead of Word.

PART

VI

CH

27

Tip from

You can use an Outlook add-on, such as ExSign, if you want more powerful signature capabilities than exist with Outlook. A trial version of ExSign is available for downloading from http://www.mokry.cz.

To create a one-line text signature to append to the messages you send, click Signatures to display the Create Signature dialog box. In that dialog box, click New, enter the text for the signature you want to use, and then click OK. Outlook displays that signature in the Signature for New Messages box. You can create as many signatures as you want in this manner. You can subsequently open the drop-down Signature for New Messages list and select a default signature. After doing that, you can open the drop-down Signature for Replies and Forwards box and select one of your signatures as the default.

SPELLING OPTIONS

Use the Spelling tab of the Options dialog box, shown in Figure 27.31, to set your preferences for spell checking.

Figure 27.31
The options in this dialog box are slightly enhanced from those in previous Outlook versions. Default settings are shown here.

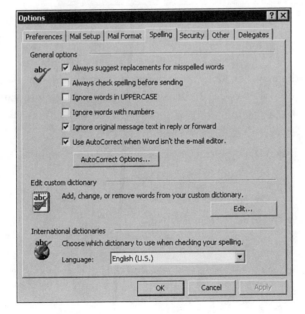

Note

Outlook shares standard and custom dictionaries with other Office applications, such as Word and Excel, but not with Outlook Express. Your custom dictionary is in the file Custom.dic.

GENERAL SPELLING OPTIONS

Check boxes in the General Options section at the top of the Spelling tab enable you to specify how you want spell checking to function. The first five option boxes are the same as those in Outlook 2000; the sixth option box is new in Outlook 2002. These boxes are self-explanatory, so they are not described here.

The AutoCorrect Settings button, new in Outlook 2002, enables you to control how Word automatically corrects certain typing errors. Click this button to display the AutoCorrect dialog box, which is the same as the one displayed when you choose Tools, AutoCorrect in Word.

EDITING A CUSTOM DICTIONARY

Click Edit in the Edit Custom Dictionary section of the Spelling tab to open a Notepad window that lists the words in your custom dictionary. You can add words to this dictionary, delete words from it, and edit existing words.

USING INTERNATIONAL DICTIONARIES

Open the Language drop-down list at the bottom of the Spelling tab and select the language you want to use for spell checking. The languages displayed are those you selected when you installed Office.

SECURITY OPTIONS

Use the Security tab of the Options dialog box, shown in Figure 27.32, to set your security preferences.

Figure 27.32
This dialog box is very similar to the corresponding dialog box in Outlook 2000.

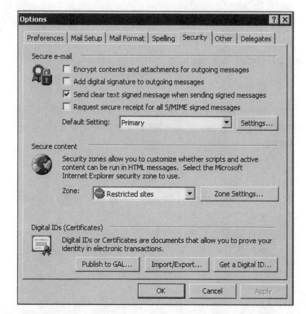

SECURING E-MAIL

You can use the Secure E-mail section at the top of the Security tab only if you have a Digital ID installed on your computer. Use this section to specify the security options you want to use for all outgoing Internet messages.

Tip from

[signature]

If you're not already familiar with digital IDs, read the sections "Sending Secure Messages on the Internet," "Sending and Receiving Digitally Signed Messages," and "Sending and Receiving Encrypted Messages," in Chapter 32, "Using Outlook Securely," before attempting to set secure e-mail options. The book *The Code Book* by Simon Singh (published by Anchor Books) is an excellent source of general information about message security.

If you already have one or more Digital IDs (also known as *certificates*) installed on your computer, the Default Settings box displays the name of the ID you're currently using. You can open the drop-down Default Setting list to select a different ID (if more than one exists on your computer).

The four check boxes near the top of the tab establish default conditions for encrypting and digitally signing messages. The choices you make here become defaults for all messages, but you can make changes for individual messages. The four check boxes are

- **Encrypt Contents and Attachments for Outgoing Messages**—This is unchecked by default.

- **Add Digital Signature to Outgoing Messages**—This is unchecked by default.

- **Send Clear Text Signed Message when Sending Signed Messages**—This is checked by default. By checking this option, you can send messages to recipients who use e-mail software that doesn't support S/MIME. These people can read your messages without verifying the digital signature.

- **Request Secure Receipt for All S/MIME Signed Messages**—This is unchecked by default.

If you don't already have a digital ID, click Settings to open a dialog box that leads you through the process of obtaining one. This process is described in detail in the section "Obtaining a Certificate," in Chapter 32.

SECURING CONTENT

The Secure Content section of the Security tab, shown previously in Figure 27.32, contains choices you can make about Internet Explorer's security zones. The choices you make here apply only to messages you receive from an Internet or intranet mail server. Security zones affect the way scripts and other active contents are handled by Outlook.

Outlook relies on some of the functionality of Internet Explorer, which is why the installation process automatically installs Internet Explorer. For detailed information about Internet Explorer's security zones, refer to a book such as *Special Edition Using Microsoft Windows Me*, published by Que.

To examine—and possibly modify—Internet zones, open the drop-down Zone list and select Internet. Then click Zone Settings. Outlook displays a message box with some information about security settings. Click OK to display the dialog box shown in Figure 27.33.

Figure 27.33
You can use this dialog box to examine the default security zones, make changes to those zones, and create your own security zones.

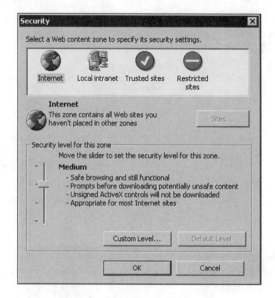

Select the zones one at a time. When you select a zone, the lower part of the dialog box shows you whether the zone has High, Medium, Medium-Low, or Low security. The text at the right of the slider summarizes what the selected security level means. You can change the selected zone's security level by dragging the slider up or down.

To restore a security zone to its default level, click Default Level (which is available only after you've changed a zone's security level).

To create a custom security zone, click Custom Level to display the dialog box shown in Figure 27.34.

→ For more detailed information about security zones, **see** "Using Security Zones," **p. 723**.

Figure 27.34
In this dialog box, you can choose how you want your custom security zone to handle various types of active message content.

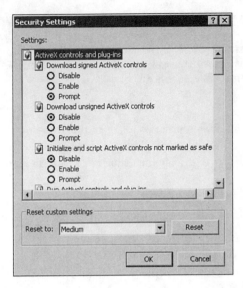

OTHER OPTIONS

Use the Other tab of the Options dialog box, shown in Figure 27.35, to set your preferences for how you want Outlook to deal with items in the Deleted Items folder, to access some advanced options, to set how you want AutoArchive to work, to customize the Preview pane, and to enable instant messaging.

Figure 27.35
The bottom section of this tab, which deals with instant messaging, is new in Outlook 2002.

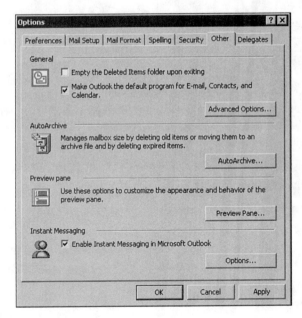

Click Options to display a dialog box in which you can set instant messaging options. For detailed information about instant messaging, see Chapter 6, "Accessing the Internet." You can also find a lot of information about instant messaging in *Special Edition Using Microsoft Windows Me*, published by Que.

→ For information about using instant messaging, **see** "Communicating Instantly," **p. 123**.

SETTING GENERAL OPTIONS

By default, the contents of your Deleted Items folder are saved when you close Outlook. The next time you open Outlook and subsequently delete items, those items are added to whatever is already in the Deleted Items folder. Over time, therefore, the Deleted Items folder can become quite large.

You can check the Empty the Deleted Items Folder upon Exiting box, which is unchecked by default, so that all items in the Deleted Items folder are permanently deleted when you close Outlook. In most cases, checking that box is a good thing to do. However, you should probably get into the habit of checking what's in your Deleted Items folder each time you prepare to close Outlook. By doing that, you'll eliminate the possibility of losing items you might want to keep.

Note

Some contracts require that all information relevant to the contract are kept. If you permanently delete items from your Deleted Items folder, you might be violating the terms of the contract under which you're working.

Click Advanced Options to display more general options in the dialog box shown in Figure 27.36.

GENERAL SETTINGS

By default, when Outlook starts it displays the Inbox Information viewer. You can open the Startup in This Folder drop-down list at the top of the Advanced Options dialog box and select a different startup folder. The available folders are

- Calendar
- Contacts
- Inbox (the default)
- Journal
- Notes
- Outlook Today
- Tasks

In many cases, Outlook Today is the best choice because it gives you an overview of your current activities.

PART

VI

CH

27

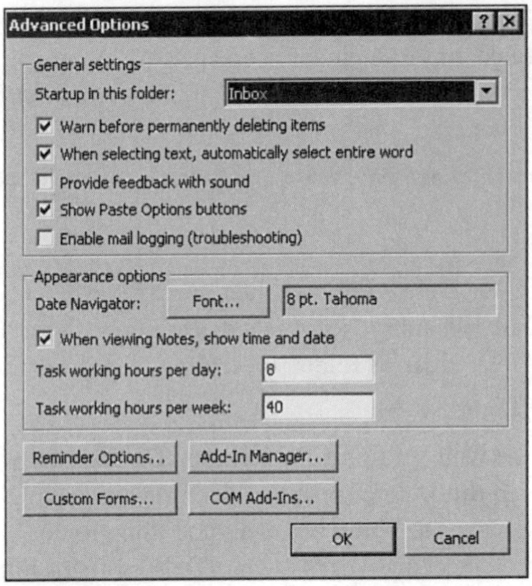

Figure 27.36
This dialog box contains several options that are new in Outlook 2002.

Three of the six check boxes in the General Settings section of the Advanced Options dialog box are new in Outlook 2002. The six check boxes are

- **Warn Before Permanently Deleting Items (checked by default)**
- **When Selecting Text, Automatically Select Entire Word**—Not available if you're using Word as your e-mail editor. If you're using Outlook's built-in editor, it is available and is checked by default.
- **Provide Feedback with Sound (unchecked by default)**
- **Show Paste Options Buttons (checked by default)**—New in Outlook 2002.
- **Enable Mail Logging (Troubleshooting) (unchecked by default)**—New in Outlook 2002.

Tip from

Gordon Prodd

Be cautious about enabling mail logging. Enable it only when you need to troubleshoot mail. Otherwise, you can quickly create a very large log file.

Log files are saved in various places. If you're running Outlook under Windows 2000, log files are saved in

- `C:\Documents and Settings\<logon name>\Local Settings\temp\OPMLOG.LOG`—Log files for MAPI, POP3, and SMTP accounts are saved here.
- `C:\Documents and Settings\<logon name>\Local Settings\Outlook Logging\<name of IMAPServer>\IMAP0.LOG, IMAP1.LOG, and so on`—Log files for IMAP accounts are saved here.

- `C:\Documents and Settings\<logon name>\Local Settings\Outlook Logging\Hotmail\Hotmail0.LOG, Hotmail1.LOG, and so on`—Log files for Hotmail accounts are saved here.

If you're running Outlook under Windows 98 or Windows Me, log files are saved in

- `C:\Windows\temp\OPMLOG.LOG`—Log files for MAPI, POP3, and SMTP accounts are saved here.

- `C:\Windows\temp\Output Logging\<name of IMAPServer>\IMAP0.LOG, IMAP1.LOG, and so on`—Log files for IMAP accounts are saved here.

- `C:\Windows\temp\Output Logging\Hotmail\Hotmail0.LOG, Hotmail1.LOG, and so on`—Log files for Hotmail accounts are saved here.

APPEARANCE OPTIONS

The choices in the Appearance Options section of the Advanced Options dialog box are the same as in Outlook 2000.

The first line in this section enables you to select a font other than the default 8-pt. Tahoma for the Calendar Information viewer's Date Navigator. You can't change the font's color, however.

If you don't want Notes to display the time and date when they were created, uncheck When Viewing Notes, Show Time and Date.

If appropriate, you can change the standard number of working hours per day and per week.

Four buttons at the bottom of the Advanced Options dialog box provide access to more specialized options.

REMINDER OPTIONS

Click Reminder Options near the bottom of the Advanced Options dialog box to display the dialog box shown in Figure 27.37.

Figure 27.37
Use this dialog box to choose whether Outlook should display a reminder and play a sound when a reminder becomes due.

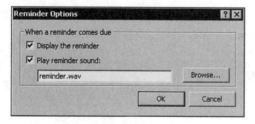

This dialog box is identical to the one in Outlook 2000. By default, the two option buttons are checked so that Outlook displays reminders and plays a sound. Uncheck either or both boxes if you prefer not to see and hear reminders.

The default sound Outlook plays when a reminder becomes due is in the file defined in the box near the bottom of the dialog box. You can click the Browse button to search your computer's folder structure to select a different sound.

Note

Outlook displays and sounds reminders only for Calendar items in the Calendar folder. If you move Calendar items to other folders, Outlook doesn't display and sound reminders for those items.

ADD-IN MANAGER

Click Add-In Manager near the bottom of the Advanced Options dialog box to display the dialog box shown in Figure 27.38.

Figure 27.38
This dialog box lists the add-ins currently installed.

This dialog box is identical to the one in Outlook 2000. The box contains a list of the add-ins currently installed on your computer. The checked add-ins are those that are activated. Unchecked add-ins are not activated.

When the dialog box is initially displayed, the first add-in is selected. You can use the down-arrow and up-arrow keys to select one add-in after another. Most add-ins have a description that is displayed under the list when that add-in is selected.

You can install add-ins in three ways:

- Install standard Outlook add-ins by opening the Windows Control Panel and choosing Add/Remove Programs. Select Outlook 2002 from the list of installed software, and then click Add/Remove. Click Add New Components and then follow the onscreen instructions.
- Install add-ins available on a disk or CD by clicking Install in the Add-In Manager dialog box.
- Install certain third-party add-ins in the same way you install other Windows applications.

Note

Some add-ins are automatically installed when you install other applications on your computer. Symantec's WinFax Pro is one application that does this.

CUSTOM FORMS

Click Custom Forms near the bottom of the Advanced Options dialog box to display the dialog box shown in Figure 27.39.

Figure 27.39
Use this dialog box to manage Outlook forms you've created.

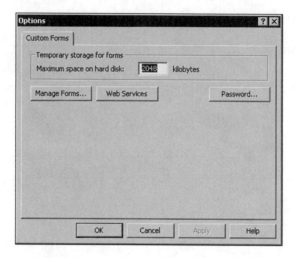

Each time you use an Outlook form, that form is stored on your hard disk in an area known as the *forms cache* so that the form is quickly available the next time you want it. By default, 2,048KB is made available for the forms cache. Although this is adequate space in many cases, if you use many forms, the cache could run out of space. When that happens, one of the forms already in the cache is removed to make room for the most recently used form.

If you use many forms and are prepared to allocate more than the default amount of space for the forms cache, you can change the size of the cache by entering a different value in the Maximum Space on Hard Disk box. By doing so, you might be able to speed up Outlook's performance.

The Options dialog box contains four buttons:

- **Web Forms**—Use this to make Web forms available.
- **Web Services**—Use this to enable the use of Outlook Web Access to be able to open messages not understood by Outlook and to activate the Web Forms link on the Actions menu.
- **Password**—Use this to change your Windows password.
- **Manage Forms**—Use this to display the Forms Manager dialog box, which you can use to copy forms, update forms, delete forms, view and modify form properties, set up forms, and save forms as files.

PART
VI

CH
27

COM ADD-INS

COM add-ins are executable files or dynamic link libraries that add extra functionality to Outlook. You can find examples of COM add-ins in the Microsoft Office Update Web site, which you can reach by choosing Help, Office on the Web. Click COM Add-ins to display a dialog box you can use to make add-ins available with Outlook.

AUTOARCHIVING OPTIONS

Outlook's AutoArchive capability moves old items into an archive file and deletes items in your wastebasket. By default, Outlook AutoArchives items of the ages listed in Table 27.2.

TABLE 27.2 DEFAULT AUTOARCHIVING AGES

Item Type	Age
Calendar	6 months
Deleted Items	2 months
Journal	6 months
Sent Items	2 months
Task	6 months

Contact, Draft, Inbox, and Note items are not AutoArchived by default.

Tip from

To change the default AutoArchive properties for a type of item, right-click the name of the folder for that type of item in the Folder List, select Properties in the context menu, and select the AutoArchive tab of the Properties dialog box.

Click AutoArchive in the Other tab of the Options dialog box to display the dialog box shown in Figure 27.40.

The first two check boxes are the same as those in Outlook 2000:

- **Run AutoArchive Every 14 Days (checked by default)**—You can change the number of days.
- **Prompt Before AutoArchive Runs (checked by default)**

By leaving Show Archive Folder in Folder List checked, as it is by default, you can easily retrieve items from the archive folder. If you uncheck this box, Outlook 2002 doesn't show the archive folder in the Folder List, as was the case in previous versions of Outlook.

The center section of the AutoArchive dialog box gives you control over what happens when AutoArchiving occurs. In previous versions of Outlook, you set the AutoArchiving age separately for each type of folder, as you can still do in Outlook 2002. In Outlook 2002, though, you also can set an AutoArchive age within Options, and then click Apply These Settings to All Folders Now to set the same AutoArchive age to all folders.

Figure 27.40
This dialog box is considerably expanded from the equivalent dialog box in Outlook 2000.

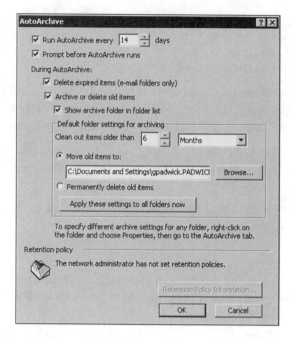

The AutoArchive dialog box, within Options, enables you to choose whether to move items to a folder or to permanently delete all items when AutoArchiving occurs, and to apply this to all types of folders, rather than having to choose for each type of folder separately.

The Retention Policy Information button at the bottom of the AutoArchive dialog box is disabled if you have installed Outlook locally on your own computer. If Outlook has been installed from your network and the network administrator has defined a policy for retaining deleted items, the Retention Policy Information button is enabled. You can click that button to display a dialog box that tells you what the installed retention policy is.

PREVIEW PANE

Click Preview Pane in the Other tab of the Options dialog box to select your preferences for how the Preview pane is displayed. Outlook displays the dialog box shown in Figure 27.41.

Figure 27.41
Use this dialog box, which is similar to the one in Outlook 2000, to customize the appearance and behavior of the Preview pane.

The first check box, Mark Messages as Read in Preview Window, is unchecked by default. Check this box if you want Outlook to mark messages as read when they have been displayed in the Preview pane for a certain period. The default period is 5 seconds, but you can change this to a different number of seconds.

The second check box, Mark Item as Read when Selection Changes, is checked by default. In this case, an item displayed in the Preview pane is automatically marked as read when you select a different item. Uncheck the box if you don't want that to happen.

The third check box, Single Key Reading Using Space Bar, is also checked by default. In this case, you can select one message after another by pressing the space bar. Uncheck this box to disable this capability.

Unlike in Outlook 2000, this dialog box doesn't provide the ability to change the font in the Preview header.

INSTANT MESSAGING

Instant messaging is a capability that's new in Outlook 2002. By default, the Enable Instant Messaging in Microsoft Outlook box at the bottom of the Other tab is not checked. Check this box to enable instant messaging.

Instant messaging uses MSN Messenger 3.5 or later. If you don't have that installed on your computer, Outlook displays a message box inviting you to download the MSN Messenger Web page. Click Yes to continue. Outlook opens Internet Explorer and, if necessary, establishes a connection to your Internet service provider. Follow the onscreen instructions to download the Web page and, when you've finished, close Internet Explorer.

Click Options to display the dialog box shown in Figure 27.42.

Figure 27.42
Use this dialog box to set your preferences for instant messaging.

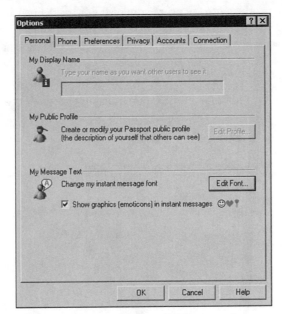

DELEGATES OPTIONS

You can use the Delegates tab of the Options dialog box to give delegates access to your Exchange Server accounts and to assign permissions to each delegate. When you first open the Delegates tab, no delegates are listed. After you've given delegates access to your accounts, the names of those delegates are listed. The Delegates tab is shown in Figure 27.43.

Figure 27.43
Use this dialog box to allow other people to send messages by way of Exchange Server on your behalf.

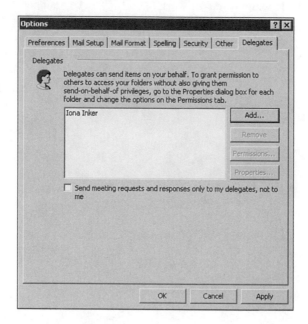

You can use these buttons at the right of the list of delegates:

- **Add**—Displays the Add Users dialog box, in which you can select delegates from the names listed in the Global Address List.

- **Remove**—Select a delegate's name, and then click this button to remove that delegate's name.

- **Permissions**—Select a delegate's name, and then click this button to display a dialog box that lists your contacts. This button isn't available if you're using Offline Folders or Personal Folders to store your Outlook items.

- **Properties**—Displays a dialog box that displays information about the selected contact. This button isn't available if you're using Offline Folders or Personal Folders to store your Outlook items.

You can check Send Meeting Requests and Reponses Only to My Delegates, Not to Me in the Delegates tab. After you do so, meeting requests and responses sent to you aren't added to your Inbox folder and aren't displayed in your Inbox Information viewer. This option is available when you give Editor permission for your Calendar folder to a delegate, and then select Delegate Receives Copies of Meeting-Related Messages Sent to Me in the Delegate Permissions dialog box.

OTHER OPTION TABS

If you install add-ins, you might see additional tabs in the Options dialog box. You can use those tabs to modify how those add-ins work.

CHAPTER 28

CREATING AND USING RULES

In this chapter

WHAT IS A RULE?

A *rule* is a set of conditions, actions, and exceptions that controls how Outlook processes and organizes messages and other Outlook items. The *conditions* determine to which types of items a rule applies; the *actions* are what the rule does; and the *exceptions* determine when a rule does not apply to certain items. Some rules work on messages you receive; other rules work on messages you send.

These two examples will help you understand the sorts of things rules can do:

- You can create a rule that forwards all messages you receive from a specific person to another person.
- You can create a rule that moves copies of messages you send to a specific person into a certain folder.

→ For an example of using rules for another purpose, **see** "Applying Colors to Items According to Their Categories," **p. 164**.

To create basic rules, click Organize in the Inbox Information viewer's Standard toolbar. To create more sophisticated rules, use Outlook's Rules Wizard.

Note

Whereas the Outlook 98 and Outlook 2000 Standard toolbars contain an icon labeled Organize, Outlook 2002 contains only an unlabeled Organize icon—it's the one immediately to the right of the Find icon.

You can create and edit rules to do things such as

- Perform an action when a message arrives
- Perform an action before a message is sent
- Move incoming messages that satisfy certain conditions into a specific folder
- Notify you when certain messages arrive
- Automatically delete messages that satisfy certain conditions
- Assign a flag to certain messages
- Automatically reply to certain messages
- Notify you when recipients read certain messages

You can combine these and other actions in many ways to create various rules, as described in the rest of this chapter. Bear in mind that Outlook restricts the amount of space for rules to 32KB, a MAPI limitation that carries over into Outlook. Although this space is adequate for most purposes, you could run up against this barrier. See the section "Managing Rules" later in this chapter for more information.

> **Note**
>
> Outlook 2000 and Outlook 2002 contain rule conditions and actions that weren't available in previous versions of Outlook.

This chapter focuses on rules that run under Outlook on your computer. If you're using Outlook as a client for Exchange Server, you can create rules that run on the server.

> **Note**
>
> In Outlook 98, rules could be used only on Internet messages received from a POP3 server. Outlook 2000 and Outlook 2002 rules, however, can also be used on messages received from an IMAP server.

→ For information about using rules for Outlook used as a client for an Exchange server, **see** "Using Server-Based Rules," **p. 449**.

USING ORGANIZE TO CREATE RULES

Chapter 17 introduces Outlook's Organize capability. That chapter describes how you can use Organize to move existing messages you've received from the Inbox folder to another folder. You also can use Organize to create rules that move new messages to a different folder when those messages arrive.

→ For information about using Organize to create rules, **see** "Organizing E-mail Messages," **p. 366**.

CREATING A RULE

Before creating a rule to move incoming messages to a folder, that folder must exist. If the folder you want to move messages to doesn't exist, follow the steps described in Chapter 14, "Managing Outlook Folders," to create a new folder.

→ For information about creating folders, **see** "Creating a New Folder," **p. 305** and "Creating Folders and Subfolders," **p. 631**.

Rules you create in Outlook that's not a client for Exchange Server always run within Outlook on your computer. In contrast, some rules you create in Outlook that is a client for Exchange Server run either within Outlook on your computer or within the server. In the case of Outlook used as an Exchange client, Outlook evaluates each rule you create. If the rule can be run in either place, Outlook gives you a choice of running the rule within the client or server.

Here's how you use Organize to create a rule that moves incoming mail to a new folder.

To create a rule that moves incoming messages to a specific folder:

 1. With the Inbox Information viewer displayed, click Organize in the viewer's Standard toolbar to display the Organize pane shown at the top of Figure 28.1.

Figure 28.1
The second line in the Organize pane assumes you want to create a rule based on the names of the sender or recipient of the currently selected e-mail item.

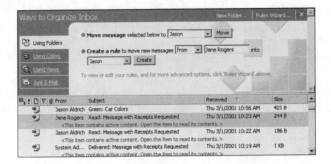

2. The first box in the second line initially contains the word "from." You're creating a rule that applies to messages from someone, so this is appropriate.

> **Note**
>
> You can open the drop-down list and select Sent To if you want to create a rule that affects messages sent to someone.

3. The second box in the second line contains the name of the sender of the currently selected message. If necessary, replace that name with the name of the sender whose messages you want the rule to apply to. You can enter the name or, if you already have a message from that person, select that message in the message headers listed below the Organize pane.

> **Tip from**
>
> Depending on various factors, a sender's name might not always appear in the same way. For example, you might sometimes see a sender's name in the From box and at other times see a sender's e-mail address. You must create a separate rule for each way a sender's name appears.

4. Open the drop-down list in the third line of the Organize pane to see a list of some of your Outlook folders, as shown in Figure 28.2.

Figure 28.2
The list contains the names of one or more custom folders that you've previously created.

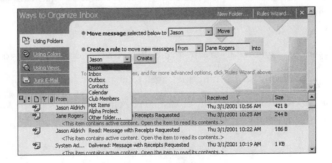

5. If the name of the folder into which you want to move incoming mail is in the list, select that name. If the name of the folder isn't in the list, select Other Folder to display the Select Folder dialog box that lists all your Outlook folders; select the folder you want to use and click OK. The name of the selected folder appears in the box at the left end of the third line in the Organize pane.

6. Click Create in the Organize pane. A message appears stating that the new rule will be applied to new messages as they are received. The message also asks whether you want "to run this rule on the current contents of the folder."

7. Click Yes if you want the rule to apply to the existing folder contents, or click No if you want the rule to apply only to new messages. After a short delay, the word Done appears to signify that the rule has been created and will be applied to all incoming messages.

8. Click the X button at the upper-right corner of the Organize pane, or click Organize in the Standard toolbar, to close the Organize pane.

After you create a rule in this way, Outlook tests each incoming message to see whether it is from the sender you specified in step 3 of the preceding procedure. If the message is from that sender, Outlook immediately moves the message into the folder you specified in step 5. If the message is not from that sender, Outlook saves the incoming message in the usual folder, normally your Inbox folder.

CREATING A RULE TO COLOR MESSAGES

You can use Organize to create rules that make message headers in the Inbox Information viewer appear in various colors according to the sender's or recipient's name. You might, for example, want all messages from your supervisor to show up in red and all messages from important customers to be blue.

Tip from

You can color *message headers* in the Sent Items folder or a custom folder that contains messages in the same way.

At the left edge of the Organize pane, click Using Colors to display the pane shown in Figure 28.3.

To color message headers:

1. The Organize pane opens with From in the first box in the top line. If you want to color message headers in your Sent Items Information viewer, open the drop-down list and select Sent To.

2. Enter the name of the person whose messages you want to color in the second box.

3. Open the drop-down list of colors and select the color you want to use.

4. To apply a color to messages already in your Inbox or Sent Items Information viewer, click Apply Color.

PART
VI

CH

28

5. If you want to apply a color to messages sent only to you, open the drop-down color list in the second line and select a color.

6. Click Turn On to apply the rule to future messages you receive or send. A few moments after you do so, the label on the Turn On button changes to Turn Off. Click that button if you want to turn off the rule.

Figure 28.3
Use this pane to color messages from specific people.

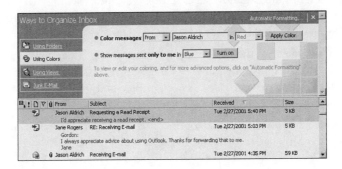

CHANGING A VIEW

The Using Views button at the left side of the Organize pane has nothing to do with creating rules. It just provides a quick way to change the view in which Outlook displays messages.

→ For detailed information about views, **see** "Using Default Views," **p. 652**.

MANAGING JUNK E-MAIL

You can use the Junk E-mail button at the left side of the Organize pane to set up how Outlook automatically processes junk e-mail.

→ For information about automatically dealing with junk e-mail, **see** "Dealing with Junk Mail," **p. 606**.

CHANGING A RULE

Although you can create additional rules in the manner just described, you can't deactivate, delete, or (with one exception) change a rule from the Organize pane. You must use the Rules Wizard to do any of these things. The remainder of this chapter describes how you can use the Rules Wizard.

The exception mentioned in the previous paragraph is this: If you use the Organize pane to create a rule that moves incoming messages from one person to a certain folder, Outlook creates a rule to do that. If you subsequently create a rule to move incoming messages from another person to the same folder, Outlook doesn't create a second rule. Instead, Outlook modifies the existing rule so that incoming messages from one person or the other are moved to the folder. However, if you choose a different folder for messages from the second person, Outlook creates a second rule.

USING THE RULES WIZARD TO MANAGE INCOMING MESSAGES

Normally, Outlook places all the messages you receive in your Inbox folder. If you receive only a few messages each day, that's no problem. However, if you're one of those people who receives many messages each day, you might prefer to organize those messages by having Outlook automatically assign certain types of messages to separate folders.

Tip from

Instead of organizing messages by saving them in various folders, you might prefer to organize messages by assigning categories to them. Subsequently, you can display messages sorted by category.

The next section describes in detail how you create a specific rule. This chapter also contains more general information about creating rules.

DELIVERING MESSAGES TO FOLDERS AUTOMATICALLY

You can use the Outlook Rules Wizard to create a rule Outlook uses to place messages that satisfy certain conditions into a custom folder you've created.

Suppose you want Outlook to save all the messages you receive in the future from a specific person in a separate folder. The first step is to create a custom folder for these messages, as described previously in the chapter. Although you don't have to, creating custom folders for mail messages as subfolders to your Inbox folder helps to keep your folder structure organized.

CREATING A RULE

Here's how you create the rule that automatically moves messages from a certain person into a specific folder.

Note

If you've worked with the Rules Wizard in previous versions of Outlook, you'll find the wizard in Outlook 2002 is quite similar. One significant difference is that additional choices are offered.

To create the rule:

1. With the Inbox Information viewer displayed, choose Tools, Rules Wizard. Outlook displays a message reminding you that rules don't act on mail sent and received using HTTP accounts (such as Hotmail). Click OK to display the first Rule Wizard window, as shown in Figure 28.4.

PART

VI

CH

28

Figure 28.4
The large box near the top of this dialog box lists the names of existing rules. The large box at the bottom contains the description of a rule selected in the top box.

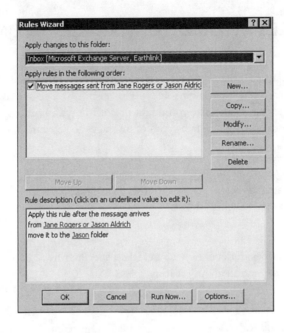

The Apply Changes to This Folder box lists the Outlook folder and the types of messages to which rules apply.

2. Click New to start creating a new rule. Outlook displays the second wizard window, shown in Figure 28.5.

Figure 28.5
The types of rules you can create are listed in the upper box.

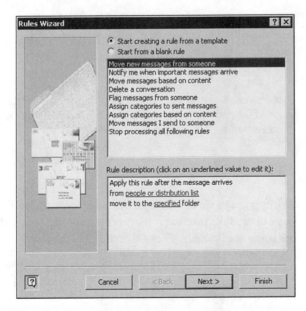

Note

The option buttons at the top of the wizard window shown in Figure 28.5 give you the option of creating a new rule based on a template, or of starting from a blank rule. The description that follows assumes you want to create a rule based on Outlook's built-in rule templates.

3. In the upper box, select the type of rule you want to create: Move New Messages from Someone in this case. A description of this rule appears in the lower box, as shown previously in Figure 28.5. The underlined words in the description (they are usually in blue or have a blue background on your monitor) require definitions.

Tip from

[signature]

The colors in which various elements within windows and dialog boxes appear depend on what you select in the Appearance tab of the Display Properties dialog box, accessible from the Windows Control Panel. Default colors are assumed throughout this book.

4. Click Next to display the next wizard window, which displays a list of conditions that must be satisfied for the rule to be applied. Each condition has a check box adjacent to it, as shown in Figure 28.6.

Figure 28.6
You can scroll through the list to see all the available conditions.

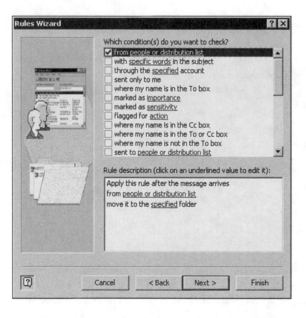

5. Check those conditions that apply. You can check as many as you like. All the checked conditions must be satisfied for the rule to be applied. In this case, the From People or Distribution List is already checked, which is what you want.

6. Click the first underlined words—People or Distribution List—in the Rule Description box. Outlook then displays a dialog box that displays a list of people in one of your address books.

7. Select one or more people to whom you want the rule to apply (or you can select one or more distribution lists). Then click From to move the selected names into the Specify the Address of the Sender box, in which, if you select more than one name, a semicolon separates names. Click OK. The name or names you select replace the underlined words in the wizard window. If you selected more than one name, the names are separated by "or" to indicate the rules apply if a message comes from any of the people specified.

Note

You might have several address books, in which case you can open the drop-down Show Names From The list and select the address book from which you want to select a name or distribution list.

8. Select the second underlined word or phrase in the lower wizard box—the word "specified" in this example. Outlook displays your folder list.

9. Select the folder into which you want Outlook to place items, and then click OK to return to the wizard window, which now looks similar to that shown in Figure 28.7.

Figure 28.7
Both the original underlined words or phrases in the lower box are replaced with your selections.

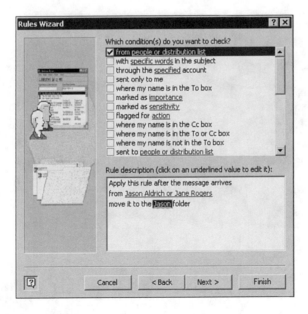

10. Click Next to display the next wizard window, in which you can choose what you want to do with messages that satisfy the conditions you've previously specified, as shown in Figure 28.8.

Figure 28.8
This window asks you what you want to do with the message. You can select one or more of the possibilities listed in the top box.

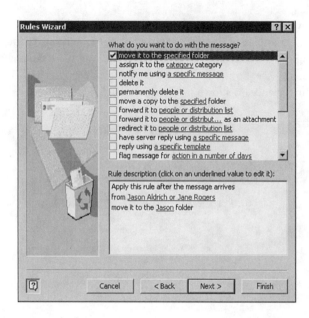

11. You probably want to move messages that satisfy the conditions you've specified in previous wizard windows to the folder you've specified. This action is already checked. You can, of course, check other actions. Notice that the description in the bottom box changes to correspond with the selection you make.

12. Click Next to display the next wizard window, shown in Figure 28.9, in which you can specify exceptions to the rule.

Figure 28.9
Use this window to select exceptions to the rule.

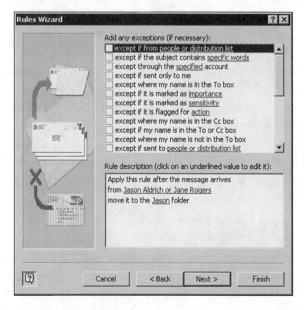

PART

VI

CH

28

13. You don't have to select any exceptions, but you can check any appropriate exceptions. When you select an exception, a description of that exception is added to the rule description in the lower box. As an example, if you want to make messages marked as high importance exceptions, scroll down the list of exceptions and check Except if It Is Marked as Importance, as shown in Figure 28.10.

Figure 28.10
Now another under-lined word (usually colored) is in the description of the rule.

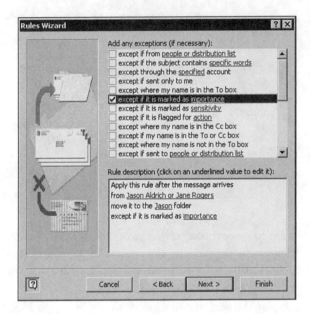

14. Click Importance in the lower box. Outlook displays the Importance dialog box, in which you can select Low, Normal, or High. Click High, and then click OK to return to the wizard window. The description now includes the importance you selected, as shown in Figure 28.11.

15. Click Next to display the final wizard window, in which you supply a name for the rule as shown in Figure 28.12.

16. Replace the suggested name in the Please Specify a Name for This Rule box with something more meaningful.

17. If you want to move messages you've previously received from the named person into the new folder, check Run This Rule Now on Messages Already in "Inbox."

18. If you want this new rule to begin testing incoming messages immediately, make sure Turn on This Rule is checked.

19. If you want the new rules to be used in all your e-mail accounts, check Create This Rule on All Accounts.

20. Click Finish to return to the first wizard window that displays the name of the rule and its final description, as shown in Figure 28.13.

Figure 28.11
The rule description now shows that messages of high importance are excluded.

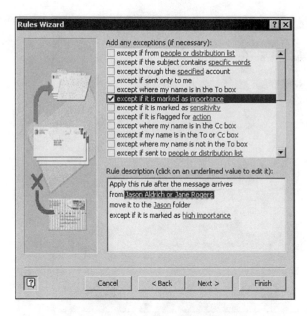

Figure 28.12
Outlook suggests the first replacement you made in the description box as the name for the new rule.

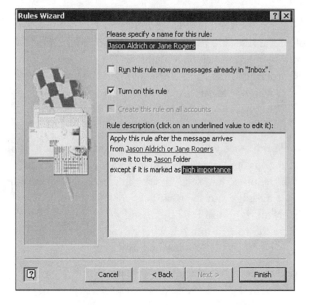

21. Click OK to close the wizard window.

Notice that the name of the rule appears in the upper box and the name is checked. Being checked, Outlook applies the rule to every message you receive and, if a message satisfies the conditions and doesn't contain anything that satisfies the exceptions, the actions of the rule occur. If you uncheck the rule name, Outlook doesn't apply the rule to incoming messages.

PART
VI

CH
28

Figure 28.13
This is how the wizard window displays the completed rule.

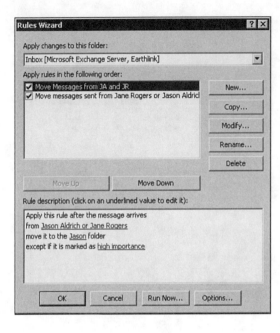

You can repeat the steps described in this section to create additional rules. After you do that, the names of all the rules are listed in the upper box of the first Rules Wizard window in alphabetical order by name. Outlook executes rules in the order in which they are listed. See the section "Reordering Rules" subsequently in this chapter for information about changing the order in which rules are executed.

TESTING A RULE

One way to test a rule is to receive a message that satisfies the rule's conditions and doesn't satisfy the rule's exceptions, and then verify that the actions of the rule occur. In the detailed example described in the preceding section, ask the person whose messages are specified in the rule to send you a message and see what happens. If the rule does what you intend, everything is probably all right. On the other hand, if the rule doesn't do what you intend, you'll have to examine the rule to find out what's wrong and then modify it, as explained in the section "Modifying a Rule," subsequently in this chapter.

Outlook offers another way to test a rule—by running it now.

APPLYING A RULE TO EXISTING MESSAGES

Normally, a rule that applies to incoming messages runs when messages are received. This was the only way to run a rule in Outlook 97 and Outlook 98. Outlook 2000 added the capability to run a rule now; this capability is also available in Outlook 2002.

Running a rule now means running a rule for messages that already exist in your folders. In the case of a rule that affects incoming messages, this means applying the rule to messages already in your Inbox folder. You can use this to test a rule you've just created and also to apply a new rule to messages that already exist in one of your folders.

> **Note**
>
> Of course, if you chose in the final wizard window to apply the rule to existing messages in a folder, you'll be able to see whether the rule works without running it now.

The rule described previously in this chapter affected incoming messages from a specific sender. If you already have messages from that sender in your Inbox, you can apply the rule to those messages.

To run a rule now:

1. Select View, Folder List, and select the folder containing messages you want to use to test the rule.
2. Select Tools, Rules Wizard to display the Rules Wizard previously shown in Figure 28.13.
3. Click Run Now to display the dialog box shown in Figure 28.14.

Figure 28.14
This dialog box shows all the available rules.

4. Check the rule or rules you want to test. Make sure all other rules are unchecked. The Run in Folder box displays the name of the folder that contains the messages you want to use for the test. You can click Browse to select a different folder.
5. Check Include Subfolders if you want to include messages in the selected folder's subfolders in the test. Usually, though, you should leave this box unchecked.
6. Open the Apply Rules To drop-down list and select All Messages, Unread Messages, or Read Messages.

7. Click Run Now to run the rule.

8. Click Close, and then click OK to close the dialog boxes.

9. If the folder list isn't already open, select View, Folder List and select the folder into which the rule should have moved messages. You should see the messages that satisfied the rule's conditions in the folder. If that's the case, your rule is working as it should. If that's not the case, you need to make changes to the rule.

MODIFYING A RULE

You can use the Rules Wizard to make changes to an existing rule.

To modify a rule:

1. With any Outlook Information viewer displayed, select Tools, Rules Wizard to display the first wizard window that shows a list of existing rules.

2. Select the rule you want to modify; then click Modify to display the wizard window shown previously in Figure 28.5, with the type of rule highlighted. Outlook assumes you want to use the selected rule as a template for the new rule.

3. Make whatever changes are necessary by selecting another type of rule in the upper box or by clicking underlined text in the lower box to make different selections. You can click Next to progress to subsequent wizard windows to make changes in them.

4. In any wizard window, click Finish to signify you've finished making changes to the rule.

CREATING OTHER TYPES OF RULES FOR MESSAGES

The preceding example used one example of a rule to explain how rules for incoming messages are created and how they work.

You can use the Rules Wizard to create many types of rules for incoming and outgoing messages. These rules are

- Move New Messages from Someone
- Notify Me when Important Messages Arrive
- Move Messages Based on Content
- Delete a Conversation
- Flag Messages from Someone
- Assign Categories to Sent Messages
- Assign Categories Based on Content
- Move Messages I Sent to Someone
- Stop Processing All Following Rules

When you choose any of these types of rules, a description of that rule appears in the lower box in the wizard window. The descriptions include underlined words or phrases (displayed in blue) that require more information. You can click the underlined words or phrases to open a dialog box in which you can enter or select the required information.

Far too many combinations of rule types and added information required exist than can be covered individually in this chapter. The preceding example of a rule that applies to incoming messages (and the example later in this chapter of a rule that applies to outgoing messages) should give you the general idea of how to create rules, and serve as examples for creating your own rules.

AUTOMATICALLY REPLYING TO MESSAGES

If you're using Outlook as a client for Exchange, you can create rules that automatically send replies to messages. For example, if you're going to be out of town for a few days, you can create a rule that detects messages from certain people, or about certain subjects, and sends a reply explaining you're away and will reply when you get back. This rule can be created to run on the server, so it works even though your computer is turned off or you've taken it with you.

Note

You can create the same rule to Outlook that isn't a client for Exchange. In this case, though, you must leave your computer on with Outlook running for the rule to operate.

Outlook uses a template for the message to be sent as a reply. Your first task, therefore, is to create the message you want sent as a reply and save it as an Outlook template.

After creating the template, follow these steps to create the rule. Because the steps are similar to those previously described, most of them are described only in outline form.

To create a rule that sends an automatic response to a message:

1. In the first Rules Wizard window, check New.
2. In the second wizard window, check Start from a Blank Rule and then select Check Messages When They Arrive.
3. In the third wizard window, check Where My Name Is in the To Box.
4. In the fourth wizard window, check Reply Using a Specific Template.
5. In the Description box, select the underlined words "A Specific Template." Outlook displays the Select a Reply Template dialog box.
6. Open the Look In drop-down list and select User Templates in File System to see a list of the templates you created.

PART
VI

CH
28

7. Select the message template you want to use for the reply; then click Open to return to the wizard window that now contains the complete file name of the template.

8. In the final wizard window, change the name Outlook proposes for the rule to something more meaningful.

9. Click Finish to save the rule. The Rules Wizard (similar to the screen shown in Figure 28.16) now contains the name of the new rule.

If, while you're away, somebody sends you a message that requests your reply be sent to someone else, the Outlook rule sends the reply to the message sender instead of to the person designated to receive the reply. For detailed information on this point, refer to the Microsoft Knowledge Base article Q196338, "Reply Rule Uses "From" Not "Reply To" Address."

CREATING A RULE BASED ON A MESSAGE

Instead of creating a rule from scratch, as described previously in this chapter, you can create a rule based on some of the information in a message you've received. For example, you might want to create a rule that applies to future messages you receive from a specific sender.

To create a rule based on a message you've received:

1. In the Inbox Information viewer, double-click a message from the person for whom you want to create a new rule to display that message in a Message form.

2. In the form's menu bar, select Actions, Create Rule. Outlook displays the first Rules Wizard window, as shown in Figure 28.15.

Figure 28.15
This window lists many conditions among which you can choose.

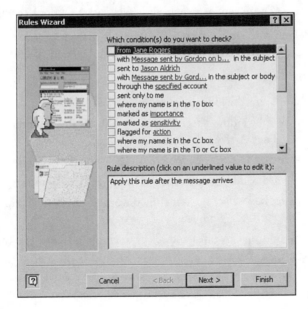

Check whichever conditions are appropriate, and then follow through the subsequent wizard windows.

CREATING RULES FOR OUTGOING MESSAGES

The process of creating rules to be applied to messages you send is similar to creating rules to be applied to incoming messages. The most frequently used rules of this type are those that save copies of certain messages you send in folders other than the usual Sent Items folder.

The following steps show how to create a rule that saves messages in which a specific word or phrase appears in the subject of the message into a folder other than the Inbox folder. Because the details of creating such a rule are the same as those described previously in this chapter, the following steps merely outline the procedure.

To create a rule that saves copies of messages you send in a specific folder:

1. In the second Rules Wizard window, select Move Messages I Send to Someone.
2. In the third wizard window, select a condition, such as With Specific Words in the Subject.
3. Click the underlined words in the Description box and replace those words with explicit words or phrases.
4. Click Next, and then define what you want to do with the message.
5. Click Next, and then define any exceptions to the rule.
6. Click Next, and then enter a name for the rule.
7. Click Finish.

MANAGING RULES

Unlike previous Outlook versions, Outlook doesn't save rules in a separate file. Rules are, in fact, saved as hidden information within the Outlook store. The Rules Wizard provides several ways in which you can manage rules, as described in the next few sections.

RENAMING A RULE

You can easily rename a rule. To do so, display the first Rules Wizard window, shown previously in Figure 28.4. Select the rule you want to rename, and then click Rename to display a dialog box in which you can edit the current name.

COPYING A RULE

A convenient way to create a new rule that's similar to an existing one is to copy the existing rule. To do so, display the first Rules Wizard window, shown previously in Figure 28.4. Select the rule you want to copy; then click Copy. Outlook adds the copied rule to the list of rules. The copy has a name starting with "Copy of" followed by the name of the rule that was copied. Click Rename to change the name to something more appropriate.

You can make changes to the rule's actions, conditions, and exceptions in much the same way you create a new rule. You can select any of the underlined words and phrases in the Rule Description box to make changes.

DELETING A RULE

To delete a rule, select it in the first Rules Wizard window, and then click Delete. Outlook displays a dialog box in which you are asked to confirm the deletion. Click Yes.

REORDERING RULES

Outlook applies rules to messages in the order in which those rules are listed in the Rules Wizard. In the case of incoming messages, Outlook applies rules to messages as they arrive in your Inbox folder. If a rule moves a message from the Inbox folder to another folder, rules are no longer applied to that message. In the case of an outgoing message, Outlook applies rules to messages as they arrive in the Sent Items folder.

Tip from

If you have created several rules and those rules are not doing what you intend, a likely reason is that the rules are being executed in the wrong order. Think through the logic implied by the order of the rules and then adjust the order of execution.

To change the order in which rules are applied to messages, display the list of rules in the first Rules Wizard window. Select a rule you want to move up or down in the list, and then click Move Up or Move Down.

EXPORTING AND IMPORTING RULES

You can export a set of rules to a file, and you can import a set of rules from a file.

Note

To copy a set of rules from one computer to another, export the rules from the first computer; then import those rules into the second computer. You can import rules from a computer running Outlook 98 or Outlook 2000, but you can't import rules from Outlook 97.

To export a set of rules:

1. Click Options in the first Rules Wizard window to display the dialog box shown in Figure 28.16.
2. Click Export Rules to display a dialog box in which you can navigate to the folder in which you want to save the exported rules.

3. Change the name of the file that will be created to something meaningful (Outlook automatically supplies .rwz as the file name extension), and then click Save to save the file.

Figure 28.16
Use this dialog box to export or import a set of rules.

Use similar steps to import rules from a file. In this case, click Import Rules in the Options dialog box to display the Import Rules From dialog box. Navigate to the Windows folder that contains the file to be imported, select the file, and click Open.

CREATING CONDITIONAL RULES

If you create several rules, Outlook normally executes the rules in the order in which they're listed in the Apply Rules in the Following Order box. You also can create a set of rules in such a way that one rule executes under certain conditions and a different rule executes under other conditions. For example, you might want to create rules that

■ Copy all messages addressed directly to you into a specific folder

■ Copy all messages that have specific subject text to a different folder

You can do this by using Stop Processing More Rules, as described in the following procedure.

You should pay close attention to what you select in the What Do You Want to Do with the Message box. For example, a significant difference exists between selecting Move It to the Specified Folder and Move a Copy to the Specified Folder. If you select the former, a message is immediately moved to another folder with the result that all subsequent rules don't act on it. On the other hand, the latter makes a copy of a message in another folder, leaving the original in the folder in which it was received. Consequently, the message is available for action by subsequent rules.

To create conditional rules that copy messages addressed to you into a specific folder and copy other messages that contain certain words or phrases in the subject to another folder:

1. If the folders into which you want to move incoming mail messages don't already exist, create them.

PART

VI

CH

28

→ For information about creating new folders, **see** "Creating Folders and Subfolders," **p. 631**.

2. Select Tools, Rules Wizard to display the first Rules Wizard dialog box, shown previously in Figure 28.4.

3. Click New to display the second wizard window.

4. Select Start from a Blank Rule and select Check Messages When They Arrive; then click Next to display the next wizard window.

5. Check Where My Name Is in the To Box, and then click Next to display the next wizard window.

6. Check Move a Copy to the Specified Folder, and then click the underlined word Specified in the Rule Description box to display the dialog box in which you can select a folder.

7. Select the folder into which you want messages addressed to you to be copied, and then click OK to return to the wizard window, in which the Rule Description box now contains the name of the folder you selected.

8. Scroll down to the bottom of the What Do You Want to Do with the Message box and check Stop Processing More Rules.

Note

At this point, the Rule Description box contains a description of your rule, such as:

```
Apply this rule after the message arrives where my name is
in the To box move
a copy to the Jason folder and stop processing more rules.
```

9. Click Next to display the next wizard window. You probably don't want any exceptions, so click Next to display the final wizard window.

10. Enter an appropriate name for the rule (such as Messages to Me); then click Finish.

That completes creating the rule that moves messages to you into a certain folder. You can see the rule's name listed in the first Rules Wizard window.

To create a rule that moves messages containing certain words or phrases in their subjects into a specific folder:

1. Click New to begin creating the second rule.

2. Select Start from a Blank Rule, select Check Messages When They Arrive, and then click Next.

3. Check the condition With Specific Words in the Subject.

4. Click the underlined words Specific Words in the Rule Description box to display the Search Text dialog box. Enter a specific word or phrase to search for in the Specify Words or Phrases to Search for in the Subject box; then click Add. The word or phrase you entered is now listed in the Search List box.

5. Enter another word or phrase in the Specify Words or Phrases to Search for in the Subject box, and then click Add. This word or phrase appears in the Search List below the first word or phrase.

6. Repeat step 5 as often as necessary to specify more words and phrases.

7. Click OK to return to the wizard window in which the Rule Description box contains the words and phrases you just specified. Notice that each word or phrase you entered in the Search Text dialog box is enclosed within quotation marks, with "or" separating one from the next. This means that the rule will detect messages containing one or more of the search words and phrases. Click Next to display the next wizard window.

8. Select Move a Copy to the Specified Folder, and then click the underlined word Specified in the Rule Description box. Select the folder into which you want to move the messages; then click OK to return to the wizard window. Click Next to open the next wizard window.

9. Select any exceptions to the rule in this window, and then click Next to open the final wizard window.

10. Enter a name for the rule; then click Finish. The two rules are now listed in the first Rules Wizard window.

You haven't quite finished yet. The Rules Wizard automatically lists rules and executes them in the order in which you created them. If you've followed the previous procedure, you have two rules: the rule that handles messages with specific words or phrases in the subject first, followed by the rule that handles messages addressed to you. If you leave the rules listed in this order, Outlook will process the rule that looks for words or phrases in the subject first and then the rule that handles messages addressed to you.

At this point, you must consider what you want to happen to a message that's addressed to you and has the words or phrases you specified in its subject. As things stand now, the first rule copies the message to a folder based on words or phrases in its subject, without regard to whether the message is addressed to you. Then the second rule runs and, if the message is addressed to you, copies the message to another folder.

If you change the order of the two rules so that the Messages to Me rule runs first, the result is different. The Messages to Me rule copies the message into the folder you specified, but the second rule doesn't run (due to Stop Processing More Rules in the Messages to Me rule). The result is that you have a copy of the message in only one of the folders.

Before leaving this subject, let's consider one more possibility. If you had included Stop Process More Rules in the rule that looks for words or phrases in the subject, and that rule is processed first, a message addressed to you with the designated words or phrases in its subject would be copied into only one of the folders.

→ For information about changing the order of rules, **see** "Reordering Rules," **p. 602**.

PART

VI

CH

28

Tip from

Although it might take some head scratching, you can set up quite complex rule processing, much like the If and Case control structures you'll be familiar with if you've done any programming. When you enable two or more conditions within a rule, all those conditions must be satisfied for the rule to run. If you want the rule to run if any one of several conditions is satisfied, you must place each condition in a separate rule. Use Stop Processing More Rules in specific rules, as described in this section, to prevent subsequent rules running.

Plan ahead before you start creating a set of conditional rules. One way to do that is to create a diagram of what you want to achieve. Then you can base the design of individual rules on that diagram.

DEALING WITH JUNK MAIL

If you use Outlook to receive Internet e-mail, you probably receive a lot of junk mail that you'd rather not have to bother with. Outlook contains a built-in filter you can turn on so that messages containing certain words and phrases in the subject or body are ignored. If you don't turn on the filter, messages containing these words and phrases are handled normally.

To see the list of words and phrases Outlook looks for, open the file named `Filters.txt`. This file is usually in a subfolder under the folder that contains Outlook. The easiest way to find it is to use the Windows Find or Search command or, from within Outlook, choose Tools, Advanced Find. Double-click the file name to open it in Windows Notepad or another text editor.

Note

The purpose of opening `Filters.txt` is to see what words and phrases Outlook uses to identify junk mail. Don't attempt to edit this file.

TURNING ON JUNK MAIL FILTERS

 With the Inbox Information viewer displayed, click Organize in the Standard toolbar. On the left side of the Organize pane, click Junk E-mail to display the pane shown in Figure 28.17.

If you looked at the contents of the `Filters.txt` file previously mentioned, you saw that the file lists two types of unwanted mail: Junk and Adult Content. You can determine how you want Outlook to handle these two types of mail. For each type, you can tell Outlook to

- Color or move the mail
- If you choose to move it, which folder to move it to

Make these selections by opening the drop-down lists in the pane and selecting from them.

After you've made your selections, click Turn On to turn on the filters. After you click Turn On, the button labels change to Turn Off. Click the Turn Off buttons to turn off the filters.

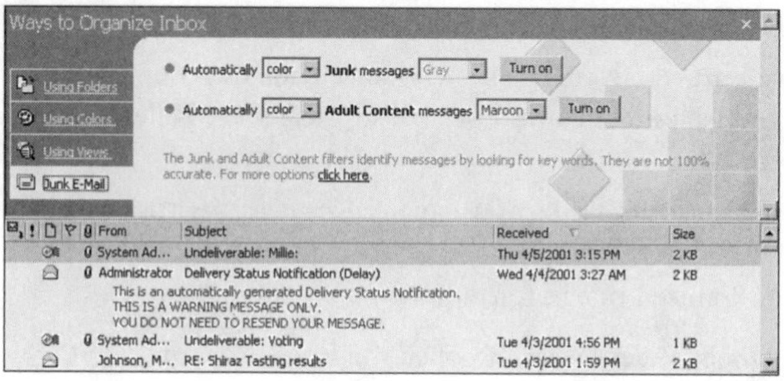

Figure 28.17
Use this pane to define how you want Outlook to handle junk e-mail.

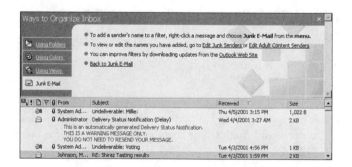

Tip from

I suggest you initially choose to color Junk and Adult Content messages. Use Outlook that way for a few days to see which type of messages Outlook detects. After that, if you're satisfied, you might prefer to have Outlook automatically send Junk and Adult Content messages to a Junk E-mail folder that Outlook automatically creates.

ADDING A SENDER TO THE JUNK OR ADULT CONTENT LIST

To add the name of a sender to the Junk or Adult Content lists, right-click a message from that sender in the Inbox Information viewer to display a context menu. Move the pointer onto Junk E-mail and click either Add to Junk Senders List or Add to Adult Content Senders List. Outlook displays a message confirming that the selected name has been added to the list you chose.

You also can add names to the Junk and Adult Content lists and remove names you previously added by displaying another view of the Organize pane. To display this view, choose Click Here in the pane shown previously in Figure 28.17. The new view is shown in Figure 28.18.

Figure 28.18
Use this pane if you want to edit your lists of Junk and Adult Content mail senders.

Click Edit Junk Senders or Edit Adult Content Senders to display a dialog box in which you can add to, or delete from, the built-in lists of senders.

IMPROVING HOW OUTLOOK HANDLES JUNK E-MAIL

So far, you've learned how to use the Organize pane to set up Outlook so that it detects junk e-mail. You can gain more control over this by using the Rules Wizard to create a customized rule.

→ For information about using the Rules Wizard to create rules, **see** "Using the Rules Wizard to Manage Incoming Messages," **p. 589**.

To create a customized rule that handles junk e-mail:

1. Choose Tools, Rules Wizard to open the Rules Wizard.

2. In the first wizard window, click New.

3. In the second wizard window, select Check Messages When They Arrive.

4. In the third wizard window, select Suspected to Be Junk E-mail or from Junk Senders.

5. Click Junk Senders. Outlook displays the Edit Junk Senders dialog box.

6. Use the Edit Junk Senders dialog box to add senders to your list or to edit or delete existing senders.

7. In the fourth wizard window, select what you want Outlook to do when it detects suspected junk e-mail. You'll probably want to select Move It to a Specified Folder.

8. Click Specified. Outlook displays a dialog box that lists your folders. Select the folder into which you want Outlook to move suspected junk e-mail.

9. In the fifth wizard window, select any exceptions to the new rule.

10. In the sixth wizard window, name the new rule and make sure it's turned on.

11. Click Finish to return to the first wizard window that lists the new rule.

You can follow an almost identical procedure to create a customized rule for detecting messages that contain suspected adult content.

CREATING RULES WITH OR CONDITIONS

Most of the rules you create by using the Rules Wizard test for only one condition, such as

- Where My Name Is in the To Box
- Sent Only to Me

However, if you examine the list of conditions offered by the Rules Wizard, you'll find some that contain the word "or." You can use these conditions to test for one thing or the other. Some examples of these are

- From People or Distribution List
- Suspected to Be Junk E-mail or from Junk Senders

TROUBLESHOOTING

RULES

If you're careful while you go through the steps of the Rules Wizard, you'll probably find that your individual rules work. But, if a rule doesn't work as you intend, it's probably because you made an incorrect selection or supplied invalid information. The only solution to this is to carefully examine each Rules Wizard window and make the necessary corrections.

After you've created several rules, those rules are listed in the first Rules Wizard window. Outlook runs those rules that are checked in the order they are listed. If you run into trouble with processing rules, the first step is to ensure that each rule works individually. You can do so by having only one rule checked at a time.

When you're satisfied that each rule runs as intended by itself, consider the order of the rules. One common problem is that a rule might move an incoming message to a folder other than the folder on which the rules operate. If this happens, subsequent rules won't operate on the message that has been moved.

You might be able to correct a problem with multiple rules by changing their order. To do this, display the list of rules in the Rules Wizard, select a rule you want to move, and then click the Move Up or Move Down button.

The most difficult rule problems to solve are those that can (and do) occur if you're using Stop Processing More Rules to create conditional rule processing.

→ For information about Stop Processing More Rules, **see** "Creating Conditional Rules," **p. 603**.

You might well find that a set of conditional rules works fine most of the time but, under some circumstances, doesn't do what you intend. Welcome to the world of computer programming! Only systematic analysis can solve these types of problems. One technique is to create a diagram (programmers call it a *flow chart*) that illustrates how you want your rules to work. Having done that, examine the details of each rule to check that each one is constructed properly.

CHAPTER 29

CUSTOMIZING OUTLOOK TODAY

In this chapter

OUTLOOK TODAY OVERVIEW

The Outlook Today window provides a concise "at-a-glance" view of your current activities in the attractive style of a Web page, as shown in Figure 29.1.

Figure 29.1
Outlook Today shows you what's on your plate.

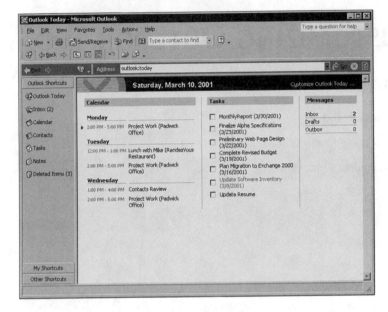

> **Note**
>
> If Outlook Today isn't displayed, click Outlook Today in the Outlook Bar.

→ For information about configuring Outlook Today to launch upon startup, **see** "Startup Options," **p. 613**.

By default, Outlook Today shows

- The activities on your calendar for today and the next few days
- Tasks that you should currently be working on
- The number of unread messages in your Inbox folder
- The number of unfinished message drafts in your Drafts folder
- The number of messages waiting to be sent in your Outbox folder

All the information displayed by Outlook Today is hyperlinked to the underlying Outlook items. You can click any information displayed by Outlook Today to see details about it. You can also check off completed tasks in Outlook Today.

But that's just Outlook Today in Outlook as it comes out of the box. You can customize Outlook Today to make it even more useful.

CHOOSING OUTLOOK TODAY'S OPTIONS

You can customize Outlook Today to suit your personal preferences. To access Outlook Today's options, click Customize Outlook Today to display the Customize Outlook Today window shown in Figure 29.2.

> **Note**
>
> Customize Outlook Today is usually at the upper-right of the Outlook Today window. In the case of the Winter style, however, it's at the bottom-right.

Figure 29.2
This window offers several choices about what Outlook Today displays.

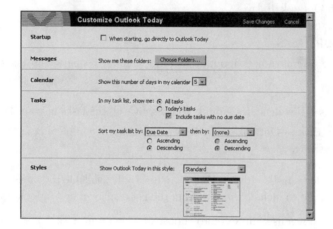

STARTUP OPTIONS

If the Startup check box is unchecked, Outlook starts up with the Information viewer specified in the Options dialog box.

> **Note**
>
> Select Tools, Options, select the Other tab, and click Advanced Options. In the Advanced Options dialog box, the Startup in This Folder contains the name of the Information viewer Outlook displays on startup.

If you want Outlook to display Outlook Today on startup, check the Startup box in the Customize Outlook Today window. After you save the changes in the Customize Outlook Today window, you can subsequently select the Other tab in the Options dialog box. There, you can click Advanced Options, where you'll see Outlook Today specified as the startup folder. Likewise, after you select Outlook Today as the startup folder in the Advanced Options dialog box, you can return to the Customize Outlook Today window, where you'll find that the Startup check box is checked.

Note

If you've had Outlook set up so that Outlook Today is the startup folder, and you then uncheck the Startup check box in Customize Outlook today, Outlook will subsequently start with the Inbox Information viewer displayed.

DISPLAYING YOUR CALENDAR ACTIVITIES

By default, Outlook Today displays activities on your calendar for five days—today and the next four days. You can open the Calendar drop-down Show list and select any number of days in the range 1–7. If your calendar contains no activities for one of those days, that day isn't listed in Outlook Today.

DISPLAYING YOUR TASKS

You can make several choices about how Outlook Today displays your tasks.

You can select

- **All Tasks**—The default. Outlook Today shows all the tasks in your Tasks folder.
- **Today's Tasks**—Outlook Today shows only those incomplete tasks that are due today or are overdue.

Check the Include Tasks with No Due Date box (only available if you've selected Today's Tasks) if you want to include those tasks in the list displayed by Outlook Today.

The two drop-down lists allow you to choose how you want tasks to be sorted. Open the Sort My Task List By drop-down list and select the primary sorting criterion from

- None
- Importance
- Due Date
- Creation Time
- Start Date

If you select any of these except None, you can open the Then By drop-down list and select a secondary sorting criterion from the same list.

You can select Ascending or Descending separately for the primary and secondary sorting criteria, as long as you haven't selected None.

SELECTING AN OUTLOOK TODAY STYLE

By default, Outlook displays Outlook Today in the Standard (three-column) format shown previously in Figure 29.1. You can open the Style drop-down list and select from these alternative styles:

- Standard
- Standard (two column)

- Standard (one column)
- Summer
- Winter

The Summer style has a yellow background; the Winter style has a white background. Both of these styles use a two-column format.

DISPLAYING MESSAGES

By default, Outlook Today displays a count of the outstanding mail items in your Inbox, Drafts, and Outbox folders.

If you've created, or have access to, other folders for Mail and Post items (including items in public folders), you can have Outlook Today display the outstanding mail in these folders, too. To do so, click the Choose Folders button in the Customize Outlook Today window to display the dialog box shown in Figure 29.3.

Figure 29.3
This dialog box shows your Outlook folder structure with the Drafts, Inbox, and Outbox folders checked.

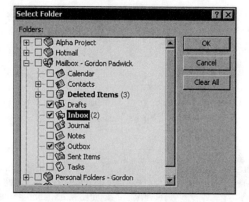

You can uncheck folders for which you don't want to see a count of outstanding mail. You can also check additional folders to have a count of outstanding Mail and Post items in those folders displayed in Outlook Today.

Note

Although you can, in the Check Folders dialog box, check folders that contain items other than Mail and Post items, Outlook Today doesn't display information about these folders.

SAVING THE OPTIONS YOU'VE SPECIFIED

After you've customized Outlook Today, as described in the preceding sections, click Save Changes to display Outlook Today with your changes incorporated.

EXTENDING OUTLOOK TODAY

You can extend Outlook Today far beyond selecting the options described in the previous section of this chapter. That's because Outlook Today is defined by HTML code, to which you have access and which you can modify.

You can customize and extend Outlook today by

- Adding text, links, and images
- Adding script
- Adding ActiveX components
- Changing styles for the background and fonts

This chapter covers only basic customization of Outlook Today. For more comprehensive information, refer to the Microsoft publication *Microsoft Outlook 2002 Deployment Kit*.

Note

This publication wasn't available at the time this book was written. It will, presumably, be available soon after Outlook 2002 is released.

BASIC CUSTOMIZATION

When you use basic customization, you save your Outlook Today page as an .htm file on your local hard disk, a shared network disk, or a Web server.

Note

To customize the Outlook Today page, you need to be familiar with the Windows registry and with HTML. Appendix F, "Working with the Windows Registry," provides an introduction to the Windows registry. For detailed information about the Windows registry, see *Using the Microsoft Windows 98 Registry* or *Microsoft Windows 2000 Registry Handbook*, both published by Que, or *Windows NT Registry*, published by New Riders. For information about HTML, refer to a book such as *Special Edition Using HTML 4, Fifth Edition*, published by Que.

The next few sections describe how you can change Outlook so that the Outlook Today window depends on a file you can edit without any special tools, instead of the default Outlwvw.dll file that isn't ordinarily editable.

OBTAINING THE OUTLOOK TODAY SOURCE CODE

Customizing involves making changes to the Outlook Today source code in the file Outlwvw.dll, which is a file that's automatically installed on your computer when you install Outlook. You need to know where that file is.

Close Outlook if it's running; then, in Windows, use Find (if you're running Windows 98 or Windows NT) or Search (if you're running Windows Me or Windows 2000) to locate the file Outlwvw.dll.

Note

> If you installed Outlook in the default location, Outlwvw.dll is in the C:\Program Files\Microsoft Office\Office10\1033 folder.

When you know where Outlwvw.dll is, you can use Internet Explorer to get the Outlook Today source code.

To get the Outlook Today source code:

1. Click the Internet Explorer icon on the Windows desktop to open Internet Explorer.

2. If Internet Explorer automatically connects you to a Web page, select File, Work Offline. Otherwise, continue to step 3.

3. Enter the following address into the Internet Explorer Address box:

   `res://C:\Program Files\Microsoft Office\Office10\1033\outlwvw.dll/outlook.htm`

Note

> The entry shown in step 3 is based on the assumption that you installed Outlook in the default folder. If that's not the case, change the path to the correct path for your computer.
>
> Note very carefully the use of forward and backward slashes. There are two forward slashes after res: and one forward slash before Outlook.htm. All others are backward slashes.

4. After you've entered the address, check it to make sure it's correct; then press Enter.

5. The Internet Explorer Error box appears because the code is not being hosted by Outlook. Click No to hide the Error box. Internet Explorer now displays Outlook Today as it appears without being linked to any data, as shown in Figure 29.4.

6. Select View, Source to display the HTML code that creates Outlook Today, part of which is shown in Figure 29.5.

7. At this point, you can select File, Print to print the HTML code for your reference.

Tip from

Gordon Padwick

> If you intend to develop a custom Outlook Today window, this code provides a good starting point.

8. Select File, Save As to open the Save As dialog box and save the file with the name Outlook.htm. Make a note of the location of the file.

Figure 29.4
This is the Outlook Today background.

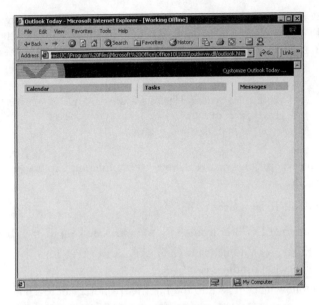

Figure 29.5
The source code is displayed in a Windows Notepad window.

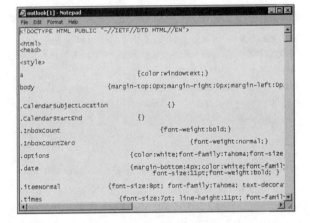

After you've saved the file, you must make three small changes. This is because the original file was designed to be saved as a .dll file and loaded with the res:// protocol. Instead, you will be using it as an .htm file and loading it with either the http:// or file:// protocol.

The text display:none occurs in three places in the file. Use Windows Notepad to search for these three and replace display:none with display:. After you've made these changes, save and close the file.

MODIFYING THE WINDOWS REGISTRY

You must make a change in the Windows registry so that Outlook Today will use the file you just created instead of Outlwvw.dll.

Caution

Always make a backup copy of the registry files before making any change to their contents. See Appendix F of this book for information about backing up the registry.

→ For general information about working with the registry, **see** "Working with the Windows Registry," **p. 799**.

To modify the registry:

1. Click Start in the Windows taskbar; then click Run to open the dialog box shown in Figure 29.6.

Figure 29.6
Use this dialog box to name the program you want to run.

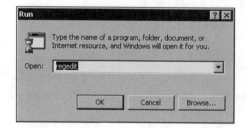

2. In the Open box, enter **regedit** and then click OK to open the Registry Editor, as shown in Figure 29.7.

Figure 29.7
The Registry Editor initially displays the My Computer tree with subtrees listed in the left pane.

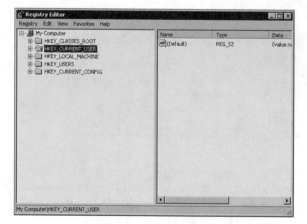

3. Expand the HKEY_CURRENT_USER subkey.

4. Continue expanding subkeys until you reach
   HKEY_CURRENT_USER\Software\Microsoft\Office\10.0\Outlook\Today

5. Select Today to see the values in that key listed in the right pane, as shown in Figure 29.8.

Figure 29.8
Look to see whether one of the values listed has the name `CustomUrl`.

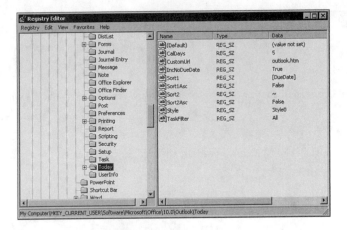

The values in this registry key correspond to the selections you made in the Customize Outlook Today window, as described previously in this chapter.

→ For information about interactive changes you can make to the Outlook Today window, **see** "Choosing Outlook Today's Options," **p. 613**.

6. Select the value named `CustomUrl`.

7. Select Edit, Modify to display the dialog box shown in Figure 29.9.

Figure 29.9
The Value Data box contains the current data in the `CustomUrl` value.

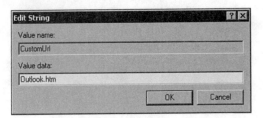

Tip from

Make a note of the current data in the URL value because you might subsequently want to restore Outlook to use the default Outlook Today window.

8. Replace the current data with the complete path name of the `Outlook.htm` file you created in the previous section, specifying the file protocol.

Note

If you saved `Outlook.htm` in the `C:\My Documents` folder, enter the new value as `File://C:\My Documents\Outlook.htm`.

Pay particular attention to using forward and backward slashes correctly.

9. Click OK. The new value for `CustomUrl` is now shown in the right pane.

10. Select Registry, Exit to close the Registry Editor.

TESTING OUTLOOK TODAY

After you've created an `Outlook.htm` file and made a change in the registry that makes Outlook Today depend on that file, you can test what happens.

Start Outlook and display Outlook Today. You should see the same Outlook Today window as you normally do. One difference, though, is that Outlook Today opens more slowly. That's because it now uses the separate .htm file instead of using the normal .dll file.

The big difference is that you can make changes to the .htm file that result in changes to what Outlook Today displays. That's something you can't do if Outlook Today runs from `Outlwvw.dll` (as it normally does).

Note

A customized Outlook Today doesn't have to be slower than the original one. After you've made changes to `Outlook.htm`, you can use a resource editor, such as Microsoft Developer Studio, to save the customized file in .dll format.

MAKING CHANGES TO OUTLOOK TODAY

The `Outlook.htm` file contains HTML code and uses Cascading Style Sheets to describe the Outlook Today page. You can modify this file in the same way you can modify any other HTML page. Details of the techniques for doing this are beyond the scope of this book. You can find general guidance in the *Microsoft Outlook 2000 Deployment Kit*. For detailed information, you'll have to consult a book about HTML that contains information about Cascading Style Sheets. One such book is *Special Edition Using HTML 4, Fifth Edition*, published by Que.

Tip from

I particularly recommend the fifth edition of *Special Edition Using HTML 4* if you're interested in working with Cascading Style Sheets.

After you've made changes to your `Outlook.htm` file, you can see the effects of those changes the next time you open Outlook Today.

DEVELOPING OUTLOOK TODAY FURTHER

This chapter provides only a broad introduction to the subject of customizing Outlook Today. Regard the Outlook Today that comes with Outlook as only an example of what Outlook Today can be.

If you're using Outlook on a home computer, you'll probably find that the default Outlook Today provides is a useful summary of your current calendar, tasks, and messages. However, if you're responsible for deploying Outlook throughout your organization, give some thought to the potential of Outlook Today.

As stated previously in this chapter, Outlook Today is an HTML page that Outlook displays. Whatever you can display on an HTML page can be displayed in Outlook Today—it's not limited to information about Outlook items, nor is it limited to information available in files on a local computer. You can use Outlook Today to present a wide variety of information to Outlook users. This information can include, but is by no means limited to

- Organization and industry news
- The current group or organization calendar
- A daily motivational message
- An up-to-date progress summary—sales statistics for marketing and sales people, bugs fixed for software people, network performance for people who support the network, orders received and orders shipped for the shipping department, and so on

In short, if information is available somewhere on your network, it can be displayed on the Outlook Today window people see when they start Outlook.

At the time this chapter was written, Microsoft hadn't published specific information about customizing Outlook Today in Outlook 2002. However, the Outlook 2000 information in the Microsoft Knowledge Base article Q236081, "Finding Information on How to Customize Outlook Today," appears to apply equally to Outlook 2002.

CHAPTER **30**

CUSTOMIZING THE FOLDER LIST

In this chapter

UNDERSTANDING OUTLOOK'S FOLDERS

If you're using Outlook, but not as a client for Exchange, Outlook saves items of information in a Personal Folders file. Although your Personal Folders file is usually on your local hard drive, it can be on any other network disk to which you have access. If you're using Outlook as a client for Exchange, Outlook can save items of information in a Personal Folders file on a local or network disk, and it can also save items in the Exchange store.

Whether you've set up Outlook to save items on a local hard drive, a network drive, or the Exchange store, items are saved in a set of ten folders, with one folder for each type of Outlook item. These folders are

- **Calendar**—For Outlook items that describe dated activities
- **Contacts**—For Outlook items that contain information about people or organizations
- **Deleted Items**—For Outlook items you've deleted from other Outlook folders
- **Drafts**—For messages you're working on but aren't ready to send
- **Inbox**—For messages you've received
- **Journal**—For Outlook items that record information about messages you've sent to, and received from, specific people; Office files you've worked with; and various other activities
- **Notes**—For Outlook items you create to save temporary information
- **Outbox**—A temporary place where Outlook saves messages you've created until a connection to a mail server is available
- **Sent Items**—For copies of messages you've sent
- **Tasks**—For tasks you've created for yourself, asked other people to accept, or accepted from other people

You can create additional folders, and you can create subfolders below the original ten folders and below any other folders you create. This chapter explains how to create additional folders.

> **Note**
>
> A folder is space on a disk that is a container for information. Within the context of Windows, a folder contains files or other folders, all of which can be seen by Windows Explorer. Within the Outlook context, a folder is space within a Personal Folders file or Exchange store that contains Outlook items and other Outlook folders and also can be used to store Windows files.

Each Outlook folder can contain one type of Outlook item, other Outlook folders, and files. If you attempt to save an Outlook item of one type in an Outlook folder that's intended for Outlook items of a different type, Outlook automatically converts the item being saved into an Outlook item of the type the folder holds. For example, if you drag a

Message item into a folder that holds Calendar items, Outlook saves the Message item as a Calendar item.

Note

> The process of creating one type of Outlook item from a different type of Outlook item is known as *AutoCreate*.

Although an Outlook folder can contain Outlook items of only one type, it can contain Outlook subfolders that contain Outlook items of a different type.

Note

> Public folders, even though they can be accessed by Outlook, are Exchange Server folders. These folders can contain any type of Outlook item.

EXAMINING THE OUTLOOK FOLDER LIST

With any Outlook Information viewer displayed, select View, Folder List to see a list of Outlook folders. If you've just installed Outlook, you'll see a list of folders similar to that shown in Figure 30.1.

Figure 30.1
This is a list of folders similar to what you might see if you're using Outlook as a client for an Exchange server.

Note

> The Folder List shown in Figure 30.1 is typical of what you'll have after installing Outlook as a client for an Exchange server and subsequently creating a Personal Folders file. After installing Outlook not as a client for an Exchange server, you'll have only a Personal Folders file.

After you, or other people, have been working with Outlook for a while, you might see many more folders than shown in Figure 30.1.

The folders are arranged in a tree structure with the root name at the top. This root name represents a Personal Folders file or an Exchange store. The folders in which Outlook saves items are listed under the root name.

Note

If you see only a root name, that name has a small box containing a + sign at the left. Click that box to expand the root so the Outlook folders are displayed. After you've expanded the root, the small box contains a – sign. You can click that box to collapse the list of Outlook folders. After you've done so, the small box contains a + sign.

In Figure 30.1, the name of the root is Outlook Today - [Mailbox - Gordon Padwick]. This indicates that the Outlook folders are in an Exchange store. You'll see roots with names similar to this only if you're using Outlook as a client for an Exchange server. Instead of "Gordon Padwick" you'll see your own name or whatever other name the Exchange administrator gave to your Exchange mailbox.

If you installed Outlook not as a client for an Exchange server, the name of the root is usually "Outlook Today - [Personal Folders]."

Note

The default name Outlook uses for your Personal Folders file is "Personal Folders." You can change that name to something different, such as "Master Folders." In that case, the name for the root folder in the Folder List would be "Outlook Today - [Master Folders]."

Note

If you're using Personal Folders files or an Exchange store you created while using a previous version of Outlook, the names for root folders might be different from what's described here. For example, the name of your Personal Folders file might just be "Personal Folders."

You can select any folder name in the list to see the Outlook items in that folder listed in an Information viewer in the right pane. You can also right-click a folder name to display that folder's context menu, as described subsequently in this chapter.

→ A folder's context menu provides a convenient way to do many things with a folder. **See** "Using a Folder's Context Menu," **p. 631**.

To hide the list of folders, click the X at the right end of the Folder List's title bar, or select View, Folder List.

DISPLAYING A TEMPORARY FOLDER LIST

The Folder List that's displayed when you select View, Folder List, as described in the preceding section, remains displayed until you hide it either by clicking the X in the list's title bar or by selecting View, Folder List again.

You can also display the Folder List by displaying any Outlook Information viewer and then clicking that Information viewer's name. The Folder List you get by doing this, shown in Figure 30.2, is almost identical to the one shown in Figure 30.1.

Figure 30.2
The Folder List shown here has a pushpin icon at the right end of its title bar.

Pushpin

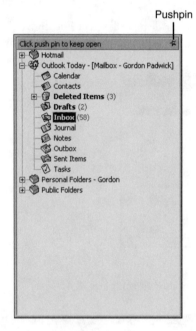

This Folder List is temporary—it disappears when you click anywhere in the right pane or when you select a folder in the list. You can use this Folder List only for selecting a folder. You can't right-click a folder name to display its context menu.

You can easily convert a temporary Folder List to the more permanent one described in the preceding section. To do so, click the pushpin in its title bar.

ACTIVATING AN OUTLOOK LOCATION

The Folder List shown in Figures 30.1 and 30.2 contains several root names. Notice that the icon at the left of one of the root names has a small image of a house superimposed on it. The superimposed house indicates that the root is the default location where Outlook currently saves items. That's of little significance if you have only one root—in that case, only one location exists where Outlook can save items, so you don't need to be shown which location that is.

CREATING ADDITIONAL PERSONAL FOLDERS FILES

You can have several Personal Folders files, each containing many folders. In Outlook used as a client for an Exchange server, you always have your Exchange mailbox as a root; in addition, you might have one or more Personal Folders files.

To create a Personal Folders file:

1. With any Outlook Information viewer displayed, select File, move the pointer onto New, and select Outlook Data File to display the dialog box shown in Figure 30.3.

Figure 30.3
This dialog box lists the types of local storage available. This version of Outlook offers only one type of storage.

2. Click OK to display the dialog box shown in Figure 30.4.

Figure 30.4
Use this dialog box to specify the new Personal Folders file.

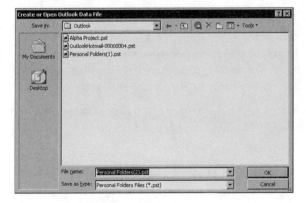

3. The Save In box contains the name of the Windows folder within which Outlook proposes to save the new Personal Folders file. You can navigate to a different folder if you want.

4. In the File Name box, replace the proposed name with a more meaningful name. The name you enter here is the name used for the new Personal Folders file within the Windows file structure.

5. Click OK to close the dialog box and display the dialog box shown in Figure 30.5.

Figure 30.5
The File box at the top of this dialog box contains the complete path of the new Personal Folders file.

Create Microsoft Personal Folders

File: C:\Documents and Settings\gpadwick.PADWICK

Name: Personal Folders

Encryption Setting
- ○ No Encryption
- ● Compressible Encryption
- ○ Best Encryption

Password
- Password:
- Verify Password:
- ☐ Save this password in your password list

[OK]   [Cancel]   [Help]

6. Replace the text in the Name box with a meaningful name for the new Personal Folders file. The name you enter here is used within Outlook to identify the file. It can be the same as, or different from, the name you entered in step 4.

7. Select an encryption setting.

8. If you want to protect the new Personal Folders file with a password, enter a password in the Password box and enter the same password in the Verify Password box.

9. Normally, leave Save This Password in Your Password List unchecked. Saving your password largely defeats the purpose of protecting your file with a password.

10. Click OK to create the new folder.

The next time you open your Folder List, you'll see the name of the new folder listed. If you click the + at the left of its name to see the individual folders the file contains, you'll find that it contains only a Deleted Items folder. If you subsequently designate this folder as your default Outlook store, Outlook automatically creates the ten standard folders in it (nine in addition to the Deleted Items folder).

DESIGNATING A DEFAULT OUTLOOK STORE

Figure 30.1 shows a Folder List for Outlook (used as a client for an Exchange server) that contains one Personal Folders file and two Exchange stores (one for your personal Outlook items and one for public folders). One of these four root folders has the house superimposed over its icon. That's the default store in which Outlook is currently set to save items.

If you have two or more sets of Outlook folders, you need to be able to select which set Outlook uses as the location to save items. The set of folders in which Outlook saves items is known as the *default store*.

To specify the place in which Outlook saves items:

1. Select Tools, E-mail Accounts to display the first E-mail Accounts dialog box, which opens with View or Change Existing E-mail Accounts selected. Click Next to display the second E-mail Accounts dialog box, shown in Figure 30.6.

Figure 30.6
The box at the bottom left indicates where Outlook currently saves items.

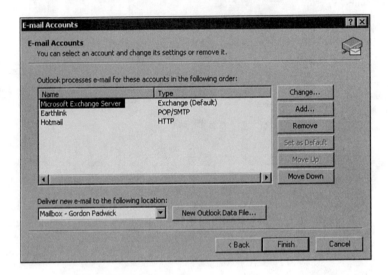

Note

Although the box's label refers only to E-mail, Outlook saves all types of items in the named location.

2. Open the drop-down Deliver New E-mail to the Following Location list.

3. Select the location where you want Outlook to save items, and then click Finish. Outlook displays a message stating that the new location will take effect the next time you start Outlook.

4. Close the message box, exit from Outlook, and restart Outlook. At the beginning of startup, Outlook displays a message stating The location messages are delivered to has changed.... Click Yes to allow startup to proceed.

5. You can, if you want, confirm that Outlook now uses the new storage location. Select View, Folder List and observe that the root of the location you selected in step 3 now has the house symbol superimposed on its icon. Alternatively, select Tools, E-mail Accounts, press Next to display the dialog box previously shown in Figure 30.6, and observe that the new location is named in the Deliver New E-mail to the Following Location box.

Subsequently, when you create new Outlook items and save them, they are saved in the folder you just designated as your default store.

USING A FOLDER'S CONTEXT MENU

Many of the remaining sections of this chapter refer to a folder's context menu. You can display a folder's context menu by right-clicking that folder's name in the Folder List. Figure 30.7 shows a typical context menu.

PART

VI

CH

30

Figure 30.7
Many of the items in the context menu contain the name of the folder you selected.

	Open
	Open In New Window
	Send Link to This Folder
	Advanced Find...
	Move "Contacts"...
	Copy "Contacts"...
	Delete "Contacts"
	Rename "Contacts"...
	New Folder...
	Add to Outlook Bar
	Mark All as Read
	Properties

Several of the items in a context menu are not available for Outlook's built-in folders. This is because you can move, delete, or rename only folders you create, not Outlook's built-in folders. With the exception of Send Link to This Folder, all the context menu items are available for folders and subfolders you create. Send Link to This Folder is available only for public folders. Figure 30.9 is an example of a context menu for a folder you've created.

CREATING FOLDERS AND SUBFOLDERS

Within an Outlook storage location—a Personal Folders file or an Exchange store—you can create as many Outlook folders as you need, and you can create subfolders within existing folders.

The reasons you create additional Outlook folders are the same as those for creating Windows folders. You save information so that you can access it when you need to do so. Accessing information might be simplified if you have the information organized into separate folders.

→ You can use two ways, and combinations of those two ways, to organize Outlook items. One way is to save items in specific folders. The other way is to assign categories to items. To learn more about how to do this, **see** "How Categories Are Assigned to Items," **p. 408**.

CREATING A NEW FOLDER OR SUBFOLDER

The procedure that's described here creates folders and subfolders within the current default location. The first step, if you have more than one Outlook storage location available, is to make sure the location in which you want to create a folder or subfolder is the default.

→ For information about making a specific store the default in which Outlook saves items, **see** "Activating an Outlook Location," **p. 627**.

Tip from

[signature]

You can drag folders and subfolders you create, but not Outlook's default folders, to different places within the folder structure.

To create a folder or subfolder:

1. With any Outlook Information viewer displayed, select File, move the pointer onto Folder, and select New Folder to display the dialog box shown in Figure 30.8. Alternatively, right-click a folder name in the Folder List to display the folder's context menu; then select New Folder.

Figure 30.8
Use this dialog box to name the new Outlook folder, specify the types of items it will contain, and specify the folder's location.

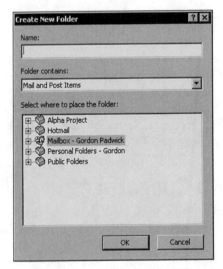

2. Enter a name for the new folder in the Name box. The name you enter must be different from the name of any folder that currently exists within the branch of the folder tree in which you intend to place the new folder.

3. If you intend the new folder to contain Outlook items other than Mail and Post items, open the drop-down Folder Contains list and select an appropriate item type. You can't create item types other than those available in the list: Calendar, Contact, Journal, Mail and Post, Note, and Task items.

4. If you want to place the new folder directly under a root, in the Select Where to Place the Folder box, select that root. Alternatively, if you want to make the new folder a child of an existing folder, expand the appropriate root folder and, if necessary, the folders under it until you reach the folder you want; then select that folder.

5. Click OK. Outlook asks whether you want to place a shortcut to the new folder on the Outlook Bar. Click Yes or No according to your preference.

6. If you want, you can select View, Folder List to confirm that the new folder exists in the position you intended within the Folder List.

CREATING A FOLDER SHORTCUT IN THE OUTLOOK BAR

When you create a new folder or subfolder, Outlook offers to create a shortcut in the Outlook Bar, as mentioned in step 5 of the preceding procedure. If you decline to create a shortcut at that time, you can subsequently create a shortcut in the Outlook Bar.

Select the Outlook Bar group in which you want to create the shortcut. Then, in the Folder List, right-click the folder or subfolder for which you want to create the shortcut to display its context menu. Select Add to Outlook Bar in the context menu. The shortcut immediately appears in the Outlook Bar.

Here's an alternative way to create an Outlook Bar shortcut for a folder you've created: Display the Folder List. Select the Outlook Bar group into which you want to place the new shortcut, and then drag the folder name from the Folder List into the Outlook Bar. The new shortcut appears in the Outlook Bar when you release the mouse button.

→ For more detailed information about creating shortcuts in the Outlook Bar, **see** "Adding Shortcut Icons to an Outlook Bar Group," **p. 497**.

To remove a shortcut from the Outlook Bar, right-click the shortcut icon in the Outlook Bar to display its context menu; then click Remove from Outlook Bar. Outlook asks you to confirm that you want to remove the shortcut. Click Yes.

DELETING A FOLDER OR SUBFOLDER

You can delete a folder or subfolder you've created but not one of Outlook's built-in folders. There are several ways to delete a folder. When you delete a folder, Outlook moves that folder and its contents into the Deleted Items folder. In each case, start by displaying the Folder List.

To delete a folder or subfolder by using that folder's context menu:

1. Right-click the folder you want to delete to display its context menu, shown in Figure 30.9.

2. Select Delete in the context menu. Outlook asks you to confirm that you want to delete the folder and its contents.

3. Click Yes. The folder immediately disappears from the Folder List.

Figure 30.9
Notice that, with only one exception, all items in the context menu for a folder you've created are available.

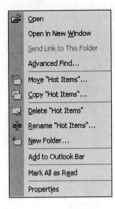

To delete a folder or subfolder by using the File menu:

1. Select the folder or subfolder you want to delete.

2. Select File, and move the pointer onto Folder to display the menu shown in Figure 30.10.

Figure 30.10
The menu contains these items if you selected a folder or subfolder you created.

> **Note**
>
> The Move, Delete, and Rename menu items are not available if you previously selected one of Outlook's built-in folders.

3. Select Delete. Outlook asks you to confirm that you really want to delete the selected folder and move all its contents into the Deleted Items folder. Click Yes to continue.

To delete a folder or subfolder by dragging it into the Deleted Items folder:

1. Select the Outlook Shortcuts group in the Outlook Bar and, if necessary, scroll down so that the Deleted Items shortcut is visible.

2. Drag the folder you want to delete from the Folder List onto the Deleted Items shortcut in the Outlook Bar. The folder name disappears from the Folder List as soon as you release the mouse button.

> **Note**
>
> When you delete a folder or subfolder, Outlook moves that folder and its contents into the Deleted Items folder. The deleted folder becomes a subfolder of the Deleted Items folder. You can, if necessary, drag the folder and its contents from the Deleted Items folder back into its original (or a different) place in the folder structure.

MOVING AND COPYING A FOLDER OR SUBFOLDER

The easiest way to move or copy a folder is by dragging within the Folder List. Select View, Folder List to display the Folder List. Drag the folder or subfolder you want to move or copy to the new place in the Folder List. By default, Outlook moves the folder. To copy the folder, hold down Ctrl while you drag.

> **Note**
>
> The preceding paragraph described conventional dragging (with the left mouse button held down). If you hold down the right mouse button while you drag, Outlook displays a menu when you release the mouse button. In that menu, you can select Move, Copy, or Cancel.

> **Note**
>
> When you copy a folder, the copy has the same name as the original. Outlook lets you have two or more folders or subfolders with the same name, provided those folders are not in the same branch of the folder structure.
>
> Outlook also lets you copy, but not move, the built-in folders.

An alternative way to move or copy a folder is to select File, move the pointer onto Move Folder (not available for Outlook's built-in folders) or Copy Folder to display a dialog box in which you can select the place in the folder structure to which you want to move or copy the folder.

COPYING A FOLDER DESIGN

You can copy the various Permissions, Rules, Description, Forms, and Views properties of one folder, as described subsequently in this chapter, to another folder.

To copy the design of a folder:

1. Display the Folder List and select the folder to which you want to copy the properties of another folder.

2. Select File, move the pointer onto Folder, and select Copy Folder Design to display a dialog box similar to that shown in Figure 30.11.

3. Expand the root folder that contains the folder that has the properties you want to copy; then select that folder to display the dialog box shown in Figure 30.12.

Figure 30.11
This dialog box shows the folder structure with all the roots collapsed.

Figure 30.12
Use this dialog box to check the properties you want to copy to another folder.

4. Check any combination of Permissions, Rules, Description, Forms, and Views that you want to copy.

5. Click OK. Outlook displays a message saying that the target folder's existing properties will be replaced by the new properties. Click Yes. Outlook copies the folder design.

SETTING FOLDER PROPERTIES

Each Outlook folder has a set of properties you can customize. To display a folder's properties, right-click a shortcut icon in the Outlook Bar or right-click a folder name in the Folder List to display the folder's context menu. In the context menu, select Properties to display the folder's Properties dialog box, shown in Figure 30.13.

Figure 30.13
The Properties dialog box opens with the General tab selected.

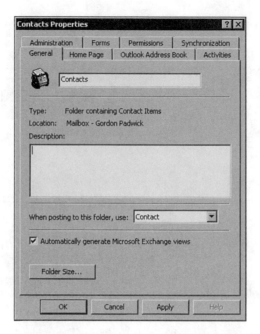

Note

The Properties dialog box shown in Figure 30.13 is for a Contacts folder in an Exchange store. A Properties dialog box for a folder in a Personal Folders file has fewer tabs.

SETTING THE GENERAL PROPERTIES

The box at the top of the dialog box contains the name of the folder. You can't change the name of Outlook's built-in folders, but you can change the name of a folder or subfolder you've created.

The text in the Type and Location labels describe the purpose (type) of the folder and its location. You can't change the text in these labels.

The Description box initially is empty. You can enter text in that box to provide information about the folder. There's no need to do so for Outlook's built-in folders, but you might want to do so for folders and subfolders you create.

The When Posting to This Folder, Use box contains the name of the form associated with the folder. For example, if you're looking at the properties of a Contacts folder, the form name displayed is Contact because that's the default form you use when you create a Contact item. You usually won't change to a different form in the case of Outlook's built-in folders.

If you have created folders, you might also have created custom forms to use for entering data into those folders. If that's the case, you can open the When Posting to This Folder,

Use drop-down list and select Forms. That takes you to the dialog box shown in Figure 30.14.

Figure 30.14
You can select a form from the Standard Forms Library shown here or open the Look In drop-down list to select a form in another forms library.

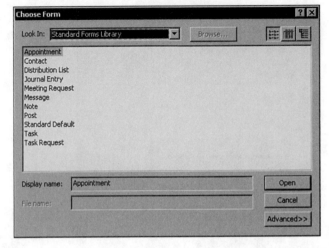

Although the Automatically Generate Microsoft Exchange Views check box in the General tab of the Properties dialog box is available for all folders, it is generally applicable only to public folders in the Exchange store. Check this box for public folders you want to make accessible to people who use Exchange Client as a client for Exchange Server.

Note

Exchange Client is an application that was available prior to Outlook. That application is still used by some people to access their Exchange stores.

The Folder Size button has nothing to do with setting a folder's properties. You can click this button to open the dialog box shown in Figure 30.15.

SETTING THE HOME PAGE PROPERTIES

Select the Home Page tab to associate a folder with a Web page or other page defined by HTML code. When you do this, Outlook uses the rendering and security services of Internet Explorer to display the HTML-defined page in a folder's Information viewer.

You can see this happening when you display Outlook Today. What you see in Outlook Today is actually a page defined by HTML code. To get an insight into this, right-click Outlook Today in the Outlook Bar to see its context menu. Click Properties, and select the Home Page tab. The Show Home Page by Default for This Folder box is checked; if you've installed Office XP in the default folders, the address of the home page is res:\C:Program Files\Microsoft Office\Office\1033\Outlwvw.dll/outlook.htm, which is the location of an HTML file on your hard disk. See Chapter 29, "Customizing Outlook Today," for more information on this topic.

Figure 30.15
This dialog box displays the size of the folder and also the sizes of any subfolders it contains.

→ For more information about working with HTML files, **see** "Obtaining the Outlook Today Source Code," **p. 616**.

For any folder, you can enter the address of an HTML page and check Show Home Page by Default for This Folder. After you do so, when you select that folder either in the Outlook Bar or the Folder List, Outlook displays the HTML page instead of the normal Information viewer. This isn't something you should do with Outlook's built-in folders because that would mean you can't see the items in those folders in the Information viewer.

In a workgroup situation, you might find it useful to create a shared folder that displays a Web page. You can demonstrate this capability if you're working at a computer that can connect to the Internet. Do the following.

To display a Web page in an Outlook Information viewer:

1. Create an Outlook folder. Name it Home (or any other name you prefer), accept the default Mail items for what it contains, and save the folder anywhere in your Folder List.

→ There's more detailed information about creating folders previously in this chapter. **See** "Creating a New Folder or Subfolder," **p. 632**.

2. Right-click the new folder in the Folder List, select Properties in the context menu, and select the Home Page tab.

3. Initially, the Show Home Page by Default for This Folder check box is unavailable and the insertion point is in the text box. In the text box, enter

`http://www.quehelp.com` (the address of the Que Publishing home page) or another Web page address. As soon as you start typing, the check box becomes available.

4. Check the check box.

5. Click OK to close the dialog box.

This procedure creates an Outlook folder that has a Web page associated with it.

Select the new folder in the Outlook Bar (if you created a shortcut icon for the new page) or in the Folder List. Your computer is automatically connected to the Internet, and the Web page you specified for the folder is displayed in the folder's Information viewer.

The preceding procedure is intended merely to give you a quick way to understand the significance of the Home Page tab in the Properties dialog box. How you use this capability in practice depends on your needs. You need to understand that

- You can create any number of folders or subfolders and associate an HTML page with each of them.

- Each HTML page can contain any type of information and can be linked to other HTML pages.

- The associated HTML pages can be anywhere—on the Web (as in the example), on your local hard disk, or on a network disk to which you have access.

The Restore Defaults button in the Home Page tab of the Properties dialog box removes the check mark from the Show Home Page by Default for This Folder check box and removes the Web page address from the text box. Thereafter, the folder provides normal access to Outlook items.

SETTING AUTOARCHIVE PROPERTIES

All folders except those designated to hold Contact items have an AutoArchive tab, similar to the one shown in Figure 30.16.

By default, AutoArchiving is turned on. Outlook defines a specific aging period for each type of item. When AutoArchiving occurs, items older than the aging period are archived. Also, by default, Outlook saves archived items in a folder named `Archive.pst`.

In this dialog box, you can

- Turn off AutoArchiving

- Change the aging period for the items in the folder

- Specify the Windows folder in which archived items are saved

- Choose to delete, instead of save, archived items

→ To learn how to control AutoArchiving, **see** "Managing AutoArchiving," **p. 396**.

Figure 30.16
Use this tab to specify how Outlook AutoArchives items in a folder.

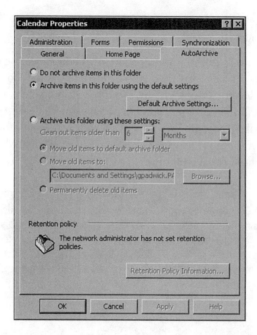

SETTING OUTLOOK ADDRESS BOOK PROPERTIES

The Properties dialog box for the Contacts folder has two tabs not available for other folders: Outlook Address Book and Activities. The Outlook Address Book tab is shown in Figure 30.17.

Figure 30.17
Use this tab to designate a Contacts folder as an e-mail address book.

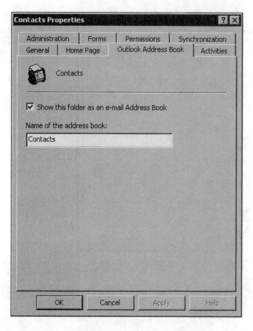

With Show This Folder as an E-mail Address Book checked, you can use the Outlook items in the Contacts folder to address e-mail.

By default, Outlook proposes to give the address book that contains information about your contacts the name Contacts. That's okay if you have only one Outlook folder for contacts. If you have two or more folders for Contact items, though, you should change the name to something more meaningful. For example, you might have one folder in which you keep information about personal friends, another folder in which you keep information about business contacts, and another folder in which you keep information about members of a club. If you do that, you should give each of these address books an appropriate name.

Tip from

Although Outlook allows you to keep any number of Contacts folders, and some people recommend that you do so, in my experience it's best to use only one Contacts folder. Rather than keeping various types of contacts in various folders, you should assign categories to contacts. By doing that, if a contact belongs in two or more groups, you can assign two or more categories instead of duplicating the contact information in two or more folders.

The other Properties tab that's unique to Contacts folders is Activities, shown in Figure 30.18.

Figure 30.18
You can use this tab to define how you want to save contact activities.

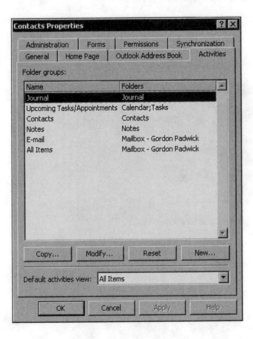

→ To learn more about tracking activities, **see** "Tracking a Contact's Activities," **p. 187.**

The Activities tab initially lists folders Outlook can search for information about your contacts' activities. You can click the buttons at the bottom of the dialog box for these purposes:

- **Copy**—To make a copy of a selected folder group
- **Modify**—To change the name of a selected folder group and to add folders to, and remove folders from, that group
- **Reset**—To reset the contents of a selected folder group to their original state
- **New**—To create a new folder group

Open the Default Activities View drop-down list and select the default view that's displayed in the Contact form's Activities tab.

SETTING ADMINISTRATION PROPERTIES

Most of the boxes in the Administration tab are unavailable if you're looking at properties for a folder in your Personal Folders file, one of your folders in the Exchange store, or a public folder in the Exchange store for which you don't have administrative permissions. Figure 30.19 shows such a tab.

Figure 30.19
This is the Administration tab for a folder in an Exchange store.

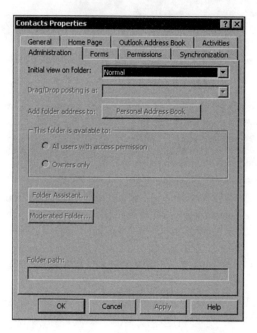

In this case, only the Initial View on Folder drop-down list is available. Although it might appear otherwise, this setting applies only to the initial view for a shared public folder. You can open the drop-down list and select a view that appears when someone opens the folder. If that person chooses a different view, that view is what the person sees.

If you look at the properties of an Exchange public folder for which you do have administrative permissions and select the Administration tab, the tab is displayed as shown in Figure 30.20.

Figure 30.20
This is the Administration tab for an Exchange public folder for which you have administrative permissions.

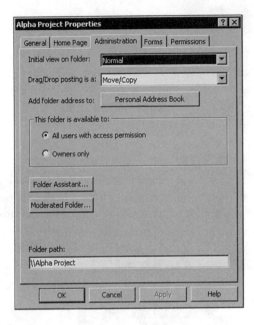

Open the drop-down Drag/Drop Posting Is A list. You can open the Drag/Drop Posting Is A drop-down list and select from the following:

- **Move/Copy**—This formats a moved or copied item as it was in the original location. The person who posted the item remains as the owner of the item. The item contains no reference to the person who moved or copied the item.

- **Forward**—This formats a moved or copied item as a forwarded item. The item appears to be from the person who moved or copied it, and that person is shown as the owner of the item.

You can click Personal Address Book to add the folder address book to your Personal Address Book.

In the This Folder Is Available to section, select an option button according to whether you want the folder to be accessible to all users who have access permission or only to people who have owner permission.

Tip from

The purpose of making the folder available only to people with owner permission is to allow you to limit access to the folder to yourself while you're creating it. After the folder has been created, you should make the folder available to people to whom you grant access permissions.

Click Folder Assistant to create rules for processing items posted in the folder.

→ For information about creating server-based rules, **see** "Using Server-Based Rules," **p. 449**.

Click Moderated Folder if the public folder is to be a moderated folder. See Chapter 23, "Using Exchange Server to Share Information," for information about setting up a moderated bulletin board.

→ To find out how to use a public folder as a moderated bulletin board, **see** "Using a Public Folder As a Moderated Bulletin Board," **p. 465**.

Folder Path displays the location of the folder.

SETTING FORMS PROPERTIES

All Outlook items have an associated default form, which you can use to create an item and also to view information in an item. In addition to the default form, you can create any number of forms for special purposes. For example, you might find it useful to have a special form for creating Contact items for club members or family members.

After you've created custom forms, you must make those forms available for use with specific folders. The Forms tab of the Properties dialog box displays the names of custom forms available to a folder, as shown in Figure 30.21.

Figure 30.21
The Forms Associated with This Folder box initially is empty because no custom forms are associated with the folder.

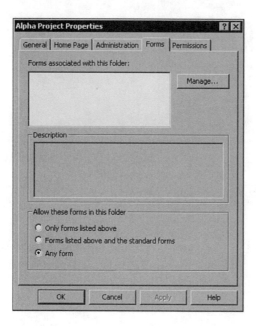

To associate custom forms with a folder:

1. Click Manage in the Forms tab to display the dialog box shown in Figure 30.22.

Figure 30.22
You can use this dialog box to select forms in a forms library and associate those forms with a folder.

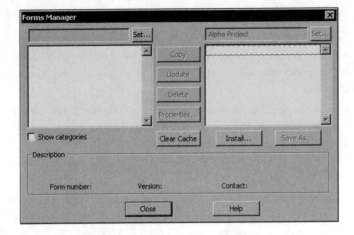

2. Click Set to display the dialog box shown in Figure 30.23.

Figure 30.23
Select a forms library in this dialog box.

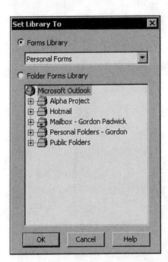

3. Select Forms Library; then open the drop-down list of forms libraries. Unless you have created forms libraries, the only one listed is Personal Forms. Select the forms library in which you've saved custom forms.

Note

Alternatively, you can select Folder Forms Library and then select a folder from some other place, such as a public folder (if you're using Outlook as a client for Exchange).

4. After you've selected a forms library, click OK to return to the Forms Manager dialog box, which now shows the forms library you selected, as shown in Figure 30.24.

Figure 30.24
The left box in this dialog box lists the custom forms in the selected forms library.

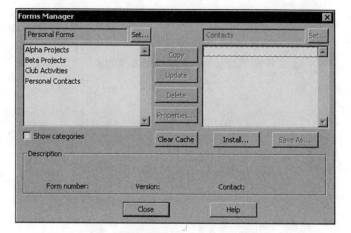

5. Select the form you want to make available to the current folder; then click Copy. The selected form is now listed in the right box.

6. Repeat step 5 to make additional forms available to the folder.

7. Click Close to return to the Forms tab, which now lists the forms available to the folder.

Note

This chapter describes only the principal use of the Forms Manager dialog box. Click Help in that dialog box for information about the purposes of the various buttons and the check box.

When you select a custom form in the Forms tab, the Description box contains a description of that form if you saved a description when you published the form. You can't change a form's description in this tab.

The Allow These Forms in This Folder section at the bottom of the Forms tab contains three option buttons that aren't available for your personal folders. They are available if you're working with public folders. Select an option button according to which forms are to be used with the selected folder.

SETTING PERMISSIONS PROPERTIES

The Permissions tab, shown in Figure 30.25, is available for a public folder you own. You can use this tab to grant permissions to other people to have access to the folder.

→ For details on granting and denying permissions, **see** "Giving People Access to a Public Folder," **p. 457**.

→ For more information about folder properties, **see** "Using Folder Properties," **p. 314**.

Figure 30.25
Use this dialog box to grant permissions to a public folder you own.

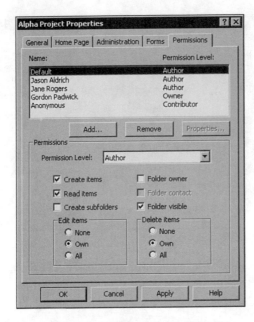

SETTING SYNCHRONIZATION PROPERTIES

The Synchronization tab, an example of which is shown in Figure 30.26 (available only when you're working with properties of a folder in the Exchange store) enables you to control synchronization between an offline folder and a folder in your Exchange store.

Figure 30.26
The Statistics for This Folder section summarizes the current synchronization status.

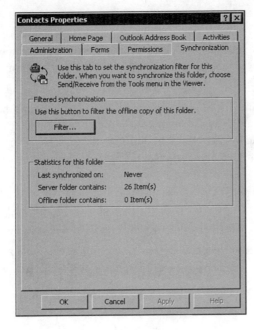

By default, all items in an offline folder are synchronized with the items in the parent Exchange store folder. If you want to synchronize only certain items in the offline folder, click Filter to display the dialog box shown in Figure 30.27.

Figure 30.27
You can use this dialog box to control which offline folder items are to be synchronized with the Exchange store folders.

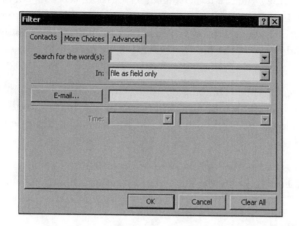

The Filter dialog box shown in Figure 30.27 is identical to the Find dialog box described in Chapter 17, "Finding and Organizing Outlook Items." Use the Filter dialog box in the same way that you use the Find dialog box.

→ For information about using the Find dialog box, **see** "Using Advanced Find to Find Words and Phrases," **p. 341**.

TROUBLESHOOTING

FOLDERS

If you create several Personal Folders files and neglect to give them specific Outlook names (even though the files have different names within the Windows file structure), Outlook's Folder List will show these files all with the same name—Personal Folders. This presents a problem because you don't know which is which.

To solve this problem, display the Folder List and, within one of the Personal Folders files, select one of the folders it contains. When you do that, you'll see the items within that folder. The items you see should be enough to tell you which Personal Folders file you've selected. Next, right-click the root of that folder to display its context menu, and in that menu select Properties to display the Properties dialog box with the General tab selected. Select Advanced and, in that dialog box, change the name of the Personal Folders file to something that describes its contents (such as Toastmasters). When you close the dialog boxes to return to the Folder List, you'll see that the Personal Folders file now has the new name instead of the generic name.

You can repeat this process to give each of your Personal Folders files a specific name.

As you've seen in this chapter, each Personal Folders file has two names: its name within the Windows file structure and the name by which it's known within Outlook. You might run into the situation in which Outlook can't find a Personal Folders file because the file's name within the Windows file structure has changed, its location has changed, or the file has become corrupted. In that case, when you attempt to access the folder from within Outlook, you'll see a message that states `Unable to display the folder`. That sentence is followed by the complete path name of the file Outlook is unable to find. Make a careful note of that path name.

If you've been meticulous about backing up your Windows files, you should be able to find the file among your backup files. In that case, copy the backup file into its original location. Now, Outlook should be able to find and use the file as it was at the time you created the most recent backup.

Another possibility is that you've moved files within your Windows file structure. In that case, use Windows Find to locate the file and restore it to its original path.

CHAPTER 31

CREATING VIEWS AND PRINT STYLES

In this chapter

SEEING OUTLOOK ITEMS

Many of the preceding chapters in this book contain examples of how you can use Outlook's Information viewers to display Outlook items. Some chapters contain information about printing Outlook items. Now, we turn to detailed information about how Outlook displays and prints items.

USING DEFAULT VIEWS

Outlook out-of-the-box has various ways to display and print items you've saved. The ways you can display items are known as *views*; the ways you can print items are known as *print styles*. Each print style is based on a view.

Each type of Outlook item can be displayed in various views. Each view of a particular type of item can be printed based on several print styles. Although most of the examples in this chapter refer specifically to Contact items, the methods described apply to items in general (except where noted otherwise).

Outlook can display items you've saved in five types of views:

- **Table view**—A view in which items are displayed in a table with one row for each item. The information about each item is displayed in columns of the table. All Outlook items can be displayed and printed in a Table view. Figure 31.1 shows a typical Table view.

- **Timeline view**—A view in which items are displayed chronologically according to the date when they were created or received. This view can be scaled to show a day, week, or month at a time. All Outlook items can be displayed in a Timeline view. Timeline views cannot be printed. Figure 31.2 shows a typical Timeline view.

- **Card view**—A view in which items are displayed as they might appear on traditional index cards. Though primarily intended for Contact items, this view can be used to display and print other types of Outlook items. Figure 31.3 shows a typical Card view.

- **Day/Week/Month view**—A view in which items are displayed in a day, week, or month calendar. Though primarily intended for Calendar items, this view can be used to display and print other types of Outlook items. Figure 31.4 shows a typical Day/Week/Month view.

- **Icon view**—A view in which items are displayed as icons. This view is primarily intended for use with Notes items; it doesn't seem to be useful for other types of Outlook items. Figure 31.5 shows a typical Icon view.

VIEWING OUTLOOK ITEMS

Outlook out-of-the-box contains various ways of viewing each type of item. To view items, select the type of item you want to view in the Outlook Bar or Folder List. Then select View, move the pointer onto Current View to display a list of views, and select the view you want Outlook to display. The default views are listed in Table 31.1, together with the default print styles available for each view.

→ For detailed information about print styles, **see** "Using Print Styles," **p. 682**.

Figure 31.1
This is a typical Table view of Contact items. The top row of the table contains field names.

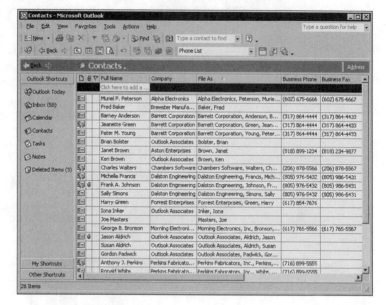

Figure 31.2
This is a typical Timeline view of Journal items.

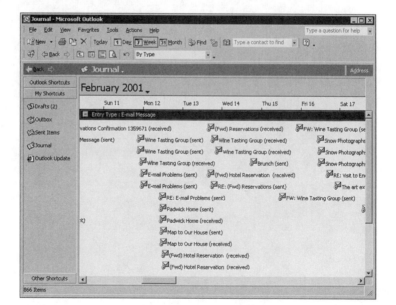

Figure 31.3
This is a typical Card view of Contact items.

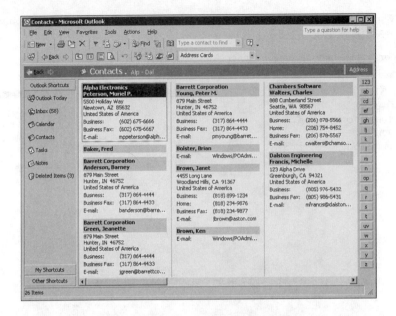

Figure 31.4
This is a typical Day/Week/Month view of Calendar items.

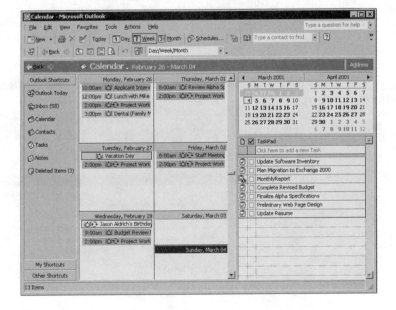

Figure 31.5
This is a typical Icon view of Notes items.

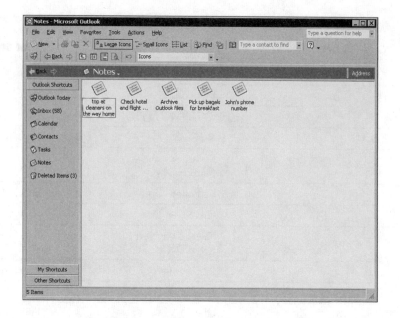

TABLE 31.1 DEFAULT OUTLOOK VIEWS

Outlook Item	View	Print Styles
Calenda Tri-fold, Calendarr	Day/Week/Month	Daily, Weekly, Monthly, Details, Memo
	Day/Week/Month with AutoPreview	Daily, Weekly, Monthly, Tri-fold, Calendar Details, Memo
	Active Appointments	Table, Memo
	Events	Table, Memo
	Annual Events	Table, Memo
	Recurring Appointments	Table, Memo
	By Category	Table, Memo
Contacts	Address Cards	Card, Small Booklet, Medium Booklet, Memo, Phone Directory
	Detailed Address Cards	Card, Small Booklet, Medium Booklet, Memo, Phone Directory
	Phone List	Table, Memo
	By Category	Table, Memo

TABLE 31.1   CONTINUED

Outlook Item	View	Print Styles
	By Company	Table, Memo
	By Location	Table, Memo
	By Follow-Up Flag	Table, Memo
Inbox	Messages	Table, Memo
	Messages with AutoPreview	Table, Memo
	By Follow-Up Flag	Table, Memo
	Last Seven Days	Table, Memo
	Flagged for Next Seven Days	Table, Memo
	By Conversation Topic	Table, Memo
	By Sender	Table, Memo
	Unread Messages	Table, Memo
	Sent To	Table, Memo
	Message Timeline	see tip
Journal	By Type	see tip
	By Contact	see tip
	By Category	see tip
	Entry List	Table, Memo
	Last Seven Days	Table, Memo
	Phone Calls	Table, Memo
Tasks	Simple List	Table, Memo
	Detailed List	Table, Memo
	Active Tasks	Table, Memo
	Next Seven Days	Table, Memo
	Overdue Tasks	Table, Memo
	By Category	Table, Memo
	Assignment	Table, Memo
	By Person Responsible	Table, Memo
	Completed Tasks	Table, Memo
	Task Timeline	see tip

Deleted Items, Drafts, Outbox, and Sent Items have the same views as the Inbox.

Tip from

Timeline views cannot be printed as such. However, you can select one or more items in a Timeline view and print those items in Memo style.

UNDERSTANDING WHAT'S IN A VIEW

Each view contains information about one type of Outlook item but only some of the fields of information about each item. Some views contain information about only those items that satisfy certain conditions.

Tip from

Views that contain only those items that satisfy certain conditions are known as *filtered*. For example, the Last Seven Days Inbox view is a filtered view because it contains only the e-mail you've received during the last seven days. All filtered views contain the phrase `Filter Applied` at the right end of the view's banner.

To understand how you find out what a particular view displays, we'll use the Address Cards view of Contact items as an example. Outlook displays Contact items in the Address Cards view, as previously shown in Figure 31.3. The information displayed in Card view contains all your Contact items but only some of the information for each contact.

To see which fields of information are displayed in the Card view:

1. Select Contacts in the Outlook Bar to display the Contacts Information viewer.
2. Select View, move the pointer onto Current View, and click Address Cards. Now you have the Address Cards view of Contacts displayed.
3. Select View, move the pointer onto Current View, and click Customize Current View to display the dialog box shown in Figure 31.6.

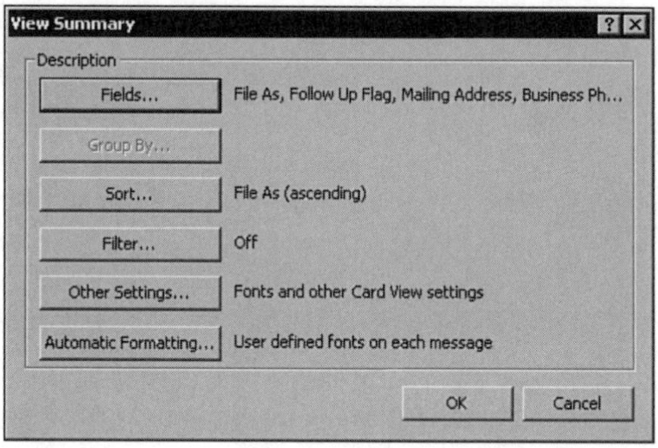

Figure 31.6
You can click the buttons near the left edge of this dialog box to get information about the current view.

4. Click Fields to display the Show Fields dialog box shown in Figure 31.7.

Figure 31.7
The list on the right shows the names of fields that are displayed (but only if they contain data) in the Card view.

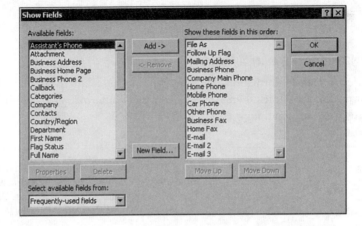

5. Click Cancel to return to the View Summary dialog box shown previously in Figure 31.6.

Tip from

In the View Summary dialog box, Group By is not available. For some views, you can click Group By to see how items are grouped in the view. You can click Sort to see how items are sorted (ascending order by File As name in this case), and Filter to see how items are filtered (Off indicates items aren't filtered). The Other Settings and Automatic Formatting buttons provide other ways you can control the appearance of a view.

6. Click Cancel to close the dialog box.

→ For information about the six buttons in the View Summary dialog box, see the next section.

MODIFYING A VIEW

You can modify any of Outlook's default views, and you can create additional views. This section covers modifying a default view, primarily using the Phone List view of Contact items as an example.

Note

You can use all the techniques described here to modify Table views. Some of these techniques are not available in other types of views.

To display the Phone List view, start with any Contacts Information viewer displayed; then select View, move the pointer onto Current View, and click Phone List. Outlook displays the view shown in Figure 31.8.

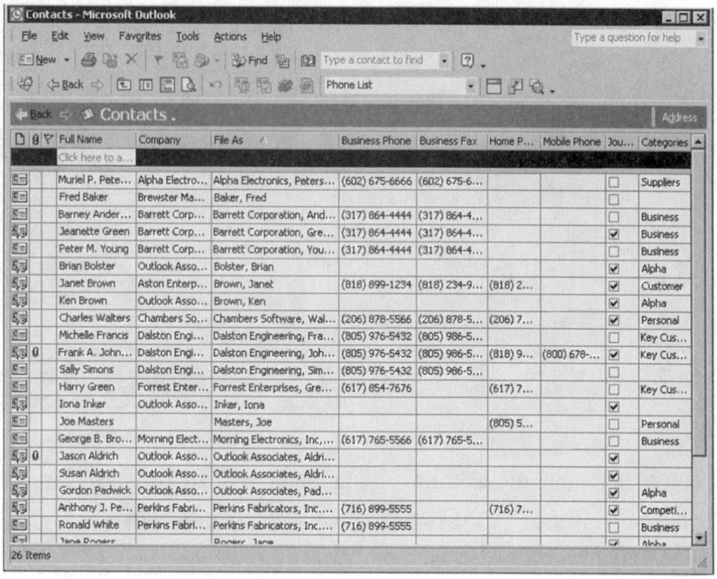

PART

VI

CH

31

Figure 31.8
The Phone List view is a table that lists some of your contacts' phone numbers.

CHANGING THE WIDTH OF COLUMNS

By default, Outlook displays this Table view (and other Table views) with the width of each column compressed so that all fields are partially visible. You can change the width of individual columns by pointing onto the vertical line that separates one column name from the next and dragging to the right or left. If you increase the width of one column, Outlook automatically decreases the width of other columns so that at least a part of each column is visible.

You can add a horizontal scroll bar at the bottom of a Table view. You have to add a horizontal scroll bar separately for each Table view. After you do so, you can set the width of any column to whatever you like without affecting the width of other columns. If you increase the width of columns, some columns are no longer visible, but you can use the scroll bar to see them.

To add a horizontal scroll bar to a Table view:

1. With a Table view displayed, select View, move the pointer onto Current View, and click Customize Current View to display the View Summary dialog box previously shown in Figure 31.6.

2. Click Other Settings to display the dialog box shown in Figure 31.9.

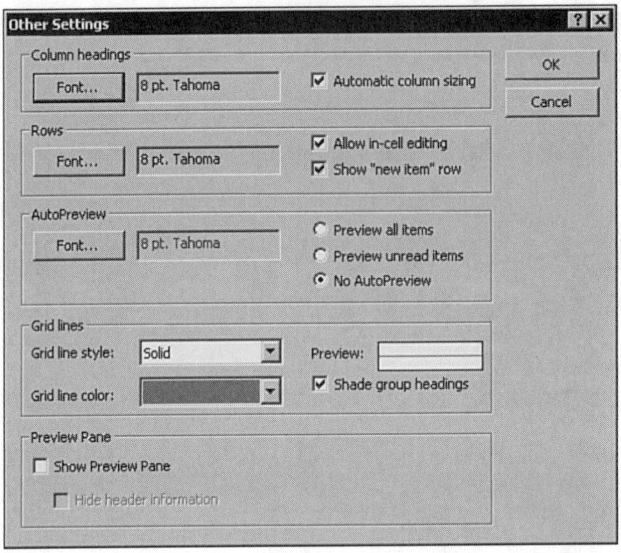

Figure 31.9
Use this dialog box to change the appearance of a Table view.

3. Uncheck Automatic Column Sizing, and click OK twice to close the dialog boxes.

4. Make one of the fields wider by dragging a vertical separator in the table's title row. The Table view now has a scroll bar at the bottom.

You can now increase the width of one or more columns without affecting the width of other columns, as shown in Figure 31.10.

Figure 31.10
You can use the horizontal scroll bar at the bottom of the Table view to see hidden columns.

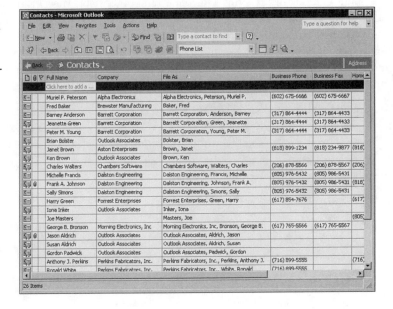

All the columns in a Card view have the same width. You can change the width of the columns in this view by dragging one of the vertical lines that separate one column from the next. By dragging one of these vertical lines, you change the width of all the columns.

CHANGING THE ORDER IN WHICH ITEMS ARE LISTED

Table views initially list information about Outlook items in a table in the order you created (or received) those items.

Note

You can use the method described here to change the order of any type of Outlook item displayed in a Table view.

You can change the order in which contacts are listed in the Phone List view by clicking in the title of a column. For example, click the title of the File As column to list the contacts alphabetically by File As name. After you do so, the items are immediately listed in File As order and a gray triangle at the top of the File As column indicates the File As field is being used to control the sort order.

→ For information about a contact's File As name, **see** "Entering a Contact's Name, Job Title, and Company," **p. 143**.

Initially, the gray triangle points upward to indicate that items are listed in ascending order. You can click the File As column heading again to reverse the sort order. After you do that, the triangle points down and the Contact items are listed in reverse (descending) alphabetical order. Click the column heading again to go back to ascending order.

You can click any column heading to make it the column that controls sort order. Click once for ascending sort order, click again for descending sort order, and click once more to go back to ascending sort order.

→ Another way to change the order in which items are listed is to sort items. You can use this with Table and other types of views. **See** "Sorting Items," **p. 672**.

CHANGING THE FIELDS DISPLAYED IN A VIEW

Each view displays only some of the fields of information available for Outlook items. To see which fields are displayed in the current view, select View, move the pointer onto Current View, and click Customize Current View to display the View Summary dialog box previously shown in Figure 31.6.

You can use this dialog box to control which fields the view displays and the order in which those fields are displayed.

CHANGING THE ORDER OF FIELDS IN A VIEW

You can use several methods to change the order in which fields are displayed in a view. You can use the first two methods described here to change the order of fields displayed in any Table or Card view.

To change the order in which fields are displayed in a Table or Card view:

1. In the View Summary dialog box shown previously in Figure 31.6, click Fields to display the Show Fields dialog box, previously shown in Figure 31.7.

2. Select the field you want to move in the Show These Fields in This Order list at the right. When you do so, the Move Up and Move Down buttons become available.

Note

Only the Move Down button is available if you select the top item in the list. Only the Move Up button is available if you select the bottom item in the list.

3. Click Move Up or Move Down to change the position of the selected field in the list.

Here's another way to change the order of fields in a Table or Card view.

To change the order in which fields are displayed in a Table or Card view:

1. In the View Summary dialog box shown previously in Figure 31.6, click Fields to display the Show Fields dialog box, previously shown in Figure 31.7.

2. In the Show These Fields in This Order list at the right, point onto the field you want to move.

3. Drag up or down to move the field to a different position in the list.

In a Table view (but not in any other view), you can change the order of columns by dragging column titles.

To change the order of columns in a Table view:

1. Display a Table view of Outlook items, such as the Phone List view of Contact items, previously shown in Figure 31.1.

2. Point onto the title of a column you want to move.

3. Drag to the left or to the right until two red arrows appear above and below the left edge of the new position for the column you want to move.

4. Release the mouse button. The column moves to the new position.

REMOVING FIELDS FROM A VIEW

You can use the Show Fields dialog box, previously shown in Figure 31.7, to remove fields from those that are displayed in the view.

To remove one or more fields from a view:

1. Select the field or fields you want to remove from the view in the Show These Fields in This Order list.

2. Click Remove. Outlook immediately deletes the selected field from the list at the right and inserts that field in the Available Fields list at the left (in its correct alphabetical order).

3. Click OK twice to close the dialog boxes and display the Table view that no longer contains the field you removed.

Another way to remove a column from a Table view is to drag the column heading up. As you drag, a large X appears over the field name. When you release the mouse button, the entire column disappears from the table.

Yet another way to remove a column from a Table view is to right-click a field name at the top of a column to display the context menu shown in Figure 31.11. Click Remove This Column in the context menu.

Figure 31.11
This is the context menu that's displayed when you right-click a column heading.

PART
VI

CH
31

ADDING A FIELD TO A VIEW

You can use the Show Fields dialog box, previously shown in Figure 31.7, to add fields to a view.

To add one or more fields to a view:

1. Select the field in the Show These Fields in This Order list after which you want the inserted field (or fields) to be inserted.

2. Select the fields you want to add in the Available Fields list.

3. Click Add. Outlook deletes the selected fields from the Available Fields list and inserts those fields into the Show These Fields in This Order list.

4. Click OK twice to close the dialog boxes and display the Table view that now includes the fields you added.

When you open the Show Fields dialog box, the Available Fields list on the left contains only frequently used fields—the Select Available Fields From box at the bottom-left of the dialog box confirms that. You can open the Select Available Fields From drop-down list and select one of these groups of fields:

- Frequently Used fields
- Address fields
- E-mail fields
- Fax/Other Number fields
- Miscellaneous fields
- Name fields
- Personal fields
- Phone Number fields
- All Document fields
- All Mail fields
- All Post fields
- All Task fields
- All Journal fields
- All Note fields
- All Distribution List fields
- User-Defined Fields in Folder
- Forms

You can select any item in the list. When you select any except the last (Forms), a list of fields appears in the Available Fields box. You can select any field and click Add to add that field to the bottom of the Show These Fields in This Order list.

When you select Forms in the drop-down Select Available Fields From list, Outlook displays the dialog box shown in Figure 31.12.

Figure 31.12
Use this dialog box to select a form.

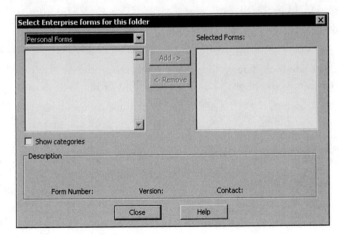

Tip from

Outlook contains many standard forms, such as the Message form, in which you create messages. You can import forms from Microsoft and other sources and also create your own forms as described in "Enhancing Outlook's Capabilities," a bonus Web chapter found at www.quehelp.com.

Most forms contain fields you can add into a Table view of Outlook items.

To select a field from a form:

1. In the Select Enterprise Forms for This Folder dialog box, open the unnamed drop-down list at the upper-left and select Personal Forms if you want to select fields from a form you've imported or created, or select Applications Forms if you want to select fields from one of Outlook's standard forms. After you do that, the box below the drop-down list contains a list of available forms.

2. Select a form from which you want to select fields, and click Add to add that form to the Selected Forms list on the right.

3. Repeat step 2 as often as necessary to add more forms into the Selected Forms list.

Note

You can remove one or more forms from the Selected Forms list by selecting forms and selecting Remove.

4. Select one or more forms in the Selected Forms list; then click Close to return to the Show Fields dialog box. The fields from the selected forms are listed in the Available Fields list.

5. Select one or more fields you want to add into the Table view and click Add.

Another way to insert a field into a Table view is to use the Field Chooser. To display the Field Chooser, right-click anywhere in the table heading to display the context menu previously shown in Figure 31.11. Select Field Chooser in the context menu to display the Field Chooser, shown in Figure 31.13.

You can open the drop-down list of field types at the top of the Field Chooser to display various lists of fields. Drag any field from the Field Chooser into the table heading and place it wherever you want. A new column appears when you release the mouse button.

CREATING A NEW FIELD

You are not limited to the information fields supplied with Outlook or available in forms. You can create your own fields.

To create a new field:

1. In the View Summary dialog box shown previously in Figure 31.6, click Fields to display the Show Fields dialog box shown previously in Figure 31.7.

2. Click New Field to display the dialog box shown in Figure 31.14.

Figure 31.13
The Field Chooser initially lists fields from the frequently used fields set.

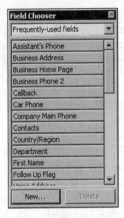

Figure 31.14
Use this dialog box to create a new field.

3. In the Name box, enter a name for the new field.

4. Open the drop-down Type list and select a type for the new field.

5. Open the drop-down Format list and select a format for the new field.

6. Click OK. The new field appears in the Show These Fields in This Order box.

→ For detailed information about creating fields, **see** the bonus Web chapter "Enhancing Outlook's Capabilities," found at www.quehelp.com.

GROUPING ITEMS

The Phone List view of Contact items shows a single list of items. Other views, such as the By Category view, arrange items in groups. For example, the By Category view of Contact items groups contacts by categories. Figure 31.15 shows the Alpha category expanded and other categories collapsed.

→ For detailed information about Outlook's categories, **see** "Using Categories and Entry Types," **p. 403**.

> **Note**
>
> If you assign more than one category to an Outlook item, that item appears in each of the categories assigned to it. A single item to which several categories are assigned is listed in each of those category groups.

Figure 31.15
Each category has a header that contains the category name. Individual categories can be expanded to show all the items in that category.

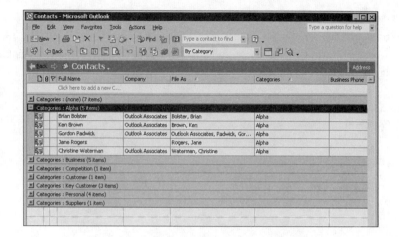

Initially, this view shows only category headers. Each category header has a small box at the left containing + to indicate there are items within that category. Each category header contains the name of the category and the number of items in that category. Click the + to display all the items within the category.

The header of each expanded category (that shows all the items in that category) has a small square containing — at the left. Click that small square to collapse the category so that only the header is visible.

Another way to expand and collapse groups is to select View and move the pointer onto Expand/Collapse Groups. You can click

- **Collapse This Group**—Collapses a selected group
- **Expand This Group**—Expands a selected group
- **Collapse All**—Collapses all groups
- **Expand All**—Expands all groups

You can modify grouping in existing views by

- Adding grouping to views that are originally not grouped
- Changing grouping in views that are originally grouped

This can be done in two ways: in a dialog box or visually. The next two sections show how you can add grouping to an originally ungrouped view, using the Phone List view of Contact items as an example.

Note

You can create as many as four levels of groupings.

USING A DIALOG BOX TO SET UP ONE LEVEL OF GROUPING

With the Contacts Information viewer displayed in the Phone List view, select View, move the pointer onto Current View, and click Customize Current View. Click Group By to display the dialog box shown in Figure 31.16.

Figure 31.16
The Group Items By box contains (none) to indicate that no grouping is in effect.

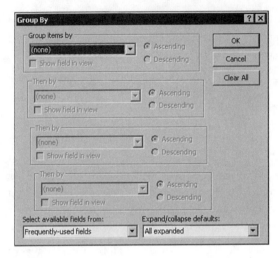

To set up one level of grouping:

1. Open the drop-down Group Items By list to display a list of fields in Contact items. This list contains all the fields in Contact items, not just those displayed in the view you're currently working with.

2. Scroll down the list of fields and select the field by which you want to group items. For example, if you want to group Contacts by company name, select the Company field. The Group By dialog box now appears as shown in Figure 31.17.

Tip from

Gordon Padwick

You can group by fields that are not displayed in the view. If necessary, you can open the Select Available Fields From drop-down list at the bottom of the dialog box to select a field that is not in the Frequently-used Fields list.

---

3. By default, Outlook proposes to show the field the items will be grouped by as a column in the table. This isn't necessary because the group name appears in each group header. Normally, you should uncheck the Show Field in View box.

4. Leave the Ascending option button selected if you want groups to be listed in ascending order. Select the Descending option button to list groups in descending order.

5. Outlook proposes to display the view with all groups expanded. You can open the drop-down Expand/Collapse Defaults list and select All Expanded, All Collapsed, or As Last Viewed.

6. Click OK to return to the View Summary dialog box that now displays how items are grouped, as shown in Figure 31.18.

Figure 31.17
The grouping field you selected now appears in the Group Items By box.

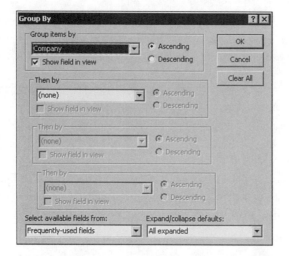

Figure 31.18
The text at the right of the Group By button in the View Summary dialog box shows how items are grouped.

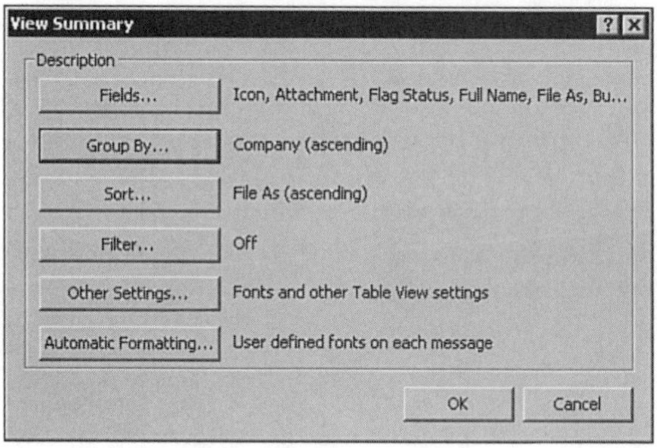

To see how items are grouped in the table, click OK to close the View Summary dialog box. The table is now similar to that previously shown in Figure 31.15.

USING A DIALOG BOX TO SET UP MULTIPLE LEVELS OF GROUPING

The preceding procedure showed how to group items at one level, such as by category or company name. You can choose to group items with groups to as many as four levels. For example, if you have Contacts that work for companies in various countries, you might find it convenient to group contacts by category and, for each category, by company, and for each company, by country.

Figure 31.17 shows the Group By dialog box after you've defined the first level of grouping. Notice that in the dialog box the Then By section is enabled. You can open the Then By drop-down list and select a field by which you want items to be grouped within the first level of grouping. If you wanted to group items by company and then by category, you would select Category for the second level of grouping.

After you've selected a field for second-level grouping, the third section of the dialog box becomes available and you can select a field for third-level grouping. That makes the fourth section of the dialog box available, in which you can select a field for fourth-level grouping.

Note

To clear all grouping, click Clear All in the Group By dialog box.

VISUALLY SETTING UP GROUPING

This example also uses the Phone List view of Contact items. If you've followed the previous section to set up grouping for the Phone List view, click Clear All in the Group By dialog box so you can follow what comes next.

To set up grouping visually:

1. With the Contacts Information viewer displayed and the Phone List view selected, select View, move the pointer onto Toolbars, and click Advanced to display the Advanced toolbar.

2. In the Advanced toolbar, click Group By Box (the third button from the right). When you do that, a row appears at the top of the Contacts table, as shown in Figure 31.19.

Note

You also can display the extra row by right-clicking any field name at the top of the table. This is convenient if you don't have the Advanced toolbar displayed.

Group By Box

Figure 31.19
The extra row at the top of the table is where grouping fields are shown.

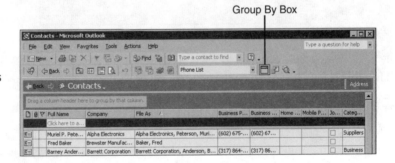

3. To group by a field, drag that field from the column heading in the table into the grouping row. For example, to group the table by the Company field, drag the

Company column heading into the grouping row. After you've done that, the table appears as shown in Figure 31.20.

Figure 31.20
The table is now grouped, with the name of the grouping field above the column titles.

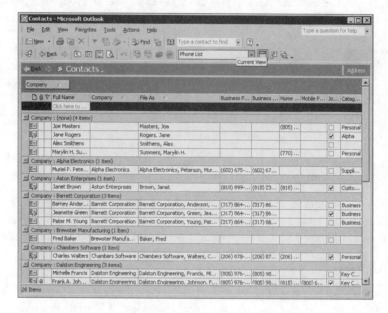

4. To create a second level of grouping, drag another field into the grouping row, as shown in Figure 31.21.

Figure 31.21
The table now has two levels of grouping.

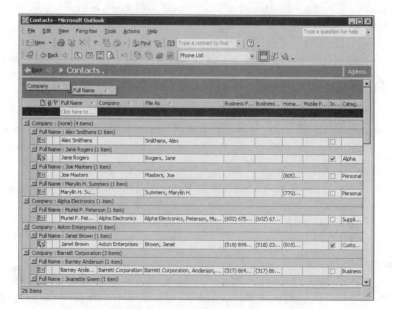

5. If necessary, repeat step 4 to create one or two additional levels of grouping.

When you're working visually, you can undo each level of grouping by dragging a group name from the grouping row back into its original position as a column title.

Note

After creating groups in the Group By dialog box (previously shown in Figure 31.16), you can click Group By Box in the Advanced toolbar to display grouping. Also, after creating groups with the Group By Box button, you can modify or clear those groups in the Group By dialog box.

To remove the Group By box at the top of a Table view, click Group By Box in the Advanced toolbar. This has no effect on the grouping in the view.

The visual method of grouping just described allows you to group only on fields displayed in the table. You can group on other fields by displaying the Field Chooser, previously shown in Figure 31.13, and dragging a field from there into the Group By box.

SORTING ITEMS

Unless a particular sort order is specified, a view displays items in the order they were created or received. For example, the Phone List view of Contact items doesn't initially have a sort order specified, so it lists items in the order they were created. The Address Cards view of Contact items, on the other hand, is defined to display items in alphabetical order by File As name.

→ You can sort a Table view based on a single field by clicking a column header. **See** "Changing the Order in Which Items Are Listed," **p. 661**.

You can create a sort order for items displayed in a table with up to four levels of sorting. To see how this works, we'll use the Phone List view of Contact items as an example.

To sort Contact items in the Phone List view:

1. Display the Contacts Information viewer with the Phone List view selected.
2. Select View, move the pointer onto Current View, and click Customize Current View to display the View Summary dialog box previously shown in Figure 31.6.
3. Click Sort to display the dialog box shown in Figure 31.22.
4. Open the drop-down Sort Items By list and select the field by which you want items to be sorted. For example, if you want items to be sorted by Company, select the Company field.

Tip from

Gordon Padwick

You are not limited to sorting by fields that are displayed in the view. If necessary, you can open the Select Available Fields From drop-down list. From here, you select the group of fields from which you want to select the field by which items are to be sorted.

Figure 31.22
The Sort Items By box initially shows (none) to indicate that items are not sorted.

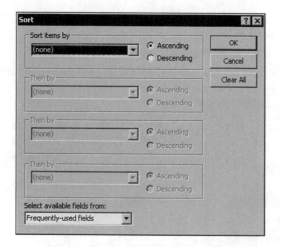

5. Select the Ascending option button if you want items to be listed in ascending order, or select the Descending option button if you want items to be listed in descending order.

This procedure explains how to specify only one level of sorting.

→ You can select up to four levels of sorting, just as you can select up to four levels of grouping. **See** "Using a Dialog Box to Set Up Multiple Levels of Grouping," **p. 669**.

FILTERING ITEMS

You can choose to filter items in a view so that a view shows only those items that satisfy certain conditions. If you have the Calendar Information viewer displayed with the Phone List view selected, the View Summary dialog box, previously shown in Figure 31.6, has Off at the right of the Filter button. This means the view doesn't filter items, so it displays all the items in the Calendar folder.

The following example illustrates how you can create a filter, in this case so that the Phone List shows only phone numbers for a certain company.

To filter a view:

1. In the View Summary dialog box, click Filter to display the dialog box shown in Figure 31.23.

→ For detailed information about using the Advanced Find dialog box, **see** "Using Advanced Find to Find Words and Phrases," **p. 341**.

Note

The left tab in this dialog box has the name of the type of item you're working with, Contacts in this case.

PART

VI

CH

31

2. In the Search for the Word(s) box, enter a word or phrase that appears in a particular field of items you want to have included. For example, if you want to list only items that include a specific company name, enter that company name.

3. Open the drop-down In list and select the field in which the name or phrase you entered in step 2 appears. For example, if the name or phrase appears in the Company field, select Company Field Only.

4. If you want to filter by an e-mail address, click E-mail to display the Select Names dialog box, select the name of a person, and click OK to return to the Filter dialog box.

5. Click OK to return to the View Summary dialog box, as shown in Figure 31.24.

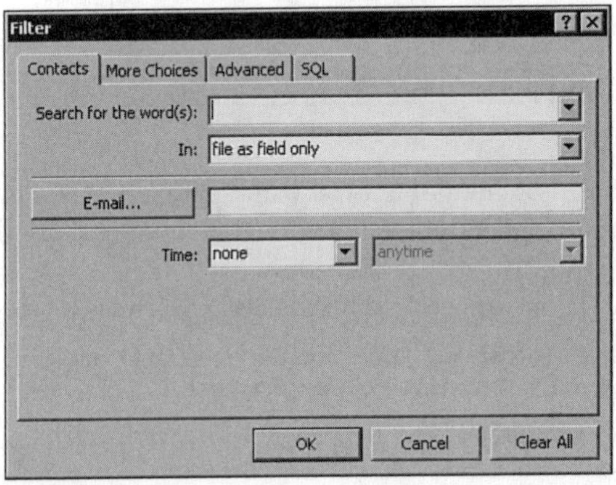

Figure 31.23
The Filter dialog box is similar to the Advanced Find dialog box.

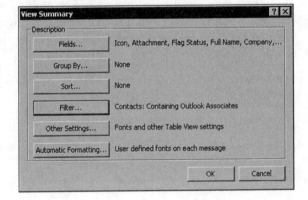

Figure 31.24
A summary of the filter you specified appears at the right of the Filter button in the View Summary dialog box.

6. Click OK to close the dialog box and display the filtered view, as shown in Figure 31.25.

Figure 31.25
The Information viewer now contains only those items that satisfy the filter condition.

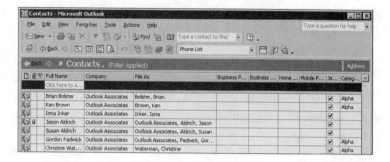

Tip from

When an Information viewer is displaying a filtered view, the words `Filter Applied` appear in the viewer's banner, as shown in Figure 31.25. This is to remind you that the viewer probably isn't displaying all the items in the corresponding folder.

The preceding sequence of steps is only a very simple example of how you can set up filters. You can use the More Choices, Advanced, and SQL tabs in the Filter dialog box to create more sophisticated filters.

→ You can create more complex filters using the same methods you employ when using Advanced Find. **See** "Using Advanced Find to Find Words and Phrases," **p. 341**.

To remove a filter from a view, open the Filter dialog box and delete the filter criteria. Click OK twice to return to the Information viewer that now displays all items in the corresponding folder, and without `Filter Applied` in the banner.

CREATING OTHER SETTINGS

The Other Settings button in the View Summary dialog box gives you access to a dialog box in which you can select fonts and various other aspects of a table's appearance.

To change a table's appearance, display the View Summary dialog box and click Other Settings to display the dialog box shown in Figure 31.26.

In this dialog box, you can

- **Change the font used for column headings**—Click Font in the Column Headings section of the dialog box to display a Font dialog box that's similar to the standard Windows Font dialog box. You can use this to select a font name, style, and size, but not effects or color.

- **Change the font used for rows in a table**—Click Font in the Rows section of the dialog box to display a Font dialog box that's similar to the standard Windows Font dialog box. You can use this to select a font name, style, and size, but not effects or color.

- **Change the font used for the AutoPreview**—Click Font in the AutoPreview section of the dialog box to display a font dialog box that's similar to the standard Windows Font dialog box. You can use this dialog box to select a font name, style, size, effects, and color.

- **Control the width of table columns**—By default, Outlook creates tables with the width of columns set so that all columns are displayed, which, in most cases, results in columns containing truncated text. You can uncheck the Automatic Column Sizing box in the Column Headings section of the dialog box so you can adjust column widths and show as many or as few columns as you want. After you do that, a horizontal scroll bar appears at the bottom of the table; you can use that scroll bar to see hidden columns.

- **Allow or disallow in-cell editing**—By default, Outlook allows in-cell editing, which means you can edit the contents of fields in the displayed table. Uncheck Allow In-cell Editing in the Rows section of the dialog box to make the table read-only.

- **Allow or disallow creating new items from within a table**—By default, you can't add new items from within a table. To allow adding new items from within a table, check Show "New Item" Row in the Rows section of the dialog box. After you do that, an empty row is displayed at the top of the table; you can use that row to create a new item.

- **Enable use of AutoPreview for Message and Calendar items**—By default, No AutoPreview is selected. You can select Preview All Items or Preview Unread Items in the AutoPreview section of the dialog box.

- **Choose whether grid lines are displayed in tables**—Use the Grid Lines section of the dialog box to control whether Outlook displays grid lines in the table and, if it does, the color of those grid lines. Open the Grid Line Style drop-down list and select a style. Open the Grid Line Color drop-down list and select a color. The Preview box on the right shows an example of the style and color you've selected.

- **To display group headings with a white background, uncheck the Shade Group Headings box**—When you select grouping, by default Outlook displays the group headings with a gray background.

- **Display Message and Calendar items with or without a Preview pane**—Check the Show Preview Pane box if you want to display a Preview pane. After you check that box, check Hide Header Information if you don't want to display the Preview pane header.

AUTOMATIC FORMATTING

The Automatic Formatting button in the View Summary dialog box provides access to rules that determine how certain kinds of items are displayed. The available rules depend on the types of items you're working with. All rules may not necessarily apply to your particular Outlook configuration.

→ To learn more about rules, **see** "Creating and Using Rules," **p. 583**.

To understand how these formatting rules work, we'll use the Inbox Information viewer as an example.

Figure 31.26
Use this dialog box to control a view's appearance.

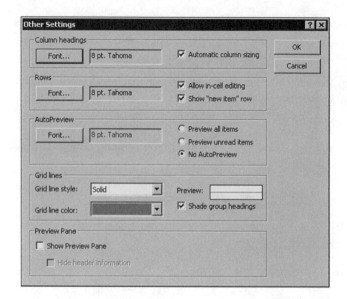

PART

VI

CH

31

With the Inbox Information viewer displayed and with the Messages view selected, select View, move the pointer onto Current View, and click Customize Current View to display the View Summary dialog box. Click Automatic Formatting to display the dialog box shown in Figure 31.27.

Figure 31.27
This is the Automatic Formatting dialog box, showing the default rules for messages.

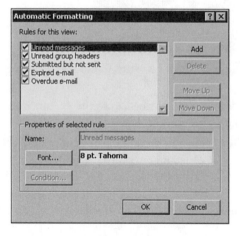

The rules in this dialog box control how Outlook displays messages in the Inbox Information viewer. Each of these rules controls how certain types of messages are displayed in the viewer. Select each rule in turn to see how it controls the display of messages. For example, if you select the Unread Messages rule, as shown in Figure 31.27, you see that unread messages are displayed in black using the 8-point Tacoma font.

You can change the font specified by each rule. With a rule selected, click Font to display the standard Windows Font dialog box, in which you can select a font name, style, size, and color.

You can create your own formatting rules to control how Outlook displays messages that satisfy certain criteria.

To create a formatting rule:

1. In the Automatic Formatting dialog box, click Add to modify the appearance of the dialog box, as shown in Figure 31.28.

Figure 31.28
A new rule appears in the list, tentatively named Untitled.

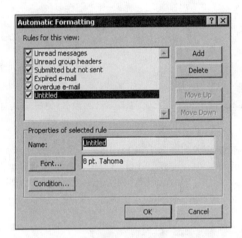

2. Change the name in the Name box to an appropriate name.

3. Click Font and select a font in which you want Outlook to display messages that satisfy the new criteria.

4. Click Condition to display the Filter dialog box, which is similar to that shown previously in Figure 31.23, but without the SQL tab.

5. Use the Filter dialog box to define the conditions that must be satisfied. For example, you might want the rule to apply to messages from a certain person, or messages in which a certain word appears in the Subject box. See Chapter 17, "Finding and Organizing Outlook Items," for detailed information about this dialog box.

→ For detailed information about using Advanced Find, **see** "Using Advanced Find to Find Words and Phrases," **p. 341**.

6. Click OK to return to the Automatic Formatting dialog box. Now the new formatting rule is listed.

To delete a rule you've created, select that rule and click Delete. You can't delete the default Outlook rules (although you can modify them).

RESETTING A VIEW TO ITS ORIGINAL STATE

If you've modified one of the views supplied with Outlook, the modified view is what Outlook subsequently uses. To go back to the original, unmodified view, you can reset the modified view to its original state.

To reset a view to its original state:

1. Display an Information viewer that displays the type of items for which you want to reset a view.

2. Select View, move the pointer onto Current View, and click Define Views to display the dialog box shown in Figure 31.29.

Figure 31.29
This dialog box lists all the views available for the type of item you selected.

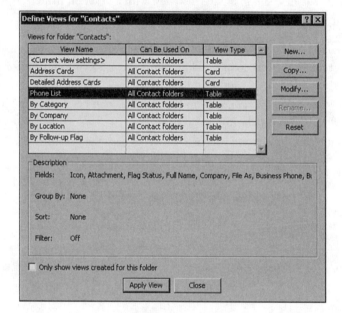

PART
VI
CH
31

3. Select the view you want to reset. If you select a view supplied with Outlook, the bottom button at the right is labeled Reset. That button is not available if you haven't modified the view; it is available if you have modified the view. If the view you select is one you've created, the bottom button is labeled Delete.

4. Click Reset. Outlook asks you to confirm that you want to reset the view to its original settings. Click OK.

CREATING CUSTOM VIEWS

The preceding information describes how you can modify the default Outlook views of items. You can also create your own custom views.

Note

If you're setting up Outlook for other people to use, you can prohibit access to the default Outlook views and make only the custom views you've created available.

→ For information about prohibiting access to Outlook's standard views, **see** "Making Only Custom Views Available," **p. 682**.

CREATING A CUSTOM VIEW BASED ON AN EXISTING VIEW

You can define a custom view based on an existing view, or you can define a custom view from scratch. If the custom view you want to create is similar to an existing view, it's easier to start from that view and then save that view with a different name.

To create a custom view based on an existing view:

1. Start by displaying an Information viewer that displays the items you want to display in the custom view. For example, if you want to create a custom view for Contact items, display a Contact Information viewer.

2. Select View, move the pointer onto Current View, and click Define Views to display the dialog box previously shown in Figure 31.29.

3. Select the existing view on which you want to base the custom view.

4. Click Copy to display the dialog box shown in Figure 31.30.

Figure 31.30
Use this dialog box to provide a name for the new view and also to select how you want the view to be used.

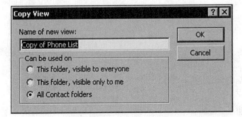

5. Replace the view name in the Name of New View box with an appropriate name for the new view.

6. Select the option button in the Can Be Used On section of the dialog box, according to how you want the new view to be used:

   - **This Folder, Visible to Everyone**—The view is available only for the folder in which it was created and can be used by everyone who has permission to access that folder.

   - **This Folder, Visible Only to Me**—The view is available only for the folder in which it was created and can be used only by the person who created the view.

   - **All Contact Folders**—The view is available in all Contact folders. If you're creating a view for Outlook items other than Contact items, the word Contact is replaced by the appropriate item name.

7. Click OK to display the View Summary dialog box, in which you can choose the settings for the new view. In this dialog box, you can refine what's shown in the new view, using the methods described previously in the "Modifying a View" section of this chapter.

After you've finished making the changes to the view, you have a new view with the name you chose in step 5.

CREATING A NEW VIEW FROM SCRATCH

You can create a new view without basing it on an existing view.

To create a new view from scratch:

1. Start by displaying an Information viewer that displays the items you want to display in the custom view. For example, if you want to create a custom view for Contact items, display a Contact Information viewer.

2. Select View, move the pointer onto Current View, and click Define Views to display the dialog box previously shown in Figure 31.29.

3. Click New to display the dialog box shown in Figure 31.31.

PART
VI
CH
31

Figure 31.31
Enter a name for the new view and select its type in this dialog box.

4. Replace New View in the Name of New View box with an appropriate name.

5. In the Type of View list, select the type of view you want to create.

6. In the Can Be Used On section of the dialog box, select an option button according to how you want the view to be used.

7. Click OK to display the View Summary dialog box, shown previously in Figure 31.6, in which you can specify the settings for the new view.

MAKING ONLY CUSTOM VIEWS AVAILABLE

You can set up Outlook so that it makes available only custom views you've created, not the default views that come with Outlook. This is done separately for each type of Outlook item.

To make only custom views available for one type of Outlook item, start by displaying an Information viewer that displays one type of Outlook item. Select View, move the pointer onto Current View, and click Define Views to display the dialog box previously shown in Figure 31.29. Check the Only Show Views Created for This Folder box.

Subsequently, when a user clicks View and moves the pointer onto Current View, the only views available are the custom views.

DELETING A VIEW

You can delete a view you've created, but you can't delete any of the default Outlook views.

To delete a view, start by displaying any Information viewer that shows the Outlook item type for which you want to delete a view. Select View, move the pointer onto Current View, and click Define Views to display the dialog box previously shown in Figure 31.29. Select the view you want to delete. If you select a view you've created, the bottom button on the right is labeled Delete. Click Delete to delete the selected view. Outlook asks you to confirm that you want to delete the view. Click Yes.

USING PRINT STYLES

Outlook provides many ways in which you can print Outlook items. Depending on the type of item you've selected, you can choose among several print styles to control how printed pages are formatted. Each print style is based on a view.

Outlook has built-in print styles for each of its views, as listed previously in Table 31.1. As that table shows, all views except Timeline views have the Memo print style available, and all Table views have a Table print style. In addition, Day/Week/Month Calendar views have several ways in which you can print calendars in the traditional calendar format; Card views of Contact items have index-card and booklet print styles.

You can modify the supplied print styles and supplement them by creating custom print styles. As described later in this chapter, if Outlook doesn't allow you to print in the format you need, you can export Outlook items to other applications and use the printing capabilities in them.

→ For more information about printing Outlook items, **see** "Using Other Applications and Utilities to Print Outlook Items," **p. 693**.

PRINTING TABLE VIEWS OF OUTLOOK ITEMS

With the Contacts Information viewer selected, you can choose among several Table views, such as the Phone List view used as an example in much of this chapter. You can choose the built-in Table or Memo print style to print this view. After you've selected a print style, you can make modifications to it.

The Table print style prints a table as it appears in a table Information viewer. In contrast, the Memo print style prints items in the format shown in Figure 31.32. Using the Table or Memo print style, you can print all the items displayed in the Information viewer, or you can select certain items to be printed. If you want to print only certain items, select those items before step 1 in the following procedure.

Figure 31.32
This is an example of how Outlook prints a Contact item in the Memo print style.

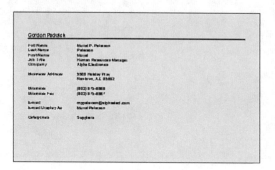

PART

VI

CH

31

To select and modify the Table print style for a Table view:

1. With a Table view, such as the Phone List view of Contact items, selected, select File and move the pointer onto Page Setup to display the menu that contains Table Style, Menu Style, and Define Print Styles.

Note

The third item in the menu, Define Print Styles, is used when you create a custom print style. Creating custom print styles is dealt with subsequently in this chapter.

2. Click Table Style to display the dialog box shown in Figure 31.33. The Format tab initially is selected.

3. The Fonts section of this dialog box shows the default fonts in which column headings and rows of the table are printed. You can click Font to change the default font name, style, and size for column headings in a dialog box similar to the standard Windows Font dialog box. You also can click Font to change the font for rows of the table.

Note

The Print Using Gray Shading box has no effect on tables that are based on a view that isn't grouped. If the view is grouped, such as the By Category view, and the Print Using Gray Shading box is checked, the group headers are printed with a gray background; if it isn't checked, the group headers are printed with a white background.

Figure 31.33
The Preview section at the top of this dialog box shows a picture of the print style.

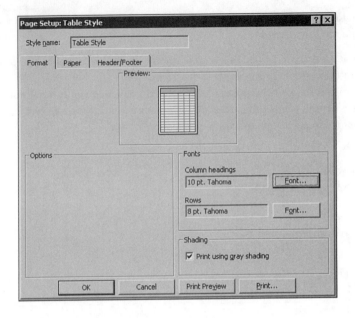

4. Select the Paper tab, shown in Figure 31.34.

Figure 31.34
Use this tab to select the size of the paper on which the table will be printed and the layout on that paper.

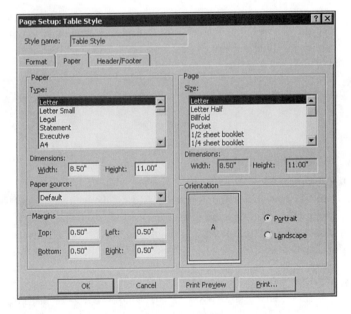

5. In the Paper section of this dialog box, select the type of paper in the Type list. The Width and Height boxes show the dimensions of the selected paper. If you're using non-standard paper, you can enter the appropriate width and height in those boxes.

The image in the Orientation section shows a scaled view of the paper. If your printer has more than one paper source, open the drop-down Paper Source list and select a source.

6. In the Page section of the dialog box, select how you want the printed image to be laid out on the paper. The image in the Orientation section shows a scaled view of the layout; the width and height boxes show the size of the printed image.

7. In the Margins section of the dialog box, enter the sizes of the margins.

8. In the Orientation section of the dialog box, select Portrait or Landscape.

9. Select the Header/Footer tab shown in Figure 31.35.

Figure 31.35
By default, Outlook prints your name, the page number, and the current date below the printed image.

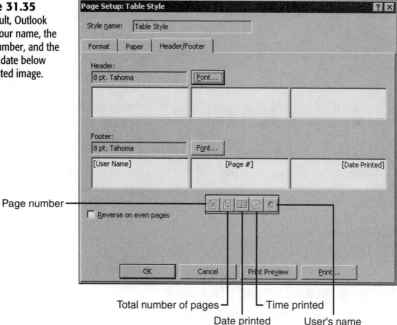

PART

VI

CH

31

10. You can enter text or any combination of five fields of information into any of the three positions in the header and into any of the three positions in the footer. Enter fields by clicking the buttons near the bottom of the dialog box. Click one of the Font buttons to select a font name, style, and size for the header and footer. To reverse the order of the header and footer sections on even pages, check the Reverse on Even Pages box.

11. If you want to see an enlarged preview of a printed page, click Print Preview.

12. Click Print Preview if you want to return to the Print Preview dialog box, or click Print to print the table. If you click Print, Outlook displays a dialog box such as that shown in Figure 31.36.

Figure 31.36
Your dialog box might be somewhat different from the one shown here, depending on the type of printer you're using.

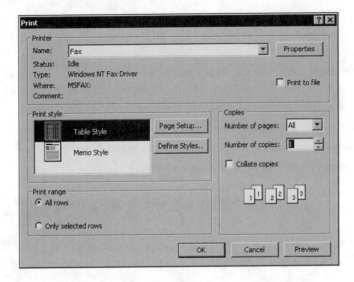

13. Most of the selections in this dialog box are similar to those available when you're printing other Windows documents. Notice that you can select All Rows or Only Selected Rows. Click OK to print the table.

Selecting the Memo style and using it to print a table is similar to using a Table print style. The only significant difference is in the Print dialog box. Instead of selecting All Rows or Only Selected Rows, you can check two check boxes:

- Start Each Item on a New Page
- Print Attached Files with Item(s)

PRINTING CALENDAR VIEWS OF OUTLOOK ITEMS

With the Day/Week/Month view of your calendar displayed in the Calendar Information viewer, you can print your daily, weekly, or monthly calendar (you can also print Calendar items using the Memo print style).

The Daily, Weekly, and Monthly print styles print calendars in almost the same way they appear in the Calendar Information viewer. Figures 38.37, 38.38, and 38.39 show previews of printed calendar pages.

Setting up the Daily, Weekly, or Monthly print style is similar to setting up the Table print style, previously described in this chapter. One difference is in the Format tab of the Page Setup dialog box. Figure 31.40 shows the Format tab for the Daily print style.

The Weekly and Monthly print styles have similar choices in the Page Setup and Print dialog boxes.

Figure 31.37
This is a preview of a typical calendar page to be printed using the Daily print style.

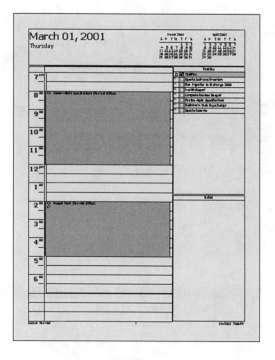

Figure 31.38
This is a preview of a typical calendar page to be printed using the Weekly print style.

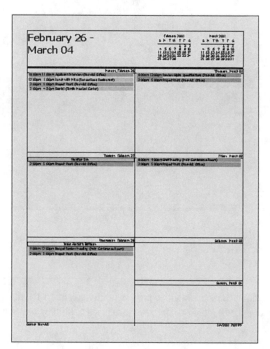

PART

VI

CH

31

Figure 31.39
This is a preview of a typical calendar page to be printed using the Monthly print style.

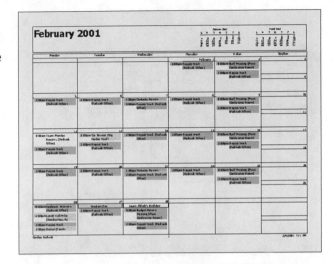

Figure 31.40
You can choose what you want to include in a printed daily calendar.

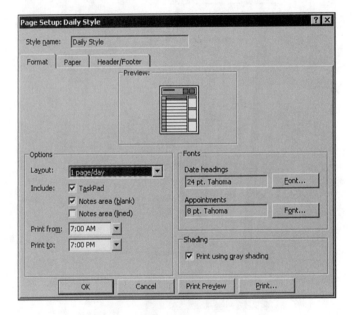

Another difference in the Print dialog box is shown in Figure 31.41.

<table>
<tr><td>**Note**</td><td>When you're using the Monthly print style, Outlook offers the ability to print exactly one month per page. Also, you have the choice of printing or not printing weekend days.</td></tr>
</table>

Figure 31.41
You can choose the range of dates to print and whether to print items marked as private.

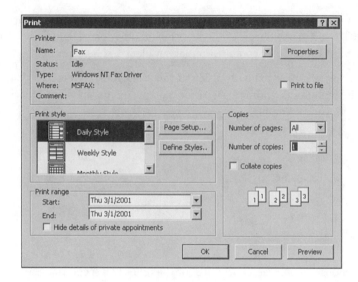

Tri-fold style is another built-in print style for use with Calendar items. This style divides the printed page into three sections—you can choose what is printed on each page.

Figure 31.42 shows the Format tab of the Page Setup dialog box after you select the Tri-fold style.

Figure 31.42
The Preview section at the top of this dialog box illustrates how the printed page is arranged in three sections.

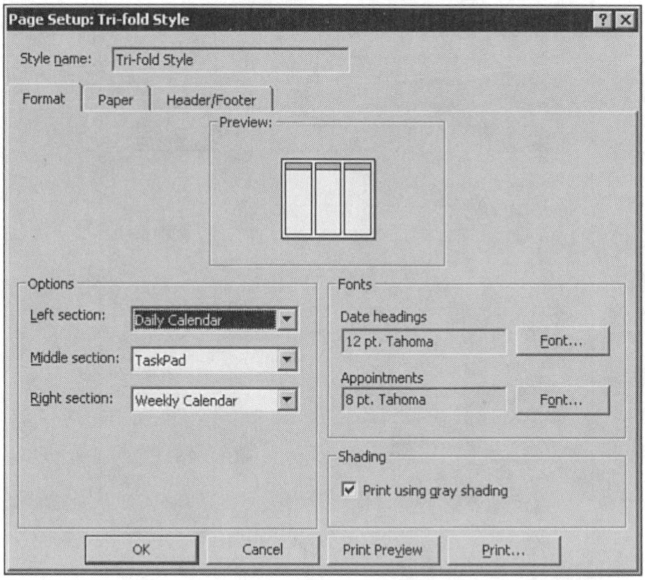

PART
VI

CH
31

You can use this print style to print a calendar that provides a detailed view of your day in one panel, a summarized view of the month in another panel, and your to-do list in the third panel. Various other combinations are available.

The Options section at the bottom-left of this dialog box is where you can select what goes into each section of the printed page. For example, if you open the Left Section drop-down list, you can choose among

- Daily Calendar
- Weekly Calendar
- Monthly Calendar
- TaskPad
- Notes (blank)
- Notes (lined)

You can choose among the same items for the other two sections.

The Calendar Details style is yet another built-in print style for calendars. This style prints details about one or more selected Calendar items. This print style is useful, for example, if you have an Appointment item for which you have entered a lot of notes. Using this print style, you can print all your notes on one or more pages, as shown in Figure 31.43.

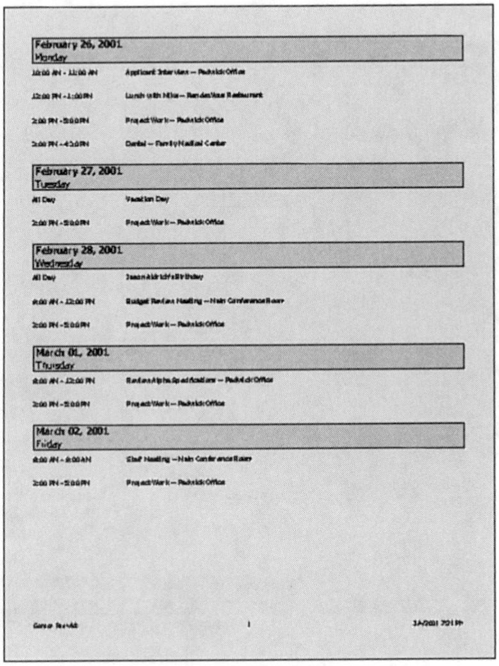

Figure 31.43
This is the preview of a page based on the Calendar Details style.

PRINTING CONTACT VIEWS OF OUTLOOK ITEMS

Just as Outlook has built-in views appropriate for Calendar items, so it has built-in views appropriate for Contact items. These are the Card, Small Booklet, Medium Booklet, and Phone Directory print styles (you can also print Contact items using the Memo print style).

You can use the Card print style to print Contact items as they might appear on traditional index cards. When you select this style, the Page Setup dialog box's Format tab initially assumes you want to print contact information on ordinary paper.

You can specify

- Whether items follow one another in columns or each item starts a new page
- The number of columns on a page
- How many blank pages to print at the end (for you to temporarily pencil in new contacts)
- Whether you want letter tabs to be printed at the edge of pages
- Whether each alphabetical section should have a heading

You can use the Paper tab of this dialog box to choose paper that is particularly appropriate for printing cards. In addition to standard paper sizes, you can select among several paper and card sizes suitable for printing cards, including standard index cards and various papers from Avery that can be used to print index cards on laser and inkjet printers.

The Small Booklet and Large Booklet print styles provide the capability to print Contact items on pages with eight or four sections, so that the pages can be folded into booklet form.

The Phone Directory print style prints Contact items in a similar format to a typical phone book. You can specify how many columns are to be on a page.

CREATING CUSTOM PRINT STYLES

So far, you have seen how you can select a built-in print style, modify it somewhat, and use it to print Outlook items. But what if you want to use a modified version of a built-in print style regularly? You must be wondering whether you have to repeat the modification each time you want to print items. No, you don't. You can solve this problem in two ways:

- You can save the modified print style. In this case, you no longer have the original built-in print style.
- You can save the modified print style as a custom print style. In that case, you have both the original built-in print style and the modified print style.

To keep things simple, we'll use the Table print style as an example. However, what follows applies to all print styles.

To create a custom print style:

1. Display the Information viewer that contains the Outlook items for which you want to create a print style. Select the view you want to use as the basis for the new print style. For example, display the Contacts Information viewer and select the Phone List view.

2. Select File, move the pointer onto Page Setup, and click Define Print Styles to display the dialog box in which you can select one of the available print styles.

3. Select the print style, such as Table Style, on which you want to base the custom view.

4. If you want to change the built-in view, click Edit. If you want to create a new view based on the built-in view, click Copy. After you click Copy, Outlook displays the dialog box shown in Figure 31.44.

Figure 31.44
This dialog box is the same one you see when you're temporarily modifying a built-in print style.

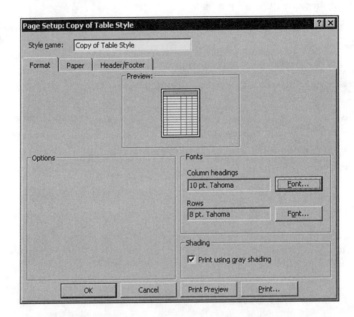

Note

If you had chosen Edit instead of Copy, the Style Name box would have contained the name of the built-in style (and would not be available for editing), instead of showing the print style as a copy of the built-in print style.

5. Edit the name in the Style Name box to create an appropriate name for your custom style.

6. Make whatever changes are necessary in the Format, Paper, and Header/Footer tabs of the Page Setup dialog box to create the new print style.

7. Click OK to save the custom print style and return to the Define Print Styles dialog box.

RESETTING AND DELETING PRINT STYLES

The Define Print Styles dialog box lists the built-in print styles and any custom print styles you've created. If you select a built-in print style, the bottom button is named Reset. After you've modified a built-in print style, you can click that button to reset a built-in print style to its original state.

If you select a custom print style you've created, the bottom button is named Delete. You can click that button to delete a custom print style.

USING OTHER APPLICATIONS AND UTILITIES TO PRINT OUTLOOK ITEMS

Although the variety of print styles provided by Outlook is extensive, you might have printing requirements that Outlook doesn't satisfy.

One way to obtain more printing flexibility is to export Outlook items into another application and use that application's printing capabilities. For example, you can export Outlook items into an Access table and then design an Access report that prints the Outlook items. Consult a book about Access, such as *Special Edition Using Microsoft Access 2002*, for information about creating Access reports.

TROUBLESHOOTING

VIEWS AND PRINT STYLES

While working with custom views, you must remember that each view you create is for items of a specific type. If you've created a custom view for your Inbox folder, that view can be used only for Mail items. In addition to using the new view for your Inbox folder, you can also use it for your Outbox and Sent Items folders, but not, for example, for your Calendar and Contacts folders. If you want to have a similar view for various types of Outlook items, you must create separate views for the appropriate Outlook folders.

It's also important to remember that a custom view can be made available in three ways. If you, or someone else, can't find a view, that might be because, although the view exists, it's not available in the current circumstances. You can select

- **This Folder, Visible to Everyone**—The view is available only in the folder in which it is created and is available to everyone who has permission to access the folder.
- **This Folder, Visible Only to Me**—The view is available only in the folder in which it is created and only to the person who created the view.
- **All Folders of a Specific Type**—The view is available in all folders of a specific type. For example, if you create a view for Mail folders, you can select All Mail Folders so the view is available in any folder that contains Mail items and is available to everyone.

After you've created a view, you can't change its availability.

SECURITY CONSIDERATIONS

CHAPTER 32

USING OUTLOOK SECURELY

In this chapter

STORING AND SHARING INFORMATION

Outlook provides facilities for saving and sharing information. If you use Outlook on a standalone computer to which only you have access and which doesn't have a modem, your concerns about security are that Outlook accurately saves the information you enter and returns that information when you need it—and that no one steals your computer.

You probably don't use Outlook like that. If you use Outlook on a standalone computer, you probably have a modem and use Outlook to send and receive e-mail by way of the Internet or another e-mail service. If you use Outlook on a networked computer, you can share information in many ways.

When you use Outlook on a computer that's connected either by way of a phone line or a LAN to other computers, several issues arise. These include

- Can you be sure that information you want to keep private can't be accessed by other people?
- Can you be sure that information you want to share with other people is accessible only by those people with whom you want to share that information?
- When you send an e-mail message, can you be sure that message is received by, and only received by, the people to whom you addressed it?
- When people receive a message from you, can you be sure the message hasn't been tampered with?
- When you receive an e-mail message, can you be sure that message was actually sent by the person from whom it appears to be sent?
- When you receive an e-mail message, can you be sure the message hasn't been tampered with?
- Can you be sure that viruses aren't introduced into your computer?

These and other questions are addressed in this chapter.

SECURING YOUR COMPUTER

There is no such thing as absolute security. However, there's a lot you can do to make your security close to impenetrable. The degree to which you are willing to adopt these measures depends on the value of the information stored on your computer and to which your computer has access.

Subsequently in this chapter you'll read about certificates. It's particularly important to secure your computer if you have a certificate. If your computer is not secure, other people can obtain copies of your certificate and then pass themselves off as you.

→ You can use certificates to authenticate and encrypt messages. **See** "Sending Secure Messages on the Internet," **p. 704**.

PHYSICALLY SECURING YOUR COMPUTER

Physically securing your computer means preventing unauthorized people from gaining access to it. If you're using a desktop computer, that might mean keeping it in a vault that's as difficult to get into as a bank's vault. In less demanding situations, it's usually adequate to keep your computer in a room that's always locked when you're not there.

An alternative is to replace the hard drive in your computer with a removable hard drive. When you're finished working, you can remove the hard drive and either keep it with you or put it in a safe.

Note

> You can't protect your data by deleting files from your hard disk because deleting removes only an index entry that points to where the data is stored. You, or someone else, can easily recover deleted files.

Laptop computers are a particular problem as far as security is concerned. Short of chaining the computer to your body, there's really no way to eliminate the possibility of the computer being stolen with all your valuable data on its hard disk. If you use a laptop and have data that must not be accessible to other people, make sure you keep that data only on a removable disk. Keep that disk in your personal possession, not plugged into the computer.

PREVENTING ACCESS TO YOUR COMPUTER

The preceding section addressed the issues of preventing people from gaining access to your computer. Those methods are probably too extreme in most environments. What do you do if you live in a cubicle to which many people have access while you're at lunch or in a meeting?

One possibility is to use a so-called screensaver. Although modern monitors don't seem to need any help to prevent ghost images being permanently registered on their screens, you can use a screensaver to blank out your screen while you're away from your computer. You, or someone else, can see information on the screen again only by entering a password.

Even though a screensaver can prevent a casual intruder from using your computer, it won't deter a skilled hacker.

Running under Windows 2000, Windows Me, Windows NT, or Windows 98, you can set up accounts that can be accessed only by entering a username and password. This is in contrast to Windows 95, which uses a username and password only to determine a user's Windows settings.

Note

> You can lock a computer that runs under Windows 2000. To do so, press Ctrl+Alt+Delete to display the Windows Security dialog box, and click Lock Computer to prevent access to any programs or files. To regain access, press Ctrl+Alt+Delete to display the Unlock Computer dialog box in which you must enter your password.

CREATING PRIVATE OUTLOOK ITEMS

When you create an Outlook item, you can mark that item as private. After doing so, the item is displayed just like any other Outlook item when you display Outlook items in an Information viewer. However, if someone else with whom you have shared your Outlook folder opens that folder, that person will see that the item exists but won't be able to see any information about it.

For example, if you allow your administrative assistant to have access to your Calendar, you can create an appointment and mark it private. Subsequently, your administrative assistant can see that you have blocked out time on your calendar but can't see the details of that item.

Tip from

In Outlook used as a client for an Exchange server, you can allow a delegate to see items you've marked as private. To do so, select Tools, Options, and select the Delegates tab. Select a delegate, and then click Permissions. Check Delegate Can See My Private Items.

CONTROLLING ACCESS TO FOLDERS

Access to Outlook folders differs according to where you store your Outlook items. You can save items in a Personal Folders file or, if you use Outlook as a client for an Exchange server, in an Offline Folders file or in the Exchange store.

WORKING WITH A PERSONAL FOLDERS FILE

There's nothing to prevent anyone who has access to your computer from copying a Personal Folders file. As mentioned previously in this chapter, you can protect all your files by requiring a password to start the operating system. You also can password-protect individual Personal Folders (.pst) files.

To create a password for a Personal Folders file, display the Folder List, right-click the root of the file you want to protect, and select Properties in the context menu to display the Personal Folders Properties dialog box. Click Advanced to display the dialog box shown in Figure 32.1.

Figure 32.1
This dialog box displays information about your Personal Folders file.

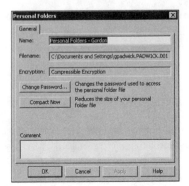

This dialog box shows

- **The Name**—This is Personal Folders, by which the file is known within Outlook. You can change that name from Personal Folders to something else.
- **The Path of the file**—You can't change that.
- **The fact that Compressible Encryption is used to save Outlook items within the file**—You can't change that.

Note

You can select an encryption level for a Personal Folders file only at the time you create that file. Although you can't change the encryption for the existing Personal Folders file, you can create another Personal Folders file and set it to Best Encryption. You can designate the new file as your default personal store.

→ For information about creating Personal Folders files and choosing one of them to be the default, **see** "Creating a Personal Folders File," **p. 311**.

Initially, Outlook creates your Personal Folders file without a password. To provide protection for your Outlook items saved in your Personal Folders file, you can protect the file with a password.

To protect your Personal Folders file with a password:

1. In the Personal Folders dialog box shown in Figure 32.1, click Change Password to display the dialog box shown in Figure 32.2.

Figure 32.2
Use this dialog box to designate a password.

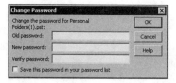

2. If you haven't previously designated a password for the Personal Folders file, leave the Old Password box empty. If you have previously password-protected your Personal Folders file, enter that password in the Old Password box.
3. Enter the new password in the New Password box. Outlook remembers the characters you enter but displays asterisks in the box.
4. Enter the new password again in the Verify Password box.

Note

Passwords are case sensitive. You must enter the same combination of uppercase and lowercase characters in both boxes. Later, when you use the password to gain access to your Outlook items, you must use the correct combination of uppercase and lowercase characters.

5. Leave the Save This Password in Your Password List box unchecked. Click OK. If you enter exactly the same characters in the New Password and Verify Password boxes, Outlook accepts the new password and closes the dialog box. If you don't enter the same characters in both boxes, Outlook tells you that both boxes must have the same content; you must correct that problem by reentering the password in both boxes.

6. Click OK three times to close the dialog boxes.

7. Select File, Exit to close Outlook.

The next time you start Outlook, you see the dialog box shown in Figure 32.3.

Figure 32.3
You must enter your password before Outlook will start.

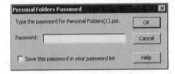

Tip from

Gordon Padwick

> If you enter the wrong password, Outlook displays a message about that. Click OK to close the message box; then enter the correct password.
>
> If you click Cancel in the dialog box shown in Figure 32.3, Outlook will open but won't be able to open the password-protected Personal Folders file.

Caution

> The security achieved by using passwords is only as good as the security of those passwords. Select passwords that can't easily be guessed, that contain alphabetic and numeric characters, and that consist of at least eight (preferably more) characters. Use a different password for each purpose so that, if someone does discover one of your passwords, that person doesn't have access to everything you've protected. Ideally, you shouldn't write down your passwords, but, if you do, keep the paper in a very secure place.

USING OUTLOOK AS A CLIENT FOR AN EXCHANGE SERVER

If you're using Outlook as a client for an Exchange server, you have access to any number of Personal Folders files and Offline Folders files on your local hard drive, and also to Outlook folders within the Exchange store. You can control access to any folder that you own in the Exchange store—your own Outlook folders and public folders for which you have Owner permissions.

→ For information about granting permission to access your Outlook folders and the public folders you own in the Exchange store, **see** "Delegating Access to Your Folders," **p. 445** and "Giving People Access to a Public Folder," **p. 457.**

LOGGING ON

Outlook provides password protection for access to mail servers. If you're concerned about other people reading e-mail addressed to you, you should set up your e-mail accounts so a password is required before Outlook will connect to a mail server. In many cases, you don't have any choice about this because mail servers are usually set up to require a password.

LOGGING ON TO AN INTERNET MAIL SERVER

If you have an Internet e-mail account, you can set up Dial-up Networking so it automatically supplies your password when you attempt to connect to the server, or so you have to provide the password each time you attempt to connect. Having your password automatically supplied is convenient, but it presents a security risk. If your computer is accessible to other people, it's generally better not to have Dial-up Networking automatically supply the password.

LOGGING ON TO AN EXCHANGE SERVER

If you're using Outlook as a client for an Exchange server, by default when you start Outlook, it automatically connects to Outlook folders in the Exchange store.

To require a password to access an Exchange server:

1. Select Tools, E-mail Accounts to display the first E-mail Accounts dialog box. With View or Change Existing E-mail Accounts selected, click Next to display the second E-mail Accounts dialog box. Select the Microsoft Exchange Server account, and then click Change. In the resulting dialog box, click More Settings to display the Microsoft Exchange Server dialog box. Select the Advanced tab shown in Figure 32.4.

PART

VII

CH

32

Figure 32.4
Use this dialog box to control access to the Exchange server.

Note

By default, Password Authentication is displayed in the Logon Network Security box. This means that the same password you use to log on to the server is used to log you on to the Exchange Server—convenient, but a possible security risk.

2. Open the drop-down Logon Network Security list and select None.

3. Click OK to close the dialog box and return to the E-mail Accounts dialog box. Click Next, and then click Finish. Select File, Exit to close Outlook.

The next time you start Outlook and attempt to connect to the Exchanger server, you'll see the dialog box shown in Figure 32.5.

Figure 32.5
You must supply your user name, password, and domain name before Outlook will connect to the Exchange server.

Subsequently, when you log on, the User Name and Domain Name boxes already contain the required information. You only need to enter your password.

SENDING SECURE MESSAGES ON THE INTERNET

Even though the Internet is convenient to use, you might wonder how secure it is and what you can do to enhance the security of your Internet communications. For normal communications, the Internet seems to be at least as secure as postal mail. Although it's not unusual to hear about mail being stolen from postal mail boxes, it's rare to hear about e-mail messages being stolen.

If the messages you send and receive contain confidential information, you should consider enhancing e-mail security by using a certificate. Outlook fully supports the use of certificates. Microsoft recommends VeriSign as a source of certificates, so this chapter focuses on certificates issued by that company. VeriSign calls certificates *Digital IDs*.

Note

Certificates rely on the Secure Multipurpose Internet Mail Extensions (S/MIME) protocol that Outlook supports. You can send secure e-mail messages to, and receive secure e-mail messages from, people who use Outlook or other e-mail programs that support S/MIME. E-mail programs that support S/MIME include Outlook, Outlook Express, Netscape Messenger, Deming, Frontier, Pre-mail, Opensoft, Connectsoft, and Eudora.

For information about certificates in general and VeriSign's products in particular, go to the Web site: http://www.verisign.com.

UNDERSTANDING CERTIFICATES

A certificate serves two purposes—authentication and encryption:

- **Authentication**—Means you can send messages to other people and those people can have a high level of confidence that the messages they receive really are from you, and that those messages haven't been tampered with in any way. Authentication also means other people can send messages to you and you can have the same confidence that the messages you receive are really from the apparent senders and are the messages those people actually sent.

- **Encryption**—The process of converting plain text into an encoded form. If you have a certificate, you can encrypt your messages so that only a recipient who knows how to decrypt those messages can read them. Likewise, other people can send encrypted messages to you.

When you receive a certificate, you get two keys: your private key and your public key. The *private* key is just that—private. It's an entry in the Windows registry on your computer that's protected by a password. Your private key is created on your computer and resides only there. It is not known to the organization or person who issued the certificate. Your private key is used to create digital signatures and to decrypt messages encrypted with the corresponding public key.

The *public* key, on the other hand, is a file you can make freely available to other people. You must provide your public key to people before they can send you encrypted messages. Your public key is used to encrypt messages that can be decrypted by your private key.

Note

The private key and matching public key are sometimes referred to as a *key pair*.

After you've installed a certificate on your computer, you're ready to send secure mail. If you want to send encrypted mail to someone, you must have that person's public key. Here are some important facts about using a certificate:

- When you send a message secured by your certificate, a recipient who uses an e-mail program that supports S/MIME can verify the message is really from you and hasn't been tampered with by anyone else.

- When people send you messages secured by their certificates, you can verify the message is really from the apparent sender and hasn't been tampered with.

- To send an encrypted message a recipient can decrypt, you must have the recipient's public key in the Contact item for that recipient in your Contacts folder.

- For other people to send you encrypted messages you can decrypt, those people must have your public key.

OBTAINING A CERTIFICATE

You can use Outlook to obtain a certificate from VeriSign or other providers. VeriSign offers a 60-day trial version at no cost or a subscription that, at the time this book was written, was available for $14.95 per year.

PART

VII

CH

32

To get a certificate from VeriSign, you have to connect to VeriSign's Web site. You must, of course, have Outlook set up to connect to the Internet.

Note   VeriSign uses the term *Digital ID* as a brand name for certificates.

To obtain a VeriSign Digital ID:

1. With any Outlook Information viewer displayed, select Tools, Options and select the Security tab shown in Figure 32.6.

Figure 32.6
The Security tab provides access to Outlook's security options.

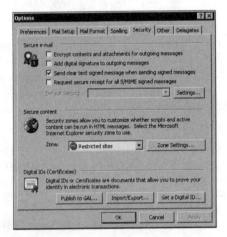

2. Click Get a Digital ID. Outlook offers VeriSign, GlobalSign, British Telecommunications, and Thawte as certifying authorities. This chapter assumes you chose VeriSign because that organization is Microsoft's preferred certificate provider.

3. Click Verisign, Inc to access the Verisign site, from which you can obtain a Digital ID. You can choose to receive a Class 1 Digital ID for which there is an annual charge ($14.95 at the time this chapter was written) or a more limited Digital ID for a free 60-day trial.

4. Follow the instructions there to apply for either an evaluation or annual subscription to a Digital ID and for installing that Digital ID on your computer.

Note   A short while after you apply for a Digital ID, you'll receive an e-mail message confirming that your application has been accepted and instructing you how to proceed. You must install the Digital ID on the same computer you used to apply for the Digital ID. As explained later in this chapter, you can subsequently move your Digital ID from one computer to another.

5. The confirming message contains a Web address you must access. Access that site and enter the PIN the message contains to download your Digital ID.

6. After you've done that, start Outlook and select Tools, Options; then select the Security tab in the Options dialog box.

7. Check Add Digital Signature to Outgoing Messages, and click Settings to display the dialog box shown in Figure 32.7.

Figure 32.7
You can use this dialog box to establish one or more security settings.

8. Enter a name for your first set of security settings in the Security Settings Name box.

9. If you intend to use this security setting for Internet e-mail, accept the default S/MIME in the Secure Message Format box. If you intend to use this security setting for Exchange e-mail, open the drop-down Secure Message Format list and select Exchange Server Security.

10. Check the Default Security Setting for This Secure Message Format box if you want to make the current settings the default for the Secure Message Format you selected in step 9.

11. Check the Default Security Setting for All Secure Messages box if you want to make the current settings the default for all secure messages if you use S/MIME and Exchange Server Security secure message formats.

12. In the Certificates and Algorithms section of the Change Security Settings dialog box, click Choose in the Signing Certificate row to display the Select Certificate dialog box shown in Figure 32.8.

13. Select the certificate you want to use. After doing that, you can (but don't have to) click View Certificate to see detailed information about that certificate. Click OK to accept the selected certificate and return to the Change Security Settings dialog box, which now displays the name of the certificate in the Signing Certificate and Encryption Certificate boxes.

PART
VII

CH

32

Figure 32.8
This dialog box lists all the certificates installed on your computer. Only one certificate is shown in this example.

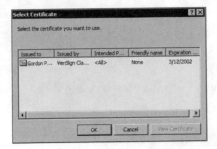

> **Note**
>
> The Hash Algorithm and Encryption Algorithm boxes specify the mathematical formulas used to digitally sign and encrypt messages. You shouldn't normally change the default values in these boxes.
>
> The Send These Certificates with Signed Messages box is checked by default so that digitally signed messages you send contain a copy of your public key. By doing this, you enable message recipients to send you encrypted messages.

14. Click OK to return to the Security tab of the Options dialog box, and click OK to close that dialog box.

The information in this section dealt only with having a single certificate (Digital ID). If you work in an environment in which a high level of security is required, you might have more than one certificate and use each for a different purpose. By doing that, you can ensure that if one of your certificates becomes compromised, others remain secure.

SETTING THE SECURITY LEVEL FOR YOUR PRIVATE KEY

During the process of installing your private key, you'll be asked to select a security level. Three security levels are available:

- **High**—Click this if you want to password-protect your private key. You'll be asked for the password each time you use your private key.

- **Medium**—Click this if you don't want to password-protect your private key. Outlook displays a message each time you use your private key.

- **Low**—Click this if you want to be able to use your private key without being asked for a password and without Outlook displaying a message.

MAKING A BACKUP COPY OF YOUR DIGITAL ID

There are two reasons you would want to make a backup copy of your Digital ID:

- So you can restore your Digital ID if it becomes corrupted on your hard disk

- So you can move your Digital ID to another computer or hard disk

You normally should save a copy of your Digital ID on a floppy disk and keep that disk in a secure place.

To make a copy of your Digital ID:

1. With any Outlook Information viewer displayed, select Tools, Options to display the Options dialog box and select the Security tab, shown previously in Figure 32.6.

2. Click Import/Export to display the dialog box shown in Figure 32.9.

Figure 32.9
Use this dialog box to import or export a Digital ID.

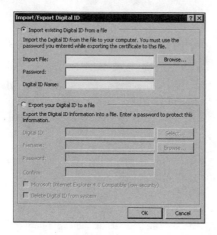

3. Select Export Your Digital ID to a File; then click Select to display the Select Cerificate dialog box, in which you can select the certificate you want to copy.

4. Select the Digital ID you want to export; then click OK to return to the Import/Export Digital ID dialog box in which the Digital ID box now contains the name of the Digital ID you selected in the previous step.

5. Click Browse to display the Locate Security Profile dialog box, use it to navigate to the location where you want to save the Digital ID, and enter a name for the file that will contain the Digital ID. Click Save to return to the Import/Export Digital ID dialog box in which the Filename box now contains the path for the file.

6. Enter a password for the file in the Password box, and enter the same password in the Confirm box.

Note

A password is required. Outlook won't let you export a Digital ID to a file without a password.

7. Leave the two check boxes near the bottom of the Import/Export Digital ID dialog box unchecked.

8. Click OK to export the Digital ID to a file. Outlook displays a message stating An application is requesting access to a Protected item. Click OK to continue. Outlook saves the file with .pfx as its file name extension.

Tip from

If someone else gains access to the backup copy of your Digital ID, that person could import your Digital ID onto another computer. For that reason, you should protect the backup file with a password and keep the backup disk in a secure place.

REMOVING YOUR DIGITAL ID FROM A COMPUTER

When the time comes to replace your hard disk with another one, you must remember to remove your Digital ID from the old disk. Otherwise, if someone else inherits your old hard disk, that person also inherits your Digital ID. Likewise, if you replace your computer with a new one, remember to remove your Digital ID before you pass your old computer on to someone else.

To remove your Digital ID, follow the first six steps in the preceding procedure. Then select Delete Digital ID from System, and click OK.

Tip from

"Removing" doesn't really remove information from your hard disk—it just makes that information inaccessible by normal means. Techniques are available to recover information you might have removed.

In high-security environments, any disk that contains, or has contained, confidential information that's removed from a computer should be physically destroyed to avoid any possibility that information can be recovered.

IMPORTING YOUR DIGITAL ID FROM A BACKUP DISK

The process of importing your Digital ID from a backup disk is similar to the process of exporting your Digital ID.

To import your Digital ID:

1. With any Outlook Information viewer displayed, select Tools, Options to display the Options dialog box and select the Security tab, shown previously in Figure 32.6.

2. Click Import/Export Digital ID to display the dialog box previously shown in Figure 32.9.

3. Select Import Existing Digital ID from a File.

4. In the Import File box, enter the full path name of the file you want to import. Alternatively, click Browse, navigate to the disk that contains the file, select the file, and click Open to return to the Import/Export Security Information and Digital ID dialog box.

5. In the Password box, enter the password of the saved file.

6. In the Digital ID Name box, enter the name by which you want Outlook to refer to your Digital ID. You can use any name, but your own name or mailbox name is appropriate.

7. Click OK to import the Digital ID.

ADDING DIGITAL ID BUTTONS TO THE MESSAGE FORM'S TOOLBAR

If you're using Outlook's native editor, you can add two Digital ID buttons to the Message form's Standard toolbar. After doing so, you can readily see whether your digital signature and encryption are turned on or off, and also enable and disable those options.

Note

If you're using Word as your message editor, you can't customize the toolbar in the manner described in this section.

To add Digital ID buttons to the Message form's Standard toolbar with the native Outlook editor in use:

1. With the Inbox Information viewer displayed, click New in the Standard toolbar to display the Message form.

2. Select View, move the pointer onto Toolbars, and click Customize. Select the Commands tab, scroll down the Categories box, and select Standard, as shown in Figure 32.10.

Figure 32.10
The Commands box contains a list of commands in the Standard category.

3. Scroll down to the bottom of the list of commands.

4. Drag the Encrypt Message Contents and Attachments command and the Digitally Sign Message command into the Message form's Standard toolbar.

5. Click Close to close the Customize dialog box. The Message form's Standard toolbar now contains the two added buttons, as shown in Figure 32.11.

Encrypt message contents and attachments

Digitally sign message

Figure 32.11
This is the Message form's Standard toolbar with the two Digital ID buttons added and with the Encryption button disabled and the Digitally Sign Message button enabled.

When encryption and digital signing are turned off, the two buttons have normal gray backgrounds. The buttons have bright backgrounds when those options are enabled. Click a button to change from disabled to enabled and vice versa.

SENDING AND RECEIVING DIGITALLY SIGNED MESSAGES

You can set up Outlook so that the default is to send all your messages with a digital signature, or so the default is to send all your messages without a digital signature. Whichever you choose as the default, you can turn the digital signature off or on for each message.

CHOOSING DIGITAL SIGNATURES AS THE DEFAULT

If you expect to digitally sign most of the messages you send, you should set this as a default.

With any Outlook Information viewer displayed, select Tools, Options to display the Options dialog box. Select the Security tab previously shown in Figure 32.6, and check Add Digital Signature to Outgoing Messages. If you want people who use e-mail applications that don't support S/MIME signatures to be able to read your messages, check Send Clear Text Signed Messages.

Note

If you leave the Send Clear Text Signed Messages unchecked, only recipients who use an e-mail application that supports S/MIME signatures will be able to read your messages. Those people will also be able to verify that the message actually came from you and has not been tampered with.

If you check the Send Clear Text Signed Messages box, all recipients (whether they use an application that supports S/MIME or not) will be able to read your messages. Recipients who don't use an application that supports S/MIME won't be able to verify that the message actually came from you, nor can they be certain the message hasn't been tampered with.

EXAMINING AND CHANGING SECURITY SETTINGS

Your Digital ID has certain security settings. You can examine and change these settings by clicking Settings (in the Security tab of the Options dialog box) to display the dialog box shown in Figure 32.12.

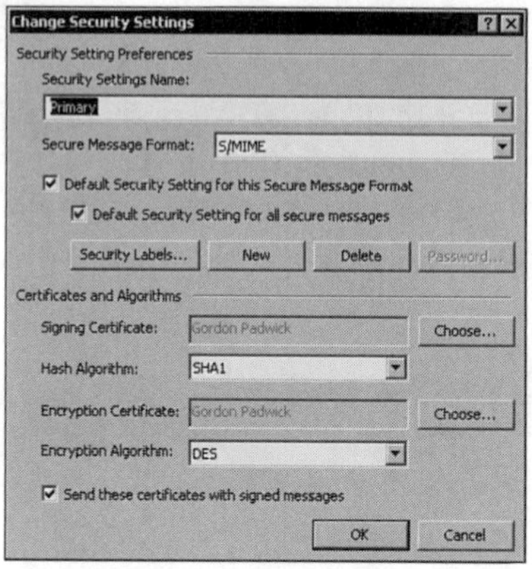

Figure 32.12
You can use this dialog box to change your security settings and create new settings.

You can change the Digital ID settings as follows:

- To change the default name of your security settings, edit the name in the Security Settings Name box.
- Open the Secure Message Format drop-down list and select S/MIME if you will use the current settings for Internet or intranet e-mail. If you're using Outlook as a client for an Exchange server and will be using that messaging system, open the drop-down Secure Message Format list and select Exchange Server Security.
- Check or uncheck Default Security Setting for This Secure Message Format.
- Click Security Labels if you want to set and configure security label settings.
- Leave Default Security Setting for All Secure Messages checked to make the current security settings the default if you use Exchange and S/MIME.
- If you want to create another security setting, click New. Outlook removes the name in the Security Settings Name box. Enter a name for the new setting in that box and select a Secure Message Format.
- If you want to delete a security setting, select that setting and click Delete.
- By default, the Signing Certificate box contains the name of your Digital ID. If you have more than one Digital ID, click Choose to open the Select a Certificate dialog box, in which you can select the certificate you want to use for signing messages in the current set of security settings.
- Leave the Hash Algorithm as the default SHA-1 unless you have a specific reason for changing it. If that's the case, open the drop-down list and select a different algorithm.

- By default, the Encryption Certificate box contains the name of your Digital ID. If you have more than one Digital ID, click Choose to open the Select a Certificate dialog box, in which you can select the certificate you want to use for encrypting messages in the current security settings.

- Leave the Encryption Algorithm as the default DES unless you have a specific reason for changing it. If that's the case, open the drop-down list and select a different algorithm.

- If you want to send your public key with messages, check the Send These Certificates with Signed Messages box. You should check this box if you want people to whom you send messages to be able to send you encrypted messages. This box is not available if you select Exchange Server Security as the Secure Message Format.

CREATING NEW SECURITY SETTINGS

The preceding section assumed you needed just one set of security settings. You can have more than one set.

Starting from the Security tab in the Options dialog box, click Settings to display the Change Security Settings dialog box shown previously in Figure 32.12. In that dialog box, click New to clear all the boxes. You can now name and select security settings for another set.

When you have two or more named sets of security settings, you can open the drop-down Security Settings Name list to select the set you want to use.

DELETING A SET OF SECURITY SETTINGS

To delete a set of security settings, select that set and then click Delete.

SENDING A DIGITALLY SIGNED MESSAGE

When you send a digitally signed message, that message contains your digital signature. The message recipient who uses an e-mail program that supports S/MIME can examine that signature to verify the message actually came from you. This works because only a computer on which your Digital ID is installed can send a message that contains your digital signature.

A digitally signed message contains the original message and an encrypted version of that message. When the message is received by a computer on which the e-mail program supports S/MIME, the original message and encrypted message are compared to ensure they are identical. Any difference between the two indicates that someone has tampered with the message.

After you've set the default to send messages with a digital signature, create a message to be sent in the normal way. If you're using the Outlook native editor and have added Digital ID buttons to the Message form's toolbar, you can click the Digitally Sign Message button to turn digital signing on or off, as shown previously in Figure 32.11.

→ For information about creating Digital ID buttons in the Message form's toolbar, **see** "Adding Digital ID Buttons to the Message Form's Toolbar," **p. 711.**

If you're using Word as your e-mail editor (or if you're using the native editor and haven't added Digital ID buttons to the Message form's toolbar), click Options to display the Message Options dialog box; then click Security Settings to display the dialog box shown in Figure 32.13. Make sure Add Digital Signature to This Message either is checked, if you want to add a Digital ID to the current message, or is unchecked, if you don't want the current message to have a Digital ID.

Figure 32.13
The two check boxes near the top of this dialog box initially show you default settings.

PART
VII
CH
32

Note

If you use the Rich Text format to create a message and send that message as a secure message using your S/MIME digital signature, Outlook automatically changes the message format to HTML to ensure the correct processing of your digital signature. As a result, some of the message formatting might be lost. The format change occurs when you click Send in the Message form.

Messages you create in Plain Text format are sent in Plain Text format. Messages you create in HTML format are sent in HTML format.

After you've sent a digitally signed message, you can see that message in your Sent Items folder. It is identified as a message that was sent with a digital signature by the red ribbon on the message symbol. Also, if you open the sent message in a Message form, the header contains the red ribbon.

RECEIVING DIGITALLY SIGNED MESSAGES

Some of the people to whom you send digitally signed messages might be using an e-mail program that supports S/MIME; others might not. Three possibilities exist:

- A recipient uses an e-mail application that supports S/MIME.
- A recipient uses an e-mail application that doesn't support S/MIME and you haven't checked Send Clear Text Signed Message in the Security tab of the Options dialog box.
- A recipient uses an e-mail application that doesn't support S/MIME and you have checked Send Clear Text Signed Message in the Security tab of the Options dialog box.

→ For information about the Send Clear Text Signed Message option, **see** "Choosing Digital Signatures As the Default," **p. 712**.

RECEIVING A DIGITALLY SIGNED MESSAGE ON A COMPUTER THAT SUPPORTS S/MIME

The Inbox Information viewer initially displays the header for a secure message with a red ribbon superimposed on the message symbol. When you select the message header, the Preview pane's header contains a red ribbon near its right edge.

You can double-click the message to display it in the Message form, as shown in Figure 32.14.

Figure 32.14
The ribbon (red on your screen) at the right side of the message header indicates the message is secure.

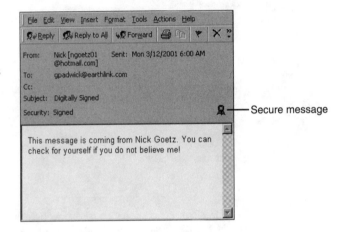

Secure message

If you want to verify the identity of the sender, follow these steps:

1. With the received message displayed in a Message form, select File, Properties to display the Security Properties dialog box. Select the Security tab shown in Figure 32.15.

Note
All five items in this dialog box should be checked if the message is fully authenticated.

2. To obtain more information about the sender, click View Signing Certificate to display the View Certificate dialog box, in which you can examine information about the sender's Digital ID.

Tip from

As an alternative to those two steps, you can click the red ribbon in the Message form's header to display a dialog box that's similar to the one shown in Figure 32.14.

Figure 32.15
This dialog box confirms, or does not confirm, the authenticity of the message.

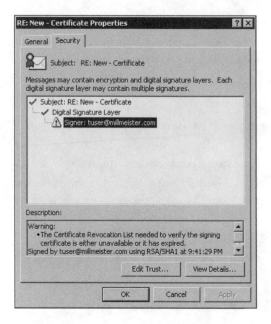

RECEIVING A DIGITALLY SIGNED MESSAGE ON A COMPUTER THAT DOES NOT SUPPORT S/MIME

Two possibilities exist, depending on how the sender set up Outlook, to send digitally signed messages:

- If the sender chose to send the message with Send Clear Text Signed Messages not enabled, recipients who use an e-mail program that does not support S/MIME to receive messages are not able to read digitally signed messages.

- If the sender chose to send the message with Send Clear Text Signed Messages enabled, recipients who use an e-mail program that does not support S/MIME are able to read digitally signed messages but are not able to verify the authenticity of those messages.

→ For information about setting up Outlook with Send Clear Text Signed Messages enabled, **see** "Choosing Digital Signatures As the Default," **p. 712**.

SENDING AND RECEIVING ENCRYPTED MESSAGES

Sending an encrypted message is similar to sending a secure message. However, you must have a person's public key in your Contacts folder to send an encrypted message to that person. This is because the encryption is based on information in the recipient's Digital ID.

GETTING PUBLIC KEYS

You must have a person's public key to send a secure message. For example, if you want to send an encrypted message to John Aldrich, you must have John Aldrich's public key and add that key to the John Aldrich item in your Contacts folder. The following paragraphs explain how you obtain the public key and add that key to a Contact item.

PART

VII

CH

32

GETTING A PUBLIC KEY FROM ANOTHER PERSON

The easiest way to get another person's public key is to ask that person to send you a message that includes his public key. When you receive that message, proceed as follows.

To add a public key to an existing Contact item or create a new Contact item that contains a public key:

1. Double-click the message that contains the sender's public key to display that message in a Message form.
2. Right-click the sender's name in the Message form to display a context menu.
3. Click Add to Contacts to display a Contact form that shows the sender's name and e-mail address. Select the Certificates tab shown in Figure 32.16.

Figure 32.16
The Certificates tab contains the name of the sender's Digital ID.

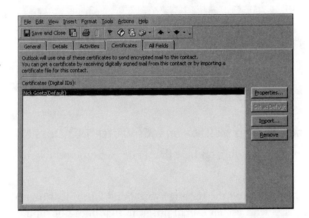

4. Click Save and Close to save the Contact item that contains the sender's public key. If a Contact item for the sender already exists, Outlook displays the Duplicate Contact Detected dialog box, in which you can select whether you want to create a new Contact item or update the existing item by adding the certificate to it.

After following these steps, you have the sender's public key, which you can use to send encrypted messages to that person.

DOWNLOADING A PUBLIC KEY

You can obtain public keys from the VeriSign Web page, `https://digitalid.verisign.com/services/client/index.html`, shown in Figure 32.17.

To download someone's public key:

1. Enter the person's e-mail address in the first box.
2. Click Valid—only valid public keys are of any use to you.
3. Click Search (not shown in the figure). After several seconds, the name of the person you're searching for is displayed together with details of that person's Digital ID.

4. Click the person's name to display a page that contains detailed information. Scroll to the bottom of that page and click Download. The page shown in Figure 32.18 is displayed.

Figure 32.17
Use this page to specify the e-mail address of the person whose public key you need.

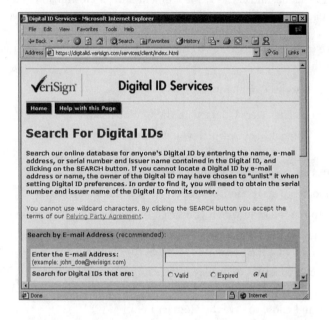

Figure 32.18
Be sure to select the format you need before downloading the public key.

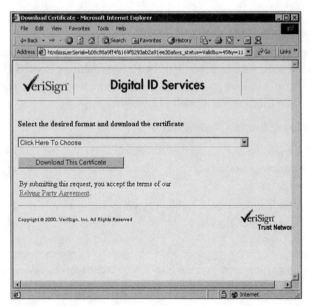

5. Open the Click Here to Choose drop-down list and select Someone Else's Digital ID for Microsoft IE (4.0 or Later)/Outlook Express/Outlook.

PART
VII
CH
32

6. Click Download This Certificate. The File Download dialog box proposes to Save This File to Disk, which is what you want to do. Click OK to open the Save As dialog box.

7. Navigate to the folder in which you want to save the public key, change the file name to the contact's name, and click OK. A moment later, a Download Complete message appears. Click OK.

Now you have to add the public key to the item in your Contacts folder that contains information about the person.

To add a public key to a Contact item:

1. Open Outlook and select Contacts in the Outlook Bar.

2. Locate the Contact item to which you want to add a public key.

3. Double-click the Contact item to open the item in a Contact form. Select the Certificates tab previously shown in Figure 32.16.

4. Click Import to display the Locate Security Profile dialog box.

5. Navigate to the folder in which you saved the public key you previously downloaded.

6. Select the public key for the contact and click Open. The public key is now listed in the Certificates (Digital IDs) box and the Properties button becomes available.

7. You can click Properties to display information about the public key. This step is not required.

8. Click Save and Close to save the Contact item.

IMPORTING PUBLIC KEYS FROM OUTLOOK EXPRESS

If, prior to using Outlook, you've been using Outlook Express to send secure messages, you have one or more public keys in your Outlook Express Address Book. When you import that address book into Outlook, public keys are not imported with the rest of the contact information. You must import each public key separately.

To export a public key from Outlook Express:

1. In Outlook Express, select Tools, Address Book to display the Outlook Express Address Book, which lists your contacts. Those whose public keys you already have are marked with red ribbons.

2. Double-click the contact whose public key you want to export to display that contact's properties. Select the Digital IDs tab.

Tip from

Gordon Padwick

If you have more than one entry in your Outlook Express Address Book for a contact, be sure you select the one that contains the contact's public key.

---

3. Select the public key you want to export; then click Export.

4. Enter the full path name for the file in which you want to save the exported public key; then click Save. Outlook Express saves the file.

Note

Outlook Express automatically provides the file name extension .cer.

→ After you've exported a public key from Outlook Express, use the procedure described previously in this chapter to add that public key to the appropriate Outlook Contact item. **See** "Getting a Public Key from Another Person," **p. 718**.

CHANGING THE TRUST STATUS OF A PUBLIC KEY

When you import someone's public key into that person's contact item, that public key has a trust status associated with it. Ideally, you should be able to absolutely trust Digital IDs, but that isn't necessarily the case.

To trust a Digital ID, you must have complete confidence that

■ The Digital ID was properly issued. This means the issuing authority verified the identity of the person to whom the Digital ID was issued, never issues the same Digital ID to more than one person, and keeps Digital IDs completely confidential.

■ The person to whom the Digital ID was issued makes sure no one else can obtain a copy of that Digital ID.

When a Digital ID is issued by a trusted certifying authority, such as VeriSign, you can be sure that the Digital ID was properly issued. Only if the person to whom the Digital ID was issued installed it on a secure computer and, if a backup is made, that backup is kept in a secure place, can you be sure that the Digital ID can be trusted.

PART

VII

CH

32

Note

Individual people usually get their Digital IDs from a reliable certifying authority, such as VeriSign. However, you might come across Digital IDs issued by individuals or organizations you don't necessarily trust.

Three trust status levels are available:

■ **Inherit Trust from Issuer**—This, the default, provides the same trust status as the one associated with the organization or person who issued the person's Digital ID.

■ **Explicitly Trust This Certificate**—This trust status says you trust the source, irrespective of who issued the person's Digital ID.

■ **Explicitly Don't Trust This Certificate**—This trust status says you distrust the source, irrespective of who issued the person's Digital ID.

To examine or change the trust status of a public key after you've added it to a Contact item:

1. With the Contacts Information viewer displayed, double-click the contact to display it in a Contact form. Select the Certificates tab previously shown in Figure 32.16, but this time with one or more certificates listed. Select the public key for which you want to examine or change the trust status.

2. Click Properties to display the Certificate Properties dialog box. Select the Trust tab, shown in Figure 32.19.

Figure 32.19
This dialog box shows the Trust status of the Digital ID.

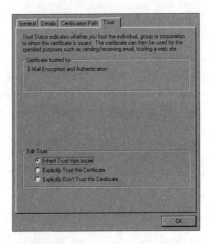

3. To change the trust status, click the appropriate option button in the Edit Trust section near the bottom of the dialog box.

SENDING AN ENCRYPTED MESSAGE

To send an encrypted message, create the message in the usual way. If you're using the native Outlook editor and have created Digital ID buttons in the Message form's toolbar, click the Encrypt Message Contents and Attachments button on the Standard toolbar, as shown previously in Figure 32.11; then send the message in the normal way.

→ For information about creating Digital ID buttons in the Message form's toolbar, **see** "Adding Digital ID Buttons to the Message Form's Toolbar," **p. 711**.

Note

You can also enable or disable encryption by checking or unchecking the Encrypt Message Contents and Attachments button in the Message Options dialog box. You must use this method if you're using Word as your editor, or if you're using the native editor and haven't created Digital ID buttons in the Message form's toolbar.

After you send an encrypted message, you can see that message in the Sent Items Information viewer. The message symbol is marked with the blue padlock to indicate it was sent as an encrypted message.

If you double-click the message to display it in a Message form, the form's header contains the blue padlock to indicate that the message was sent encrypted.

Receiving an Encrypted Message

When you receive an encrypted message, the message header appears in your Inbox Information viewer with a blue padlock symbol superimposed on the message icon. When you select the message header, the Preview pane doesn't display the message; instead, it states `Encrypted or encoded messages cannot be shown in the Preview Pane. Open the message to read it`. After you double-click the message header to display it in the Message form, a blue padlock symbol at the right side of the form's header indicates that the message was encrypted.

Note

Encrypted messages can be decrypted only if you're using e-mail software, such as Outlook, that supports S/MIME.

Using Security Zones

Incoming e-mail messages and Web pages you access can contain scripts that run on your computer. Although most of these scripts are useful, some can either accidentally or deliberately damage files on your hard disk. By taking advantage of security zones, you can control what happens when you receive messages or access Web pages that contain scripts. By choosing an appropriate zone for each Web page you access, you can prevent potentially damaging content from being downloaded or receive a warning before potentially damaging content is downloaded.

You can choose among four zones:

- **Local Intranet Zone**—For sites on a local intranet that you completely trust
- **Trusted Sites Zone**—For sites outside your local intranet that you completely trust
- **Internet Zone**—For most Web sites
- **Restricted Sites Zone**—For sites you don't trust

By default, each zone has a security level assigned to it, as listed in Table 32.1.

TABLE 32.1   DEFAULT SECURITY LEVELS FOR ZONES

Zone	Security Level
Local Intranet Zone	Medium
Trusted Sites Zone	Low

TABLE 32.1 CONTINUED	
Zone	**Security Level**
Internet Zone	Medium
Restricted Sites Zone	High

You can change the security level for any zone.

The effect of each security level is defined in Table 32.2.

TABLE 32.2 EFFECTS OF SECURITY LEVELS	
Level	**Effect**
High	All potentially damaging content is not downloaded to your computer.
Medium	Outlook warns you before running any potentially damaging content.
Low	Outlook accepts potentially damaging content without giving you any warning.
Custom	It's up to you to specify how Outlook handles potentially damaging content.

You're probably wondering exactly what type of potentially damaging content security levels are concerned with and exactly what zones do about potentially damaging content.

The message content and other activities that security levels detect are listed in these categories:

- ActiveX controls and plug-ins
- Cookies
- Downloads
- Java
- Miscellaneous
- Scripting
- User authentication

CHANGING THE SECURITY LEVEL FOR A ZONE

You can change the security level for each zone to other than the default. For example, you might have such complete confidence in your local intranet that you want to change its security level to Low.

To change the security level of a zone:

1. In the Options dialog box, select the Security tab, shown previously in Figure 32.6.
2. Click Zone Settings. Outlook displays a warning message about changing security settings. Click OK to display the dialog box shown in Figure 32.20.

Figure 32.20
This is the dialog box you use to work with security zones.

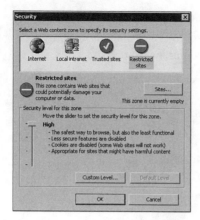

3. Select one of the four zones in the box at the top of the dialog box.

4. Move the slider at the left side of the box to set the security level for that zone.

5. To customize the security level, click Custom Level to display the dialog box shown in Figure 32.21.

Figure 32.21
This is the beginning of a list of available security settings.

6. Select Disable, Enable, or Prompt for each security setting. Alternatively, you can open the Reset To drop-down list and select a preset combination.

RESTORING A ZONE'S DEFAULT SECURITY LEVEL

To restore a zone's security level to the default, click Default Level.

ASSIGNING WEB SITES TO ZONES

When you first start using Outlook, no Web sites are assigned to any zones. By default, Outlook assumes the use of the Internet Zone, so you are warned before Outlook runs any potentially damaging content.

ASSIGNING SITES TO THE LOCAL INTRANET ZONE

You define what type of sites you want to assign to the Local Intranet Zone. You can also assign sites that are outside your local intranet to this zone.

To assign types of intranet sites and sites outside your intranet to this zone:

1. In the Security dialog box, select Local Intranet.
2. Click Sites to display the dialog box shown in Figure 32.22.

Figure 32.22
You can check any combination of the check boxes in this dialog box.

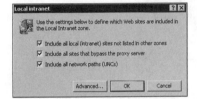

3. By default, all three check boxes are checked. Uncheck any that are inappropriate.
4. Click Advanced to display the dialog box shown in Figure 32.23.

Figure 32.23
Use this dialog box to assign specific Web sites to the zone.

5. Enter the complete URL of a site in the Add This Web Site to the Zone box, and then click Add. The URL you entered is added to the list of sites in the Web Sites box.
6. Repeat step 5 to add more URLs.
7. For added security, check the Require Server Verification (https:) for All Sites in This Zone. By doing that, Outlook will use the Local Intranet Zone for sites in the Web Sites box that are accessed by a secure server.

Note
To remove a site, select that site in the Web Sites box, and then click Remove.

ASSIGNING SITES TO THE TRUSTED SITES ZONE

You can assign any Web sites to the Trusted Sites Zone.

To assign sites to this zone:

1. In the Security dialog box, select Trusted Sites.
2. Click Sites to display the Trusted Sites Zone dialog box, which is similar to the one previously shown in Figure 32.23.
3. Enter a URL in the Add This Web Site to the Zone box, and then click Add. The site is added to the list in the Web Sites box.
4. For added security, you can check Require Server Verification (https:) for All Sites in This Zone. After you do so, Outlook will use the Trusted Sites Zone only for sites that are accessed by a secure server.

ASSIGNING SITES TO THE INTERNET ZONE

You can't add specific sites to the Internet Zone. Outlook automatically assigns sites that aren't assigned to another zone to the Internet Zone.

ASSIGNING SITES TO THE RESTRICTED SITES ZONE

Assign sites to the Restricted Sites Zone in the same way that you add sites to the Trusted Sites Zone, as previously described.

SECURITY IN EXCHANGE SERVER

The sections of this chapter that cover authenticated and encrypted messages focused on Internet messages. Most of that material also applies to messaging in the Exchange environment. Security is managed by key pairs (each user having a public and private key) in the same way it's managed for Internet messages.

In this case, though, instead of using an external source—such as VeriSign—for keys, keys are generated within the Exchange server. The Exchange administrator uses Key Management Server, a component of Exchange Server, to create and manage keys.

From a user's perspective, there's little difference between using authentication and encryption for Exchange and Internet messages. One key point to note, though, is that when using the Change Security Settings dialog box—previously shown in Figure 32.12—to specify security settings, you should open the drop-down Secure Message Format list and select Exchange Server Security.

For detailed information about administering and using security in an Exchange messaging environment, see *Special Edition Using Microsoft Exchange Server 5.5* or *Special Edition Using Microsoft Exchange Server 2000*, both published by Que.

PART

VII

CH

32

PROTECTING AGAINST VIRUSES

Unfortunately, some people are motivated to cause harm to computers. One of the ways they do this is to create viruses that can be hidden within attachments to e-mail messages. These viruses consist of macros, scripts, and other executable files that run when an attachment is opened. To protect your computer from the damage these macros can do, be very careful about opening attachments to messages.

Even if you receive a message from a source you trust, you can't be sure attachments to that message are free from viruses. That's because some of the sources you trust might unknowingly have viruses that automatically attach themselves to messages those sources send.

Here are some hints about how you can attempt to prevent viruses from infecting your computer:

- Install virus protection software on your computer and frequently (once a week or more often) update that software so that it detects the most recently introduced viruses. Run your virus protection program at least once a day.

- Instead of opening attachments to e-mail, save those attachments as files. Then use your virus protection program to examine each file. Open each file only after the virus protection program assures you that no viruses are present or, if it detects viruses, removes them.

Outlook provides some level of protection against viruses. You can activate this by selecting Tools, moving the pointer onto Macro, and then clicking Security to display the dialog box shown in Figure 32.24.

Figure 32.24
Text in this dialog box explains the three security levels.

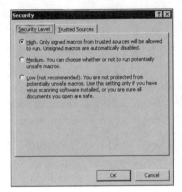

By default, Outlook uses Medium security. Although this does, indeed, provide you with a high level of protection against viruses, it might prevent you from opening attachments you need. It's up to you to select the level of security you need.

TROUBLESHOOTING

SECURITY

Take care to remember a password you assign to a Personal Folders file because, without the correct password, you won't have access to folders within the file. If you do forget a password, the only thing you can do is remove the Personal Folders file from the Folder List and then delete the corresponding Windows file. Subsequently, you can create a new Personal Folders file, but the Outlook items in the original file are permanently lost.

It's important to protect your computer from viruses, not only to protect your own computer, but also not to unwittingly become a source of sending viruses to other people. There's no perfect way to protect your computer from viruses, so you must adopt a compromise. At one extreme, you could refuse to allow anything to be copied to your hard drive, but that's not practical because you wouldn't have anything for your computer to use. At the other extreme, you could load or download whatever's available, but that virtually guarantees virus problems. Outlook offers some help in choosing which attachments you can open.

Outlook looks at message attachments and classifies them as Level 1 or Level 2:

- **Level 1**—Outlook blocks all executable attachments, such as those that have file name extensions such as .bat, .exe, .js, and .vbs. When you receive an attachment of this type, you'll see the paperclip icon to let you know the message has attachments, but you won't be able to open those attachments.

- **Level 2**— Outlooks detects suspicious attachments other than those in Level 1. When you receive an attachment of this type, you'll see the paperclip icon to let you know the message has attachments. You can double-click an attachment and then decide whether you want to save that attachment. After saving it, you can decide what you want to do with it. You should use your virus program to examine it for viruses before opening it.

PART VIII

APPENDIXES

INSTALLING AND MAINTAINING OUTLOOK 2002

In this appendix

SYSTEM REQUIREMENTS

To experience acceptable performance from Office XP, Microsoft recommends:

- An x86-compatible PC with a Pentium (or better) processor clocked at 166MHz or higher. Microsoft recommends at least a P5 90MHz processor.
- At least 32MB of RAM if you're running Outlook under Windows 98 or Windows Me and at least 64MB of RAM if you're running Outlook under Windows NT or Windows 2000. You might need more RAM if you want to use more than one Office application simultaneously.
- At least 350MB of free space on your hard drive. An extra 50MB of space is required for each additional language user interface.
- A CD-ROM drive (Office XP is not available on floppy disks) for local installation, or a network connection to a server for LAN-based installation.
- A video board and VGA color monitor capable of displaying at least 256 colors (Super VGA or better is recommended) at 800×600 pixel resolution.
- A Microsoft Mouse (or compatible) pointing device.
- A modem capable of communicating at 9600bps or more (at least 28.8Kbps is recommended) if you intend to use Outlook to send and receive messages by way of a phone line.
- Microsoft Windows 98, Windows NT 4 (with at least Service Pack 6a installed), Windows 2000, or Me. Office XP is not compatible with Windows 3.x, Windows NT 3.5x, or Windows 95.

You'll gain considerably better performance from Office XP if you have a computer that exceeds the recommended specifications. If you have a fast computer (a Pentium II that runs at 300MHz or faster, and has 128MB or more of RAM), you'll probably be very satisfied with the performance of Office XP.

Note If you intend to use the installation rollback features of Office XP, set aside at least another 100MB of disk space.

INSTALLING OFFICE XP

Outlook is usually installed with the rest of the Office XP components. You can, however, purchase Outlook 2002 separately and install it without the other Office XP components.

Note Unlike Outlook 98 and Outlook 2000, both of which were installed with one of three possible service options, Outlook 2002 has unified e-mail accounts and is installed in only one way. If you previously had Outlook 98 or Outlook 2000 installed on your computer, Outlook 2002 is automatically installed with the same e-mail accounts you previously used. If you install Outlook 2002 on a computer that didn't previously have a version of Outlook installed, the installation process gives you the opportunity to create e-mail accounts.

The procedure in the following steps describes what occurs if you haven't previously had Office installed on your computer.

The following procedure describes how to install Office XP, including Outlook, from a CD-ROM. Consult your network administrator if you want to install from a server.

Note

Prior to installing Office XP (or most other applications), make sure that no other programs are running. Especially make sure that any antivirus programs are disabled during the installation process.

To install Office XP:

1. Insert the Office XP CD-ROM into your CD-ROM drive. After a few seconds, a window similar to the one shown in Figure A.1 appears.

   If the window doesn't appear, choose Start in the Windows taskbar, move the pointer onto Settings, and choose Control Panel. In the Control Panel, choose Add/Remove Programs; then, with the Install/Uninstall tab selected, choose Install in Windows 98 or Windows Me, or Add New Programs in Windows 2000.

   Windows 98 or Windows Me displays the Install Program from Floppy Disk or CD-ROM window. Click Next, and then, in the Run Installation window, click Finish. After a few seconds, a window similar to the one shown in Figure A.1 is displayed.

   Windows 2000 displays a window in which you can choose to Add a Program from CD-ROM or Floppy Disk or Add Programs from Microsoft. Choose CD or Floppy to display a window in which you are told to insert the CD-ROM. Insert the CD-ROM and click Next to display the Run Installation Program window. Click Finish. After a few seconds, a window similar to the one shown in Figure A.1 is displayed.

APP

A

Note

You might see a message saying that your Windows installer has been updated and you must reboot your system. Click OK and then reboot your system.

Tip from

[signature]

You'll find the Product Key on your disc package. To discourage people from borrowing or stealing your discs, you should store the discs and the packages in separate places.

Figure A.1
To minimize the risk of software piracy, the Office installation procedure requires you to enter the Product Key before you can continue the installation process.

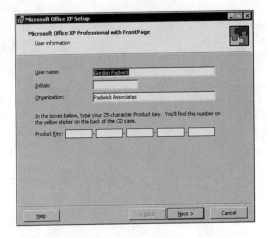

Some editions of Office XP are supplied with two Product Keys. To install Office in the normal manner, enter the Office Product Key.

2. If necessary, correct the information displayed in the User Name, Initials, and Organization boxes.

3. Enter the Product Key, and then click Next to display a window in which you can read the End-User License Agreement.

4. Read the end-user license agreement. If you agree to it, select I Accept the Terms in the License Agreement. Click Next to display the window shown in Figure A.2.

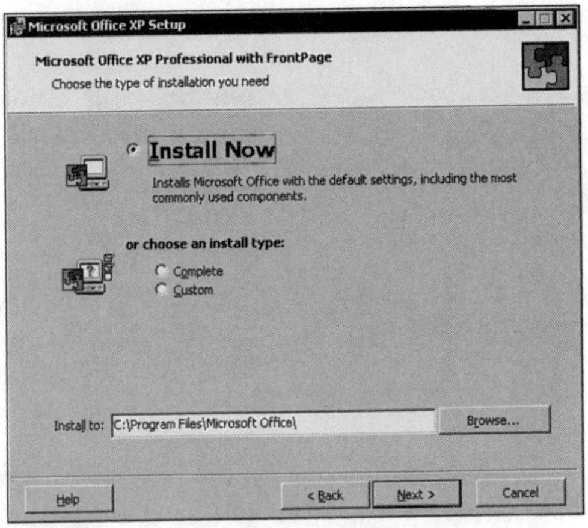

Figure A.2
Choose how you want to install Office XP.

5. At this stage, you have a choice: Install Now, which installs Office with the default settings and with commonly used components; Complete; or Custom. The first time you install Office XP, it's usually best to choose Install Now. Later, you can customize your Office XP installation. Choose Install Now and then click Next to display the window shown in Figure A.3.

Figure A.3
This window lists the Office XP applications available for installation.

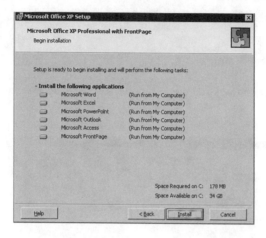

Note

All the applications available on your Office CD are listed. The applications listed depend on which edition of Office you're installing. The list you see might differ from that shown in Figure A.3. If, in step 5, you chose Install Now or Complete, you can't change which applications will be installed. However, if you chose Custom, a somewhat different window is displayed; you can use that window to select which of the Office applications will be installed.

APP

A

6. Click the Install button to initiate the installation process, which takes approximately 15–20 minutes. During that time, a progress bar and text let you know what is happening.

Note

If nothing seems to be happening for a minute or two, be patient. You'll probably see the screen flicker from time to time. Eventually, the installation process will get to the next step.

7. When the installation process is complete, an information box confirms that the installation is complete.

Notice that the installation process creates an Outlook shortcut icon on your Windows desktop.

RUNNING OUTLOOK 2002 FOR THE FIRST TIME

Double-click the Microsoft Outlook icon on the Windows desktop to start Outlook.

> **Note**
>
> The procedure described here is what happens the first time you run Outlook 2002 after you've installed it, if you have a previous version of Outlook installed on your computer. The procedure is slightly different if you've not had a previous version of Outlook installed.

The first time you start Outlook, the first Outlook 2002 Startup Wizard window shown in Figure A.4 appears.

Figure A.4
This is the first of a series of wizard windows that guide you through the process of configuring Outlook.

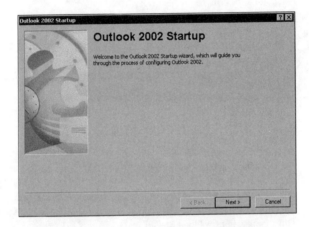

To configure Outlook:

1. With the first wizard window displayed, click Next to display the second wizard window, shown in Figure A.5.

Figure A.5
This screen gives you the opportunity to decide whether you want Outlook to be a client for an e-mail server.

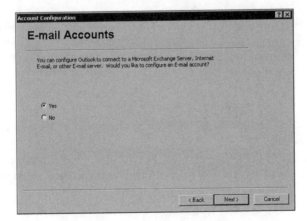

2. In all probability, you want to use Outlook for e-mail, so leave the default Yes selected. If you want to use Outlook only as a personal information manager, click No. Click Next to display the window shown in Figure A.6.

Figure A.6
This window, displayed only if you chose Yes in the previous window, lists the various types of e-mail servers for which Outlook can be a client.

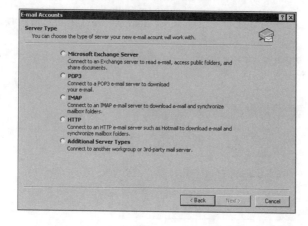

Note

POP3 is the protocol used by most Internet e-mail servers.

3. Select one of the types of e-mail servers for which you want Outlook to be a client. Click Next to display the window shown in Figure A.7.

Figure A.7
This is the window displayed if you chose to make Outlook a client for a POP3 e-mail server.

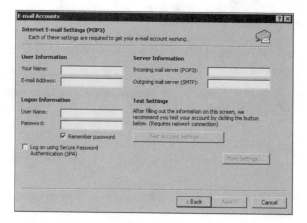

App

A

Note

If you chose a different type of e-mail server in step 3, you'll see a window that's different from that in Figure A.7.

4. Follow through the sequence of windows to set up the e-mail account. Detailed information about setting up e-mail accounts is given in various chapters of this book.

→ For information about setting up an Internet e-mail account, **see** "Creating a POP3 Account for Internet E-mail," **p. 49** and "Creating an IMAP Account for Internet E-mail," **p. 56**. For information about setting up an Exchange Server e-mail account, **see** "Setting Up Outlook As an Exchange Client," **p. 428**. For information about setting up Outlook as a client for Hotmail, **see** "Creating an HTTP Account for Hotmail," **p. 56**.

5. After you've finished setting up the e-mail account, Outlook displays the dialog box shown in Figure A.8.

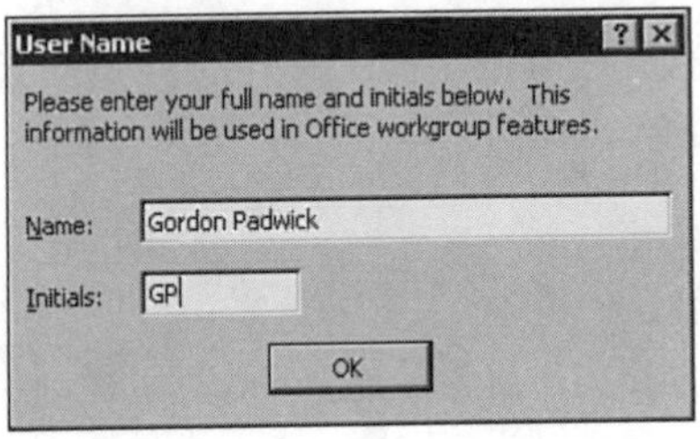

Figure A.8
Enter your name and initials in this dialog box for subsequent use by Office workgroup components.

The Startup Wizard leads you through the process of creating one account. You can subsequently create additional accounts.

→ For information about setting up accounts, **see** "Creating E-mail Accounts," **p. 47**.

INSTALLING ADD-INS

When you install Outlook, you have access to many communication and information capabilities. Outlook comes with additional capabilities (known as *add-ins*) that you can install. In addition to the add-ins supplied with Outlook, more add-ins (some are called *add-ons*) are available from Microsoft and other suppliers.

Most add-ins are installed by the method described in the following steps. However, some add-ins are installed from the Control Panel in the same way as Windows applications.

To install an add-in:

1. With any Outlook Information viewer displayed, choose Tools, Options. Select the Other tab.
2. Choose Advanced Options, and then choose Add-In Manager to display the dialog box shown in Figure A.9.

Note

The single add-in listed in this box is checked to indicate it's enabled for use. You can disable an installed add-in by unchecking it.

3. Click the Install button to display the dialog box shown in Figure A.10.

Figure A.9
This dialog box lists the add-ins already installed.

Figure A.10
This dialog box lists add-ins available for installation.

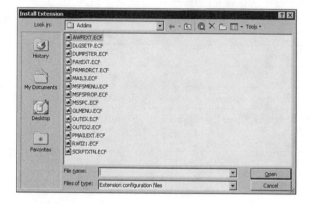

The dialog box shown in Figure A.10 lists the add-ins supplied with Outlook. If you want to install an add-in from another source, navigate to the folder that contains the add-in file.

APP
A

4. Select the add-in you want to install, and click Open to return to the Add-In Manager dialog box, in which the new add-in is listed and checked.

The dialog box shown in Figure A.10 lists available add-ins by file name. Table A.1 relates file names to the functions of add-ins.

TABLE A.1   ADD-IN FILE NAMES

Add-In	File Name
Delegate Access	Dlgsetp.ecf
Exchange Extensions Commands	Outex.ecf
Exchange Extensions Property Pages	Outex2.ecf
NetMeeting Extensions	Nmexchex.ecf
TeamStatus Form	Olmenu.ecf

TABLE A.1   CONTINUED

Add-In	File Name
Rules Wizard	Rwiz1.ecf
Mail 3.0 Extensions	Mail3.ecf
Deleted Item Recovery	Dumpster.ecf
Server Scripting	scrptxtn.ecf
Internet Mail	Minet.ecf
Net Folders	Fldpub.ecf
Fax Extension	Faxext.ecf
cc:Mail Menu Extension	Ccmxp.ecf
Microsoft Fax	Awfext.ecf
Microsoft Mail 3.x Menu Extensions	Msfsmenu.ecf
Microsoft Mail 3.x Property Sheet Extensions	Msfsprop.ecf
Schedule+	Msspc.ecf
Windows CE Support	Pmailext.ecf
Outlook Forms Redirector	Frmrdrct.ecf

Note

All these add-ins also were supplied with Outlook 2000. However, four add-ins supplied with Outlook 2000 are not available with Outlook 2002, namely

- Team Manager Support (Mtmolmnu.ecf)
- Digital Security (Etexch.ecf)
- The Microsoft Network (Msn.ecf)
- CompuServe E-mail (Cserve.ecf)

You can open add-in (.ecf) files with a standard text editor (such as Windows NotePad) to gather more information about them. Under no circumstances, though, should you modify them. Doing so can cause an add-in to function incorrectly (or not at all). Also, be aware that simply installing an add-in with the Add-in Manager does not necessarily add the functions of the add-in to Outlook. Many are dependent on other components (such as transports), without which they will not operate. An excellent example of this is Exchange add-ins, which must have the Exchange Server service installed and functioning. See Appendix D, "Outlook Resources," for information about sources of Outlook add-ins.

RESTORING OUTLOOK 2002 TO THE FIRST-RUN CONDITION

After you, or a user you're trying to help, have been using Outlook for a while and have modified it to suit your personal needs, you might want to restore it to what it was when you first installed it. One case of this is if you acquire a new computer and are generous enough to pass on your old computer to a new user; in that case, you probably want the new person to inherit a virgin Outlook, rather than your customized version.

You might think that you can simply uninstall Office and then reinstall it to get Outlook (as well as the other Office applications) back to its original state, but that doesn't work. The reason it doesn't work is that all Office applications save many of their setup conditions in the Windows registry. Although uninstalling Office removes the Office files, it doesn't restore the registry to the condition it was before Office was installed. After you uninstall Office and then reinstall it, the related registry keys are the same as they were before you performed the uninstall. The result is that the new Office installation (Outlook included) has most of the customizations you made before you installed.

So, what's the answer? Unfortunately, there's no simple solution. Microsoft has published some Knowledge Base articles that describe how to reset previous versions of Outlook to a first-run condition:

- Q171161 "Outlook 97: How to Reset Outlook to a First-Run Condition"
- Q181055 "Outlook 98: How to Reset Outlook to a First-Run Condition"
- Q197653 "Outlook 2000: How to Reset Outlook to a First-Run Condition"

Presumably, a similar Knowledge Base article will become available soon after Outlook 2002 is released.

→ To find out how to use the Microsoft Knowledge Base, **see** "Finding Information in the Microsoft Knowledge Base," **p. 781**.

APP

A

OUTLOOK'S FILES, FOLDERS, FIELDS, AND REGISTRY KEYS

In this appendix

WHERE OUTLOOK SAVES INFORMATION

Outlook saves configuration information and Outlook items in many places and files. The data you see in Outlook, such as e-mail, appointments, tasks, reminders, and so on, are saved in a Personal Folders file with a .PST extension. This file can have any name, but most often it has the same name as the Outlook profile you use. Some configuration and customization information is kept in separate files with specific file extensions, and some is kept in the Windows registry. This appendix provides details about where this information is stored.

Information also is available in the Office Resource Kit about all the files and registry keys that Outlook uses. This information is in the form of Excel workbook files.

OUTLOOK FILES

Outlook saves various kinds of information in files with standard file name extensions. Also, Outlook can import files from, and export files to, various applications, each of which have specific file name extensions. The files in which Outlook saves its configuration and customization data are listed in Table B.1. Many of the other file name extensions you might encounter while working with Outlook are listed in Table B.2.

TABLE B.1   OUTLOOK CONFIGURATION AND CUSTOMIZATION FILES

File	Outlook Information
Adult Content Senders.txt	Additions to the Adult Content Senders rule
Exception List.txt	Exceptions to the Junk Senders rule
Extend.dat	List of Outlook extensions and add-ins
Frmcache.dat	Forms cache
Junk Senders.txt	Additions to the Junk Senders rule
<profile name>.fav	Outlook Bar shortcuts
<profile name>.nick	Names for the Automatic Name Check feature
Outcmd.dat	Customizations to menus and toolbars
OutlPrnt	Print settings
VbaProject.OTM	Macro and VBA code
Views.dat	Some of the information on custom views
Outlbar.inf	Setup file for the Outlook Bar structure

Note

In Table B.1, <profile name> signifies the name of your Outlook Profile.

TABLE B.2   OUTLOOK FILE NAME EXTENSIONS

Extension	Information Contained
.cal	Schedule+ 1.0 files
.cfg	Form setup files
.chm	Help file
.csv	Comma-separated values files (Windows)
.dat	Menu and view settings
.dbf	ACT!, FoxPro, and dBASE files
.dic	Spelling dictionary files
.dll	Application extensions
.doc	Word files
.ecf	Extension configuration files
.eco	ECCO files
.exe	Executable files
.fav	Outlook Bar shortcuts
.fdm	Form message files
.htm	HTML files
.html	HTML and stationery files
.ics	iCalendar files
.inf	Profile settings
.mdb	Access files
.msg	Messages dragged onto the Windows desktop
.nick	Nicknames
.ocx	ActiveX controls
.oft	Outlook templates
.org, .or2	Lotus Organizer files
.oss	Saved searches
.ost	Offline storage files
.pab	Personal address book
.pag	Saved toolbox page
.pst	Personal folder and AutoArchive files
.rhc	Remote mail header file
.rtf	Document saved in rich text format
.sc2	Schedule+ interchange files

APP

B

TABLE B.2 CONTINUED	
Extension	**Information Contained**
.scd	Schedule+ 7x files
.srs	Send/receive settings
.stf	Setup Table files
.txt	Tab-separated values files, comma-separated values files (DOS), and text files
.vcf	vCard files
.vcs	vCalendar files
.vfb	Free/busy files
.wab	Windows Address Book
.xls	Excel files
.xnk	Folder shortcuts

OUTLOOK FOLDERS

Outlook saves items in various folders within a Personal Folders file or an Exchange store. Some customization information, such as the information for customized views, is also saved in the same files. The standard folders are listed in Table B.3.

TABLE B.3 STANDARD OUTLOOK FOLDERS	
Folder Name	**Items Contained**
Calendar	Appointments, events, and meetings.
Contacts	Information about people and organizations.
Deleted Items	Items deleted from other folders.
Inbox	Messages received from a mail or fax server.
Journal	Activities saved in the Journal.
Junk E-mail	This folder is created if the Junk E-mail or Adult Content Rules are enabled.
Notes	Notes.
Outbox	Messages waiting to be sent.
Sent Items	Items sent to a mail or fax server.
Tasks	Tasks created, assigned to others, and received as assignments.

OUTLOOK FIELDS

Outlook maintains a database that contains various tables of information. Each table contains many fields that have the data you see in the various Outlook forms. Some fields are used in only one table, whereas others are used in more than one table. Table B.4 lists all the data fields available in Outlook.

Tip from

You can create an unlimited number of custom fields in addition to the standard fields listed here.

TABLE B.4 OUTLOOK DATA FIELDS

Field Name	Data Type	Write	Notes	Calendar	Contact	Journal	Mail	Note	Post	Task	Document
% Complete	Number	N	Percentage of task completed.							X	
Abstract	Text	Y	Document abstract.								X
Account	Text	Y	Description of account.		X						
Actual Work	Duration	Y	Time spent on task. Saved in minutes.							X	
Address Selected	Text	N	Displayed address.		X						
Address Selector	Internal	Y	Current address name.		X						
All Day Event	Yes/No	Y	If set to Yes, the Duration field is set to 1440 minutes.	X							
Anniversary	Date/Time	Y	When this field has a value, a Calendar item is attached to a Contact, and the Attachment field is set to Yes.		X						
Assigned	Internal	N	0 - not assigned 1 - assigned by me 2 - assigned to me							X	
Assistant's Name	Text	Y	Name of assistant.		X						
Assistant's Phone	Text	Y	Phone number of assistant.		X						
Attachment	Internal	N	For Contact: Yes when Birthday or Anniversary date is provided. Otherwise No.	X	X	X	X		X	X	
Author	Text	N	Original document author.								X

Field Name	Data Type	Write	Notes	Calendar	Contact	Journal	Mail	Note	Post	Task	Document
Auto Forwarded	Yes/No	N	Yes if item received as result of autoforwarding. Otherwise No.	X			X				
BCC	Internal	N	Names of blind copy recipients.				X				
Billing Information	Text	Y	Information about person or organization to be billed.	X	X	X	X		X	X	
Birthday	Date/Time	Y	For Contact, when a birthday date is provided, a Calendar item is attached to the Contact and the Attachment field is set to Yes.		X						
Business Address	Text	N	Complete business address. Combination of individual business address fields.		X						
Business Address City	Text	Y	Business address city.	X	X						
Business Address Country	Text	Y	Business address country.		X						
Business Address PO Box	Text	Y	Business address post office box.		X						
Business Address Postal Code	Text	Y	Business address postal code.		X						
Business Address State	Text	Y	Business address state.		X						
Business Address Street	Text	Y	Business address street address.		X						

TABLE B.4 CONTINUED

Field Name	Data Type	Write	Notes	Calendar	Contact	Journal	Mail	Note	Post	Task	Document
Business Fax	Text	Y	Business fax number.		X						
Business Home Page	Text	Y	Business URL.		X						
Business Phone	Text	Y	Business first phone number.		X						
Business Phone 2	Text	Y	Business second phone number.		X						
Bytes	Number	N	Document size.								X
Callback	Text	Y	Callback phone number.		X						
Car Phone	Text	Y	Contact's car phone number.		X						
Categories	Keywords	Y	Multiple categories are separated by commas.	X	X	X	X	X	X	X	X
Category	Text	N	Document category.								X
CC	Internal	N	Names of copy recipients.				X				
Changed By	Text	N					X				
Characters	Integer	N	Characters in document.								X
Check Address	Internal	N			X						
Check In Time	Date/Time	N									X
Check Name	Internal	N			X						
Children	Keywords	Y	Names of children.		X						
City	Text	Y	Home city name.		X						
Color	Internal	Y	0 - Blue 1 - Green 2 - Pink 3 - Yellow 4 - White					X			

Field Name	Data Type	Write	Notes	Calendar	Contact	Journal	Mail	Note	Post	Task	Document
Comment	Text	Y									X
Comments	Text	N	Document comments.								X
Company	Text	Y	Company or organization name.		X	X				X	
Company	Keywords	N	Company or organization name.								X
Company and Full Name	Text	Y			X						
Company Main Phone	Text	Y	Company or organization main phone number.		X						
Complete	Yes/No	Y	Whether task is complete.							X	
Computer Network Name	Text	Y	Name of computer network.		X						
Contact	Keywords	N				X					
Contact	Keywords	Y								X	
Contacts	Internal	N	Contacts' names.	X	X	X	X	X		X	
Content Class	Text	N	Type of item.	X	X	X	X	X	X	X	X
Content Language	Text	N									
Content Length	Integer	N									
Content Type	Text	N									X
Conversation	Text	N	Value of the Subject field in the first message of conversation.	X			X		X	X	
Country/Region	Text	Y	Home country.		X						

TABLE B.4   CONTINUED

Field Name	Data Type	Write	Notes	Calendar	Contact	Journal	Mail	Note	Post	Task	Document
Created	Date/Time	N	Date and time item was created.	X	X	X	X	X	X	X	
Creation Time	Date/Time	N	Date and time document created.								X
Customer ID	Text	Y	Customer identification.		X						
Date Completed	Date/Time	Y	Date and time task completed.							X	
Defer Until	Date/Time	Y	Date and time message to be delivered.				X		X		
Delete After Submit	Yes/No	N	Whether copy of task request should be kept.				X			X	
Department	Text	Y	Department name.		X						
Directory Server	Text	Y	Name of directory server.	X							
Distribution List Name	Text	N	Name of distribution list.		X						
Do Not AutoArchive	Yes/No	Y	Whether to AutoArchive item.	X		X	X	X	X	X	
Document Posted	Date/Time	N									X
Document Printed	Date/Time	N									X
Document Routed	Date/Time	N									X
Document Saved	Date/Time	N									X
Document Subject	Test	N	Subject of document.								X

Field Name	Data Type	Write	Notes	Calendar	Contact	Journal	Mail	Note	Post	Task	Document
Due By	Date/Time	N	Date and time action associated with a message flag is to be completed. When this field has a value, the Flag Status field is set to 2.	X			X				
Due Date	Date/Time	Y	Date and time task is due.							X	
Duration	Duration	N	Minutes. 1440 for All Day Events. Otherwise, the difference between the End Time and the Start Time.	X		X					
E-mail	Text	Y	First e-mail address.		X						
E-mail 2	Text	Y	Second e-mail address.		X						
E-mail 3	Text	Y	Third e-mail address.		X						
E-mail Account	Text	Y					X				
E-mail Display As	Text	N	Displayed name for first e-mail address.		X						
E-mail Original Display Name	Text	N	Actual first e-mail address.		X						
E-mail Selected	Text	N	Displayed e-mail address.		X						
E-mail Selector	Internal	Y	Name of selected e-mail address: E-mail, E-mail 2, or E-mail 3.		X						
E-mail 2 Display As	Text	N	Displayed name for second e-mail address.		X						
E-mail 2 Original Display Name	Text	N	Actual second e-mail address.		X						

APP

B

TABLE B.4 CONTINUED

Field Name	Data Type	Write	Notes	Calendar	Contact	Journal	Mail	Note	Post	Task	Document
E-mail 3 Display As	Text	N	Displayed name for third e-mail address.		X						X
E-mail 3 Original Display Name	Text	N	Actual third e-mail address.		X						
Edit Time	Number	N	Minutes spent editing document.								X
End	Date/Time	Y	End date and time.	X		X					
Entry Type	Text	N	Type of entry for Journal item (selected from list).			X					
Etag	Text	N									X
Event Address	Text	Y		X							
Expires	Date/Time	Y	Date and time message expires.				X		X		
File As	Text	N	Name under which Contact item is filed.		X						
First Name	Text	Y	Contact's first name.		X						
Flag Status	Internal	Y	0 - Normal 1 - Completed 2 - Flagged		X		X				
Follow Up Flag	Text	Y	Follow-up text.		X		X				
FTP Site	Text	Y	FTP site name.		X						
From	Internal	N	Message sender.				X		X		
Full Name	Text	Y	Title, first name, second name, last name, and suffix.		X						

Field Name	Data Type	Write	Notes	Calendar	Contact	Journal	Mail	Note	Post	Task	Document
Full Name and Company	Text	N			X						
Gender	Internal	Y	0 - Unspecified 1 - Female 2 - Male		X						
Government ID Number	Text	Y	Government identification.		X						
Have Replies Sent To	Internal	N	Signifies replies are to be sent to someone other than the sender.				X				
Header Status	Internal	N					X		X		
Hidden	Yes/No	Y									X
Hidden Slides	Integer	N	Hidden PowerPoint slides.								X
Hobbies	Text	Y	Hobbies and interests.		X						
Home Address	Text	N	Complete home address. Combination of individual home address fields.		X						
Home Address City	Text	Y	Home address city.		X						
Home Address Country	Text	Y	Home address country.		X						
Home Address PO Box	Text	Y	Home address post office box.		X						
Home Address Postal Code	Text	Y	Home address postal code.		X						

TABLE B.4 CONTINUED

Field Name	Data Type	Write	Notes	Calendar	Contact	Journal	Mail	Note	Post	Task	Document
Home Address State	Text	Y	Home address state.		X						
Home Address Street	Text	Y	Home address street address.		X						
Home Fax	Text	Y	Home fax number.		X						
Home Phone	Text	Y	Home phone number.		X						
Home Phone 2	Text	Y	Second home phone number.		X						
Icon	Internal	N	Icon exists.	X	X	X	X	X	X	X	
ID	Text	N									X
IM Address	Text	Y	Instant messaging address.		X						
Importance	Internal	Y	0 - Low Importance 1 - Normal Importance 2 - High Importance	X			X		X		
In Folder	Text	N	Name of folder that contains item.	X	X	X	X	X	X	X	
Initials	Text	N	Contact's initials.		X						
Internet Free/ Busy Address	Text	Y			X						
ISDN	Text	Y	ISDN phone number.		X						
Job Title	Text	Y	Job title.		X						
Journal	Yes/No	Y	Whether contact activities are to be journaled.		X						
Junk E-mail Type	Internal	Y					X				
Keywords	Keywords	N	Document keywords.				X				X

Field Name	Data Type	Write	Notes	Calendar	Contact	Journal	Mail	Note	Post	Task	Document
Label	Internal	Y		X							
Language	Text	Y	Contact's language.		X						
Last Author	Text	N	Most recent editor.								X
Last Name	Text	Y	Contact's last name.		X						
Last Name and First Name	Text	N	Contact's last name and first name.		X						
Last Saved Time	Date/Time	N	Date and time document most recently saved.								X
Lines	Number	N	Lines in document.								X
Location	Text	Y	Contact's location.	X	X						
Lock Discussion	Text	N									X
Mailing Address	Integer	N	Identifies mailing address: Home (1), Business (2), or Other (3).		X						
Mailing Address Indicator	Yes/No	Y	Whether mailing address is set.		X						
Manager	Text	N	Document manager's name.								X
Manager's Name	Text	Y	Manager's name.		X						
Meeting Status	Internal	Y	0 - None 1 - Meeting organizer 2 - Tentatively accepted 3 - Accepted 4 - Declined 5 - Not yet accepted	X							
Message	Internal	N	Text of message.				X		X		
Message Class	Text	N	See list of message classes.	X	X	X	X	X	X	X	

APP

B

TABLE B.4 CONTINUED

Field Name	Data Type	Write	Notes	Calendar	Contact	Journal	Mail	Note	Post	Task	Document
Message Flag	Text	Y	Action associated with message flag. When an action exists, the Flag Status field is set to 2.				X				
Middle Name	Text	Y	Middle name.		X						
Mileage	Text	Y	Mileage information.	X	X	X	X		X	X	
Mobile Phone	Text	Y	Mobile phone number.		X						
Modified	Date/Time	N	Last time item modified.	X	X	X	X	X	X	X	
Multimedia Clips	Text	N	File names of multimedia clips.								X
NetMeeting AutoStart	Yes/No	Y	Whether NetMeeting should start automatically at reminder time.	X							
NetMeeting Office Document Path	Text	Y		X							
NetMeeting Organizer E-mail	Text	Y		X							
Nickname	Text	Y	Contact's nickname.		X						
Notes	Internal	N	Text in notes box.	X	X	X				X	X
Office Location	Text	Y	Contact's office location.		X						
Online Meeting	Yes/No	Y		X							
Online Meeting Type	Integer	N	NetMeeting (0), Windows Media Services (1), or Exchange Conferencing (2).	X							

Field Name	Data Type	Write	Notes	Calendar	Contact	Journal	Mail	Note	Post	Task	Document
Optional Attendees	Text	N	Names of optional attendees at meeting or appointment (each name separated from next by a semicolon).	X							
Organizational ID Number	Text	Y	Contact's organization ID number.		X						
Organizer	Text	N	Organizer of meeting or appointment.	X							
Originator Delivery Requested	Yes/No	N					X				
Other Address	Text	N	Complete Other address. Combination of individual Other address fields.		X						
Other Address City	Text	Y	Other address city.		X						
Other Address Country	Text	Y	Other address country.		X						
Other Address PO Box	Text	Y	Other address post office box.		X						
Other Address Postal Code	Text	Y	Other address postal code.		X						
Other Address State	Text	Y	Other address state.		X						
Other Address Street	Text	Y	Other address street address.		X						
Other Fax	Text	Y	Other fax number.		X						

TABLE B.4   CONTINUED

Field Name	Data Type	Write	Notes	Calendar	Contact	Journal	Mail	Note	Post	Task	Document
Other Phone	Text	Y	Other first phone number.		X						
Outlook Internal Version	Integer	N	For administrative use only.	X	X	X	X	X	X	X	
Outlook Version	Text	N	Outlook version in which item created.	X	X	X	X	X	X	X	
Owner	Text	Y	Task owner's name.							X	
Pager	Text	Y	Pager phone number.		X						
Pages	Integer	N	Number of document pages.								X
Paragraphs	Integer	N	Number of document paragraphs.								X
Percent Complete	Number	N								X	
Personal Home Page	Text	Y	Contact's personal URL.		X						
Phone 1 Selected	Text	Y	First phone number.		X						
Phone 1 Selector	Internal	N	First phone number name.		X						
Phone 2 Selected	Text	Y	Second phone number.		X						
Phone 2 Selector	Internal	N	Second phone number name.		X						
Phone 3 Selected	Text	Y	Third phone number.		X						
Phone 3 Selector	Internal	N	Third phone number name.		X						
Phone 4 Selected	Text	Y	Fourth phone number.		X						
Phone 4 Selector	Internal	N	Fourth phone number name.		X						
Phone 5 Selected	Text	Y	Fifth phone number.		X						
Phone 5 Selector	Internal	N	Fifth phone number name.		X						

Field Name	Data Type	Write	Notes	Calendar	Contact	Journal	Mail	Note	Post	Task	Document
Phone 6 Selected	Text	Y	Sixth phone number.		X						
Phone 6 Selector	Internal	N	Sixth phone number name.		X						
Phone 7 Selected	Text	Y	Seventh phone number.		X						
Phone 7 Selector	Internal	N	Seventh phone number name.		X						
Phone 8 Selected	Text	Y	Eighth phone number.		X						
Phone 8 Selector	Internal	N	Eighth phone number name.		X						
PO Box	Text	Y	PO Box number.		X						
Presentation Format	Text	N	PowerPoint presentation format.								X
Primary Phone	Text	Y	Primary phone number.		X						X
Printed	Date/Time	N	Date and time last printed.								
Priority	Internal	Y	0 - Low 1 - Normal 2 - High							X	
Private	Yes/No	Y	0 - Not private 1 - Private	X	X		X	X	X	X	
Profession	Text	Y	Contact's profession.		X						
Radio Phone	Text	Y	Radio phone number.		X						
Read	Internal	N	Whether an item has been read.	X	X	X	X	X	X	X	
Read Only	Yes/No	N									X
Receipt Requested	Yes/No	N					X				
Received	Date/Time	N	Date and time message received by recipient's mail box.				X		X		

TABLE B.4 CONTINUED

Field Name	Data Type	Write	Notes	Calendar	Contact	Journal	Mail	Note	Post	Task	Document
Received Representing Name	Text	N			X						
Recipient Name	Text	N								X	
Recipient No Reassign	Yes/No	N								X	
Recipients Allowed	Yes/No	N								X	
Recurrence	Internal	Y	0 - None 1 - Daily 2 - Weekly 3 - Monthly 4 - Yearly	X						X	
Recurrence Pattern	Text	N	Combination of values in Recurrence, Start, and End fields.	X						X	
Recurrence Range End	Date/Time	N	Last date and time of recurring item.	X						X	
Recurrence Range Start	Date/Time	N	First date and time of recurring item.	X						X	
Recurring	Yes/No	N	Whether item is recurring.	X						X	
Referred By	Text	Y	Name of person who referred contact.		X						
Relevance	Integer	Y					X				
Remind Beforehand	Yes/No	Y	Whether a reminder is activated.	X						X	
Reminder	Yes/No	Y	Whether a reminder is set.	X	X					X	

Field Name	Data Type	Write	Notes	Calendar	Contact	Journal	Mail	Note	Post	Task	Document
Reminder Override Default	Yes/No	Y	Yes - use reminder defaults set in Options. No - use values in Reminder Beforehand, Reminder Sound, and Reminder Sound File fields.	X						X	
Reminder Sound	Yes/No	Y	Whether a sound is played as a reminder.	X						X	
Reminder Sound File	Text	Y	Path of reminder sound file.	X						X	
Reminder Time	Date/Time	Y	Date and time for reminder.	X	X					X	
Reminder Topic	Text	Y	Reminder topic.	X	X						
Remote Status	Number	N	Remote mail header status: 0 - None 1 - Marked 2 - Marked for download 3 - Marked for copy				X		X		
Request Status	Number	N	Assigned task status: 0 - None 1 - Not responded 2 - Accepted 3 - Declined							X	
Requested By	Text	N								X	
Required Attendees	Internal	N	Names of required attendees at meeting or appointment (multiple names separated by semicolons).	X							
Resource Type	Text	N									X

TABLE B.4 CONTINUED

Field Name	Data Type	Write	Notes	Calendar	Contact	Journal	Mail	Note	Post	Task	Document
Resources	Internal	N		X							
Response Requested	Yes/No	Y		X							
Retrieval Time	Number	N	Time taken to download a message (in minutes) by Remote Mail.				X		X		
Revision Number	Text	N	Document revision number.								X
Role	Text	Y	Contact's role.							X	
Schedule+ Priority	Text	Y	Priority in Schedule+.							X	
Send Plain Text Only	Yes/No	Y			X						
Sensitivity	Internal	Y	0 - Normal 1 - Personal 2 - Private 3 - Confidential	X	X	X	X		X	X	
Sent	Date/Time	N	Date and time message sent to Outbox.				X		X		
Show Time As	Internal	Y	0 - Free 1 - Tentative 2 - Busy 3 - Out of office	X							
Signed By	Text	N					X				
Size	Internal	N	Bytes occupied by item.	X	X	X	X	X	X	X	
Slides	Integer	N	Number of slides in presentation.								X
Spouse	Text	Y	Name of spouse.		X						

Field Name	Data Type	Write	Notes	Calendar	Contact	Journal	Mail	Note	Post	Task	Document
Start	Date/Time	Y	Item start time.	X		X					
Start Date	Date/Time	Y	Start date and time.							X	
State	Text	Y	Contact's state.		X						
Status	Number	Y	Task status: 0 - Not started 1 - In progress 2 - Completed 3 - Waiting for someone else 4 - Deferred							X	
Street Address	Text	N	Contact's street address.		X						
Subject	Text	Y	Subject of item. For contact, if Full Name field is empty, value of File As field is used.	X	X	X	X	X	X	X	
Suffix	Text	Y	Contact's suffix.		X						
Supplemental Lock	Keywords	N									X
Team Task	Yes/No	Y	Whether team task.							X	
Telex	Text	Y	Telex number.		X						
Template	Text	N	Document template.								X
Title	Text	Y	Contact's title.		X						
To	Internal	N	Names of message recipients.				X				
Total Work	Number	Y	Time task is expected to take (saved in minutes).							X	

TABLE B.4 CONTINUED

Field Name	Data Type	Write	Notes	Calendar	Contact	Journal	Mail	Note	Post	Task	Document
Tracking Status	Internal	N	1 - Delivered 5 - Read 6 - Not read				X				
TTY/TTD Phone	Text	Y	Contact's TTY/TTD number.		X						
UID	Text	N									X
Unread	Yes/No	N		X			X		X	X	
User Certificate	Text	N	User certificate.		X						
User Field 1	Text	Y	User-defined text.		X						
User Field 2	Text	Y	User-defined text.		X						
User Field 3	Text	Y	User-defined text.		X						
User Field 4	Text	Y	User-defined text.		X						
Voting Response	Text	N					X				
Web Page	Text	Y	URL.		X						
Words	Integer	N	Number of words in document.								X
Zip/Postal Code	Text	Y	Contact's ZIP or postal code.		X						

MESSAGE CLASSES

In Outlook, each item is an object that has a message class. The class defines the properties of the object and how that object behaves. One of the most significant properties is the form that's used to display the object.

The Outlook message classes are listed in Table B.5.

TABLE B.5   OUTLOOK MESSAGE CLASSES

Class ID	Item Type
`IPM.Activity`	Create journal entry.
`IPM.Appointment`	Create appointment.
`IPM.Contact`	Create contact.
`IPM.DistList`	Create distribution lists.
`IPM.Document`	Create document.
`IPM`	The specified form cannot be found.
`IPM.Note`	Create e-mail message.
`IPM.Note.IMC.Notification`	Create a report from the Exchange Server gateway to the Internet.
`IPM.Note.Rules.Oof.Template.Microsoft`	Show out-of-office templates.
`IPM.Note.Rules.Oof.Template.Microsoft`	Show out-of-office templates.
`IPM.Note.Rules.ReplyTemplate.Microsoft`	Edit rule reply template.
`IPM.Note.Secure`	Send encrypted note.
`IPM.Note.Secure.Sign`	Send digitally signed note.
`IPM.OLE.Class`	Create an exception to a recurrence series.
`IPM.Outlook.Recall`	Retrieve sent message from recipient's inbox.
`IPM.Post`	Post note in folder.
`IPM.Recall.Report`	Create a message recall report.
`IPM Remote`	Represent Remote Mail message header.
`IPM.Report`	Report item status.
`IPM.Resend`	Resend failed message.
`IPM.Schedule.Meeting.Canceled`	Send meeting cancellation.
`IPM.Schedule.Meeting.Request`	Create meeting request.
`IPM.Schedule.Meeting.Resp.Neg`	Create decline meeting response.
`IPM.Schedule.Meeting.Resp.Pos`	Create accept meeting response.

APP

B

TABLE B.5   CONTINUED

Class ID	Item Type
IPM Schedule.Meeting.Resp.Tent	Create tentative meeting response.
IPM.StickyNote	Create note.
IPM.Task	Create task.
IPM.TaskRequest	Create task request.
IPM.TaskRequest.Accept	Create task request accept response.
IPM.TaskRequest.Decline	Create task request decline response.
IPM.TaskRequest.Update	Create update to task request.

OUTLOOK REGISTRY KEYS

In addition to the files listed previously in this appendix, Outlook saves information in the Windows registry—a database that contains setup information for Windows and applications that run under Windows, as well as information about Windows users.

The registry database is maintained in several files, but you can access the information in those files by using the Registry Editor utility without having to be aware of the files that contain the information. Appendix F, "Working with the Windows Registry," contains information about how you can use the Registry Editor to examine and modify setup information in the registry.

→ To learn more about examining and modifying setup information, **see** "Working with the Windows Registry," **p. 799**.

When you use the Registry Editor to examine the registry, it looks much like a set of folders and subfolders. Instead of folders and subfolders, however, the structure consists of keys and subkeys. Just as subfolders are referred to as folders in the Windows file system, subkeys in the registry structure usually are referred to as keys.

Table B.6 lists some of the principal registry keys that control Outlook for the current user. A complete list is available in the Office Resource Kit. See the file Regkey.xls.

Note

All the keys in Table B.6 are in the HKEY_CURRENT_USER\Software\Microsoft\ section of the registry. A key listed as Office\10.0\Outlook would have a full path in the Registry of HKEY_CURRENT_USER\Software\Microsoft\Office\10.0\ Outlook.

Some of the keys listed in Table B.6 are visible in the registry only after you've performed an operation that makes use of those keys.

TABLE B.6   OUTLOOK KEYS

Key	Outlook Item
`Office\10.0\Outlook`	General Outlook key
`Office\10.0\Outlook\Appointment`	Appointments
`Office\10.0\Outlook\AutoConfiguration`	Directories
`Office\10.0\Outlook\Categories`	Master Category list
`Office\10.0\Outlook\Contact`	Contacts folders
`Office\10.0\Outlook\CustomizableAlerts`	Web settings
`Office\10.0\Outlook\DistList`	Distribution lists
`Office\10.0\Outlook\Forms`	Default form
`Office\10.0\Outlook\Journal`	Journal log files
`Office\10.0\Outlook\JournalEntry`	Journal entry frame
`Office\10.0\Outlook\Message`	Message frame
`Office\10.0\Outlook\Note`	Note frame
`Office\10.0\Outlook\Office Explorer`	Explorer settings
`Office\10.0\Outlook\Office Finder`	Finder settings
`Office\10.0\Outlook\Options`	Outlook Options settings
`Office\10.0\Outlook\Preferences`	Outlook Preferences settings
`Office\10.0\Outlook\Printing`	Print settings
`Office\10.0\Outlook\Setup`	Setup information
`Office\10.0\Outlook\Task`	Task frame
`Office\10.0\Outlook\Today`	Outlook Today settings
`Office\10.0\Outlook\UserInfo`	User information
`Shared Tools\Outlook\Journaling`	Settings for applications and items to be Journaled
`WAB\Server Properties`	Account information for other mail services, such as LDAP

APP

B

Note

Additional information relating to Table B.6 is also located in the registry keys and sub-keys under `HKEY_LOCAL_MACHINE\Software\Microsoft\Exchange`.

BACKING UP OUTLOOK

A complete backup of Outlook consists of more than just making a copy of your Personal Folders. In addition to copying the .PST files you use, you also need to copy the other files listed previously in this appendix. Copying the recommended files enables you to retain the customizations that have been performed to make Outlook look and work the way you want. Making an export copy of the registry keys listed previously preserves the Outlook settings and customizations that are not kept in separate files.

To learn more about backing up Outlook, look in the Microsoft Knowledge Base at articles Q195719 and Q196492. These articles were written for Outlook 2000, but most of the information applies to Outlook 2002. In addition, Knowledge Base articles specifically written for Outlook 10 will be available soon. More information on backing up Outlook is available at http://www.slipstick.com/config/backup.htm.

Microsoft has indicated that it might make available a utility or Outlook add-in that will back up Outlook. If this utility is created, it will be available at the Office Update Web site.

C

OUTLOOK'S SYMBOLS

In this appendix

WHAT ARE SYMBOLS FOR?

Outlook uses symbols to provide information about items. For example, a symbol that looks like a closed envelope indicates a message item is unread, whereas a symbol that looks like an open envelope indicates a message has been read.

The tables in this appendix list the symbols most frequently used with Outlook's items.

SYMBOLS FOR CALENDAR ITEMS

Table C.1 lists the symbols used for Calendar items.

TABLE C.1   CALENDAR SYMBOLS

Image	Meaning
	Appointment.
	Click to see items that don't fit into current view.
	Meeting.
	Meeting request.
	Recurring appointment.
	Recurring meeting.
	Recurring appointment or meeting.
	Reminder for appointment or meeting.
	Private appointment or meeting.
	Start time for appointment or meeting.
	End time for appointment or meeting.
	Calendar item has attachment.

SYMBOLS FOR CONTACT ITEMS

Table C.2 lists the symbols used for contact items.

TABLE C.2	CONTACT SYMBOLS
Image	**Meaning**
	Activities for contacts are recorded in journal.
	Contact item.
	Contact item has attachment.
	Contact flagged for follow-up.
	Contact follow-up complete.
	Distribution list.

SYMBOLS FOR MESSAGE ITEMS

Table C.3 lists the symbols used for message items.

TABLE C.3	MESSAGE SYMBOLS
Image	**Meaning**
	High importance message.
	Low importance message.
	Read message.
	Unread message.
	Forwarded message.
	Replied to message.
	Saved or unsent message.
	Encrypted message.
	Digitally signed message.
	Invalid signed message.

TABLE C.3   CONTINUED

Image	Meaning
	Microsoft Mail 3.x form.
	Meeting request.
	Accepted meeting request.
	Tentatively accepted meeting request.
	Declined meeting request.
	Canceled meeting.
	Task request.
	Accepted task.
	Declined task.
	Message has attachment.
	Message flagged for follow-up.
	Message follow-up complete.

SYMBOLS FOR JOURNAL ITEMS

Table C.4 lists the symbols used for Journal items.

TABLE C.4   JOURNAL SYMBOLS

Image	Meaning
	Appointment.
	Appointment request, appointment response, meeting, meeting request, meeting response.
	Meeting canceled.
	Conversation.
	Document.
	E-mail message.

TABLE C.4	CONTINUED
Image	**Meaning**
	Fax.
	Letter.
	Microsoft Access database file.
	Microsoft Excel workbook file.
	Microsoft PowerPoint presentation.
	Microsoft Word document.
	Note.
	Phone call.
	Task.
	Task request, task response.
	Remote session.
	Journal item has an attachment.

SYMBOLS FOR TASK ITEMS

Table C.5 lists the symbols used for task items.

TABLE C.5	TASK SYMBOLS
Image	**Meaning**
	Accepted task.
	Completed task.
	Declined task.
	High importance task.
	Low importance task.
	Recurring task.

TABLE C.5 CONTINUED

Image	Meaning
	Task.
	Task assigned to another person.
	Task assigned to you.
	Task has an attachment.
	Uncompleted task.

OUTLOOK RESOURCES

In this appendix

This appendix lists some of the resources I've found useful while working with Outlook.

RESOURCES AVAILABLE ON THE WORLD WIDE WEB

The World Wide Web provides comprehensive resources for information about Outlook and related subjects. Some of the sites I've found useful are listed here. Many of these sites provide links to other related sites. You probably won't have the time to explore these sites in depth, but I suggest you make a preliminary visit to each of them to gain an idea of what's available.

Note

> The sources listed here are just a sampling of the many Internet sites in which you can find access to answers to your Outlook and communications questions. I encourage you to use search engines, such as Alta Vista (`http://www.altavista.com`) or Google (`http://www.google.com`), to search for information about specific subjects.

- **amazon.com**—This is a Web site maintained by the most popular online book store. You can use this site to find books on any subject, including Outlook. The site contains information about, and reviews of, many books. You can, of course, use this site to purchase books:
  `http://www.amazon.com`

- **Helen Feddema's Home Page**—This Web site contains many useful examples of Visual Basic code that customizes Outlook and also links Outlook to other Office applications:
  `http://www.ulster.net/~hfeddema/`

- **Que Publishing**—Contains information about books published by Que. You can download sample chapters of many books, get technical information from resource centers, and much more:
  `http://www.quepublishing.com` and `http://www.quehelp.com`

- **Microsoft Office Home Page**—You can use this site to find information about any Microsoft Office product, including Outlook. The site has many links that take you to detailed information:
  `http://www.microsoft.com/office/`

- **Microsoft Outlook Home Page**—This site contains links to Outlook-specific information. One of these links leads you to information about Outlook add-ins available from many sources. If any upgrades for Outlook become available from Microsoft, you'll probably find them on this site:
  `http://www.microsoft.com/outlook/`

- **Microsoft Technical Support**—This site provides access to Microsoft's Knowledge Base (a collection of some 200,000 technical articles) and other resources:
  `http://support.microsoft.com/support/`

See the next section "Finding Information in the Microsoft Knowledge Base," to see how you can find answers to your questions in the Microsoft Knowledge Base.

- **Outlook Downloads**—This site contains Outlook add-ins available from Microsoft for downloading:

  `http://search.officeupdate.Microsoft.com/downloadCatalog/default.asp?product=Outlook`

- **Slipstick Systems Exchange Center**—Probably the best and most complete source of information about Outlook and Exchange. The site contains many articles about specific topics together with links to other sources of information:

  `http://www.slipstick.com`

- **whatis.com**—This site contains an enormous amount of information about computer-related topics in general, including messaging. If you ever want to find out what a word or acronym means, you'll find it here:

  `http://whatis.com`

FINDING INFORMATION IN THE MICROSOFT KNOWLEDGE BASE

To access the Microsoft Knowledge Base, go to

`http://support.Microsoft.com/`

The site initially displays the Knowledge Base home page. From this page, you can access many thousands of articles about Microsoft products and their uses.

To find information about a specific product, such as Outlook:

1. Open the drop-down My Search Is About list and choose a product.
2. Accept the default Keyword Search Using item under I Want to Search By.
3. Open the drop-down Keyword Search Using list and choose among Any Word, All Words, Exact Phrase, or Boolean Expression.
4. Enter search words or an expression in the My Question Is box.
5. Further down in the Knowledge Base Search screen you can choose whether you want to search in the full text of articles (the default) or only in their titles. You also can choose whether you want the results of the search to display the title and an excerpt from each article (the default) or only article titles.
6. Choose Go to find Knowledge Base articles that match your request.

The Knowledge Base responds by displaying a list of up to 200 articles that contain information relating to what you asked for. You can select any one of those articles to see it in full. With the article displayed, you can choose Print to print the article.

Tip from

[signature]

> Instead of printing Knowledge Base articles, I suggest you save the ones in which you're interested on your hard disk, a Zip disk, or a writeable CD. By doing that, you save a lot of printer supplies (paper and print cartridges) and still have rapid access to the articles in the future.

If you want to download a specific Knowledge Base article for which you know the reference number, such as one of the articles referred to in this book, choose Specific Article ID Number under I Want to Search By. Then, enter the article number, such as "Q197653" (without the quotation marks) in the My Question Is box, and choose Go.

Alternatively, to access a specific Knowledge Base article, such as article number Q197653, you can enter

```
http://support.Microsoft.com/support/kb/articles/q197/6/53.asp
```

in your browser's Address box. Notice that, in this case, you must insert a forward slash after the third and fourth characters of the article's number.

BOOKS

The following is a list of books that contain detailed information about Outlook and related topics. The books listed here are those available before the introduction of Outlook 2000. By the time you read this book, you'll be able to find updated books about Outlook 10. In addition to the books listed here, you can find many more books about Outlook listed by online book stores, such as Amazon, Barnes and Noble, and others.

Building Applications with Microsoft Outlook 2000. Randy Byrne. Microsoft Press, ISBN: 0-73560-581-5.

Mastering Microsoft Outlook 2000. Gini Courter et al. Sybex, ISBN: 0-7821-7472-0.

Microsoft Exchange User's Guide. Sue Mosher. Duke, ISBN: 1-882419-52-9.

Microsoft Office 97 Visual Basic Programmer's Guide. Microsoft Press, ISBN: 1-57231-340-4.

Microsoft Outlook E-mail and Fax Guide. Sue Mosher. Duke, ISBN: 1-882419-82-0.

Microsoft Windows 2000 Registry Handbook. Jerry Honeycutt. Que, ISBN 0-7897-1674-7.

Programming Microsoft Outlook and Microsoft Exchange. Thomas Rizzo. Microsoft Press, ISBN: 0-73560-509-2.

Special Edition Using Microsoft Exchange Server 2000. Kent Joshi et al. Que, ISBN: 0-7897-2278-X.

Special Edition Using Microsoft Internet Explorer 4. Jim O'Donnell and Eric Ladd. Que, ISBN: 0-7897-1046-3.

Special Edition Using Microsoft Outlook 97. Gordon Padwick et al. Que, ISBN: 0-7897-1096-X.

Special Edition Using Microsoft Outlook 2000. Gordon Padwick et al. Que, ISBN: 0-7897-1909-6.

Using Outlook 98. Gordon Padwick et al. Que, ISBN: 0-7897-1516-3.

Using the Windows 98 Registry. Jerry Honeycutt. Que, ISBN: 0-7897-1658-5.

VBA Developer's Handbook. Ken Getz and Mike Gilbert. Sybex, ISBN: 0-7821-1951-4.

Visual Basic for Applications Unleashed. Paul McFedries. Sams Publishing, ISBN: 0-672-31046-5.

Windows NT Registry. Sandra Osborne. New Riders Professional, ISBN: 1-5620-5941-6.

APPENDIX

OUTLOOK SHORTCUT KEYS

In this appendix

SPEED YOUR WORK BY LEARNING SHORTCUTS

Because Outlook has a graphical interface, many people primarily use a mouse (or another pointing device) to control Outlook. However, using keyboard shortcuts is often faster and more convenient. You can speed up your work with Outlook by learning a few of the shortcuts listed in this appendix. For example, if you make frequent use of timelines, using keyboard shortcuts is often much faster than using the mouse.

Note

Many of the Outlook shortcuts perform the same, or similar, functions in other Office applications.

This appendix summarizes many of the shortcuts available in Outlook in tables, some of which refer to *controls*. Here's a reminder: A control is an element on a form or dialog box that displays information or that can be used to input information. Controls include such things as text boxes, drop-down lists, check boxes, groups of option buttons, and command buttons.

WORKING WITH OUTLOOK ITEMS

Table E.1 lists keyboard shortcuts for general use while you're working with Outlook items.

TABLE E.1   GENERAL-USE OUTLOOK ITEM SHORTCUTS

Task	Shortcut
Cancel current operation	Esc
Display ScreenTip for active item	Shift+F1
Expand selected group	+ (numeric keypad)
Collapse selected group	- (numeric keypad)
Select item	Enter
Turn on editing in a field	F2
Move from item to item	Up arrow Down arrow Left arrow Right arrow
Switch to next tab stop	Ctrl+Tab or Ctrl+Page Down
Switch to previous tab stop	Ctrl+Shift+Tab or Ctrl+Page Up
Display address book	Ctrl+Shift+B
Dial	Ctrl+Shift+D
Use Advanced Find	Ctrl+Shift+F

Task	Shortcut
Flag for follow-up	Ctrl+Shift+G
Create new Office document	Ctrl+Shift+H
Next item (with item open)	Ctrl+Shift+>
Previous item (with item open)	Ctrl+Shift+<
Mark as read	Ctrl+Q
Reply to mail message	Ctrl+R
Reply all to mail message	Ctrl+Shift+R
Switch case for selected text in RTF messages	Shift+F3
Switch between panes (folder list, information viewer, and preview pane)	F6 or Ctrl+Shift+Tab

Table E.2 lists keyboard shortcuts for adding World Wide Web information to items.

TABLE E.2   WEB SHORTCUTS FOR OUTLOOK ITEMS

Task	Shortcut
Edit a URL within a message	Ctrl+left mouse button
Locate link browser (Specify the browser program that will open URLs)	Shift+left mouse button
Insert a hyperlink	Ctrl+K (Word as e-mail editor)

Table E.3 lists keyboard shortcuts for applying formatting to items in rich text format or HTML mail items. In each case, select the text you want to format and then press the shortcut keys.

TABLE E.3   SHORTCUTS FOR APPLYING FORMATTING

Task	Shortcut
Make bold	Ctrl+B
Add bullets	Ctrl+Shift+L
Center	Ctrl+E
Italicize	Ctrl+I
Increase indent	Ctrl+T
Decrease indent	Ctrl+Shift+T
Left align	Ctrl+L
Underline	Ctrl+U

TABLE E.3   CONTINUED

Task	Shortcut
Increase font size	Ctrl+]
Decrease font size	Ctrl+[
Clear formatting	Ctrl+Shift+Z or Ctrl+Spacebar

Table E.4 lists keyboard shortcuts for creating items and files.

TABLE E.4   SHORTCUTS FOR CREATING ITEMS AND FILES

Task	Shortcut
Create an appointment	Ctrl+Shift+A
Create a contact	Ctrl+Shift+C
Create a folder	Ctrl+Shift+E
Create a journal entry	Ctrl+Shift+J
Create a distribution list	Ctrl+Shift+L
Create a message	Ctrl+Shift+M
Create a meeting request	Ctrl+Shift+Q
Create a note	Ctrl+Shift+N
Find people	Ctrl+Shift+P
Create a task	Ctrl+Shift+K
Post in this folder	Ctrl+Shift+S
Create a task request	Ctrl+Shift+U

Table E.5 lists keyboard shortcuts for managing menus. To select any menu command, hold down the Alt key while you press the underlined character in the menu item's name. You can use the same technique to select something on a form or in a dialog box.

TABLE E.5   SOME COMMONLY USED MENU SHORTCUTS

Task	Shortcut
Save	Ctrl+S or Shift+F12
Save and close (contact, appointment, journal, and task items)	Alt+S
Send (mail item using default account)	Alt+S
Save as	F12
Go to folder	Ctrl+Y

Task	Shortcut
Go to Inbox folder	Shift+Ctrl+I
Post to a folder	Ctrl+Shift+S
Print	Ctrl+P
Create a new message	Ctrl+N
Cut to the Clipboard	Ctrl+X or Shift+Delete
Copy to the Clipboard	Ctrl+C or Ctrl+Insert
Copy item	Ctrl+Shift+Y
Paste from the Clipboard	Ctrl+V or Shift+Insert
Move item	Ctrl+Shift+V
Check names (in default editor)	Ctrl+K
Check names	Alt+K
Undo	Ctrl+Z or Alt+Backspace
Delete	Ctrl+D
Select all	Ctrl+A
Display context menu	Shift+F10
Display program control menu when menu bar is active	Spacebar
Display program icon menu	Alt+Spacebar
Select next command on menu	Down arrow
Select previous command on menu	Up arrow
Select menu to the left	Left arrow
Select menu to the right	Right arrow
Select first command on menu	Home
Select last command on menu	End
Make menu bar active	F10
Move between toolbars	Shift+Ctrl+Tab
Advanced find	F3
Find items (while main Outlook window is active)	Ctrl+Shift+F F4
Find text (while an item is open)	F4
Find next	Shift+F4
Refresh	F5

APP

E

TABLE E.5 CONTINUED

Task	Shortcut
Check spelling	F7
Display Favorites menu (while main Outlook window is active)	Alt+O
Display format menu (while an item is open)	Alt+O
Close print preview	Alt+C
Accept (within item)	Alt+C
Decline	Alt+D
Forward	Ctrl+F
Check for new mail	Ctrl+M
Send, post, or invite all (not Word)	Ctrl+Enter
Close menu and submenu (if open)	Alt
Close menu and submenu	Esc
Delete highlighted item in information viewer	Del

Table E.6 lists keyboard shortcuts for moving around in a dialog box. These shortcuts act on the selected control or group within a dialog box. You can select a control by holding down Alt while pressing the underlined character in the control's name.

TABLE E.6 DIALOG BOX SHORTCUTS

Task	Shortcut
Switch to next tab stop	Ctrl+Tab
Switch to previous tab stop	Ctrl+Shift+Tab
Move to next option or option group	Tab
Move to previous option or option group	Shift+Tab
Move to next item in drop-down list	Down arrow
Move to previous item in drop-down list	Up arrow
Perform action assigned to button	Spacebar
Select or clear check box	Spacebar
Open a drop-down list	Alt+Down arrow
Close a drop-down list	Alt+Up arrow or Esc

Table E.7 lists keyboard shortcuts you can use while working in a text box. The shortcuts are available when you've selected a text box in a form or dialog box. Moving refers to the position of the insertion point within the text box.

TABLE E.7   TEXT BOX SHORTCUTS FOR OUTLOOK ITEMS

Task	Shortcut
Move to beginning of text box	Home
Move to end of text box	End
Move one character to the left	Left arrow
Move one character to the right	Right arrow
Select from insertion point to beginning	Shift+Home
Select from insertion point to end	Shift+End
Select or unselect one character to the left	Shift+Left arrow
Select or unselect one character to the right	Shift+Right arrow
Select or unselect one word to the left	Ctrl+Shift+Left arrow
Select or unselect one word to the right	Ctrl+Shift+Right arrow

Table E.8 lists keyboard shortcuts for working with print preview.

TABLE E.8   PRINT PREVIEW SHORTCUTS

Task	Shortcut
Open print preview	Ctrl+F2
Print from print preview	Alt+P
Print preview page setup	Alt+S, or Alt+U
Zoom	Alt+Z
Display next page	PageDown
Display previous page	PageUp
Display first page	Ctrl+Up arrow or Home
Display last page	Ctrl+Down arrow or End

Table E.9 lists keyboard shortcuts for working with Windows.

TABLE E.9   WINDOWS SHORTCUTS

Task	Shortcut
Switch to next program	Alt+Tab
Switch to previous program	Alt+Shift+Tab

APP

E

TABLE E.9 CONTINUED	
Task	**Shortcut**
Move to next window	Alt+Shift+Esc
Display Start menu	Ctrl+Esc
End active program	Ctrl+Shift+Delete
Move to next pane	F6
Move to previous pane	Shift+F6
Close Outlook window	Alt+F4

Table E.10 lists keyboard shortcuts for working in the Card view of a contact (or other) item. Select a Card view of an Outlook item to use these shortcuts.

TABLE E.10 CARD VIEW SHORTCUTS	
Task	**Shortcut**
Select next card	Down arrow
Select previous card	Up arrow
Select first card	Home
Select last card	End
Select first card on current page	PageUp
Select first card on next page	PageDown
Select closest card in next column	Right arrow
Select closest card in previous column	Left arrow
Select or unselect active card	Ctrl+Spacebar
Extend selection to next card	Ctrl+Shift+Down arrow
Extend selection to previous card	Ctrl+Shift+Up arrow
Extend selection to next card and unselect previous cards	Shift+Down arrow
Extend selection to previous card and unselect subsequent cards	Shift+Up arrow
Extend selection to last card	Shift+End
Extend selection to first card	Shift+Home
Extend selection to last card on previous page	Shift+PageUp
Extend selection to first card on next page	Shift+PageDown

Table E.11 lists keyboard shortcuts for moving between cards. These shortcuts move to another card without changing which card is selected. Select a card before using these shortcuts.

TABLE E.11 CARD VIEW SHORTCUTS

Task	Shortcut
Move to next card	Ctrl+Down arrow
Move to previous card	Ctrl+Up arrow
Move to first card	Ctrl+Home
Move to last card	Ctrl+End
Move to first card on previous page	Ctrl+PageUp
Move to first card on next page	Ctrl+PageDown
Move to closest card in previous column	Ctrl+Left arrow
Move to closest card in next column	Ctrl+Right arrow
Move to field in active card	F2
Move to specific card by which cards are sorted	Type one or more characters of the name

Table E.12 lists keyboard shortcuts for moving between fields in a selected card.

TABLE E.12 SHORTCUTS FOR MOVING BETWEEN FIELDS IN A CARD

Task	Shortcut
Select first or next field in a card	Tab or Enter
Select previous field in a card	Shift+Tab
Add line to multiline field	Enter

Table E.13 lists general keyboard shortcuts for working with day/week/month views of calendar items.

TABLE E.13 GENERAL SHORTCUTS FOR CALENDAR ITEMS

Task	Shortcut
View 1–10 days (0 for 10 days)	Alt+<n>
Switch to weeks	Alt+-
Switch to months	Alt+=
Move between Calendar, TaskPad, and folder list	Ctrl+Tab or F6

TABLE E.13   CONTINUED

Task	Shortcut
Select next appointment	Tab
Select previous appointment	Shift+Tab
Go to next day	Right arrow
Go to previous day	Left arrow
Go to same day in next week in Daily and Work Week views	Alt+Down arrow
Go to same day in previous week in Daily and Work Week views	Alt+Up arrow
Move selected item to same day in next weekin Monthly view	Alt+Down arrow
Move selected into to same day in previous week in Monthly view	Alt+Up arrow
Move from item to item	Tab

Table E.14 lists keyboard shortcuts for working in the Day view.

TABLE E.14   DAY VIEW SHORTCUTS

Task	Shortcut
Select beginning of workday	Home
Select end of workday	End
Select previous block of time	Up arrow
Select next block of time	Down arrow
Select block of time at top of screen	PageUp
Select block of time at bottom of screen	PageDown
Extend selected time	Shift+Up arrow
Reduce selected time	Shift+Down arrow
Move selected appointment back	Alt+Up arrow
Move selected appointment forward	Alt+Down arrow
Move start of selected appointment	Alt+Shift+Up arrow
Move end of selected appointment	Alt+Shift+Down arrow

Table E.15 lists keyboard shortcuts for working in a table.

TABLE E.15   TABLE SHORTCUTS

Task	Shortcut
Select next item	Down arrow
Select previous item	Up arrow
Go to next item without changing selection	Ctrl+Down arrow
Go to previous item after changing selection	Ctrl+Up arrow
Go to first item	Home
Go to last item	End
Go to item at bottom of screen	PageDown
Go to item at top of screen	PageUp
Extend select item(s) by one	Shift+Up arrow
Reduce selected item(s) by one	Shift+Down arrow
Open item	Enter
Select all items	Ctrl+A

Table E.16 lists keyboard shortcuts for working with groups in a table.

TABLE E.16   SHORTCUTS FOR GROUPS IN A TABLE

Task	Shortcut
Expand group	Enter or Right arrow
Collapse group	Enter or Left arrow
Select previous group (with all groups collapsed)	Up arrow
Select next group (with all groups collapsed)	Down arrow
Select first group	Home
Select last group	End
Select first item in expanded group	Right arrow

Table E.17 lists keyboard shortcuts for moving around in a timeline when an item is selected.

TABLE E.17   TIMELINE SHORTCUTS WITH ITEM SELECTED

Task	Shortcut
Select previous item	Left arrow
Select next item	Right arrow
Select adjacent previous items	Shift+Left arrow
Select adjacent subsequent items	Shift+Right arrow
Select nonadjacent previous items	Ctrl+Left arrow+Spacebar
Select nonadjacent subsequent items	Ctrl+Right arrow+Spacebar
Open selected item	Enter
Display items one screen above	PageUp
Display items one screen below	PageDown
Select first item	Home
Select last item	End
Display and select first item	Ctrl+Home
Display and select last item	Ctrl+End

Table E.18 lists keyboard shortcuts for moving around in a timeline when a group is selected.

TABLE E.18   TIMELINE SHORTCUTS WITH GROUP SELECTED

Task	Shortcut
Expand group	Enter or Right arrow
Collapse group	Enter or Left arrow
Select previous group	Up arrow
Select next group	Down arrow
Select first group	Home
Select last group	End
Select first onscreen item in expanded group	Right arrow
Move back one increment of time	Left arrow
Move forward one increment of time	Right arrow
Switch from upper to lower time scale	Tab
Switch from lower to upper time scale	Shift+Tab
Select first onscreen item or first group (with lower time scale selected)	Tab

Table E.19 lists keyboard shortcuts for the Date Navigator.

TABLE E.19   DATE NAVIGATOR SHORTCUTS

Task	Shortcut
Go to first day of current week	Alt+Home
Go to last day of current week	Alt+End
Go to same day in previous week	Alt+Up arrow
Go to same day in next week	Alt+Down arrow
Go to first day of current month	Alt+PageUp
Go to last day of current month	Alt+PageDown

Table E.20 lists keyboard shortcuts for moving around in command bars.

TABLE E.20   COMMAND BAR SHORTCUTS

Task	Shortcut
Activate menu bar	F10
Select next toolbar	Ctrl+Tab
Select previous toolbar	Ctrl+Shift+Tab
Select next button or menu	Tab
Select previous button or menu	Shift+Tab
Open selected menu	Enter
Perform action of selected button	Enter
Enter text in selected text box	Enter
Select option from drop-down list or menu	Up arrow or Down arrow, then Enter

Table E.21 lists keyboard shortcuts for the File Open and Insert File dialog boxes.

TABLE E.21   FILE OPEN AND INSERT FILE SHORTCUTS

Task	Shortcut
Return to previously viewed folder	Alt+1
Up one folder level	Alt+2
Search the Web	Alt+3
Delete current selection	Alt+4

APP

E

TABLE E.21   CONTINUED

Task	Shortcut
Create new folder	Alt+5
Change view	Alt+6
Open Tools menu	Alt+7

Table E.22 lists keyboard shortcuts for the Office Assistant.

TABLE E.22   SHORTCUTS FOR THE OFFICE ASSISTANT

Task	Shortcut
Open Macro Selector	Alt+F8
Open VBA Development Environment	Alt+F11
Select Help topic <n>	Alt+<n>
See more Help topics	Alt+Down arrow
See previous Help topics	Alt+Up arrow
Close Office Assistant message	Esc
Get Help from Office Assistant	F1
Display next tip	Alt+N
Display previous tip	Alt+B
Close tips	Esc

WORKING WITH THE WINDOWS REGISTRY

In this appendix

WHY WORK WITH THE REGISTRY?

You might wonder why a book about Outlook contains information about the Windows registry, also known as the registration database. The reason is that Outlook saves a lot of information in the registry. For example, the categories in your personal Master Category List are saved in the registry, as described in Chapter 20, "Using Categories and Entry Types." Although you don't need to be concerned with the registry while you use Outlook in your daily work, some customizing tasks can be performed only by working with the registry. If you want to copy a personal Master Category List from one computer to another, you must copy information from one computer's registry to the other computer's registry.

Quite often, when you consult articles about Outlook in the Microsoft Knowledge Base, or on the TechNet CD-ROM, you'll come across techniques that require you to make changes within the Windows registry.

This appendix provides an introduction to the Windows registry, including the information you need to make changes to the registry when you receive detailed instructions, such as those in various chapters of this book and in information from Microsoft and other software providers.

WHAT IS THE REGISTRY?

The registry is a database that exists in files on your hard disk. Each computer that runs Windows 98, Windows Me, Windows NT, or Windows 2000 has a registry. The registry contains information about your computer hardware, the operating system, applications (such as Outlook) that run under Windows, and computer users.

Although the information in the registry is in several files (*many* files in the case of Windows NT and Windows 2000), you don't have to be concerned with how these files are structured. That's because Windows contains various tools for displaying and modifying what's in the registry.

The registries for the four operating systems have similar structures, although some of the contents are different.

BACKING UP AND RESTORING THE REGISTRY

Before you attempt to make any changes to the registry, you should create a backup copy of the registry files. This is because the operation of your computer, when running under Windows, depends on information in the registry. If you inadvertently corrupt your registry, you might not be able to start Windows. It's a very wise precaution, therefore, to create a backup copy of your registry before you begin to make any changes to it.

Having said that, you also should know that Windows automatically keeps a backup of the registry. Rather than relying on that, though, it's much safer to create your own registry backup. In Windows 98 and Windows Me, you can access the registry backup by starting in MS-DOS mode and then entering the command scanreg /restore.

Windows NT also has a means to use the backup registry. Soon after you begin to start Windows NT, a message inviting you to press spacebar now to invoke hardware profile/last known good menu appears. You have only a second or so to press the spacebar. Microsoft says that this procedure restores your registry to its state when you last successfully started your computer.

One way to save a copy of the registry is to export the entire registry to a text file. This method is described in detail in this appendix, in the section "Copying a Registry Key from One Computer to Another." Be aware, though, that if you're using a computer that has Windows profiles for two or more users, this method exports only the registry data associated with the user who is currently logged on.

BACKING UP THE WINDOWS NT REGISTRY

The Windows NT 4.0 registry is contained in too many files to make saving these files individually very practical. The Windows NT Workstation Resource Kit, available from Microsoft, contains a backup utility—regback.exe—that you can use to create a backup of the Windows NT registry.

APP

F

BACKING UP THE WINDOWS 2000 REGISTRY

Windows 2000 doesn't offer a means to back up only the registry. It does, however, provide a means to back up the system state data, which includes the registry and other system components. From the Windows desktop, select Start, Programs, Accessories, System Tools, Backup to display the initial Backup window. At this point, you can choose to use either the Backup Wizard or the Backup tab. In either case, select to back up only the system state data.

You can't back up to the same drive that contains the system state data. Instead, use a removable medium, such as magnetic tape, a 250MB Iomega Zip disk, or a writeable CD. Note that the backup data consists of more than 220MB, so a 100MB Zip disk isn't large enough.

RESTORING THE REGISTRY

The only time you should need to restore the registry is after it becomes so corrupted that Windows won't start. If that ever happens, I hope you've followed the wise practice of always having an up-to-date Emergency Repair Disk. Use the Emergency Repair Disk to start the computer and subsequently, in the case of Windows 98, use Windows Explorer to copy the backup files into their original location on your hard disk.

In the case of Windows NT, after you've started Windows from the Emergency Repair Disk, you can use Regrest.exe (included in the Windows NT Workstation Resource Kit) to restore your registry.

For Windows 2000, after you've started Windows from the Emergency Repair Disk, use the backup utility to restore the system state data.

EXAMINING THE REGISTRY

The Registry Editor utility (Regedit.exe) is automatically installed on your computer when you install Windows. You can use this utility to examine and, if necessary, make changes to the registry.

To open Regedit, select Start on the Windows Taskbar; then select Run in the Start menu to display the Run dialog box.

Enter **Regedit** in the Open box, and then click OK. The Registry Editor initially opens, as shown in Figure F.1.

Figure F.1
The Registry Editor window contains two panes.

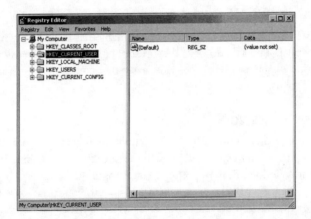

The left pane shows the registry tree with the tree name—My Computer—at the top. Under the tree name are the names of several subtrees. The names of most of the subtrees are the same for Windows 98, Windows Me, Windows NT, and Windows 2000.

> **Note**
>
> A tree consists of subtrees. Subtrees have keys, and keys have subkeys. The word branch is used to refer to any level of a tree and all the subordinate subkeys of that level.

You can expand a subtree by clicking the small box that contains a plus sign at the left of the subtree name, as shown in Figure F.2.

After you've expanded a subtree, the small square at the left of its name contains a minus sign. You can click that square to compress the list of keys.

Figure F.2
The HKEY_
CURRENT_USER
subtree is expanded
here to show the keys
it contains.

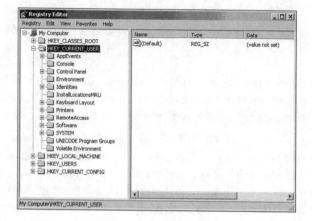

The items contained within a subtree are known as *keys*. Each key can contain a value, or subkeys, or both. A key that contains one or more subkeys has a small square containing a plus sign at the left of its name. The subkeys are revealed when you click that square.

Many keys contain several levels of subkeys. Figure F.3 shows two levels of subkeys under the Software key.

Figure F.3
The Command
Processor subkey is
selected to show the
values it contains.

You can select any key or subkey by clicking it. After you do so, the right pane of the Registry Editor window displays the values contained in that key or subkey, as shown in Figure F.4. Notice also that the status bar at the bottom of the Registry Editor window contains complete information about the path through the tree to get to the selected subkey, much as file pathnames are defined.

> **Note**
> You can drag the border between the two panes to make either of them wider.

The right pane contains two columns. The left column contains the names of various data items; the right column contains the actual value in each data item. You can change the width of the columns by dragging the vertical separator bar at the top of the pane.

Although you can see the values a key or subkey contains, it's rarely clear what these values are for or what would happen if you changed one. To the best of my knowledge, Microsoft hasn't published a definitive list of keys and the values they contain. Neither does any other software provider publish detailed information about the registry entries created when their software is installed. However, in this book and in such resources as Microsoft Knowledge Base articles, when information about making changes to the registry is provided, detailed information about the registry keys and their values is included.

> **Note**
> To obtain much more detailed information about the registry, see books such as *Using the Microsoft Windows 98 Registry* and *Windows 2000 Registry Handbook*, both by Jerry Honeycutt and published by Que.

When you've finished examining the registry, select Registry, Exit to close the Registry Editor.

FINDING INFORMATION IN THE REGISTRY

If you know the path to the subkey you want to see, you can drill down into the registry by expanding the appropriate tree, expanding a key, and successively expanding subkeys. If you don't know the path, you can use the Registry Editor's Find capability.

Using the Find capability, you can search the registry for the names of keys and subkeys, names of values, or actual text values. You can search the entire registry, or a key and the subkeys below that key.

> **Note**
> When you use Find in the Registry Editor to search for the value of keys, you can search only for text values. In previous versions of Outlook, the value of the registry key that contains the names of Outlook categories was stored as text, so you could use Find to locate a key that contained a specific category. In Outlook 2002, however, the value of the registry key that contains categories is stored as a binary value, so you can't use Find to locate a key that contains a specific category.

You might be interested to search through the entire registry to see whether Outlook sub-keys exist, which they do. To do this, start by selecting the top of the tree (My Computer);

then select Edit, Find (or press Ctrl+F) to open the dialog box shown in Figure F.4. If you want to search only a part of the registry, such as those keys and subkeys in the HKEY_LOCAL_MACHINE subtree, start by selecting that subtree.

Figure F.4
Use the Find dialog box to define what you want to find in the registry.

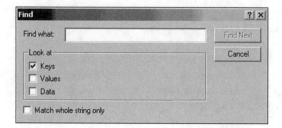

Enter the text you want to find in the Find What box. For example, if you want to find keys named Outlook, enter **Outlook** (you don't have to be concerned about upper- and lower-case). The Find Next button becomes enabled as soon as you enter one character in the Find What box.

You can select to search key names, value names, or value data, or any combination of these. To search only for key names, check only the Keys check box. Click Find Next to initiate the search.

After a short delay, the Registry Editor locates the first key or subkey named Outlook, and displays that part of the tree, as shown in Figure F.5.

Figure F.5
The tree automatically expands to the level necessary to display the key that's found.

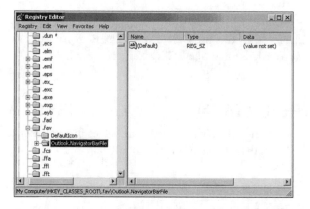

In this case, you know the Outlook subkey contains other subkeys because the square at the left of the subkey name contains a plus sign. You can click the square to see the subkeys within Outlook. Notice also that the status bar at the bottom of the window displays the complete path to the found subkey. In this case, that's

My Computer\HKEY_CLASSES_ROOT\.fav\Outlook.NavigatorBarFile

To find the next occurrence of a subkey named Outlook, select Edit, Find Next (or press F3). If you continue pressing F3, you'll find many subkeys named Outlook and others that have Outlook as part of their names.

ADDING AND DELETING SUBKEYS

Caution

Never add, delete, or change a key or subkey unless you know exactly what you're doing. Even if you think you know what you're doing, create a backup of your registry before making any changes.

The procedure for creating a new key is quite simple.

To add a new subkey, follow these steps:

1. Select the key or subkey for which you want to create a new subkey.
2. Select Edit, move the pointer onto New, and select Key. The new key appears in the correct position in the tree with a temporary name.
3. Change the temporary name to the appropriate name, and then press Enter.

The procedure to delete a key is even simpler.

To delete a subkey, follow these steps:

1. Select the subkey you want to delete.
2. Select Edit, Delete (or press the Delete key). The Registry Editor asks you to confirm that you want to delete the subkey. Click Yes to proceed.

CHANGING THE DATA IN A KEY OR SUBKEY VALUE

A common task is to change the data in one of the values in a key. For example, to add entry types to Outlook's default list, as explained in Chapter 20, you must modify the subkey:

HKEY_LOCAL_MACHINE\SOFTWARE\Microsoft\Shared Tools\Outlook\Journaling

→ For detailed information about changing Outlook's default list of entry types, **see** "Creating New Entry Types," **p. 413**.

Caution

The next few paragraphs are intended to show you how to change a value in a registry key. Never make any changes to registry values unless you have first backed up the registry and you know what you are doing.

When you select a subkey, you'll see the values it contains, the type of each value, and the data in each value, as shown in Figure F.6.

Figure F.6
This is an example of some values in a key.

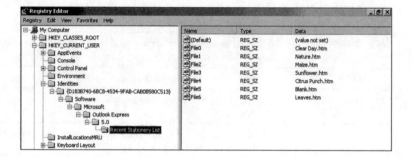

To change a value, select that value's name in the right pane, and then select Edit, Modify to display the Edit String dialog box shown in Figure F.7.

Figure F.7
You can use normal editing techniques to change the value displayed in the Value Data box.

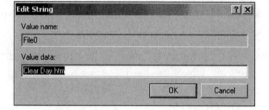

After you've edited the text, click OK to close the dialog box.

MANAGING VALUES IN A SUBKEY

You can add values to a subkey, and you can delete values from a subkey.

ADDING A VALUE TO A SUBKEY

Windows 98 Registry keys can contain the first three types of values listed in Table F.1. Windows NT and Windows 2000 Registry keys can contain the five types of values in the table.

TABLE F.1   TYPES OF VALUES IN A SUBKEY

Value Type	Explanation
REG_BINARY	Raw binary data. Binary data is represented by a series of hexadecimal bytes.
REG_DWORD	A special case of binary data that always consists of four bytes displayed in binary, hexadecimal, or decimal format.
REG_EXPAND_SZ	A string value that applications can change on-the-fly.
REG_MULTI_SZ	A multiple string. Contains multiple string values separated by null characters.
REG_SZ	Alphanumeric text. String values are enclosed within double quotation marks. An empty string value consists of two consecutive double quotation marks.

To add a value to a subkey, start by selecting it. Select Edit and move the pointer onto New. Select String Value, Binary Value, or DWord Value. As you're following instructions about adding a value to a subkey, those instructions will tell you which value type to choose. When you select a value type, the new value appears in the right pane with a temporary name. Change the temporary name to the name you want to use.

After creating a new value, you can change the data in that value using the method described in the previous section, "Changing the Data in a Key or Subkey Value."

DELETING A VALUE IN A KEY OR SUBKEY

To delete a value in a key or subkey, select the name of the value in the right pane. Then select Edit, Delete (or press the Delete key).

COPYING A REGISTRY KEY FROM ONE COMPUTER TO ANOTHER

You easily can copy a registry key, its subordinate subkeys, and the values in those subkeys to a file, and subsequently copy the information in that file into another computer's registry.

Caution

The information given here is based on the assumption that the source and target computers are using the same operating system (such as Windows 98) and the same version of Outlook (such as Outlook 2000). There are differences between the detailed structure of the registry in Windows 98, Windows Me, Windows NT, and Windows 2000. Also, there are differences between the directory keys created when you install the various versions of Outlook.

The amount of data in a typical registry key or subkey is usually quite small and can be copied to a floppy disk.

To copy a registry key, its subkeys, and the values in those subkeys to a file:

1. In the Registry Editor, select the registry key you want to copy to a file.
2. Select Registry, Export Registry File to display the dialog box shown in Figure F.8.

Figure F.8
Use the Export
Registry File dialog
box to define what
you want to export
and the location to
which you want to
export it.

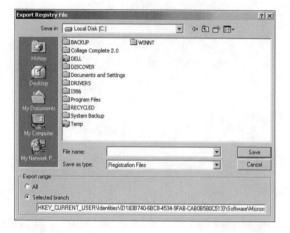

3. Navigate to the drive and folder in which you want to save the file.
4. Enter a name for the exported file in the File Name box. The Registry Editor automatically provides the extension .reg to exported registry files.
5. By default, the Registry Editor proposes to export only the selected branch of the registry tree. If you want to export the entire registry, select All in the Export Range section of the dialog box.
6. Click Save to save the file.

After saving the file, you can import the file into another computer's registry.

To import a file into the registry:

1. Open the Registry Editor on the target computer.
2. Select Registry, Import Registry File to display the dialog box shown in Figure F.9.

Figure F.9
Use the Import
Registry File dialog
box to locate the file
to be imported.

3. Navigate to find the file you want to import into the registry and select that file.

4. Click Open to import the file. A message appears telling you that the file has been successfully imported.

GLOSSARY

This glossary lists terms and abbreviations you might come across while you're working with Outlook. It doesn't provide broad definitions that necessarily apply in other environments. You can find definitions of other terms used in Office applications at `http://support.Microsoft.com/support/Office/OFF2K/Gloss.asp`.

Account See *User Account*.

Activity An appointment, event, or meeting. Activities can be one-time or recurring.

Add-In A software component available from Microsoft that can be added into Outlook to provide extra functionality.

Add-On A software component available from a third-party that can be added to Outlook to provide extra functionality. Outlook treats add-ons in the same manner as add-ins.

Address Book A generic term that refers to one or more files or folders supported by Outlook, Exchange Server, or Internet directory services that contain information about people, organizations, and other contacts. These files and folders include the Global Address List, Internet directory services, the Outlook Address List, personal address books, and address books in third-party applications. See also *Global Address List*, *Internet Directory Service*, *Outlook Address List*, and *Personal Address Book*.

Administrator The person who controls a workgroup, LAN, or service (such as Exchange Server).

Age The length of time since an Outlook item was created or modified.

America Online (AOL) An organization that offers information and communication facilities to computer users. AOL is an Internet service provider. See *Internet Service Provider*.

American Standard Code for Information Interchange (ASCII) A code that represents letters, numbers, punctuation marks, and certain other characters by numeric values. Standard ASCII code provides for 128 characters; extended ASCII code provides for 256 characters.

AOL See *America Online*.

API See *Applications Programming Interface*.

Applications Programming Interface (API) A set of functions that can be used by programs running under Windows.

Appointment   A period blocked for a specific purpose in an Outlook user's calendar.

Archive   A file containing Outlook items that are older than a specific age. When Outlook archives items, it moves those items from current folders to an archive folder.

ASCII   See *American Standard Code for Information Interchange*.

ATAPI   See *AT Attachment Protocol Interface*.

AT Attachment Protocol Interface (ATAPI)   The protocol used by AT (and later) computers to communicate with CD-ROM and tape drives. Don't confuse the ATAPI protocol with the TAP and TAPI protocols. See also *Telelocator Alpha-Paging Protocol* and *Telephony Applications Programming Interface*.

Attachment   A file, Outlook item, or object that is linked to, or contained in, an Outlook item. Files, items, and objects can be attached to messages, contacts, appointments, tasks, and so on.

AutoAddress   Outlook's capability to separate an address into street, city, state, postal code, and country fields.

AutoArchive   Outlook's capability of moving items of a specific age from a Personal Folders file into an archive file.

AutoCreate   Outlook's capability to automatically convert an item of one type into an item of another type. For example, you can create a Task item by dragging a Message item into the Tasks folder.

AutoDate   Outlook's capability to convert a description of a date into a specific calendar date.

AutoJournal   Outlook's capability to automatically create journal items that record activities involving specific contacts and access to Office files.

AutoName   Outlook's capability to separate a person's full name into first name, middle name, and last name fields.

AutoName Check   Outlook's capability to verify that names entered into To, Cc, and Bcc fields exist in an address book.

AutoPreview   Outlook's capability to display the first three lines of a message without the user having to open the message.

AutoSave   Outlook's capability to automatically save data to a file at predetermined intervals.

Balloon   The message box used by the Office Assistant to display information.

Banner   The bar across the top of an Information viewer. The banner contains the name of the folder that contains the items displayed in the viewer.

BASIC   See *Beginners All-Purpose Symbolic Instruction Code*.

Basic Input/Output System (BIOS)   A set of routines, usually in ROM, that support the transfer of information between such computer hardware components as the processor, keyboard, disks, memory, and monitor.

BCC   See *Blind Carbon Copy*.

Beginners All-Purpose Symbolic Instruction Code (BASIC)   A high-level programming language initially developed as a means to teach programming. It has subsequently been developed into such programming languages as Visual Basic, Visual Basic for Applications (VBA), and Visual Basic Script (VBS).

BIOS   See *Basic Input/Output System*.

Blind Carbon Copy (BCC)   A copy of a message that is sent without the recipient's name appearing on the copies other people receive. The word "carbon" comes from the carbon paper that was used to make copies on a typewriter.

Boolean Search   A database search that uses Boolean operators (usually AND and OR) to combine words or phrases to search for. Searching for "cat AND dog" finds items that contain both "cat" and "dog"; searching for "cat OR dog" finds items that contain either "cat" or "dog", or both words.

Branch   The Windows registry has a tree-like structure. Sections of the structure are referred to as branches.

Browser   An application that's used to find information on the World Wide Web.

Calendar   A component of Outlook in which users plan their activities. See also *Activity*. Also, the Outlook Information viewer that displays activities. Outlook saves Calendar items in the Calendar folder. See also *Information Viewer*.

Carbon Copy (CC)   The name of a person to whom an e-mail message is copied. The CC names are included on the messages sent to all recipients. The word "carbon" comes from the carbon paper that was used to make copies on a typewriter.

Card View   One of the formats in which Outlook displays or prints contact information. This view is similar to how information about people is presented on conventional index cards.

Category   An identifier for an Outlook item. One or more categories can be assigned to each item.

CC   See *Carbon Copy*.

CDO   See *Collaboration Data Object*.

Certificate   A digital identification used to send secure messages by way of the Internet or other communication system. See also *Key*.

Client   A computer, or software running on that computer, that accesses data or services on another computer.

Client/Server   A LAN configuration in which one or more computers (servers) provide services to users' computers (clients).

Collaboration Data Object (CDO)   A set of technologies which implement messaging and collaboration functionality in an application. CDO was previously known as Active Messaging and OLE Messaging.

Command Bar   A menu bar or toolbar.

Compress   To reduce the size of a file. See also *Zipped File*.

CompuServe   An organization that offers information and communication facilities to computer users. Outlook can send and receive CompuServe e-mail messages.

Contact   A person or organization. Outlook maintains a list of contacts in the Contacts folder. Each contact item contains information about one contact.

Contact List   The list of contacts maintained by Outlook.

Contacts   The Outlook Information viewer that displays information about contacts. Items displayed in this Information viewer are stored in the Contacts folder. See also *Information Viewer*.

Context Menu   A menu displayed when you right-click an object in a window. One of the most useful items in context menus is Properties, which you can use to see and change an object's properties. A context menu is also known as a *shortcut menu*.

Control   An object on a form, used to obtain user input and display output. Controls available in Outlook are: CheckBox, ComboBox, CommandButton, Frame, Image, Label, ListBox, MultiPage, OptionButton, ScrollBar, SpinButton, TabStrip, Textbox, and ToggleButton.

Control Panel   A window in Outlook that provides access to the fundamental components of Windows. To access the Control Panel, choose Start in the Windows taskbar, choose Settings in the Start menu, and choose Control Panel.

Conversation   A sequence of related messages, often known as a *thread*. Each message in a conversation has the same conversation name. See also *Subject*.

Corporate/Workgroup E-mail Service (C/W)   An Outlook 98 and Outlook 2000 installation that includes capabilities to use various messaging systems, in addition to the Internet, for e-mail. It also provides personal information management capabilities. Compare with Internet Only E-mail Service. Unified messaging in Outlook 2002 eliminates the need for separate Corporate/Workgroup and Internet Only installations. See also *Internet Only E-mail Service*.

C/W   See *Corporate/Workgroup E-mail Service*.

Data File   A file that contains one or more folders, each of which contains Outlook items. See also *Personal Folders File*.

Data Link   See *Timex Data Link*.

Date Navigator   The section of the Calendar Information viewer that shows one or more complete months. You can use the Date Navigator to move rapidly to specific dates.

Decrypt   To restore encrypted information to its original intelligible form. See also *Encryption*.

Deleted Items   The folder that contains items that have been deleted from other Outlook folders. Also the name of the information viewer in which deleted items are displayed. See also *Information Viewer*.

Desktop   The screen that first appears when you log on to Windows. The desktop contains shortcut icons that provide access to frequently used programs, documents, and printers.

Dial-Up Networking (DUN)   Connecting to a network by way of a dialed connection over telephone lines.

Dialog Box   A window displayed by an operating system or application that solicits a response from the user.

Digital Dashboard   An enhanced version of the Outlook Today window that displays information from various sources. These sources include files on a local drive or drive accessed by way of a network, as well as Web or intranet sites.

Digital Signature   See *Certificate*.

Directory   A means of locating e-mail addresses. See also *Lightweight Directory Access Protocol*. The word *directory* previously referred to a container for files on a disk; the word *folder* is now used for that purpose.

Distribution List   A list of people to whom a message is to be sent. Outlook stores distribution lists in the Contacts folder.

DLL   See *Dynamic-Link Library*.

DNS   See *Domain Name Service*.

Document   Something created in an Office application, such as a table created in Access, text created in Word, a workbook created in Excel, or a presentation created in PowerPoint.

Domain   A group of computers on a Windows NT or Windows 2000 network that shares a directory database.

Domain Name Service (DNS)   A service provided by a DNS server that translates hostnames into their corresponding IP addresses.

Draft   A version of a message that has been prepared to be sent, but might require revision. Outlook saves draft messages in the Drafts folder.

Drafts   An Outlook folder in which drafts of messages are saved. Also the name of the information viewer in which drafts are displayed. See *Information Viewer*.

Drag and Drop   The capability to select an object created in one Office application and use the mouse to drag that object into another application. Drag and drop also can be used to create one type of Outlook item from another, such as creating a Task item from a Message item (known as *AutoCreate*).

DTMF   See *Dual Tone Multiple-Frequency*.

Dual Tone Multiple-Frequency (DTMF)   An international signaling standard for telephone digits. When you press a button on your telephone, a dual tone is transmitted. The same dual tone is generated when you use your modem to place a call. Numeric pagers decode DTMF signals to display numbers.

DUN   See *Dial-Up Networking*.

Dynamic-Link Library (DLL)   An operating system capability that enables programs to dynamically exchange information and commands.

E-mail   A message sent from one person to one or more other people, each of whom uses a computer or other appliance. Most messages consist only of text, but messages can include any type of information that can be created on a computer. Users who exchange e-mail messages can use the same computer, be part of a workgroup, be interconnected by way of a LAN or WAN, or use a messaging service provider to access the Internet. See also *Local Area Network* and *Wide Area Network*.

Embedded Object   An object included within another object. The included data consists of the object's native data and presentation data.

Encryption   A means of limiting access to data by converting the data into an apparently meaningless form. Only people who have the key to the encryption can reverse the process (decryption) to make the data meaningful.

Event   In general, something that happens and is recognized by the computer so an appropriate action can be taken. In Outlook, an event is an activity that occupies one or more days but does not require the user to block time.

Exchange   See *Exchange Server*.

Exchange Client   An e-mail client application in Windows 95 and Windows NT that provides access to Exchange messages. Provides messaging capabilities similar to those in Outlook, but does not contain scheduling capabilities. Microsoft now refers to Exchange Client as *Windows Messaging*.

Exchange Server   An e-mail and collaboration server that runs under Windows NT Server and Windows 2000 Server. An Exchange Server administrator creates accounts for users. Users can access those accounts by creating corresponding e-mail accounts within Outlook.

Exchange Store   Disk space controlled by Exchange Server, which contains users' mail boxes and information in public folders.

Favorites A folder that contains shortcuts to items, documents, folders, and Uniform Resource Locators (URLs).

Fax An abbreviation of "facsimile." A method of transmitting text and graphics over telephone lines in digital form. Outlook can send and receive fax messages if the appropriate add-ons are installed.

Fax Viewer A facility that can display outgoing fax messages.

Field An area of memory that contains a specific type of information. Outlook uses a separate field for each type of information it deals with; fields are used for such information as First Name, Middle Name, Last Name, Street Address, City, and so on. Controls are used to display the contents of fields on forms and to print contents of fields in reports. See also *Control*.

Field Chooser A list of fields that can be used to add fields to a form.

Field Type The type of data a field can contain. Each Outlook field can contain one of the following types of data: combination, currency, date/time, duration, formula, integer, keywords, number, percent, text, and yes/no.

File The basic unit of storage on such media as disks and tape.

File Transfer Protocol (FTP) A common method of sending files from one computer to another by way of the Internet.

Filter An Outlook facility used to access information that satisfies certain specified criteria. The specified criteria refer to contents of fields. Filters can be used to find items that contain certain text in text fields, certain dates (or ranges of dates) in date fields, and certain values (or ranges of values) in numeric fields.

Firewall An application that protects a LAN or an individual computer from unauthorized outside access.

Flag An indication in a message that some follow-up activity is necessary. Messages are indicated as flagged by the flag symbol in the Flag Status column of the message list.

Folder A container for information. Outlook 2002 uses a Personal Folders file as a container for folders. This file contains several folders—one for each type of item. Each folder contains either subfolders or items of a specific type. Users can augment the initial folder structure by adding folders and a hierarchy of subfolders.

Form A window used to display and collect information. Outlook provides forms for such purposes as creating and viewing messages, appointments, and contact information. Some of these forms can be modified to suit custom needs. You can create custom forms.

Forward To send a received message, including attachments, to someone else.

FTP See *File Transfer Protocol*.

Function A unit of program code that can be accessed from other code, performs some operation, and returns a value to the code from which it was accessed.

GAL   See *Global Address List*.

Gateway   A capability to transmit data from one information system to another. For example, a gateway enables the exchange of messages between an Internet message server and the CompuServe messaging system.

Global Address List (GAL)   A list of e-mail and other addresses maintained on a mail server.

GMT   See *Greenwich Mean Time*.

Greenwich Mean Time (GMT)   The current time as it is in Greenwich (London, England). Now known as *Universal Coordinated Time*.

Group   To separate items displayed in a list or timeline into sections, each of which contains items with a common characteristic. For example, a list of contacts can be grouped by category, company, or other characteristics.

HTML   See *Hypertext Markup Language*.

HTTP   See *Hypertext Transport Protocol*.

Hypertext   Text that contains links to other information in the same document or to information in other documents.

Hypertext Markup Language (HTML)   A language used to create hypertext documents for use on the World Wide Web. Outlook includes the capability to send and receive messages created in HTML format. HTML messages can include graphically rich text, including images and links. These messages can be read by users who have any HTML-compliant client.

Hypertext Transport Protocol (HTTP)   The protocol used for sending hypertext documents on the Internet.

iCalendar   A format for sending and receiving free/busy information by way of the Internet. Outlook supports iCalendar.

IMAP4   See *Internet Message Access Protocol 4*.

IMO   See *Internet Only E-mail Service*.

Importance   In Outlook and other messaging systems, messages automatically have normal importance. They can be marked to have high or low importance.

Inbox   The Outlook Information viewer that displays messages received but not moved to another folder. Items displayed in this Information viewer are stored in the Inbox folder. See also *Information Viewer*.

Inf   See *Information File*.

InfoBar   A box that appears in some Outlook forms to alert users to special conditions. For example, if you use the Appointment form to create a new appointment for a time in the past, an InfoBar appears stating This appointment occurs in the past. InfoBars have a yellow background to attract attention.

Information File (Inf)   A file that defines how an application or a component of an application is to be installed. For example, the Outlbar.inf file defines the default installation of the Outlook Bar.

Information Store   See *Store*.

Information Viewer   The section of an Outlook window that displays a specific type of item. Each Information viewer displays items from a specific folder or subfolder.

Integrated Services Digital Network (ISDN)   A communications system by which many types of information can be transmitted at high speed over telephone lines.

IntelliSense   The capability of the Office Assistant to offer assistance with a user's current task.

Internet   A worldwide, interconnected system of computers that provides information and communication services.

Internet Directory Service   An address book available on the Internet that uses the *Lightweight Directory Access Protocol*. You can set up Outlook to access Internet Directory Services.

Internet Explorer   An Internet browser available from Microsoft. Outlook depends on some facilities within Internet Explorer. Because of that, Internet Explorer is automatically installed with Outlook, even if you don't use Internet Explorer as your primary Internet browser.

Internet Message Access Protocol 4 (IMAP4)   An industry-standard protocol used to access remote computers by way of dial-up connections. This protocol offers more capabilities than the Point-to-Point Protocol and the Serial Line Internet Protocol. Some Internet service providers use this protocol. See also *Point-to-Point Protocol (PPP)* and *Serial Line Internet Protocol (SLIP)*. Outlook includes support for this protocol.

Internet Only E-mail Service   An installation of Outlook 98 and Outlook 2000 that provides Internet and intranet e-mail and personal information management capabilities. Also known as Internet Mail Only (IMO). Unified messaging in Outlook 2002 eliminates the need for separate Corporate/Workgroup and Internet Only installations.

Internet Protocol (IP)   The protocol that controls message routing on the Internet.

Internet Read Receipt   An Internet read receipt is created when a recipient reads a message. Outlook supports the Internet read-receipt standard.

Internet Service Provider (ISP)   An organization that provides access to the Internet.

Intranet   An Internet-like environment accessible only within an organization.

IP   See *Internet Protocol*.

ISDN   See *Integrated Services Digital Network*.

ISP   See *Internet Service Provider*.

Item   A unit of information in Outlook. E-mail messages, appointments, contacts, tasks, journal entries, and notes are all items.

Journal   The Outlook facility for creating Journal items that automatically record such activities as working with Office files and sending and receiving e-mail messages. Users can manually record other activities as Journal entry items. Also the Outlook Information viewer that displays Journal items. Items displayed in this information viewer are stored in the Journal folder. See also *Information Viewer*.

Key   A digital code used to authenticate and encrypt e-mail messages. Each person who sends a message has access to the recipients' public keys. To authenticate a message or decrypt it, recipients use their private keys. A key is also known as a *certificate*.

Also a part of the Windows registry structure that contains information about computer hardware or software settings.

LAN   See *Local Area Network*.

LDAP   See *Lightweight Directory Access Protocol*.

Legacy   Something passed on from the old days. Legacy applications and files are those designed for old computers, but are still used by people with modern computing systems.

Lightweight Directory Access Protocol (LDAP)   A simplified (lightweight) version of the Directory Access Protocol. LDAP is a directory service used by Outlook, as well as other e-mail clients, to access directories of e-mail addresses. This protocol can be used to find users on the Internet or on a corporate intranet.

Linked Object   An object included within another object. The included data consists of the object's presentation data and a reference to its native data. See also *Native Data* and *Presentation Data*.

Local Access Phone Number   A phone number, usually within your local calling area, that provides access to an Internet service provider without incurring toll or long distance charges.

Local Area Network (LAN)   A computer network limited to a small area, such as one building or group of buildings.

Location   The place where an appointment, event, or meeting is to occur.

Log   A record of specific types of events. For example, Outlook can create an event log that marks the completion of each CompuServe e-mail session.

Mail Client   A computer, or the software running on a computer, that can receive e-mail from, and send e-mail to, a mail server.

Mail Server   A computer, or the software running on a computer, that provides mail services to mail clients. These services include storing messages sent by mail clients until the recipient mail clients retrieve those messages.

Mailbox   The space on a mail server dedicated to storing messages intended for a specific mail user.

Mailing List   See *Distribution List*.

MAPI   See *Messaging Application Programming Interface*.

Master Category List   A list of categories from which a user can choose to assign one or more categories for each item.

Meeting   In Outlook, a period blocked by two or more users for the purpose of a face-to-face or other type of meeting.

Menu Bar   The row immediately under the title bar in a window that contains menu names. The items in each menu are displayed by choosing the menu name. A menu bar is a component of *Command Bars*.

Message   Any piece of information sent from one person to one or more other people. A message usually, but not necessarily, originates from and is received by a computer. E-mail, voice mail, and fax are the principal methods of sending messages. Messages can be received by other devices, such as alphanumeric pagers and Internet appliances.

Message Class   A field within any type of Outlook item that specifies the form to be used when the item is displayed.

Message Status   An indication, marked by a flag, of something special about a message.

Messaging   The practice of communicating by means of electronic messages.

Messaging Application Programming Interface (MAPI)   A set of API functions and an OLE interface that Outlook and other messaging clients use to interface with message service providers.

Method   An action defined within an object. Each of Outlook's objects contains certain methods.

MHTML   See *Multilingual Hypertext Markup Language*.

Microsoft Exchange   See *Exchange Client* and *Exchange Server*.

Microsoft Fax   A set of API functions Outlook and other Windows applications can use to send and receive fax messages.

Microsoft Mail   A set of API functions Outlook and other Windows applications can use to send and receive e-mail messages within a workgroup.

Microsoft Network   A system that offers information and communication facilities to computer users. Outlook can send and receive Microsoft Network e-mail.

Microsoft Office XP   The applications suite released in 2001 that contains Outlook 2002. Other applications in the suite are Microsoft Access, Microsoft Excel, Microsoft PowerPoint, and Microsoft Word.

Microsoft Outlook   A desktop information manager that includes comprehensive messaging, scheduling, and information management facilities.

Microsoft Outlook Express   An application, provided with Internet Explorer, that provides e-mail facilities and allows access to newsgroups.

Microsoft Outlook Web Access (OWA)   A Web mail client that can access Exchange Server mailboxes and Public Folders.

Microsoft Project   An application used to plan, control, and track the progress of projects.

Microsoft Team Manager   An application used to allocate tasks among team members to coordinate the work of those members.

Microsoft Word   A word processor that is Outlook's default e-mail editor.

MIME   See *Multipurpose Internet Mail Extensions*.

Modem   A device that converts digital information into analog (sound) suitable for transmission over telephone lines, and also converts incoming analog (sound) information into digital form. The word is derived from Modulator/Demodulator.

Multilingual Hypertext Markup Language (MHTML)   An embedded browser and gateway service that permits browsing in Web documents containing non-English characters, such as those used in the Chinese, Greek, Japanese, and Russian languages.

Multipurpose Internet Mail Extensions (MIME)   A protocol for e-mail messages that enables those messages to include attachments such as pictures and computer code. See also *S/MIME*.

My Computer   An icon on the Windows desktop that provides access to folders on any disk on an Outlook user's computer and to disks that other network users have made available for sharing.

My Documents   A folder that contains a list of documents created in, or modified by, an Office application running under Windows. See also *Personal Folders*.

Native Data   One of the two types of data associated with an OLE object (the other type is Presentation Data). Native data consists of all the data needed by an application to edit the object. See also *Presentation Data*.

Navigator   An Internet browser available from Netscape.

NetBEUI   See *NetBIOS Extended User Interface*.

NetBIOS   See *Network Basic Input/Output System*.

NetBIOS Extended User Interface   Provides data transport services for communication between computers.

NetMeeting A Microsoft application that supports communications sessions between two or more Internet users. Also, a name used for that communication. During a NetMeeting, users can exchange text, sound, graphics, and video.

Network Interconnected computers. In a client/server network, a server provides services to clients (individual users). In a peer-to-peer network, any computer can act as a client or a server.

Network Basic Input/Output System (NetBIOS) Establishes communication between computers in a network.

Network Interface Card (NIC) A circuit board or other assembly that connects a computer to a network. Each computer must have a network interface card to be part of a network.

Network News Transport Protocol (NNTP) A protocol used to post, distribute, and retrieve messages on the Internet or corporate intranets. Outlook includes an Internet Newsreader that's shared with Internet Explorer.

News Server A computer on which newsgroup messages are stored. Many news servers are open for anyone to access, but some are private and allow access only to people who are registered and can provide a registered username and password.

Newsgroup A collection of messages posted on a news server. Subject to permissions given by the newsgroup administrator, people who access a newsgroup can read messages and post their own messages. All the newsgroups available on the Internet are collectively known as Usenet. See also *News Server*.

NIC See *Network Interface Card*.

NNTP See *Network News Transport Protocol*.

No E-mail An installation of Outlook 98 and Outlook 2000 that provides personal information management capabilities, but no capability to send and receive e-mail.

Node A computer, printer, or other device connected to a network.

Note A type of Outlook item. A note consists of data that subsequently will be used for any other purpose. Notes are generally used for temporary information.

Notes The Outlook Information viewer that displays notes. Items displayed in this Information viewer are stored in the Notes folder. See also *Information Viewer*.

Object An entity that can contain data and have properties and methods. OLE associates presentation data and native data with objects. Outlook, and other Office applications, contains a hierarchical structure of objects known as an object model. See also *Object Model*.

Object Linking and Embedding (OLE) The technology by which objects can be embedded into, or linked to, other objects. Outlook uses OLE to incorporate various kinds of objects into messages and other items.

Object Model   The structure of an application in terms of its objects and their interrelationships. Often represented graphically. See also *Object*.

Off Hook   The condition in which a telephone or modem is connected to a telephone line. The term comes from the days of old-fashioned telephones that had a receiver hanging on a hook. To use the telephone, a person took the receiver off the hook. See also *On Hook*.

Office Assistant   The animated icon that can be displayed in an Outlook window to provide help with whatever task a user is attempting.

Offline Store File (OST)   A file on a user's computer that contains a copy of information in that user's Exchange store.

On Hook   The condition in which a telephone or modem is not connected to a telephone line. See also *Off Hook*.

Organize   In Outlook, the capability to move items into specific folders according to the content of those items.

OST   See *Offline Store File*.

Out of Office Assistant   A facility within Exchange Server that automatically answers or forwards messages. This facility is available in Outlook only when the current e-mail account connects to an Exchange Server and a network connection to that Exchange Server is available.

Outbox   The Outlook Information viewer that displays messages created but not sent. Items displayed in this Information viewer are stored in the Outbox folder. See also *Information Viewer*.

Outlook   See *Microsoft Outlook*.

Outlook Address List   An Outlook folder that contains information about people and organizations.

Outlook Bar   The bar at the left side of Outlook's Information viewers that contains shortcuts to Information viewers and other folders. See also *Information Viewer*.

Outlook Express   See *Microsoft Outlook Express*.

Outlook Today   An Outlook window that provides a summary of information relevant to the current day and next few days.

Outlook Web Access (OWA)   See *Microsoft Outlook Web Access*.

OWA   See *Microsoft Outlook Web Access*.

Package Definition File (PDF)   A file used by the Microsoft System Management Server to control remote installation of applications.

Pane   An area within a window that contains related information. See also *Preview Pane*.

Password   A private sequence of characters a user types to gain access to a computer, to specific applications running on a computer, and to specific files. In Outlook, information services can be set up so that a password is necessary to use them.

Password Authentication   The process by which a server verifies the validity of a user's password.

PDF   See *Package Definition File*. The abbreviation PDF is also used for Portable Document Format, the format used by Adobe's Acrobat Reader.

Peer-to-Peer Network   A network in which each connected computer can be a client and a server.

Permission   A permission allows a user to have access to a shared resource, such as a disk drive or a printer. See also *Right*.

Personal Address Book   An address book that contains an Outlook user's personal list of people's names and information about those people. A Personal Address Book can be used to create distribution lists.

Personal Folders   The set of folders in which Outlook stores items. Outlook creates a separate folder for each type of item. Users can add their own hierarchies of folders and subfolders and subsequently move items from one to another.

Personal Folders File (PST)   A file that contains folders in which Outlook stores items.

Personal Information Manager (PIM)   An application used to save and manage personal information, including a calendar, an address book, and a to-do list. Outlook acts as a personal information manager as well as a means of sending and receiving messages.

PIM   See *Personal Information Manager*.

Point-to-Point Protocol (PPP)   An industry-standard protocol used to access remote computers by way of dial-up connections. Many Internet service providers use this protocol. See also *Internet Message Access Protocol 4 (IMAP4)* and *Serial Line Internet Protocol (SLIP)*.

Polling   The process of periodically connecting to a messaging service to ascertain whether messages are waiting and, if so, to move those messages into the Inbox. At the same time, any messages for that service waiting in the Outbox are sent.

POP3   See *Post Office Protocol 3*.

Post   To place a message on a public folder on a server such as Exchange Server, or on a news server.

Post Office Protocol 3 (POP3)   A messaging protocol commonly used by Internet messaging service providers. Messages you receive are transmitted in POP3 format. Outlook includes support for this protocol.

Postoffice   A facility on a network that maintains information, including mailbox addresses, about each user and manages the process of sending and receiving messages.

PPP   See *Point-to-Point Protocol*.

Presentation Data   One of the two types of data associated with an OLE object (the other type is Native Data). Presentation data consists of all the data needed by an application to render the object on a display device. See also *Native Data*.

Preview Pane   The area within Outlook's Inbox Information viewer that contains previews of received messages. See also *Information Viewer*.

Private   Items, such as appointments and contacts, that are marked so they are available only to the person who created them.

Profile   A set of information that defines how a specific person uses Outlook. A profile defines the information services to be used and passwords required to access those services. Each profile can be protected by a password.

Project   See *Microsoft Project*.

Property   A characteristic of an icon, a form, or an object on a form. Properties include such characteristics as a name, the position of an object on a form, the font used by the object, and various settings.

Protocol   A set of rules that defines how computers communicate. A protocol can contain other protocols.

PST   See *Personal Folders File*.

Public Folder   A folder maintained on a server, such as Exchange Server, that can be accessed by users who have access to the server.

RAM   See *Random Access Memory*.

Random Access Memory (RAM)   The memory within a computer in which currently executing programs and information being processed is stored.

RAS   See *Remote Access Service*.

Read Receipt   See *Internet Read Receipt*.

Real-time Clock   The clock within a computer that keeps track of the current date and time.

Recall   The capability to retrieve a message that has been sent. Under some circumstances, Outlook can recall messages that recipients haven't yet read.

Recipient   A person (mailbox) to whom a message is addressed.

Recurring   An appointment, an event, or a meeting that occurs regularly.

Registration Database   See *Registry*.

Registry   Windows files that maintain up-to-date information about a computer's hardware and software configuration, and also about users. Outlook's profiles, Master Category Lists, and other information are maintained in the registry. The registry has a tree-like structure; branches of the tree contain keys, many of which are divided into subkey components. Also known as the Registration Database.

Reminder A visual or an audible warning Outlook gives a certain time before an item is due. Outlook can provide reminders before appointments, meetings, events, and task due dates.

Remote Access Service (RAS) In Windows NT, the capability of a client computer to access a server by way of a dialed telephone connection, and the capability of a server to be accessed in this way. Also known as Dial-up Networking.

Remote Mail The facility for working with e-mail at a computer that is not connected permanently to a mail server.

Replication The process of maintaining up-to-date copies of data in various locations, such as on a local computer and a server.

Resolve The process by which Outlook checks the message recipient names entered into a Message form by comparing them with names in address books and automatically uses the appropriate e-mail address.

Resource A facility (such as a conference room) or a piece of equipment (such as a projector) that can be scheduled for use at a meeting. In some applications, such as Project, people are referred to as resources.

Rich Text Format (RTF) A method of formatting text so that documents can be transferred between various applications running on different platforms. Outlook can use RTF.

RichEdit One of the text editors available within Outlook for creating and editing messages.

Right A right gives a user access to a domain or a computer. See also *Permission*.

RTC See *Real-time Clock*.

RTF See *Rich Text Format*.

Rule A directive for how messages are to be handled by Outlook or Exchange Server. In Outlook, the Rules Wizard leads you through the process of creating rules.

S/MIME See *Secure Multipurpose Internet Mail Extensions*.

Schedule+ A scheduling application provided with Office 95 and now superseded by the scheduling facilities within Outlook. Schedule+ was supplied in some versions of Exchange Server.

Search Engine An application that searches the Internet to find pages and newsgroups that contain information that matches specific criteria.

Secure Multipurpose Internet Mail Extensions (S/MIME) An extension of the MIME protocol that incorporates security provisions. The implementation of S/MIME in Outlook includes digital signing and encryption.

Sender   The person who sends a message, or the person on behalf of whom a message is sent.

Sensitivity   In Outlook, messages normally have normal sensitivity. A sender can mark a message as having personal, private, or confidential sensitivity. A message recipient cannot change the sensitivity.

Sent Item   A message that has been sent to a mail server. Outlook automatically moves items that have been sent from the Outbox subfolder to the Sent Items folder.

Sent Items   The Outlook Information viewer that displays messages that have been sent. Items displayed in this Information viewer are stored in the Sent Items folder. See also *Information Viewer*.

Serial Line Internet Protocol (SLIP)   An industry-standard protocol used to access remote computers by way of dial-up connections. Some Internet service providers use this protocol. See also *Internet Message Access Protocol 4 (IMAP4)* and *Point-to-Point Protocol (PPP)*.

Server   A computer, or the software running on that computer, that provides services to client computers. One server computer can have several server applications; for example, a server computer running under Windows NT Server or Windows 2000 Server can provide SQL Server and Exchange Server (and other) services.

Service Provider   An organization that provides access to a computer-related service. An Internet service provider (ISP) provides access to the Internet.

Shared Folder   A folder on a server to which several or many users have access so they can share information.

Shortcut   A link to information in a folder or to an application.

Signature   Text that Outlook can automatically incorporate into all messages you send. Most often used to sign messages.

Simple Mail Transport Protocol (SMTP)   A protocol used by the Internet for transmitting messages. Messages you send are submitted to an e-mail server in SMTP format. Outlook includes support for this protocol.

SLIP   See *Serial Line Internet Protocol*.

SMTP   See *Simple Mail Transport Protocol*.

Snail Mail   A slang name for conventional mail delivered by a traditional postal service.

Spam   Unsolicited and unwanted e-mail.

Stationery   A pattern or background that Outlook can add to the messages you send by way of the Internet or an intranet.

Status Bar   The row at the bottom of a window that displays certain information about what is displayed in the rest of the window. The status bar at the bottom of Outlook's Information viewers displays the number of items in the displayed viewer. See also *Information Viewer*.

Status Report   Information about the progress of a task assigned to another person.

Store   The location within a computer's file system where information is stored.

Subfolder   A component of a folder. In Outlook, a folder can have many subfolders. Each subfolder contains items of a specific type and can contain other subfolders.

Subject   A brief description of an appointment, an event, a meeting, or a message. The subject of the first message in a conversation becomes the conversation name. See also *Conversation.*

Subkey   A component of a Windows registry key.

Subscribe   To become a regular user of a facility. By subscribing to a newsgroup, you easily can find that newsgroup.

Swap   To move data between memory (RAM) and disk. Swapping allows an operating system to have access to much more memory than actually exists as physical RAM. See also *RAM.*

Synchronize   To copy data from one folder to another so both folders contain the most recent data. Data is often synchronized between a server and a client.

System State Data   In Windows 2000, a term used to collectively refer to these system components: the registry, the COM+ Class Registration database, boot files (including system files), the Certificate Services database, the Active Directory directory service, the SysVol directory, and Cluster service information.

System Tray   A box at the right end of the Windows taskbar that can contain the current time and icons that provide access to the battery meter, dial-up networking monitor, fax monitor, mouse properties, PC Card status, volume control, and other facilities.

Table   Information arranged in rows and columns. In Outlook, a Table view displays items with one item in each row. Each column contains information in a specific field.

TAP   See *Telelocator Alpha-Paging Protocol.*

TAPI   See *Telephony Applications Programming Interface.*

Task   An Outlook item that describes something to be done. A task can have a due date and start date. The person who creates a task item can assign that task to another person. A person who receives an assigned task can accept or reject the assignment and can reassign it to someone else.

Taskbar   The bottom row of the Windows desktop that displays the Start button and buttons representing each active application.

TaskPad   The pane at the bottom-left of the Calendar Information viewer that contains a list of current tasks. See also *Information Viewer.*

Tasks   The Outlook Information viewer that displays Information about tasks. Items displayed in this Information viewer are stored in the Tasks folder. See also *Information Viewer.*

TCP   See *Transmission Control Protocol*.

TCP/IP   See *Transmission Control Protocol/Internet Protocol*.

Team Manager   See *Microsoft Team Manager*.

Telelocator Alpha-Paging Protocol (TAP)   A protocol used by alphanumeric pagers. Alphanumeric pagers decode information received in the TAP protocol and display that information on their screens. Don't confuse the TAP protocol with the ATAPI and TAPI protocols. See also *AT Attachment Protocol Interface* and *Telephony Applications Programming Interface*.

Telephony Applications Programming Interface (TAPI)   A protocol that controls how Windows applications interact with the telephone system. Don't confuse the TAPI protocol with the ATAPI and TAP protocols. See also *AT Attachment Protocol Interface* and *Telelocator Alpha-Paging Protocol*.

Template   An Outlook item that can be used as the basis for creating other items.

Thread   Related messages in a newsgroup or bulletin board. See also *Conversation*.

Timeline   A view of Journal and other items displayed in relation to time.

Timex Data Link   A protocol for transmitting information to a Timex Data Link watch and to other compatible devices.

Toolbar   The row (usually under the menu bar) containing buttons that provide quick access to often-used facilities. Toolbars are components of *command bars*.

ToolTip   The temporary box that appears under a toolbar button to identify that button.

Transmission Control Protocol (TCP)   The protocol that controls the delivery of sequenced data.

Transmission Control Protocol/Internet Protocol (TCP/IP)   A combination of the TCP and IP protocols that controls message routing and delivery.

Transport   Software that provides a reliable connection between one message protocol and another.

Tree   A term used to describe the structure of the Windows registry.

UCT   See *Universal Coordinated Time*.

UNC   See *Universal Naming Convention*.

Uniform Resource Locator (URL)   The address of a resource on the World Wide Web.

Universal Coordinated Time (UCT)   An international, geography-independent way of specifying time. UCT was formerly known as Greenwich Mean Time (GMT).

Universal Inbox   See *Inbox*.

Universal Naming Convention (UNC)   A format for naming files and resources on a network. The format is

`\\servername\path\resourcename`

or

`\\servername\path\filename`

URL   See *Uniform Resource Locator*.

Usenet   See *Newsgroup*.

User   A person using Outlook or another application.

User Account   A person having access to a network is said to have a user account.

UUENCODE   A utility that converts binary information into 7-bit ASCII characters. After conversion, these characters can be transmitted using a text-only e-mail system. At the receiving end, the UUDECODE utility is used to convert the text back into binary format. This system has been mostly replaced by the MIME format. UUENCODE also is used as a name for the format in which converted messages are transmitted. See also *Multipurpose Internet Mail Extensions*.

VB   See *Visual Basic*.

VBA   See *Visual Basic for Applications*.

VBE   See *Visual Basic Editor*.

VBS   See *Visual Basic Scripting Edition*.

vCalendar   A format by which meeting request information can be sent and received by way of the Internet. Outlook supports vCalendar.

vCard   A format by which contact information can be sent and received by way of the Internet. Outlook supports vCard.

View   A manner in which Outlook displays information in an Information viewer. A user can select from several standard views and also create custom views. Outlook uses views as the basis of formats for printing items.

Visual Basic (VB)   A programming environment (much more than a programming language) based on *BASIC*, which can be used to create Windows applications.

Visual Basic Editor (VBE)   The programming environment in which Visual Basic and Visual Basic for Applications code is created and edited.

Visual Basic for Applications (VBA)   Dialects of Visual Basic that are tailored for developing applications for Office components (Access, Excel, PowerPoint, and Word). Visual Basic for Applications also is used for customizing Outlook at the application level.

Visual Basic Scripting Edition (VBS)   A subset of Visual Basic for Applications, originally developed for working with hypertext documents, that now is also used for developing extended capabilities in Outlook forms.

Voting   A capability of Outlook and other MAPI-compatible applications for sending a message in which recipients are asked to reply indicating their choice among two or more answers to a question.

WAN   See *Wide Area Network*.

Web Folder   An Outlook facility that keeps track of information you've accessed on the World Wide Web.

Web Page   A group of related HTML documents, together with associated databases, files, and scripts, accessible by way of the World Wide Web.

Wide Area Network (WAN)   A network that covers an area larger than a single building.

Wildcard   A character that represents one or more other characters. "$" used as a wildcard represents any one character; "*" used as a wildcard represents any number of characters.

Window   An area of a display screen that provides access to an operating system or application and contains information relating to that system or application.

Windows Messaging System (WMS)   A predecessor of Outlook that was also known as Exchange Client.

Wizard   A sequence of windows that helps users step through what might otherwise be a complex operation.

WMS   See *Windows Messaging System*.

Word   See *Microsoft Word*.

WordMail   A name used to refer to the Word word processor when it is used as the Outlook e-mail editor.

Workgroup   Two or more people using Windows whose computers are connected to form a peer-to-peer network.

World Wide Web (WWW)   Hypertext servers interconnected by way of the Internet that give users access to text, graphics, video, and sound files.

WWW   See *World Wide Web*.

Zip Drive   A disk drive that accepts a removable disk capable of storing 100MB or more of information. Zip drives are supplied by Iomega Corporation.

Zipped File   A file compressed in a format introduced by PkWare. Within the Windows environment, DynaZip (available from Inner Media) and WinZip (available from WinZip Computing) are generally used to create zipped files.

INDEX

Y

Z